Best Reference Books
1970-1980

BEST
REFERENCE BOOKS
1970-1980

Titles of Lasting Value Selected from
American Reference Books Annual

Edited by
Susan Holte
and
Bohdan S. Wynar

Libraries Unlimited, Inc.
Littleton, Colorado
1981

Library of Congress Cataloging in Publication Data

Main entry under title:

SAN FRANCISCO
PUBLIC LIBRARY

Best reference books, 1970-1980.

87- 11

   Includes index.
   1. Reference books--Reviews. 2. Reference books--
Bibliography.   I. Holte, Susan, 1947-   . II. Wynar,
Bohdan S.   III. American reference books annual.
Z1035.1.B534   028.1'2   81-5788
ISBN 0-87287-255-6   AACR2

TABLE OF CONTENTS

INTRODUCTION xv
CONTRIBUTORS xvii
JOURNALS CITED xxiv

1 – GENERAL REFERENCE WORKS

Bibliography 1
    Bibliographic guides, 1; National and trade bibliographies: United
    States, 4; Great Britain, 7; other countries, 8
Periodicals and Serials 11
Publishing and Bookselling 15
    Dictionaries, 15; Directories, 15; Price guides, 17; Copyright, 18
Encyclopedias 19
Directories 21
Handbooks 24
Abbreviations 28
Alternative Information Sources 29
Government Publications 29
Style Manuals 34
Biography 35
    Bibliographies, 35; Indexes, 35; International, 39; United States, 41;
    Foreign countries, 42

2 – LIBRARY SCIENCE

General Works 48
Bibliographies 48
Dictionaries and Encyclopedias 49
Directories 51
Handbooks 54
Periodicals 58
Selection Aids 59
    General, 59; College libraries, 61; School libraries, 62
Biography 65

3 – SOCIAL SCIENCES AND AREA STUDIES

Social Sciences 66
    Bibliographies, 66; Encyclopedias, 67
Area Studies 67
    Comprehensive works, 67; Africa, 68; Asia: comprehensive works, 70;
    China, 70; India, 71; Australasia, 72; Canada, 73; Eastern Europe and
    the Soviet Union, 73; Great Britain, 75; Latin America, 76; Middle
    East and North Africa, 77; United States, 79

4 — HISTORY

Archaeology 81
World History 83
    General works, 83; Atlases, 84; Bibliographies, 86; Chronologies,
    86; Encyclopedias, 87
United States 90
    General works, 90; Atlases, 90; Bibliographies, 92; Dictionaries and
    encyclopedias, 95; Directories, 96; Indexes, 98; Biography, 99
Africa 99
Asia 100
Canada 102
Germany 102
Great Britain 103
Italy 105
Latin America 106
Russia 106

5 — ETHNIC STUDIES

Comprehensive Works 108
Individual Groups 110
    Blacks, 110; Jews, 113; Native Americans, 115; Puerto Ricans, 115;
    Slavic Americans, 116

6 — GENEALOGY AND HERALDRY

Comprehensive Works 117
Genealogy 117
    General works, 117; United States, 118; Great Britain, 118
Heraldry 119
Names 121

7 — POLITICAL SCIENCE

General Works 123
Dictionaries 123
Handbooks 124
U.S. Government 126
    Dictionaries and encyclopedias, 126; Federal government, 127; State
    government, 129; Local government, 130; Biography, 131
Communism 131
Fascism 133
International Relations 133

8 — LAW

General Works...135
Bibliographies 135
Dictionaries 136
Sources and Documents...137
Biography 138

9 — GEOGRAPHY

Atlases..140
    World, 140; United States, 143; Africa, 144; Canada, 145; Central
America, 145; China, 145
Bibliographies 146
Dictionaries 149
Directories 150
Place Names...150

10 — EDUCATION

Bibliographies 152
Dictionaries and Encyclopedias..156
Directories 160
Indexes 161
Biography...162
Instructional Materials..163

11 — RECREATION AND SPORTS

Bibliographies 166
Dictionaries and Encyclopedias..166
Baseball...167
Basketball...168
Football and Soccer..168
Games...169
Golf...171
Hockey 171
Hunting and Fishing...172
Motor Sports..172
Sailing 173
Skiing 173
Swimming...174
Tennis 174

12 – SOCIOLOGY

Bibliographies 175
Directories 175
Encyclopedias 176
Aging 176
Marriage and the Family 177
Prisons 178

13 – WOMEN'S STUDIES

General Works 180
Bibliographies 182
Biography 183

14 – ANTHROPOLOGY AND ETHNOLOGY

Atlases 184
Bibliographies 184
Encyclopedias 185
Handbooks 187

15 – STATISTICS AND DEMOGRAPHY

General Works 190
Dictionaries and Encyclopedias 190

16 – ECONOMICS AND BUSINESS

Atlases 192
Bibliographies 192
Dictionaries and Encyclopedias 194
Directories 195
Accounting 198
Advertising 199
Finance and Banking 199
Insurance 200
Labor 200
Management 201
Real Estate 201

17 – FINE ARTS

Bibliographies 203
Dictionaries 204
Encyclopedias 205

Indexes 207
Biography 207
Architecture 209
Graphic Arts 210
Painting 211
Sculpture 214

18 — APPLIED ARTS

General Works 216
Dictionaries and Encyclopedias 216
Collecting 218
    Antiques, 218; Coins and currency, 220; Firearms, 223; Glass, 224;
    Other collectibles, 225
Crafts 226
    Bibliographies, 226; Encyclopedias, 226; Ceramics, 227; Needlework,
    228; Textiles, 229; Woodworking, 230
Photography 230

19 — MUSIC

General Works 232
Bibliographies 232
Dictionaries and Encyclopedias 234
Indexes 236
Instruments 236
Opera 237
Popular Music 239
Biography 241

20 — THEATRE

General Works 244
Bibliographies 245
Dictionaries and Encyclopedias 246
Directories 248
Indexes 249
Biography 251

21 — FILMS

General Works 254
Dictionaries and Encyclopedias 256
Filmographies 258

22 – RELIGION

General Works..262
Atlases...262
Bibliographies..264
Dictionaries..264
Encyclopedias...269
Bible Studies...270

23 – PHILOSOPHY

Philosophy..277

24 – MYTHOLOGY, FOLKLORE AND POPULAR CUSTOMS

Mythology and Folklore..281
Popular Customs...284

25 – LINGUISTICS

Bibliographies..287
English Language Dictionaries...287
    General works, 287; Comprehensive, 288; School and college, 289;
Historical, 294; Slang, 296; Synonyms and antonyms, 297; Foreign
terms, 299; Grammar and usage, 300
Foreign Language Dictionaries...301
    Arabic, 301; Chinese, 302; Czechoslovakian, 302; Egyptian
hieroglyphic, 302; French, 303; German, 304; Indonesian, 305;
Italian, 305; Latin, 306; Persian, 306; Polish, 307; Russian, 307;
Serbo-Croatian, 308; Spanish, 308; Yiddish, 309

26 – COMMUNICATION

Communication..310

27 – LITERATURE

General Works..312
Bibliographies...313
Dictionaries and Encyclopedias...317
Indexes..320
Biography..321
Children's Literature..324
    General works, 324; Bibliographies, 325; Indexes, 329; Biography, 331
Comics...332
Mystery and Crime Fiction..333

Poetry..334
Science Fiction and Fantasy Literature................................335
> Bibliographies, 335; Encyclopedias, 336; Indexes, 338

American Literature..339
> General works, 339; Bibliographies, 340; Fiction, 342; Biography, 343

British Literature..343
> Bibliographies, 343; Handbooks, 345; Fiction, 345; Biography, 347

Canadian Literature..347
Caribbean Literature...347
Classical Greek and Roman Literature.................................348
French Literature..349
German Literature...350
Hungarian Literature...351
Italian Literature..351
Latin American Literature...352
Oriental Literature...353
Slavic Literature..353
Spanish Literature...354

28 – SCIENCE AND TECHNOLOGY – GENERAL

General Works...355
Bibliographies..355
Dictionaries and Encyclopedias.......................................357
Biography..359

29 – MATHEMATICS

Mathematics..362

30 – ASTRONOMY

Atlases...365
Dictionaries and Encyclopedias.......................................365
Handbooks...367

31 – CHEMISTRY

Bibliographies..371
Dictionaries..372
Encyclopedias..373
Biography..375

32 – PHYSICS

Physics..377

33 — NATURAL HISTORY AND BIOLOGY

General Works..379
Bibliographies 380
Dictionaries and Encyclopedias.....................................380

34 — BOTANY

Bibliographies 382
Dictionaries 382
Cultivated Plants..383
Endangered Plants..384
Flowers 384
Grasses 387
Herbs..387
Mosses and Fungi...387
Trees 388

35 — ZOOLOGY

Encyclopedias 391
Birds 394
Fishes 398
Insects..398
Mammals 400
Mollusks...401
Reptiles and Amphibians..402

36 — ENVIRONMENTAL SCIENCE AND ENERGY RESOURCES

Bibliographies 404
Dictionaries and Encyclopedias.....................................404
Directories 408
Handbooks..408

37 — EARTH SCIENCES

Encyclopedias 411
Geology..412
Hydrology 415
Meteorology..415
Mineralogy...416
Oceanography 418
Soil Science...419

38 — PSYCHOLOGY

Bibliographies 420
Dictionaries and Encyclopedias 421
Mental Health 423
Parapsychology and the Occult 423

39 — MEDICAL SCIENCE

Bibliographies 427
Dictionaries and Encyclopedias 429
Directories 434
Handbooks 435
Popular Medical Guides 435
Pharmacology 437

40 — AGRICULTURE

Beverages 441
Domestic Animals 442
Foods and Cooking 444
Horticulture 446
Veterinary Medicine 449

41 — ENGINEERING AND TECHNOLOGY

Chemical Engineering 450
Construction 450
Computer Technology 451
Electrical Engineering 451
Mechanical Engineering 451
Transportation 452

42 — MILITARY SCIENCE

Almanacs 454
Atlases 454
Bibliographies 456
Dictionaries and Encyclopedias 457
Directories 459
Biography 460

Index 461

INTRODUCTION

Best Reference Books 1970-1980 provides a selection of 920 reference titles determined by the editors to be of lasting value to libraries of all types. Works appearing in this selection include those of a specialized nature, which will be of particular value to larger libraries, as well as those of wider appeal, which will be useful to smaller as well as large and medium-sized libraries. This volume was designed to be used as a selection tool for existing libraries looking for gaps in their collections and for new libraries just beginning to build a reference collection.

These titles were selected from 12 volumes of *American Reference Books Annual,* the comprehensive annual reviewing service for reference books published in the United States. The 12 volumes of ARBA published since 1970 have provided reviews of a total of 20,553 titles. Reference books reviewed in ARBA include dictionaries, encyclopedias, directories, bibliographies, guides, concordances, atlases, and other types of "ready reference" tools, as well as foreign reference titles that have an exclusive distributor in the United States. Government documents and reprints are reviewed in ARBA on a highly selective basis. As a matter of editorial policy, the following categories of reference books are not reviewed in ARBA: reference titles of less than 48 pages; books published by vanity presses; those produced by the author as publisher; and certain types of reference materials published by library staffs for internal use. With a few exceptions, serial publications have been excluded from *Best Reference Books,* as well as travel guides, and, in the area of literature, reference titles that deal with individual authors. These editorial decisions were made in order to keep this volume to a manageable size and thus make it more useful to smaller libraries.

The first edition of *Best Reference Books,* published in 1976, presented a selection of 818 reference titles covering the years 1970 to 1976. All titles included in the first edition have been reevaluated, and, if necessary, revised for this new edition; a total of 471 titles from the first edition have been retained and 449 new titles were added. A small number of titles published in 1969 which in our judgment represent substantial contributions to the literature have been included in this edition.

Reviews for the titles included in this volume were prepared by 290 subject specialists throughout the United States and Canada who review for ARBA. Editorial notes have been added to many of these reviews to indicate new editions, added volumes, other changes since the original review was published, as well as additional titles that may prove useful. Many reviews have been re-edited or completely rewritten to bring the information up to date and to reflect a title's value in view of more recent publications in that subject area. Reviews signed by two contributors are in most cases composite reviews, which were prepared from two reviews pertaining to two different editions or two separate volumes of a particular work. Unsigned reviews were written by the editors. Complete bibliographic and ordering information is provided for each title. Prices for all titles have been updated to December 1980, and those citations lacking price information are presumed to be out of print. References to reviews published in periodicals (e.g., *Library Journal, Wilson Library Bulletin,* etc.) are appended to the reviews.

Although this is a selection of "best reference books," critical comments provided in the original ARBA reviews have been retained. Thus, this volume follows the same policy as ARBA, providing critical appraisals of the titles, since even superior works may be deficient in one respect or another. In many cases, the reviews evaluate and compare a work in relation to other titles of a similar nature.

We wish to express our gratitude to the many ARBA contributors whose reviews appear in *Best Reference Books*. The contributors and their affiliations are listed on the pages following this introduction. We would also like to thank the following members of the Libraries Unlimited staff for contributing their talents to this volume: Judy Caraghar, Mary Alice Deveny, Beverley Hanson, Janet Littlefield, Robynn Moon, Melissa Mullins, Louise Stwalley, and Stephanie Van Bogart.

Susan Holte
Bohdan S. Wynar

CONTRIBUTORS

RICHARD G. AKEROYD, JR., Asst. City Librarian and Director of Public Services, Denver Public Library, CO

WALTER C. ALLEN, Assoc. Professor, Graduate School of Library Science, Univ. of Illinois, Urbana

RAO ALURI, Division of Librarianship, Emory Univ., Atlanta, GA

MOHAMMED M. AMAN, Dean, School of Library Science, Univ. of Wisconsin, Milwaukee

ROBERT H. AMUNDSON, Dept. of Sociology/Anthropology, Loretto Heights College, Denver, CO

FRANK J. ANDERSON, Director, Sandor Teszler Library, Wofford College, Spartanburg, SC

MARGARET ANDERSON, Assoc. Professor, Faculty of Library Science, Univ. of Toronto

CHARLES R. ANDREWS, Dean of Library Services, Hofstra Univ., Hempstead, NY

MARTIN ANDREWS, Dept. of Psychology, St. Johns Univ., Collegeville, MN

THEODORA ANDREWS, Pharmacy, Nursing, and Health Sciences Librarian, and Professor of Library Science, Purdue Univ., West Lafayette, IN

HENRY T. ARMISTEAD, Head, Collection Development, Scott Memorial Library, Thomas Jefferson Univ., Philadelphia

ANDY ARMITAGE, Director, Owen Sound Public Library, Owen Sound, ON

JUDITH ARMSTRONG, Director, Walker Library, Drury College, Springfield, MO

PAULINE A. ATHERTON, Professor, School of Information Studies, Syracuse Univ., NY

THEODORE M. AVERY, JR., formerly of Brooklyn Public Library, NY

DORIS H. BANKS, Public Services Librarian, Whitworth College, Spokane, WA

CHARLA LEIBENGUTH BANNER, Science Librarian, Butler Univ., Indianapolis, IN

MARY A. BANNER, College of Library Science, Univ. of Kentucky, Lexington

GARY D. BARBER, Coordinator of Reference Services, Daniel A. Reed Library, State Univ. College, Fredonia, NY

JOYCE L. BARNUM, Reference Division, Univ. of Washington Library, Seattle

THOMAS BAUHS, Dept. of Learning Resources, Northwest Missouri State Univ., Maryville

JANE A. BENSON, Reference Librarian, Kent State Univ. Libraries, Kent, OH

ROBERT C. BERRING, Assoc. Librarian, Harvard Law Library, Cambridge, MA

JULIE BICHTELER, Assoc. Professor, Graduate School of Library Science, Univ. of Texas, Austin

ALEXANDER S. BIRKOS, General Manager, Mercury Book Co., Mount Shasta, CA

FAY M. BLAKE, School of Library and Information Science, Univ. of California, Berkeley

RON BLAZEK, Assoc. Professor, School of Library Science, Florida State Univ., Tallahassee

JAMES E. BOBICK, Coordinator of Science Libraries, Temple Univ., Philadelphia

NANCY G. BOLES, Curator of Manuscripts, Maryland Historical Society, Baltimore

PEGGY CLOSSEY BOONE, Librarian, Joseph A. Leonard Jr. High School, Old Town, ME

VLADIMIR T. BOROVANSKY, Arizona State Univ. Library, Tempe

WILLIAM BRACE, Assoc. Professor, Graduate School of Library Science, Rosary College, River Forest, IL

PAUL BREED, Univ. Bibliographer, Wayne State Univ., Detroit, MI

DEBORAH JANE BREWER, Managing Editor, Plastics Design Forum, Denver, CO

DAVID W. BRUNTON, Englewood, CO

CHARLES R. BRYANT, Curator, Southeast Asia Collection, Yale Univ., New Haven, CT

RICHARD M. BUCK, Asst. to the Chief, Performing Arts Research Center, New York Public Library at Lincoln Center

CHESTER S. BUNNELL, Law Library, Univ. of Mississippi, University

HELEN M. BURNS, formerly Chief Law Librarian, Federal Reserve Bank of New York

JOAN E. BURNS, Principal Art Librarian, Art and Music Dept., Public Library of Newark, NJ

LOIS BUTTLAR, Asst. to the Director, Center for the Study of Ethnic Publications, Kent State Univ., OH

HANS E. BYNAGLE, Director of Library and Asst. Professor of Philosophy, Friends Univ., Wichita, KS

JERRY CAO, Asst. Professor, School of Library Science, Univ. of Southern California, Los Angeles

DAVID R. CARAGHAR, associated with Associated Landscape Contractors of Colorado and American Landscape Contractors Assoc., Englewood

JUDY GAY CARAGHAR, Staff, Libraries Unlimited, Inc.

CAROL JEAN CARLSON, Manager, Publications Center, Travenol Laboratories, Morton Grove, IL

GENEVIEVE M. CASEY, Professor, Division of Library Science, Wayne State Univ., Detroit, MI

JEFFERSON D. CASKEY, Professor of Library Science and Instructional Media, Western Kentucky Univ., Bowling Green

JOSEPH H. CATAIO, Chicago, IL

RAFAEL CATALA, Hampton, NJ

RICHARD R. CENTING, English, Communications & Theatre Graduate Library, Ohio State Univ., Columbus

FRANCES NEEL CHENEY, Professor Emeritus, School of Library Science, George Peabody College for Teachers, Nashville, TN

JOSEPH J. CHOUINARD, Music Librarian, Reed Library, State Univ. College, Fredonia, NY

DONALD B. CLEVELAND, Assoc. Professor, School of Library and Information Sciences, North Texas State Univ., Denton

CECIL F. CLOTFELTER, Asst. Director, Eastern New Mexico Univ. Library, Portales

MARY CLOTFELTER, Instructor, Library Science, Eastern New Mexico Univ., Portales

HARRIETTE M. CLUXTON, Director of Medical Library Services, Noah van Cleef Medical Memorial Library, Illinois Masonic Medical Center, Chicago

CHARLES WM. CONAWAY, School of Library Science, Florida State Univ., Tallahassee

PAUL B. CORS, Collection Development Librarian, Univ. of Wyoming Library, Laramie

JAMES R. CRAWFORD, Free-lance writer, Chicago

MILTON H. CROUCH, Asst. Director for Reader Services, Bailey/Howe Library, Univ. of Vermont, Burlington

ROYLENE G. CUNNINGHAM, Santa Paula Memorial Hospital, Santa Paula, CA

KATHERINE CVELJO, Assoc. Professor, School of Library and Information Science, North Texas State Univ., Denton

WILLIAM J. DANE, Supervising Art and Music Librarian, Public Library of Newark, NJ

DONALD G. DAVIS, JR., Assoc. Professor, Graduate School of Library Science, Univ. of Texas, Austin

DOMINIQUE-RENÉ DE LERMA, Professor of Music, Morgan State Univ., Baltimore, MD

ADRIAAN DE WIT, Assoc. Professor of French, Kent State Univ., Kent, OH

WINIFRED F. DEAN, Reference/Bibliographer, Social Sciences, Cleveland State Univ. Libraries, OH

ELIE M. DICK, Marketing Planning Supervisor, 3M Company, St. Paul, MN

RUTH DIEBOLD, Finkelstein Memorial Library, Spring Valley, NY

ROBERT K. DIKEMAN, Asst. Professor, Division of Library Science, San Jose State Univ., CA

AMITY DOERING, Reference and Information Librarian, Free Library of Philadelphia

PETER DOIRON, Woodbridge Public Library, NJ

LAMIA DOUMATO, National Gallery of Art, Library and Study Center, Washington, DC

RONALD F. DOW, Director, Graduate Business School Library, New York Univ.

JEROME DROST, Assoc. Librarian, Lockwood Library, State Univ. of New York, Buffalo

PAUL Z. DuBOIS, Director, Trenton State College Library, NJ

SUSAN EBERSHOFF-COLES, Librarian (Supervisor of Technical Services), Indianapolis-Marion County Public Library, IN

DAVID EGGENBERGER, Director, Publications, U.S. National Archives and Records Service, Washington, DC

DONALD L. EHRESMANN, Assoc. Professor, History of Architecture and Art, Univ. of Illinois, Chicago

JULIA M. EHRESMANN, Instructor, William Rainey Harper College, Palatine, IL

JOHN W. EICHENSEHER, Asst. Professor of Accounting, Univ. of Illinois, Urbana

DONALD EMPSON, Reference Librarian, Minnesota Historical Society, St. Paul

JONATHON ERLEN, History of Medicine Librarian and Asst. Professor, Univ. of Texas Health Science Center, Dallas

JUDITH ANN ERLEN, Assoc. Professor of Nursing, Texas Woman's Univ., Dallas

G. EDWARD EVANS, Professor, Graduate School of Library and Information Science, Univ. of California, Los Angeles

MARY ANN MILLS-EVANS, Englewood, CO

CHARLES FARLEY, Kansas City Public Library, MO

ADELE M. FASICK, Professor, Faculty of Library Science, Univ. of Toronto

VALMAI FENSTER, Asst. Professor, Library School, Univ. of Wisconsin, Madison

P. WILLIAM FILBY, formerly Director, Maryland Historical Society, Baltimore

DONALD D. FOOS, Staff, Libraries Unlimited, Inc.

GREGORY T. FOUTS, Asst. Professor, Dept. of Psychology, Univ. of Denver, CO

NORMAN FRANKEL, Library Science Librarian, Western Michigan Univ., Kalamazoo

CAROLE FRANKLIN, Music Librarian, Pennsylvania State Univ., University Park

MICHAEL STUART FREEMAN, Chief, Reference Services, Dartmouth College Library, Hanover, NH

STEPHEN M. FRY, Head, Music Library, Schoenberg Hall, Univ. of California, Los Angeles

BETTY GAY, Asst. to Central Library Director, Los Angeles Public Library, CA

PRISCILLA C. GEAHIGAN, Asst. Management and Economics Librarian, Krannert Library, Purdue Univ., West Lafayette, IN

JUDITH G. GERBER, Solar Energy Research Institute, Golden, CO

EDWIN S. GLEAVES, Chair, Department of Library Science, George Peabody College, Vanderbilt Univ., Nashville, TN

RUTH I. GORDON, Director, IMC-Library Services, Lassen County, CA

FRANK WM. GOUDY, Asst. Professor, Univ. Libraries, Western Illinois Univ., Macomb

RICHARD A. GRAY, Louisville, KY

SUZANNE K. GRAY, Coordinator of Science, Boston Public Library, MA

RICHARD W. GREFRATH, Reference Librarian, Univ. of Nevada Library, Reno

HELEN GREGORY, Children's Librarian, Albion Public Library, Albion, MI

LAUREL GROTZINGER, Dean, Graduate College, and Chief Research Officer, Western Michigan Univ., Kalamazoo

LEONARD GRUNDT, Professor, A. Holly Patterson Library, Nassau Community College, Garden City, NY

LAURA GUTIÉRREZ-WITT, Head Librarian, Benson Collection, Univ. of Texas, Austin

RICHARD P. HALGIN, Dept. of Psychology, Univ. of Massachusetts, Amherst

EDWARD J. HALL, JR., Asst. Professor of Library Administration, Kent State Univ., OH

ELIZABETH C. HALL, Senior Librarian, The Horticultural Society of New York

THOMAS S. HARDING, Librarian Emeritus, Washburn Univ. of Topeka, KS

ROBERT D. HARLAN, Professor, School of Library and Information Studies, Univ. of California, Berkeley

PATRICIA C. HARPOLE, Chief, Reference Library, Minnesota Historical Society, St. Paul

CHAUNCY D. HARRIS, Samuel N. Harper Distinguished Service Professor of Geography, Univ. of Chicago

MICHAEL H. HARRIS, Professor, College of Library Science, Univ. of Kentucky, Lexington

RUTH DAHLGREN HARTMAN, Dept. of Librarianship, Central Washington Univ., Ellensburg

ANN J. HARWELL, Toronto, ON

JOY HASTINGS, Manager, Information Center, Hunt-Wesson Foods, Fullerton, CA

ROBERT J. HAVLIK, Univ. Engineering Librarian, Univ. of Notre Dame, Notre Dame, IN

CAROLYN J. HENDERSON, Asst. Library Personnel Officer, Stanford Univ. Library School, CA

ROSEMARY HENDERSON, Director, Learning Resources, Coffeyville Community Jr. College, KS

PETER HERNON, Asst. Professor, School of Library and Information Science, Simmons College, Boston, MA

DORALYN J. HICKEY, Professor, School of Library and Information Sciences, North Texas State Univ., Denton

JAMES M. HILLARD, Librarian, Citadel Memorial Library, Charleston, SC

GEORGE V. HODOWANEC, Director, William Allen White Library, Emporia State Univ., Emporia, KS

SUSAN C. HOLTE, Staff, Libraries Unlimited, Inc.

JIMMIE H. HOOVER, Head, Government Documents Dept., Louisiana State Univ. Library, Baton Rouge

SHIRLEY L. HOPKINSON, Professor, Library Science, California State Univ., San Jose

BARBARA M. HOWES, Asst. Science Librarian, Butler Univ., Indianapolis, IN

SAMUEL T. HUANG, McKusick Law Library, Univ. of South Dakota, Vermillion

DAVID ISAAK, General Librarian, Univ. of Victoria, Victoria, BC

JOHN C. JAHODA, Assoc. Professor of Biology, Bridgewater State College, MA

PEGGY JAY, Instructor, National College of Business-Denver Extension, CO

MAGGIE JOHNSON, Coordinator, Government Documents Div., Missouri State Library, Jefferson City

ROGER A. JONES, Trade Documentation Adviser, International Trade Centre, New York, NY

IVAN L. KALDOR, Professor, School of Library and Information Science, State Univ. of New York, Geneseo

MARGARET KAMINSKI, Public Relations Dept., Detroit Public Library, MI

DORIS FLAX KAPLAN, Reference Dept., Univ. of Maine at Orono

THOMAS A. KAREL, Reference Librarian, Rider College Library, Lawrenceville, NJ
SHARAD KARKHANIS, Professor, Kingsborough Community College, Brooklyn, NY
DEAN H. KELLER, Head, Special Collections, Kent State Univ. Libraries, OH
RICHARD J. KELLY, Asst. Professor and Asst. Reference Head, Univ. of Minnesota Library,
    Minneapolis
BARBARA E. KEMP, Asst. Head, Undergraduate Library, Univ. of Michigan, Ann Arbor
MICHAEL KERESZTESI, Assoc. Professor of Library Science, Wayne State Univ., Detroit
MARTIN KESSELMAN, Science Librarian, Bobst Library, New York Univ.
EUGENE L. KEYSER, Denver, CO
LOUIS KIRALDI, Dwight B. Waldo Library, Western Michigan Univ., Kalamazoo
BRETT A. KIRKPATRICK, Acting Librarian, New York Academy of Medicine, NY
PHILIP H. KITCHENS, Engineering Librarian, Univ. of Alabama, University
SARAH E. KUHLMAN, formerly Staff, Libraries Unlimited, Inc.
SUSAN BEVERLY KUKLIN, Director of Law Library and Asst. Professor of Law, DePaul
    College of Law, Chicago, IL
COLBY H. KULLMAN, Dept. of English, Univ. of Kansas, Lawrence
MARY LARSGAARD, Map Librarian, Arthur Lakes Library, Colorado School of Mines, Golden
NORMAN LEDERER, Lower Columbia College, Longview, WA
DONALD J. LEHNUS, Assoc. Professor, Graduate School of Library and Information
    Sciences, Univ. of Mississippi, University
DOROTHY E. LITT, Flushing, NY
DAVID W. LITTLEFIELD, Subject Cataloging Director, Processing Dept., Library of Congress,
    Washington, DC
JANET H. LITTLEFIELD, Staff, Libraries Unlimited, Inc.
KOERT C. LOOMIS, JR., Denver, CO
JAY K. LUCKER, Director of Libraries, Massachusetts Institute of Technology, Cambridge
DEBORAH S. LUECK, Englewood, CO
H. ROBERT MALINOWSKY, Assoc. Dean of Libraries, Univ. of Kansas, Lawrence
CHARLES W. MANN, Special Collections, Pennsylvania State Univ. Library, University Park
EDWARD MAPP, Dean of Faculty, Borough of Manhattan Community College, City Univ. of
    New York
BARBARA MARCONI, Hiawathaland Library Cooperative, Sault Sainte Marie, MI
LORRAINE MATHIES, Head, Education and Psychology Library, Univ. of California, Los Angeles
GEORGE LOUIS MAYER, Senior Principal Librarian, Library and Museum of the Performing
    Arts, New York Public Library
THERESA MAYLONE, Information Specialist, General Foods, White Plains, NY
STEVEN J. MAYOVER, Head, Films Dept., Northeast Regional Library, Free Library of
    Philadelphia, PA
JAMES P. McCABE, Librarian, Allentown College of Saint Francis De Sales Library, Center
    Valley, PA
KATHRYN McCHESNEY, Asst. Professor, School of Library Science, Kent State Univ., OH
STANLEY JOE McCORD, Director, Univ. of Houston Victoria Campus Library, Victoria College,
    Victoria, TX
KATHLEEN McCULLOUGH, Bibliographer, School of Humanities, Social Science and Education,
    and Assoc. Professor of Library Science, Purdue Univ., West Lafayette, IN
JOSEPH McDONALD, Doctoral candidate, Drexel Univ., Philadelphia
LAURA H. McGUIRE, Documents Librarian, Eastern New Mexico Univ. Library, Portales
GIL McNAMEE, Head, Business Library, San Francisco Public Library, CA
SHIRLEY MILLER, Reference Librarian, Kalamazoo Public Library, MI
JOSEPH H. MOREHEAD, Assoc. Professor, School of Library and Information Sciences,
    State Univ. of New York, Albany
JOHN MORGAN, Reference Librarian, Univ. of Toledo, OH
WALTER L. NEWSOME, Documents Librarian, Univ. of Virginia Library, Charlottesville
GAIL M. NICHOLS, International and Foreign Documents Librarian, Univ. of California, Berkeley
SUZINE HAR NICOLESCU, Dept. of Library Science, Medgar Evers College, Brooklyn, NY
ERIC R. NITSCHKE, Reference Librarian, Robert W. Woodruff Library, Emory Univ.,
    Atlanta, GA
CLEON ROBERT NIXON, III, Free-lance writer, Platteville, WI
MARGARET NORDEN, Reference Librarian, Falk Library of the Health Professions, Univ. of
    Pittsburgh, PA
DENNIS NORTH, Head Librarian, Regis Educational Corp., Denver, CO
MARSHALL E. NUNN, Reference Librarian, Glendale Community College, CA

JEANNE OSBORN, Professor, School of Library Science, Univ. of Iowa, Iowa City
HARRY S. OTTERSON, JR., Buffalo, NY
ELLIOT S. PALAIS, Reference Librarian, Arizona State Univ. Library, Tempe
ROBERTA R. PALEN, Head, Documents Div., Univ. Library, Texas A&M Univ., College Station
MAUREEN PASTINE, Head, Undergraduate Library, Univ. of Illinois, Urbana
DEBORAH PEARSON, Asst. Librarian and Instructor, Lancaster Library, Longwood College, Farmville, VA
JAVIER PEÑALOSA, Asst. Professor of Biology, Boston Univ., MA
SHARON S. PETERSON, San Diego, CA
MIRIAM POLLET, Head, Reference Dept., Downstate Medical Center Library, Brooklyn, NY
NANCY J. PRUETT, Head, Geology-Geophysics Library, Univ. of California, Los Angeles
GARY R. PURCELL, Professor, Graduate School of Library and Information Science, Univ. of Tennessee, Knoxville
RANDY RAFFERTY, Asst. Professor and Humanities Reference Librarian, Mississippi State Univ. Library, Mississippi State
F. W. RAMEY, Staff, Libraries Unlimited, Inc.
MARGERY READ, Maine Hospital Assoc., Castine
BARBARA A. RICE, Coordinator, Bibliographic Development, State Univ. of New York, Albany
JOHN V. RICHARDSON, JR., Asst. Professor, Graduate School of Library and Information Science, Univ. of California, Los Angeles
EDWARD A. RICHTER, Reference Librarian, Eastern New Mexico Univ., Portales
PHILIP R. RIDER, Instructor of English, Northern Illinois Univ., DeKalb
JOHN R. RITER, JR., Dept. of Chemistry, Univ. of Denver, CO
WILLIAM C. ROBINSON, Assoc. Professor, Graduate School of Library and Information Science, Univ. of Tennessee, Knoxville
A. ROBERT ROGERS, Dean, School of Library Science, Kent State Univ., OH
JIM ROGINSKI, Marketing Director, Children's Books, G. P. Putnam's Sons, Coward-McCann, New York
DAVID ROSENBAUM, Reference Librarian, Education Library, G. Flint Purdy Library, Wayne State Univ., Detroit, MI
JUDITH ROSENBERG, formerly Children's Librarian, Ayers Branch, Akron Public Library, OH
KENYON C. ROSENBERG, Chief, Input Processing Division, U.S. Dept. of Commerce, National Technical Information Service, Springfield, VA
RICHARD H. ROSICHAN, Director, Heed Univ. Library, Hollywood, FL
STEVE RYBICKI, Center Campus Library, Macomb County Community College, Mount Clemens, MI
JULIA SABINE, formerly Special Asst. to the Director, Munson-Williams-Proctor Institute, Utica, NY
LINDA SCHALLAN, Researcher, *People's Almanac*, Santa Monica, CA
WILLIAM Z. SCHENCK, Head, Acquisitions Dept., Wilson Library, Univ. of North Carolina, Chapel Hill
R. G. SCHIPF, Science Librarian, Univ. of Montana, Missoula
SYD SCHOENWETTER, formerly Bird Cinematographer and Recordist, Brooklyn, NY
LORRAINE SCHULTE, Corporate Technical Library, Upjohn Company, Kalamazoo, MI
ELEANOR ELVING SCHWARTZ, Assoc. Professor, Coordinator, Library/Media Program, Dept. of Communication Sciences, Kean College of New Jersey, Union
LeROY C. SCHWARZKOPF, Government Documents Librarian, McKeldin Library, Univ. of Maryland, College Park
RALPH L. SCOTT, Reference Librarian — Bibliographer, East Carolina Univ. Library, Greenville, NC
ROBERT A. SEAL, Director for Administrative Services, Univ. of Virginia Library, Charlottesville
LILLIAN L. SHAPIRO, School Library Consultant, New York, NY
JANET SHEETS, Reference Dept., Baylor Univ. Library, Waco, TX
GERALD R. SHIELDS, Asst. Dean, School of Information and Library Studies, State Univ. of New York, Buffalo
BRUCE A. SHUMAN, Assoc. Professor, Dept. of Library Science, Queens College, Flushing, NY
JACQUELINE D. SISSON (d.), Head, Fine Arts Library and Assoc. Professor, Ohio State Univ., Columbus
MARY R. SIVE, Editor, *Media Monitor*, Pearl River, NY
ANN SKENE-MELVIN, Toronto, ON

DAVID SKENE-MELVIN, Publications Coordinator, Historical Planning and Research Branch, Ministry of Culture and Recreation, Toronto

STANLEY J. SLOTE, Library Consultant, White Plains, NY

SALLY S. SMALL, Head Librarian, Berks Campus, Pennsylvania State Univ., Reading

ROMAINE S. SOMERVILLE, Director, Maryland Historical Society Library, Baltimore

MILUSE SOUDEK, Subject Specialist for Psychology/Philosophy, and Assoc. Professor, Northern Illinois Univ. Libraries, DeKalb

LAWRENCE E. SPELLMAN, Curator of Maps, Princeton Univ. Library, NJ

BERNARD SPILKA, Dept. of Psychology, Univ. of Denver, CO

JOSEPH W. SPRUG, Library Director, St. Edward's Univ., Austin, TX

LEE STEINBERG, Asst. Branch Librarian, Williamsburgh Branch, Brooklyn Public Library, NY

JERRY E. STEPHENS, Assoc. Law Librarian, Univ. of Kansas, Lawrence

NORMAN D. STEVENS, Univ. Librarian, Univ. of Connecticut, Storrs

ROLLAND E. STEVENS, Professor, Graduate School of Library Science, Univ. of Illinois, Urbana

ARTHUR H. STICKNEY, Merrick, NY

ESTHER F. STINEMAN, formerly Librarian-at-Large for Women's Studies, Memorial Library, Univ. of Wisconsin, Madison

LEON J. STOUT, Pennsylvania State Collection Archivist, Pattee Library, Pennsylvania State Univ., University Park

LOUISE STWALLEY, Staff, Libraries Unlimited, Inc.

SUSAN F. SUDDUTH, Librarian/Marketing Analyst, IMA, Inc., Sherman Oaks, CA

NORMAN E. TANIS, Director of Libraries, California State Univ., Northridge

D. BERNARD THEALL, Assoc. Professor of Library Science, Catholic Univ. of America, Washington, DC

DENNIS THOMISON, Assoc. Professor, Dept. of Library Science, Univ. of Southern California, Los Angeles

LAWRENCE S. THOMPSON, Professor of Classics, Classics Dept., Univ. of Kentucky, Lexington

SUSAN THORPE, Zionsville, IN

BRUCE H. TIFFNEY, Dept. of Biology, Yale Univ., New Haven, CT

ANDREW G. TOROK, Asst. Professor, Dept. of Library Science, Northern Illinois Univ., DeKalb

PEGGY M. TOZER, Director, Library, Eastern New Mexico Univ., Portales

DEAN TUDOR, Chairman, Library Arts Dept., Ryerson Polytechnical Institute, Toronto

ROBERT F. VAN BENTHUYSEN, Library Director, Guggenheim Memorial Library, Monmouth College, West Long Branch, NJ

BARBARA VAN DEVENTER, State Documents Librarian, Stanford Univ. Libraries, CA

ALBERT C. VARA, Asst. Librarian, Business Library, Temple Univ., Philadelphia

KATHLEEN J. VOIGT, Head, Reference Dept., Carlson Library, Univ. of Toledo, OH

ROBERT L. WAGNER, Reference and Information Librarian, Free Library of Philadelphia

MARY JO WALKER, University Archivist and Special Collections Librarian, Eastern New Mexico Univ., Portales

DEDERICK C. WARD, Geology Librarian, Univ. of Illinois, Urbana

HANS H. WEBER, Library Consultant, Riverside, CA

HARRY WEIHS, Principal, Quan, Carruthers, King & Quan Consultants, Toronto

ROBERT L. WELKER, Professor and Chairman of the English Dept., Univ. of Alabama, Huntsville

ERWIN K. WELSCH, Social Studies Bibliographer, Memorial Library, Univ. of Wisconsin, Madison

JOHN ROBERT WHEAT, Reference Librarian, Austin Public Library, TX

WAYNE A. WIEGAND, Asst. Professor, College of Library Science, Univ. of Kentucky, Lexington

JOHN G. WILLIAMSON, Director, St. Mary's College of Maryland Library, St. Mary's City

PAUL A. WINCKLER, Professor, Palmer Graduate Library School, Long Island Univ., NY

GLENN R. WITTIG, Ph.D. candidate, School of Library Science, Univ. of Michigan, Ann Arbor

FRANCIS J. WITTY, Professor, Dept. of Library Science, Catholic Univ. of America, Washington, DC

MARDA WOODBURY, Research Ventures, Berkeley, CA

JOAN H. WORLEY, Reference Librarian, Univ. of Tennessee, Knoxville

IRVING WORTIS, Humanities Librarian, Trenton State College, NJ

KIETH C. WRIGHT, Chairman, Library Science/Educational Technology Division, School of Education, Univ. of North Carolina, Greensboro

ANNA T. WYNAR, Program Officer, Handicapped Student Services, Kent State Univ., OH

BOHDAN S. WYNAR, President, Libraries Unlimited, Inc., Littleton, CO

CHRISTINE GEHRT WYNAR, President, Corona Press, Littleton, CO

LUBOMYR R. WYNAR, Professor, School of Library Science, and Director, Program for the Study of Ethnic Publications in the United States, Kent State Univ., OH

SALLY WYNKOOP, Manager of Marketing and Information Services, Revenue Sharing Advisory Service, Washington, DC

VIRGINIA E. YAGELLO, Head, Chemistry and Physics Libraries, Ohio State Univ., Columbus

A. NEIL YERKEY, Asst. Professor, School of Information and Library Studies, State Univ. of New York, Buffalo

WILLIAM C. YOUNG (d.), Author, Lawrence, KS

SAMIR M. ZOGHBY, Asst. Head, African Section, Library of Congress, Washington, DC

JOURNALS CITED

FORM OF CITATION	JOURNAL TITLE
BL	Booklist
Choice	Choice
C&RL	College & Research Libraries
JAL	Journal of Academic Librarianship
LJ	Library Journal
RQ	RQ
SLJ	School Library Journal
WLB	Wilson Library Bulletin

1 GENERAL REFERENCE WORKS

BIBLIOGRAPHY

BIBLIOGRAPHIC GUIDES

1. **Books in Series in the United States.** 2nd ed. New York, R. R. Bowker, 1979. 3273p. $57.50. LC 76-41665. ISBN 0-8352-1081-2. ISSN 0000-0515.

This well-received reference source is substantially larger than the first edition (1977), where inclusion was limited to the years 1966-1975. With the date of publication no longer a criterion for inclusion, the second edition provides a much-needed retrospective coverage for all known series (with the exception of series intended for children, elementary and high school textbooks in series, U.S. government publications unless reprinted by a trade publisher, and certain categories of publishers series as defined in "criteria for inclusion" in the preface). Reprints and most publishers' series are included.

The three basic sections, a series index (alphabetical by series title, then by series number), an author index, and a title index (individual volume title), are followed by a subject index to series and a listing of publishers' abbreviations (with addresses). *Books in Series*, providing access to some 113,000 titles in 10,837 series issued by 1,270 publishers, far surpasses E. Baer's *Titles in Series*, 3rd ed. (Scarecrow, 1978. 4v. $95.00/set) in coverage, especially of U.S. imprints. [R: ARBA 80, p. 1; LJ, 1 June 79, p. 1243]

2. Sheehy, Eugene P., comp. **Guide to Reference Books.** 9th ed. With the assistance of Rita G. Keckeissen and Eileen McIlvaine. Chicago, American Library Association, 1976. 1015p. index. $30.00. LC 76-11751. ISBN 0-8389-0205-7.

3. Sheehy, Eugene P., ed. **Guide to Reference Books, Ninth Edition: First Supplement.** Chicago, American Library Association, 1980. 305p. index. $15.00pa. LC 79-20541. ISBN 0-8389-0294-4.

The ninth edition of *Guide to Reference Books* provides some 10,000 entries—an increase of 2,500 over the eighth edition. Most entries conform to those appearing on Library of Congress printed cards, and Library of Congress class marks are supplied with the entries when these appeared on the printed cards. There are also a few changes in arrangement and coverage. The "Societies" section has been eliminated, and much of the material from this section has been absorbed into the subsection "Associations, Societies, and Academies" under "Social Sciences." In the "Literature" section, individual author bibliographies and concordances are less extensively covered, being limited now only to major literary figures. This change is justified in the preface by mention of today's proliferation of both types of reference works.

For all practical purposes the cut-off date is 1973, and the compiler notes that "the total number of 1974 items included is disappointingly small" (p. x). Mr. Sheehy also indicates that "with Miss Winchell's gracious permission, much of the text of the previous edition is used without alteration. Although additions and changes have been made wherever they were necessary or deemed helpful, many of the annotations have been carried forward unchanged from the eighth edition and its supplements" (p. ix). No special search was made for reprint editions, which means that "reprints are listed if they are in the collections of the Columbia University Libraries or if Library of Congress cards for reprint editions were encountered in the verification process" (p. x).

To these general introductory comments provided in the preface we might add that this edition omits citations to reviews, although there is no explanation of why this practice was dropped. A significant number of annotations and bibliographical citations carry over errors from previous supplements or the eighth edition, and one also occasionally finds new errors. Apparently in order to accommodate more titles, many of the annotations are brief—sometimes to the point of being meaningless; and the greater part of them are descriptive rather than evaluative.

The ninth edition is printed on paper of good quality, margins are wide, and the book lies flat when opened. The index was found to be reliable. In spite of its several shortcomings, Mr. Sheehy's edition adequately maintains the long tradition of *Guide to Reference Books*, and this work can be safely recommended for libraries of all types. It will serve the uninitiated rather well.

Ed. note: The first *Supplement* to the ninth edition updates the material to October 1978, including new publications between 1974 and 1978 and those earlier noted as "in progress," and attempts to include works omitted from the basic *Guide*. The structure is identical to the basic work. Coverage is proportionate to the output of publishers during the period 1974-1978, and an increase in titles on women, ethnic groups, blacks, energy, film, and the American Revolution reflects changing emphases in publication concerns during that time span. Most practices followed by the *Guide* are repeated in the *Supplement*. The *Supplement* differs from the *Guide* in providing approximate price information and relying heavily on CIP information for entries, rather than LC printed cards. It remains a disturbing fact that the standard *Guide to Reference Books* lags behind the actual publication of reference materials by about two years. [R: ARBA 77, p. 3; C&RL, May 77, p. 262; Choice, June 77, p. 516; JAL, Mar 77, p. 37; LJ, 15 Dec 76, p. 2560; WLB, Jan 77, p. 442; BL, 15 Apr 80, p. 1177]   Arthur H. Stickney
                                                                  Bohdan S. Wynar

4. Walford, A. J., ed. **Guide to Reference Material: Volume 1, Science and Technology.** 3rd ed. London, The Library Association; distr., New York, R. R. Bowker, 1973. 615p. index.

5. Walford, A. J., ed. **Guide to Reference Material: Volume 2, Social & Historical Sciences, Philosophy & Religion.** 3rd ed. London, The Library Association; distr., Chicago, American Library Association, 1975. 647p. index. $35.00. ISBN 0-85365-088-8.

6. Walford, A. J., ed. **Guide to Reference Material: Volume 3, Generalities, Languages, the Arts and Literature.** 3rd ed. London, The Library Association; distr., Chicago, American Library Association, 1977. 710p. index. $35.00. ISBN 0-85365-409-3.

The three volumes comprising Walford's third edition of this standard British counterpart to the American *Guide to Reference Books*, now edited by Eugene P. Sheehy (see the preceding entry), were published sequentially in 1973, 1975, and 1977. Totalled, the Walford volumes provide main entries for some 13,000-plus books with some 1,000 "subsumed entries"—works that are mentioned in the annotations and given access through the index. From a *Booklist* sampling it can be estimated that some 13% of the cited books were published in the United States, 31% in the United Kingdom, 5% were joint U.S.-United Kingdom publications, and the remaining 51% were published in other countries. The bibliographic citations routinely contain UDC numbers and the price in pounds. The normal annotation in Walford is descriptive, not critical, lengthier than the average annotation in Sheehy, and frequently contains references to other works and to journal reviews of the item. There are inter-volume cross references from volumes 2 and 3 to preceding volumes in the set. Each volume has a subject index and an author-title index. The third volume has a cumulated subject index, but no cumulated author-title index.

Walford has a better balance of selection and a more comprehensive coverage than Sheehy. The quantity of American publications included is comparable, but coverage of British, European, and foreign imprints is far stronger in Walford. It is also stronger on more recent titles. There is much duplication between the works, but there are also important differences in selection. Walford's annotations are longer and more descriptive than Sheehy's, but are marred by frequent factual and typographical errors—especially for non-British imprints. Sheehy's work is much more accurate. The indexes for Walford are unhappily deficient. The title index is an index only to title main entries; there is no access to other kinds of titles. Added entries for editors are often missed. The subject index provides only the sketchiest kind of subject access. Index reference is only to page number, which especially increases the difficulty in locating indexed "subsumed entries," which are buried in the body of the annotations. Missed index references are frequent. There is no cumulated index to authors or titles. Sheehy's index is exemplary by comparison.

In summary, Sheehy and Walford ought to be regarded as complementary works, each having certain strengths that help to make up for the deficiencies of the other.

Ed. note: The new fourth edition of volume 1 (London, The Library Association; distr., Chicago, American Library Association. 697p. index. $55.00) was published in 1980. It contains entries for some 5,000 items, over 1,000 of which are subsumed. Among newer subjects included are biochemistry, environmental pollution, energy, consumer science, microcomputers, and Islamic science. A detailed review of this volume can be found in *American Reference Books Annual 1981* (Littleton, CO, Libraries Unlimited, 1981). Publication of volumes 2 and 3 of the fourth edition is projected for 1982 and 1984, respectively. [R: BL, 15 Dec 73, p. 393; Choice, Dec 73, p. 1536; C&RL, July 74, p. 251; RQ, Winter 73, p. 180; ARBA 77, p. 7; BL, 15 Apr 76, p. 1208; ARBA 79, p. 3]

Arthur H. Stickney

7.   Wynar, Bohdan S., ed. **Reference Books in Paperback: An Annotated Guide.** 2nd ed. Littleton, CO, Libraries Unlimited, 1976. 317p. $15.00. index. LC 76-44238. ISBN 0-87287-166-5.

Prepared as a guide to inexpensive reference materials suitable for home use, school libraries, and public and college libraries, the second edition of *Reference Books in Paperback* selects and describes 715 reference books; an additional 1,500 titles are referred to within the annotations. The topical chapters are arranged alphabetically from agriculture to zoology and are subdivided by type of material. The author-title and subject indexes provide access to all the numbered main entries as well as to the authors and titles mentioned in the annotations.

The guide provides comparisons to related titles in both paperback and hardcover. The 282 text pages of the second edition have been completely reworked to include hundreds of new titles; out-of-print or superseded works have been dropped. The price criterion has been dropped in selecting paperbacks for this edition due to the continuing upward movement of book prices. Some paperbacks with rather substantial prices are now included, yet these editions represent a saving over the cost of the hardcover editions. The third edition of *Reference Books in Paperback*, now in preparation, will provide coverage through 1980. [R: ARBA 77, p. 9; Choice, Apr 77, p. 184; LJ, 15 Dec 76, p. 2560; WLB, Feb 77, p. 541]

NATIONAL AND TRADE BIBLIOGRAPHIES

United States

8.   **American Book Publishing Record Cumulative 1950-1977: An American National Bibliography.** New York, R. R. Bowker, 1978. 15v. index. $1,500.00/set. LC 66-19741. ISBN 0-8352-1094-4. ISSN 0002-7707.

The massive *American Book Publishing Record Cumulative 1950-1977* is not merely a cumulation of 28 years of *ABPR*, but includes thousands of titles from MARC tapes (1968-) and the *National Union Catalog* from 1950-1968. The result is a subject arrangement of over 920,000 books, providing bibliographic and cataloging information for each. The first 10 volumes of the 15-volume set include nonfiction titles arranged by Dewey Decimal Classification numbers. Volume 11 lists adult and juvenile fiction by main entry. Titles not classified by DDC numbers are arranged alphabetically by main entry in volume 12. Author, title, and subject indexes comprise volumes 13, 14, and 15, and complete the set. Whenever available, information included represents Library of Congress cataloging, and lists author, title, publication date and place, publisher, collation, series statement, LC number, DDC number, price (if available), ISBN, and subject tracings and added entries. Each volume also includes a "table of relocations of Dewey Decimal Classifications Numbers" to show changes from the various editions of Dewey used in the past, so that obsolete classifications can be updated.

The set seems to contain very few errors, although occasional misprints do occur. The sections for "Annual Report" and "Report" in the title index contain many useless citations. The computer seemed to have great difficulty alphabetizing titles beginning with numbers — the section involving one thousand (1,000), one hundred (100), and variations thereof is mind-boggling. Twentieth-century dates (1900-1999) and numbers in the nineties suffer the same confusion.

The few shortcomings of the set are far outweighed by the many potential uses. *ABPR Cumulative* will be used in the reference department to find books on a particular subject (the subject index uses LC tracings as headings), more books by a certain author, or just to find out who wrote a certain title. But the set is equally valuable to the cataloging department, especially those unable to afford such tools as the *National Union Catalog* or the *Combined Index to the Library of Congress Classification Schedules*. The cataloging information can be assumed to be reliable, and can be used to convert DDC to LC, to revise outdated cataloging, locate appropriate subject tracings, and a variety of other cataloging tasks. The set will also have applications to interlibrary loan and collection development. Despite the set's seemingly high price, most libraries will find such a variety of uses for *ABPR Cumulative* that it will be a necessary acquisition. [R: ARBA 80, p. 3; BL, 15 July 78, p. 1753; Choice, Nov 79, p. 1147; C&RL, July 79, p. 358; LJ, July 79, p. 1442; RQ, Fall 79, p. 79]   Janet H. Littlefield

9.   **A Checklist of American Imprints, 1820-1829. Title Index. Author Index.** Comp. by M. Frances Cooper. Metuchen, NJ, Scarecrow, 1972, 1973. 562p. 172p. $19.00 (Title Index); $8.00 (Author Index). ISBN 0-8108-0513-8 (Title Index); 0-8108-0567-7 (Author Index).

10.   **A Checklist of American Imprints for 1831: Items 5610-10775.** Scott Bruntjen and Carol Bruntjen, comps. Metuchen, NJ, Scarecrow, 1975. 429p. $17.00. LC 64-11784. ISBN 0-8108-0828-5.

11.   **A Checklist of American Imprints for 1832: Items 10776-17207.** Scott Bruntjen and Carol Bruntjen, comps. Metuchen, NJ, Scarecrow, 1977. 523p. $22.00. LC 64-11784. ISBN 0-8108-1019-0.

12.   **A Checklist of American Imprints for 1833: Items 17208-22795.** Scott Bruntjen and Carol Bruntjen, comps. Metuchen, NJ, Scarecrow, 1979. 478p. $25.00. LC 64-11784. ISBN 0-8108-1191-X.

It has been 22 years since the first volume of *American Imprints*, familiarly known as Shaw and Shoemaker, appeared. The aim of its initial compilers, Ralph Shaw and Richard Shoemaker, was to fill the gap in American national bibliography by continuing the work begun by Charles Evans. Shaw and Shoemaker's first volume, *American Bibliography: A Preliminary Checklist* (1958), covered the year 1801 and their series continued to cover each year through 1819. In 1964, Shaw dropped out of the project and Shoemaker continued the work under the title *Checklist of American Imprints*. As each volume from 1820 to 1825 appeared, Shoemaker modified the original precept of the project, which had been to depend solely upon printed sources and catalogs for compiling entries. This policy had led to numerous duplications of titles and the listing of nonexistent ones. From the 1821 volume and continuing, in addition to noting author, title, place of publication and publisher, selected locations of books were added, and, for rare titles, actual copies were examined. This approach resulted in improved reliability and usefulness of the *Checklist* as a reference tool. Shoemaker died in 1970, before he could complete the volumes for 1828 and 1829. These volumes and that for 1830 were seen through the press by Dr. Gayle Cooper. The series is now in the hands of Scott and Carol Bruntjen. The work will be continued until it covers the years through 1875, when it will be complete.

The *Title Index* for 1820-1829 was compiled by M. Frances Cooper and published in 1972. It affords easy access to the more than 41,000 entries in the *Checklist* for the years covered. The *Author Index*, also compiled by M. Frances Cooper, was published in 1973 and follows the example set by Shaw and Shoemaker in their index to *American Bibliography*. Over 500 corrections deal with duplicate entries, multiple listings, misdatings, etc. The volumes for 1831, 1832, and 1833 follow the format of previous volumes. This series is considered an important tool in American bibliography. [R: Choice, Sept 73, p. 942; ARBA 76, p. 36; Choice, Jan 76, p. 1420; ARBA 78, p. 4; ARBA '80, p. 4]

13.   Shipton, Clifford K., and James E. Mooney. **National Index of American Imprints through 1800: The Short-Title Evans.** Worcester, MA, American Antiquarian Society and Barre Publishers, 1969. 2v. 1028p. $45.00. LC 69-11248. ISBN 0-8271-6908-6.

This compilation is a great boon to all students of American culture. It is a by-product of the Early American Microprint Project, which undertook to reproduce on micro-card all non-serial works printed in America before 1801. The basic guide or index for this project was Charles Evans' *American Bibliography*, which listed 39,162 items for this period. But the percentage of "ghosts" listed by Evans was estimated to be 1 in 10 and, in the intervening years since its publication, an additional 10,035 titles had turned up. The project underlined the need for a less cumbersome and more trustworthy and timely index than that provided by the 13 volumes of Evans. Finally the Microprint cards themselves provided the means by which such an index could be produced.

The *National Index*, handsomely bound on good paper and supervised by the leading authority in the field, is, in essence, an inventory. The compilers' rigid insistence on examining the books directly retired many ghosts and enabled the compilers to correct title mistranscriptions, remove faulty attributions, and incorporate much new information. The 49,197 entries are arranged in a single alphabetical list, including short titles, places of publication, dates, a single location, the Evans number, and, in many cases, a brief note on attributions, imperfect copies, or unlocated items. Of course, more titles will turn up for this period, but "not in Evans" has been superseded by "not in the *National Index*," thus paying tribute to a work which measures up to the standards we associate with the American Antiquarian Society. [R: ARBA 71, pp. 6-7]   Charles W. Mann

14.   Tanselle, G. Thomas. **Guide to the Study of United States Imprints.** Cambridge, MA, Harvard University Press, 1971. 2v. index. $50.00. LC 79-143232. ISBN 0-674-36761-8.

This comprehensive work, prepared in the tradition of McMurtrie's record of American imprints, serves as a standard guide to the study of the principal material dealing with printing and publishing in this country. The material is arranged in nine broad subject categories: regional lists (imprints of particular localities); genre lists (arranged by types, e.g., accounting books, almanacs, architecture books); author lists (subdivided by localities); copyright records; catalogues; book trade directories; and "supplementary studies" listing studies of individual printers and publishers, general studies, and checklists of secondary material. The appendix provides a listing of 250 titles that constitute a basic collection on this subject. As one would expect in a work of this type, the basic approach is chronological, and the bibliographical description of all titles listed is, of course, complete. There is an excellent index to facilitate the use of this work, which should be of interest to many libraries as well as to scholars of American civilization as represented in the printed word. Needless to say, the enormous value of this guide is only emphasized by the fact that, in spite of the great bulk of research in this field during the last decade, there is nothing comparable to this guide, which was prepared in accordance with sound principles of scholarship. [R: ARBA 72, p. 20]   Bohdan S. Wynar

15.   Thompson, Lawrence S., ed. **The New Sabin: Books Described by Joseph Sabin and His Successors, Now Described Again on the Basis of Examination of Originals, and Fully Indexed by Title, Subject, Joint Authors and Institutions and Agencies, Volume I.** Troy, NY, Whitston, 1974. 1v. in 2 pts. $25.00(pt.1); [pt.2-o.p.]. LC 73-85960. ISBN 0-87875-049-5(pt.1).

16.   Thompson, Lawrence S. **The New Sabin: Books Described by Joseph Sabin and His Successors, Now Described Again on the Basis of Examination of Originals, and Fully Indexed by Title, Subject, Joint Authors, and Institutions and Agencies, Volume II.** Troy, NY, Whitston, 1975. 1v. in 2 pts. $25.00(pt.1); [pt.2-o.p.]. LC 73-85960. ISBN 0-87875-060-6(pt.1).

17.   Thompson, Lawrence S. **The New Sabin: Books Described by Joseph Sabin and His Successors, Now Described Again on the Basis of Examination of Originals, and Fully Indexed by Title, Subject, Joint Authors, and Institutions and Agencies, Volume III.** Troy, NY, Whitston, 1976. 1v. in 2 pts. $25.00(pt.1); [pt.2-o.p.]. LC 73-85960. ISBN 0-87875-103-3(pt.1).

18.   Thompson, Lawrence S. **The New Sabin: Books Described by Joseph Sabin and His Successors, Now Described Again on the Basis of Examination of Originals, and Fully Indexed by Title, Subject, Joint Authors, and Institutions and Agencies, Volume IV.** Troy, NY, Whitston, 1977. $25.00. LC 73-85960. ISBN 0-87875-134-3.

19.   Thompson, Lawrence S. **The New Sabin: Books Described by Joseph Sabin and His Successors, Now Described Again on the Basis of Examination of Originals, and Fully Indexed by Title, Subject, Joint Authors, and Institutions and Agencies, Volume V.** Troy,

NY, Whitston, 1979. 2v. $25.00(vol. 5); $30.00(index). LC 73-85960. ISBN 0-87875-153-X(vol. 5); 0-87875-154-8(index).

In 1867 Joseph Sabin inaugurated his monumental *Bibliotheca Americana, a Dictionary of Books Relating to America, from Its Discovery to the Present Time*, a work acknowledged as the most important scholarly enterprise in the history of American bibliography. An immense undertaking, it was not completed until long after Sabin's death in 1936.

The *New Sabin* is a wholly new series of bibliographies, planned as a continuing effort to verify and expand on Sabin's enterprise. The titles in volumes 1-4 have been drawn from various microform sources; volume 5 lists and describes only items from Sabin's work. Each volume is organized alphabetically and stands independently of the other volumes. The entries are in Library of Congress format. A cumulative index to joint author, title, corporate entry, and LC subject headings formed "Part 2" of each of the first three volumes. Those indexes are subsumed in the *Cumulative Index to Entries 1-13513*, which was published contemporaneously with volume 5, but is no longer called "Part 2."

The *New Sabin* is a very ambitious project. Its reliance on the varying decisions of LC cataloging practice imposes inherent limitations (e.g., a lack of geographic subject headings, the inconsistencies that have plagued LC cataloging decisions over the years). In spite of its inability to fully achieve its very ambitious aims, or perhaps even the scholarly standards of the original Sabin, the *New Sabin* provides a major bibliographic resource in American studies and belongs in those institutions engaged in a high level of scholarship in fields that demand access to unusual materials in Americana. [R: C&RL, Jan 75, p. 81; RQ, Spring 75, p. 267; RQ, Winter 76, p. 188; ARBA 77, pp. 11, 12; LJ, July 79, p. 1443]

Arthur H. Stickney

Great Britain

20. **The British Library General Catalogue of Printed Books to 1975, Volume 1: A-ACHEB.** New York, K. G. Saur; London, Clive Bingley, 1979. 509p. $28,440.00/set (standing order); $23,040.00/set (prepaid); $79.00/vol. (standing order); $64.00/vol. (prepaid). LC 79-40543. ISBN 0-85157-520-X(set); 0-85157-521-8(v. 1).

Most larger libraries already have the *General Catalogue of Printed Books*, published by the British Museum (now the British Library) during 1959-66 (photolithographic edition in 263 volumes), as well as the first, second, and third supplements. The present edition of the *General Catalogue* will cumulate in one alphabetical sequence the main set and its supplements, incorporating numerous additions and corrections made by the British Library staff up to February 1979 for the letter "A." According to the introduction, it is hoped that this editorial work will continue ahead of the publishing schedule so that, for example, the letter "Z" will be corrected prior to the anticipated publication of the final volume in 1984. The projected publication schedule is approximately 72 volumes per year, with completion of this large-scale project expected in 1984 or 1985. Approximately 900,000 titles not included in the main set or its supplements will be included in this new edition, and, judging from the first volume, the legibility of the text is much superior to the original edition.

Most larger libraries should welcome this project; it is not as comprehensive as the well-known *National Union Catalog, Pre-1956 Imprints*, but both important catalogs will supplement each other. The publisher is to be congratulated for this ambitious undertaking. It is a very important bibliographic work, reflecting holdings of one of the best collections in the world, and is especially strong in Western European imprints. [R: ARBA 80, p. 7]

Bohdan S. Wynar

21. **Short-Title Catalogue of Books Printed in England, Scotland, & Ireland and of English Books Printed Abroad 1475-1640. Volume 2, I-Z.** 2nd ed., rev. and enl. First comp. by A. W. Pollard and G. R. Redgrave. London, Bibliographical Society; distr., New York, Oxford University Press, 1976. 494p. $135.00pa. ISBN 0-19-721790-7.

22. **Short-Title Catalogue of Books Printed in England, Scotland, Ireland, Wales, and British America and of English Books Printed in Other Countries, 1641-1700, Volume 1.** 2nd rev. and enl. ed. Donald Wing, comp. New York, Modern Language Association of America, 1972. 642p. $80.00. ISBN 0-87352-044-0.

This revision of the indispensable *Short-Title Catalogue* was begun over 25 years ago by William A. Jackson. Upon his death in 1964 his principal assistant, Katharine Pantzer, continued his work and has completed it. Since Jackson's most recent attention had been to the last part of the alphabet, and since Miss Pantzer had personally overseen this later portion of the work, it was decided to issue volume 2 of the revised edition first. Volume 1 is to be published in 1980, and a third volume, containing an index to printers and booksellers and corrections and additions, is promised at a later date.

The original edition of the *Short-Title Catalogue* contained over 26,000 entries; the revised edition adds about 10,000 new entries to that total. Volume 2, the letters I-Z, contains entries 14045.5 through 26143. The form of entry remains much the same as it was in the first edition; up to five locations are given for England and up to five for America, with attention to geographical distribution in each country when selecting locations. Volume 2 contains enough preliminary material to make the work usable, including a list of locations; but volume 1 will contain a detailed statement on the scope of the *Short-Title Catalogue*, will give an account of the elements of transcription and description, and will provide a list of reference books used and alluded to in the text. Volume 1 will also contain an account of the inception and progress of this revision and a full list of acknowledgments.

Wing's *Short-Title Catalogue . . . 1641-1700* was first published in three volumes, 1945-51, as a continuation of Pollard and Redgrave. It followed the same format, except that Wing used his own location symbol system. It proved to be equally invaluable for scholarship. The second edition represents an expansion and correction of the earlier publication. Unhappily, further revision was interrupted by Wing's death in 1972.

The two short-title catalogs form the most comprehensive record of English-language books for the period from 1475 to 1700. The revisions should be available in the reference departments of all but the smallest public, college, and university libraries. Allison and Goldsmith's *Titles of English Books (and of Foreign Books Printed in England): An Alphabetical Finding-List by Title of Books, Published under the Author's Name, Pseudonym or Initials* (2 vols. Archon Books, 1976, 1977) is a title index to both Pollard and Redgrave and Donald Wing's continuation. Omitted from both volumes of Allison and Goldsmith are anonymous works (which are cross referenced in the STC volumes) and corporate entries. *Titles of English Books* represents a major contribution, and is indispensable for libraries owning the STCs. [R: ARBA 77, p. 14]   Dean H. Keller
                                                                                      Arthur H. Stickney

Other Countries

23. Borchardt, D. H. **Australian Bibliography: A Guide to Printed Sources of Information.** Elmsford, NY, Pergamon Press, 1976. 270p. illus. bibliog. index. $30.00; $13.50pa. ISBN 0-08-020551-8; 0-08-020550-Xpa.

Most librarians are familiar with *Australian National Bibliography* (published four times a month, with monthly and annual cumulations since 1961) and *Australian Books in*

Print (annual since 1950). The present work provides a good overview of the bibliographic network in Australia. Material is arranged in 10 chapters. The first chapter, which briefly covers the history of libraries and library catalogs, is followed by a description of the more important encyclopedias and general reference works. The third chapter describes Australian retrospective and current bibliographies. The three following chapters deal with subject bibliographies in the social sciences, humanities, and pure and applied sciences. Brief chapters on regional bibliographies, sources of biographical information, government publications, and a general summary called "The Bibliographic Scene" conclude this useful work. Borchardt's book updates *Australian Bibliography and Bibliographic Services*, published by the Bibliographic Centre of the Australian Advisory Council on Bibliographic Services in 1960. It is a most welcome addition to the not too numerous general orientation guides pertaining to bibliographic services in individual countries. [R: ARBA 77, p. 12; RQ, Spring 78, p. 271]   Bohdan S. Wynar

   24. **Gesamtverzeichnis des deutschsprachigen Schrifttums (GV), 1911-1965: Vol. 1.** Ed. by Reinhard Oberschelp and Willi Gorzny. Munich, Verlag Dokumentation; distr., New York, K. G. Saur, 1976. 464p. $64.00. ISBN 3-7940-5600-0.

   This volume, the first edition of a projected series of about 150 volumes, is an additional part of the publisher's complete catalog of literature of the German-speaking peoples. It is intended to provide access to all printed books of German literature in print. The catalog is designed to draw into one bibliographic tool the contents of the many short-lived bibliographies which appeared in East and West Germany after World War II as well as that of the *Deutsche Nationalbibliographie* (Leipzig) and *Deutsche Bibliographie* (Frankfurt/am Main). Like its sister publication for the earlier period (1700-1910), "Gesamtverzeichnis-1911" contains alphabetically ordered, photographically duplicated citations from more than 15 titles—all containing discrete parts of the German-speaking book production. Thus it shares the strengths and weaknesses of these bibliographies. No attempt was made to include additional citations where gaps were presumably identified.

   The series, projected for completion by 1983, should be of great use in the libraries of universities where graduate research in German literature is conducted and in those academic libraries of colleges and universities with German programs which lack a substantial part of the German national bibliographies. This valuable contribution to the existing scholarship will, no doubt, quickly become a necessary tool for the student and scholar of German literature.   Edward J. Hall, Jr.

   25. **Gesamtverzeichnis des deutschsprachigen Schrifttums (GV), 1700-1910: Vol. 1.** Ed. by Peter Geils and Willi Gorzny. New York, K. G. Saur, 1979. 401p. $66.00. ISBN 3-598-30000-X.

   This volume, the first edition of a projected series of 135 volumes on German literature, is the first part of the publisher's complete catalog of German-speaking people's literature. The catalog is intended to draw into one set a multiplicity of citations from bibliographies of German literature. It contains alphabetically ordered, photographically duplicated citations from approximately 178 different titles, each containing discrete parts of the German-speaking world's book production. The catalog is intended to be as comprehensive as possible, given the constraints of compiling retrospective bibliographies. The German universal bibliography, *Deutsche Nationalbibliographie*, is considered to be "almost without exception based upon fragmentary materials of booksellers' fair catalogs, etc., and as a rule makes no allowance for additional books." The works of Heinsius, Kayser, or Hinrichs contain only parts of the book production and necessitate additional bibliographic searching, assert the editors.

Although the present publication initially met with complaints, perhaps because of the multiplicity of typefaces and large number of abbreviations and symbols, it already seems to have attained some international acknowledgement as a useful bibliographic tool. The projected set should be of great use in scholarly libraries of universities where graduate research in German literature is conducted and in those academic libraries of universities and colleges with German programs which lack a substantial part of the German national bibliographies. This valuable contribution to the existing scholarship will, no doubt, quickly become a necessary tool for the student and scholar of German literature.

Edward J. Hall, Jr.

26.   **A South African Bibliography to the Year 1925: Being a Revision and Continuation of Sidney Mendelssohn's** *South African Bibliography (1910)*. London, Mansell; distr., Salem, NH, Mansell, 1979. 4v. $367.00/set. ISBN 0-7201-0556-0/set.

Heralded as a "principal milestone" in South African bibliography, this 3,000-page compilation purports to continue Sidney Mendelssohn's pioneering two-volume *South African Bibliography* (London, Kegan Paul, 1910; repr. Boston, J. S. Canner; London, Holland Press, 1957). South Africa's counterpart to Sabin, Mendelssohn (1860-1917), a diamond magnate turned book collector and bibliographer, amassed one of the finest collections of Africana of all time. It took him 11 years to catalog his own library, which he bequeathed to the Parliament of the Union of South Africa. In his bibliography, Mendelssohn described and annotated about 7,000 items, adding also some material he had found in the major national libraries of Europe and North America.

The implicit purpose of the present work was to establish a comprehensive retrospective inventory of South Africana. While not formally enunciated anywhere, one must assume that by the term "South African bibliography" the compilers meant not only all types of printed and manuscript materials generated within the boundaries of the designated geographical area, but anything published anywhere in any language that has some bearing on the subject matter. This same criteria must have been used for the authorship of the material enumerated. The geographical designation applied here is Africa south of the Limpopo River and includes also South West Africa, the former protectorates of Bechuanaland, Basutoland, and Swaziland, as well as Madagascar and Mauritius prior to 1850. Rhodesia was left outside the scope of the effort.

Sixteen years of bibliographic toil went into the compilation of the 50,000 entries listed here, part of which represent pre-1909 items omitted from the original Mendelssohn. The holdings of many libraries of the region were checked for relevant materials in order to make the inventory as complete as possible. The project staff did not deem it necessary to go beyond 1925 because it was felt that other works provide adequate coverage for the subsequent period. No effort was spared in presenting items in the proper bibliographic format, based on the *Anglo-American Cataloging Rules*, and library locations for most items are given in the entry. The work's graphic qualities are superior.

The claim to have created here a "principal milestone in South African bibliography" is justified: a gap has been filled. For libraries with Africana research collections, this bibliography is indispensable. It is only unfortunate that an opus of this magnitude was allowed to see the light of day with such a technically inept introduction, which contains only vague statements about the exact scope of the enterprise and has little to say about selection policies and principles or the nature of the material censused.

Ed. note: Reuben Musiker's *South African Bibliography: A Survey of Bibliographies and Bibliographical Work* (Archon Books, 1970. 105p. $10.00) is a smaller but very competent volume, which serves as a much-needed model for other regional bibliographic guides.

Each chapter is presented in the form of a bibliographic survey with a bibliographical description of reference works listed in the footnotes. [R: ARBA 80, p. 144]

Michael Keresztesi

PERIODICALS AND SERIALS

27. **Book Review Digest: Author/Title Index 1905-1974.** Ed. by Leslie Dunmore-Leiber. New York, H. W. Wilson, 1976. 4v. $245.00/set. LC 75-43680. ISBN 0-8242-0589-8.

Started in 1905, BRD is an index to reviews of current fiction and nonfiction books appearing in some 70 popular periodicals and journals. An annual volume lists approximately 6,000 books. The *Author/Title Index 1905-1974* consolidates in one single alphabet reviews that appeared in all volumes, thus providing easy access to reviews of about 300,000 books as they appeared in some 150 periodicals and journals. In the prefatory note the editors admit that "inevitably in an index covering a long span of time, inconsistencies have developed. These have included variations in an author's name, in filing and spelling, and in the choice of the principal listing. Such discrepancies have been accommodated in order to make the Index a uniform work of reference." The editors also indicate that "maximum usefulness of the Index is assured with the availability of all annual volumes of *Book Review Digest*, which will be kept in print permanently." According to the "Directions for Use," title, author, and additional entries lead directly to the appropriate volume. The additional entries include compilers, editors, joint authors, translators, and illustrators. Cross references are provided (as much as possible) for variant forms of personal and institutional names; the listing of the periodicals themselves (p. ix) contains a number of cross references.

Probably the only problems this cumulative index will present are those concerned with variant forms of names—or, more specifically, with pseudonyms. No attempt has been made to identify all pseudonyms. Pseudonyms are identified only if both names appear in the index.

The page layout is good, with an appropriate use of boldface and indentions to allow easy scanning of entries. The use of this index will be limited to libraries that have BRD volumes, since each entry provides reference only to the individual BRD volume (the year, but not the pages), instead of to the original source where the review was published. All in all, this well-executed project maintains the high Wilson standards and can be recommended to all libraries that have adequate funds.

National Library Service Cumulative Book Review Index 1905-1974 (National Library Service, 1975. $390.00/set), in six volumes, lists all titles contained in *Book Review Digest* as well as reviews from *Library Journal* (1907-1974), *Saturday Review* (1924-1974), and *Choice* (1964-1974), a total of 560,000 citations. [R: ARBA 77, p. 20; BL, 1 Jan 77, p. 683; Choice, Oct 76, p. 955; LJ, 1 Sept 76, p. 1758; WLB, Oct 76, p. 185]

Bohdan S. Wynar

28. Devers, Charlotte M., Doris B. Katz, and Mary Margaret Regan, eds. **Guide to Special Issues and Indexes of Periodicals.** 2nd ed. New York, Special Libraries Association, 1976. 289p. index. $14.50. LC 75-25621. ISBN 0-87111-224-3.

This edition totals 1,256 entries, or 450 more titles than were contained in the 1966 edition. The *Guide* provides easy access to the specialized contents of selected American and Canadian trade, technical, and consumer journals. In alphabetical order by periodical title, the main text contains a detailed descriptive listing of annual special issues, features, supplementary issues, and/or sections appearing on a recurring basis, and also information on editorial and advertiser indexes. A typical entry includes the name of the periodical, its frequency, address and subscription price, the special issues or features in entry-a-line format, the date and price of the special issues, and occasionally a descriptive note.

A classified list of periodicals (under such terms as accounting, golf, journalism, travel, etc.) precedes the main section. The contents of the specials can be found through a comprehensive subject index at the end. The index is well made; typography and binding are very good. The classified list and the inclusion of Canadian titles are new features of this edition. This work will be especially useful in the business section of a public, special, or academic library. Advertisers and agencies, publishers, manufacturers, marketing specialists, and professional associations will find this to be highly useful in matters relevant to its scope. The reference librarian can use this also to answer such a question as: In what issue does *Consumer Reports* evaluate new cars? For the next issue the compilers might consider coding information on titles being included in particular periodical indexes. [R: BL, 15 Nov 76, p. 500; Choice, July/Aug 76, p. 644; LJ, 1 Apr 76, p. 882; WLB, June 76, p. 812; ARBA 77, p. 18; LJ, 1 Mar 77, p. 556]   Joseph W. Sprug

29.   Katz, Bill, and Berry G. Richards. **Magazines for Libraries: For the General Reader and School, Junior College, College, University, and Public Libraries.** 3rd ed. New York, R. R. Bowker, 1978. 937p. index. $39.95. LC 78-18541. ISBN 0-8352-0921-0.

The second edition of *Magazines for Libraries*, published in 1972, included 4,500 annotated entries as compared with the approximately 2,400 titles represented in the first edition (1969). The supplement to the second edition (published in 1974) and the main volume together provided 6,300 annotated entries, compared to the checklist of some 55,000 titles then found in *Ulrich's.*

The third edition includes annotations to 6,500 periodicals (there are some 60,000 periodicals now listed in *Ulrich's*), and approximately 75% of the titles from earlier editions are found in this edition. As is indicated in the preface, all of the annotations from the previous editions and supplement were reviewed, and about 95% of the annotations were edited and revised. Each annotation indicates the specific audience or type of library for which the magazine is best suited. The selection of periodicals in most subject areas was entrusted to numerous subject specialists, and, in this respect, there are many more contributors to this third edition than in previous editions. Berry G. Richards is now responsible for scientific and technological sections; Bill Katz, for titles in the humanities and the social sciences. In comparing the second and third editions, it is quite evident that the selection and quality of annotations are constantly improving. *Magazines for Libraries* is a well-executed work and will be of substantial assistance to libraries of all types. [R: ARBA 79, p. 8]

30.   Marshall, Joan K., comp. **Serials for Libraries: An Annotated Guide to Continuations, Annuals, Yearbooks, Almanacs, Transactions, Proceedings, Directories, Services.** Santa Barbara, CA, ABC-Clio; New York, Neal/Schuman Publishers, 1979. 494p. index. $49.75. LC 78-31144. ISBN 0-87436-280-6.

According to criteria established by the editor and the advisory editorial board, some 2,000 titles published in English and available in the United States were selected for this volume. Most serials included here are published on an annual or other regular basis; irregular serials (those not published more often than once a year) have been included "if the title contains information not available elsewhere" (p. viii). Bibliographical information includes title and former titles, ISSN, year started, frequency, publisher, address, issue examined (date, editor, number of pages, and price), and audience level, and where the volume is indexed. The brief descriptive annotations vary in length, most of them between 120 and 150 words. Author-title and subject indexes conclude this valuable publication, which will complement Bill Katz's *Magazines for Libraries* (see entry 29). Indeed, a well-executed project. [R: Choice, Nov 79, p. 1153; LJ, 1 Nov 79, p. 2290; ARBA 80, p. 11]

Bohdan S. Wynar

31. **New Serial Titles: A Union List of Serials Commencing Publication after December 31, 1949; 1950-1970 Cumulative.** New York, R. R. Bowker, 1978. $100.00 (microfilm); $250.00(Xerographic reprint). ISBN 0-8352-1105-3(microfilm); 0-8352-1106-1(Xerographic reprint).

The third edition of the *Union List of Serials*, published in five volumes in 1965, contained 156,499 entries for serial titles held by 956 libraries in the United States and Canada. The information was current up to 1949. In 1950 the Library of Congress conceived a plan for putting records of serial holdings on punched cards and the compilation of *New Serial Titles* was first issued in 1951. Today there are more than 800 cooperating libraries in the United States and Canada. Some types of material — such as government documents, annual reports, and house organs — that were not listed in the *Union List* are included in *New Serial Titles*. The serials are arranged alphabetically according to title. The basic publication is issued monthly, with quarterly and annual cumulations, as well as cumulative volumes for the years 1950-60, 1961-65, and 1966-69.

This is a reissue of the 1973 cumulation, which supersedes not only the above-mentioned cumulations, but also the quarterly issues for 1970. In addition to this material already available in printed form, the Library of Congress added for this cumulation 43,000 cards containing 13,000 revisions and 200,000 additional library holdings.

Serials are listed under entries prepared in accordance with the rules in the *A.L.A. Cataloging Rules . . .* (2nd ed., 1949) or the *Anglo-American Cataloging Rules*, following generally the form used in the *Union List of Serials*. It is indicated in the introduction that "since the entries for inclusion in this publication often may be prepared prior to their official establishment for cataloging records, new corporate entries appearing in this list may not always agree with the established form adopted subsequently. In such cases, the entries which are affected are revised so that their next appearance in a cumulative issue will be under the heading officially adopted" (p. vii). Thus, this cumulation contains a "Changes in Serials" section, covering the 1950-1970 period and including some 25,000 entries.

The following bibliographic data are provided "whenever the information is readily available" (p. vii): title, issuing body (in parentheses following the title in title entries), place of publication, beginning and ending dates, Dewey Decimal Classification number, library locations and holdings, ISSN, and code for country of publication. Entries for serials published monthly or quarterly also include frequency, address of publisher, and occasionally annual subscription price in the United States. It should be noted, however, that the statement "whenever the information is readily available" means just what it says. Over 50% of the entries for serials published quarterly or monthly do not show their frequency, and at least 40% of the entries for serials do not show their first year of publication or a closing year. There are adequate cross references — a total of 65,000, according to the description provided on page ix.

In all, this cumulation has many advantages over the previous cumulations. It will be an indispensable reference tool for larger libraries for years to come. It should be noted that the original volumes are out of print and that this set can be obtained on microfilm or Xerographic clothbound reprint.

Bohdan S. Wynar

32. **New Serial Titles 1950-1970 Subject Guide.** New York, R. R. Bowker, 1975. 2v. $138.50. LC 75-15145. ISBN 0-8352-0820-6. ISSN 0098-2237.

New Serial Titles: 1950-1970 Cumulative has been described as an indispensable reference work for years to come. The same general characterization clearly applies to the present work. However, the *Subject Guide* serves entirely different purposes.

The *Subject Guide* is arranged in modified DDC order. As a requirement of computerization, it was necessary to establish Dewey "ranges." Hence, under 150, Psychology, we are told that this number encompasses DDC numbers 150-159, including behaviorism. Headnotes preceding major number ranges helpfully list "see also" and "see" references by subject and number. Under each subject, entries are arranged first by country alphabetically and within country by title. A main entry for a serial consists of: title, ISSN, one or more DDC numbers, descriptive cataloging, and publication history. Note that entries do not include library locations, for which it is still necessary to consult *New Serial Titles*, in any of its several formats.

Indexing and other user aids include: Country Names and Codes; Subject Headings, Numerical Sequence; Subject Headings, Alphabetical Sequence; Index to Subject Headings; Correlation Table of Dewey Numbers to Subject Headings; Statistical Summaries (by subject and by country).

The reference uses to which this compilation may be put are the verification of a truncated or garbled citation to a serial whose subject or subjects are, however, known; and the identification of pertinent 1950-1970 serial titles as possible information sources. Acquisitions uses include cooperative coordination of purchasing among groups, networks, or consortia of libraries.

It lends itself beautifully to compilation of subject bibliographies, particularly those with a strong orientation to country of origin. It will serve as a research data book. Because of the prominence of the country of origin approach, it provides the raw data from which inferences — potentially significant in several fields of study — can be drawn; as measured by the launching of new serials, how active or productive are the various national groups in identifiable fields of scholarship and research? In geological sciences, for example, how do the British compare with the French, or the West Germans? The *Subject Guide* is an indispensable resource in attempting to frame answers to such questions. [R: ARBA 76, p. 43; Choice, Mar 76, p. 48; LJ, 1 Dec 75, p. 2235; RQ, Spring 76, p. 276; WLB, Jan 76, p. 413]

Richard A. Gray

33. **Sources of Serials: An International Publisher and Corporate Author Directory.** New York, R. R. Bowker, 1977. 1547p. index. (A Bowker Serials Bibliography). $52.50. LC 77-015833. ISBN 0-8352-0855-9. ISSN 0000-0523.

Sources of Serials is basically an international name authority file for all serial publishers and corporate authors included in *Ulrich's International Periodicals Directory, Irregular Serials and Annuals*, and *Ulrich's Quarterly*. The coverage is rather impressive, including 63,000 publishers and corporate authors arranged under 181 countries, with some 90,000 listings. The main section provides name of publisher or corporate author with complete address, all serial titles published or sponsored, and ISSN. There are some 4,000 cross references for variant forms of names and an alphabetical index to publisher/corporate authors.

In examining this reference source, our first impression is very positive. It seems to us that *Sources of Serials* is capable of performing an invaluable service in order departments, enabling them to locate desired serial titles under the name of publisher or sponsor, thus providing an efficient approach to the profile of publishing activities of a given publisher or corporate author. *Sources of Serials* can also be used in reference departments. Questions regarding publications of the University of Alberta, Department of Educational Foundations, for example, now can easily be answered with the assistance of this fact-finding tool.

Obviously, the coverage in the first edition cannot be perfect. There are some gaps, incomplete listings, etc. Taking into consideration the tremendous scope of this publication, however, some omissions are quite understandable; and we are sure that the second edition will remove many of the gaps and provide even more complete information for many corporate authors or corporate bodies.

Sources of Serials is a unique tool of tremendous value to libraries, research institutions, and individual scholars. It is also a well-executed book, one that shows much thought in editorial planning. A valuable member of the Ulrich "family," this directory will take its place among standard sources of bibliographic control of serial publications that quite frequently constitute 50% of budgetary spending in major academic and research institutions. [R: ARBA 78, p. 10; Choice, July 78, p. 674; C&RL, July 78, p. 301; RQ, Fall 78, p. 104; WLB, Mar 78, p. 588]   Bohdan S. Wynar

PUBLISHING AND BOOKSELLING

DICTIONARIES

34.   Collins, F. Howard. **Authors and Printers Dictionary.** 11th ed. Rev. by Stanley Beale. New York, Oxford University Press, 1973. 474p. $9.75. ISBN 0-19-211542-1.

The fact that this work is in its eleventh edition attests to its usefulness and popularity. It has frequently been revised and amended since its first appearance in 1905. Beale has completely revised and updated this edition to make it more useful for the contemporary researcher. The type has been reset, and the printing is sharp and clear.

This is a dictionary of usage rather than a dictionary of definition. The entries are in double columns, with boldface roman type for English words and boldface italic type for foreign words and phrases. At the end of each alphabetical section is a blank page for the user's own notes. American and English spellings of words are indicated. A lengthy section under "punctuation" is divided into 15 subsections, which explain the function and usage of all punctuation marks. This is a very useful work, not only for authors and printers, but for anyone (student, scholar, secretary, etc.) involved in the preparation of typewritten or printed copy. [R: ARBA 75, p. 23]   Frank J. Anderson

DIRECTORIES

35.   Brewer, Annie M., and Elizabeth A. Geiser, eds. **Book Publishers Directory: A Guide to New and Established, Private and Special Interest, Avant-Garde and Alternative, Organization and Association, Government and Institution Presses.** 2nd ed. Detroit, Gale, 1979. 668p. index. $110.00. LC 77-74820. ISBN 0-8103-0189-X.

The *Book Publishers Directory* was originally a quarterly publication. Quarterly publication was apparently abandoned after four issues. Those four issues are now termed "the first edition (1977-1978)." The second edition cumulates the four quarterlies and adds 800 new entries for a total of some 3,400 entries.

The closest thing to a statement of scope or definition that the editors provide is the subtitle, " . . . A Guide to New and Established, Private and Special Interest, Avant-Garde and Alternative, Organization and Association, Government and Institution Presses," appended by a phrase in the introduction that the directory provides "information on more than 3,400 publishing houses about which it is otherwise difficult to find much—or any—information." Coverage is limited to the United States and Canada, a fact which must be deduced from examination. As might be anticipated, the loose definition of coverage leaves much leeway in respect to comprehensiveness and selectiveness of coverage.

A check of 30 randomly selected entries against other standard directories of the publishing world, the *Literary Market Place*, the *International Directory of Little Magazines and Small Presses*, and the *Publishers' International Directory*, reveals very slight overlap (two entries each, not identical) with *LMP* and *Little Magazines and Small Presses*, and a very large (26 entries) overlap with the *Publishers' International Directory*. Despite that, the *BPD* and the *PID* are very different tools. The *PID* provides only addresses, telephone numbers, ISBNs, and very broad subject categorizations, and it has no indexes. The *BPD*, on the other hand, provides in the ideal entry (information is limited to that from questionnaires, and so is prone to irregularities), in addition to addresses, telephone, and ISBN, the names of owners and officials, number of titles published, a description of the publisher's aims, subject areas, discount rates and returns policies, affiliations, other imprints, divisions and subsidiaries, and a list of selected titles. There are a publishers index, a subject index, and a geographic index. The publishers index is almost totally redundant, providing alphabetical access to an alphabetically arranged file; its only value is in providing an occasional variant given-name access to those publishers with full personal names. The subject index provides access to potentially useful narrow subject headings, but that advantage is diminished by the practice of assigning only one subject heading to each publisher. The geographic index is unconditionally useful.

In weighing the acquisition of the *BPD* against the *PID*, one must consider the greater individual information and number of access points and limited, unpredictable coverage of the *BPD* against the comprehensive international listing and bare-bones essential information and lack of indexes of the *PID*. The *Book Publishers Directory* unquestionably fills a gap in information provision on the North American publishing industry. It will be valuable to libraries needing to provide as full an amount of information as possible on publishing outlets and sources. Libraries with serious budget restraints or a less demanding clientele could get along without it or purchase the *PID* instead. [R: ARBA 80, p. 19]

Arthur H. Stickney

36. **Information Market Place 1978-79: An International Directory of Information Products and Services.** Eusidic (European Association of Information Services) and James B. Sanders, consultant eds. New York, R. R. Bowker, 1978. 270p. index. $21.50pa. LC 78-26391. ISBN 0-8352-1079-0.

The familiar format of this new addition to the family of *Market Place* directories from R. R. Bowker will make the information contained within immediately accessible for use. Arranged in seven major categories, *Information Market Place 1978-79* is a necessary ready-reference tool for all but the smallest general collections.

The sections entitled "Information Production" and "Information Distribution" will provide the most requested answers to questions on data base publishers; printed and on-line information products; and the services of 100 on-line vendors and library and telecommunications networks worldwide. Information products are classified by subject, and each information producer is listed alphabetically with address, telephone number, and key personnel. Other particularly useful sections identify information retailers, support services and suppliers, association and government agencies, conferences and courses, and reference books, periodicals, and newsletters in the field—each with complete contact data. Completing the volume are a geographic index and a names and numbers directory for every individual and organization listed in the work. The data, collected from questionnaires, and in some instances from secondary sources (so indicated by an asterisk), meet Bowker's reliably high standards.

In spite of its detailed entries, this is a general work, considering the rapid growth of the information industry. Future editions will no doubt exceed exponentially the 270 pages of this first edition, and users requiring more comprehensive, specialized, or current information would be advised to consult such publications as Cuadra Associates' quarterly, *Directory of Online Databases.*

Ed. note: A new edition with an altered title, *Information Industry Market Place 1980-1981* (R. R. Bowker, 1980. 400p. $35.00pa.) is in preparation. [R: ARBA 80, p. 22; LJ, Aug 79, p. 1551; WLB, Apr 79, p. 588]   Theresa Maylone

PRICE GUIDES

37.   Bradley, Van Allen. **The Book Collector's Handbook of Values: 1978-1979.** 3rd rev. and enl. ed. New York, G. P. Putnam's, 1978. 590p. $25.00. LC 75-13906. ISBN 0-399-12110-2.

A third edition of this useful book price guide, coming just four years after the second, was prompted by the rapid development of book collecting as a hobby and as an investment, and a corresponding rise in book prices. It was necessary to bring the prices in the guide in line with the current market, make corrections and revisions, and expand the scope of the work.

Organized like its predecessors, the third edition of the guide lists about 18,000 British and American books from the nineteenth and twentieth centuries by author, or by title when no author is given. Bradley takes his entries from the title pages of the books he lists; thus books by Samuel Clemens will be found under "Twain, Mark" if the pseudonym is used on the title page, and Emerson's *Nature* will be found under the title since the book appeared anonymously. Cross references are provided wherever they are needed. Typical entries contain the author's full name, title of the book, a brief binding description, place and date of publication, edition, price range, and a recent auction record if it is available. Sometimes notes on limitation, variants, and later editions are provided.

Users of the *Handbook* should keep in mind that Bradley lists only books that have a retail market value of more than $25, and that the prices given are for books in *fine condition in original bindings.* The "introduction" to the first edition, reprinted here, should be read carefully, for it defines exactly what Bradley set out to do and tells what limitations were imposed. A basic bibliography of works consulted by the author is included in the "acknowledgments." [ARBA 80, p. 24]   Dean H. Keller

38.   Heard, J. Norman, Jimmie H. Hoover, and Charles F. Hamsa. **Bookman's Guide to Americana.** 7th ed. Metuchen, NJ, Scarecrow, 1977. 403p. $18.00. LC 76-51257. ISBN 0-8108-1007-7.

Intended for booksellers, collectors, and librarians, the *Bookman's Guide* seems firmly established as the standard compilation of Americana booksellers' catalogs. Users unfamiliar with its scope should note that "Americana" is understood to include North and South America. In fact, this edition claims an "unusually large number of titles relating to the Latin American republics" (p. iii).

The compilers have maintained the alphabetical arrangement of previous editions, but have included 15% more titles (8,559 items) than the sixth edition (1971). There is no mention of the overall recency of information, except that the preface indicates a cut-off date of March 1976. Assuming the compilers have maintained their earlier procedure, catalogs are two or three years old at most. Unfortunately, the compilers have chosen to delete the appendix, which lists the catalogs examined. A reasonable alternative would have been to include the source in the citation, as does McGrath in his *Bookman's Price Index* (Gale, 20v. $78.00/vol.). (Incidentally, this latter source has a similar objective but is broader in scope.) Occasional "see" references appear, and although several prices are cited for many items, the statements of physical condition are quite brief. A list of abbreviations should be given for users not on intimate terms with the out-of-print dealer's vocabulary.

Reference librarians in any type of library are called upon to assist users interested in the value of their personal collections, and, of course, acquisitions librarians may want this source to guide them in the area of Americana. [R: ARBA 78, p. 30; BL, 1 Nov 78, p. 495; LJ, 1 Apr 77, p. 789]   John V. Richardson, Jr.

39.   Mandeville, Mildred S., comp. **The Used Book Price Guide: An Aid in Ascertaining Current Prices, 1977 Supplement to the 5 Year Edition.** Kenmore, WA, Price Guide Publishers, 1977. 479p. bibliog. $39.00. LC 63-24123. ISBN 0-911182-76-17.

As indicated in the title, this volume supplements the five-year edition of the same title, published in two volumes (A-K, 1972; L-Z, 1974. $45.00/set). The supplement lists used book prices found in dealers' catalogs from 1973 to June 1977. It contains approximately 40,000 entries (compared to 74,000 in the five-year edition). Ninety-five percent of these entries are claimed to be different titles or editions than those listed in the other two volumes; the balance updates earlier entries. The entries give author, title, place and date of publication, size, type of binding, condition, dealer's code, and price in dealer's catalog. This is an extremely useful addition to an already invaluable reference for dealers, collectors, and interested librarians. [R: ARBA 79, p. 26; WLB, Jan 78, p. 427]

Carol Jean Carlson

COPYRIGHT

40.   Bush, George P., and Robert H. Dreyfuss, eds. **Technology and Copyright: Sources and Materials.** Mt. Airy, MD, Lomond Books, 1979. 552p. index. $22.50; $15.50 microfiche. LC 79-65635. ISBN 0-912338-17-2; 0-912338-18-0 microfiche.

The first edition of *Technology and Copyright* was published in 1972. Since that time, the enactment of the 1978 Copyright Law has clarified some points on the legal protection of technology; but this area remains ambiguous, and will be subject to much debate and conflicting judicial opinion. The timely second edition of *Technology and Copyright* does, as its preface states, "present the reader with reference and resource materials which will not only inform and educate, but will also provide a sense of the debate centering on the provisions of the Copyright Law relating to technology and copyright" (p. v).

Part I is an annotated bibliography, divided into subjects ranging from specific technologies (computer systems, reprography, video communications, microforms) to technological applications (education, libraries, networks and information systems, permissions and payments). The scope of each section and references to other applicable sections are given in headnotes. The bibliography is representative rather than exhaustive, but presents a balance of views expressed on the 1978 law in the context of the technological environment.

Part II is a superlative selection of reprinted articles and documents drawn from legal, technological, and information science literature. The decision of the *Williams & Wilkins* case is also reprinted. These are key papers which should be read by everyone involved in the information transfer process.

The back matter includes a list of the 101 periodicals cited, and separate name, subject, and case indexes. The work is, appropriately, issued in dual media. This is an excellent presentation, and is highly recommended for all but the smallest general collections. [R: ARBA 80, p. 25]

Theresa Maylone

41.   Miller, Jerome K. **U.S. Copyright Documents: An Annotated Collection for Use by Educators and Librarians.** Littleton, CO, Libraries Unlimited, 1980. 290p. bibliog. index. $25.00. ISBN 0-87287-239-4.

Jerome K. Miller, author of *Applying the New Copyright Law* (American Library Association, 1979), provides educators and librarians with an analysis of the Copyright Revision Act of 1976 and related congressional reports, together with the actual documents. The seven essays in part I elucidate the ambiguous concept of "fair use" and the complex regulations regarding the duplication of journal articles for reserve reading collections, the duplication of musical, pictorial, graphic, and audiovisual works by libraries and archives, interlibrary loan, registration and deposit, the reproduction of unpublished materials, and copyright warning notices.

The Copyright Revision Act of 1976 is reprinted in its entirety in part II, along with the corresponding sections of the congressional reports and related Copyright Office and American Library Association regulations, providing a convenient parallel reading of the law and its supporting documents. The editor's notes, interspersed among the passages, clarify key points of the law and refer the reader to related sections of the law. Also included in part II are the Transitional and Supplementary Provisions. A detailed index provides easy access to this practical guide to the new law.

ENCYCLOPEDIAS

42.   Kister, Kenneth F. **Encyclopedia Buying Guide: A Consumer Guide to General Encyclopedias in Print, 2nd ed.** New York, R. R. Bowker, 1978. 389p. index. $19.25. LC 76-645701. ISBN 0-8352-1059-6. ISSN 0361-1094.

The basic format of this book has not changed since the 1976 edition, although the introductory material has been expanded and generally rewritten. A separate section is devoted to the history of encyclopedias. In the sales section, Kister emphasizes consumer protection and sources of assistance for encyclopedia buyers.

The main section of the book, "Encyclopedia Profiles," covers 36 general encyclopedias currently (1978) available in the United States. As in previous editions, both children's and adult encyclopedias of more than one volume are covered. Many of the profiles now provide meaningful comparisons to other encyclopedias (in the "Summary" and "Recency" sections). For example, *Compton's* coverage of nine topics (also used in the comparison of the adult sets) is compared to that provided by *Encyclopedia International, Merit Students Encyclopedia,* and *World Book.* The topics used for comparison are reasonably chosen and current, although rather inappropriate for the children's sets: abortion, condominium housing, Eritrea, Freedom of Information Act, genetics, Mao Tse-tung, marijuana (use and laws), OPEC, solar energy, and Supreme Court (U.S.).

Titles reviewed in *Encyclopedia Buying Guide* for the first time include *Great World Encyclopedia, Hamlyn Younger Children's Encyclopedia, Purnell's First Encyclopedia in Colour* (a one-volume British children's encyclopedia), *Rand McNally's Children's Encyclopedia, Random House Encyclopedia,* and *University Desk Encyclopedia.* If the next edition shows as much improvement as this edition, we will have a new standard work for selecting encyclopedias. Future editions are now planned for three-year intervals rather than the former two-year period. [R: ARBA 79, p. 35; BL, 1 May 79, p. 1386; LJ, 1 Nov 78, p. 2176; WLB, Oct 78, p. 185]   G. Edward Evans

43.   **The New Columbia Encyclopedia.** 4th ed. Ed. by William H. Harris and Judith S. Levey. New York, Columbia University Press; distr., Philadelphia, J. B. Lippincott, 1975. 3052p. illus. $79.50; $135.00(deluxe ed.). LC 74-26686. ISBN 0-231-03572-1; 0-231-03977-8(deluxe ed.).

Since the publication of its first edition in 1935, the *Columbia Encyclopedia* has been committed to the ideal of an accurate, current volume of general reference. Until the fourth edition, however, it did not attempt to provide information for specialists in their areas of expertise — no one-volume work could possibly do that. It does now offer far more detailed expositions of scientific processes and theories than it did in editions 1, 2, and 3 (1935, 1950, and 1963, respectively).

In their introduction, the editors claim to be current as of January 1975. In general, this claim is validated by sample testing. Articles on Vietnam, Watergate, U.S.-Chinese relations, and Nobel prizes are current as of the end of 1974. Bibliographies are equally current, although citations are not as complete as librarians usually wish them to be.

Maps, placed as close as possible to relevant textual material, are clear and illuminating, as are diagrams, charts, and tables.

This edition is an excellent home reference work, but it is important as a library reference tool as well. Its subject entries are discrete and precise, and its brief discussions serve effectively as a first-order entree into a field of study both for the reference librarian and for the library user. [R: ARBA 76, p. 59; Choice, Dec 75, p. 1292; LJ, July 75, p. 1309; WLB, Nov 75, p. 263]   Richard A. Gray

44. **The Random House Encyclopedia.** James Mitchell, ed.-in-chief. New York, Random House; distr., Chicago, Encyclopaedia Britannica Educational Corp., 1977. 2v. illus. (part col.). bibliog. index. $69.95. LC 77-3447. ISBN 0-394-40730-X.

The idea of the *Colorpedia*, volume I of this new encyclopedia, was conceived by editor-in-chief James Mitchell of the British firm Mitchell Beazley, who envisioned an international encyclopedia using pictures, drawings, and maps as a primary means of transferring information from the book to the reader. Since 1975 he has also worked with editorial director Jess Stein, editor-in-chief of the *Random House Dictionary*. This work will appear in Canada and England under the title *The Joy of Knowledge*.

The *Colorpedia*, designed to cover the whole of human knowledge, is arranged under seven categories: The Universe, Earth, Life on Earth, Man, History and Culture, Man and Science, and Man and Machines, each introduced by a brief essay by a well-known scholar. The content is further classified under 896 specific topics, each treated in 1,400 words of commentary and detailed captions for the small, highly colored illustrations, which often seem crowded, though they occupy more space than the text. Also, the captions, which do not duplicate the text, often use more words than the commentary, and in very small type. The topics range from "preventive medicine" to "bread and pasta." Advice is sometimes included, such as how to remember difficult things, found under "memory and recall." There are many "see also" references. Some topics lend themselves readily to the pictorial treatment — e.g., "spiders and scorpions." "What is philosophy?" (and its "see also" references), however, seems not as well suited to the pictorial approach; its many illustrations are less useful. Thus, the strict uniformity of treatment of each topic has its limitations.

The second volume, the *Alphapedia*, contains 25,000 very briefly treated entries for concepts, people, and places, with frequent references to the *Colorpedia*, serving as its only index. These follow a time chart of 23 two-page spreads giving a chronological approach to five broad areas: religion and philosophy; music; literature; art and architecture; and science and technology. Though the arrangement is convenient, the type is too small for easy use. The body of the volume is useful chiefly for quick identification. Biographical entries cover a wide range of nationalities and occupations, from early caliphs to contemporary American jazzmen and sports figures, with American presidents more fully treated than other biographees. There are some notable omissions, among them Will Durant and artists Stuart Davis and Charles Demuth. Geographical coverage is good for countries and American states; each of these entries concludes with a profile giving pertinent and up-to-date information. The geographical coverage is augmented by an appended atlas, whose double-spread maps are small but clear, with good world coverage and an index of 21,000 names. Many smaller places are omitted, which is to be expected in such a work. Scientific terms are more fully treated than in recent unabridged dictionaries. The appended bibliography, arranged like the *Colorpedia*, organizes about 1,500 recent English-language books and periodicals for reference and general reading. A section on flags of the world follows.

The *Alphapedia* resembles the *University Desk Encyclopedia* (E. P. Dutton, 1977. 1055p. $69.95) in both format and coverage, although *Random House* generally gives more detail (with the exception of sketches in science and technology). While the *UDE* is convenient to use and well illustrated, the added features of the *Random House Encyclopedia* offer more information for the same price. This new encyclopedia will be useful as a quick reference source and for pictorial representations of a wide range of subjects. Its organization provides two approaches to these. Persons seeking more text and fewer pictures may prefer the *New Columbia Encyclopedia* (see entry 43). [R: ARBA 78, p. 41; Choice, Mar 78, p. 48; LJ, 1 Nov 77, p. 2252; WLB, Jan 78, p. 428]   Frances Neel Cheney

DIRECTORIES

45.   Ethridge, James M., ed. **The Directory of Directories: An Annotated Guide to Business and Industrial Directories, Professional and Scientific Rosters, and Other Lists and Guides of All Kinds.** 1st ed. Cecilia Ann Marlow, assistant ed. Detroit, Information Enterprises; distr., Detroit, Gale, 1980. 722p. index. $56.00. ISBN 0-8103-0270-5.

The *Directory of Directories* is based on the six 1977-78 issues of Gale's *Directory Information Service*, and describes some 5,200 directories, of which 1,400 are new listings. All of the older entries were updated, and in the process, of course, some were found to be defunct; these are listed in the title index as "Discontinued."

"Directories contain addresses" is the guideline for selection of entries. Of course, many contain other information as well, but all are characterized by lengthy listings and minimal textual matter. Limited-interest directories of small local clubs, etc., have been omitted. The entries are listed under 15 subject headings covering businesses, professions, religion, education, leisure and recreation, etc. Title and subject indexes complete the volume; the indexes are printed on colored paper for convenience. Entries are numbered consecutively and contain full title and subtitle, publisher's address, telephone number, description of contents, arrangement, information included in entries, frequency of publication, number of pages, indexes, price, editor's name, and ISSN. The *DOD* is similar in format and appearance to its complementary publication, the *Encyclopedia of Associations*. More convenient than the serial *Directory Information Service*, the *Directory of Directories* is an important new tool for most libraries.   Janet H. Littlefield

46.   Gadney, Alan. **Gadney's Guide to 1800 International Contests, Festivals & Grants in Film & Video, Photography, TV-Radio Broadcasting, Writing, Poetry, Playwriting, Journalism.** Carolyn L. Porter and Mary M. Gadney, associate eds. Glendale, CA, Festival Publications, 1978. 578p. index. $22.95; $15.95pa. LC 77-089041. ISBN 0-930828-01-1; 0-930828-00-3pa.

For individuals working in those (and associated) fields listed in the title, this guide provides an excellent, and perhaps unique, place to begin the complex process required to either seek financial assistance for proposed works, or to enter completed works in contests, festivals, exhibitions, or similar events. The editors have done an incredible amount of painstaking and detailed work, which will in turn save prospective entrants the endless hours of research and frustration usually required to simply identify the appropriate and/or desirable places to submit their works or proposals. With over 1,800 contest/grant sources included, *Gadney's Guide* provides sufficient detail and cross referencing to allow for informed evaluation and comparison *before* sending away for the necessary entry requirements, restrictions, deadlines, and procedures. In general, this guide can be expected to take a place beside such standard reference works in this area as the Foundation Center's various guides and directories, the *Catalog of Federal Domestic Assistance*, and the *Annual Register of Grant Support*, particularly if its planned revisions and updates are accomplished.

The *Guide* is divided into six chapters or "media divisions": film; video/audio/tv-audio broadcasting; photography; writing/print journalism; general (all media); and additions (all media). These chapters are further divided into 166 "special interest" subcategories. The 1,888 contests/grants included in the *Guide* are then distributed among these subcategories. At the beginning of each subcategory is a brief introductory section, which gives the specific content of the subcategory, definitions where appropriate, and cross references. For each contest/grant event listed, the following specific information is provided: current address; month/season held; an introductory descriptive paragraph; technical entry regulations; eligibility requirements; entry fees; awards; judging aspects and catch clauses; and deadlines.

Also included is an introduction, with a detailed description of the organization and use of the *Guide* and some helpful hints for the submission of entries and proposals. In addition, there are two valuable indexes: an alphabetical event/sponsor/award index, and a subject/category index to the 166 special interest subcategories. [R: ARBA 80, p. 34; LJ, 15 May 79, p. 1127]   Richard G. Akeroyd, Jr.

47.   Hodson, H. V. **The International Foundation Directory.** 2nd ed., rev. and enl. Detroit, Gale, 1979. 378p. index. $55.00. LC 79-23803. ISBN 0-8103-2018-5.

This is a revised and updated edition of the 1974 first edition. With coverage limited to permanent charitable foundations that are independent of some other institution, it excludes most government and religious institutional foundations. The scope also excludes U.S. foundations and comprises primarily those foundations that operate on an international basis, with some selected large national foundations included. The second edition lists 686 foundations, compared to some 1,000 foundations in the first edition (possibly reflecting the decline of the independent charitable foundation as a viable institution outside of the United States). However, the second edition includes some 100 foundations not listed in the first edition.

The arrangement is alphabetical by country, and then by the name of the foundation. Each entry provides the name of the foundation or trust, its address, the date it was founded, a brief history, a description of its aims and activities, financial data, officers, and publications. There are indexes to foundation names and subjects.

While limited in coverage by its definition, this is a useful supplement to the biennially published *Foundation Directory* (7th ed. Columbia University Press, 1979. 615p. $40.00), which provides coverage of the 3,100 largest U.S. foundations for those larger collections that require such additional information.   Arthur H. Stickney

48.   Hudson, Kenneth, and Ann Nicholls. **The Directory of World Museums.** New York, Columbia University Press, 1975. 864p. bibliog. index. $75.00. LC 74-21772. ISBN 0-231-03907-7.

Before reading the editors' delightful introduction, this reviewer had no clear idea of how extraordinarily difficult it is to define "museum" in a logically satisfying way. On reflection, however, it is obvious that numerous criteria intrude to deflect the cause of rigorous definition. Among these are permanence (of staff, of establishment, of collections) and animation versus physicality (e.g., are zoos and botanical gardens museums?).

The editors report beautifully on their struggles in the realm of defining logic, and then they give us six precisely defined negative criteria. The 22,000 institutions that survived the exclusionary thrusts of the following are the ones included: 1) no museum without a permanent collection; 2) no zoos or botanical gardens; 3) no historic houses without appropriate furnishings; 4) no historic site which is only a historic site; 5) no collection which exists solely for purposes of propaganda (e.g., The Turkish Museum of Greek Atrocities in Cyprus); 6) no collection without a serious collection (e.g., Ripley's "Believe It or Not" Museums in the United States).

Entries are arranged by country, then by city, and then alphabetically by *English* name. Specific informational elements in each entry are address, brief characterization of holdings, and hours of opening. Most country sections are preceded by a brief essay describing or explaining the state of museums in that country.

This directory had the full cooperation of the International Council of Museums in Paris. It is certainly the most comprehensive directory of its kind ever to be issued. Moreover, its reference value is greatly enhanced by a lengthy and minutely detailed classified index of specialized and outstanding collections, according to which it is possible to identify museums by every conceivable field of special collecting interest.

The work is subject to negative criticism on only one ground. The basic arrangement is by country, then by city. This principle of arrangement works well for most countries—there is, after all, only one London, one Paris, and one Nuremburg. But applied to the United States (itself a massive section containing about one-fourth of the 22,000 entries), it causes inconveniences. A case in point is Rochester. There is, as it happens, a Rochester in Michigan, one in Minnesota, and still another in New York. The result is that all museums in all three cities are interfiled in one alphabetic sequence. It would appear that U.S. entries require a modification of the arrangement scheme—to state and then city. Irritating though it may be to users, this is a minor flaw in an excellent reference book. [R: ARBA 76, p. 62; Choice, Oct 75, p. 980; LJ, 15 Apr 75, p. 746; WLB, May 75, p. 673]

Richard A. Gray

49. Palmer, Archie M., ed. **Research Centers Directory: A Guide to University-Related and Other Nonprofit Research Organizations Established on a Permanent Basis and Carrying on Continuing Research Programs in Agriculture, Business, Conservation, Education, Engineering and Technology, Government, Law, Life Sciences, Social Sciences, and Humanities.** Assisted by Laura E. Bryant. 6th ed. Detroit, Gale, 1979. 1121p. index. $110.00. LC 60-14807. ISBN 0-8103-0454-6.

The sixth edition of this now indispensable directory is the final one under the editorship of Archie Palmer. It follows the format of the last edition, with entries for 6,268 research centers in the United States and Canada, an increase of nearly 800, grouped under 16 subject headings, the largest of which is the "life sciences." About 1,500 new research centers appear for the first time in this work, according to the editor. Each serially numbered entry includes up to 15 categories of useful information, depending on the depth of data the publisher is provided. In this edition, the many centers known also by the name of parent institutions receive abbreviated descriptions under those names and cross references to the entry under their official names. The expected indexes—institutional, name, and subject—provide good access. As with other major Gale directories, one asks: how did we survive without them for so long?

Donald G. Davis, Jr.

50. Wasserman, Paul, managing ed. **Awards, Honors, & Prizes: Volume 1, United States and Canada.** Associate ed., Janice McLean. 4th ed. Detroit, Gale, 1978. 700p. index. $58.00. LC 78-16691. ISBN 0-8103-0378-7.

Since its first edition in 1969, this exhaustive and accurate source has increased in coverage, with volume 1 listing 5,254 awards, honors, and prizes—1,000 more than in the third edition. This may be accounted for in part by their ever-increasing number and by the addition of a new category, "better-known competitions and events in which winning is the sole objective, as opposed to awards for service, achievement, etc., which are incidental or professional endeavors, and which continue to comprise the bulk of this volume," such as the Davis Cup and the Kentucky Derby. Information on exact title, purpose, form, frequency, and status (active or inactive) in most cases was supplied by the sponsoring organization, under which the directory is arranged. A subject index reveals over 40 awards in library science, plus many more listed under seven "see also" references. Also retained is an alphabetical index to names of awards. The volume for United States and Canada is supplemented by one for international and foreign awards, the fourth edition of which is now in preparation. [R: ARBA 80, p. 41]   Frances Neel Cheney

HANDBOOKS

51.   **Great Treasury of Western Thought: A Compendium of Important Statements on Man and His Institutions by the Great Thinkers in Western History.** Ed. by Mortimer J. Adler and Charles Van Doren. New York, R. R. Bowker, 1977. 1771p. index. $32.95. LC 77-154. ISBN 0-8352-0833-8.

This work is half-way between an anthology and a book of quotations. Its 20 chapters on major themes like man, family, love, etc., are subdivided into 327 sections that contain selections in both prose and verse from over 200 authors ranging in time from classical Greece to the twentieth century. Adler, who worked on *Great Books of the Western World* and its Syntopicon some 25 years ago, was inspired by that experience to compile the present volume. The selections are longer than one finds in the usual book of quotations (generally at least 100 words) and as a rule do not duplicate what can be found in Bartlett and other standard sources. There are an author index and an alphabetical subject and proper name index of some 50,000 entries. The author index is difficult to use, despite the apparently clear explanation, because it gives only chapters and sections. If one remembers that individual quotations within a section appear in chronological order, the scope of the search is rapidly narrowed. (Authors' dates are given in the index.) The subject and proper name index is much easier to use because it gives chapter, section, and individual quotation numbers. Useful for inspirational browsing as well as reference, this book deserves a place in home, school, public, and academic libraries. [R: ARBA 78, p. 51; Choice, Jan 78, p. 1480; JAL, Nov 77, p. 305; LJ, 15 Oct 77, p. 2149; LJ, 15 Apr 78, p. 817; RQ, Spring 78, p. 268; WLB, Dec 77, p. 344]   A. Robert Rogers

52.   **The International Thesaurus of Quotations.** Comp. by Rhoda Thomas Tripp. New York, Thomas Y. Crowell, 1970. 1088p. $10.95; $11.95 (thumb-indexed). LC 73-106587. ISBN 0-690-44584-9; 0-690-44585-7 (thumb-indexed).

The quotation dictionary has two main uses: to identify remembered or partially remembered quotations, and to learn of appropriate quotations on a topic or theme. This dictionary is compiled primarily for the second use. It supplies writers, speakers, and browsers with quotations to fit a given idea. This function is fulfilled admirably by the arrangement of some 16,000 quotations under the ideas they express rather than under key words within the quotation, the method used by most other dictionaries. The selection is wide, thoughtful, and modern. More than 6,000 are of this century, including favorites from Eric Hoffer, John Kennedy, Walter Lippmann, Pearl Buck, and numerous other speakers and writers.

A comparison with six of the standard quotation dictionaries indicates that a maximum of 30% of its quotations can be found in any of them. Proverbs are included, but not slogans, old saws, and familiar phrases like "till Hell freezes over" or "an apple a day keeps the doctor away." Citations to sources are complete. In addition to an index of authors and sources and an index of the topics and ideas under which the quotations are arranged, there is a 294-page index of key words to help the user identify a particular quotation. This is less complete than we could hope for, often listing a quotation under only one of its significant words. Reference from the index to the quotation is to category and specific entry in the main section. The *International Thesaurus of Quotations* is of value in supplying both old and more recent quotations on a theme and in containing a large number of quotations not found in other dictionaries. [R: ARBA 71, p. 442; LJ, 1 Jan 71, p. 64; RQ, Spring 71, p. 282; WLB, Dec 70, p. 409]   Rolland E. Stevens

53.   Kenin, Richard, and Justin Wintle, eds. **The Dictionary of Biographical Quotation of British and American Subjects.** New York, Alfred A. Knopf, distr., New York, Random House, 1978. 860p. index. $25.00. LC 78-452. ISBN 0-394-50027-X.

For those who wish to be in on who said what about which Britons and Americans (and often when and where), the *DBQ* will serve admirably at the same time that it frustrates (one often wants more than is given). Although people from a variety of walks of life have been included, the balance goes to the literati — after all, they were the ones who not only said but wrote, and thereby preserved what was said (or a version of it). The urge is to quote; I yield: Clifton Fadiman said of Gertrude Stein that she was a "past master at the art of making nothing happen very slowly"; William Morris thought that Ralph Waldo Emerson was "one of the seven humbugs" of Christendom; and according to Oscar Wilde, Robert Browning "used poetry as a medium for writing in prose." Not all are nasty, though; many are highly lauditory. Yet the compilers have attempted, it seems, to choose a balanced selection, so that no one comes off looking too saintly — or evil, for that matter (e.g., when Al Capone states that he runs his rackets on "strictly American lines").

Not only were the *Dictionary of National Biography* and the *Dictionary of American Biography* drawn upon for this work, but numerous biographies and collections of letters offered quotations as well. Criteria seem to be the importance or notoriety of the subject in combination with a particularly apt or well-phrased observation; and over 1,000 people are discussed, often by one another. It's rather like being behind a two-way mirror at a large party and hearing everyone talking about everyone else; it's fascinating for a while, but a little will go a long way. This is, however, an exciting work, and future editions will surely bear the mark of readers' submissions. *The Dictionary of Biographical Quotation of British and American Subjects* is a worthy item to place alongside Bartlett's *Familiar Quotations* (14th ed. Little, 1968. 1750p.) or *Oxford Dictionary of Quotations* (see following entry). [R: ARBA 79, p. 49]   Koert C. Loomis, Jr.

54.   **The Oxford Dictionary of Quotations.** 3rd ed. New York, Oxford University Press, 1979. 907p. index. $29.95. LC 79-40699. ISBN 0-19-211560-X.

Appearing more than a quarter of a century after the second edition, this new *Dictionary* is a marked improvement over its predecessors. Essentially it is the first substantial revision since the original compilation, the second edition having retained most of the contents of the first. No longer included are proverbs; nursery rhymes; songs; advertisements and slogans; and, in most cases, titles of books, films, and plays. Missing also are entries for such people as Lanier, Markham, Pétain (along with his famous promise given at Verdun, "They shall not pass"), and Remarque. Readers will look in vain for "And what is so rare as a day in June?" even though some of Lowell is still retained. Cowper, Kipling, and Wordsworth, too, have been cut back.

The trimmings and deletions in the text and the index have made an essentially more useful book with the inclusion of novelists Conrad, Fitzgerald, Greene, Waugh, and even Raymond Chandler; of playwrights Beckett, Brecht, Fry, Pinter, Rattigan, and Stoppard; of poets Auden, Betjeman, Cummings, Larkin, Lowell (Amy and Robert), MacLeish, and Pound (Eliot, Frost, and Spender have been expanded); and heads of state Kennedy, Mao, and Stalin. Other luminaries like Buckminster Fuller, J. K. Galbraith, and Martin Luther King also appear.

Alphabetic arrangement by author is the same as in the earlier editions, and sections like "Anonymous," "Ballads," "the Bible," and "the Mass in Latin" are included in the alphabetical order.

The format is pleasing in a number of ways. The name of the author starting and ending each page appears in heavy type at the top. Likewise, in the 77-page section on Shakespeare, the name of the work beginning and ending each page is similarly positioned to facilitate searching. Foreign quotations have been italicized, and the ubiquitous and annoying *Ibid* has been dropped.

The index still occupies about one-third of the volume, and it, too, has been improved by the use of upper-case catchwords, more varied type fonts, and the first several letters of the author's name preceding each page number and quotation reference. Again, consideration of the user has been placed foremost.

The memorable "Introduction" by Bernard Darwin, written in 1941 for the first edition, has been reprinted here. What Mr. Darwin said then about the "innocent vanity" of quotation recognition and use holds true today: it "often helps us over the hard places in life; it gives us a warm little glow against the coldness of the world and keeps us snug and happy." [R: LJ, 1 Feb 80, pp. 395-96; WLB, Feb 80, p. 400]   Charles Andrews

55. Peter, Laurence J. **Peter's Quotations: Ideas for Our Time.** New York, William Morrow, 1977. 540p. index. $10.95. LC 77-3672. ISBN 0-688-03217-6.

Peter, the author of *The Peter Principle, The Peter Prescription, The Peter Plan*, and others, has collected a delightful selection of quotations gleaned from a lifetime of reading, observing, and listening to others. The emphasis is on quotations that have meaning in contemporary society and are expressed with brevity and wit. They are arranged under very broad subject headings, such as Ability, Beauty, Canada, Behavior, and Zoos. There is a cross-referenced Table of Subjects at the front of the volume, but it is not always easy to determine where certain quotations would appear or why. There is also an index of names and authors, which is somewhat confusing since no distinction is made between those names indexed as the source of a quote and those that appear in a quote. The sources, all undocumented, range from the standards to be found in Bartlett or Stevenson to show business personalities such as Zsa Zsa Gabor and Tom Smothers. Peter himself is extensively quoted. He has also included oral material that he originally noted at live lectures and performances or heard spoken by his friends and relatives. The lack of documentation and very broad nature of the subject categories combine to limit the work's effectiveness for certain reference situations.

Similar in style, content, and format is Rosenberg's *Quotations for the New Age* (Citadel Press, 1978. 179p. $8.95; $4.95pa.), which suffers from the same limitations of undocumented quotations, broad subject arrangement, and weak indexes. However, *Peter's* provides a wider selection of material, along with greater clarity of meaning in the chosen quotations. It is an excellent source of material for writers and speakers and is a perfect browsing item. It would definitely be useful in a reference collection and also can be recommended for personal collections. [R: ARBA 78, p. 52; BL, 1 July 78, p. 1699; LJ, 15 Sept 77, p. 1835; WLB, Jan 78, p. 422]   Barbara E. Kemp

56. Sharp, Harold S., comp. **Handbook of Pseudonyms and Personal Nicknames.** Metuchen, NJ, Scarecrow, 1972. 2v. $32.50. LC 71-189886. ISBN 0-8108-0460-3.

57. Sharp, Harold S., comp. **Handbook of Pseudonyms and Personal Nicknames: First Supplement.** Metuchen, NJ, Scarecrow, 1975. 2v. $37.50. LC 71-189886. ISBN 0-8108-0807-2.

This list of pseudonyms and personal nicknames includes in one alphabetical sequence approximately 15,000 real-name entries and about 25,000 nicknames and/or pseudonyms, most of them from the Western world, ranging in time from Aristides (c.530-468 B.C.) to Willie Mays. No authority is cited for the information given for the real names, and since the work must have extended over some years, a few dates of death are not noted, as in the case of E. L. Arnold, 1856- , and Frederick A. Atkins, 1864- , surely no longer with us. If the letter A is an adequate sampling, about a third of the main entries are authors, while among the rest are actors, musicians, popes, saints, kings, statesmen, bullfighters, military men, and many sports figures. Occasionally, conflicting information will be found, as for Ira Albridge (c.1810-67) and Ira Aldridge (c.1810-66), both identified as Negro tragedians, both with the nickname "The African Roscius," though only the latter is listed under "African Roscius" or "Roscius, The African," in this otherwise heavily cross-referenced handbook. The compiler laments the "substantial number of discrepancies in the birth dates as reported by various standard reference sources." This is the only clue to sources used, though it is obvious that many of the entries were found elsewhere.

In spite of these rather picky criticisms, this will be a ready source for pseudonyms used by dime novelists, for the many nicknames given to Hiram Ulysses Grant, better known as Ulysses S. Grant, and for the real names of many contemporary figures in the performing arts. Among publications dealing with pseudonyms and personal nicknames, no one volume is as comprehensive as this. The supplement lists 18,000 real names and some 30,000 nicknames or pseudonyms. [R: ARBA 74, p. 45; BL, 15 May 73, p. 888; Choice, May 73, p. 433; LJ, 15 Feb 73, p. 527; WLB, Apr 73, p. 70; ARBA 76, p. 240; BL, 1 Apr 76, p. 1132; LJ, 1 Oct 75, p. 1813; WLB, Dec 75, p. 325]   Frances Neel Cheney

58. Whiting, Bartlett Jere. **Early American Proverbs and Proverbial Phrases.** Cambridge, MA, Belknap Press of Harvard University Press, 1977. 555p. bibliog. index. $25.00. LC 77-2139. ISBN 0-674-21981-3.

Whiting, now retired from Harvard University where he taught from 1926 to 1975, has filled a linguistic gap—the period before 1820 in the United States, which is either not covered at all or only partially covered by previous publications in the field. Though there would appear to be some overlap with the *Oxford Dictionary of English Proverbs* (3rd ed., 1970), this is more apparent than real. Many of the same proverbs occur, but Oxford cites English and, occasionally, Scottish sources. There is some real overlap with Burton Stevenson's *Home Book of Proverbs, Maxims and Familiar Phrases* (Macmillan, 1948; reprinted in 1965 as the *Macmillan Book of Proverbs, Maxims and Familiar Phrases*), because Stevenson included American sources. But no one can rival Whiting for care and thoroughness for the period covered. It complements Archer Taylor and B. J. Whiting's *Dictionary of American Proverbs and Proverbial Phrases, 1820-1880* (Harvard, 1958). Libraries desiring comprehensive coverage of proverbs in the English language will also want to include Morris Palmer Tilley's *Dictionary of Proverbs in England in the 16th and 17th Centuries* (University of Michigan Press, 1950) and Whiting's *Proverbs, Sentences and Proverbial Phrases: From English Writings Mainly before 1500* (Harvard, 1968).

The introduction not only affords valuable insight into the method of compilation and arrangement, but contains reflections on those themes that occur most frequently in American proverbial sayings. The bibliographical references are extensive. The main body of the work is arranged alphabetically by key words. Each proverb is assigned a unique entry number (letter and number combination) and is given in its normal order, with the key word set in heavier type. Sources are then cited, in chronological order. Because the choice of key words can leave some room for dispute, there is an "Index of Important Words" (pp. 523-51) and an "Index of Proper Nouns" (pp. 553-55). To illustrate how the system works, I chose the proverb, "to kill the goose that lays the golden eggs." It is entered under "goose" as the key word, but one can also retrieve the proverb through the index under "golden" and under "egg." In the sample of proverbs checked, the system worked well. Occasionally, there is a slight departure from strict alphabetical order (e.g., entries about "teeth" are grouped where "tooth" occurs). There are cross references and many citations to other books or proverbs, like Oxford and Tilley, in this excellent collection for libraries desiring thorough coverage of proverbs. [R: ARBA 79, p. 52; Choice, June 78, p. 528; LJ, 15 Apr 78, p. 859]   A. Robert Rogers

ABBREVIATIONS

59.   **Acronyms, Initialisms, and Abbreviations Dictionary.** 6th ed. Ed. by Ellen T. Crowley. Detroit, Gale, 1978. 1,103p. $62.00. LC 78-18362. ISBN 0-8103-0503-8.

By now a standard and nearly ubiquitous reference work, the sixth edition of Ellen T. Crowley's *Acronyms, Initialisms, and Abbreviations Dictionary* is nearly 40% larger than the 1976 fifth edition, containing 178,949 entries. The *Dictionary* provides the most complete key available to alphabetical designations, contractions, abbreviations, acronyms, initialisms, and similar appellations. Arrangement in the basic volume (volume 1) is alphabetical by acronym. Each entry then provides the "definition" of the acronym.

Annual paperbound supplements keep the tool up to date. The 1980 supplement cumulates the 1979 supplement, adding some 25,000 new entries in all. The publisher terms the supplements "volume 2." Volume 3, *Reverse Acronyms, Initialisms, and Abbreviations Dictionary* (Gale, 1978. 1,100p. $68.00), is essentially a variant arrangement of volume 1's file, providing access from the alphabetically arranged complete word or term to the accepted short form, word, or term as definition. It is a "backwards" companion to the main volume.

The emphasis is on organizational names, technical terms, and governmental and educational denominations used in the United States. Coverage is much broader, however, including other fields of endeavor and selected words from Great Britain, France, Germany, the USSR, and other countries. [R: ARBA 78, p. 63; LJ, 1 Feb 79, p. 393]
Arthur H. Stickney

60.   De Sola, Ralph. **Abbreviations Dictionary.** New international 5th ed. New York, Elsevier North Holland, 1978. 654p. $28.00. LC 77-22195. ISBN 0-444-00213-8.

In its fifth edition in 20 years, this publication is a standard reference source. Perhaps the best way to explain the inclusions is to quote the subtitle: *Abbreviations, Acronyms, Anonyms, and Eponyms, Appellations, Contractions, Geographical Equivalents, Historical and Mythological Characters, Initials and Nicknames, Short Form and Slang Shortcuts, Signs and Symbols.* The *Dictionary* contains 160,000 entries, which is one-third more than the fourth edition (1974). The real value of the book lies in the fact that it assembles in one place material on the above-listed subjects, material that usually can be found only in scattered form. It could provide a user or a small library with information that might otherwise require several reference books – for example, names of diseases, common chemicals, nicknames of states, nicknames of outstanding musical compositions. Following the alphabetical listing are 50 pages of such sundry materials as international conversions simplified and proofreaders' marks. As in any volume, individual users may find omissions that would seem obvious, but, in general, coverage is very good. [R: ARBA 79, p. 53; BL, 1 Apr 79, p. 1234; Choice, Sept 78, p. 838]   Peggy M. Tozer

ALTERNATIVE INFORMATION SOURCES

61. **The Future: A Guide to Information Sources.** 2nd ed. Washington, DC, World Future Society, 1979. 722p. index. $25.00; $19.50 to members. LC 79-19398. ISBN 0-930242-07-6.

Included among the 2,200 listed information resources on the study of the future are 270 organizations, 560 individuals, 587 books and reports, 105 periodicals, 120 research projects, 280 courses and programs, and sundry films, audiotapes, games, and mixed media presentations. Still, the editors admit the list is not exhaustive. They introduce each of the 10 sections with guidelines to facilitate use.

The "Organizations" and "Individuals" sections, which comprise the bulk of the volume, are alphabetically arranged. A typical entry in the former includes organization name, address, phone number, founding date, officers, sources of support, budget, objectives and interests, major programs and projects, special facilities, and publications. An entry for the latter normally includes name, home address, phone number, profession, field of specialization, education, employment history, professional activities, and publications. A "Books and Reports" section contains a selected bibliography of 587 English-language publications, about 20% of which are annotated. The work also includes a glossary of terms (e.g., "ekistics" and "ad-hocracy") and two indexes—one geographical, which lists organizations and individuals alphabetically by country (within the United States alphabetically by state), and the other subject ("global survival macroproblem"), in which names (in regular type) and organizations (in italics) are cross-referred to other subject headings within the index.

If librarians do not have the first edition, they ought to have the second.

Wayne A. Wiegand

GOVERNMENT PUBLICATIONS

62. Andriot, John L., ed. **Guide to U.S. Government Publications.** 1978-1979 ed. McLean, VA, Documents Index, 1978. 3v. index. $250.00/set.

Andriot's *Guide* in its several editions has been of great help to documents librarians and their clientele for many years. This current edition follows the format of the 1976/77 edition by being published in hardbound volumes rather than the looseleaf format. To compensate for the loss of recency which the abandoning of looseleaf inserts effected, Andriot has included in each volume an "Appendix" section that gives new Superintendent of Documents class numbers appearing in the issues of the *Monthly Catalog* and the *Daily Depository Shipping Lists* that were too late to be incorporated into the main entries. But this fails to compensate adequately for large reorganization activity, such as the newly created Department of Education. In my judgment, the looseleaf format was a superior method of maintaining currency.

The strength of Andriot's *Guide* has been and continues to be the organization of entries by provenance. Preceding each agency there is a brief to fairly lengthy account of its creation, authority, and history. Following that is a listing of important series, serials (including periodicals), and reference works issued by each agency. Important nondepository as well as depository categories are included. Unfortunately, publications issued in microfiche only, such as the *Federal Supply Code for Manufacturers, United States and Canada* (Cataloging Handbook series H 4-1 and H 4-2), are listed by Andriot as still issued in looseleaf form. Each volume contains an agency index and a title index, arranged alphabetically by key word. Many entries are annotated, and discontinued series are interfiled by Superintendent of Documents class number along with current series. This represents a departure from the earlier looseleaf editions, which separated by volume discontinued agency publications from current ones. The user will find in the agency index "War Savings Staff, T 1.100," and the entry will show that this agency existed from 1942 to 1943 and was then abolished. This discontinued agency feature of Andriot's *Guides* has been of outstanding bibliographic usefulness.

Despite the more comprehensive publications of the United States Historical Documents Institute, specifically the *1789-1975 Checklist*, which contains on microfilm the shelflist of the Superintendent of Documents' library, Andriot's selective *Guide* is an invaluable addition to the bibliographic resources of libraries with federal government documents collections. Its relatively reasonable price makes it a necessary purchase for large depository and nondepository libraries alike. [R: ARBA 80, p. 46]   Joe Morehead

63.   Buchanan, William W., and Edna M. Kanely, comps. **Cumulative Subject Index to the Monthly Catalog of United States Government Publications, 1900-1971.** Washington, Carrollton Press, 1975. 15v. $1,260.00/set. LC 4-18088. ISBN 0-8408-0001-0.

This landmark publication in federal documents bibliography indexes more than one million publications listed in the *Monthly Catalog* from 1900 to 1971. As the title indicates, this is primarily a cumulative "subject" index to the *Monthly Catalog*. It does not contain the following entries included in the source indexes: names of persons who were beneficiaries of individual "relief" measures, and "personal authors." However, the following types of entries contained in the source indexes have been cumulated: government agency "author" entries, and title entries.

This cumulation represents a massive merging of entries in all previously published official cumulative indexes to the *Monthly Catalog*: 49 annual indexes (calendar years 1900-1905, 1935-1940, and 1961-1971; and fiscal years 1908/09-1933/34); the two decennial indexes; and one six-month index (July-December 1934). Original indexing was done for the 30 monthly issues that were not indexed, and the entries were merged.

The years 1895-1899 were not included since these catalogs had no indexing whatsoever from January 1895 through November 1897, and only monthly indexes from December 1897 through December 1899. This gap has been filled by Edna Kanely, who produced original entries for the 35 catalogs which had no indexing and merged them with the entries from the 25 monthly indexes in the two-volume *Cumulative Subject Index to the Monthly Catalog of U.S. Government Publications, 1895-1899* (Carrollton Press, 1978). With the publication of these volumes, the last indexing gap in the complete run of the GPO *Monthly Catalog* was filled.

Although the present compilation will increase the use of the *Monthly Catalog* for the period 1900-1940 and will make searches more convenient and complete, it will not eliminate the need for the *Document Catalog*, which is more comprehensive and includes many additional documents. Its indexing is generally better and in greater depth. The *Document Catalog* is also a combined catalog-index. Arranged by subject, the entries provide complete bibliographic information, and the user must look only in one place and need not consult both index and catalog listings. In those cases in which the user can narrow the search to a short time frame, the *Document Catalog* might still be preferred. However, most documents reference work concerns more recent publications, and this cumulative index is warmly welcomed since it fills a serious gap for the period 1961-1971.

Due to variations in terminology and indexing rules that have occurred over this span of 72 years, the compilers have been forced to make certain arbitrary, but eminently reasonable and practical, editorial decisions. Subject headings appear intact under their original spellings. However, this problem has been alleviated by merging many "see" and "see also" references that had disappeared over the years. The problem of subject headings in both singular and plural form, often widely separated, has been solved by combining them under either one or the other heading. In the case of series and certain types of reports, chronological and numerical listings are used rather than straight alphabetical listings.

The complete set is published in attractive, folio-size, case-bound volumes. The price may appear to be prohibitive, but when judged by its value in practical use, in time saved for librarians and other users of federal documents, and in the more exhaustive searches which it allows and encourages, the set is an outstanding bargain. [R: ARBA 75, p. 47; JAL, Jan 76, p. 26]   Susan C. Holte
LeRoy C. Schwarzkopf

64.   **Cumulative Subject Guide to U.S. Government Bibliographies, 1924-1973.** Comp. by Edna A. Kanely. Arlington, VA, Carrollton Press, 1976. 7v. $765.00/set. LC 76-43592. ISBN 0-8408-0151-3.

Carrollton Press is by now a well-known publisher of important reference sources on government documents. The *Cumulative Subject Guide, 1924-1973* is a convenience tool well worth its price. As Joseph Morehead indicates in the introduction to this set, "from 1924 to 1947, with the exception of fiscal year 1931, the *Monthly Catalog*'s annual indexes included subject entries for bibliographies that were both separate documents in themselves and references appended to publications with textual narration. But for the remaining years, only separate bibliographies were indexed. This inconsistency in indexing policy resulted in a loss of easy access to full bibliographic information. This new *Cumulative Subject Guide to U.S. Government Bibliographies, 1924-1973* remedies that bibliographic lacuna and provides the user with a single-location source for bibliographies in the full sense of the term. The volumes include some 18,000 entries citing self-contained bibliographies, but the conspicuous achievement of the *Subject Guide* is the listing of over 22,000 entries describing publications which have addended bibliographies or lists of references" (p. ix).

Entries in this *Subject Guide* are identical to those in the *Monthly Catalog*, providing full title, personal author if any, issuing agency, size, pagination, LC card number (if available), SuDocs class number, and depository item number (if applicable). There are numerous "see" and "see also" references. Thus, in consulting *Subject Guide*, one will be doing one search in a single alphabetical sequence rather than 25 separate searches in the individual volumes of the *Document Catalog*. A separate index volume arranged in SuDocs class order enables the user to have access by U.S. government author-organization, based on the principle of provenance. [R: ARBA 77, p. 67]   Bohdan S. Wynar

65.   Morehead, Joe. **Introduction to United States Public Documents.** 2nd ed. Littleton, CO, Libraries Unlimited, 1978. 377p. illus. index. (Library Science Text Series). $22.50; $13.50pa. LC 78-16866. ISBN 0-87287-186-X; 0-87287-190-8pa.

The revised second edition of *Introduction to United States Public Documents* is a noteworthy successor to Morehead's outstanding textbook published in 1975. It is extensively revised and updated, reflecting the many changes that have taken place in government publishing since 1975. New and expanded information includes current developments in GPO micropublishing; the new *Monthly Catalog* on-line with OCLC; microform distribution to depository libraries; and bibliographic control of non-depository publications, such as those of the National Technical Information Service, NASA, Defense Documentation Center, and the Department of Energy.

Chapters 1 through 4 describe the administrative machinery and bibliographic systems by which both government and libraries execute the transfer and sharing of public information (the Government Printing Office, the Superintendent of Documents, the depository library system, and non-depository publications). Chapter 5 introduces the catalogs, checklists, indexes, and guides to government documents and commercial publications. Chapters 6 through 11 discuss prominent publications generated by or in support of the activities of the five acknowledged arms of the federal establishment. (These chapters emphasize categories of materials rather than a lengthy recital of individual titles and series.) Appendix A examines a selected number of special problems in documents librarianship: federal mapping and charting activities; Census Bureau information; computer-based bibliographic series; federal audiovisual information; and microforms. Appendix B identifies the abbreviations, acronyms, citations, and popular names used in the text. The text is indexed by personal author, title/series, and subject. Illustrations of sample publications, forms, catalog entries, etc., complement the text. [R: ARBA 79, p. 61; C&RL, Jan 79, p. 76; RQ, Fall 79, p. 86]

66. Newsome, Walter L. **New Guide to Popular Government Publications: For Libraries and Home Reference.** Littleton, CO, Libraries Unlimited, 1978. 370p. index. $20.00. LC 78-12412. ISBN 0-87287-174-6.

This is a completely revised edition of *A Guide to Popular Government Publications* (1972). Newsome's *New Guide to Popular Government Publications* describes some 2,500 selected government documents of current or long-term popular interest to a wide range of readers. Publications of popular interest that have appeared since 1972 are included as are those published prior to 1972 that are still of interest and value. The reader will find listed publications on history, travel, recreation, wildlife, gardening, consumer information, child care—even art, music, and literature. Each entry contains a descriptive annotation, full bibliographic description, prices (although these are subject to change by the GPO), and order information.

New to this edition is a section on acquiring government publications, which lists GPO bookstores, gives hints on how to order from GPO, describes the services of the Consumer Information Center, and explains distribution of documents by Congress. Appendixes contain a list of guides to AV resources, selected agency catalogs, documents in commercial reprint editions, and a directory of non-GPO agencies. These features are unique to this bibliography. [R: ARBA 79, p. 62; LJ, 1 Feb 79, p. 394; SLJ, Jan 79, p. 32; WLB, Feb 79, p. 474]

67. Przebienda, Edward, ed. **Quinquennial Cumulative Personal Author Index 1971-1975, United States Government Publications Monthly Catalog.** Ann Arbor, MI, Pierian Press, 1979. 218p. $24.95. LC 4-18088. ISBN 0-87650-097-1.

This is the fifth and final volume in a set of cumulative author indexes to the *Monthly Catalog of United States Government Publications.* The first four volumes parallel the time frames of the official decennial and quinquennial cumulative indexes to the *Monthly Catalog* published by the Government Printing Office: 1941-1950, 1951-1960, 1961-1965, and 1966-1970. A GPO quinquennial cumulative index now under preparation will cover the period 1971 through June 1976, since cataloging procedures were changed to Anglo-American Cataloging Rules with the July 1976 issue.

The GPO indexes emphasize subjects, and did not include entries for personal main authors prior to 1963. The Pierian Press indexes include not only main authors, but also secondary authors and other contributors whose names are listed in the *Monthly Catalog* entries. Beginning in 1974, the *Monthly Catalog* provided separate indexes for authors, subjects, and titles. Previously, these were combined in a single alphabetical index. With the adoption of *AACR* in 1976, GPO includes in the author index not only main authors, but also joint authors and other significant contributors. Thus, the publisher decided to discontinue the series. For 1963 and later entries, its main advantage over the GPO indexes is its greater scope with secondary authors and contributors.

Entries include single authorship; coauthorship where the names of both authors are listed; and multi-authorship in which all authors are listed separately by name with the notation "et al." Names are listed as they are entered in the *Monthly Catalog*, so the same author may be listed more than once if the *Monthly Catalog* entries differ. Entries include citation to the *Monthly Catalog* year and entry number. The GPO indexes, in addition to the citation, also include the title or subject of the work. [R: ARBA 80, p. 50]

LeRoy C. Schwarzkopf

68. Rodgers, Frank. **A Guide to British Government Publications.** New York, H. W. Wilson, 1980. 750p. index. $35.00. LC 80-322. ISBN 0-8242-0617-7.

In his "Introduction," the author states that the purpose of the *Guide* "is to present a broad though necessarily selective view of the publications released by British government departments and related agencies" (p. 4). In this endeavor Rodgers has succeeded admirably. Part I of this survey covers basic background information on the British constitution and form of government, the organization and evolution of government printing and publishing, and a discussion of general catalogues and indexes.

Part II covers parliamentary documents—the journals, debates, sessional papers, statutory instruments, and other publications pursuant to the workings of the Parliament and its committees. The third and last part is the most detailed; it covers the executive agencies and their salient publications. Emphasis here is upon annual administrative reports and important statistical serials. Recent monographs are treated more selectively, with emphasis upon policy papers.

Beginning with chapter 4, there are "Selected References" at the end of each chapter. A "Glossary" at the end defines words and phrases that frequently appear in a perusal of British official documentation. A detailed index rounds out the volume.

This ambitious effort comprises 29 chapters and 750 pages. In addition to coverage of central departments, the author includes other official and quasi-official bodies such as committees, boards, councils, research laboratories, and museums. A brief account of the origins, history, and changes in function of an entity precedes its selected publications. The narrative is well written and adequate in bibliographic detail.

Clearly, this work belongs in libraries that carry good collections of the documents described or as a reference work in smaller libraries for referral purposes. It belongs on the shelf with the other guides produced by Ford, Ollé, and Pemberton.   Joe Morehead

69. **United States Government Publications, Volume I: An Author Index Representing Pre-1956 Holdings of American Libraries Reported to the National Union Catalog in the Library of Congress.** London, Mansell; distr., Salem, NH, Mansell, 1980. 543p. $992.00 (16 vol. set). ISBN 0-7201-0993-0(v.1); 0-7201-1509-4(set).

This 16-volume set is a reprint of the section with "United States" author entries in volumes 609 to 624 of the publisher's *National Union Catalog, Pre-1956 Imprints.* This section, consisting of 228,971 entries, comprises the single largest author heading in the entire 685 volumes of the *NUC*, and conveniently segregates the majority of U.S. government documents in the *NUC*.

The entries are reproduced catalog cards arranged alphabetically by author. They represent holdings of approximately 900 research libraries as reported to the *National Union Catalog* through mid-1978 for pre-1956 imprints. In addition to the wide variety of documents cataloged by the Library of Congress, cataloging in greater depth in specialized fields is provided by entries from the National Library of Medicine; National Agricultural Libraries; and libraries of the Department of Labor, Department of the Interior,

Department of Health, Education and Welfare, and the Geological Survey. Entries include location of documents, which is useful for interlibrary loan.

This set includes main entries, added entries, and cross references. It also includes many agency history cards, and it permits tracing the history of periodicals and other serials through notes on main entry cards or through cross references. The set complements and supplements the *Monthly Catalog of U.S. Government Publications* and other standard Government Printing Office indexes. Both *NUC* and GPO catalogs are selective, and far from comprehensive. *NUC* lists many publications not found in GPO catalogs, and vice versa. Both list many of the same publications, but some titles are found under different main entries due to differences in cataloging practice. The *NUC* entries include the LC classification number (but not the Superintendent of Documents number), subject headings, and other tracings. LeRoy C. Schwarzkopf

STYLE MANUALS

70. **A Manual of Style: For Authors, Editors, and Copywriters.** 12th ed., rev. Chicago, University of Chicago Press, 1969. 546p. bibliog. index. $15.00. LC 6-40582. ISBN 0-226-77008-7.

The twelfth edition of the University of Chicago's *Manual of Style* is a major revision and enlargement of the 1949 eleventh edition. The book provides a clearly presented, detailed, specific manual of editorial procedures and styling conventions. It is primarily aimed at the needs of book editors, but has application to other forms of editorial activity and to writers.

The work is organized into three major parts. Part I, "Bookmaking," details the organization of the physical book, the parts of the book, the steps in the preparation of a manuscript, including the roles of author, editor, and printer, the handling of galley proofs, and rights and permissions requirements. Part II, "Style," delineates and illustrates with examples styling conventions for the preparation of books. Part III, "Production and Printing," outlines the fundamentals of book design and typography and presents samples of various standard type styles. Included are a 30-page glossary of technical terms, an annotated bibliography, and an index.

The Chicago *Manual* is probably the most widely accepted basic styling guide used by scholarly and general publishers in all media. Even in instances in which "house style" differs from the Chicago *Manual*, the *Manual* is normally the groundwork on which the departure is based, and it is followed more often than not. In addition to providing an authoritative standard for basic styling decisions, the *Manual* provides a concise and detailed introduction to essential publishing procedures for the novice writer or editorial trainee. There are other style manuals, but none of them have the wide acceptance of the Chicago *Manual*.

The only serious flaw in the book is its difficult and frequently ineffective classification and indexing system. Quite often a needed element of information is in the text, but access to it through either the index or the detailed classified arrangement of the book is a hit-or-miss affair. The index would benefit from more specific and more numerous access points.

Kate L. Turabian's two student style manuals, *Student's Guide for Writing College Papers*, 3rd ed. (University of Chicago Press, 1969. 256p. $10.00; $3.45pa.) and *A Manual for Writers of Term Papers, Theses, and Dissertations*, 4th ed. (University of Chicago Press, 1973. 216p. $11.00; $3.95pa.), cover much of the material found in part II of the Chicago *Manual*, with appropriate elaborations and a great many more examples for the designated writing group, undergraduate and graduate students. Both have achieved wide acceptance as standard writer's style guides and can generally be relied upon as appropriate guidance for the preparation of manuscripts for publishers who adhere to the conventions of the Chicago *Manual of Style*. All three works should be available to library clientele.

Arthur H. Stickney

BIOGRAPHY

BIBLIOGRAPHIES

71. Slocum, Robert B. **Biographical Dictionaries and Related Works: An International Bibliography of Collective Biographies, Biobibliographies, Collections of Epitaphs, Selected Genealogical Works, Dictionaries of Anonyms and Pseudonyms, Historical and Specialized Dictionaries, Biographical Materials in Government Manuals, Bibliographies of Biography, Biographical Indexes, and Selected Portrait Catalogs, Second Supplement.** Detroit, Gale, 1978. 922p. index. $35.00. LC 67-27789. ISBN 0-8103-0974-2.

This *Second Supplement* to the standard international bibliography of biographical dictionaries and related works adds 3,823 citations and increases the total number of works covered in the three-volume set to 12,094 titles. The base volume was published in 1967; the first supplement in 1972. The format for this volume, similar to the earlier ones, is a division into three categories—universal; national or area; and vocational biography. The compiler also provides author, title, and subject indexes to the entries.

Complete bibliographic citations are given, including size and special features (for example, portraits and illustrations). Foreign-language publications are listed in the Latin alphabet with an English translation of the title. Brief descriptive annotations are provided. The author and title indexes provide quick access to the bibliography. The subject index is adequate, but some subject headings cite too many entries (e.g., Afro-Americans has 20) for quick use and should be subdivided. Duplicate entries for many works under the main subject heading and its various subheadings are unnecessary. The set has no cumulative index.

Although the publisher claims that this volume updates the earlier volumes, it also includes works published previously that were not cited in the earlier volumes. Therefore, the successive supplements do not indicate the publication dates of the entries included. Libraries that do biographical research will need all three volumes. [R: ARBA 79, p. 67; WLB, Sept 78, p. 88]

Sally S. Small

INDEXES

72. **Author Biographies Master Index: A Consolidated Guide to Biographical Information Concerning Authors Living and Dead as It Appears in a Selection of the Principal Biographical Dictionaries Devoted to Authors, Poets, Journalists, and Other Literary Figures.** Ed. by Dennis La Beau. 1st ed. Detroit, Gale, 1978. 2v. $90.00/set. LC 76-27212. ISBN 0-8103-1085-6.

This two-volume work indexes 140 biographical dictionaries and directories of writers, indicating which publication(s) should be consulted for information on a particular author. If there is no information available in any of the selected sources, this fact is also noted. Each of the 413,000 entries gives the author's name, dates, and the code for the indicated title(s). The 140 sources are identified, with brief annotations, in a key to the publication codes used in locating sources; they are also listed on the endsheets. The sources include most recent biographical tools in literature (with the exception of *The International Authors and Writers Who's Who*, 7th ed.; Cambridge, England: Melrose Press, 1976). Among the major sources indexed are: Gale's *Contemporary Authors* series; the St. Martin's *Contemporary Writers in the English Language* series; Scribner's *American Writers*;

the *Oxford Companions* to various literatures and genres; and the H.W. Wilson biographical series on authors.

Although a number of international and national sources are included, the coverage is especially strong for British and American authors. Each of the 140 sources chosen met the criterion to have "at least a moderate amount of biographical, critical, or career-related information on individual authors, and most include a substantial amount of information." All names in an indexed source, whether living or deceased, have been listed in ABMI. Some slight standardization of names has been done, but where an author's name differs from publication to publication, the variant forms have been used. The user is advised to be thorough, since "an individual author could have more than one listing if the various source books differ greatly in how that author's name appears." Minimal editing extends to the provision of cross references: "Cross references appearing in the publications indexed have been retained in ABMI." These are very sparse, and, for example, no references connect Lewis Carroll to Charles Lutwidge Dodgson and Charles Lutwige Dodgson; nor do his six pseudonyms link with John Creasey, although all six are entered in addition to his real name.

The introduction claims that ABMI is the largest project of its kind ever undertaken, and certainly its 140 sources, yielding 413,000 entries (but *not* individual authors), result in a more substantial list than the 50 sources (68,000 authors) cited in the *Index to Literary Biography* (Scarecrow, 1975). The latter tool does, however, index 13 foreign-language tools; ABMI, though its coverage is international, is limited to English-language tools. The *ABMI Supplement* (1980. 587p. $65.00) provides more than 182,500 citations to biographical sketches of writers appearing in 53 works of collective biography. (R: ARBA 79, p. 68; C&RL, Jan 79, p. 48; LJ, 15 Dec 78, p. 2504; RQ, Spring 79, p. 312; WLB, Dec 78, p. 344]   Deborah Jane Brewer

73. Biographical Dictionaries Master Index: A Guide to More than 725,000 Listings in over Fifty Current Who's Whos and Other Works of Collective Biography. Dennis La Beau and Gary C. Tarbert, eds. Detroit, Gale, 1975. 3v. $85.00/set. LC 75-19059. ISBN 0-8103-1077-5.

Biographical Dictionaries Master Index provides a cumulated index to the entries in 53 current biographical dictionaries. There are over 800,000 citations in all. The selection of tools indexed is focused on those providing information on contemporary Americans. Indexing of those tools is comprehensive, so that a few entries for deceased or non-American figures appear to the extent that they are included in the biographical dictionaries indexed.

The entries are listed alphabetically using the fullest name available from the source with a sub-arrangement by the individual's year of birth. The arrangement with the birth year notation helps greatly to reduce the confusion resulting from entries under variant forms of a name. However, the accuracy of the index is tied to the accuracy of the information from the indexed tools, and the searcher must always allow for the variations of proper name forms and/or birth dates in considering specific entries.

Biographical Dictionaries Master Index: First Supplement (Miranda C. Herbert and Barbara McNeil, eds. 1979. 638p. $72.00pa. [price includes 2nd supplement]) is the first of "biennial" supplements intended to provide added access to revised or new biographical reference works. It provides an additional 235,000 citations to nine revised volumes listed in the basic book and 16 additional new works through 1978. A second supplement is scheduled for publication in 1980.

Within the limits of its stated scope of covering contemporary American biographical reference works, the *Biographical Dictionaries Master Index* is an extremely valuable reference tool. If it can be faulted at all, it is in its exclusion of a number of specialized professional tools (notably in medicine and education) from the group of works indexed. In the best of all possible worlds, one would wish that similar indexes existed for international and retrospective biographical tools as well. This index, however, because of its relative comprehensiveness, clearly useful organization, and routine updating is the obvious first point of departure for biographical reference information on living Americans.

Marquis Who's Who Publications Index to All Books (Chicago, Marquis Who's Who) is an annually published index to a selection of the Marquis Who's Who publications. Its advantages over the *BDMI* publications are that it is more current in its coverage of its limited universe, and covers two or three minor tools that *BDMI* has not seen fit to include—including *Who Was Who in America* (which has its own cumulative index anyway). As the *Biographical Dictionaries Master Index* provides access to far more reference works and trails behind in its indexing of almost the same body of Marquis Who's Whos by only a year or two, it is by far the more valuable tool of the two. [R: ARBA 77, p. 71; Choice, July 76, p. 358; C&RL, July 76, p. 358; RQ, Winter 75, p. 169; WLB, Dec 75, p. 325; WLB, Oct 76, p. 186; WLB, May 80, p. 588]   Arthur H. Stickney

74. McNeil, Barbara, and Miranda C. Herbert, eds. **Historical Biographical Dictionaries Master Index.** 1st ed. Detroit, Gale, 1980. 1003p. (Gale Biographical Index Series, No. 7). $125.00. LC 80-10719. ISBN 0-8103-1089-9.

This index includes about 304,000 persons, chiefly Americans no longer living, who appear in at least one of more than 35 generally held sources of retrospective biography. Eleven of the sources are either original or reprint titles published by Gale, such as *Appleton's Cyclopaedia of American Biography*, which contains a few fictitious biographies. Only a few have broader geographical coverage, among them *McGraw-Hill Encyclopedia of World Biography* and *Dictionary of Scientific Biography*. A few include some living persons, as *Encyclopedia of American Biography*. Four, like *American Women*, give adequate coverage of women leaders. Agriculture, religion, art, and politics are also represented by biographical sources in those fields. Codes for each indexed title are conveniently printed inside front and back covers. Later editions will include additional titles.

Birth and death dates as they appear in the cited source are given for each biographee, with discrepancies shown in separate entries. Clara Barton has three, giving her birth date as 1830?, 1826, and 1821 in various sources, thus alerting the user to conflicting information. No explanation is given for why death dates are not included for all names in *Who Was Who in America*, with some entries given only a birth date. Nevertheless, this latest addition to the Gale Biographical Index Series will be a great time-saver in biographical reference work.   Frances Neel Cheney

75. Nicholsen, Margaret E. **People in Books: A Selective Guide to Biographical Literature Arranged by Vocations and Other Fields of Reader Interest. First Supplement.** New York, H. W. Wilson, 1977. 792p. index. $25.00. LC 69-15811. ISBN 0-8242-0587-1.

This "selective guide to biographical literature" drawn from a number of basic lists for public and school libraries raises the question of the aims of a second edition ("First Supplement") reference work. The main volume, published in 1969, indexes biographies and biographical writings included in 17 standard guides such as *Children's Catalog* and *The Elementary Shcool Library Collection, Standard Catalog for Public Libraries*. Many vocations as well as specific areas of interest are represented under 249 headings. Obviously, the author would attempt in this supplement to update the entries to include more recent materials in a given field, but should the author also attempt to redress the major grievances of critics of the first edition concerning format, contents, and utility, by undertaking structural changes in the work?

On both of these issues—currency and structure—some minor criticism might be made of the second edition. The preface to the book disclaims recency as a main criterion to this edition by stating that "the present volume indexes lists published from 1967 through 1971," making it by comparison actually less current than the first edition (which indexed books published through 1966) was at the time of its appearance in 1969. Although the work purports to include "the subjects of biographical writings . . . recommended for libraries serving readers of all ages," one must question the usefulness of *People in Books* as a tool for scholars. For example, from William Faulkner's entry drawn from the subject heading "Novelists (American – 20th Century)," the most recent book listed by Ms. Nicholsen was published in 1970. A check of the card catalog in a moderate-sized university library revealed five books on Faulkner published since 1970, the most recent of which appeared in 1975. This seems like a rather large omission in a 1977 reference work.

On the plus side, the book does list 344 vocational headings compared to 249 found in the 1969 edition. The taxonomic breakdown of these occupational categories includes the generic (e.g., "Philosophers") as well as the more specific (e.g., "Munitions Executives"), and headings of personal characteristics which include 41 distinctions in the category of *Victim* . . . from "Duels" to "Ghouls" to "Gout." If you can't find your malady here it isn't worth suffering from.

Five appendices to the work include: an index to all the people included in the book by country and century; a list of the general collective biographies indexed wholly or in part; an index to books of an autobiographical nature; a directory of publishers; and an index of all the individuals mentioned in the main section of the book.

A noteworthy exclusion in this era of feminist sensitivity occurs in many designated categories of the biographees. Thus, there are headings for "wives of famous men," "cowboys," "mistresses of famous men," and even a special isolated category, "women"; but conversely no "husbands of famous women," "cowgirls," "lovers of famous women." Understandably, perhaps, Nicholsen finds no need to include a special section, "men."

Overall though, the book is a meticulously researched and clearly defined index to biographical material of particular interest to school and public libraries. [R: ARBA 78, p. 64; BL, 1 Nov 78, p. 491; Choice, Sept 77, p. 834; LJ, Apr 77, p. 789; WLB, June 77, p. 816]

Esther F. Stineman

76. Ruffner, James A., ed. **Eponyms Dictionaries Index: A Reference Guide to Persons, Both Real and Imaginary, and the Terms Derived from Their Names.** Detroit, Gale, 1977. 730p. bibliog. $64.00. LC 76-20341. ISBN 0-8103-0688-3.

According to the publisher's blurb, the *Index* contains some 33,000 entries covering 20,000 eponyms ("the thing named"), together with the 13,000 personal names upon which they are based, thus indexing in one place some 100 dictionaries, encyclopedias, and word books where eponyms are defined or explained and more than 500 biographical sources (books and journal articles) containing details about the lives of persons whose names have been attached to other entities.

Each eponym entry provides the word or phrase, the person's name on which the eponym is based (noting variant spellings or uncertain connection), one of 60 broad subject categories, and citations of sources (referring back to the bibliography, pp. xiii-xxviii).

The biographical entries (for real and imaginary persons) are arranged in the same alphabetic sequence, with names, dates of birth and death, nationality, occupation, citations giving biographical details, and eponym(s) based on the person's name.

Thirty-nine of the sixty subject categories are mentioned on the title page, with the natural sciences, especially chemistry and medicine, being well covered (e.g., diseases, equations, experiments, formulas, mixtures, organs, processes, reactions, syndromes, etc.). The entire list of subject categories is not given, an unexplained omission. Several categories of eponyms are excluded by design: trade names, legal cases, geographical features, buildings, streets, and astronomical bodies and features.

This reference book will surely aid in unlocking the many treasures to be found in other books in the library, once the bibliography is checked against a library's card catalog. If eponymic questions occur frequently at the reference desk, this bibliography could also serve as a collection development tool. A very valuable addition to a reference collection. [R: ARBA 78, p. 65; BL, 15 Oct 77, p. 403; Choice, Sept 77, p. 830; LJ, 15 May 77, p. 1169; LJ, 15 Apr 78, p. 816; WLB, Sept 77, p. 91]   Pauline A. Atherton

INTERNATIONAL

77.   **Chambers's Biographical Dictionary.** Rev. ed. Ed. by J. O. Thorne and T. C. Collocott. Edinburgh, Chambers; Edison, NJ, Two Continents, 1978. 1432p. index. $25.00. LC 78-56110. ISBN 0-550-16001-9(Chambers); 0-8467-0510-9(Two Continents).

First published in 1897, this is one of the standard British biographical dictionaries. A major revision was undertaken in 1961. A minor revision was made in 1969. Since then, revisions have been confined to those landmark changes in world politics that could be encompassed in the change of a single line of text in the volume (e.g., the resignation of President Nixon) and vital changes and additions that comprise the 11-page introductory supplement to the book. So, in essence, the book is up to date through 1968/69, with a supplement that further updates it to the latest imprint date (1978). The book has some 15,000 biographies. There is British and political bias in the selection of entries, although the scope is very large.

Entries are of varying fullness. Most entries give, in addition to the usual biographical data, the published works of the biographee, and important critical works about him or her. Selection is based on the likelihood of the individual "to be looked up." There is an index to the main body of the volume from a classified subject index from items/titles uniquely associated with the biographee.

If one can overlook the minimal currentness, the lack of American entries for non-political spheres, the occasional inexplicably curt entry, and the disproportionate emphasis on political figures, this can be regarded as one of the best one-volume biographical dictionaries. If one has the 1969 edition, the minimal updating of later imprints makes their purchase problematic for all but the most punctiliously maintained collections.

A two-volume paperbound version of the 1976 imprint is available from Littlefield for $7.95. The cost saving is the only argument in favor of that edition rather than the clothbound.   Arthur H. Stickney

78.   Levy, Felice, comp. **Obituaries on File, Volume 1 (A-R).** New York, Facts on File, 1979. 514p. $75.00(2v. set). LC 79-12907. ISBN 0-87196-372-8.

Since its first appearance in 1940, *Facts on File* has provided a valuable running reference summary of the more important events that have taken place in the nation and the world. Among the more interesting sections contained in each edition of the publication is that devoted to a necrology of noteworthy persons dying during the time period covered by the edition. The names included in these lists are not only representative of the leading lights of politics, economics, business and industry, and entertainment, but also adhere to individuals whose fame may have been transitory, notorious, or downright obscure. Author T. S. Eliot (died January 4, 1965) finds a place, as does Adolf Hitler (a suicide in Berlin, April 30, 1945); but so does Clarence (Ginger) Beaumont, the first man to bat in a World Series game (died April 10, 1956), and J. Frank Honeywell, author of boys' adventure books (died August 6, 1951).

The almost 25,000 names included in the two volumes of this set cover the period 1940 through 1978, with each entry encompassing the name of the person deceased, age at the time of death, significant aspects of his or her life, date of death, and place of demise. The second volume of the set, covering persons with last names starting with S through Z, also includes lists of dates on which persons died and a comprehensive subject index, providing means of tracing persons through their major areas of renown and their geographical location. The set will be a useful acquisition for larger public and most academic libraries. [R: Choice, Apr 80, p. 204; WLB, May 80, pp. 590-91]   Norman Lederer

79.   **The McGraw-Hill Encyclopedia of World Biography.** David I. Eggenberger, ed.-in-chief. New York, McGraw-Hill, 1973. 12v. illus. (part col.). index. $340.00/set. LC 70-37402. ISBN 0-07-079633-5.

According to the introduction, this encyclopedia "has been designed to meet a growing need in school and college libraries as well as in public libraries. Written entirely by academic authorities and other specialists, and enriched with illustrations, bibliographies, study guides, and index, this work, we believe, combines more useful features for the student than any other multivolume biographical encyclopedia" (vol. 1, p. v). In other words, *EWB* was conceived primarily for the use of students. The editors have provided 5,000 biographies, averaging about 800 words in length, with a curriculum orientation. Each article is signed, and each concludes with a "further reading" section, consisting of references to study guides in volume 12 and to related articles in other volumes. An annotated bibliography of English-language books is appended to each article. Access to the material is enhanced by the 100,000-entry index located in the last volume; the last volume also contains a list of contributors, showing their institutional affiliation.

It is almost impossible to provide a formula for selection of 5,000 biographees who might be "universally appealing" to students. Inclusions (or exclusions) can be debated. With respect to politicians, Beria, head of the Soviet secret police until his execution, is included (although with an inadequate bibliography), as is Trotsky (who is provided with much better coverage). However, Benesh, the president of Czechoslovakia from 1935 to 1938 and 1940 to 1948, is treated in less detail. A comparison of the *EWB* with *Dictionary of Scientific Biography* shows that the coverage of famous scientists who have popular appeal is quite adequate. [R: ARBA 74, p. 41; BL, 1 July 74, p. 1161; Choice, Apr 74, p. 236; LJ, 15 Apr 75, p. 732]   Bohdan S. Wynar

80.   Roberts, Frank C., comp. **Obituaries from** *The Times* **1951-1960, Including an Index to All Obituaries and Tributes Appearing in** *The Times* **during the Years 1951-1960.** Reading, England, Newspaper Archive Developments; Westport, CT, Meckler Books, a division of Microform Review, 1979. 896p. index. $85.00. LC 79-12743. ISBN 0-930466-16-0(Meckler).

The first of a three-volume set (vol. II, 1961-70 and vol. III, 1971-75 were published in 1975 and 1978, respectively), compiled by Frank Roberts, this work provides biographical information on 1,450 persons whose deaths occurred during the period 1951-60. It is noted in the preface that there is some overlap with the relevant volume of the *Dictionary of National Biography*, but even so, some 57% of the notices provided here refer to British subjects who were not included in the *DNB*, or to foreigners ineligible for inclusion. For some of these, from Europe and Latin America, other English-language biographical detail may be hard to find.

As source material for historical research, these obituaries, written at the time of their subjects' death, reflect contemporary opinion based on contemporary knowledge, and so provide a picture of the individual's perceived role in society. That perception of individual importance may well alter as research and new discoveries reveal fresh information concerning their activities and influence is recognized by the compilers in a somewhat unfortunate way. The preface contains the following statement: "It will be noticed that there are a number of obituaries which have not been republished, of figures who might have been expected to appear, where we considered that the original obituary notice, written with knowledge available at the time, might be misleading." While the omission of such notices preserves the *Times'* reputation for high standards of objective, impartial reporting, historians in search of biographical detail will need the corrected or completed information, and most probably, the contemporary assessment as well. One may still access the persons omitted through the index, which does list all obituaries and tributes published during the period, and gain access to this information, but only if one can find a full back file of the *Times.*

Historians and biographers will find all three volumes of this record useful, both for accurate factual information concerning their subjects, and some understanding of how they may have been viewed by their contemporaries. [ARBA 80, p. 52]

Margaret Anderson

81. **Webster's Biographical Dictionary.** Springfield, MA, G. & C. Merriam, 1980. 1697p. $15.00. LC 79-23607. ISBN 0-87779-443-X.

Since its first appearance in 1943, there have been many editions of this work, although they should perhaps be called reprintings, since few changes were made from one edition to another. The present edition contains some 40,000 biographical sketches—approximately the same number as in the 1943 edition. Nevertheless, there are still some glaring omissions. For example, there are no entries for Golda Meir, Ian Smith, or Suharto. Because coverage of American public figures is less than impressive, one will need to consult *Webster's American Biographies* (1979. 1233p. $15.00), which provides more detailed information for some 3,000 notable Americans.

The editors point out in the preface that "the length of a biography is no measure of the relative importance of the person treated, but rather an indication of editorial judgment of material most likely to prove useful to consultants" (pp. v-vi). This editorial judgment seems to be in need of revision, as the work still has serious shortcomings. *Webster's Biographical Dictionary* is a fine universal dictionary, but it should be better.

Susan C. Holte
Bohdan S. Wynar

UNITED STATES

82. **Concise Dictionary of American Biography.** 3rd ed. New York, Scribner's, 1980. 1333p. $55.00. LC 80-13892. ISBN 0-684-16631-3.

The first edition of the *Concise DAB* extended to December 31, 1940, and included at least minimal entries for every person represented in the parent set and the two supplements to that date. The second and third editions continue that coverage. The third edition comprises in alphabetical sequence entries (some 17,000) from the parent set and the first six supplements. In includes, therefore, all of the *DAB*'s selection of outstanding Americans who died prior to 1961.

Entries range from minimal (birth, death, one or two descriptive phrases) to median (more extended than minimal, but only presenting highlights) to extended (reserved for the most important figures). The ratio of compression is approximately 14:1, but that varies according to the subject. The *DAB*, of course, is the preeminent work in its field for United States history, and any library not owning it, or the first *Concise*, should certainly purchase this volume. If the first *Concise* is available along with the third, fourth, fifth, and sixth supplements, then this might not be needed. But for any busy reference desk, this would be extremely handy and authoritative insofar as it goes. This reviewer had hopes of seeing full birth and death dates being supplied instead of only years, but perhaps that will happen in the next edition of this valuable condensation. [R: ARBA 78, p. 67; Choice, Sept 77, p. 827; LJ, 15 Feb 77, p. 476; WLB, May 77, p. 782]   Koert C. Loomis, Jr.

83.   **Notable American Women 1607-1950: A Biographical Dictionary.** Edward T. James, ed. Cambridge, MA, Harvard University Press, 1971. 3v. $75.00; $25.00pa. LC 76-152274. ISBN 0-674-62731-8; ISBN 0-674-62734-2pa.

This biographical dictionary, the first large-scale scholarly work in its field, was prepared under the auspices of Radcliffe College. A total of 1,359 biographical sketches is included, and the entries are patterned after the well-known *Dictionary of American Biography*.

According to the preface, "for each biography the editors endeavored to find an author with special knowledge of the subject or of her field. Seven hundred and thirty-eight contributors were enlisted, the scholarly community making a generous response in time and effort for which the modest honorarium was a purely token recompense. The few unsigned articles are the product of editorial collaboration. The length of the article varies according to the importance of the individual, the complexity of her career, and the availability of the material: the two longest (more than 7,000 words) are the biographies of Mary Baker Eddy, founder of the Church of Christ, Scientist, and author Harriet Beecher Stowe; the shortest is the 400-word sketch of the colonial printer Ann Timothy." It should also be pointed out that "only one group of women, the wives of the presidents of the United States, were admitted to *Notable American Women* on their husbands' credentials. For the others the criterion was distinction in their own right of more than local significance." The women appearing in the *Dictionary of American Biography* who were omitted in this biographical dictionary are "mostly individuals who seemed to have lost significance with the passage of time or . . . marginal figures about whom so little material was available that there seemed no point in attempting a fresh sketch."

Articles are evaluative and are accompanied by bibliographies that list both primary and secondary material. A classified list of selected biographies is appended, including names of 17 librarians. An authoritative, scholarly work for women's history. [R: ARBA 72, p. 93; BL, 15 July 72, p. 948; Choice, Apr 72, p. 196; C&RL, July 72, p. 320; LJ, 1 Sept 71, p. 2589; LJ, 15 Mar 72, p. 1003; WLB, Feb 72, p. 543]

FOREIGN COUNTRIES

84.   **Australian Dictionary of Biography, Volume 7: 1891-1939, A-Ch.** Bede Nairn and Geoffrey Serle, general eds. Carlton, Victoria, Melbourne University Press; distr., Forest Grove, OR, International Scholarly Book Services, 1979. 647p. bibliog. $37.50. ISBN 0-522-84185-6.

The *Australian Dictionary of Biography* is a projected 12-volume compilation of biographical sketches, of which 6 volumes, covering the first two periods and the years 1788 through 1890, have already been published. When completed, the project will include some 7,000 sketches.

Volume 7, the first of six volumes to cover the "Third Period," 1891 to 1939, contains 658 entries written by 469 authors. As in earlier volumes, the selection of names for inclusion appears to have been based on sound scholarship and high standards, and to portray a cross section of Australian life of the period. Many of the subjects of the biographies were leaders in politics, business, the armed services, the professions, the arts, and the labor movement. A good sampling of representatives of ethnic and social minorities is included. There also are a few sketches of innovators, notorieties, eccentrics, and other intriguing characters.

Sketches range in length from under a page to seven pages. All are signed and include a short list of reference sources, personal data, and information on careers or other contributions. Author sketches give summaries of their works. All are well written, readable, and manage to convey a wealth of information in a relatively short space. Contributors were nominated by seven working committees set up on a regional basis plus one for the armed services. About one-half of the contributors are members of university staffs; others are judges, medical practitioners, librarians, musicians, publishers, etc. [ARBA 80, p. 185]

Shirley L. Hopkinson

85. Baylen, Joseph O., and Norbert J. Gossman, eds. **Biographical Dictionary of Modern British Radicals, Volume 1: 1770-1830.** Sussex, England, Harvester Press; Atlantic Highlands, NJ, Humanities Press, 1979. 565p. index. $91.00. ISBN 0-85527-404-2 (Harvester); 0-391-00914-1 (Humanities).

According to the intentions of its editors (two American professors of history), this new biographical dictionary is intended to "supplement and in some cases correct the biographical sketches in the *Dictionary of National Biography*." A six-page introduction sets forth the aims and limitations of the dictionary and provides a brief historical background. The term "radical" receives a fairly broad interpretation and is meant to include anyone who advocated a substantial change in Britain's political, economic, and social institutions. For this volume, very similar in format to the venerable *DNB*, 214 such radicals have been chosen.

Each entry begins with a short paragraph that identifies the individual, placing him (only five women were selected) within the political, social, or cultural movements of the time. The biographical sketch itself ranges in length from one-half page to seven pages, and concludes with a short bibliography (in narrative form, rather than merely a listing of sources). Some of the lengthier sketches are for Robert Owen, Thomas Paine, David Ricardo, William Blake, Charles James Fox (a leader of parliamentary opposition), and William Roscoe (a reformer and leader in the abolition movement). Some other well-known names merit lesser consideration: Percy Bysshe Shelley, John Witherspoon, William Hazlitt, Jeremy Bentham, and, surprisingly, Josiah Wedgwood.

Since most of the important figures are adequately treated in the *DNB*, the chief value of this volume for libraries lies in the information provided about the less widely known radicals. Ralph Eddowes is an appropriate example. He was a reformer in the city of Chester before emigrating to the United States, where he became an important Unitarian leader. He is not mentioned at all in the *DNB*, but rates 6 pages in *Modern British Radicals.* Likewise, William Duckett (an Irish supporter of the French Revolution) and John McCreery (a printer and organizer) received only short entries in the *DNB*, but have 5 and 6 pages, respectively, in *MBR*. However, a few of the radicals fared much better in the *DNB*: Fox received 17 pages, compared to 5 in *MBR*; and there are 18 pages for O'Connell, and 10 pages for Paine.

The entries in *Modern British Radicals* are signed, and a list of contributors (with academic affiliations) is included. There is an index, which is nothing more than a table of contents for the volume. For libraries with extensive research holdings in British history, there are cross references to entries in the *Dictionary of Labour Biography.* Two additional volumes are scheduled for publication in 1980, which will extend the dictionary's coverage through 1970. Judging from volume 1, this set should be an important acquisition for most academic libraries. Unfortunately, the inordinately high price tag will probably restrict availability to only the largest research libraries. [R: ARBA 80, p. 188]   Thomas A. Karel

86. Boorman, Howard L., ed. **Biographical Dictionary of Republican China.** New York, Columbia University Press, 1967-1971. 4v. map. bibliog. index. $32.50ea.(v.1, 2, 3);

$37.50(v.4). LC 67-12006. ISBN 0-231-08955-4(v.1); 0-231-08956-1(v.2); 0-231-08957-0 (v.3); 0-231-08958-9(v.4).

This comprehensive directory is the most important biographical work on Republican China available in English. Chinese personal names are romanized according to the Wade-Giles system and alphabetically arranged in the Chinese style—i.e., surname first. However, a few biographies (e.g., Chiang Kai-shek) appear under the name most familiar to Western readers. For the few biographies of Japanese subjects, the Hepburn romanization system is used. Each biography begins with a brief summary of the subject's most recognized contributions or attainments. Biographies include both personal and career information, but emphasis is on the latter. Articles are not signed and bibliographies are not appended. However, the bulk of volume IV is the bibliography for the set. Names are listed in the same sequence in which they appear in the text and the bibliography for each is given, including both works by the subject of the article, if any, and sources used in preparing the article. *The Biographical Dictionary of Republican China: A Personal Name Index* (Janet Krompart, ed. Columbia University Press, 1979. $25.00) is volume V of the set. It provides complete indexing of all persons mentioned in the four-volume dictionary, with extensive cross references and a thorough bibliography.

More than 10 years in preparation, the *Biographical Dictionary of Republican China* is executed according to sound traditions of modern scholarship; it will remain for years the standard source on the subject. The two-volume *Dictionary of Ming Biography* (Columbia University Press, 1976. $100.00/set), which includes 650 biographies with emphasis on rulers and officials, complements Boorman's work by extending coverage to the fourteenth century. [R: WLB, Mar 69, p. 673; Choice, Sept 70, p. 817; ARBA 71, p. 77; ARBA 72, p. 94; Choice, Apr 72, p. 195; WLB, Apr 72, p. 741]

87. Boylan, Henry. **A Dictionary of Irish Biography.** New York, Barnes & Noble, a division of Harper & Row, 1978. 385p. bibliog. $25.00. LC 79-102572. ISBN 0-06-490620-5.

The first comprehensive biographical dictionary of Ireland to appear in 50 years, the *Dictionary of Irish Biography* will be a valuable addition to collections of Irish reference materials. John S. Crone produced the *Concise Dictionary of Irish Biography* (New York, Longman) in 1928, and Alfred Webb wrote the standard *Compendium of Irish Biography* in 1878 (repr., Humanities Press, 1970). Both earlier biographical dictionaries could be considered more comprehensive than Boylan, up to the dates of publication. Boylan, however, had to sacrifice minor figures in Irish history to allow inclusion of important twentieth-century personalities. The introduction carefully explains how selections were made, and discusses the difficulties in determining the selection criteria. The comprehensiveness of individual entries varies, of course, depending not only on the importance of the person, but on the source materials available. The *Dictionary of Irish Biography* will find an important place in most collections of biographical reference works. [R: ARBA 80, p. 53, Choice, June 79, p. 506]   Janet H. Littlefield

88. **Dictionary of Canadian Biography. Volume IV, 1771-1800.** Toronto and Buffalo, University of Toronto Press, 1979. 913p. index. $35.00. ISBN 0-8020-3351-2.

Unlike the basic sets of the *DNB* and *DAB*, the *DCB* is being arranged (and published) in chronological units by death dates (but arranged alphabetically within by personage). Also, to take advantage of the wealth of material being made available to scholars from diverse sources, the *DCB* is now a non-sequential publication. Thus far, volumes 1-3 (1000-1770 A.D.) were published from 1966 to 1974 and effectively cover the French regime in Canada. Volumes 9 and 10 (1861-1880), published from 1972 to 1976, cover the political turbulence of the Confederation period. Volume 4 presents 504 biographies for the period 1771-1800.

The whole project, which should be completed by the turn of the century, is financed by a mixture of government fundings, private bequests, and sales. Its aim: to create original and authoritative biographies that are readable, critical, and interpretive. Criteria for inclusion obviously include importance to the nation's growth and conceptualization. For the student there are copious bibliographies, a full name index, and cross references to other people and other volumes. Volumes 5 to 8 and 11 are on the way, extending the scope through 1890.

Ed. note: Supplementing these volumes is the *Macmillan Dictionary of Canadian Biography*, 4th ed. (Macmillan of Canada, 1978. 914p. $49.95), which extends coverage, on a much smaller scale, through 1976, providing over 5,000 biographies of persons who influenced Canadian history. Dean Tudor

89. **Dictionary of National Biography.** Ed. by S. P. Sen. Calcutta, Institute of Historical Studies; distr., Columbia, MO, South Asia Books, 1972. 4v. $120.00/set (sold only as a set; standing order arrangement). LC 72-906859. ISBN 0-88386-030-9.

According to the preface, this four-volume dictionary is "the first attempt of its kind in India, on the lines of similar works in other countries." The four volumes cover the period 1800 to 1947 and include about 1,400 entries for Indians and for foreigners who made India their home and who "made some tangible contribution to national life." Articles of varying length cover living as well as deceased individuals and are signed. Most of the 350 contributors are historians in Indian universities. Selected bibliographies are appended to longer articles and emphasize Indian-language materials. The work is extensively cross referenced. An important contribution in an area where nothing comparable exists. [R: ARBA 74, p. 45; Choice, June 73, p. 596; C&RL, Jan 74, p. 36]

90. **The Dictionary of National Biography: The Compact Edition.** Complete text reproduced micrographically. New York, Oxford University Press, 1975. 2v. index. $149.00 (in slipcase with magnifying glass). ISBN 0-19-865102-3.

The *Dictionary of National Biography (DNB)* is the first major biographical tool of the English-speaking world. There were other British biographies, but none whose scope or completeness could match the *DNB*. At first the plan was to make a universal biography, but it was decided that such an undertaking would be too impractical. The project was begun by Mr. George Smith, the publisher who took on the financial responsibility, and Sir Leslie Stephen, the editor. In 1889 Stephen resigned because of poor health and was succeeded by Sir Sidney Lee. After his retirement Stephen continued to be a major contributor; in all, he wrote 820 biographies consisting of over 1,370 pages.

The editors intended to include all noteworthy inhabitants of Great Britain, Ireland, and the Colonies, exclusive of living persons, from the earliest historical period to the time of publication. Included are Britons who lived abroad and foreigners who became British subjects during their lifetime. Important legendary figures, such as Robin Hood, are also listed. Among the names included are the very famous, the famous, and the infamous.

The *DNB* staff gathered names from a wide range of sources in historical and scientific literature and from an endless amount of miscellaneous records and reports. A preliminary list was compiled and sent to specialists of literary experience competent to write articles for the proposed dictionary. Subsequent lists were published in the *Athenaeum* and readers' comments were invited.

The contributors were urged to get their information from original sources whenever possible, especially from unpublished papers. The articles had to be accompanied by bibliographies. The average length of a biography is a little less than one page, although some run much longer (Shakespeare, 49 pages) and some are less than one column. The articles are signed with the initials of the contributor, and a key to their names is included in every volume.

On the whole, the *DNB* is praised for its scholarly approach, its good writing, and its comprehensiveness. Most of the bibliographies include private papers and records as sources. For some of the articles only secondary sources are used. Most of the entries in this category, however, are for lesser known persons of the nineteenth century about whom little information is available. The treatment is generally objective and the style is entertaining as well as informative.

Included in the basic set are 29,120 articles. At present the work has been brought up to 1960 by supplements. The compact edition of the *DNB* includes the complete and unaltered texts of the 22 volumes reissued by Oxford University Press in 1938 and the six volumes of supplements which make up the twentieth century *DNB*. The last supplement, covering 1951-1960, was published by Oxford University Press in 1971.

At this reasonable price, most libraries should now have the *DNB*; even reading it with a magnifying glass should not detract from the use of this monumental work. [R: ARBA 77, p. 79; BL, 15 July 76, p. 1626; Choice, Apr 76, p. 201]   Bohdan S. Wynar

91.   **The Encyclopaedia Africana Dictionary of African Biography (in 20 Volumes): Volume One, Ethiopia-Ghana.** New York, Reference Publications, 1977. 367p. illus. maps. index. $59.95. LC 76-17954. ISBN 0-917256-0188.

92.   **The Encyclopaedia Africana Dictionary of African Biography, Volume 2: Sierra Leone-Zaire.** Algonac, MI, Reference Publications, 1979. 372p. illus. maps. index. $59.95; $49.95/vol. on standing order. LC 76-17954. ISBN 0-917256-06-9.

The appearance of these volumes under the aegis of the *Encyclopaedia Africana* is a major publishing event. It is the first tangible outcome of W. E. B. Du Bois' dream (conceived in 1909) of a monumental synoptic work devoted to the contributions of Africa and Africans to civilization. The idea has been kept alive for more than one-half century, but not until 1961 was it possible to translate it into concrete work plans. That year, Du Bois moved to Ghana to organize and direct the project with Nkrumah's financial and moral support. Following Du Bois' death in 1963, the editorial board of the *Encyclopaedia* decided to implement the plan by publishing initially volumes of biographical articles on a country-by-country basis covering the entire sweep of African history. Subsequent financial support came from some African governments and from American and West German foundations.

The first volume brings together 146 Ethiopian and 138 Ghanian biographies, meticulously researched by leading Africanists, half of whom are African nationals associated with leading universities on the continent. Volume 2 contains 138 Sierra Leone biographies and 110 Zaire (former Belgian Congo) biographies, all of non-living persons; of the 43 contributors to the volume 39 are African scholars associated with their national universities.

The biographies in both volumes include rulers, religious leaders, politicians, intellectuals, and people from all walks of life who have influenced the course of events in these countries. All are treated in a broad historical framework in the context of events contemporary with the biographee. Articles are cross referenced and followed by substantial bibliographies both of materials in Western languages and of citations to local source materials when available. A large number of the biographies are accompanied by portraits and illustrations. Each country section is introduced with a historical essay. Other features include maps, glossaries of unfamiliar terms, and in volume 2, chronologies of past kings of pre-colonial Congo and the rulers of the early kingdom of Lunda, now southeastern

Zaire. Detailed indexes at the ends of the volumes provide excellent access to the contents of the articles.

Collectively, these biographies accomplish the project's objective, which Kenneth Kaunda, president of the Republic of Zambia, defined in the *Dictionary*'s prefatory note: "to reveal the genius of her [Africa's] people, their history, culture and institutions, their achievements as well as their shortcomings." The *Dictionary of African Biography* should be hailed as a landmark achievement in every respect. When completed (20 volumes), it will close a vast gap in our knowledge. In restoring the dignity of Africa's contribution to the civilization of mankind, it will become an effective instrument for the promotion of cultural understanding between Africa and the West. [ARBA 79, p. 173; BL, 1 Mar 78, p. 1127; Choice, Dec 78, p. 1346; ARBA 80, p. 139]   Michael Keresztesi

93.   Lewytzkyj, Borys, and Juliusz Stroynowski, eds. **Who's Who in the Socialist Countries: A Biographical Encyclopedia of 10,000 Leading Personalities in 16 Communist Countries.** 1st ed. New York, K. G. Saur; Munich, Verlag Dokumentation, 1978. 736p. $129.00. LC 78-4068. ISBN 0-89664-011-6(Saur).

As most specialists know, communist countries do not publish biographical directories of the who's who type. One can find only a minimum of biographical information in numerous Soviet or Eastern European general or subject encyclopedias, and the few directories that do exist provide information only on full and associate members of the Soviet Academy of Sciences and on the most prominent Soviet scholars. It is extremely difficult to find biographical information on Soviet or Eastern European officials, and one must search hundreds of "official sources" (usually newspapers and journals) to get bits and pieces of biographical data. As a result, biographical directories published in the West are incomplete and provide only fragmentary information. This is the case with *Who's Who in Communist China* (published already in several editions by Union Research Institute, Hong Kong); *Party and Government Officials of the Soviet Union, 1917-1967* (Scarecrow, 1969); and *The Soviet Diplomatic Corps, 1917-1967* (Scarecrow, 1970). *Who Was Who in the USSR: A Biographic Directory Containing Five Thousand and Fifteen Biographies of Prominent Soviet Historical Personalities* (compiled by the Institute for the Study of the USSR and published by Scarecrow in 1972), covering important Soviet persons no longer living, also falls into this category, although the magnitude of the project compensates somewhat for its uneven coverage.

The present volume is no exception; there are obvious gaps in its coverage. Out of 20,000 biographical sketches, at least half are of Soviet personalities, primarily government officials, party functionaries, and some prominent scholars. The information for these biographies comes primarily from Lewytzkyj's archives—clippings and notes from all available Soviet reference books, hundreds of daily and weekly Soviet newspapers, and other sources. (Lewytzkyj is the author of many books on the Soviet Union in several languages and, with the possible exception of Professor John A. Armstrong of the University of Wisconsin, has the most extensive private archives on this subject.) Somewhat weaker is the representation of biographies of people from 15 other communist countries, prepared by Professor Stroynowski, who left his native Poland in 1969. The emphasis is again on government and party officials, but there are also rather lengthy biographies on scholars, writers, and other personalities, not all of national importance. Obviously, it is much easier to obtain biographical data on Polish or Yugoslav officials than on Soviet personalities. Thus, coverage is uneven, and biographical sketches vary in length, depending on the relative importance of the biographee. Nevertheless, considering the magnitude of this work, both editors should be congratulated on preparing a unique reference work that will be of great interest to all students of Eastern European studies. [R: ARBA 79, p. 72; Choice, Dec 78, p. 1350; C&RL, July 79, p. 346; LJ, 1 Sept 78, p. 1626; WLB, Nov 78, p. 275]   Bohdan S. Wynar

2 LIBRARY SCIENCE

GENERAL WORKS

94. Katz, William A. **Introduction to Reference Work.** 3rd ed. New York, McGraw-Hill, 1978. 2v. index. (McGraw-Hill Series in Library Education). $13.95(v.1); $12.95(v.2). LC 77-12539. ISBN 0-07-033331-9(v.1); 0-07-033332-7(v.2).

Katz's well-known book remains the basic introductory textbook for library school students and reference librarians. The third edition has been substantially rewritten and updated from the second edition (1974). In the first volume, the author discusses the basic reference sources, following the traditional arrangement of different types of reference sources: bibliographies; indexing and abstracting services; encyclopedias; ready-reference sources (almanacs, yearbooks, etc.); biographical sources; dictionaries; geographical sources; and government documents. The second volume elaborates on an introductory chapter in the first volume ("The Reference Process"). It covers such topics as reference service and the information community; channels of communication interview and search; reference service and the computer (one of the most substantially revised sections); and evaluation of reference services. [R: ARBA 79, p. 146; C&RL, Nov 78, p. 509; LJ, 15 Nov 78, p. 2317]

95. Rogers, A. Robert. **The Humanities: A Selective Guide to Information Sources.** 2nd ed. Littleton, CO, Libraries Unlimited, 1980. 355p. index. (Library Science Text Series). $25.00; $14.50pa. LC 79-25335. ISBN 0-87287-206-8; 0-87287-222-X(pa.).

Rogers' text, used extensively in its first edition by library schools across the country for courses in the bibliography and literature of the humanities, is now updated and available in a revised second edition.

The Humanities is both a graduate level text and a subject reference tool in philosophy, religion, the visual and performing arts, language, and literature. Grouped by discipline, each bibliographic chapter is preceded by a chapter outlining the process of information access in each discipline: major divisions of the field, commonly used cataloging and classification practices specific to a particular discipline, contributions of professional organizations, and special subject collections. New sources have been added to the bibliographic chapters, which now annotate 1,200 works that serve either a selection or reference function; and annotations are longer and more comparative than in the first edition. A separate section has also been added which discusses multidisciplinary works.

The arrangement of the text by discipline within the humanities allows for ease of classroom use and rapid reference referral. The bibliographic chapters are indexed by author and title, and a broad subject index gives access to topics receiving more than passing mention in the textual chapters. [R: JAL, July 80, p. 186]

BIBLIOGRAPHIES

96. Jordan, Anne Harwell, and Melbourne Jordan, eds. **Cannons' Bibliography of Library Economy, 1876-1920: An Author Index with Citations.** Metuchen, NJ, Scarecrow, 1976. 473p. $20.50. LC 76-3711. ISBN 0-8108-0918-4.

For the period from 1876 through 1920, H. G. T. Cannons' *Bibliography of Library Economy* is the major "classified index to professional periodical literature in the English language" for these 44 years. It includes "articles published in the leading periodicals devoted to librarianship in the United States and Great Britain, as well as a few monographs." Cannons' presents the citations in a subject or classified arrangement, and within each grouping the material is arranged chronologically by date of publication. This was a useful arrangement for historians, but for others it meant that checking through Cannons' was a painstaking and laborious task.

Anne and Melbourne Jordan have prepared *An Author Index with Citations* to Cannons', a supplementary publication that serves "to provide further access to this material." Their work is arranged in two major units: 1) a listing of "Publications Indexed," and 2) an alphabetical listing by author's surname. Thus, the writings of Putnam, Dewey, Billings, Dana, Cutter, Spofford, Williamson, and other "historically important figures in librarianship" are now more easily accessible to students and researchers. Each entry contains the following data: author's surname, initials, title of article or monograph, name of periodical, volume number, and pagination. It would have been helpful if the date of issue had been included in these citations. However, this is a useful reference tool for librarians, library educators, library school students, and library historians.

John Burke states in the introduction that "the Jordans have improved upon the indexing of this important bibliography. Corrections were made, whenever possible, to the existing material appearing in Cannons', and a considerable number of incomplete and blind entries were rescued with appropriate changes. This book as a result, is a genuine supplement to Cannons' *Bibliography of Library Economy*, as well as a tool which makes Cannons' indexing accessible to the profession." [R: ARBA 77, p. 89; Choice, Feb 77, p. 1572; LJ, 15 Oct 76, p. 2152] Paul A. Winckler

DICTIONARIES AND ENCYCLOPEDIAS

97. **ALA World Encyclopedia of Library and Information Services.** Robert Wedgeworth, ed.; Joel Lee, associate ed. Chicago, American Library Association, 1980. 601p. illus. $85.00. LC 80-10912. ISBN 0-8389-0305-3.

From "Academic Libraries" to "Zimbabwe Rhodesia," the new *ALA World Encyclopedia of Library and Information Services* proposes to "inform and educate" students, practitioners, and the public about the field of librarianship at the international level. Following the inception of the *ALA Yearbook*, first published in 1976, the yearbook editorial staff sought an international perspective, but considered that the breadth and scope of such coverage demanded knowledge of history as well as the present status and condition of libraries, archives, and other information services in many countries. For these reasons, the new encyclopedia was conceived in 1976 and published in 1980.

This reference tool includes 452 articles, 700,000 words, 364 contributors from 145 countries, 33 editorial advisers, 300 (black and white) illustrations, and 144 statistical tables. Articles on librarianship in various countries of the world, on major historical periods, on the library as an institution, on the theory and practice of librarianship, and biographies are covered in average lengths of more than 1,000 words. Contributors were "selected for their knowledge, experience, and professional or scholarly achievements [that] lend impressive authority to the *ALA Encyclopedia*." A weakness of the encyclopedia is the differing levels of contributors' expertise. As an example, articles on library education: comparative; curriculum; history; and specialization (pp. 320-30), written by four different authors, vary in documentation and treatment. Two are well written and scholarly in nature, while the other two are speculative, superficial in nature, and cursory in content.

The Outline of Contents is organized in five principal divisions: The Library in Society; The Library as an Institution; Theory and Practice of Librarianship; Education and Research; and International Library, Information, and Bibliographic Organizations. Fritz Milkau's *Handuch der Bibliothekswissenschaft, The Encyclopedia of Library and*

Information Science, edited by Kent, Lancour, and Daily, and *The Dictionary of American Library Biography*, published by Libraries Unlimited, are mentioned for assistance in planning and setting standards for publishing the encyclopedia. A Parallel Index in the margins throughout the volume accompanies articles and provides the reader with other references.

As a new single-volume encyclopedia in the field of librarianship, this is a selectively needed item in any reference collection. The price may prohibit purchase by small libraries with limited budgets. Donald D. Foos

98. **Encyclopedia of Library and Information Science.** Allen Kent, Harold Lancour, and Jay E. Daily, executive eds. New York, Marcel Dekker, 1968- . $45.00/v. subscription. LC 68-31232. In progress.

Projected for 32 volumes, 28 volumes of which have been published to date, the *Encyclopedia of Library and Information Science* is the first attempt in English to provide encyclopedic coverage for library science. The purpose is clearly stated in the preface to the first volume. "The emphasis has been, throughout, on depth of treatment. While the contributors were urged to stress basic information, they were likewise encouraged to express their evaluative opinions as well, wherever possible, to suggest and indicate future trends as they saw them. . . . The editors are . . . committed to a 'one world' concept of their science. To this end the approach has been strongly international. . . . A more accurate description of the basic editorial policy would be that this work is not so much inter-national as it is non-national, although, admittedly, this has not been easy to accomplish."

In general, the editors have kept their promise. There is an impressive number of foreign contributors, a number of good articles on individual countries (e.g., Brazil), and many excellent pages devoted to certain aspects of library science or library development. Nevertheless, the material is of uneven quality. Articles vary in length, not necessarily reflecting the relative importance of a given topic. Some articles are quite chatty, others provide only a minimum of factual data and occasionally read like observations made by tourists visiting libraries in some strange countries. Such articles are not, unfortunately, limited to those on libraries in Botswana or the British West Indies. A good example of this treatment is found in a long article on the National Library of Austria. Much factual information is somehow lost in its chatty style, and the facts that can be ferreted out are not always accurate. There are many books and hundreds of articles about this library, but no bibliography is included with this article. Obviously, not all articles dealing with the national development of libraries are so inadequate, but, nevertheless, more editorial attention in this particular area will eliminate embarrassment.

Articles on the "home scene" are much better, although there are exceptions. For instance, an article on bookmobiles stretches out to 57 pages while, by contrast, an article on bibliography is crammed into 12 pages. Obviously, the value of printed material is measured in terms other than number of pages, but such a dramatic difference seems worth pointing out. There is a wealth of information in this encyclopedia and its purpose is to be applauded and supported, but the lack of editorial supervision remains evident. The most harmful result of this neglect of supervision seems to be that the volumes are filled with a certain amount of trivia.

Volumes 29-31 are scheduled for 1980 publication. The final volume, which will contain a detailed analytical index for the entire work, along with two supplements, is to be published in early 1981. [R: BL, 15 Feb 69, p. 601; RQ, Wint 69, p. 140; WLB, May 69, p. 907; RQ, Fall 69, p. 80; Choice, Apr 73, p. 264; ARBA 71, p. 34; ARBA 72, p. 31; ARBA 73, p. 58; ARBA 74, p. 49; ARBA 75, p. 72; ARBA 76, p. 94; ARBA 78, p. 77; ARBA 79, p. 81; ARBA 80, p. 58] Bohdan S. Wynar

99.   Harrod, Leonard Montague. **The Librarians' Glossary of Terms Used in Librarian- ship, Documentation and the Book Crafts, and Reference Book.** 4th rev. ed. Boulder, CO, Westview Press, 1977. 903p. $42.50. LC 76-52489. ISBN 0-8915-727-6.

The previous edition of *The Librarians' Glossary* was characterized as "a handbook of British terminology . . . for a British audience." The fourth edition of the *Glossary* pro- vides well-written definitions of library terms for American as well as British librarians. New terms in the fourth edition include: "Information science," glossed by Hal Borko; "PRECIS," defined by Derek Austin; and in the Supplement, *Williams & Wilkins v. the United States* discussed under the term "Fair use." The British orientation is evident in the discussion of "Cataloguing in Source," which describes the CIP program at the Library of Congress, though not by name. On the other hand, "Centralized processing" only refers to developments in the United States.

The third edition defined 784 pages of terms. In this edition, 690 terms have been added and 310 expanded, to give a total of 903 pages. It would be useful to know the number and kinds of terms that have been dropped, and the policy for such revisions (i.e., obsolescence, terminology change, etc.). The major and peripheral areas of librarianship are adequately covered, including printing, information science, bibliography, professional associations and awards (British and American), the larger library institutions, and the functional areas of acquisitions, cataloging, reference, and, to a lesser degree, manage- ment. *The Librarians' Glossary*, fourth edition, makes the effort to reach an American audience (who still lack an updated ALA glossary). Since American librarians have accepted "catalogue" in *AACR 2*, perhaps an "Anglo-American" glossary accords well with a developing trend of linguistic cooperation. [R: ARBA 79, p. 82; JAL, March 78, p. 49; LJ, 15 June 78, p. 1238]   Deborah Jane Brewer

DIRECTORIES

100.   Ash, Lee, comp. **Subject Collections: A Guide to Special Book Collections and Sub- ject Emphases as Reported by University, College, Public, and Special Libraries and Museums in the United States and Canada.** 5th ed., rev. and enl. New York, R. R. Bowker, 1978. 1184p. $72.50. LC 78-26399. ISBN 0-8352-0924-5.

This standard reference work hardly needs an introduction. The first edition was published in 1958 (17,000 entries) and the fourth in 1974 (70,000 entries). The present edi- tion has some important innovations. It has been produced with the assistance of a com- puter, enabling most participating libraries to review on previously submitted printout all of the entries that were listed for their collections under the subject headings assigned to them in the fourth edition. According to the preface, most suggestions for change, inclu- sion, or omission have been accepted by the editor. As a result, this new edition has over 2,500 new subjects, 1,000 of which are personal name collections of books or papers by or about the persons listed, and 1,500 of which are entirely new subjects. As a result of adding new subjects, some broader headings (e.g., "Microforms—Collections") have been dropped.

The fourth edition was exceedingly wasteful of space due to its repetition of identical entries. Some criticism was also raised about cross references; specifically, it was pointed out that under both "Slavic History" and "Slavic Languages and Literatures" the same rather long entry for the NYPL Slavonic Division appears. In most cases, this is no longer true in the fifth edition. The entry for NYPL under the heading "Slavic History" now has a note indicating that this collection is described in *Dictionary Catalog of the Slavonic Col- lection* (G. K. Hall, 1974); an identical note is provided under "Slavic Languages and Literatures." This approach certainly makes sense and provides additional information about more specialized reference sources.

Along with Downs' *American Library Resources: A Bibliographical Guide* and its supplement, the new edition of *Subject Collections* should be a high-priority acquisition for all types of libraries. [R: ARBA 80, p. 58; C&RL, July 79, p. 378; LJ, 1 May 79, p. 1043; WLB, Apr 79, p. 587]   Bohdan S. Wynar

101. **Directory of Special Libraries and Information Centers.** Margaret L. Young, and Harold C. Young, eds. 5th ed. Detroit, Gale, 1979. 2v. index. $110.00(v.1); $86.00(v.2). LC 79-16966(v.1); 79-16788(v.2). ISBN 0-8103-0297-7(v.1); 0-8103-0298-5(v.2).

102. **New Special Libraries: A Periodic Supplement to the Fifth Edition of Directory of Special Libraries and Information Centers, Issue No. 1- .** Margaret L. Young, and Harold C. Young, eds. Detroit, Gale, 1979- . irreg. $96.00 (inter-edition subscription). ISSN 0193-4287.

103. **Subject Directory of Special Libraries and Information Centers.** 5th ed. Margaret L. Young, and Harold C. Young, eds. Detroit, Gale, 1979. 5v. index. $200.00/set; $48.00/vol. LC 79-21711. ISBN 0-8103-0300-0(v.1); 0-8103-0301-9(v.2); 0-8103-0302-7 (v.3); 0-8103-0303-5(v.4); 0-8103-0304-5(v.5).

The fifth edition of Gale's *Directory of Special Libraries and Information Centers* covers over 14,000 libraries, including 1,200 new entries and 32,000 changes from the fourth edition. Again published in a multivolume format, volume 1 is the directory of special libraries in the United States and Canada, arranged alphabetically by sponsoring institution, with numbered entries listing name of sponsoring institution, name of library (if distinctive), address and telephone number, name of person in charge, founding date, staff size, special subject collections and scope of collection as a whole, size of holdings, number of serial titles received, services to outside inquirers, automated library systems, network memberships, publications issued by library, special catalogs and indexes maintained, and names and titles of professional supervisory staff. Volume 2, *Geographic and Personnel Indexes*, provides access to libraries by state or province (subarranged by city), and in a second index, by names of personnel associated with the libraries.

New Special Libraries: A Periodic Supplement to the Fifth Edition forms volume 3, and lists alphabetically libraries identified after completion of the main *Directory*, as well as libraries that have undergone substantial reorganization and require new entries. *New Special Libraries* will appear periodically until publication of the new sixth edition.

The *Subject Directory of Special Libraries and Information Centers* complements the *Directory* and *New Special Libraries*, providing information on the over 14,000 special libraries in the United States and Canada. Each of the five volumes represents a major subject area: business and law libraries; education and information science libraries; health science libraries; social science and humanities libraries; and science and technology libraries. These five areas are further divided into 27 subject sections, with United States and Canadian libraries listed separately under each subject heading. Each of the five volumes can be purchased separately, allowing specialized information centers access to data about similar centers without the necessity of purchasing the entire set. For each listing, all the information contained in the entry in the *Directory of Special Libraries* is repeated, making referral to the original entry unnecessary. Over two dozen facts about each library are included (whenever available), ranging from the official name of the facility, address, and phone number, to collection statistics and policies regarding use of the collection.

The *Directory of Special Libraries* is again recommended as the most comprehensive source of information about special libraries available. Researchers, reference librarians, and interlibrary loan departments will find all three titles valuable. [R: ARBA 80, pp. 83-84]   Janet H. Littlefield

104. Kruzas, Anthony T., ed. **Encyclopedia of Information Systems and Services.** Linda Varekamp Sullivan and John Schmittroth, Jr., associate eds. 3rd ed. Detroit, Gale, 1978. 1030p. index. $135.00. LC 78-14575. ISBN 0-8103-0940-8.

The first edition of this well-known work (containing 833 entries and 1,109 pages) was published in 1971, and the second edition (containing 1,750 entries and 1,271 pages) was published in 1974. The third edition is also substantially enlarged, providing 2,094 entries for some 2,500 organizations, including over 400 foreign organizations. As in previous editions, this volume covers computer service companies, publishers, libraries, professional societies, government agencies, research organizations, information centers, and other organizations that produce, process, store, and use bibliographic and nonbibliographic information. Not included are printed commercial and legal services, libraries with traditional reference services only, computer and micrographic hardware manufacturers and distributors, general purpose data management systems, and similar organizations. Eighteen indexes facilitate the use of this volume; in addition to the combined index to organizations, systems, and services, there are separate indexes for data producers and publishers, library and information networks, micrographic applications and services, etc.

New Information Systems and Services: A Periodic Supplement to the Third Edition of Encyclopedia of Information Systems and Services (Gale, 1979- . irregular. $70.00/inter-edition subscription) has the same scope and format of the base volume, but it incorporates all the headings into a single comprehensive index, adding 234 entries for: 1) recently established organizations, systems, and services; 2) new products and extended services initiated by organizations listed in the third edition; 3) organizations and services overlooked in the third edition; and 4) organizations that have undergone substantial changes since their appearance in the third edition. New data bases available from online vendors and computerized information services available in libraries are provided. The *Supplement* also includes new online systems and listings for new information technologies, such as viewdata and teletext systems. [R: ARBA 79, p. 85; BL, 1 May 79, p. 1388]

Andrew G. Torok
Bohdan S. Wynar

105. Lewanski, Richard C., comp. **Subject Collections in European Libraries.** 2nd ed. New York, R. R. Bowker, 1978. 495p. index. $57.00. ISBN 0-85935-011-8.

Intended as a companion volume to Lee Ash's *Subject Collections* (entry 100), this work is somewhat improved and substantially enlarged (12,000 entries) in comparison to the first edition published in 1965 (8,000 entries). It is arranged by subject, using the Dewey Decimal Classification, and the information is based on a questionnaire mailed to some 10,000 libraries selected from national and local library directories and other sources. According to the preface, only about 25% of the libraries answered the questionnaire; consequently, most of the information included in this volume is based on secondary sources. Each entry includes the following data: name of institution, address, director (when given), year established, special items, size of collection, and restrictions in use, if any. This new edition occasionally includes hours of service, availability of photocopying facilities, and types of catalogs or periodicals published by a given institution. The volume concludes with a rather inadequate subject index, which serves as a kind of alphabetical key to the classification scheme.

The listing for Ukrainian literature (p. 362) includes 11 entries. The largest library in Ukraine, Tsentral'na Naukova Biblioteka of the Academy of Sciences of the Ukrainian SSR in Kiev, is listed; however, the information provided is not always accurate. Some of the errors were probably made in typing or copying from the rather obsolete directory, *Biblioteky Ukrains'koi SSR. Dovidnyk* [Libraries of Ukrainian SSR. Directory] (Kharkiv, 1969). Thus, much of the information is taken word for word from the above-mentioned source, e.g., name of the director (now deceased), quantity of mss., music scores, picture prints, patents, etc. Lewanski indicates general holdings of this library as 4 million items (should be 6 million, according to *Biblioteky Ukrains'koi SSR. Dovidnyk*, and is now actually over 7 million). Interestingly enough, the same library is listed again under Ukrainian history (p. 449); this entry lists the library's holdings as 5 million and mostly repeats the information provided in the section under literature.

If Lewanski correctly lists some of the special collections for leading literary figures (e.g., Kotsiubyns'kyi) under literature, it is unnecessary to list them again in the historical section. Instead, special collections of prominent Ukrainian historians (e.g., Lazarevs'kyi or M. Hrushevs'kyi) should be listed only in the historical section. Of the 11 entries given for Ukrainian literature, some are simply not pertinent. Thus, Knyzhkova Palata Ukrains'koi SSR (Ukrainian Book Chamber) is an equivalent to the All-Union Book Chamber in Moscow, specializing in bibliographical work (primarily preparing Ukrainian national bibliographies as well as some trade bibliographies). The same is true of some smaller libraries, e.g., libraries of certain institutes of education listed by the compiler. Most large university libraries are not listed, e.g., Kiev, Odessa, etc. As a matter of fact, Lenin Library in Moscow, the largest Soviet library, contains a rather significant collection in Ukrainian literature, as do other libraries in the Soviet Union outside of Ukraine.

Such errors in fact or interpretation can be found in other subjects, which simply illustrates the difficulty in executing a project of this magnitude. These difficulties notwithstanding, the work provides a beginning point from which to locate special collections. It should be recommended to all academic libraries. [R: ARBA 80, p. 62; C&RL, July 79, p. 391; JAL, May 79, p. 111; LJ, 1 June 79, p. 1231]   Bohdan S. Wynar

HANDBOOKS

106.   Chan, Lois Mai. **Immroth's Guide to the Library of Congress Classification.** 3rd ed. Littleton, CO, Libraries Unlimited, 1980. 402p. index. (Library Science Text Series). $25.00; $14.50pa. LC 80-16981. ISBN 0-87287-224-6; 0-87287-235-1(pa.).

Lois Chan's revision updates Immroth's *Guide to the Library of Congress Classification* by elucidating changes in policies and practices that have taken place since 1971 and by incorporating examples and instructive analysis of recently published schedules and revisions of schedules.

Chapters 1-4 treat the development and purpose of the classification, the general principles and characteristics, the notation (including Cutter number) applicable to the entire system, and the use of the tables. Chapter 5, which discusses individual classes, has been completely revised and enlarged; and chapter 6, on special types of library materials, is new to this edition.

Examples are included throughout. Many are new, and those retained from the second edition have been checked against the Library of Congress shelflist to ensure validity. The appendix now contains only those tables that are used throughout the system but printed in only a few of the schedules, and tables that have undergone significant change or revision.

107.   Chan, Lois Mai. **Library of Congress Subject Headings: Principles and Application.** Littleton, CO, Libraries Unlimited, 1978. 347p. bibliog. index. (Research Studies in Library Science, No. 15). $22.50. LC 78-9497. ISBN 0-87287-187-8.

Since the 1951 publication of David Haykin's *Subject Headings: A Practical Guide*, many changes in the formation, structure, and application of subject headings have taken place. Chan's new text re-examines the underlying principles of LC subject headings and describes current subject cataloging practices of the Library of Congress. Advances in both the theory and techniques of information retrieval through subject analysis, not previously brought together in one text, are presented along with practical suggestions for their implementation. The approach is descriptive rather than prescriptive; no attempt is made to formulate any rules. Rather, the book is an analysis of principles and a description of current practice. Part 1, "Principles, Form and Structure," covers topics such as forms of headings, subdivisions, cross references, and proper names in subject headings. Part 2, "Application," provides guidelines for cataloging special types of materials and for items in subject areas requiring special treatment—for instance, music, art, and legal materials. Numerous card samples and examples occur throughout the text. Appended are current information on free-floating subdivisions, abbreviations, capitalization, punctuation, and filing; a bibliography; and subject index.

Much more limited in scope is Joan Marshall's *On Equal Terms: A Thesaurus for Nonsexist Indexing and Cataloging* (Neal-Schuman; distr., ABC-Clio, 1977. 152p. $14.95; $9.50pa.). This work is a constructive first step toward the correction of some of the sexist, racial, and ethnic biases in the Library of Congress subject headings. It is to be hoped that Ms. Marshall's significant effort will be expanded and supplemented in the future. Though there is a question whether LCSH will adopt all of Marshall's suggestions, her contribution should certainly give subject catalogers some viable alternatives to the perpetuation of prejudicial and stereotypical terminology. [R: ARBA 79, p. 133; C&RL, Mar 79, p. 167; JAL, Jan 79, p. 457; LJ, 1 Dec 78, p. 2395; RQ, Spr 79, p. 301]   Doralyn J. Hickey
Bohdan S. Wynar

108.   Duckett, Kenneth W. **Modern Manuscripts: A Practical Manual for Their Management, Care, and Use.** Nashville, TN, American Association for State and Local History, 1975. 375p. illus. bibliog. index. $16.00. LC 75-5717. ISBN 0-910050-16-3.

This is the most thorough, concise, clearly written, and logically organized practical guide available to the curator of manuscripts. Duckett modestly claims that it is aimed at the novice curator, but certainly the experienced manuscript librarian will find much of interest and value in the book. In nine chapters the author considers manuscript collecting, administration, acquisitions, physical care and conservation, establishing bibliographic control, information retrieval (automation, the computer, and microphotography), non-manuscript material, use of collections, and public service. Each chapter concludes with a very useful discussion of selected readings, and the notes for each chapter contain a wealth of information. There are three useful appendixes: Plans, Records Center Carton and Flat-Storage Box; Table of Equivalents; and Perpetual Calendar. Other additions are directories of associations, publications, equipment, supplies and services, a list of facsimiles, a glossary, and an excellent bibliography (pp. 345-69). There is an index, the illustrations are apt, and the book is well printed and sturdily bound. [R: ARBA 77, p. 180; Choice, Feb 76, p. 1556; C&RL, May 76, p. 276; LQ, July 76, p. 319]   Dean H. Keller

109.   Irvine, Betty Jo. **Slide Libraries: A Guide for Academic Institutions, Museums, and Special Collections.** With the assistance of P. Eileen Fry. 2nd ed. Littleton, CO, Libraries Unlimited, 1979. 321p. illus. index. $22.50. LC 79-17354. ISBN 0-87287-202-5.

Irvine's pioneering work, *Slide Libraries*, out of print and unavailable to slide curators, art librarians, and media professionals for several years, has been fully revised and enlarged in this second edition. Among the expanded topics are automation applications for slide collections, the development of standardized cataloging and classification applications, and sophisticated indexing techniques utilizing both manual and machine systems. A new section has been devoted to a subject that was only mentioned in the 1974 edition—environmental controls and preservation measures for slides.

Slide Libraries presents a comprehensive overview of the establishment and management of slide libraries: administration and staffing, classification and cataloging, use of standard library techniques and tools, equipment and supplies, storage and access systems, planning for physical facilities, projection systems, and acquisition, production methods, and equipment. The text is supplemented by a 35-page classified bibliography, a directory of distributors and manufacturers of equipment and supplies, and a directory of slide sources. Illustrating the volume are 50 figures, 29 diagrams, and 19 photographs. [R: ARBA 80, p. 85]

110. Muench, Eugene V. **Biomedical Subject Headings.** 2nd ed. Hamden, CT, Shoe String Press, 1979. 774p. $52.50. LC 78-27206. ISBN 0-208-01747.

Standardization of subject headings has long been a controversial topic as far as specialized collections are concerned. However, in this era of machine-readable data bases, it might appear as if several problems had been resolved through the production of authorized sources such as MARC. Unfortunately, in the field of medicine, the National Library of Medicine pioneered early in its own cataloging data base (now known as CATLINE), and the two systems are based on different subject heading lists. As the "Introduction" to Muench's volume notes, "the purpose of this comparative listing of these two controlled vocabularies is to state precisely where they are alike and where they are different and to enable librarians to convert this information from one system to the other to suit the objectives of the local library."

The work, now in its second edition (the first was issued in 1971), is arranged in three parts: 1) the main section of the tool, an alphabetical list of MeSH headings followed by LC equivalents or cross references to other MeSH terms; 2) a 10-page list of "Subheadings," i.e., MeSH terms with LC equivalents, and 3) a list of LC subject headings, with MeSH equivalents when those headings do not fall into the alphabetical sequence. Five caveats are also noted: 1) the major source for this volume was the alphabetic list of the *Index Medicus* MeSH, i.e., the large type headings (certain small type terms which occur as "see under" cross references have been included but the "user is advised to consult the introduction to MeSH"); 2) alpha-numeric symbols (A1-B4) refer to the categorized list (trees) materials, which are not found in this volume although there is a list of "Categories and Subcategories"; 3) since MeSH was produced for a specialized field, it usually excludes the word "medical" while the LC list often uses it to provide specificity; 4) certain concepts are obviously handled differently in the two sources; and 5) MeSH makes heavier use of inverted subject headings.

It is hard to question the value of this work for a cataloguer who must make appropriate and consistent selections in terminology. Moreover, the editor notes, "With the increasing sophistication of computer software and hardware, technical processing in libraries will become fully automated. The ultimate value of this work lies in a computer interface between these two controlled vocabularies." In addition, of course, the reference librarian will invariably find the tool useful in effectively searching either a computer or manual data base.   Laurel Grotzinger

111. Pacey, Philip. **Art Library Manual: A Guide to Resources and Practice.** New York, published in association with the Art Libraries Society by R. R. Bowker, 1977. 423p. index. $26.50. LC 77-70290. ISBN 0-85935-054-1.

Delving into nearly all the major areas of art librarianship, this manual is by far one of the finest published to date. Although all but two of the contributors are British and a few of the chapters pertain to collections in areas that should be covered by all art libraries but are not, most of the text is just as pertinent to North American librarians as they are to the British. Sponsored by the original Art Libraries Society (ARLIS) in Great Britain, each chapter is written by erudite librarians. Space does not allow individual critiques of the chapters, and even though each reader will have preferences for the subject matter of some chapters over others, they are all a well-balanced mixture of procedures and bibliographic essays that are uniformly well written, specific, and informative. There is no better way of describing the contents than to simply list the chapter titles: general art; bibliographies; quick reference material; the art book; museum and gallery publications; exhibition catalogs; sales catalogs and the art market; standards and patents; trade literature; periodicals and serials; abstracts and indexes; theses; primary sources; out-of-print materials; reprints; microforms; sound recordings; video and film; slides and filmstrips; photographs and reproductions of works of art; photographs as works of art; printed ephemera; book design and illustration; artists' books and book art; loan collections of original works of art; illustrations. Included in two brief appendices are lists of sources of information and conservation. Primary sources are defined as original manuscripts such as letters and documents; therefore, this chapter is concerned with archival materials and not printed primary sources. Little is said about collecting early printed guide books and other such essential tools.

Each chapter could well be expanded into a single volume, but in every case the authors delve into specifics, not theories. Art librarians, no matter how knowledgable, will find this guide an excellent refresher course. The *Art Library Manual* will certainly become the main textbook for art librarianship courses. It should also be available to all library users and to library administrators responsible for establishing materials and staffing budgets, since the authors lucidly state the unique problems universally encountered by art librarians. [R: ARBA 78, p. 139; Choice, Dec 77, p. 1337; JAL, Sept 78, p. 223; LJ, 15 Jan 78, p. 146; RQ, Spring 78, p. 267]   Jacqueline D. Sisson

112.   Saffady, William. **Micrographics.** Littleton, CO, Libraries Unlimited, 1978. 238p. bibliog. index. (Library Science Text Series). $22.50. LC 78-1309. ISBN 0-87287-175-4.

This introductory textbook is designed for practicing librarians and library school students who want a systematic presentation of the basic facets of micrographics as applied to library work. The first chapter introduces the topic of microforms and libraries, presenting an overview of major areas of application. The subsequent eight chapters discuss types of microforms and their uses; microfilm production and duplication; computer-output microfilm (COM); micropublishing; the use of microforms in the library, including types of readers and reader/printers; bibliographic control of microforms; microform storage and retrieval systems; and a look at the future of micrographics in the library. Numerous illustrations and photographs accompany the text, and extensive references conclude each chapter. A six-page glossary defines essential terms used throughout the book. A 10-page selected bibliography on library applications of micrographics and a detailed index round out the work. [R: ARBA 79, p. 166; C&RL, Nov 78, p. 497; LJ, 15 Nov 78, p. 2318]

113.   Velleman, Ruth A. **Serving Physically Disabled People: An Information Handbook for All Libraries.** New York, R. R. Bowker, 1979. 392p. bibliog. index. $17.50. LC 79-17082. ISBN 0-8352-1167-3.

Serving Physically Disabled People is arranged in four parts. Part 1 introduces physically disabled people, including social attitudes and definition of specific disabilities. Part 2 describes the civil rights now enacted into law on behalf of disabled persons. This part lists sources of inexpensive materials available to libraries, as well as basic illustrated barrier-free design criteria for library facilities. Specific needs of the blind and deaf are discussed by Dr. Hanan C. Selvin and Ms. Alice Hagemeyer, respectively. Part 3 gives an overview of rehabilitation history and philosophy, as well as a list of materials for a model rehabilitation library. Part 4 discusses school and university libraries in the context of the development of special education and library services to students with special needs. A suggested core special education collection is included. Appendices provide information on professional and volunteer agencies, independent living centers, national rehabilitation associations, research and training centers, and other related centers. Since many rehabilitation and information facilities are federally funded, the reader is advised to check listings against the latest changes in the federal system.

The book is based on Ms. Velleman's experience at the Human Resources School, her national workshop and consultant experience in this field, and her teaching experience at the Palmer Graduate Library School of Long Island University. The book is a benchwork of library services for the physically disabled as of 1979. There is no comparable work.

Kieth C. Wright

114. Wynar, Bohdan S. **Introduction to Cataloging and Classification.** 6th ed. With the assistance of Arlene Taylor Dowell and Jeanne Osborn. Littleton, CO, Libraries Unlimited, 1980. 657p. $25.00; $15.50pa. LC 80-16462. ISBN 0-87287-220-3; 0-87287-221-1(pa.).

Introduction to Cataloging and Classification has been for years the standard professional text. For this important sixth edition the text has been completely revised to treat *AACR 2, DDC 19*, and *Sears 11* in one volume. Each is discussed in depth and is amply illustrated with excerpts and examples of its application.

Part I provides an overview of cataloging. Part II is a specific and careful treatment of descriptive analysis, following the mnemonic structure of *AACR 2*, chapter by chapter. For each type of material, or condition or pattern of publication, selected basic rules are illustrated with elements from sample bibliographic descriptions. These elements are added, rule by rule, until a complete bibliographic record has been presented. All available LC implementation decisions have been noted.

Part III, "Subject Analysis," examines *DDC 19*, and discusses other classification systems. Separate chapters carefully present *LCSH 8* and *Sears* subject headings (11th edition), as well as other types of verbal subject analysis.

Part IV treats the organization and maintenance of catalog and library services, including shelflist filing and authority files; PRECIS; and centralized processing networks such as OCLC.

The fifth edition of *Introduction to Cataloging and Classification* remains in print for those libraries using *AACR 1* and *DDC 18*. [R: BL, 15 Nov 80]

PERIODICALS

115. **Library of Congress Cataloging Service: Bulletins 1-125, with a Comprehensive Subject Index.** Ed. by Helen Savage. Detroit, Gale, 1980. 2v. index. $78.00. LC 79-25343. ISBN 0-8103-1103-8.

Lives there a cataloger with soul so dead that he/she will not welcome this reprint? Most of us, or our libraries, are on the *Cataloging Service Bulletins* mailing list, but few of us were around when it first appeared in June 1945. Many did not start to read it faithfully until it began to announce and discuss official AACR rule additions and changes in 1967. It had, of course, offered a similar service since 1953 for the earlier "red book" and "green book" rules. Such material makes the earlier issues seem largely outdated and antiquarian, but an occasional announcement or definition gives useful insights into modern standardized practice, as affected by the paternalistic leadership of the Library of Congress. For instance, the initial issue gave news of certain LC-approved transliteration tables. Thenceforward, publication of what are now termed "Romanization tables" has regularly followed each LC adoption for a different non-Roman script.

The photo-reproductions are slightly reduced in size from their originals. Some pages of early issues show less than perfect visual quality, but it is nearly carping to say so, for all are completely legible. Growth in scope and coverage is implicit in the fitting of bulletins 1 through 106 (1945 to mid-1973) into volume 1, whereas bulletins 107 through 125 (December 1973 to spring 1978) comprise, with the 38-page index, an equally bulky volume 2. Tables of contents were inaugurated with bulletin 104 (May 1972) — a further evidence of increasing size and complexity. LC publication and distribution announcements were carried from the first. Local, national, and international committee and conference decisions, particularly those affecting descriptive practices (e.g., ISBD) are frequent. LC directives for applying both its own and the Dewey Decimal classifications have burgeoned, as have explanations and lists or tables of changes for LC subject headings and LC shelf-listing practices. The index includes both topical headings and rule-number entries.

This collection is sensibly limited to those issues published under the original form of the name. A "new" series took over in the summer of 1978, changing nothing of format and content, differing only in its addition of the word *Bulletin* to the title proper, and in its reversion to number "1" for its first issue. This purely technical change in bibliographic identification reflects the impact of AACR and the International Serials Data System on the form of the title entry. It was the logical time to provide catalogers full retrospective control of their much-thumbed, incomplete, unbound sets. Untidy shelves can be emptied to accumulate a second, continuingly useful, serial generation.   Jeanne Osborn

SELECTION AIDS

GENERAL

116.   Gardner, Richard K., and Phyllis Grumm, eds. **Choice: A Classified Cumulation. Volumes I-IX.** Assisted by Julia Johnson. Totowa, NJ, Rowman and Littlefield, 1976-1977. 9v. index. $395.00/set; $49.50(index). ISBN 0-87471-792-2(set); 0-87471-897-X(index).

During the first 10 years of its existence, *Choice* published reviews of 58,700 books. This set represents a 10-year interpolated edition of *Choice* with the following breakdown: volume 1 — reference and bibliography, library science, general works, humanities, art, communication arts, and sports and recreation; volume 2 — language and literature; volume 3 — literature (cont'd), performing arts, philosophy, and religion; volume 4 — science and technology; volume 5 — engineering and technology; volume 6 — history; volume 7 — history (cont'd), geography, description and travel, law, political science; volume 8 — education, psychology, sociology, anthropology; and volume 9 — index.

Most librarians are quite familiar with *Choice*. Reviews range between 75 and 175 words apiece, with an occasional review somewhat longer. The length of the review does not necessarily reflect the relative importance of a given book. Contrary to the prevailing practice in scholarly journals and also in several of the reviewing media for the library profession (e.g., *School Library Journal* and *Library Journal*), reviews in *Choice* are not signed. In all fairness to *Choice*, it must be added that most reviews in *Booklist* are also unsigned. The whole question of signed reviews versus unsigned is a topic that needs continued discussion in the profession.

One of the more serious weaknesses is *Choice*'s coverage of materials in library science. The second chapter of volume I, "Library Science/Bibliography/Research" (pp. 349-53), contains 32 reviews — several of which do not pertain at all to library science. Why *Choice* avoids reviewing professional literature is puzzling.

This cumulation of *Choice* reviews serves a number of very useful purposes, primarily in the area of collection development. In this respect, the index volume is most crucial, providing author, title, and subject access. The title and author indexes provide citations to both the original volumes of *Choice* and to the volumes of the classified cumulation represented in this work. A helpful feature is the "see" and "see also" references that are provided when the *Choice* entry appears in variant form or when the *Choice* entry differs from the Library of Congress entry. It should be noted that cross references in the author and title indexes are limited to personal names; thus, it is necessary to consult the *National Union Catalog* for additional variations.

The subject index unfortunately has major flaws. There is no explanation of how it was designed. Apparently it provides references only to those subject categories found in monthly issues of *Choice*. Those subject headings appear to have been developed erratically and suffer from the lack of adherence to any standard subject terms authority file or thesaurus. Cross references are characterized by unpredictable omissions. The subject index is very brief (four pages). Altogether it is difficult to use and of marginal value. If this set is reprinted again, we would highly recommend the preparation of a useful index that will do justice to this important compilation. [R: ARBA 77, p. 105; ARBA 79, p. 90; BL, 15 May 77, p. 1450; BL, 1 Mar 79, p. 1116; RQ, Fall 77, p. 75; WLB, Mar 77, p. 604; WLB, Jan 78, p. 426]   Bohdan S. Wynar

117. **The New York Times Book Review Index, 1896-1970.** New York, New York Times and Arno Press, 1973. 5v. $600.00/set. LC 68-57778.

The *New York Times* re-issued the entire *Book Review* series (from October 10, 1896 through 1968) in 125 bound volumes. This index was designed to accompany those volumes and to provide the means for their effective use. Subsequent volumes of the *Book Review* have been individually indexed. The index covers virtually everything that was printed in the *Book Review*, including reviews, essays, biographical sketches, letters to the editor, brief commentaries, notes, and anecdotal items; it can be used with either the bound volumes or the microfilm copies of the *New York Times*.

Volume 1 is an author index (with author defined as the person who wrote the book, not the one who wrote the review). It is arranged alphabetically and lists main authors, associate authors, corporate bodies, editors, illustrators, translators, and authors of prefaces or introductions. The title is given in parentheses after the author, followed by the name of the reviewer (preceded by R) and the citation (e.g., 1934, June 3, p. 18). Bonus features of this volume are the inclusion of pseudonyms (sometimes with cross references to legal name and sometimes with duplicate entries), and the addition of birth and death dates or titles of nobility when they are necessary to avoid confusion. If many titles by the same author are listed, they appear in alphabetical, not chronological, order.

Volume 2 contains the title index. Entries are made under titles, collective titles of multivolume works, and subtitles. Furthermore, permuted title entries provide access through each significant word in the title. Every significant mention of a title is indexed; if the book is reviewed, mentioned in an essay, or referred to in a letter to the editor, it is indexed. The author's name and citation follow the title.

Volume 3, entitled "Byline Index," indexes reviews, essayists, columnists, and writers of letters to the editor. For reviews, the personal name is followed by the title of the work, the author, and the citation. For other items, the person's name is followed by a brief abstract and the citation.

Volume 4 is a subject index. The subject entries conform to *The Times Thesaurus of Descriptors*, with exceptions and modifications where necessary. This volume indexes primarily essays, reviews of non-fiction works, and comments and letters. The introduction states that "reviews of fiction may be included [in the subject index] under certain circumstances," but these circumstances are not explained. Thus, the user should not rely on this index as a subject approach to fiction.

Volume 5 is entitled "Category Index." In this volume works are classed by the following genres: anthologies, article and essay collections, children's fiction, children's nonfiction, criticism and belles lettres, drama, humor and cartoons, mystery, detective and spy fiction, nature and wildlife books, poetry, reference works, science fiction, self-help books, short stories, travel books, and westerns. Entries under these headings, arranged chronologically by year and date of the *Book Review* issue, are limited to reviews only. "General fiction, biography, history, and the descriptive or analytical literature on current affairs were excluded from this listing. Since these have always been the principal fields [of books reviewed], a separate listing here would not have revealed anything new and would have been largely redundant." Users of this index may not agree with that. Historical fiction is not one of the categories included, nor is it discussed as one purposely omitted. Certainly the genre is an important one that should not have been overlooked.

The New York Times Book Review Index is a major reference work. The *Book Review* section of the *New York Times* reflects the literary, political, social, artistic, and scientific trends in American life, and this comprehensive index provides the key to that vast source. [R: ARBA 75, p. 82; BL, 15 Dec 73, p. 404; Choice, May 74, p. 413; WLB, Mar 74, p. 593]

Sally Wynkoop

COLLEGE LIBRARIES

118.   **Books for College Libraries: A Core Collection of 40,000 Titles.** 2nd ed. Chicago, American Library Association, 1975. 6v. index. $70.00pa./set. LC 74-13743. ISBN 0-8389-0178-6.

The present work, known as *BCL II*, is, of course, the successor to *BCL I* (Chicago, American Library Association, 1967). The number of 40,000 titles (the actual count is 38,651) was chosen because it represents four-fifths of the 50,000 minimum that the 1959 ALA Standards require for even the smallest four-year academic library. The remaining one-fifth, or 10,000 titles, each individual college is expected to choose in accordance with its own particular curricular needs.

The authority for the selections rested in a group of teaching scholars, specialist librarians, and staff members of professional associations, many of whom were *Choice* reviewers. Working from *BCL I* as a base, the *BCL II* team expanded, pruned, and modified the list as necessary. In most cases, final selections represented a consensus of contributor opinion.

The editors admit to a liberal arts bias, an admission that was absolutely necessary, given the extreme thinness of the offerings in science and technology. Part of the reason for this comparative neglect of science is the stress that *BCL II* places on monographs. There are no periodicals and only a scant few serials. Since·science, even at the undergraduate level, places its prime reliance on serials, the science sections are inevitably meager.

The arrangement is by modified LC classification. A modification was used to effect a coherent structure of the bibliography in five paperbound parts: I, Humanities; II, Language and Literature; III, History; IV, Social Sciences; V, Psychology, Science, Technology, Bibliography (LC's "Z" class). Volume VI is an author and a title index. The entries are LC catalog cards in *run-on* style, hence the elements or fields are identical to those of LC cards.

The root questions, of course, are: how good is selection? And has ACRL really identified four-fifths of the 50,000 titles that every four-year academic library worthy of the name must have?

On prima facie grounds, the effort itself seems presumptuous. Therefore, one is justified in viewing the results with skepticism. It was noted above that the editors concede the thinness of their science offerings; however, the situation is worse than even they imagine it to be. There are serious gaps in basic science monographs, particularly in reference works. Because of the decision against including serials, no abstracting and indexing services are cited, an omission which for science reference is almost fatal. Serials aside, the number of monographs cited in the various "Z" categories relevant to science is suspiciously low.

The books cited under the several subheadings of library science are both insufficient in number and unbalanced. Under Z678-686 (Library Administration), there are precisely four titles, two of which deal with library architecture. Other library science sections, Z675 and Z710-715 (Reference Circulation), not only contain citations to books that are inappropriate to the small college library (e.g., Wilson and Tauber's *The University Library*) but neglect titles of high relevance. Section Z710-715 lists only one book on reference, Gates' *Guide to the Use of Books and Libraries*. The selection of professional literature is definitely not appropriate to the needs of the managers and staff members of libraries with collections in the 50,000-volume range. Nevertheless, in spite of these difficulties, *BCL II* is a standard work and can be used in acquisition departments as a checklist for evaluating possible gaps in existing collections. [R: ARBA 76, p. 100; BL, 1 May 76, p. 1284; C&RL, Jan 76, p. 71; LJ, 1 Mar 76, p. 672; RQ, Fall 76, p. 77; WLB, Nov 75, p. 262]   Richard A. Gray

SCHOOL LIBRARIES

119.   **Books for Secondary School Libraries.** 5th ed. Comp. by a committee of librarians from member schools of the National Association of Independent Schools. New York, R. R. Bowker, 1976. 526p. index. $15.95. LC 75-37836. ISBN 0-8352-0836-2.

Over 6,000 non-fiction titles are listed as valuable for secondary school libraries. While this volume attempts to cover topics of immediate concern (Arab-Israeli relationship; ecology; population) and adolescent interests (birth control; yoga; women's liberation movement), the major criterion for inclusion is material for the college-bound student. One finds no representative titles on comics, nothing by Charles Schulz. Biography is not classified as a separate section but is integrated into subject areas — a decision that will not please everyone. The largest number of titles is under "Geography, Travel and History"; the next largest is under "Literature," followed by the "Social Sciences." "Science," represented by 597 titles, seems meager, and "Language," with 36 titles, is a bit light.

There is a directory of publishers and an author, subject, title index that provides access to a specific title by entry number (this does not always work, as in the reference to James Baldwin, which brings the reader to Lomax's *American Ballads and Folk-Songs*). More serious, in my opinion, is the decision to omit all fiction because "[it is] so heavily dependent upon the taste and needs of a library's users." Certain fiction is a *sine qua non* for all secondary schools and, bypassing even the standard classical writers, a list like this could safely include fiction by Salinger, Lessing, Arnow, Doctorow, Updike, and Drabble. Coverage of foreign literature is good, and references to recommended series are useful.

The NAIS list will be useful in secondary school libraries but cannot be considered a first priority for *all* high schools in the way that Wynar's *Guide to Reference Books for School Media Centers* is (see entry 123). This selection tool will be most directly related to the kind of collection usually found in preparatory and private schools. [R: ARBA 77, p. 122; BL, 15 Oct 76, p. 316]   Lillian L. Shapiro

120.   Brown, Lucy Gregor. **Core Media Collection for Elementary Schools.** 2nd ed. Assisted by Betty McDavid. New York, R. R. Bowker, 1978. 224p. index. $18.95. LC 78-11674. ISBN 0-8352-1096-0.

The 1,400 or so titles in *Core Media Collection* all received favorable reviews in professional journals, won awards, or are recommended by the editor and other media specialists. Most are also fairly recent releases (1973-1977), making this an excellent tool against which to check one's own collection or the current offerings of media producers.

An alphabetical subject arrangement (employing Sears List of Subject Headings) is supplemented by a title index. Each entry refers to reviews in one or more of 67 reviewing sources and supplies full annotations, including Dewey Decimal number, grade level, release date, price, and a contents synopsis. Though some materials are recommended for grades through 8, and even higher, the bulk of the collection is intended for K-6. Filmstrips predominate, but films, filmloops, recordings (no musical recordings), and other visuals are also found. Most curricular areas are represented (though under "Reproduction," we can only find out about baby chicks and brown trout). The balance seems to be a bit heavy on the side of language arts and natural history, but this probably reflects what is on the market. There are plenty of entries on such high-interest topics as nutrition, art, values, vocational guidance, and the metric system.

Media specialists will want to know how *Core Media Collection* compares with *The Elementary School Library Collection*, now in its twelfth edition, and at present on a biennial revision schedule (see entry 122). Spot checks reveal little overlapping, and the number and fullness of entries are comparable. *Core Media Collection* is a small, easy-to-use volume. Whether a media center owns *The Elementary School Library Collection* or not, this is a recommended purchase, especially if not too much time elapses between editions. [R: ARBA 80, p. 66; Choice, May 79, p. 363; JAL, May 79, p. 103; WLB, April 79, p. 588]

Mary R. Sive

121. Haviland, Virginia, comp. **Children's Literature: A Guide to Reference Sources, Second Supplement.** With the assistance of Margaret N. Coughlan. Washington, Library of Congress; distr., Washington, GPO, 1977. 413p. illus. index. $7.75. LC 66-62734. ISBN 0-8444-0215-X. S/N 030-001-00075-3.

Arranged as the previous two volumes in this ongoing series, selective journal articles and books have been annotated in a numbered order, from the general topic to the specific. This volume lists those pieces appearing from about 1970 through 1974. The eight categories from the first two volumes ("History and Criticism," "Authorship," "Illustration," "Bibliography," "Books and Children," "The Library and Children's Books," "International Studies," and "National Studies") have not changed. Of the major categories, "International Studies" has been expanded the most. Subdivisions of categories appearing for the first time are "Selection of Nonprint Materials" (in "The Library and Children's Books"), "Research in Children's Literature" (in "Books and Children"), "Translation" (in "International Studies"), and "French Canada" (in "National Studies"). There are a total of 929 annotations, as compared to 1,073 in the first volume and 746 in the second. The index covers only those numbered annotations in this volume, a pattern set with the first two books.

Highly selective in annotated material and directing themselves primarily toward librarians, Haviland and Coughlan do masterful work in pulling together scattered articles and other works from around the world and organizing them into a usable form. Allied fields of children's literature and research (reading studies, dissertations, English literature studies) are peripherally mentioned, if at all. Expansion of children's literature-related articles located in larger works and beyond the library field would be welcomed. For instance, John Tebbel's *History of Book Publishing in the United States* and its sections on children's book publishing are lacking, while a library-oriented book such as *Issues in Children's Book Selection* has been annotated and subdivided. As new volumes in the series are published, a comprehensive index including all previously published volumes would be an asset. This will be a necessary purchase for all who purchased the first two volumes.

Institutions not owning these volumes would be wise to get them. This is the only source of material with this scope and depth on the subject in a readily available form. [R: ARBA 79, p. 116; BL, 15 July 78, p. 1739; WLB, Sept 78, p. 87]   Jim Roginski

122.   Winkel, Lois, ed. **The Elementary School Library Collection: A Guide to Books and Other Media, Phases 1-2-3.** 12th ed. Newark, NJ, Bro-Dart Foundation, 1979. 1096p. index. $39.95. LC 79-10366. ISBN 0-912654-11-2.

The twelfth edition, under new editorship, gives the appearance of a carefully weeded and revised core collection for elementary media centers. The purpose, scope, and selection criteria are unchanged, although some shifts in emphasis may be noted. The introduction specifies the policies followed for selecting individual items and for achieving balance among various formats, subject areas, and interest/reading levels.

In terms of numbers, the twelfth edition represents a net increase of 378 items over the eleventh edition; the additions are for 285 books, 32 periodicals, and 185 AV items. The reference collection is the only category of book materials to decrease (172 versus 201). Among AV categories there is a decrease in all formats except phonodiscs, sound filmstrips, and pictures. The continuous downward trend in the use of captioned filmstrips is demonstrated by reduction of these materials to only 10 items. Sound filmstrips jumped by 88 items to a total of 985 entries in the twelfth edition.

The editor states that over 1,000 titles recommended in the eleventh edition were dropped. Many of these were lost due to the severe cutbacks in publishers' backlists. Other deletions resulted from the editor's strict reevaluation of all entries, including long-held standard titles. The poetry section is one such area that demonstrates the process. An examination of the 820s showed 44 entries in the eleventh edition and 41 in the twelfth edition; 10 titles were dropped and 7 added. The deletions include titles such as Untermeyer's *Golden Treasury of Poetry*, De la Mare's *Tom Tiddler's Ground*, and Milne's *Christopher Robin Book of Verse*. The decision to drop items if they are substantially duplicated by other titles seems to work well in this section. Such weeding allows space for new titles, which, on the whole, are more tuned to interests of today's youngsters.

Other rearrangements and changes include integration of professional periodicals into the professional collection, an effort to increase the number of basic materials for Canadian users, and more emphasis on various minority groups. Format has been altered to a more easily handled size of 8½ by 11 inches. Legibility has been enhanced by choice of a more opaque paper, which decreases the distraction of show-through.

In summation, the twelfth edition provides a larger basic collection than previous editions, and one which is at the same time a more strictly evaluated selection. The twelfth edition is recommended for all elementary schools. [ARBA 80, p. 67; BL, 15 Apr 79, p. 1321]
                                         Christine Gehrt Wynar

123.   Wynar, Christine L. **Guide to Reference Books for School Media Centers.** Littleton, CO, Libraries Unlimited, 1973. 473p. index. $19.50. LC 73-87523. ISBN 0-87287-069-3.

The guide contains 2,575 annotated entries arranged under 53 subjects. The first two sections describe 182 basic tools for locating print and non-print media and for evaluation and selection of media. Entries give full bibliographic descriptions and prices plus descriptive and evaluative annotations. References to reviews in major reviewing media and standard recommended lists and catalogs are appended to the annotations. A full author-title-subject index provides access to all entries and to hundreds of related titles mentioned in the annotations. The guide suggests reference books for use by students K-12 and for the professional needs of teachers and librarians in elementary and secondary schools.

Ed. note: The second edition is due for publication in May 1981. [R: ARBA 74, p. 64; BL, 1 Feb 74, p. 558; RQ, Summer 74, p. 370; WLB, Feb 74, p. 508]

BIOGRAPHY

124. **Dictionary of American Library Biography.** George S. Bobinski, Jesse Hauk Shera, and Bohdan S. Wynar, eds. Littleton, CO, Libraries Unlimited, 1978. 596p. index. $85.00. LC 77-28791. ISBN 0-87287-180-0.

The publication of *Dictionary of American Library Biography* marks the culmination of five years of planning, research, writing, and editorial work by the editorial board of *DALB*, over 200 contributors throughout the library community, and the staff of Libraries Unlimited, Inc. *DALB*, the first scholarly dictionary of past American library leaders, contains thoroughly researched, original biographical sketches of 300 outstanding men and women who, in large measure, founded and built this country's libraries, professional associations, and library education programs, and who developed basic bibliographic tools and information networks.

Selected for inclusion in *DALB* were those individuals who made contributions of national significance to American library development, whose writings influenced library trends and activities, who held positions of national importance, who made major achievements in special fields of librarianship, or who affected American libraries through their significant scholarly, philanthropic, legislative, or governmental support or activity. To insure proper historical perspective, only those people deceased as of June 30, 1976, are included. Probably the first biographical dictionary of its kind for any profession in the United States, *DALB* is a significant contribution to library history, making it possible to gain the historical perspective necessary to better interpret the profession's present resources and their origins. [R: ARBA 79, p. 94; C&RL, Sept 78, p. 403; JAL, Jan 79, p. 457; LJ, 1 Sept 78, p. 1575; RQ, Spring 79, p. 301; WLB, Sept 78, p. 89]

3 SOCIAL SCIENCES AND AREA STUDIES

SOCIAL SCIENCES

BIBLIOGRAPHIES

125.   **A London Bibliography of the Social Sciences: Twelfth Supplement 1977, Volume XXXV.** London, Mansell; distr., Salem, NH, Mansell, 1978. 402p. (British Library of Political and Economic Science). $49.50. ISBN 0-7201-0829-2. ISSN 0076-051X.

The twelfth supplement of *A London Bibliography of the Social Sciences* contains additions during 1977 to the British Library of Political and Economic Science and the Edward Fry Library of International Law, both located at the London School of Economics. It follows the same subject arrangement as the previous supplements and is produced by means of computer typesetting. In order to make a proper use of this major reference source, one has to consult a comprehensive "list of subject headings used in the bibliography arranged under topics," which is appended at the end of the volume. Taking into consideration that *LBSS* is the major international bibliography in the social sciences and constitutes an indispensable tool in any major academic library, the user and librarian would expect to find a complete bibliographical citation of the listed entry. However, this is not the case, and the name of the publishing house is still excluded. The preface is too brief to have any special meaning and does not provide necessary information concerning non-English publications excluded from this important reference tool.

Lubomyr R. Wynar

126.   White, Carl M., and associates. **Sources of Information in the Social Sciences: A Guide to the Literature.** 2nd ed. Chicago, American Library Association, 1973. 702p. index. $25.00. LC 73-9825. ISBN 0-8389-0134-4.

The first edition of this bibliographical guide (1964) gained a deserved recognition among social scientists and bibliographers. The present updated and revised edition is similar in structure to its predecessor. This guide includes separate chapters on social science literature, history, geography, economics and business administration, sociology, anthropology, education, and political science. Each chapter consists of two basic parts — a subject introduction, written by a subject specialist, that introduces the user to the historical development and subject structure of the discipline, and a strictly reference-bibliographical section, usually prepared by the subject bibliographer. All reference entries contain adequate descriptive or critical annotations. The chapter on geography is new to this edition, and the present index shows a marked improvement over that of the first edition. In his preface, Dr. White states that the main objective of this edition is "to make it easier to get at knowledge and information of importance to us all . . . to throw light on the workings of the social science information system, and to support subject bibliography as a branch of the study" (p. xiii).

In general, the editor accomplished his objectives. However, a few critical remarks are in order. White's guide is international in scope — but the history section's emphasis on English publications renders it rather parochial. The bibliographical section is also confused and not adequately updated. The section on "Specialized Guides" (B320-B337) includes both *Guide to the Records in the National Archives* and Miller's *The Negro in America*. There should be a separate section on archival reference publications and on minority and ethnic groups in the United States. In the section on "Reviews of the Literature" (pp. 108-109) there is no listing of Long's comprehensive chronology, *The Civil*

War Day by Day (1971), or H. Bengton's *Introduction to Ancient History* (1970). Again, the auxiliary historical sciences, except for skimpy coverage of genealogy and heraldry, are omitted. A more representative and balanced selection of relevant titles is needed in future editions. Despite its shortcomings, this is an important guide. [R: ARBA 75, p. 142; BL, 1 Mar 75, p. 701; Choice, Apr 74, p. 240; C&RL, July 74, p. 248; C&RL, Sept 74, p. 372; RQ, Winter 74, p. 184; WLB, Apr 74, p. 675]   Lubomyr R. Wynar

ENCYCLOPEDIAS

127. **International Encyclopedia of the Social Sciences Biographical Supplement.** New York, Free Press, a division of Macmillan Publishing, 1979. 768p. $75.00(suppl. to the 17v. ed. of IESS); $70.00(suppl. to the 8v. ed. of IESS). ISBN 0-02-895510-2(suppl. to 17v. ed.); 0-02-895690-7(suppl. to 8v. ed.).

Biographies of the 215 most important figures in current social sciences are included in this volume. The *Biographical Supplement* updates the original 17-volume *International Encyclopedia of the Social Sciences* (*IESS*) (Macmillan, 1968. $495.00/set). *IESS* includes only eminent social scientists who were deceased or had reached the age of 75, and therefore does not include many modern social scientists; the *Supplement* follows the same criteria. Social science fields represented are: anthropology, criminology, demography, economics, history, linguistics, philosophy, political science and legal theory, psychology and psychiatry, religion, sociology, and statistics. Each biography is a signed work of original scholarship, written by a leading social scientist. Entries contain basic biographical information, as well as an indepth discussion of the subject's work, contributions, and influence on other scholars. Most entries contain two bibliographies: one of the subject's own work, and another of works related to the subject. The *Biographical Supplement* is available in two formats, to accompany the 17-volume *IESS*, or the 8-volume *IESS*. [R: ARBA 80, p. 136]

AREA STUDIES

COMPREHENSIVE WORKS

128. Kurian, George Thomas. **Encyclopedia of the Third World.** New York, Facts on File, 1978. 2v. illus. maps. bibliog. index. $85.00/set. LC 78-6812. ISBN 0-87196-398-1(v.1); 0-87196-399-X(v.2); 0-685-95032-8(set).

According to the editor, this encyclopedia "provides a compact, balanced and objective description of the dominant political, economic and social systems of 114 countries of the world" (preface, p. viii). Indeed, this reference tool may be regarded as the most comprehensive current encyclopedic work covering Third World nations. George Kurian, a noted historian and lexicographer, developed a special classification system (pp. ix-xvii) covering a wide range of encyclopedic information for each country, including a basic fact sheet, location of area, weather, population, ethnic composition, languages, religions, colonial experience, constitution and government, civil service, local government, foreign policy, parliament, political parties, economy, budget, finance, agriculture, energy, foreign commerce, transportation, mining, education, legal system, law enforcement, food, a brief glossary, a chronology, and a bibliographical section. In addition, each encyclopedic entry includes a political map and an organizational governmental chart for each country. A separate chapter covers international organizations, and the appendices include various comparative statistical tables pertaining to population and political and economic developments of Third World countries. A selective bibliography and a comprehensive index conclude this valuable reference tool.

The data for this publication were obtained from various international and national government documents as well as from secondary reference sources, and statistical information is current as of 1978. Included in this work are 114 states designated as "Third World" nations. The author's definition of the Third World and his criteria of inclusion or exclusion of various countries are rather confusing. China, Taiwan, and Rhodesia are excluded for reasons not explained, as are Yugoslavia and Albania, while Cuba, which may be considered a political and economic satellite of the Soviet Union (the "Second World") is included, even though it does not fit the author's formula of "non-aligned nation."

From the reference point of view, the *Encyclopedia of the Third World* overlaps with statistical data provided by such established encyclopedic compendiums as the 1978 and 1979 *Europa Year Book, Statesman's Yearbook*, the *Worldmark Encyclopedia of Nations*, and similar international-in-scope reference titles. However, taking into consideration the increased influence of the Third World nations in the world, this encyclopedia will find its users. The work is well executed, and its editor deserves our gratitude. [R: ARBA 80, p. 137; Choice, June 79, p. 510; LJ, 15 Jan 79, p. 179; LJ, 15 Apr 79, p. 886; RQ, Fall 79, p. 85; WLB, Apr 79, p. 587]   Lubomyr R. Wynar

AFRICA

129.   **African Encyclopedia.** New York, Oxford University Press, 1974. 554p. illus. maps. index. $14.95. ISBN 0-19-913178-3.

This is a comprehensive compilation of 1,850 articles by 137 contributors, copiously illustrated and blessed with a 4,000-item index. A major contribution of the work is that it is Africa-oriented: illustrations are presented in an African context, and the work provides a continental view of Africa.

There are some minor shortcomings that could be corrected in a future edition. Not all changes in city names have been included. The general map shows Fort Lamy, and not N'Djamena, while the Chad map (p. 121) shows Sarh. The general map and the Gambia map (p. 220) show Banjul, while the Senegal map (p. 450) shows Bathurst. The dates of all historical and contemporary figures should be added. It is confusing to see an entry for Usuman dan Fodio, with appropriate dates, when there are no dates for his brother Abdullahi and no dates for President Barre, Bai Bureh, Hamad of Macina, Kayira, and many others. An effort should be made to include the synonyms of African language names. "Fulfulde" is included in the index, but the more correct "Bamana" is not. "More" is commonly written "Moré" and not "Moore" (p. 156). If Aimé Césaire is cited, shouldn't Léon G. Damas be included? He was one of the founders of Negritude, and he played a role in the formative stages of African politics. Ali Mazrui is as important on today's scene as his forefathers were on theirs (p. 333). There are some confusing typographical errors: Ibrahim al-Salahi becomes Salami (p. 65) and Egangaki appears as Ekangani (p. 366). The picture of the Beirut harbor seems to belong to the 1920s (p. 299). And finally, each article should be signed by the contributor. In spite of these details, the *African Encyclopedia* is a useful, balanced, continent-wide, and Africa-centered reference tool of particular importance to the high school and undergraduate university audience.

Ed. note: The Encyclopedia of Africa (Franklin Watts, 1976. 223p. $14.90), a colorful and attractive one-volume work, is excellent for browsing and suitable for a general audience. However, it is of little value as a reference source because of its thematic arrangement. [R: ARBA 75, p. 154; BL, 1 Oct 74, p. 195; Choice, Mar 75, p. 43; LJ, 15 Sept 74]
                                                                Samir M. Zoghby

130.   Duignan, Peter, and L. H. Gann. **Colonialism in Africa, 1870-1960. Volume 5, A Bibliographic Guide to Colonialism in Sub-Saharan Africa.** New York, Cambridge University Press, 1974. 532p. index. $51.95. LC 75-77289. ISBN 0-521-07859-8.

The two authors, both Senior Fellows of the Hoover Institution, have compiled a massive and thorough bibliography that should serve both librarians and researchers. The authors preface the work with an interesting introductory essay on the development of historical research into colonialism, and on the institutions established by the European powers to study Africa. The bibliography itself is divided into three sections. Part I, "Guide to Reference Materials," lists organizations concerned with African studies, general guides to African research, and library and archive collections that are important to the study of African colonialism. Collections in Western Europe, America, and Africa are included. The section concludes with a collection of bibliographies on Africa. The second part, "Subject Guide for Africa in General," an annotated list of important works on Africa, is divided into 15 subject areas (demography, economics, education, etc.). This section is quite selective, listing only the more important titles. The third part, "Area Guide," contains a much more detailed annotated list of works relating to all aspects of colonialism. This section cites bibliographies, serials, atlases, and reference works arranged by colonial power, region, and country (British Africa—West Africa—Nigeria). There is an extensive index that includes author and title information to all cited works.

Although 1969 was the original cut-off date for inclusion, important works published up to 1972 are included. Because of its interdisciplinary approach to the study of colonialism, this is a valuable book for all major fields of study that are concerned with Africa from 1870 to 1960. The inclusion of works in all Western European languages makes this work valuable for even the most sophisticated researcher. The scope, organization, access, and 2,500-plus annotations combine to make this book an important and very useful addition to the field of African studies.

Other volumes in the *Colonialism in Africa, 1870-1960* series include: volume 1, *History and Politics of Colonialism, 1870-1914*; volume 2, *History and Politics of Colonialism, 1914-1960*; volume 3, *Profiles of Change: African Society and Colonial Rule*; and volume 4, *Economics of Colonialism.* [R: ARBA 75, p. 144; Choice, Oct 74, p. 1108; LQ, Apr 75, p. 225]   William Z. Schenck

131.   Rosenthal, Eric, comp. and ed. **Encyclopaedia of Southern Africa.** 6th ed. New York, Frederick Warne, 1973. 662p. illus. (part col.). maps. index. LC 75-114791. ISBN 0-7232-1487-5.

This is a most detailed and informative encyclopedia on South Africa, despite the compiler's somewhat emphatic claim that "this is an encyclopaedia of *Southern* not merely *South* Africa." The bibliography includes about 5,000 abundantly illustrated entries. It contains 11 colored plates, seven maps, a number of photographs, and 22 main topical articles.

The compiler's claim is not substantiated; about 680 entries relate to white South Africans or individuals identified with the country, while there are references to only about 50 Bantu Africans, 51 white and three black Rhodesians, three Zambians, two black Mozambicans, three personalities from Botswana, and two from Swaziland. There are approximately 1,295 references to geographical locations in South Africa proper or territories under its control, and only 28 for Botswana, 13 for Lesotho, 84 for Rhodesia, 27 for Zambia, and 14 for Swaziland. The author has also cleverly woven the history of white settlement into the notes on the various geographical locations in South Africa. There are 41 references to African tribes within the South African orbit, but only four from Rhodesia and two from Mozambique. A number of hardly important towns and villages are cited, such as Umbumbulu with a population of "60, including 30 Whites." The complex question of South West Africa is treated in a relatively cavalier way. The paternalistic attitude toward blacks comes through in a citation about a Bantu leader, which reads: "Mr. Justice de Waal described Champion as 'in many respects a remarkable man' " (p. 107).

If one adopts the premise that this is an encyclopedia on South Africa, and on a given segment of its society, then this work is indeed a remarkable one. [R: ARBA 75, p. 156; BL, 1 Mar 74, p. 702]   Samir M. Zoghby

ASIA

Comprehensive Works

132. **Far Eastern Serials.** Chicago, Far Eastern Library, University of Chicago; distr., Chicago, Photoduplications Department, University of Chicago Library, 1977. 370p. (Reference List, No. 2). $8.00pa.

This catalog of serial titles published in China, Japan, and Korea, or dealing substantially with those countries, lists approximately 5,000 titles, including periodicals, newsletters, directories, annual reports, statistical reports, and newspapers available in the University of Chicago Libraries. A wide range of disciplines is represented, but the emphasis of the collection is on history, the humanities, and social sciences.

The catalog is divided into four sections by language, with further subdivision of each section into a main list and a list of addenda. Each subsection is arranged alphabetically by romanized title. Bibliographical information provided, besides the romanized title, includes the title in characters, Western-language title (if any), place of publication and inclusive publication dates, followed by the call number and holdings of the University of Chicago Libraries. Western-language titles for Japanese- and Chinese-language journals are listed in the Western-language section with reference to the romanized title of the main entries listed in the Chinese or Japanese sections.

The Far Eastern Library of the University of Chicago is one of the oldest and largest special collections on East Asia in North America. This comprehensive and well-edited catalog of East Asian serials is an important reference tool for other special collections on the area.   Charles R. Bryant

China

133. **An Annotated Bibliography of Selected Chinese Reference Works.** 3rd ed. Compiled by Ssu-yü Teng and Knight Biggerstaff. Cambridge, MA, Harvard University Press, 1971. 250p. glossary. index. (Harvard-Yenching Institute Studies). $8.00pa. LC 77-150012. ISBN 0-674-03851-7.

The original *Annotated Bibliography of Selected Chinese Reference Works* was published in China as monograph no. 12 of the *Yenching Journal of Chinese Studies*, 1936, subsidized by the Harvard-Yenching Institute. The second edition appeared in 1950 as the second volume of these Harvard-Yenching Institute Studies. This third edition, bearing the same number, is substantially revised and enlarged, adding nearly 200 new titles, including 25 written in Japanese. Some 100 titles that appeared in the second edition have been dropped because they have been superseded by newer works. The format of the second edition has been retained, and the material is arranged under eight broad subject categories: bibliographies, encyclopedias, dictionaries, geographical works, biographical works, tables, yearbooks, and Sinological indexes. All entries provide complete bibliographical description with excellent annotations that should serve as a model for critical evaluation of foreign reference works. The emphasis is on new material, since *Contemporary China: A Research Guide*, by Peter Berton and Eugene Wu (Hoover Institution, 1967. $22.50), covers reference works published during the 1950s and 1960s. All in all, this is an excellent bibliographical guide that will be of substantial assistance to subject specialists in this area. [R: ARBA 72, p. 107; Choice, Mar 72, p. 48; WLB, Jan 72, p. 449]

134. Kaplan, Fredric M., Julian M. Sobin, and Stephen Andors. **Encyclopedia of China Today.** Fair Lawn, NJ, Eurasia Press; New York, Harper & Row, 1979. 336p. illus. maps. bibliog. index. $27.50. LC 77-6886. ISBN 0-06-012256-0.

The authors of this work have attempted to bring together in one volume information on a wide range of topics concerning the People's Republic of China (PRC). Their ability to combine comprehensive coverage with conciseness and accuracy stands out in a subject area witnessing an increasing quantity of publications. Topics covered range from geography, politics, and economics (with brief descriptions of all major industries) to language, education, and medicine, with indexes providing easy access to specific subjects. This traditional encyclopedic approach is augmented by chapters describing the mechanics of gaining access to the PRC via both direct travel and the printed word. Biographies of 54 prominent figures in the PRC make up an early chapter, and photographs, maps, charts, and tables abound.

This volume is the work of a new generation of China scholars significantly less constrained by cold war rhetoric than their predecessors. (An introduction written by a member of the older generation, John Service, succinctly captures this change in outlook.) Besides providing practical guidance for the potential tourist or trader, the *Encyclopedia* should prove useful to both the interested observer of major shifts in international relations who may be struggling to comprehend the volatile image China presents to the Western world and the serious student searching for primary source materials emanating from PRC. This work provides an excellent summary of events in China from 1949 to the end of the 1970s. [R: ARBA 80, p. 148; LJ, 1 Dec 78, p. 2439; WLB, May 79, p. 652]

John W. Eichenseher

135. Skinner, G. William, and others, eds. **Modern Chinese Society: An Analytical Bibliography.** Stanford, CA, Stanford University Press, 1973. 3v. $35.00(v.1); $38.00(v.2); $32.00(v.3). LC 70-130831. ISBN 0-8047-0751-0(v.1); 0-8047-0752-9(v.2); 0-8047-0753-7(v.3).

This is the most comprehensive bibliography on China published so far, with a total of about 31,500 entries. The volumes are divided on the basis of language: vol. 1 covers publications in Western languages (1644-1972); vol. 2, publications in Chinese (1644-1969); and vol. 3, publications in Japanese (1644-1971). The project was initiated in 1963 by the Social Science Research Council's Subcommittee on Research on Chinese Society. The purpose of the project was to cover the modern period (1644 to the present) of Chinese history, concentrating on writings in Western languages, Chinese, and Japanese. The voluminous writings in Russian and the excellent Russian bibliographies are not included. [R: ARBA 75, p. 149; Choice, Sept 74, p. 918; WLB, May 74, p. 767]

India

136. Gidwani, N. N., and K. Navalani, comps. and eds. **A Guide to Reference Materials on India.** Jaipur, India, Saraswati Publications, 1974; distr., Columbia, MO, South Asia Books, 1976. 2v. index. $75.00/set. LC 74-901997. ISBN 0-88386-578-5.

The present work is by far the most comprehensive bibliographical guide to Indian reference sources. H. D. Sharma's *Indian Reference Sources: An Annotated Guide to Indian Reference Books*, published in 1972, described 2,200 reference books published in recent decades. According to the introduction to the present work, the compilers decided not to be selective and to provide complete coverage of all existing reference materials as far as this was possible. A rough count shows that this guide contains over 25,000 entries for all types of reference books, including many internally produced library catalogs, indexes, handbooks of 48 pages and less, etc. The material is arranged by broad form or subject categories—e.g., bibliographies, current abstracting and indexing periodicals in India, catalogs, manuscripts, union catalogs of periodical holdings, followed by subject-oriented chapters (e.g., journalism, natural sciences, mathematics, astronomy). In addition, all major chapters are subdivided by more specific subject headings. Thus, under sociology we find such subject descriptors as culture, cultural relations with foreign countries, social and technical change, etc. Most entries provide fairly complete bibliographical information—author, title and subtitle, imprint, and pagination. In addition to monographic material, the reader will find here many serials (with open or closed entries) and some analytical entries—primarily for bibliographies or indexes published in periodicals. Most entries are briefly annotated, with occasional references to published reviews for a given work. A fairly detailed alphabetical author and subject index concludes this impressive work.

The guide does have shortcomings. Numerous Soviet works dealing with India are not represented, and the bibliographical detail provided for the more important Indian works is not always complete—e.g., A. K. Mukherjee's *Manual of Reference Work* (p. 2) or P. K. Mukerji's *Indian Literature in China and the Far East* (p. 3), to cite only a few examples from the first three pages. Nevertheless, this is a monumental undertaking. It is unfortunate that the quality of paper and binding is very poor; the set will not last long in heavy library use. Highly recommended for all larger collections in this country. [R: ARBA 77, p. 165]   Bohdan S. Wynar

AUSTRALASIA

137. **Encyclopaedia of Papua and New Guinea.** Peter Ryan, gen. ed. Victoria, Melbourne University Press; distr., Portland, OR, International Scholarly Book Services, 1972. 3v. illus. maps. index. $75.00. ISBN 0-522-84025-6.

Published by Melbourne University in association with the University of Papua and New Guinea, this comprehensive work covers all important subjects relating to Papua New Guinea. The official name of Papua New Guinea was adopted following unification of the two former territories at the time this encyclopedia went to press. It was decided to retain the original title because the work covers the time when these areas were under separate names.

All entries are arranged in one alphabet, and authors of the signed articles are identified in the third volume. Most entries are lengthy comprehensive discussions of the topic. For example, see Education, which covers nearly 50 pages and includes sections on the history of education, education of indigenous groups, influence of religious missions, etc. The article on art is very well balanced, including numerous photos (unfortunately all in black and white). Almost every entry contains bibliographic citations. There are entries on all aspects of Papua New Guinea, such as persons, animals, diseases, economics, customs of the peoples, law, etc. One serious drawback is the treatment of the indigenous peoples: "Abau. People of the Central District," followed by a bibliographic source. In other words, these specific entries tell virtually nothing about the various indigenous groups; one finds more detailed information on them in the broader headings such as Initiation or Education.

The encyclopedia itself is in two volumes. Volume 3 (83 pages) contains a chronology of 1971 events, a gazetteer of place names, an index (only 50 pages), a fold-out map, and other supplementary data. One hopes that the incomplete index can be improved for the next edition. An essential work on this subject. [R: ARBA 73, p. 137; C&RL, Jan 73, p. 67; LJ, 15 Nov 72, p. 3696]

138.   Learmonth, Andrew T., and Agnes M. Learmonth. **Encyclopaedia of Australia.** New York, Warne, 1969. 606p. illus. $10.00. LC 69-11019.

Primarily designed for young adults and students, this handy volume includes over 2,700 entries with 50 main articles supplemented by color plates, black-and-white photographs, line drawings, and some 20 maps. Articles incorporating information and commentary cover such subjects as the arts, biography, history and geography. Many articles provide references to additional readings. With information current as of 1968, the *Encyclopaedia* is obviously somewhat dated, but it and the more comprehensive 10-volume *Australian Encyclopedia* (Michigan State University Press, 1958) remain the only substantial encyclopedias of Australia. [R: ARBA 70, p. 28; LJ, 15 Apr 70, p. 1439]

CANADA

139.   Ryder, Dorothy E., ed. **Canadian Reference Sources: A Selective Guide.** Ottawa, Canadian Library Association, 1973. 185p. index. $10.00. ISBN 0-88802-093-7.

140.   Ryder, Dorothy E., ed. **Canadian Reference Sources: Supplement.** Ottawa, Canadian Library Association, 1975. 121p. index. $7.00pa. ISBN 0-88802-106-2.

According to the introduction, the purpose of this work is "to provide librarians and students with a guide to Canadian reference material. It is a selective guide only, and does not aim at completeness. The material covers Canada in general, the 10 provinces, the territories, and three cities—Ottawa, Montreal, and Toronto. No geographical area smaller than a province, with the exception of the three cities named, is considered" (p. iii).

The arrangement and treatment of material are quite similar to what is found in Winchell: complete bibliographical information, plus brief descriptive annotations. No price is indicated, and there are no references to published reviews. Although this work is very useful, a more comprehensive approach would be an improvement.

The *Supplement* to *Canadian Reference Sources* adds new works and editions published up to December 1973. The work follows the same format as the previous volume. The scope has been enlarged to include "a few personal bibliographies and material dealing with areas smaller than the provinces" (p. i). Four pages of corrections and additions to the main volume are provided. While this new supplement adds greatly to the already useful *Canadian Reference Sources*, it is hoped that a new edition incorporating both volumes and future additions will be forthcoming. [R: ARBA 74, p. 3; BL, 15 May 74, p. 1015; Choice, Oct 73, p. 1159; C&RL, Jan 74, p. 65; C&RL, July 74, p. 242; LJ, 1 Dec 73, p. 3532; ARBA 76, p. 35]   Chester S. Bunnell
                                                                                                                Bohdan S. Wynar

EASTERN EUROPE AND THE SOVIET UNION

141.   Bakó, Elemér. **Guide to Hungarian Studies.** Stanford, CA, Hoover Institution Press, 1973. 2v. illus. index. (Hoover Institution Bibliographical Series, No. 52). $35.00. LC 79-152422. ISBN 0-8179-2521-X.

This massive, two-volume guide offers 4,426 bibliographical entries describing special reference works, periodicals, monographs, and journal articles devoted to Hungarian history, culture, and economics. A brief sketch of the history of Hungarian intellectual life (pp. 3-21) is followed by a two-part chronology of Hungarian political, military, cultural, economic, and social history (pp. 25-145). Preliminaries also include a useful list of Hungarian abbreviations, with English equivalents for each term (pp. 147-51). Bibliographical entries in the main body of the work fall into 20 categories: 1) History of the Hungarian Book; 2) Cultural Life and Institutions; 3) General Works; 4) Statistical Research; 5) The Land; 6) The People; 7) History and Historiography; 8) Constitution and Legislation; 9) Government and Politics; 10) Social Life; 11) Economics; 12) Religion and Church Affairs; 13) Language; 14) Literature; 15) Fine Arts and Music; 16) Education; 17) Science; 18) Press and Publishing; 19) Hungarians Abroad; 20) Hungary and the United States.

A system of cross references facilitates access to works devoted to more than one subject. Two indexes — one to periodical titles and another to personal names — close the second volume. The bibliography section includes sources in Hungarian, English, French, German, and Latin. Hungarian titles are followed by their English translations. The Bakó work is a significant addition to Hungarica collections. [R: ARBA 75, p. 150; Choice, Sept 74, p. 907]   Ivan L. Kaldor

142. Horak, Stephan M., comp. **Russia, the USSR, and Eastern Europe: A Bibliographic Guide to English Language Publications, 1964-1974**. Ed. by Rosemary Neiswender. Littleton, CO, Libraries Unlimited, 1978. 488p. index. $25.00. LC 77-20696. ISBN 0-87287-178-9.

No comprehensive survey of studies in English relating to the Soviet Union and Eastern Europe has appeared since Paul Horecky's *Russia and the Soviet Union: A Bibliographic Guide to Western Publications* (1965) and his companion volumes, *East Central Europe* (1969) and *Southeastern Europe* (1969). Horak's new guide is designed to update bibliographic coverage of these areas in the social sciences and humanities by bringing together an annotated listing of significant titles published from 1964 to 1974. The approximately 1,600 entries are accompanied by critical annotations excerpted (and in some cases adapted) from reviews published in major United States and British Slavic journals. In instances where no published reviews were found, annotations have been supplied by the compiler. (Full bibliographic citations are also given for the quoted reviews.) The index includes authors, compilers, editors, and translators. [R: ARBA 79, p. 189; Choice, Feb 79, p. 1642; C&RL, July 79, p. 351; LJ, 1 Nov 78, p. 2229; RQ, Spring 79, p. 307; WLB, Dec 78, p. 348]

143. Horecky, Paul L., ed. **East Central Europe: A Guide to Basic Publications**. Chicago, University of Chicago Press, 1969. 956p. index. $39.00. LC 70-79472. ISBN 0-226-35189-0.

144. Horecky, Paul L., ed. **Southeastern Europe: A Guide to Basic Publications**. Chicago, University of Chicago Press, 1969. 755p. index. $31.00. LC 73-110336. ISBN 0-226-35190-4.

With these two companion guides to the standard sources for two East-European geographical areas, Dr. Horecky provides the library profession with the most comprehensive guide ever attempted. He was assisted in this difficult task by a number of well-known subject specialists, responsible for individual sections, whose names and professional positions are listed in both volumes. In terms of scope and organization of material, the volumes are almost identical.

The first volume, *East Central Europe*, covers Czechoslovakia, East Germany (including a separate section on Lusatians and Polabians), Hungary, Poland, plus a general section dealing with the publications "which pertain either to two or more countries of the area or to subjects for which a consolidated rather than separate presentation by countries seemed indicated." In this general section the reader will find such topics as general reference aids and bibliographies, and general works on Slavic language or literature. The material for each country is presented under uniform subject categories: general reference aids and bibliographies, the land, the people, history, the state, the economy, the society, and intellectual and cultural life. Coverage is international, with emphasis on monographic material, but important serial publications and occasionally articles of special significance are also included. All entries are annotated, frequently with critical comments and references to similar works.

The second volume, *Southeastern Europe*, covers Albania, Bulgaria, Greece, Romania, and Yugoslavia and has identical arrangement. Both volumes list over 6,000 entries, but the main value of this work is not its quantity, but the well-designed criteria for selection. In this respect, the two volumes omit very little. The third part of the first volume is an index of authors and publishers, with rather unique information for scholars. [R: ARBA 71, p. 84-85; Choice, July 70, p. 670; C&RL, July 70, p. 278; LJ, July 70, p. 2449; WLB, June 70, p. 1067; Choice, July 70, p. 670; C&RL, Nov 70, p. 418; LJ, July 70, p. 2449; WLB, June 70, p. 1067]   Bohdan S. Wynar

145. **Ukraine: A Concise Encyclopaedia. Volume 2.** Prepared by Shevchenko Scientific Society. Edited by Volodymyr Kubijovych. Toronto, Buffalo, published for the Ukrainian National Association by University of Toronto Press, 1971. 1394p. illus. (some col.). maps. index. $60.00; $94.50/set. ISBN 0-8020-3261-3(v.2).

A Concise Encyclopaedia is a revised and substantially enlarged version of the three-volume work published in Ukrainian in 1949 by the Shevchenko Scientific Society in Munich. The first volume, published in 1963, covers physical geography and natural history, population, ethnography, language, history, culture, and literature.

The present, concluding volume provides information on law; Ukrainian church; education and research institutions; libraries, archives, and museums; book publishing and the press; the arts; music and choreography; theater and cinema; national economy; health, medical services, and physical culture; and military science. There is also a separate chapter on Ukrainians abroad. Several hundred noted scholars cooperated in this project; all articles are signed, with appended bibliographical listings of additional sources of information. The material is arranged under broad subject categories as noted above, with numerous subdivisions, and some 800 illustrations are integrated with the narrative.

The first volume of this work, which is probably the most authoritative single source on the Ukraine and its history in the English language, received most favorable reviews in many professional journals, including *Slavic Review*. The second volume retains the distinguished tradition of its predecessor, providing a well-balanced and impressive presentation of the subjects covered. Both volumes offer a wealth of information. [R: ARBA 72, p. 114]

GREAT BRITAIN

146. Ward, William S. **British Periodicals and Newspapers, 1789-1832: A Bibliography of Secondary Sources.** Lexington, University Press of Kentucky, 1972. 387p. index. $25.50. LC 74-190536. ISBN 0-8131-1271-0.

This is a sequel to Ward's *Index and Finding List of Serials Published in the British Isles, 1789-1832*, which was published in 1953. In the present work the author attempts to "provide a bibliography of the books and articles that have been written about the newspapers and periodicals listed in that *Index.*" Recorded here are all sorts of writings that deal with the history of these newspapers and periodicals, with the men who wrote for them or who edited them or produced them, and with the "public that read them and the government that was concerned with their impact upon the times."

The work contains a unit that lists general bibliographies and bibliographical studies and general studies, both arranged alphabetically by author. This is followed by units on periodicals, arranged under name of journal; people, arranged by surname; and places, arranged by place-name. The final unit includes material on printing, production, advertising, freedom of the press, etc. There are some brief annotations for a few of the entries. The indexes are most complete and are arranged in three units: authors, subjects, and library catalogs and union lists.

A specialized, but useful, guide whose aim is to "disentomb as many of these memoirs and books and articles as possible and thereby make it easier for those who come hereafter to discover what others have already said and done." [R: ARBA 74, p. 12; Choice, May 73, p. 434]   Paul A. Winckler

LATIN AMERICA

147. Comitas, Lambros. **Caribbeana 1900-1965: A Topical Bibliography.** Seattle, University of Washington Press, 1970 (c.1968). 909p. $18.50. LC 68-14239. ISBN 0-295-73970-3.

A unique bibliography of twentieth-century publications on the non-Hispanic Caribbean islands and mainland territories. Unannotated, it is deliberately unselective, except for the requirement of a minimal level of scholarly value. The 7,000 references include books, monographs, reports, periodical articles, unpublished theses, and "authored" government documents. Entries were drawn mainly from the scholarly libraries and special collections of New York City (locations are cited). Supplementary searching was done in various libraries and collections in the West Indies, London, and Canada. Nothing was included without examination, even references from the nearly 700 periodicals. The compiler's limited claim to have included "most of the scholarly writings" in this field is perhaps modest, but probably just (given that the large and important class of agency-produced documents is intentionally omitted).

The arrangement consists of 10 major themes subdivided into topic-chapters (67 in all). It has virtually no subject limitations, covering all topics of possible interest to social scientists (the primary audience). The expected topics are all here under cultural, historical, political, socioeconomic, and environmental science categories, but there also are such imaginative topic-chapter headings as: Values and Norms; Cultural Continuities and Acculturation; Ethnohealth and Ethnomedicine; West Indians Abroad; and Theory and Methodology.

There are author and geographic indexes, but no subject index (or keyword or catch-title index). Some help is provided by the coding of the unannotated entires to bring out additional subject aspects. There are other useful codings and marginal cues, part of a splendid format. [R: ARBA 71, p. 83]   David Rosenbaum

148. Delpar, Helen, ed. **Encyclopedia of Latin America.** New York, McGraw-Hill, 1974. 651p. illus. $36.50. LC 74-1036. ISBN 0-07-055645-8.

Many hard-to-find facts on such topics as population, political parties, trade, communism, transportation, etc., are included in this alphabetically arranged encyclopedia. All the information is in a very concise form; most articles are less than half a page in length, but some run to two or three pages. The 1,600 articles are signed and many are accompanied by bibliographies. There is a general article on each of the 18 Spanish-speaking republics, plus Brazil, Haiti, and Puerto Rico; these articles cover history, geography, industry, and culture. The *Encyclopedia* seems to be particularly rich in biographies;

included are political figures, writers, musicians, and artists of all kinds, both living and dead. According to the editor, "efforts were made to include . . . every vital subject or person related to each country's history and position in the world." This can be considered an excellent one-volume reference work for identifying Latin Americans and as a source for statistics on many aspects of Latin America. [R: ARBA 75, p. 155; BL, 15 May 75, p. 971; Choice, May 75, p. 368; C&RL, July 75, p. 316; LJ, 15 Mar 75, p. 568; LJ, 15 Apr 75, p. 732; WLB, May 75, p. 674]   Donald J. Lehnus

149. Gropp, Arthur E. **A Bibliography of Latin American Bibliographies Published in Periodicals.** Metuchen, NJ, Scarecrow, 1976. 2v. index. $40.00/set. LC 75-32552. ISBN 0-8108-0838-2.

A distinguished author, compiler, and librarian of Latin American material, Gropp presents impressive credentials to undertake this ambitious index of bibliographies published in 1,044 periodicals. Represented in the 9,729 entries are not only bibliographical articles but also important bibliographies that accompany articles. The latter feature is certainly one of the work's most valuable inclusions. The cut-off date is 1965, with most of the entries being selected from periodicals published during the preceding 30 years. In scope the bibliography is comprehensive. Arranged alphabetically by subject (agriculture to zoology) and form (e.g., archives, bibliography, indexes, maps), each section is then arranged by main entry (which is preponderantly author). An extensive index of 160 pages provides full author and subject access.

This work and Gropp's earlier *Bibliography of Latin American Bibliographies* (1968) and its 1971 supplement provide comprehensive, convenient, and reliable access to a large body of material found in disparate and sometimes fugitive sources. Recommended for scholarly collections. [R: ARBA 77, p. 174; Choice, Oct 76, p. 958; C&RL, Jan 77, p. 46; LJ, 1 May 76, p. 1104; RQ, Winter 76, p. 185]   Robert D. Harlan

MIDDLE EAST AND NORTH AFRICA

150. **Arab Islamic Bibliography: The Middle East Library Committee Guide.** Ed. by Diana Grimwood-Jones, Derek Hopwood, and J. D. Pearson. Based on Guiseppe Gabrieli's *Manuale di bibliografia musulmana.* Sussex, England, Harvester Press; Atlantic Highlands, NJ, Humanities Press, 1977. 292p. index. $51.00. LC 76-51397. ISBN 0-85527-384-4(Harvester); 0-391-00691-6(Humanities).

Since its publication in 1916, Guiseppe Gabrieli's *Manuale di bibliografia musulmana* has received much-deserved acclaim as a standard work on this subject. The present work, the product of a group of noted scholars, retains much of the material from the original publication, supplementing this with more recent information. The original structure of Gabrieli's *Manuale* is, generally speaking, retained; the work covers bibliographies, encyclopedias, and other reference works; Arabic grammars; genealogy, biographical dictionaries and who's whos; the press and periodicals; maps and atlases; Arabic geographical names; festschrifts; scientific expeditions; orientalism and orientalists; institutions; Arabic manuscripts; Arabic papyri; archives; Arabic epigraphy; Muslim numismatics; Arabic printing and book production; libraries; and a directory of booksellers. Each section has a brief narrative introduciton, followed by a listing of pertinent materials. All entries provide adequate bibliographic citations; many contain brief notes (e.g., Arabic Grammars); and some (e.g., Encyclopedias and Reference Works) have more detailed annotations, occasionally relating a given work to similar titles. The volume concludes with an index of authors and titles of anonymous works. Other works on this subject include the prestigious

Index Islamicus, several publications sponsored by the Library of Congress, and Littlefield's *The Islamic Near East and North Africa* (see entry 152). [R: ARBA 78, p. 150; Choice, May 78, p. 369]   Bohdan S. Wynar

151.   **Encyclopedia of Zionism and Israel.** Ed. by Raphael Patai. New York, Herzl Press and McGraw-Hill, 1971. 2v. illus. bibliog. $44.50. LC 68-55271. ISBN 0-07-079635-1.

Recent years have witnessed a number of scholarly reference materials about Israel and Jewish problems in general, including such notable works as *Encyclopaedia Judaica*. The present work deals primarily with the Zionist movement, and with its nearly 3,000 signed articles written by some 285 contributing authors it constitutes probably the most authoritative single source on this subject. The history of this interesting project is described in some detail in the preface. Originally, it was envisioned as a "Zionist Encyclopedia." Gradually, during the process of preparation, its scope was substantially enlarged and it was agreed that since "Zionism and Israel were so closely intertwined, the nature of material to be covered in the encyclopedia required that they be given equal attention." Thus, both subjects receive adequate coverage, and the reader will find here not only a well-documented presentation of the history of the Zionist movement in various countries, but also a description of Zionist institutions in Israel integrated with Israel's political and social history, cultural customs, governmental agencies, Jewish immigration, etc. In addition to articles that, generally speaking, may be described as topical (e.g., "Belgium, Zionism in," or "Architecture and Planning in Israel"), there are a number of biographical articles, primarily on Zionist leaders and Israeli statesmen and public officials. The third category consists of articles of a geographic nature, describing major cities, towns, regions, etc. Most of them are rather brief.

To this reviewer, some of the best documented articles are "Crime in Israel" and "Foreign Aid Program in Israel," while, on the other hand, such topics as "Assimilation" or even "Anti-Semitism" seem to be rather brief, considering the availability of material on both subjects. For most major countries (e.g., Germany, Russia, the United States), the encyclopedia presents well-written surveys of inter-relations between Zionism and Israel. There are separate articles for immigrants from various countries (e.g., Bulgarian Jews in Israel, German Jews in Israel). It is probably unfortunate that even the major articles do not contain bibliographical listings referring the reader to additional sources of information. A selected bibliography is appended at the end of the second volume, but as one might expect it is limited to monographic works. The text is accompanied by many black-and-white illustrations.

On the whole, *Encyclopedia of Zionism and Israel* is a modern reference work that presents a wealth of information and a well-balanced treatment of the different subjects. It is one of the best sources available on this subject today. [R: ARBA 72, p. 113; BL, 1 July 72, p. 913; LJ, 1 Nov 71, p. 3594; RQ, Fall 71, p. 74]   Bohdan S. Wynar

152.   Littlefield, David W. **The Islamic Near East and North Africa: An Annotated Guide to Books in English for Non-Specialists.** Littleton, CO, Libraries Unlimited, 1977. 375p. index. LC 76-218. ISBN 0-87287-159-2.

The main part of the book contains a basic collection of 1,166 titles documenting the major aspects of Near Eastern history and life and representing the main disciplines through which the region is studied. Included are: bibliographies; reference books; biographies; pictorial works; guidebooks; travelogs, old and new; documentary collections; language textbooks; medieval and nineteenth-century primary sources; and translations of literary and other works from Arabic, Hebrew, Persian, and Turkish.

The book is divided into two parts. "General Works" includes topical chapters: history and politics, international relations, biography, civilization, language and literature, society, education, economy, description and travel, religion, Islam.

"Individual Countries," the second part, covers over 25 nations, including Afghanistan, Cyprus, Egypt, Iran, Israel and Palestine, Lebanon, Turkey, and Algeria. There is an extensive separate section dealing with the Arab-Israeli conflict. Each chapter concerned with an individual country is subdivided by topics such as history and politics, biography, society, economy, description and travel, and guidebooks.

The annotations describe and evaluate each book as to its contents, its value as a source of information or pleasure, its contribution to understanding of the subject, its reliability, and the audience and educational level for which it is most appropriate. Priority codes are assigned to the most basic works in key fields to indicate suggested order of purchase or reading and to point out the kind of library (smaller, medium-sized, and larger public and college libraries) for which they are most suitable. Over 500 titles of more advanced or specialized works for further reading are included within the annotations.

Contained within the appendix are: four core collections (small and medium-sized public and college libraries); a list of works that will give the serious general reader a start at systematic study of the region and its people; a basic student library, including paperbacks; and a list for businessmen providing a brief overview of the area and quick reading on basic issues relevant to business relations with Arab and other Near Eastern nations. [R: ARBA 78, p. 151; Choice, June 77, p. 514; LJ, 15 Apr 77, p. 903; LJ, 15 Apr 78, p. 816; RQ, Fall 77, p. 80; WLB, May 77, p. 781]

UNITED STATES

153. Lamar, Howard R., ed. **The Reader's Encyclopedia of the American West.** New York, Thomas Y. Crowell, 1977. 1306p. illus. $24.95. LC 76-17236. ISBN 0-690-00008-1.

Howard R. Lamar is to be congratulated on a splendid job of assembling the essays of over 200 contributors into a book as informative as it is well written and easy to use. Given the central role in the formation of American character that many historians assign to the frontier experience, such a one-volume quick reference is indeed welcome, especially this one, which covers the West of myth and reality, of early Indian days, and present controversies over use of natural resources. The editor recognizes that the definition of "the West" has changed over the course of United States history, and entries demonstrate this; for instance, a summary of the circumstances surrounding the formation of each of the states is provided, since they were all, at one time, frontier territory.

The 2,400 entries are arranged alphabetically, and cross references are generous. Coverage includes Indian-white relations, expansion, trapping, mining, livestock raising, and the rise of Texas and Mormon Utah as subcultures. Additionally, there is coverage of the effect that the idea of the West has had on the arts—literature, music, theater, photography, films, etc. Coverage of Indians is not exhaustive, but articles on the historic tribes, on most of the significant Indian-white contacts, and on prominent Indians do reflect current scholarship. Coverage of other ethnic groups (Basque, Mexican, Chinese, Japanese, etc.) is provided, as are articles on various linguistic phenomena associated with these and other groups. Contemporary concerns are reflected in the articles on the aerospace industry, the oil industry, and the film industry. Articles are of two types, overview and specific topic, the latter predominating.

The articles are concise, often witty, and always densely packed with information. If differing views of a situation are current, or if views have changed over the years, this is indicated in remarkably even-handed summaries. The article on Latter-Day Saints (Mormons) contains a paragraph on the Mountain Meadow Massacre that is a model of what such an entry can be, if researched and written with care. The article on Zane Grey places him perfectly. The articles on Franklin, Jefferson, and Washington emphasize their roles in and concerns with the settlement of "the West" and are refreshing in the change in perspective that is provided. Women are covered, and not simply the notorious, though this coverage might be expanded in a future edition.

As to quibbles, a clearer explanation of possible motives for the Sand Creek Massacre would have helped. And in the article on the·Shakers, more specific mention might have been made of the fact that they have almost died as a sect because they deliberately do not procreate; this was only hinted at. The article on the oil industry should surely have mentioned oil shale, given the billions of dollars already spent and potentially involved.

On balance, though, this is a superb job and would benefit the collection of any library, especially those with works that only concern the historical West, as it will bring them up to date very pleasurably. [R: ARBA 78, p. 169; C&RL, July 78, p. 307; LJ, 15 Feb 78, p. 450; LJ, 15 Apr 78, p. 819; WLB, Apr 78, p. 651]   Koert C. Loomis, Jr.

154.   U.S. Library of Congress. General Reference and Bibliography Division. **A Guide to the Study of the United States of America: Representative Books Reflecting the Development of American Life and Thought. Supplement 1956-1965.** Prep. under the direction of Roy P. Basler. Washington, GPO, 1976. 526p. index. $12.00. LC 60-600009. ISBN 0-8444-0164-1. S/N 030-001-00042-7.

"When the *Guide to the Study of the United States of America* was published in 1960, the Library anticipated updating it with supplements or revisions. A supplement covering books published during the decade 1956-65 was decided upon, and a guideline limiting its contents to approximately half the number of entries contained in the 1960 *Guide* was adopted" (p.ix). After some 16 years, the Library finally overcame its numerous setbacks, changes of editors, and other problems, and managed to publish a highly selective descriptive listing of 2,943 entries dealing with major topics in American studies. A second supplement, covering books published during the decade 1966-1975, is now being compiled by the Library, which wisely has given no hint of its possible completion date.

The supplement, with slight variations, follows the structure, style, and selection criteria of the main volume. An omission is the list of selected readings in American studies. The scope and purpose of the *Guide* are broad: to meet the requirements of serious readers, students seeking orientation, and librarians engaged in developing collections about the United States, and to spread before readers a panorama of life in the United States, past and present. Books were selected on the basis of their value as an expression of life in the United States. Entries are grouped in 32 broad chapters covering a wide range of subjects from literature and language to law, politics, and libraries. Entries usually supply full bibliographic data, plus LC card number and LC classification number. Annotations are primarily descriptive notes; occasionally other titles are cited and contrasted in the annotations.

The value of the supplement as an orienting reading guide or collection-building tool is severely limited by the age of the selections. Readers are left to trace their own paths through the ever-increasing book production on American life and thought from 1966 to the present. Libraries will want to add this book to their collections, but it will serve more as a selective checklist for accessing the collection of older materials than as a reading guide. Students will find more timely, although highly selective, works listed in such guides as R. Walker's *American Studies: Topics and Sources* (Greenwood Press, 1976. 393p. $21.25). [R: ARBA 77, p. 173; Choice, June 77, p. 517]   Christine Gehrt Wynar

4 HISTORY

ARCHAEOLOGY

155. Avi-Yonah, Michael, and Ephraim Stern, eds. **Encyclopedia of Archaeological Excavations in the Holy Land, Volume 4.** Englewood Cliffs, NJ, Prentice-Hall, 1978. 1v. (various paging). illus. (part col.). maps. index. $25.00. LC 73-14997. ISBN 0-13-275149-6.

This is the last volume of the four-volume work, prepared in cooperation with a number of internationally known experts. The *Encyclopedia* painstakingly describes and analyzes all of the important archaeological excavations done during the past 100 or more years in the Holy Land. Each article is illustrated with black-and-white or color photographs, diagrams, and maps. Included in each section are identification, a history of the site, a history of the explorations and excavations, finds, and a bibliography. This is indeed a fine, scholarly work, essential for both laypersons and archaeologists interested in Holy Land sites. [R: ARBA 80, p. 160]   Susan C. Holte

156. Charles-Picard, Gilbert, ed. **Larousse Encyclopedia of Archaeology.** Trans. by Anne Ward. New York, Putnam's, 1972. 432p. index. illus. $25.00. LC 76-179972. ISBN 0-600-75451-2.

The *Larousse Encyclopedia of Archaeology* was first published in France in 1969. Designed as an authoritative reference book for students of archaeology and for laymen, it discusses archaeology as a field of study and surveys archaeological sites throughout the world.

The book is beautifully illustrated with 40 color plates and 600 monochrome photos. At the end are a bibliography for further reading (subdivided by topics) and an index to names, places, and subjects, with italics referring to illustrations. The two main parts of the encyclopedia are "Archaeology at Work" and "The Recovery of the Past." Part 1 contains six chapters defining archaeology, explaining the survival of relics, how sites are located and excavated, and how scientists date and restore finds and publish the collected data. Part 2, geographically arranged, describes the work and discoveries of famous archaeologists in various parts of the world. These 12 chapters cover work in prehistoric archaeology, ancient Western Asia, the Nile, the Aegean world, Greece, the Etruscans, the Romans, Europe, the Americas, India, Southeast Asia, and China. All articles are signed by specialists.

A second volume aimed at the amateur is Leonard Cottrell's *Concise Encyclopedia of Archaeology* (2nd ed., Hawthorn Books, 1971. 430p.), which includes articles written by 48 eminent authorities in the field, covering cities and civilizations, trends and techniques, and ancient languages and their decipherment. Coverage is worldwide, although it should be noted that there is little information on the archaeology of classical Greece and Rome, since this is discussed extensively in other sources. [R: ARBA 73, p. 172; BL, 1 Jan 73, p. 425; BL, 15 Jan 73, p. 489; Choice, Mar 73, p. 62; LJ, 1 May 73, p. 1471; WLB, May 73, p. 793]

157. Stillwell, Richard, ed. **The Princeton Encyclopedia of Classical Sites.** Princeton, NJ, Princeton University Press, 1976. 1019p. illus. maps. (col.). $135.00. LC 75-30210. ISBN 0-691-03542-3.

The text of this huge encyclopedic dictionary contains at least 1,000,000 words, and lists classical sites extending from Scotland to the Sudan and from Morocco to Pakistan. Chronologically, its limits are from the eighth century B.C. to about the sixth A.D.; it excludes both Byzantine and late Christian classical sites. The 400 authors who describe the 2,800 sites are both classicists and archaeologists; they come from all over Europe and America, and in many cases they seem to be the best qualified living experts. Entries vary in length from a few lines to Nash's 9,000-word description of ancient Rome. Each site is identified and located by map; if the information is available, the history of the site is summarized and modern excavations noted. Every entry has some bibliography. The bibliographies, which are highly selective, stress technical rather than popular works and include books and articles in most of the written languages of modern Europe. There are a few slight misprints. Some of the sites are relatively unimportant, and it seems that at least one, Bolsena, excavated in recent years by the French School at Rome, has been overlooked. All in all, this is an extraordinary book, useful especially to scholars and serious students.

Ed. note: On a much smaller scale, but covering the same subject, is the *Atlas of Classical Archaeology* (McGraw-Hill, 1977. 256p.). Editor M. I. Finley, along with 11 contributors, discusses 13 geographic-historical areas in the Mediterranean region "inhabited or dominated by Greeks and Romans in historic times" (p. 10), roughly 1000 B.C.-A.D. 500. Over 100 sites are described in both historic and contemporary contexts. Discussions of most sites are accompanied by photographs, and there are brief bibliographies for each site, including scholarly and foreign-language material. For its price ($22.50) and size (256p.), the *Atlas* is the likely alternative purchase for those unable to afford *The Princeton Encyclopedia*. [R: ARBA 77, p. 180; BL, 1 Feb 77, p. 854; Choice, Dec 76, p. 1278; LJ, 1 Oct 76, p. 2050; WLB, Feb 77, p. 541]   Theodore M. Avery, Jr.

158.   Taylor, R. E., and Clement W. Meighan. **Chronologies in New World Archaeology.** New York, Academic Press, 1978. 587p. illus. index. (Studies in Archeology). $49.50. LC 78-2039. ISBN 0-12-685750-4.

In 1966, *Chronologies in Old World Archaeology* (R. W. Ehrich, ed., University of Chicago Press) was published. It took 12 years of planning and work to produce the New World volume. Eighteen of the leading New World archaeologists prepared essays of 30 to 40 pages that summarize the chronology of 13 archaeological regions (Western and Sub-Arctic; Eastern United States; Diablo Range; North American Plains; Great Basin; American Southwest; California; Western Mesoamerica, Pre-A.D. 900, and 900-1520 A.D.; and Eastern Mesoamerica, Lower Central America, the Caribbean, and Northern Chile).

Experts will note some significant gaps in the geographical coverage, especially for South America. However, most of the gaps are partially filled by Gordon Wiley's 50-page essay, "A Summary Scan." Wiley is undeniably qualified to undertake such a task, since he has already compiled two monumental works on New World archaeology. R. E. Taylor's opening essay, "Dating Methods in New World Archaeology," provides a concise summary of the techniques employed in dating New World archaeological sites. Each article concludes with a short bibliography of relevant books and articles. The index covers places, sites, and cultural terms but excludes personal names. A must for colleges and universities with programs in New World archaeology. [R: ARBA 80, p. 162; Choice, Dec 78, p. 1422]
                                                                                          G. Edward Evans

159.   Whitehouse, David, and Ruth Whitehouse. **Archaeological Atlas of the World.** San Francisco, W. H. Freeman, 1975. 272p. illus. index. $24.50; $11.00pa. LC 75-2028. ISBN 0-7167-0274-6; 0-7167-0273-8pa.

Two scholars produced a useful and needed atlas of prehistoric and proto-historic archaeological sites. The 103 maps, drawn by John Woodcock and Shalom Schatten and superimposed by a grid numbering scheme used in the site index, pinpoint about 5,000 sites. Maps, ranging from one-half to double-page size, are in sepia and white with topological features indicated. Site types (e.g., caves, settlements, etc.) are differentiated by black symbols. A very brief introduction covering the development and methodology of archaeology is followed by seven sections of maps: paleolithic sites in the Old World; Africa; Western Asia; the Mediterranean Basin; Europe with Russia; South and East Asia; Australasia and the Pacific; and the Americas. Each section and each map has brief explanatory material and brief reading lists. Although the work is intended for professionals and laymen, its chief value will be to student and amateur archaeologists. Recommended for all but the smallest public and school libraries, and as a must for academic libraries. [R: ARBA 77, p. 180; BL, 1 June 76, p. 1423; Choice, Nov 75, p. 1146]

Kathryn McChesney

WORLD HISTORY

GENERAL WORKS

160.   Barzun, Jacques, and Henry F. Graff. **The Modern Researcher.** 3rd ed. New York, Harcourt, Brace, Jovanovich, 1977. 378p. bibliog. index. $12.95; $9.95pa. LC 76-25777. ISBN 0-15-562511-X.

This standard work is primarily addressed to students of history, but should be read by anyone in the social sciences and humanities, and not only for the lucid intelligence displayed herein. In this edition, the chapter on fact-finding explains the necessary steps to take in order to efficiently tap data banks, joint repositories, etc. The bibliography of reference books has been revised to account for works published between 1970 and 1977, again with the balance in history. Other disciplines have a few basic works indicated. Selection is of uniformly high quality.

The authors discuss rumor and fraud, and their new guidelines on lecturing are a model of conciseness that would bear reading and application by many an experienced speaker. A brief survey of the "sister disciplines" (including cliometrics) provides an idea of the breadth of historical inquiry. All in all, the third edition is as timely as the first edition was, and perhaps more needed now than then. This reviewer was also delighted to note that his favorite statement from the previous edition has not been deleted: "A Bachelor or Master of Arts who has not fully mastered the alphabet should study it and practice its use" (p. 20, N.). Nothing escapes the authors' attention, and this revision should be in every library, especially at this price. [R: ARBA 78, p. 174; C&RL, July 77, p. 331; LJ, 15 Dec 76, p. 2560]

Koert C. Loomis, Jr.

161.   Iggers, Georg G., and Harold T. Parker, eds. **International Handbook of Historical Studies: Contemporary Research and Theory.** Westport, CT, Greenwood Press, 1979. 452p. bibliog. index. $35.00. LC 79-7061. ISBN 0-313-21367-4.

Twenty-four history professors and scholars from eight countries contributed to this collection of writings on contemporary historical methodology. All but 3 of the 23 contributions were written expressly for this volume. Iggers wrote the introduction, and Parker made "some concluding observations." Part I ("Some Methodological Reorientations") contains 8 articles on such topics as the philosophy and theory of history, the use of linguistics, demography, and psychology in historiography, and economic and social history. Part II ("Reorientation of Historical Studies: Regional and National Developments") is made up of 15 articles on historiography in such diverse places as the United States, Japan, Great Britain, Germany, Italy, USSR, China, Rumania, Latin America, India, and Africa. An extensive bibliography accompanies each article, and a four-page "Select Bibliography on Historiography" is appended at the end of the book.

There is an index to personal names and journal titles mentioned in the 23 contributions. This collection of articles is a very good guide to the many facets of current historiography in many parts of the world and is recommended for all college and university libraries, as well as large public libraries.   Donald J. Lehnus

162.   Poulton, Helen J., and Marguerite S. Howland. **The Historian's Handbook: A Descriptive Guide to Reference Works.** Norman, University of Oklahoma Press, 1977. 304p. index. $14.95; $7.95pa. LC 71-165774. ISBN 0-8061-0985-8.

Intended for students of history as a conveniently arranged handbook to basic source material, this work should provide substantial assistance for the uninitiated. The following topics are covered: the library and its catalog; national library catalogs and national and trade bibliographies; guides, manuals, and bibliographies; encyclopedias, dictionaries, and chronologies; almanacs, yearbooks, statistical handbooks, and current surveys; serials and newspapers; geographical aids — including bibliographies, indexes, gazetteers, etc.; biographical materials; primary sources and dissertations; legal sources; and government publications. The material is presented in the form of bibliographical essays, with some 970 titles mentioned in the text. The coverage is international, and the reader will find here a good sampling of basic reference materials pertaining not only to the United States but also to Great Britain, Latin America, the Soviet Union, the Far East, etc. Unfortunately, Western European countries and the Soviet Union receive rather sketchy coverage, which is probably the only serious drawback of this otherwise satisfactory handbook.

Bohdan S. Wynar

ATLASES

163.   Barraclough, Geoffrey, ed. **The Times Atlas of World History.** Maplewood, NJ, Hammond, 1978. 360p. illus. (col.). maps. index. $70.00. LC 78-5403. ISBN 0-8437-1125-6.

The authority of this new atlas is backed by its publishers, Times Books Ltd. and Hammond; its editor, the well-known Geoffrey Barraclough; and an impressive list of contributors representing Great Britain, the United States, and Australia. It is an all new production containing some 130 plates (600 maps and illustrations) and 300,000 words of narrative, glossary, and index. The *Atlas* aims to present a view of historical geography that is worldwide in conception and presentation and to avoid "Eurocentricity." National histories, changes in political boundaries, and particular events are given less emphasis than are broad movements, such as religions and great civilizations. A 12-page world chronology precedes the atlas sections. At the end are a glossary and an index of historical place names. The seven sections of the atlas are: 1) the world of early man; 2) the first civilisations; 3) the classical civilisations of Eurasia; 4) the world of divided regions; 5) the world of the emerging West; 6) the age of European dominance; 7) the age of global civilisation. The maps are large, well designed and colored, and easy to read.

The aim of depicting the broad sweeps of historical movements for students and nonspecialists is successfully achieved. The selectivity enforced on the compressed text will not satisfy all readers and will not substitute for detailed historical atlases or for texts on specific topics. For example, discussion of "The Russian Revolution" omits nationalism as an issue and bypasses the independent status of Ukraine during this time. Except for some detail on maps, Ukraine is ignored in the survey of "Russian" historical development. Another limitation of the *Atlas* acknowledged by the editor is the sparse coverage of contemporary problems, e.g., the Middle East. In summary, the *Atlas* is overall a fine popular work offering simplified depictions of complex regional or topical problems, and it should be useful in all types of libraries. [R: ARBA 79, p. 287; Choice, Mar 79, p. 60; C&RL, July 79, p. 352; LJ, 15 Apr 79, p. 889; WLB, Jan 79, p. 406]   Christine Gehrt Wynar

164.   Darby, H. C., and Harold Fullard, eds. **The New Cambridge Modern History: Volume XIV, Atlas.** New York, Cambridge University Press, 1970. 319p. maps. bibliog. index. $65.00; $19.95pa. ISBN 0-521-09908-0.

The *Atlas* was designed to accompany *The New Cambridge Modern History*. However, it can stand alone as a useful adjunct to the study of modern history, whatever text might be used. The compilers have done an excellent job of presenting a balanced coverage, and the atlas depicts the world as it was at various times in the modern era. There are maps of Europe, North America, Latin America, Africa, the Far East, and Australasia. The 288 maps are essentially political, but thematic maps are also included, and all have been newly compiled for this atlas, with reproduction done by a lithographic process that gives them a sharp and clean appearance. Typography is well selected and is crisp and sharp; the color work is pleasing and excellently registered. Maps within groups are arranged in chronological sequence and are reproduced on the same scale so that the user can make meaningful comparisons. Projection is not indicated for every map, but the editors have selected those projections which were most useful for the presentation of particular data.

A 31-page short subject index facilitates access to the cartographic data, and a 3-page short title bibliography will be useful to scholars. There is no text.

The only criticism that might be leveled would be the size of the volume, which had to be scaled to match the other volumes in the set. It is difficult to print a minutely detailed map on a 6x9-inch page, and a folio volume would have been preferred. On the other hand, the compact size makes it easy to handle. [R: ARBA 71, p. 105; Choice, Apr 71, p. 204; LJ, 1 May 71, p. 1597; WLB, Feb 71, p. 597]   Frank J. Anderson

165.   Platt, Colin. **The Atlas of Medieval Man.** New York, St. Martin's Press, 1980 (c.1979). 256p. illus. (part col.). index. $22.50. LC 79-65611. ISBN 0-312-15993-0.

Colin Platt has done much more than produce a new atlas. Instead, he has created a beautifully illustrated, analytical encyclopedia of the Middle Ages. He has analyzed each of the five centuries between 1000 and 1400 A.D. Each century constitutes a major division, with sections on historical context and material culture. With the latter, art and architecture are emphasized. Although science is not neglected, it is relegated to a minor role until the fifteenth century, when the invention of printing promoted a greater diffusion of knowledge. At the same time, developments in navigational techniques and vessels made possible the voyages of discovery near the end of this century.

A commendable feature of Platt's atlas is that he has avoided Europocentrism. Developments in each century are narrated for each of the major global regions: Western Europe, Far East, South-East Asia, India, Near East, Eastern Europe, Africa, and the Americas. The atlas traces the historical evolution of each region with a large number of maps, as well as illustrations of buildings and works of art created during these 500 years.

The Atlas of Medieval Man belongs in every academic library and in most public libraries. It will probably receive its optimum use as part of the collection on medieval history, rather than with the atlas collections.   Thomas S. Harding

166.   Shepherd, William R. **Shepherd's Historical Atlas.** 9th ed., rev. and updated. New York, Harper and Row, 1973 (c.1964). 115p. illus. maps. index. $22.50. LC Map 64-26. ISBN 0-06-013846-7.

Beginning with the old through new kingdoms of ancient Egypt (ca.3000-525 B.C.), Shepherd's superb atlas progresses in chronological arrangement to the European community in 1973, covering all periods and continents. All maps of the seventh edition (1929) have been reprinted, and eight more, prepared by C. S. Hammond & Company, have been appended to cover the period 1930 to 1973. However, it would be more accurate to limit this latter date to the mid-1960s, as one map of Europe cannot suffice to convey world history between then and 1973.

The Index and Index-Supplement provide thorough and detailed references to the maps. Locations are coded to correspond to latitude/longitude grids, as well as to page numbers for the maps. Variations in names, including classical and medieval Latin, and spellings of localities are noted or cross referenced. The two indexes together list names that appear in the original edition and those that are omitted from it, and update the work to 1929. The indexes do not cover the eight new maps.

Typography is generally quite excellent, only occasionally fading, shadowing, or being inadequately revised (as apparent on the map "Central Europe about 1786"). Color and cartography are superior, especially in the basic work. There is no text. [R: ARBA 75, p. 172; WLB, May 74, p. 767]   Peggy Jay

BIBLIOGRAPHIES

167.   Caenegem, R. C. van. **Guide to the Sources of Medieval History.** With the collaboration of F. L. Ganshoff. Amsterdam, New York, Elsevier/North-Holland, 1978. 428p. index. (Europe in the Middle Ages: Selected Studies, Vol. 2). $56.00. LC 77-7455. ISBN 0-7204-0743-5.

The *Guide to the Sources of Medieval History* is partly based on the *Kurze Quellenkunde des Westeuropäischen Mittelalters* and is more comprehensive than Paetow's *Guide to the Study of Medieval History.* The text consists of five parts: "Typology of the Sources of Medieval History" (narrative sources, treatises, fiscal and economic records); "Libraries and Archives" (description of important library catalogs); "Great Collections and Repertories of Sources" (historical introduction and enumeration of sources from 16 countries); "Reference Works for the Study of Medieval Texts" (linguistic works and ready reference sources); and "Bibliographical Introduction to the Auxiliary Sciences of History" (diplomatic, palaeography, epigraphy, etc.). The emphasis is on Western European sources, occasionally including some materials from Poland or Czechoslovakia, but not Russia. This is by far the best current work on this subject, and for Eastern Europe it can be supplemented by J. Macurek's *Dějepisectví evropského východu* (Prague, 1946) or *Sovetskaia istoriografiia Kievskoi Rusi* (Leningrad, 1978). Highly recommended for all universities.

James Powell's *Medieval Studies: An Introduction* (Syracuse University Press, 1976. 389p. $22.00; $9.95pa.) is a useful starting point for student research into Western culture before 1500 A.D. The 10 bibliographic chapters cover various aspects of medieval studies, summarizing the state of current knowledge and pointing out trends in recent scholarship. Major reference tools on each topic are described. [R: ARBA 80, p. 163; C&RL, Jan 79, p. 54]   Bohdan S. Wynar

CHRONOLOGIES

168.   De Ford, Miriam Allen, and Joan S. Jackson. **Who Was When? A Dictionary of Contemporaries.** 3rd ed. New York, H. W. Wilson, 1976. 184p. $30.00. LC 76-2404. ISBN 0-8242-0532-4.

The first edition of this work was published in 1940, the second in 1950. This third edition of the well-known quick reference dictionary provides access to some 10,000 celebrated individuals from 500 B.C. through 1974. Information is provided through a chronological approach. The years are listed along the left margin of each page, and the remainder of the page lists 11 categories of endeavor. Names of people are listed in appropriate subject categories at the years of their birth and the years of their death. Thus, contemporaries are aligned in two dimensions: by date (whether birth or death) and by broad field of activity. Between the birth and death dates of any individual can be found the names and dates of those in the same field as that individual, or in any other area of activity. The index lists each person mentioned in the chronology, giving birth and death dates for each (these dates, of course, serve as location devices for the chronological listings). [R: ARBA 77, p. 185; BL, 15 July 77, p. 1751; Choice, Mar 77, p. 42; WLB, Dec 76, p. 364]

169. Freeman-Grenville, G. S. P. **Chronology of World History: A Calendar of Principal Events from 3000 BC to AD 1976.** 2nd ed. London, Rex Collings; distr., Totowa, NJ, Rowman and Littlefield, 1978. 746p. index. $40.00. ISBN 0-901-72067-4.

This work, in its second edition, is a chronology of world history from 3100 B.C. to 1976 (the first edition encompasses 3100 B.C. to 1973), with an emphasis on developments and dates outside of the Western world. This allows the user to compare the events of Europe with those that were contemporaneously taking place elsewhere in the world. This second edition includes some items omitted earlier, and some 2,000 new entries, many of which are in the column headed "Religion and Culture."

Like S. H. Steinberg's *Historical Tables 58 BC-AD 1972* and *The People's Chronology*, this source attempts to record major historical and cultural events. But, unlike Steinberg's *Historical Tables* and like *The People's Chronology*, Freeman-Grenville includes a detailed and comprehensive index, which is an integral part of the work. The arrangement of Freeman-Grenville is particularly impressive. Like Steinberg and unlike *The People's Chronology*, the information is arranged in a tabular fashion in six columns. This allows the user to see events taking place around the world at the same time, producing a "pictorial effect of the *camera-obscura*." But unlike Steinberg's chronology, this one devotes the first five columns to the geographical headings which were most prominent during particular eras; the sixth column is devoted to religion and culture. Steinberg, on the other hand, is somewhat inconsistent in his method of treatment.

Freeman-Grenville contains no bibliography and no justificatory footnotes. Some abbreviations are used frequently; a key for these appears in the front of the text. The *Oxford Atlas* is used as a standard for the geographic names contained within the text. For personal names some arbitrary decisions have been made, but generally the usage of the best English authors has been followed.

It appears that this is the best chronology of its kind available at the present time. While others, containing a broader spectrum of information, are available, none are as contemporary or as easily accessible as this one. Therefore, for the user who wants to find world events at a glance, this source is highly recommended.　　　　Mary A. Banner
Michael H. Harris

ENCYCLOPEDIAS

170. Langer, William L. **An Encyclopedia of World History: Ancient, Medieval, and Modern, Chronologically Arranged.** 5th ed. rev. and enl. Boston, Houghton Mifflin, 1972. 1569p. illus. maps. genealogical tables. index. $19.95. LC 68-14147. ISBN 0-395-13592-3.

The outlines in this work provide a historical chronology for important events that occurred in various places throughout the world from prehistoric times through 1970. The broad periods are subdivided geographically, and events are concisely described. The fourth revised edition (1968) was a major revision in which more material was added to the prehistory section, including information on new dating techniques; and sections on art, literature, thought, and science and technology were also incorporated. Cross references were improved and better genealogical tables were prepared. Lists of emperors, popes, and rulers are included. Fifty-seven outline maps and 104 genealogical tables are included in the fifth edition.

The fifth edition (1972) brings the chronologies up to January 1, 1971, incorporating events in the Middle East, Southeast Asia, the cultural revolution in China, the emergence of Japan as a prime industrial power, the increase in the number of states gaining their independence, the youth revolt and drastic changes in educational systems, and race conflicts. An extensive index supplies access to names of events, places, and people mentioned in the text. It should be noted that Langer's *New Illustrated Encyclopedia of World History* (Abrams, 1975. 1362p. $65.00), in two volumes, varies from the work above only in its lavish illustrations. There is no evidence of textual revision.

Ed. note: Morris' *Harper Encyclopedia of the Modern World* (Harper and Row, 1970. 1271p. $20.00) resembles Langer's *Encyclopedia* in general make-up. Because coverage is limited to the past two centuries, it provides greater detail and clearer descriptions for events of the period than does Langer. For coverage of the recent era, it is to be preferred to Langer's work. [R: ARBA 73, p. 153; BL, 15 July 72, p. 985, 999; RQ, Summer 73, p. 407] Christine Gehrt Wynar

171. Parrish, Thomas, ed. **The Simon and Schuster Encyclopedia of World War II.** Chief consultant ed., S. L. A. Marshall. New York, Simon and Schuster, 1978. 767p. illus. (part col.). maps. bibliog. index. (A Cord Communications Book). $29.95. LC 78-9590. ISBN 0-671-24277-6.

We are used to claims that a book is the ultimate in a certain field, and certainly the *Simon and Schuster Encyclopedia of World War II* makes these claims — with good reason. Consider the statistics: 4,000 entries, 700,000 words, a comprehensive index; 200 maps and photographs. It maintains that the treatment of strategy, campaigns, battles, heroes, traitors, generals and admirals, statesmen, and scientists is comprehensive, and this is true. There are copious notes on code names, intelligence secrets, and double agents, but with the revelations from ULTRA, the book is well behind this history. Of course this may be an unfair comment, because with its exquisite map diagrams, superb photographs, and a formidable list of consulting editors and contributing writers, this book could not fail. It answers all the questions that the reference desk would expect to get, and as such is a must for most libraries. It is a huge book, but beautifully designed and printed. [R: ARBA 80, p. 165; BL, 1 May 79, p. 1399; Choice, June 79, p. 512; LJ, 1 Jan 79, p. 94; LJ, 15 Apr 79, p. 889; WLB, May 79, p. 652] P. William Filby

172. Taylor, A. J. P., and J. M. Roberts, eds. **20th Century.** 1979 ed. rev. by R. W. Cross, and others. Milwaukee, WI, Purnell Reference Books, a division of Macdonald-Raintree, 1979. 20v. illus. (part col.). bibliog. index. $299.50. LC 78-27424. ISBN 0-8393-6079-7(library binding).

The 1979 edition of *20th Century* is an updating of a 10-volume set published and copyrighted in 1971, 1972 under the title *Purnell's History of the 20th Century.* The set is an illustrated history of world social and political events from the opening of the twentieth century to the present. A substantial amount of material is new to this edition. New topics include race, terrorism, politics in Africa and the Middle East, sport and leisure, women, energy crisis, and civil rights in the United States. Not found were topics such as Helsinki Accords (except brief citation of the treaty) and the human rights movement. Organization of the set is chronological. Volume 1 opens with an examination of Europe as the world's overlord and concludes in volume 20 with events of the 1970s. The November 1978 Jonestown, Guyana tragedy is included as the last article in volume 20.

About 20 signed articles subsumed under four or five chapters are in each volume. At the beginning of each chapter, a chronology by theme(s) and topic(s) is printed in one column, e.g., chapter 1 lists chronologies for Africa (1886-1902), Society in Great Britain (1857-1912), Science and Invention (1845-1909), and General (1883-1902); chapter 98, "Society and the Media," lists the Women's Movement (1898-1976). A period is explored from a number of angles that may cover political and military activity in a single country or continent, social changes and movements that cut across geographical boundaries, and international events that engage most of the world's governments. Some attention is given to the arts, music, literature, science, and popular culture, but the emphasis of the set is on the illustrated chronology and interpretation of world political, military, and economic events.

The library edition has a reinforced binding for heavy use and is side sewn. The physical set contains 20 volumes, continuously paged (2,832 pages, or about 140 pages per volume). The previous edition in 10 volumes is estimated to be some 300 pages shorter. The original 96 chapters were expanded to 99. The 8½x11-inch pages are fully illustrated, using some 5,000 black-and-white photos, reproductions of paintings, cartoons, maps, and other contemporary illustrative material. A few maps and graphics were created for the set. Both selection and reproduction of the illustrations are of high quality.

Volume 1 contains a complete list of the contents of the set arranged by volume and chapter. A general index, bibliography, and list of contributors (which notes their affiliations, publications, and cites their articles in the set) are appended to volume 20. The general index is, at best, a finding device for individual names, specific events, and topics. A few cross references are employed, and some entries, for example "USSR" and "War," bring together many scattered references. Approach by theme, however, seems weakened to almost uselessness. Index entries are set in very small type, and those consisting of subentries are run-on and difficult to read. There are no citations to sources used or to additional readings following the articles, but the set includes a bibliography. The plan of the bibliography is changed from the chapter and article arrangement used in the original edition to a thematic approach. Thus, one finds over one-half page of selected books on diplomacy (one of the 16 themes). The selections are all in English and include some U.S. imprints. Any such limited selection is open to criticism, and future revisions may find a different approach to suggested readings.

The contributors to this set represent many reliable and authoritative writers and scholars. The editor-in-chief, A. J. P. Taylor, authored the volume on the twentieth century in the *Oxford History of England*. Most of the over 250 contributors are British scholars and journalists.

The text attempts to synthesize and interpret the main political events and movements in international affairs in the past 70 years for the general public. The constricted space allotted to text (over one-half the space is used for illustration) demands a kaleidoscope approach to most subjects. Considering such difficulties, the authors and editors do provide a fairly balanced presentation for nonscholarly purposes. In summation, this is an attractive and well-organized illustrated history of the twentieth-century world, suggested especially as a pictorial source for school and public libraries. [R: ARBA 80, p. 165]

Christine Gehrt Wynar

UNITED STATES

GENERAL WORKS

173.   Adams, James Truslow, ed. **Album of American History.** New York, Scribner's, 1969. 6v. illus. index. $35.00/v.; $165.00/set. LC 74-91746.

James Truslow Adams, one of America's most noteworthy historians and essayists, edited the well-known *Dictionary of American History* and *The Atlas of American History.* The first edition of this work was published in 1944-49 (5v.). Many scholars cooperated in the preparation and organization of the articles. To obtain the pictorial material used in these volumes the editors have searched museums, libraries, private collections, and public institutions of the country.

Volume 1 covers the colonial period. Around 1,600 pictures are presented, many of them previously unknown. In reissuing this volume, the editors have revised 62 of the pages, providing improved pictorial treatments of the original subjects. The second volume illustrates the years 1783 to 1853, roughly the period of westward expansion. In some 1,300 pictures of various types, with brief text, it presents a chronological panorama of American politics, economic development, social life, and customs. The third volume covers 1853-1893 and volume 4, 1893-1917. The fifth volume presents the pictorial history of the United States between the years 1917 and 1953. The sixth volume contains pictures illustrative of various phases of the years 1953 to 1968; it was edited by J. G. E. Hopkins. Like the previous volumes, it provides a pictorial chronicle of this period, coveirng in five chapters various aspects of American cultural and political life. This last volume also contains a general index to volumes 1 through 6. An excellent work printed from new plates with some 6,300 pictures. [R: ARBA 71, p. 106; WLB, Dec 70, p. 409]

Bohdan S. Wynar

174.   Commager, Henry Steele, ed. **Documents of American History.** 9th ed. Englewood Cliffs, NJ, Prentice-Hall, 1973. 2v. index. $12.95pa.(v.1); $12.95pa.(v.2). LC 73-11490. ISBN 0-13-216994-0(v.1); 0-13-217000-0(v.2).

Though it had been more than five years since the last edition of this basic reference tool was published, the ninth edition adds little in content. In fact, the first volume of the seventh edition, which this reviewer had at hand for comparison, duplicates exactly volume I of the ninth edition. Volume II of the ninth differs from volume II of the eighth only in that several documents (focusing mainly on civil rights and civil disobedience) have been dropped in order to make room for documents of the period from 1965 through mid-1973.

But for these exceptions, the ninth edition is almost a carbon copy of its predecessors. Commager still includes documents of an official/quasi-official nature, which he calls part of the country's "official record." Each document is preceded by a brief background note and an even briefer suggested bibliography. Treatment is chronological, beginning in volume I with the "Privileges and Prerogatives Granted Columbus" on April 30, 1492, and ending in volume II with *Miller vs. California,* the June 21, 1973, Supreme Court decision on obscenity. Volume II also repeats the Constitution in an appendix. [R: ARBA 75, p. 173; WLB, Nov 74, p. 249]

Wayne A. Wiegand

ATLASES

175.   **Atlas of the American Revolution.** Map selection and commentary by Kenneth Nebenzahl. Narrative text by Don Higginbotham. New York, Rand McNally, 1974. 218p. illus. (col.). maps. index. $50.00. LC 74-6976. ISBN 0-528-83018-X.

This is a large, lavish, and colorful recapitulation of the Revolutionary War, its antecedents, actions, and outcome. Map commentary is by Kenneth Nebenzahl, internationally acclaimed rare map expert, and narrative text by Don Higginbotham, author of *The War of American Independence.*

The work is woven around a germane selection of over 70 superbly reproduced maps/map insets originally drawn during or very shortly after noteworthy military events of the period (e.g., Bunker Hill, Bemis Heights, Yorktown). These are arranged chronologically by theater of war to depict and accentuate their tactical or strategic import from the standpoint of what happened and how it influenced the colonial struggle for self-rule. Each map is accompanied by cogent notes on its cartographic information content. All are interconnected intelligibly by a sprightly 40,000-word account of the times, concentrating on the activities of individual political and military leaders. The source of each map is indicated. More than 100 illustrations of contemporary portraits, views, cartoons, broadsides, and other printed items exert an impact on the reader that is both stimulating and instructive.

Maps, text, and illustrations are printed on quality stock and are positioned with an aesthetic sense of visual balance and contrast that is rarely encountered in volumes of this type. An appendix lists alphabetically all major American, French, British, and Hessian participants. The index contains approximately 600 entries keyed, as appropriate, to Higginbotham's text, Nebenzahl's map observations, and/or the maps themselves. The sole drawback of the atlas is the omission of a bibliography or suggested reading list. Summation: outstanding political, social, and military portrait of the American Revolution limned by mapmakers of the period with significant appeal to both browser and researcher. [R: ARBA 75, p. 177; BL, 1 Apr 75, p. 822; Choice, Feb 75, p. 1758; LJ, 15 Nov 74, p. 2691; RQ, Spring 75, p. 265; WLB, Dec 74, p. 314]   Lawrence E. Spellman

176.   Cappon, Lester J., ed.-in-chief, and others. **Atlas of Early American History: The Revolutionary Era, 1760-1790.** Princeton, published for The Newberry Library and The Institute of Early American History and Culture by Princeton University Press, 1976. 157p. illus. maps. (col.). index. $150.00. LC 75-2982. ISBN 0-691-04634-4.

American colonialists have long anticipated the publication of this volume, and they will not be disappointed with the results. A decade and a half of planning and eight years of research have culminated in the production of a volume of unsurpassed excellence.

The *Atlas of Early American History* contains 286 newly executed maps, 271 of them in color, based upon the best available cartographic evidence. These maps clearly and beautifully present a range of subject matter that is impressive in its completeness. Every conceivable aspect of colonial economic, social, and political life is touched upon. Particularly noteworthy is the treatment of the War of the Revolution. A series of 24 maps spotlight areas of military action, rather than individual battles. This innovation, depicting the level of military activity in each area over time, is far more useful in providing an understanding of the strategy of the conflict than separate battle maps would be.

The full value of this atlas, however, is not only in the cartographic record it provides. The accompanying text provides detailed explanation and analysis of each of the map series, including citations to relevant primary and secondary materials. Taken together, maps and text provide a basic education in the life of colonial America from 1760 to 1790. This work, superb in both concept and execution, supplants for its time period the earlier efforts of James T. Adams and Charles O. Paullin. It is a must acquisition for all research and university libraries and archival repositories, and it should be given serious consideration by most public libraries regardless of size. One is left with the wish that the authors will not cease with this volume but will provide similar works covering the early colonial years. [R: ARBA 77, p. 190; BL, 1 Oct 77, p. 317; Choice, Nov 76, p. 1115; LJ, 15 Nov 76, p. 2357; WLB, Nov 76, p. 262]   Robert L. Wagner

177. Jackson, Kenneth T. **Atlas of American History.** Rev. ed. New York, Scribner's, 1978. 294p. illus. maps. index. $45.00. LC 77-76851. ISBN 0-684-15052-2.

The first edition of this work, published in 1943, appeared with James Truslow Adams as editor-in-chief, the first name on the title page. This revised volume contains 198 maps; 51 are new, and all others have been updated. However, in an age of lavish atlases and encyclopedias, the black-and-white maps seem stark. Most of the new maps relate to twentieth-century developments and to current interest topics (women's movement, race riots, etc.). The *Atlas* is intended to be used with the *Dictionary of American History*, and the new edition should provide a new lease on life for this standard, but aging, reference work. [R: ARBA 79, p. 206; Choice, Sept 78, p. 842; LJ, 15 May 78, p. 1051; RQ, Spring 79, p. 310; WLB, June 78, p. 810]   G. Edward Evans

178. Marshall, Douglas W., and Howard H. Peckham. **Campaigns of the American Revolution: An Atlas of Manuscript Maps.** Ann Arbor, University of Michigan Press; Maplewood, NJ, Hammond, 1976. 138p. illus. (part col.). index. $25.00. LC 75-13657. ISBN 0-472-23300-9(University of Michigan); 0-8437-3125-7(Hammond).

This atlas, a genuine contribution to the burgeoning corpus of bicentennial literature, deserves a place in all American libraries. The maps range from crude field sketches to high examples of cartographic art which were produced after the heat of battle as a record of the events. The rare maps reproduced in this volume are principally from the splendid collection of the William L. Clements Library of the University of Michigan and are not ordinarily seen by persons other than the specialist scholars who use that collection. Douglas Marshall, who is curator of maps at the Clements Library and coordinator of the university's program in the history of discovery, has written several books on American maps and cartographic history. His collaborator on *Campaigns of the American Revolution*, Howard Peckham, is the director of the Clements Library and a professor of history at the University of Michigan; he has written a number of books about the American Revolution.

The authors have selected 56 maps that show the scope and progress of our war for independence—from Lexington to Concord in 1775 through the events at Yorktown, New London, and Pensacola which occurred in 1781. For each year of the war they present a narrative overview of the situation at that time, which precedes the maps of the campaigns for the year. The maps show the topography and the disposition of opposing forces. A page or two of text carries us through the events and is related to the map. Thus, the book is a military history of the war illustrated with contemporary maps. Comments about map makers and the state of the cartographic art are included in the pages. The thesis of the volume is the importance of maps to military operations as shown by these campaigns. A few words from the final paragraph of the book are worth quoting, *viz.*: "Although it was the larger issues of ends and means which defeated the British army, inadequate maps contributed to the problem." The flow of the narrative is not impeded by a clutter of footnotes, but the scholar will find that each map, including the endpaper maps, is carefully described in the section headed "Sources" (pp. 130-36). A two-page, four-column index, printed in highly legible boldface type, completes the volume. Impeccable printing and color registration, as befits the Hammond reputation. Nicely bound in cloth over heavyweight boards. Highly recommended. [R: ARBA 77, p. 191]   Frank J. Anderson

BIBLIOGRAPHIES

179. Harrison, Cynthia E., ed. **Women in American History: A Bibliography.** Pamela R. Byrne, managing ed. Santa Barbara, CA, ABC-Clio Press, 1979. 374p. index. (Clio Bibliography Series, No. 5). $62.50. LC 78-26194. ISBN 0-87436-260-1.

The idea behind the excellent tool *Women in American History*, edited and introduced by social historians who have written extensively about American women, is so good that it is surprising that no one thought of doing it until now. Searching volumes 1 through 14 of the American Bibliographical Center's *America: History and Life*, a major historical abstracting service, yielded nearly 3,400 relevant abstracts from a pool of 64,000. Historian Anne Firor Scott writes that this search "brought in every article even remotely touching upon the subjects of family or sex . . . from dozens of fields: sociology, anthropology, literature, demography, religion, economics, statistics, comparative studies, medicine, psychology, politics—to list a few."

Without a doubt, this is *the* source for scholarly periodical literature about women with a historical and interdisciplinary emphasis. The abstracts, in the main, are meaty, the index a pleasure to use. Browsing the index one finds references to every aspect of women-related scholarship: the American Revolution, actresses, clothing, communes, eugenics, labor unions, polygamy, travel accounts—in a word, the scope of social history. Personal names surface readily, and the subject index is particularly fine in locating materials state by state. In the 25 or so entries under "Colorado," one finds the range from suffrage to "Baby Doe" Tabor of silver mining fame. Because the abstracts are substantial, users will have a fair idea of whether an article is useful or not, certainly a help for people requiring interlibrary loan assistance in getting the actual articles.

Scholarly periodical literature about women has posed a particular access problem for women's studies students and scholars, and for social historians. *Women in American History* provides the best coverage to date of the academic journals, and one looks for periodic updates of this landmark project.　　　　　　　　　　　　　Esther F. Stineman

180.　**Harvard Guide to American History**. Rev. ed. Ed. by Frank Freidel, with the assistance of Richard K. Showman. Cambridge, MA, Belknap Press of Harvard University Press, 1974. 2v. index. $45.00. LC 72-81272. ISBN 0-674-37560-2.

The last edition of this standard work was published in 1954. This edition has been expanded into two volumes. Volume 1 includes sections on research methods and materials, biographies and personal records, comprehensive and area histories, and histories of special subjects. Volume 2 is arranged chronologically, beginning with "America to 1789" and ending with "Twentieth Century." It should be noted that the cut-off date for inclusion of both books and articles was June 30, 1970.

The first chapter, "Research, Writing, and Publication," includes essays on history as a literary art, research, writing for publication (including guidelines for style, proof-reading, and indexing), and book reviewing. In this chapter, a discussion of bibliographies notes the elements that should appear in bibliographical citations. But the entries in this work do not follow their own guidelines. Neither place of publication nor publishers' names are included in citations. (The 1954 edition did include place of publication, but not publisher.)

Some inconsistencies are still evident in this edition, and the updating seems to have been done on a random basis. In the section on government publications, *Checklist '70* is included, but *CIS/Index* and *Government Reference Books*, two serial publications that began in 1970, are not. Similar examples can be found in other sections.

The two volumes are indexed by authors and subjects. More detail in the subject index would have been helpful. A specific example is the list of individual biographies arranged by names. These names are not indexed. A title index would also have been a helpful feature.

As a standard general orientation guide, the *Harvard Guide to American History* is impressive. Nevertheless, one hopes that future editions will be published at more frequent intervals, and that more bibliographic detail will be provided in entries. [R: ARBA 75, p. 173; Choice, Dec 74, p. 1456; C&RL, Jan 75, p. 66; RQ, Spring 75, p. 260; WLB, Nov 74, p. 249]   Sally Wynkoop

181.   Howes, Wright, comp. **U.S.iana (1650-1950): A Selective Bibliography in Which Are Described 11,620 Uncommon and Significant Books Relating to the Continental Portion of the United States.** Rev. and enl. ed. New York, R. R. Bowker for the Newberry Library, 1978 (c1962). 652p. $40.00. LC 62-10988. ISBN 0-8352-0103-1.

This is the third reprinting of the second (1962) edition. It is a well-made book, suitable for heavy reference use, with type so clean and clear that it could have been composed anew. An annotated bibliography of 11,620 titles encompassing 300 years needs some boundary lines. The subtitle has delimited the selectivity of compiler Howes, who has excluded all books (and booklets) of less than 24 pages. More important is the subject matter limitation: only those books relating to human affairs, and within that circumference, each volume had to be factual, serious, and basically historical. (Howes called the compilation task "almost the lowest possible form of literary endeavor.")

Each main entry gives author, title, place and date of publication, size and number of volumes, pagination, number of maps, etc., and six codes indicating levels of market value from $10 to $1,000. Except for the somewhat outdated money figures, the bibliographic information should be of interest to antiquarian book collectors and sellers, historians, librarians, and American history buffs. [R: ARBA 80, p. 172]   David Eggenberger

182.   Masterson, James R., and Joyce E. Eberly, comps. **Writings on American History, 1961.** Millwood, NY, KTO Press, a division of Kraus-Thomson Organization, 1978. 2v. index. $55.00. LC 75-22257. ISBN 0-527-09252-0.

Writings on American History, 1961 will probably be the final volume of a noble and important subject bibliography, to be completed under the direct supervision of the National Historical Publications Commission and published as part of the American Historical Association's *Annual Report.* This classified list of books and articles in United States history covers most years since 1902 (the exceptions are 1904-1905 and 1941-1947) and is now complete through 1961.

The 1961 *Writings* cites every book and article published during 1961 "that has any considerable value for study and research pertaining to the history of the United States from primitive times to the recent past." The bibliography is divided into four sections: 1) writings pertaining to the historical profession, 2) writings concerning the United States as a whole, 3) writings pertaining to single regions, states, territories or dependencies of the United States, and 4) publications that are placed in the category "unclassified and miscellaneous history." Book and article titles that clearly indicate both the nature and the dates of their subject matter are cited without annotation. Titles that are adequate except for dates of subject matter are cited with bracketed dates. All other titles are provided with brief annotations. Notations ("biblio." and "notes") were made for articles and books having bibliographies and bibliographic footnotes.

As users of this bibliography know, the index section of the *Writings* varies somewhat from year to year. In the 1961 *Writings*, the index is a name, place, and subject index; many of the previous volumes, including the *Writings on American History, 1960*, have a name and place index but no other subject breakdown within the index. Among the subjects indexed in this volume are ethnic groups, religious sects, and a variety of social, political, industrial, and philosophical movements in history. However, the "contents" section for *Writings 1961* is abbreviated and does not serve as a complete outline to the work. The 1960 *Writings* has 414 page references in its table of contents, the 1961 *Writings*, 23 page references. All libraries owning all or part of this bibliography will wish to purchase this important reference work.

Ed. note: Writings on American History 1962-73: A Subject Bibliography of Articles (KTO Press, 1976. 4v. $275.00/set) is intended to fill the gap between the 1961 volume and the new annual series by James Dougherty commencing in 1973. It is useful for that reason alone, but has some basic flaws that make it compare poorly to the 1948-1961 series or the recent *America: History and Life* (ABC-Clio). First, the coverage is confined to journal articles only, some 33,000 citations from 510 journals. The citations are not annotated, so that cryptic citations go unexplained. The geographic and subject category headings are very broad, to the effect that tracking down a specific article becomes a task of scanning. One slight advantage over the 1948-1961 series is the addition of a chronological listing. In sum, while it does add significantly to the body of literature covered by *America: History and Life*, its imprecise index headings, lack of annotations, scope limitations, and high price make it a poor alternative when only one or the other title can be purchased. [R: ARBA 80, p. 173; LJ, 15 Apr 79, p. 939]   Milton H. Crouch

DICTIONARIES AND ENCYCLOPEDIAS

183.   Boatner, Mark Mayo, III. **Encyclopedia of the American Revolution.** Bicentennial ed. New York, McKay, 1974. 1290p. illus. maps. index. $25.00. LC 73-91868. ISBN 0-679-50440-0.

Colonel Boatner, a noted military historian, author of *Civil War Dictionary, Landmarks of the American Revolution*, and other historical works, has prepared another outstanding reference work on the American Revolution. The encyclopedia, which covers the period from 1763 to 1783, contains alphabetically arranged articles on people, issues, and events of the American Revolutionary period. The volume contains a number of maps, diagrams, and genealogical charts, which increase the reference value of this encyclopedia. The author thoroughly covers the political, military, and diplomatic aspects of the Revolution and provides a reliable presentation of all important historical events. Many encyclopedic entries constitute biographical sketches of statemen, diplomats, and officers. All entries contain necessary cross references. The author also provides a useful bibliography and a short-title index. [R: ARBA 75, p. 177; Choice, Dec 74, p. 1453; WLB, Nov 74, p. 249]   Lubomyr R. Wynar

184.   **Dictionary of American History.** Rev. ed. New York, Scribner's, 1976. 8v. index. $370.00. LC 76-6735. ISBN 0-684-13856-5.

For many years the *Dictionary of American History*, edited by the distinguished historian James Truslow Adams, has been the standard and the most comprehensive work on this subject. It was published in five volumes by Scribner's in 1940, then reprinted with minor changes until 1961, when a supplement was issued to extend and expand the first edition. The emphasis was on political, economic, social and cultural history; biography was omitted in order not to overlap with *Dictionary of American Biography*. There are also two companion volumes to the *Dictionary*—namely, *Album of American History* (Scribner's, 1969. 6v.; see entry 173) and *Atlas of American History* (Scribner's, 1978; see entry 177).

This revised edition constitutes a substantial revision and enlargement of the *Dictionary*. New material is quite evident in such areas as aspects of technology, history of the arts, and much better coverage of such topics as American Indians and blacks. There are new articles on such timely subjects as the American Civil Liberties Union, Arab-American relations, the Central Intelligence Agency, the civil rights movement, etc.

According to the publisher's claim, this new edition contains 1,200 completely rewritten articles and 4,500 substantially reedited or updated articles; there are some 500 new subjects not represented in the previous edition. The total number of articles in this new edition is now 6,200, written by approximately 800 authors. The number of cross references has also been increased. Like the previous edition, the *Dictionary* has articles of varying length — from a short paragraph (e.g., ABC Conference) to several pages (e.g., the 11-page article on agriculture). Longer articles are subdivided chronologically and, if necessary, by specific aspects of the given subject. The article on agriculture, for example, consists of an essay on the history of American agriculture, followed by a discussion of such topics as farm tenancy, agricultural societies and farm organizations, agricultural policies and legislation, federal farm credit agencies, Department of Agriculture, farm periodicals, scientific aid to agriculture, agricultural experiment stations, and agricultural education. Most articles contain bibliographies, but, unfortunately, in most cases the bibliographical citations indicate only the author and title (and the source for a periodical article) but not the year of publication or the publisher.

The *Dictionary of American History* belongs to the category of monumental works, and it will serve well libraries and scholars for many years to come. It is a truly outstanding work. [R: ARBA 77, p. 194; BL, 15 July 77, p. 1745; Choice, Dec 76, p. 1267; LJ, July 77, p. 1479; RQ, Summer 77, p. 343; WLB, Nov 76, p. 261]   Bohdan S. Wynar

185. Morris, Richard Brandon, and Jeffrey Brandon Morris, eds. **Encyclopedia of American History.** Bicentennial 5th ed. New York, Harper and Row, 1976. 1245p. illus. maps. index. $29.95. LC 74-15839. ISBN 0-06-013081-4.

The updated fifth edition follows the basic chronological arrangement of the previous editions (1953, 1961, 1965, and 1970) but shows significant improvement. Its purpose still is to "provide in a single handy volume the essential historical facts about American life and institutions," although its coverage is now much more comprehensive — even more so than can be judged from the number of pages (the 1970 edition had 850 pages). There are new sections on popular music, dance, and mass media, plus additional coverage of minorities, ethnic groups, and women. The biographical section, of questionable value since there are so many other biographical sources, has been enlarged to 500 sketches. Supplementary material from the previous edition has now been integrated into the body of the text, which is now relatively free of errors of fact or interpretation. There are still some minor errors in the list of American colleges founded before the Revolution, and sections that were not updated (regrettably) contain some confused paragraphs. The illustrations are also poor, which seems to be a typical feature of this work.

Nevertheless, this edition has been greatly improved. It serves as the standard source on this subject and is highly recommended to all types of libraries. [R: ARBA 77, p. 195; BL, 15 Apr 77, p. 195; Choice, July/Aug 76, p. 647; C&RL, July 76, p. 367; LJ, 1 Mar 76, p. 705; WLB, Apr 76, p. 649]   Bohdan S. Wynar

DIRECTORIES

186. **Directory of Archives and Manuscript Repositories in the United States.** Washington, U.S. General Services Administration, National Archives and Records Service, National Historical Publications and Records Commission, 1978. 905p. index. $25.00. LC 78-23870.

It has been almost 20 years since the first edition of this book was published (P. H. Hamer's *A Guide to Archives and Manuscripts in the United States*). The number of repositories in the present edition (3,250) is almost triple the number found in the 1961 edition. Part of the increase in number is due to new repositories being established; however, most of it is the result of greater cooperation on the part of existing agencies. The new edition was prepared using a data base concept; now that the program is operative (it began in 1974), NHPRC hopes to provide editions more frequently.

Each entry consists of the following information: name and address of archive, telephone number, hours of service, access, user fees, copying facilities available, material solicited, holdings, bibliographic references (especially to Hamer), and published guides or finding aids published since 1958. Each archive has a unique "access code," which represents the state, city, and institution (e.g., CA 421-40 represents CA — California, 421 — Los Angeles, 40 — Arnold Schoenberg Institute Archives). The access code is used in place of page numbers in the index and special lists. The main body of the directory is arranged alphabetically by state. The major special list is arranged by type of repository: corporate, federal, local government, local history, medical, museum, organization, "other" institutions, public library, religious institution, special research institution, state archive, state department, state historical society, university archive, university department, or university library. The 125-page index covers persons, titles, subjects, and institutions.

The major criticism this reviewer has of the book is that the space allowed for describing the holdings is too small. Thus, the amount of information a researcher can derive from this material is very limited. Nevertheless, this edition was long overdue and will be welcomed by all serious researchers and scholars.

Ed. note: John Raimo's *Guide to Manuscripts Relating to America in Great Britain and Ireland* (Meckler Books, 1979. 467p. $79.50) describes over 300,000 manuscripts relating to American History and literature, providing mailing addresses for all but a few entries. An excellent, detailed index facilitates access to even the most esoteric references. A very useful tool within the limits of its scope. [R: ARBA 80, p. 168; Choice, July 79, p. 652; C&RL, July 79, p. 345; LJ, 1 May 79, p. 1043; WLB, Apr 79, p. 587]

G. Edward Evans

187. U.S. Department of the Interior. National Park Service. **The National Register of Historic Places, 1976.** Ronald M. Greenberg, ed.-in-chief. Washington, GPO, 1976. 961p. illus. index. $13.00. LC 76-10861. S/N 024-005-00645-1.

The National Register is one of several preservation programs that are administered by the National Park Service; these programs include the Historic American Buildings Survey, the Historic American Engineering Record, the National Historic Landmarks program, and architectural and archaeological technical assistance programs. Federal programs in historic preservation, which date back to the Antiquities Act of 1906, received more administrative attention later with the creation of the National Park Service. The first full-scale national program for designating national historic landmarks was made possible by passage of the Historic Sites Act of 1935. In 1966 the National Historic Preservation Act codified the national register of historic properties and broadened the scope of the register to include state and local properties as well as those of national significance.

The ground-swell of interest in preserving local and regional historic landmarks is thoroughly documented in this edition of the *National Register*. It has grown from 1,500 properties in 1969, consisting primarily of national historic landmarks, to some 12,000 properties in June 1976. Included are properties that have a quality of significance in American history, architecture, and culture: prehistoric archaeological sites, eighteenth-century missions and forts, canals, furnaces, covered bridges, government structures, dwellings, and neighborhood districts such as a barrio in San Antonio or the original waterfront warehouse district in Boston. Generally excluded are cemeteries, graves, birthplaces, religious properties, and structures that have been moved or reconstructed that have achieved significance within the past 50 years. The 1976 edition contains descriptions of all properties added to the *National Register* through December 31, 1974. It replaces the 1972 edition and the Supplement (1974). Names and locations of properties in the *National Register* are published annually in the *Federal Register*; additions are published on the first Tuesday of each month. Arrangement is by state, then by county, city, or area; individual entries are listed alphabetically by name of landmark. A one-page survey of the key historical sites and landmarks and their relation to the historical and cultural development of the state prefaces each state section. An outline map of each state's counties, accompanied by three pages of black-and-white photos of landmarks, is also included. Entries, printed in three-column pages, give location, name, address, date of construction and architect, description and significance (about 20 to 50 words), ownership, and accessibility to the public. Codes for survey designations are recorded for many entries. An index locates the name of the property by state code and page and the architect by page only. The volume is handsomely designed and printed and includes a useful collection of photos and some architectural sketches; decorative end sheets reprinted from the atlas volume of *Washington's Life* (1805) add to the visual quality of the book.

The *National Register* is an essential reference source for public libraries that need to provide information on existing landmarks to preservation groups and to travellers; school libraries will find it an exceptional source for a wide range of reference queries. That all academic institutions will need to acquire it is obvious. [R: ARBA 77, p. 197]

Christine Gehrt Wynar

INDEXES

188. Butler, John P., comp. **Index, The Papers of the Continental Congress, 1774-1789.** Washington, U.S. General Services Administration, National Archives; distr., Washington, GPO, 1978. 5v. $85.00/set. LC 78-23783. S/N 022-002-00065-1.

Index, The Papers of the Continental Congress, 1774-1789 will be a welcome guide to over 1 million cubic feet or records stored in the National Archives. Researchers have had microfilm access to the Papers, consisting of the records of the two Continental Congresses, the Confederation Congress, and the Constitutional Convention, but there has been no complete index. A result of an American Bicentennial project, the five-volume set is a companion to the *Index to the Journals of the Continental Congress*, published in 1976. The Papers consist of about 50,000 documents, or 170,000 pages, bound in 518 bindings. They are not arranged to reflect the identity, structure, or function of each of the yearly Congresses, but are bound chiefly by type of document—journals, committee reports, and correspondence—and subarranged chronologically or alphabetically. Access to the microfilmed collection has been difficult since past indexes have been sketchy.

The present index is four volumes accompanied by a one-volume chronology that lists all the documents in sequence. Items to be indexed were sorted with the aid of a specially designed computer program, SPINDEX II. Entries under an index term are arranged chronologically, and include document description and reference to the location on microfilm. The document description includes the name of the originator of the document, the name of the recipient of the document, and the number of manuscript pages. If appropriate, also included are the place from which the document was sent, and the type or category of the item. Dates are as accurate as possible, but occasionally a supplied date or "no date" is used. Name index terms are complete if the information is available, but often no full name has been recorded; variant spellings are entered under the preferred spelling. Numerous cross references are included, relating overlapping subjects, variant spellings of names, and specialized items, such as connecting military units with their commanders, and congressional delegations with the proper state.

This comprehensive index is a needed addition to the bibliographic control of early U.S. documents. Librarians and researchers, including genealogists, will find it a useful tool. [R: ARBA 80, p. 177]

Janet H. Littlefield

BIOGRAPHY

189. Warner, Ezra J., and W. Buck Yearns. **Biographical Register of the Confederate Congress.** Baton Rouge, Louisiana State University Press, 1975. 319p. illus. bibliog. $20.00. LC 74-77329. ISBN 0-8071-0092-7.

In their introduction, the compilers acknowledge that the Confederate Congresses were, for the most part, impotent, almost ceremonial gatherings. So inconsequential did Confederate congressmen consider their legislative service that, after the War, surviving members often suppressed accounts and memoirs. Certainly no member rose to fame and prominence *because* he was a senator or representative.

Nonetheless, this scholarly volume, with its alphabetically arranged series of biographies of all men who served in the three Confederate Congresses (the Provisional Congress in five sessions from February 4, 1861, to February 17, 1862; the First Congress in four sessions from February 18, 1862, to February 17, 1864; and the Second Congress in two sessions from May 2, 1864, to March 18, 1865) fills a gap in our knowledge of Southern Civil War history.

Each biographical sketch is itself a solid piece of historical research. Moreover, because of the fact already alluded to that ex-members were not proud of their legislative service, the research effort was extraordinarily difficult. All possibly relevant primary and secondary sources were combed for clues. Often the only source that yielded hard biographical data was the 1850 Census, the first census to record heads of households by name.

Sources are cited at the end of most sketches; those that lack source citations were compiled from such standard sources as the *Biographical Directory of the American Congress.* The latter work was particularly fruitful because many of the men who served as Confederate legislators had previously served in the U.S. Congress.

The work concludes with four appendixes (Sessions of the Confederate Congress, Standing Committees, Membership, and Maps of Occupied Confederate Territory, 1861-1864), and a bibliography of the manuscripts, newspapers, government documents, and other materials used as sources.

Ed. note: For biographies of Confederate leaders—military, political, economic, and social—one should consult Jon L. Wakelyn's *Biographical Dictionary of the Confederacy* (Greenwood Press, 1977. 601p. $29.95). Taken mostly from secondary sources, the 651 biographies serve as a valuable quantitative study as well as an excellent one-volume reference work. [R: ARBA 76, p. 195; Choice, Feb 76, p. 1554; LJ, 15 Mar 76, p. 803]
Richard A. Gray

AFRICA

190. Fage, J. D. **An Atlas of African History.** 2nd ed. New York, Africana Publishing, a division of Holmes & Meier Publishers, 1978. 1v. (unpaged). illus. maps. index. $29.00; $14.50pa. LC 78-16131. ISBN 0-8419-0429-4; 0-8419-0430-8pa.

The second edition contains 71 maps; 21 are completely new, and many of those included in the first edition (1958) have been changed considerably. The 20 years that have elapsed between the two editions have wrought seismic transformation on the political and social landscape of Africa. At the same time, spectacular advances in archaeological and anthropological research have accumulated a mass of new knowledge of Africa's past, forcing us to revise many previously held truths. The need to reflect these new developments was the chief motivating factor in the redesigning of the atlas.

The work encompasses the entire sweep of African history from ancient times to 1975. The majority of the maps are segmented, graphically illustrating events by region and by historical period. Thematically, they are reasonably well balanced, giving the strongest coverage to the eighteenth, nineteenth, and twentieth centuries. The subjects dealt with include European exploration, conquest, settlement, and economic development. Half of the 18 continental maps depict patterns of alien rule in Africa from 1830 to 1965.

The conception of African history permeating the maps is clearly Euro-centric, and the successive struggles of Africans against foreign domination are not highlighted. Otherwise, the maps are superbly informative, crammed with facts and data that are easily retrievable through the index. For the most part, the maps are drawn in black and white and are of good graphic quality, although some of them seem to be somewhat crowded. One could lament the meager treatment of the anthropological, archaeological, and linguistic aspects of Africa, but even with these shortcomings, it would be difficult to imagine studying African history on the college level without the aid of this atlas. [R: ARBA 80, p. 184; LJ, 1 Apr 79, p. 816]   Michael Keresztesi

191.   Freeman-Grenville, G. S. P. **Chronology of African History.** New York, Oxford University Press, 1973. 312p. index. $17.95. ISBN 0-19-913174-0.

The purpose of this extensive and well-researched reference work is to provide a time framework for African history. Starting around 1000 B.C., the volume lists in tabular form all important events that occurred in Africa. The starting date has been set arbitrarily to avoid duplicating previous chronologies on Egyptian history. From 1000 B.C. to A.D. 599, four columns are listed, giving comparative dates for Egypt, the Sudan and Eastern Africa; Northern and Western Africa; Western Asia; and Europe. From A.D. 600 to 1399, the columns change to reflect the development of Africa, listing Egypt and the Sudan, Northern Africa, Africa south of the Sahara, and other countries. After 1400, when knowledge of African history becomes more extensive, there are six columns (three per page), dividing Africa into its four geographic regions, plus Central Africa and other countries. The last column is included in each time period to give better perspective to events in Africa.

The majority of entries in this book are after 1500, when the author could rely on independent sources for verification of dates. Entries before this time are limited due to lack of verification methods and the still limited knowledge of early African history. An excellent index helps to make this a useful volume for both the casual student and the advanced researcher. [R: ARBA 75, p. 188; Choice, Sept 74, p. 910]   William Z. Schenck

ASIA

192.   Burgess, James. **The Chronology of Indian History: Medieval & Modern.** Delhi, India, Cosmo Publications, 1972; distr. Forest Grove, OR, International Scholarly Book Services, 1973. 483p. index.

One of the encouraging trends in Indian publishing in the late 1960s and early 1970s was the reprinting of outstanding works that had been out of print for several years. These two volumes of *Chronology of Indian History* are a result of that trend. Volume 1, which covers the period from the earliest times to the sixteenth century and which was written by C. Mabel Duff (Mrs. W. R. Rickmers), was first published in 1899. James Burgess' second volume, covering the medieval and modern period, was originally issued in 1912.

In view of the complexities of Indian history, the extensive Hindu literature, and the accumulated material scattered through hundreds of English and foreign volumes and periodicals, one must admire the authors for their scholarship and hard work in giving us this systematic chronology of Indian history. Volume 1 begins with the year 3102 B.C. and ends with 1530 A.D.; volume II picks up from 1492 A.D. and concludes with 1894 A.D. Within entries, civil material is given first, then literary dates. When several events occur under the same date, they are roughly grouped according to their relative importance. Events in northern India generally take precedence over those of southern India. Each entry is accompanied by references to the sources from which it is derived. A 50-page appendix in volume I contains a rare collection of lists of the dynasties ruling throughout India, giving the names of the rulers in a chronological order. To facilitate use, each volume has a detailed index.

Ed. note: Volume 2 is available under the title *The Chronology of Modern India, 1494-1894* from Irish Academic Press. [R: ARBA 74, p. 120]   Sharad Karkhanis

193.   **A Historical Atlas of South Asia.** Joseph E. Schwartzberg, and others, eds. Chicago, University of Chicago Press, 1978. 352p. illus. (part col.). maps. bibliog. index. (Association for Asian Studies Reference Series, No. 2). $150.00. LC 77-81713. ISBN 0-226-74221-0.

A long-awaited and much anticipated work, this atlas sets high standards. It is a cartographic record of South Asia (Afghanistan to Burma; India to the Maldives), from the Stone Age to the present. Some 650 maps, most in color, as well as hundreds of chronological charts, tables, photographs, and drawings accompany the text.

Arrangement follows a general chronological format, beginning with "the physical stage" and prehistory, and following regional history to the present, concluding with social and cultural evolution, modern demographic and economic evolution, and settlement patterns. The text is comprehensive, not only explaining the maps but providing a brief history of the period, sources used, shortcomings of the data, essential findings, and references to related maps in the atlas. The index contains some 15,000 items and is thoroughly cross referenced. Over 4,000 items appear in the classified bibliography, making it a valuable reference tool in itself. Five unbound inserts accompany the *Atlas*: two overlay transparencies, two chronological charts, and a political survey chart. Beautifully printed and sturdily bound, the *Historical Atlas of South Asia* will be a necessary acquisition in most large libraries, regardless of price. [R: ARBA 80, p. 185; Choice, Apr 79, p. 204; C&RL, July 79, p. 352; LJ, 15 Mar 79, p. 717]   Janet H. Littlefield

194.   Lu, David John. **Sources of Japanese History.** New York, McGraw-Hill, 1974. 2v. index. $13.95/v.; $9.95/v.pa. LC 73-6890. ISBN 0-07-038902-2(v.1); 0-07-038903-9(v.2).

This is a two-volume compilation of primary source materials for the study of Japanese social, intellectual, economic, and political history. The first volume covers the period from the prehistoric, mythological era through the middle of the Tokugawa regime (early eighteenth century). The second volume covers the period from the decay of the Tokugawa system during the early years of the nineteenth century to the present time, with emphasis on the events of the past 125 years. The compiler, a professor of history and director of the Center for Japanese Studies at Bucknell University, has done a thorough job of selecting representative writings to reflect the spirit of each age and to portray the life styles of the people.

In the first volume, chapter introductions give background information on the period and on subjects illustrated by the readings. The compiler has carefully avoided duplication of existing sources available in this country, and more than three-fourths of the documents have been translated into English for the first time. Some were written by commoners and minor officials and record everyday matters and business transactions. A number are excerpts from religious works and government directives. Some are folk tales and poems. An appendix to the first volume translates Japanese weights and measures into both metric and U.S. equivalents, and a brief glossary translates Japanese terms and names into English.

In volume 2 the documents, or excerpts from documents, are arranged in eight chapters, each portraying a particular period in time; a ninth chapter contains the Nobel lecture of Kawabata Yasunari, given in 1968. The documents and writings range from imperial edicts, constitutions, and treaties to wartime diaries of students and housewives, public opinion surveys, and questions from a qualifying examination for a position in a newspaper company. Complete bibliographical citations for all documents are given in footnotes that accompany each chapter. The compiler's introductions and supplementary notes add greatly to the usefulness of the material, and the introductions provide a running commentary and serve to tie all the material together.

This carefully prepared work will be of primary interest to students and teachers of Japanese history and civilization. Its arrangement and detailed index will make it useful also as a quick reference tool for information on many subjects within its overall scope. [R: ARBA 75, p. 188; Choice, June 74, p. 654]   Shirley L. Hopkinson

CANADA

195.   Thibault, Claude. **Bibliographia Canadiana.** Don Mills, Ontario, Academic Press, 1973. 795p. index. $25.00. ISBN 0-7747-3054-4.

The 25,660 entries in this classified bibliography make it *the* Canadian history bibliography. Entries are up to date through 1970 for books and 1969 for periodical articles.

Two main criteria were used: the first was that genealogical, biographical, local, or provincial works were to be omitted; the second was that the works should indicate "the trend of interpretation which had taken place in Canadian history since the middle of the nineteenth century." The arrangement is primarily under three main chronological headings: "The French Colonial Regime," "British North America, 1713-1867," "The Dominion of Canada, 1867-1967." The first section, "Tools of Research," is divided into 1) primary sources (i.e., guides to manuscript and archival collections, collections of printed documents, government publications), 2) general secondary sources (e.g., bibliographies, encyclopedias, atlases), and 3) historiography. [R: ARBA 75, p. 189; C&RL, Jan 74, p. 44; RQ, Fall 74, p. 71]

GERMANY

196.   Fest, Wilfried. **Dictionary of German History 1806-1945.** New York, St. Martin's Press, 1978. 189p. $18.50. LC 78-54658. ISBN 0-86043-108-8.

This concise dictionary contains over 700 entries pertaining to Germany's political, economic, and social history from the collapse of the Holy Roman Empire to the destruction of the German Third Reich in 1945. All entries are arranged in straight alphabetical sequence. The text is well written and provides clear and brief description of major personalities and events (treaties, wars, agreements, institutions, and other topics). The author excluded literary, cultural, ecclesiastical, and scientific German history.

The *Dictionary* consists of two major parts: articles (pp. 1-184), and a chronological table (pp. 185-89). In his introduction, Fest states that "due to limitations of space, the omission of some interesting topics was unavoidable" (preface, p. i). However, he fails to explain his criteria of exclusion or inclusion of those important topics. This results in a rather highly selective and uneven coverage of various relevant historical topics. For instance, on page 174 one finds the entry "Weltpolitik," which is defined as a "German version of imperialist policy." On the other hand, there is no entry for German "Ostpolitik," which is essential in explaining this German expansionist policy. There is no entry for Friedrich Ratzel (1844-1904), who exercised a major influence on the formation of Nazi ideology. These are just a few illustrations of omissions of important topics. However, one has to remember that this is not a comprehensive dictionary of German modern history. Therefore, this reviewer considers this publication a valuable reference tool for public and academic libraries. [R: ARBA 80, p. 187; Choice, June 79, p. 508; RQ, Fall 79, p. 84]

Lubomyr R. Wynar

197. Snyder, Louis L. **Encyclopedia of the Third Reich.** New York, McGraw-Hill, 1976. 410p. illus. bibliog. $26.50. LC 75-25740. ISBN 0-07-059525-9.

The heart of this work is the German Third Reich of 1933-1945. But, included also are those significant people and events preceding the establishment of the regime as well as those immediately following its destruction. Politicians, artists, military leaders, battles, weapons, domestic events, songs, slogans, and philosophy are among the ingredients of this compilation of facts about the Nazi era.

Subjects are treated in articles that vary in length from a few lines to several pages. The length of any article is consistent with its subject and the size and plan of the volume. While not exhaustive studies, the articles are not so abbreviated as to be useless by reason of generality or inaccurate by reason of omission. German is used for the main entries of most non-biographical articles, with cross references from the English version or versions of the term. This approach at first seems awkward, but in sum it is quite practical and increases the value of the work as a key to references in either language. The ample cross references from article to article ensure that terms are not left undefined or individuals unidentified. This network of cross references is extremely complete.

Most of the biographical articles, and some others, cite at least one source of additional information. Illustrations are sharp and well placed. A chronology of events, from Hitler's birth to the Nuremberg trials, begins the work, and an unannotated bibliography of books and articles concludes it. This is a fine example of a one-volume subject encyclopedia. [R: ARBA 77, p. 205; BL, 15 Feb 77, p. 922; Choice, Oct 76, p. 962; C&RL, Jan 77, p. 53; LJ, 1 Apr 76, p. 881; LJ, 15 Apr 77, p. 877; WLB, Sept 76, p. 86]

Eric R. Nitschke

GREAT BRITAIN

198. Brown, Lucy M., and Ian R. Christie, eds. **Bibliography of British History 1789-1851.** Issued under the direction of the American Historical Association and the Royal Historical Society of Great Britain. New York, Oxford University Press, 1977. 759p. index. $59.00. ISBN 0-19-822390-0.

In 1915 Charles Gross' massive landmark, *Sources and Literature of English History from the Earliest Times to about 1485,* was posthumously published. With that as a groundwork, the Royal Historical Society of Great Britain and the American Historical Association established a joint committee to sponsor the compilation of companion bibliographies to cover all of British history. The Tudor and Stuart volumes were published respectively in 1933 and 1928, and subsequently revised in 1959 and 1970; the eighteenth-century volume was published in 1951 and reprinted in 1977, the 1851-1914 volume in 1976. Gross' original bibliography was revised, expanded, and published in a second edition in 1975.

All are selected, selectively annotated bibliographies of primary and secondary materials covering all aspects of history—in its broadest interpretation—within the specified period. Books, pamphlets, documents, articles, and papers are all encompassed with the bibliographies. Each work is organized by a detailed classification scheme, and additional access is provided by an author and subject index. Each is monumental for its specified time period, although the volumes achieve varying degrees of success in approaching the high standard set by the original Gross, which in its revised and expanded edition remains the preeminent work in the series.

The present volume provides coverage of contemporary manuscript and printed material during the period 1789-1851. It is an excellent tool for those engaged in the study of British history of the first half of the nineteenth century.

All volumes in this series are indispensable to scholars of British history, literature, or social sciences. No other subject bibliographies on British history match them in authority or scope. [R: ARBA 78, p. 200; BL, 15 Oct 77, p. 396; Choice, Sept 77, p. 826; RQ, Spring 78, p. 271; WLB, June 77, p. 814]   Arthur H. Stickney

199.   Guth, De Lloyd J. **Late-Medieval England, 1377-1485.** New York, published for the Conference on British Studies by Cambridge University Press, 1976. 143p. index. (Conference on British Studies Bibliographical Handbooks). $14.95. LC 75-23845. ISBN 0-521-20877-7.

This bibliography is the sixth of the series published in association with the Conference on British Studies. Covering English and Welsh history between the reigns of Richard II and Richard III, it is limited to 2,500 published significant books, articles, and standard texts, including primary and secondary sources. Similar to other volumes of the series, it is divided into 14 thematic categories, with brief annotations and cross references. The many cross references are in entries of given authors. Due to the time period, the religious history section, as expected, is the largest category.

The other volumes in this series are: *Modern England, 1901-1970*; *Restoration England, 1660-1689*; *Anglo-Norman England, 1066-1154*; *Tudor England, 1485-1603*; and *Bibliographical Handbook on Tudor England, 1485-1603.* All are selected collections of significant primary and secondary materials, each including 1,800-2,500 entries and an index to authors, editors, and translators. Literature per se is excluded. The lack of subject indexing diminishes somewhat from the utility of the volumes; nevertheless, they form excellent supplements to the more ambitious bibliographies sponsored by the joint committee of the Royal Historical Society of Great Britain and the American Historical Association (see entry 198), and will serve the needs of scholars of the given time periods with less demanding research needs. [R: ARBA 77, p. 209; Choice, Dec 76, p. 1270]

Maureen Pastine
Arthur H. Stickney

200.   Morrill, J. S. **Seventeenth-Century Britain, 1603-1714.** Hamden, CT, Archon; Folkestone, England, Dawson, 1980. 189p. index. (Critical Bibliographies in Modern History, Vol. 2). $17.50. ISBN 0-208-01785-2(Archon).

This bibliography of 879 books and 478 articles is one of the most helpful guides available to the history of the period from the accession of James I to the death of Anne. It is not, nor is it intended to be, a complete bibliography. The articles, without annotation, are grouped in an appendix — almost as an afterthought. Morrill is primarily interested in organizing and annotating books, and it is this work which makes the bibliography valuable.

The 11 chapters cover the following topics: general; government; political history; political and constitutional thought; military and naval affairs; ecclesiastical history; economic history; social history; local studies; cultural history; Scotland, Ireland, and Wales. Each chapter is further subdivided. Books are then grouped, and for each group there is a discursive and sometimes lengthy annotation. There is an introduction to each chapter and an index of authors and editors.

Morrill has written a rare thing — a readable bibliography. He does not attempt to write impartial annotations; rather, he makes the judgments of a seasoned scholar, pointing out both the gold and the dross. The annotations are refreshingly frank. One book is "a very dry-as-dust exegesis," another "contains some of the worst distortions of evidence, some of the least credible assumptions and some of the most banal statements ever committed to paper by a professor of history." Another "is a masterpiece too little used nowadays." Morrill is not merely contumacious or cantankerous; most scholars will agree with his judgments, and most students will find them helpful.

A final point—every person who aspires to compile a bibliography should read Morrill's preface. It is a clear exposition of the purpose and method of the book and a wonderfully frank admission of the compiler's shortcomings and biases.   Philip R. Rider

201. **Writings on British History 1901-1933: Volume V, 1895-1914. Appendix (Parts 1 and 2).** Compiled by the Royal Historical Society. London, Jonathan Cape; distr., Totowa, NJ, Biblio Distribution Centre, 1970. 2v. $45.00. ISBN 0-389-01367-6.

The fifth volume of the series *Writings on British History* was edited for the Royal Historical Society by the late Professor H. Hale Bellot. A most comprehensive bibliography, it covers books and articles on the history of Great Britain from about 450 A.D. to 1914, published during the years 1901 to 1933. Excluded are items published by learned societies of Great Britain.

This international bibliography is arranged by various types of histories and by special subjects. The bibliographical description of book entries excludes the name of the publisher. The first part covers political, economic, social, cultural, ecclesiastical, science, and military history. Special sections list publications on foreign relations (subdivided chronologically), English local history, British Empire (divided by geo-political units), and historical sources. Part 2 includes a biography (collective and individual), an appendix containing a select list of publications in the years 1914-1933 on British history since 1914, and an author index.

Previous volumes cover *Auxiliary Sciences and General Works* (v.1, 1968), *The Middle Ages, 450-1485* (v.2, 1968), *The Tudor and Stuart Periods, 1485-1714* (v.3, 1968), and *The Eighteenth Century, 1714-1815*, 2 parts (v.4, 1969). [R: ARBA 71, p. 121]

Lubomyr R. Wynar

ITALY

202. **The New Century Italian Renaissance Encyclopedia.** Ed. by Catherine B. Avery. New York, Appleton-Century-Crofts, 1972. 978p. illus. $42.95. LC 76-181735. ISBN 0-390-66950-X.

Comparison with *Dictionary of the Renaissance*, edited by Frederick M. Schweitzer (New York, Philosophical Library, 1967. $15.00), reveals similarity in scope, but the encyclopedia covers most topics in much more depth and detail from Dante's birth to the close of the sixteenth century. Biographical entries predominate in both works. *New Century* is also well illustrated. In addition to numerous black-and-white reproductions in the text, there are 12 color plates and 32 pages of black-and-white plates. The latter are arranged in groups to give a chronological survey, but are not directly keyed to pages in the text. This did not prove to be a problem with the items sampled because the text contained entries for all the artists in the normal alphabetical sequence. When more than one form of a name has been used in the past, cross references are provided to the form chosen. Resumes of some literary works are included. There are also general articles of some length on topics like architecture (five pages), painting (five pages), and sculpture (four pages). The one area apparently neglected is music. No entries were found for "music," "musical instruments," "madrigal," "motet," or "polyphony," and only the briefest treatment of "ars nova." Apart from this and the lack of a bibliography, the book is a superb reference tool. [R: ARBA 73, p. 170; BL, 15 May 72, p. 793; BL, 1 Oct 72, p. 105; LJ, 1 Feb 72, p. 485; RQ, Fall 72, p. 85]   A. Robert Rogers

LATIN AMERICA

203.   Griffin, Charles C., ed. **Latin America: A Guide to the Historical Literature.** Austin, University of Texas Press, 1971. 700p. index. (Conference on Latin American History, No. 4). LC 71-165916. ISBN 0-292-70089-X.

This comprehensive guide contains 7,087 entries providing full bibliographical description of titles listed plus brief evaluative annotations. The basic organization of material is chronological, with main divisions devoted to the colonial, independence, and post-independence periods. Within these major parts, separate sections deal with the various geographical areas. The major parts are preceded by sections that include reference materials and works of a general nature. The organization of these sections and of Part II, International Relations, is topical and geographical rather than chronological.

It should be noted that this guide has a long history, having originated at a meeting in the Library of Congress jointly sponsored by the Hispanic Foundation and the Joint Committee on Latin American Studies of the American Council of Learned Societies and the Social Science Research Council in April 1962. At that time, a group of invited specialists discussed the general structure of this undertaking; most of the suggestions were later adopted by the editor and advisory editorial board. As a result we have at our disposal a cooperative work of high professional caliber, which will serve for years to come as the standard guide to the historical literature of Latin America. [R: ARBA 72, p. 143; Choice, Sept 72, p. 791; C&RL, July 72, p. 326; WLB, June 72, p. 927]

RUSSIA

204.   Pushkarev, Sergei G., comp. **Dictionary of Russian Historical Terms from the Eleventh Century to 1917.** Edited by George Vernadsky and Ralph T. Fisher, Jr. New Haven, Yale University Press, 1970. 199p. $18.50. LC 73-81426. ISBN 0-300-01136-9.

The dictionary is "designed to assist English-speaking readers to understand the specialized terms they encounter in Russian historical sources and in English-language works on Russia." It includes approximately 2,000 terms from areas of political, ecclesiastical, military, economic, social, legal, and cultural history. Excluded are biographical data and geographical names. The terms in this dictionary are not limited only to Russian history. In many instances they are related to Belorussian and Ukrainian history.

In the reviewer's opinion, the compiler should present a clearer and more objective concept of historical terminology and periodization of Russian, Belorussian, and Ukrainian history. Considering that this is the first attempt to compile such a dictionary in English, however, there is no doubt that it will assist American historians and graduate students in their research. [R: ARBA 71, p. 126; Choice, Nov 70, p. 1223; LJ, July 70, p. 2451]   Lubomyr R. Wynar

205.   **A Source Book for Russian History from Early Times to 1917.** Ed. by George Vernadsky, sr. ed., and Ralph T. Fisher, Jr., managing ed. Alan D. Ferguson, Andrew Lossky, and Sergei Pushkarev, comps. New Haven, CT, Yale University Press, 1972. 3v. $20.00/v.; $60.00/set. LC 70-115369. ISBN 0-300-01602-5(set).

The purpose of this comprehensive work is to provide in English translation representative excerpts from primary sources pertaining to Russian history from early times to

March 1917. The arrangement of material combines chronological and topical groupings, following the usual presentation of Russian history in most textbooks. Thus, the first chapter opens with introductory comments on pre-Kievan beginnings, by George Vernadsky, followed by excerpts from Procopius, Jordanes, Mauricius, etc., and concluding with Nestor's *Primary Chronicle.* Chapter 2, "Kievan Russia, Tenth to Twelfth Centuries," provides excerpts from the *Laurentian Chronicle* concerning Oleg's establishment in Kiev in 882 and the campaign against Byzantium in 907. This is followed by the treaty of Oleg with Byzantium, as transmitted in the *Laurentian Chronicle* for 911. All in all, the three volumes contain some 700 distinct sources pertaining to political, legal, and administrative history; economic history; social, cultural, and intellectual history, etc.

In addition to Russian history, the editors present some documents related to the history of the Lithuanian state and to Ukrainian history (primarily in the first volume). It should be noted that about 75% of the material has not been previously published in English translation, which means that the present work will be invaluable for all students of Eastern Europe.

The only major criticism concerns certain terminology used by the editors. The introduction points out that the companion volume, *Dictionary of Russian Historical Terms* (see entry 204), provides explanations for the Russian terms that appear in the book. Both Pushkarev and the *Source Book* use the term "Kievan Russia" instead of "Kievan Rus'." Even such well-known Soviet historians as Grekov (see his work *Kiev Rus'*) and Tikhomirov (*The Towns of Ancient Rus'*) use "Rus'" as the political designation for the above-mentioned period. Pushkarev is, of course, aware of this, and we are somewhat at a loss to understand some of the political implications presented in this otherwise excellent work. [R: ARBA 73, p. 170; Choice, Apr 73, p. 347; LJ, 1 Feb 73, p. 420]

Bohdan S. Wynar

5 ETHNIC STUDIES

COMPREHENSIVE WORKS

206.   Buttlar, Lois, and Lubomyr R. Wynar. **Building Ethnic Collections: An Annotated Guide for School Media Centers and Public Libraries.** Littleton, CO, Libraries Unlimited, 1977. 434p. index. $22.50. LC 76-55398. ISBN 0-87287-130-4.

This annotated guide is a major selection aid for public and school libraries and university collections supporting research on American ethnic groups. Listed are books and nonprint materials dealing with over 40 distinct ethnic groups. Part 1 describes general titles on ethnicity; part 2 contains selective bibliographies on individual groups such as American Indians, Appalachian Americans, British Americans, Japanese Americans, etc. Materials for each section are subdivided by five categories: reference sources, curriculum materials, nonfiction, fiction, and audiovisual (films, filmstrips, posters, study prints, slides, transparencies). In all, 2,300 titles are annotated. [R: ARBA 78, p. 203; JAL, Sept 77, p. 237; RQ, Spring 78, p. 261; SLJ, Dec 77, p. 36; WLB, Sept 77, p. 90]

207.   Katz, Zev, ed. **Handbook of Major Soviet Nationalities.** New York, Free Press, 1975. 481p. illus. index. $25.00. LC 74-10458. ISBN 0-02-917090-7.

Until recently American and European sovietologists focused their research primarily on Russia and the Russian people, ignoring the non-Russian nationalities in the Soviet Union. In many instances the Soviet Union was identified as "Russia" and the various nationalities that compose the Soviet Union as "Russians." In reality, the Russians presently comprise only 53.5% of the Soviet population. The present handbook constitutes the first major reference compendium of major Soviet nationality groups. It consists of four major parts: 1) The Slavs (Russians, Ukrainians, and Belorussians); 2) The Baltics (Estonians, Latvians, and Lithuanians); 3) The Transcaucasians (Armenians, Georgians, and Azerbaidzhanis); 4) Central Asia (Kazakhs, Kirgiz, Turkmen, Uzbeks, Tadzhiks); 5) Other Nationalities (Jews, Tatars, and Moldavians). The appendix contains comprehensive statistical data on all national republics and nationalities in the Soviet Union. The whole project was executed at the Center for International Studies at the Massachusetts Institute of Technology. Chapters were written by subject specialists; each chapter contains data on territory, economy, history, demography, culture, external relations, media, educational and scientific institutions, national attitudes, and present manifestation of nationalism. Except for the chapter on Russians, they follow a uniform outline and contain extensive statistical data, plus selective bibliographies pertaining to individual nationalities. The presentation in this handbook is precise and objective, and the material is better organized than that in G. Shopflin's handbook, *Soviet Union and Eastern Europe* (Praeger, 1970).

The introduction, which is written by Richard Pipes, deals with the nationality problem in the Soviet Union. It is hard to accept his hypothesis that the most important single element that keeps ethnic feelings alive in the USSR is "competition for resources and services" (pp. 3-4). In this reviewer's opinion, the major vital force among the various nationalities in the Soviet Union is their own national, historical, and cultural tradition, which is different from the Russian, as well as their struggle against Russian discrimination policies in the Soviet Union. It should also be pointed out that Pipes' usage of the term "Great Russian" is obsolete and misleading; the first chapter of this handbook, however, is correctly entitled "Russia and Russians."

Any future edition of this valuable encyclopedic work should include a brief subdivision on the religion of each nationality, since religion constitutes an important element of the life of the people. Also, maps for individual Soviet republics should be added. In general, this is a well-executed project.

In view of the rather biased interpretation of Soviet nationalities and their histories in *The New Encyclopaedia Britannica* (1974) and many other reference sources dealing with the Soviet Union, the present handbook will serve as a basic reference tool for all academic and public libraries.   Lubomyr R. Wynar

208. **Makers of America.** Wayne Moquin, ed. Chicago, Encyclopedia Britannica, 1971. 10v. illus. index. $117.00/set. LC 74-129355. ISBN 0-87827-000-0.

This impressive set is probably one of the most important reference sources on ethnic pluralism in the United States. The material is arranged in chronological order: Vol. 1, The Firstcomers, 1536-1800; Vol. 2, Builders of a New Nation, 1801-1848; Vol. 3, Seekers after Freedom, 1849-1870; Vol. 4, Seekers after Wealth, 1871-1890; Vol. 5, Natives and Aliens, 1891-1903; Vol. 6, The New Immigrants, 1904-1913; Vol. 7, Hyphenated Americans, 1914-1924; Vol. 8, Children of the Melting Pot, 1925-1938; Vol. 9, Refugees and Victims, 1939-1954; and Vol. 10, Emergent Minorities, 1955-1970. The set contains 731 selections from letters, diaries, newspaper editorials, and other contemporary sources describing various activities of minority groups, their organizations, important religious groups, etc. *Makers of America* is not a history of immigration in the traditional sense of the term, but a collection of primary sources that will support such a history, showing the diversity of Americans in as many ways and from as many points of view as possible. As it is indicated in the introduction, "*Makers of America* is primarily designed to illustrate issues of ethnic pluralism, immigration, nativism, and race, along with legal, political, social, and cultural matters pertinent thereto. . . . As much as possible the editors have endeavored to call attention to broader issues of American history by the use of readings. . . ." To support such objectives the set is well indexed, with a number of primary and secondary indexes, including ethnic index, proper name index, topical index, author-source index, and illustration index. [R: ARBA 72, p. 129; RQ, Winter 71, p. 169]

209. Wynar, Lubomyr R. **Encyclopedic Directory of Ethnic Organizations in the United States.** With the assistance of Lois Buttlar and Anna T. Wynar. Littleton, CO, Libraries Unlimited, 1975. 440p. index. $25.00. LC 75-28150. ISBN 0-87287-120-7.

This is the only comprehensive encyclopedic guide to major ethnic organizations in the United States. In all, it includes 1,475 organizations, representing 73 ethnic groups. A separate section provides a selective listing of major multi-ethnic and research-oriented non-ethnic organizations involved in the study of ethnicity.

The *Encyclopedic Directory* lists major cultural, religious, fraternal, political, educational, professional, scholarly, youth, and other ethnic organizations. Entries, arranged alphabetically by ethnic groups with the necessary cross references, provide the following information: name of organization, address, phone number, principal officers, staff, date founded, scope, branches, membership, nature of the organization, publications, affiliations, and additional descriptive information.,

The emergence of ethnic awareness has resulted in an emphasis on the study of the ethnic heritage of Americans within the curriculum of our universities, colleges, and public schools. The wealth of information contained in this *Encyclopedic Directory* makes it a valuable source of information for governmental agencies, historians, and sociologists engaged in the study of American ethnicity. A comprehensive alphabetical index of names of organizations concludes this important reference guide. [R: ARBA 76, p. 219; BL, 15 July 76, p. 1617; Choice, Apr 76, p. 210; LJ, 15 May 76, p. 1202; RQ, Spring 76, p. 283; WLB, Jan 76, p. 410]

210. Wynar, Lubomyr R., and Anna T. Wynar. **Encyclopedic Directory of Ethnic Newspapers and Periodicals in the United States.** 2nd ed. Littleton, CO, Libraries Unlimited, 1976. 248p. index. $20.00. LC 76-23317. ISBN 0-87287-154-1.

The second edition of the *Encyclopedic Directory of Ethnic Newspapers and Periodicals in the United States* is based on a comprehensive survey of the ethnic press conducted by Lubomyr Wynar, who is director of the Center for the Study of Ethnic Publications, Kent State University. Many of the 977 publications indexed were not listed in the 1972 edition. The present directory covers the publications of 63 ethnic groups, including Albanian, Arabic, Armenian, Byelorussian, Chinese, Croatian, Czech, Danish, Dutch, German, Hungarian, Jewish, Korean, Latvian, Polish, Portuguese, Russian, Slovak, Spanish, Turkish, Ukrainian, and Welsh, among many others. In addition, this revised edition contains information on the presses of eight groups not included in the earlier directory: Argentinian, Basque, Egyptian, East Indian, Iranian, Irish, Pakistani, and Scottish. New sections devoted to the Asian press, the Scandinavian press, and multi-ethnic publications have been added in the second edition.

The present *Encyclopedic Directory* consists of 51 sections. Entries are arranged in two categories within each ethnic group: native language and bilingual publications, and publications in English. Information provided for each publication includes title (with English translation), starting date, language of publication, sponsoring organization, frequency, circulation, subscription rate, and name, address, and telephone number of editor or editorial office. A brief description of the objectives and scope of the publication is also included.

In addition to the listings by ethnic groups, the directory includes an appendix of statistical data on the publications for each ethnic group and an alphabetical index of titles. An essay "Nature of the Ethnic Press" deals with the historical development and role of the ethnic press, types of publications, and the present status of ethnic publications. [R: ARBA 77, p. 221; Choice, Feb 77, p. 1578; WLB, Dec 76, p. 362]

INDIVIDUAL GROUPS

BLACKS

211. Fisher, Mary L., comp. **The Negro in America: A Bibliography.** 2nd ed. rev. and enl. With a foreword by Thomas F. Pettigrew. Originally compiled by Elizabeth W. Miller. Cambridge, MA, Harvard University Press, 1970. 315p. index. $17.50; $4.95pa. LC 71-120319. ISBN 0-674-60703-1; 0-674-60702-3pa.

The first edition, edited by Elizabeth W. Miller, was published in 1966. The second revised edition, considerably enlarged, contains some 6,500 entries for books, serials, articles, pamphlets, and government documents representing, for the most part, a selection of the literature from 1954 to February 1970. Reprints, dissertations, and most newspaper articles are omitted. The entries are arranged under 20 chapters and are subdivided by broad headings. Full bibliographic description is provided for articles; however, the entries for books omit pages. Brief annotations are provided where titles are not self-explanatory. The scope is enlarged to give greater coverage to black history (including historiography), folklore and literature, and biography. Civil rights protest is now in two sections: materials up to 1965 and since 1965. Given more emphasis is the issue of black nationalism, which covers background, theory, Panthers, Muslims, and response and resistance. Other additions and enlargements include black theater, dance, the arts and music, references to language and idiom, and Negro-Jewish relations. *The Negro in America* provides detailed coverage of the social sciences and is oriented to the needs of researchers.

Szwed and Abrahams' *Afro-American Folk Culture: An Annotated Bibliography of Materials from North, Central and South America and the West Indies* (2v. Philadelphia, Institute for the Study of Human Issues, 1978. $55.00/set) provides more detailed and current information on Afro-American (and Afro-Hispanic) culture. Although not exhaustive, it is the most comprehensive title available on the subject, covering, among other topics, music, language, dance, games, religion, physical mannerisms, biographies, food, and drama. [R: ARBA 72, p. 276]

212. **Handbook of Black Librarianship.** Comp. and ed. by E. J. Josey and Ann Allen Shockley. Littleton, CO, Libraries Unlimited, 1977. 392p. index. $25.00. LC 77-21817. ISBN 0-87287-179-7.

The *Handbook of Black Librarianship*, compiled and edited by two distinguished librarians, defines black Americans' contributions to American libraries in the past and present. The *Handbook* contains 37 topical essays and resource lists, arranged in seven major sections: Pioneers and Landmark Episodes; Early Library Organization; Contemporary Black Librarianship; Vital Issues in Black Librarianship; Significant Books and Periodicals for Black Collections; African Resources; Afro-American Resources. Seven directories follow the main part of the text: Undergraduate Library School Departments in Predominantly Black Colleges and Universities; Predominantly Black Graduate Library Schools; Libraries of Public Library Systems Serving Predominantly Black Communities; Black Academic Libraries; Additional Libraries Named for Afro-Americans; Selective List of Black-Owned Bookstores; Black Book Publishers.

Historical material in the first two sections includes, among the eight articles, a chronology of events in black librarianship, 1808-1977; a history of the Hampton Institute Library School; and descriptions of five early black library organizations.

Contemporary black librarianship is well covered by 11 articles encompassing topics such as the Black Caucus of ALA, statistics on black libraries and librarians, and library services to black Americans.

A special feature of the *Handbook* is the identification and description of resources for African and Afro-American studies. Here are found lists of reference books and periodicals reflecting the black experience and several articles dealing with black authors, best sellers, and black librarians as writers. Black resources in U.S. libraries, archives, oral history programs, and museums are also discussed and described. [R: ARBA 78, p. 81; BL, 15 May 78, p. 1519; C&RL, May 78, p. 223; JAL, Sept 78, p. 229]

213. Hatch, James V., and OMANii Abdullah, comps. **Black Playwrights, 1823-1977: An Annotated Bibliography of Plays.** New York, R. R. Bowker, 1977. 319p. index. $19.95. LC 77-11890. ISBN 0-8352-1032-4.

The work was "designed for directors and producers in search of plays to meet their specific production requirements and for scholars and researchers who are seeking historical data," and it "lists over 2700 plays by approximately 900 black American playwrights" (preface, p. xi). The focus is on plays written by Afro-Americans from 1823 to 1977; the editors have attempted inclusiveness to the point of listing plays that may have not been published and on which they have very little information. They invite additional data and corrections.

The entries are careful and precise, with 11 possible items for any given play. These are: author, title(s), dates, genre, description, cast, length, productions, publication, library sources, and permissions. The entries are concise and contain many abbreviations, which are carefully keyed in the front. Many well-known playwrights are listed, such as Ed Bullins, Lorraine Hansberry, and Joseph A. Walker, as well as many much less known. The work is very thorough. Following the main section are three valuable bibliographies (books and sources on black drama and its theatre artists; anthologies; and dissertations and theses) and three appendices: taped interviews in the oral history library of the Hatch-Billips Archives; awards to black theatre artists; and addresses of playwrights, agents, and agencies. A title index, including alternate titles, is included. All in all, the compilation is a valuable addition to theatre bibliography and well nigh indispensable for its subject and purpose. [R: ARBA 79, p. 493; BL, 1 July 78, p. 1695; Choice, Mar 79, p. 54; C&RL, July 78, p. 304; LJ, July 78, p. 1386; WLB, June 78, p. 808]   Richard M. Buck

214.   Ploski, Harry A., and Warren Marr, comps. and eds. **The Negro Almanac: A Reference Work on the Afro American.** Bicentennial ed. New York, Bellwether, 1976. 1206p. illus. $59.95. LC 75-24805.

First published in 1967, the *Negro Almanac* is considered the most important single-volume ready reference source about blacks. The second edition was published in 1971, and this "Bicentennial edition" continues the fine tradition of its predecessors, reflecting "a singular awareness of the expanding directions of the black cultural and social experience." It covers a wide range of topics, both historical and current—marriage, women, employment, history, civil rights, education, music, etc. There is a considerable updating in this edition. For example, the section on black women contains 64 articles, as opposed to 43 in the second edition, and substantial enlargement is seen in "Black Classical Musicians." Some sections now have new titles and have been restructured (thus, instead of "Africa: The Changing Continent," the new edition uses the title "Africa: The Emerging Nations"). There are biographical sketches within many of the articles. The chronology records events from 1600 to 1976. Most of the articles indicate revision and updating, and some new photos have been added. This is indeed a professionally executed volume, with credit due to its editor, Harry A. Ploski, a noted educator and psychologist. [R: ARBA 77, p. 223; BL, 15 Nov 76, p. 501; Choice, May 77, p. 350; LJ, 1 Mar 77, p. 594]   Bohdan S. Wynar

215.   Rush, Theressa Gunnels, Carol Fairbanks Myers, and Esther Spring Arata. **Black American Writers Past and Present: A Biographical and Bibliographical Dictionary.** Metuchen, NJ, Scarecrow, 1975. 2v. illus. $32.50. LC 74-28400. ISBN 0-8108-0785-8.

Previous work by one of the authors (Myers) on a book entitled *Black Power in the Arts* (Flint, MI, The Mott Foundation, 1970) convinced her and later her co-authors of the need for a dictionary, ideally as comprehensive as possible, of all black writers, past and present, of poetry, drama, fiction, children's literature, and criticism. While stressing writers in these categories, the work also includes those who have written nonfiction that is used in black studies curricula and writers from Africa and the West Indies who either live or publish in the United States.

The entries are arranged in straight alphabetical order. Their components are biographical information (supplied exclusively by the living author, and through secondary sources for deceased writers); bibliographies of writings; citations for work published in anthologies or periodicals; and finally, biographies and critical studies. Here an effort at comprehensiveness was made for minor writers only. The work concludes with a general bibliography and two appendixes, which list, respectively, black and white critics, historians, and editors.

Unquestionably, this is the most comprehensive dictionary of its kind to be issued. Nonetheless, its execution could easily have been improved. Many of its entries are so very brief that they become meaningless. An example on page 175, quoted in full: "CORBO, Dominic R., Jr. *Novel: Hard Ground* New York: Vantage, 1954." Corbo was evidently uncooperative with the compilers, who nevertheless could have made some effort to supply from secondary sources information not to be extracted from him.

The underlying criterion for inclusion in the book was the fact of having had something published. No qualitative standards of any kind were used. Frankly, I think this was a mistake. The corpus of black American literature has now become so large that qualitative standards are needed if one is to make sense of it. Fascination with sheer numbers should give way to reasoned criticism and discriminating judgment. [R: ARBA 76, p. 591; BL, 1 Oct 76, p. 279; Choice, Jan 76, p. 1426; LJ, 1 Sept 75, p. 1537; LJ, 15 Apr 76, p. 968; RQ, Fall 75, p. 80, WLB, Oct 75, p. 118]   Richard A. Gray

216.   Smythe, Mabel M., ed. **The Black American Reference Book.** Englewood Cliffs, NJ, Prentice-Hall, 1976. 1026p. illus. index. $29.95. LC 75-26511. ISBN 0-13-077586-X.

The first edition of this work, edited by John P. Davis and published under the title *The American Negro Reference Book* (Prentice-Hall, 1966. 969p.), was acclaimed as a comprehensive and reliable reference source, covering black history and black contributions in all fields of American life—agriculture, politics, the arts. The articles, arranged by subject, emphasized sociological aspects, including status of various black groups, family life, women, the effect of prejudice, religion, economic position, and legal status of blacks. Many articles showed appropriate citations to further readings on a given subject.

This edition contains 30 lengthy articles covering many aspects of the black experience: history, black women, black workers, education, religion, the black professional, protest, blacks in the American theatre, in the armed forces, in sports. The 38 authors who contributed the essays are identified at the front of the book, and a detailed index concludes the work. Overall, this edition maintains the fine reputation of the 1966 edition and is certainly one of the best reference sources on blacks. [R: ARBA 77, p. 224; BL, 1 July 77, p. 1673; LJ, 1 Mar 77, p. 591; WLB, Nov 76, p. 263]   Bohdan S. Wynar

217.   Tudor, Dean, and Nancy Tudor. **Black Music.** Littleton, CO, Libraries Unlimited, 1979. 262p. index. (American Popular Music on Elpee). $22.50. LC 78-15563. ISBN 0-87287-147-9.

Black Music is a survey of and a buying guide to the best and most enduring of recorded black music currently available on long-playing discs and tapes. The authors have selected both old and new recordings that they feel should be in a collection representative of black music. As part of the introductory material, the authors outline a suggested order of purchasing tailored to various needs and budgets.

The authors' essay, "Introduction to Popular Music," surveys popular music as a twentieth-century art form made available to the masses through records, discussing the recording industry as well as styles of popular music. The 1,300 entries in this guide are grouped first by style: blues, rhythm 'n' blues, gospel, soul, and reggae. The development of each style is discussed in the introduction to that section, noting memorable performers and originators of special styles. Books and periodicals concerning each style, with full bibliographic citations, are listed at the end of the book. Each style is subdivided into anthologies, groups, and individual performers. All relevant order information and annotations averaging 300 words accompany the entries. Discs considered "first purchase" recordings from which to build a collection are starred. Completing the volume are directories of labels and specialist record stores, and an artists index. This annotated selection tool aids libraries and individual collectors in basing their choices on informed evaluation. [R: ARBA 80, p. 443; LJ, 15 Apr 79, p. 940; WLB, May 79, p. 655]

JEWS

218.   **Encyclopaedia Judaica.** Jerusalem, Encyclopaedia Judaica; New York, Macmillan, 1972. 16v. illus. (part col.). index. $500.00. LC 72-177492.

Encyclopaedia Judaica includes 25,000 entries, 11 million words, and over 8,000 illustrations in color and black and white, plus hundreds of maps, charts, tables, diagrams, and other illustrative material. In addition to the 2,000 contributors, there are many divisional and departmental editors. The editor-in-chief was Professor Cecil Roth, until his death in 1970; he was succeeded by Dr. Geoffrey Wigoder, who served from 1966 to 1970 as deputy editor-in-chief. All articles are signed with initials, and identification is provided in the first volume, where one also finds a lengthy introduction, an index, and other supplementary material.

The criteria of selection are discussed in the introduction. The goal was comprehensive coverage of all subjects and areas related to Jews. Thus, there are many long articles on modern and historical Israel, Zionism, arts and sciences, philosophy, the Bible, Yiddish literature, Jews and their contributions to individual countries, etc. There are a number of so-called "capsule" entries—"to expand the scope of biographical entries, especially covering the participation of Jews in world culture" (p. 7). It should be noted, however, that many biographies found in other encyclopedias have been omitted in the *Judaica*. Longer articles are subdivided by specific topics; thus, "Synagogue" (vol. 15, pp. 579-630) has eight main subdivisions plus some 30 sections, all represented in an outline preceding the article. There are extensive bibliographies appended to each article, and, in most cases, the coverage is well balanced.

Probably the only serious drawback to this encyclopedia is its index (some 250,000 entries), which is incomplete and hard to use. In addition, compared to the rest of this lavishly produced encyclopedia, it is not easy to read and contains a number of typographical errors. In general, the treatment of most subjects is highly authoritative and well balanced. Occasionally, there are some ideologically inspired colorings, especially with respect to more recent political events or the history of Jewish minorities in individual countries (notably in Eastern Europe). But this is probably to be expected, since this is, after all, a national Jewish encyclopedia; even scholars are entitled to their opinions. All in all, this is a monumental work; it will be envied by the many nations that do not have anything even close to it.

The *Encyclopaedic Dictionary of Judaica* (Jerusalem, Keter Publishing House; distr., New York, Leon Amiel, 1974. 673p. $29.95) is a complementary volume to the *Encyclopaedia Judaica*, containing 15,000 entries covering broad aspects of Jewish culture, history, and literature. Most articles represent a condensed treatment of subjects found in the *Encyclopaedia*, with special emphasis on topics of current interest, Jewish contributions to world culture, population statistics, Jewish customs, and Israel. The *Encyclopaedic Dictionary of Judaica* is well indexed, well illustrated, professionally executed, and highly recommended for use as a mini-encyclopedia in schools and homes. [R: ARBA 73, p. 136; BL, 1 Nov 72, p. 209; Choice, Oct 72, p. 948; C&RL, July 72, p. 321; LJ, Aug 72, p. 2562; LJ, 15 Apr 73, p. 1244; WLB, 21 Dec 72, p. 12]   Bohdan S. Wynar

219. **Who's Who in American Jewry: Incorporating** *The Directory of American Jewish Institutions.* 1980 ed. Los Angeles, Standard Who's Who, 1980. 726p. $87.50. ISSN 0196-8009.

A handy, one-volume biographical directory containing over 6,000 entries for notable Jewish men and women in the United States and Canada. According to the editor, the principle underlying the selection criteria "has been to choose Jewish men and women who have achieved distinction in a particular field of human endeavor or who hold leadership positions in the Jewish or national community" (preface, p. iv). The present volume consists of two major parts: a biographical section and the Directory of American Jewish Institutions. The Directory is arranged by state and covers over 9,000 Jewish institutions. *Who's Who in American Jewry* constitutes a major reference work on American Jewry and is recommended for large academic and public libraries.   Lubomyr R. Wynar

NATIVE AMERICANS

220. Stensland, Anna Lee. **Literature by and about the American Indian: An Annotated Bibliography.** With contributions by Aune M. Fadum. 2nd ed. Urbana, IL, National Council of Teachers of English, 1979. 382p. index. $6.75pa.; $6.00 (NCTE members). LC 79-18073. ISBN 0-8141-2984-6.

The second edition of *Literature by and about the American Indian* reflects the increase of interest in and publication about Native American culture and heritage. The number of annotated titles, 775, is more than double that of the 1973 edition. New to this edition is the inclusion of more than 200 books for elementary grade level children, prepared by Aune M. Fadum. Works about Indians in Alaska, Canada, and Mexico are now represented. The outstanding feature of Stensland's bibliography is her adherence to the principle of selecting works that deal honestly with Indian life, whether written by Native Americans or others. As in the first edition, the primary emphasis is on literature — myth, legend, poetry, fiction, and biography, although other areas are not neglected. An important section in the book deals with teaching the literature of the American Indian. The second edition is an essential purchase for all types of libraries. [R: ARBA 80, p. 206]   Christine Gehrt Wynar

221. Washburn, Wilcomb E. **The American Indian and the United States: A Documentary History.** New York, Random House, 1973. 4v. illus. map. index. $135.00. LC 72-10259. ISBN 0-394-47283-7.

Wounded Knee "II" was a symbol of the long-standing conflict between the American Indians and the government of the United States, not just the Sioux nation and the United States. Dr. Washburn draws together, in four impressive volumes, the documentary evidence relating to this conflict. He uses five sources to illustrate how the problems developed: 1) reports of commissions of Indian affairs (vols. 1 and 2), 2) congressional debates on Indian affairs (vols. 2 and 3), 3) acts, ordinances, and proclamations (vol. 3), 4) Indian treaties (vols. 3 and 4), and 5) legal decisions (vol. 4).

Each section is arranged in chronological order with a one- or two-page introduction by Dr. Washburn. The introductory statement provides an overview of the material and some indication as to how items were selected for inclusion. Every entry has a brief paragraph that provides the basic background about the item. All major aspects of the five types of documents are covered, and there are interesting sidelights that provide a fuller view. While individuals may disagree with some items selected for inclusion, the total result is excellent. One could not hope to find a better overview of the situation.

It must be pointed out that this *is* a documentary history, which means that it presents the case of the United States government — and *not* the Indians' case. The Indians' point of view is frequently indicated in Dr. Washburn's opening paragraph for an entry — for example, on page 81: "Commissioner Dole's report for 1862 discussed the problems in the Northern Superintendency caused by the depredations of the Sioux, who had been goaded to an outbreak by an insensitive Government."

Access to this very important work is provided by a 92-page index. No matter what limitations can be identified for this set, the fact remains it must be considered *the* best basic general reference work on the subject. [R: ARBA 75, p. 179; BL, 15 Oct 74, p. 248; Choice, June 74, p. 665; LJ, 15 Apr 74, p. 1116; WLB, May 74, p. 766]   G. Edward Evans

PUERTO RICANS

222. Herrera, Diane, ed. **Puerto Ricans and Other Minority Groups in the Continental United States: An Annotated Bibliography.** Detroit, Blaine Ethridge — Books, 1979. 397p. index. $30.00. LC 78-27314. ISBN 0-87917-067-0.

This bibliography, originally published as *Puerto Ricans in the United States: A Review of the Literature* (a Title VII, Bilingual Education Act, project), was intended to review all available literature on the experiences of Puerto Rican children within the United States educational system on the mainland. Although the scope was expanded to include materials of historical, sociological, economic, and anthropological relevance, the emphasis remained on topics of interest to educators, such as those related to teacher education, educational and psychological testing, learning styles, and bicultural education. Other groups included in the bibliography are Mexican Americans, blacks, Cubans, American Indians, Jews, etc.

The original bibliography reprinted here includes 2,155 entries (complete through December 1972); the new edition also includes a supplementary bibliography by Francesco Cordasco of approximately 250 titles. Unfortunately, only about 15% of these titles bear post-1972 publication dates. For this reason, it seems that the title of the bibliography should indicate the dates of coverage, as the 1979 publication date might lead researchers to expect this reference guide to include more current items than it does.

Arrangement of the bibliography is in four sections. Part I is entitled "Bibliographies" and includes a total of 58 guides to material on Puerto Rican and other Spanish-speaking minorities, but with a majority of materials on language, linguistics, and bilingualism. Part II, "The Puerto Rican Child in the American System," covers books and articles that are anthologies or are related to general topics, Puerto Ricans in Puerto Rico and the mainland, educational opportunities, socioeconomic and cultural characteristics, or those that are studies pertaining to the bilingual/bicultural child, intellectual development, testing, academic achievement, and educational programs and materials for Puerto Rican and other non-English-speaking students. Part III, "The Puerto Rican Experience on the Mainland," includes demographic studies; social, psychological, and anthropological studies; and the Puerto Rican experience in literature. Part IV lists "Unpublished Materials." An index to authors is provided, but because of the scope of coverage here, a subject index is demanded. It would be particularly useful to identify entries related to other minority groups covered, e.g., Mexicans, Cubans, etc.

The bibliography is a comprehensive tool for materials about Puerto Ricans and the education of Puerto Rican and other non-English-speaking children published through 1972. This edition has a new and informative 14-page foreword by Francesco Cordasco that stresses the importance of bilingual/bicultural education. This guide would be extremely useful for researchers studying Spanish-speaking minority groups, bilingual education, cultural differences in educational testing and measurement, and cognitive style as it is related to ethnicity. [R: ARBA 80, p. 194; Choice, July 79, p. 648; LJ, 1 June 79, p. 1244]   Lois Buttlar

SLAVIC AMERICANS

223. Wynar, Lubomyr R. **Slavic Ethnic Libraries, Museums and Archives in the United States: A Guide and Directory.** With the assistance of Pat Kleeberger. Chicago, American Library Association. Association of College and Research Libraries, 1980. 164p. index. $14.00pa.(ACRL members); $17.50pa.(non-ACRL members). LC 80-18034.

This is the first comprehensive directory of cultural resources found in Slavic ethnic museums, libraries, and archives in the United States. It identifies institutions representing more than 10 Slavic groups, and provides a multi-cultural section covering several ethnic groups and/or research institutions concerned with ethnicity. Institutions are listed alphabetically, and for each the following information is provided: address, phone, date of inception, sponsor, personnel, scope, staff, annual visitors, admission fee, publications produced by the institution, objectives, and a description of the collection. A useful tool for researchers, educators, and librarians.

6 GENEALOGY AND HERALDRY

COMPREHENSIVE WORKS

224. Filby, P. William, comp. **American & British Genealogy & Heraldry: A Selected List of Books.** 2nd ed. Chicago, American Library Association, 1975. 467p. index. $25.00. LC 75-29383. ISBN 0-8389-0203-0.

The first edition of this valuable guide, published in 1970, contained about 1,800 entries. The present edition is updated and expanded. Its major objective is to: 1) serve as a reference manual for librarians and individuals interested in heraldry and genealogy; 2) serve as a selection aid to the librarian; and 3) provide the family searcher with a list of basic sources. The guide contains over 5,000 annotated entries related to genealogy and heraldry covering the United States, Latin America, Canada, Great Britain, and British Island areas. The chapter on the United States includes an extensive reference section (bibliographies, atlases, censuses, etc.) and separate sections on states listed in alphabetical order. Annotations are brief and to the point. The inclusion of definitive articles that appeared in genealogical and historical journals broadened the source basis of this valuable reference tool. It is hoped that in the next edition Filby will be successful in including major foreign genealogical and heraldic sources as well as prices for all listed publications that are in print. This outstanding publication is recommended to all public and academic libraries. [R: ARBA 77, p. 232; BL, 1 May 77, p. 1372; Choice, Nov 76, p. 1116; WLB, Sept 76, p. 92]   Lubomyr R. Wynar

GENEALOGY

GENERAL WORKS

225. Barrow, Geoffrey B. **The Genealogist's Guide.** Chicago, American Library Association, 1977. 205p. $12.50. LC 77-83833. ISBN 0-8389-3203-7.

In 1903 George W. Marshall issued the fourth edition of his *Genealogist's Guide*, containing lists of pedigrees in all printed books and periodicals. This monumental work was reprinted by Genealogical Publishing Company (Baltimore) in 1973. In 1953, John B. Whitmore published his *Genealogical Guide*, which contained pedigrees published in Great Britain from 1900 to 1950, with corrigenda to Marshall, but unaccountably, the Society of Genealogists (London) has refused permission to reprint even though it has long been out of print. Geoffrey Barrow has now brought the collection to 1975, with corrigenda and addenda to the former works, and thus the story is more complete. Like the former compilations, Barrow's book is essential, and it is hoped that soon Whitmore's will be made available so that libraries can have this three-volume unique and essential tool. [R: ARBA 79, p. 236]   P. William Filby

226. Kaminkow, Marion J., ed. **Genealogies in the Library of Congress: A Bibliography.** Baltimore, Magna Carta Book Co., 1972. 2v. $150.00. LC 74-187078. ISBN 0-910946-15-9.

227. Kaminkow, Marion J., ed. **Genealogies in the Library of Congress: A Bibliography. Supplement 1972-1976.** Baltimore, Magna Carta Book Co., 1977. 285p. $25.00. LC 74-187078. ISBN 0-910946-19-1.

The supplement updates the two-volume set published in 1972. The preface and editor's note are repeated unchanged in each volume. Together the set supersedes the various editions of *American and English Genealogies in the Library of Congress* and provides over 23,000 genealogical entries and 30,000 cross references. The supplement alone includes 2,798 new entries for books added between 1972 and 1976. The alphabetical arrangement is by family surname for both the bibliographical entries and the cross references. Title, place, publisher, author, and LC card and call numbers are included. Comprehensive and easy to use, this work is a major starting point for identifying and approaching American, English, Canadian, Latin American, European, and Asian genealogical sources. [R: ARBA 73, p. 173; LJ, July 72, p. 2376; LJ, 15 Apr 73, p. 1243; ARBA 78, p. 214; LJ, 1 Apr 77, p. 789]   Jimmie H. Hoover

UNITED STATES

228. Greenwood, Val D. **The Researcher's Guide to American Genealogy.** Baltimore, Genealogical, 1973; distr. New York, Scribner's, 1974. 535p. illus. $22.50. LC 73-6902. ISBN 0-8063-0560-6.

Books and records available anywhere in the country are listed here and examined in detail; areas and states are fully covered. The author is not satisfied with merely listing records; he generally gives basic background for their presence and discusses methods of research. Milton Rubincam, himself the author of genealogical manuals, comments in his eulogistic introduction that the guide has long been needed and that "Mr. Greenwood delves deeply into the historical background of our records systems, providing us especially with an understanding of the legal aspects of genealogical research." The only objection to this important book is its unwieldy size – large octavo, 535 pages! [R: ARBA 74, p. 131; Choice, Jan 74, p. 1698; LJ, 15 June 74, p. 1692]   P. William Filby

229. Rose, James, and Alice Eichholz. **Black Genesis.** Detroit, Gale, 1978. 326p. index. (Gale Genealogy and Local History Series, Vol. 1). $28.00. LC 77-74819. ISBN 0-8103-1400-2.

If this were only a bibliography of published materials on Afro-American genealogical research, it would be worth consideration by all persons engaged in black-American studies. As it is, the compilers have included an exceptionally large number of unica, simultaneously providing the location of these materials. In addition, the volume's contents of both published and manuscript material are carefully classified by subject and geographical area, and the supplemental features include detailed data on genealogical libraries and federal archives and records centers, concluding with indexes by author, title, and subject. A few family histories are provided, as well as facsimiles of early sources. The introduction provides serious assistance for scholars engaged in genealogical research. With acknowledgement to the inspiration of Alex Haley (whose search for Kunta Kinte would have been enormously easier had this book been available to him), the authors have provided research stimuli in genealogy, sociology, economics, demography, and history, with substantial reference value in all areas. A remarkable work of great potential influence. [R: ARBA 80, p. 213]   Dominique-René de Lerma

GREAT BRITAIN

230. Hamilton-Edwards, Gerald. **In Search of British Ancestry.** 3rd ed. Baltimore, Genealogical, 1974. 296p. $15.00. LC 74-9346. ISBN 0-8063-0628-9.

In 1967 Mr. Hamilton-Edwards brought out a book that was of great assistance to those wishing to trace British forebears and that has become the standard book for American research. The third edition adds items that were suggested to the author or that he has discovered in his own researches.

All types of records are discussed, with details of the record offices in Ireland, Wales, and Scotland. To the average researcher and also to the professional, the records held by the Public Record Office in London are of particular value, but they are not easy to find or to understand, largely because so many were the products of the established church. One, for instance, the Prerogative Court of Canterbury, collected vital papers for years. Their value is scarcely known to American researchers, yet with the thousands of names in wills, marriage lists, inventories, etc., they are of prime interest. These and many other idiosyncrasies are discussed. Above all, the bibliography is certainly the finest to be found in any book of genealogy; nothing has escaped the author. It is also an excellent study of British history. [R: ARBA 75, p. 206]   P. William Filby

231. Hamilton-Edwards, Gerald. **In Search of Scottish Ancestry.** Baltimore, Genealogical, 1972. 252p. illus. $10.00. LC 72-86. ISBN 0-8063-0506-1.

Mr. Hamilton-Edwards' book on Scottish ancestry is, without question, the best book on Scottish genealogy for the researcher yet to be produced. The author deals extensively with basic places of research and shows himself to be adept in the use of all types of registers.

There are chapters on surnames and Christian names, tax and census lists. Genealogists working on Scottish records will meet with words and phrases not seen elsewhere, and the glossary will be of great value to Americans who must delve into commissariat and other early lists. Nonconformist and other parish lists are equally difficult to find and to understand, but with this outstanding work, which overlooks no aspect of Scottish genealogy, the American will find his work made easier. There is also an introduction to Scottish history. Again, this outstanding bibliography is the best produced so far. [R: ARBA 73, p. 180; LJ, 15 Jan 73, p. 151; RQ, Fall 72, p. 97]   P. William Filby

232. Montague-Smith, Patrick, ed. **Debrett's Peerage and Baronetage, with Her Majesty's Royal Warrant Holders 1980.** London, Debrett's Peerage; distr. Detroit, Gale, 1979. 1v. (various paging). illus. (part col.). $110.00. LC 78-69894. ISBN 0-8103-0949-1.

The first new edition since 1976, *Debrett's Peerage* is now being distributed by the Gale Research Company. *Debrett's*, the long-established authority on British nobility, was "founded in 1769, renamed Debrett in 1802." This huge volume contains articles discussing the Royal Family, the peerage, the Privy Council, Scottish Lords of Session, the baronetage, chiefs of names and clans in Scotland, and chieftans in Ireland. The major portion of the book consists of alphabetically arranged articles, illustrated with coats of arms, "concerning every living male descended in the male line from the first Peer and of all living females being issued of males so descended" (p. P25). A separate section discusses the baronetage in a similar manner. Each biography lists the title, the individual's name, birthdate, education, marriage, and brief biographical data. Living relatives are listed, as well as collateral branches now living. Predecessors are traced to the creation of the title. *Debrett's* is rather complicated to use and assumes some knowledge of British nobility, but it is an invaluable tool for genealogists and historians.   Janet H. Littlefield

HERALDRY

233. **Boutell's Heraldry.** Rev. by J. P. Brooke-Little. New York, Frederick Warne, 1978. 357p. illus. (part col.). bibliog. index. $25.00. LC 73-75030. ISBN 0-7232-2096-4.

Heraldry is defined as an auxiliary historical science of "armorial bearings" or coats of arms. It describes and interprets various coats of arms according to the research methods of heraldry. Usually, heraldry is related to genealogy and vexillology.

Boutell's Heraldry is considered a standard text on heraldry. It consists of 25 chapters, a critical bibliography, a glossary, and an index, with 28 color plates and numerous figures illustrating the text. The emphasis is placed on British heraldry. Probably the weakest section of this publication is the chapter pertaining to the "Commonwealth and Foreign Heraldry," which is very limited in its coverage of European heraldry. The same limitation applies to the "Critical Bibliography" (pp. 292-302), which excludes even P. William Filby's *American & British Genealogy & Heraldry*, an extensive bibliographical guide. The present revised edition features recent changes in corporate and ecclesiastical heraldry. It is hoped that the future edition of this important text will incorporate more comprehensive interpretation of non-British heraldry. The same recommendation pertains to its bibliographic section. [R: ARBA 80, p. 217]   Lubomyr R. Wynar

234.   Brooke-Little, J. P. **An Heraldic Alphabet.** New York, Arco, 1973. 224p. illus. (part col.). $8.95. LC 72-95468. ISBN 0-668-002941-2.

A dictionary of 1,000 terms, with drawings accompanying many of the definitions. One of the best features of this book is the sensible manner in which Brooke-Little (Richmond Herald of Arms and, therefore, a top authority) has attempted to solve the orthographical questions. For the beginner (and the professional), many heraldic words make little or no sense, partly because of the peculiar spelling. While Brooke-Little does not claim to have solved all the problems, his anglicizing of many endings will be useful.

The chapters that precede the alphabet concern heralds and the birth of heraldry, the development and law of arms, and the grammar of heraldry. As might be expected, all of these are authoritative and useful. One of the best points about the book is its size. Heraldists always expect a weighty tome — and they usually get it — but Brooke-Little has deliberately cut the book to smaller size without sacrificing anything of value.

Ed. note: See also Franklyn and Tanner's *Encyclopaedic Dictionary of Heraldry* (Pergamon, 1970), which includes foreign heraldry. [R: ARBA 74, p. 139; BL, 15 Oct 73, p. 206; Choice, Jan 74, p. 1696; LJ, Aug 73, p. 2261; LJ, 15 Apr 74, p. 1098; WLB, Nov 73, p. 264]   P. William Filby

235.   Burke, Sir John Bernard. **The General Armory of England, Scotland, Ireland, and Wales.** Baltimore, Genealogical, 1976. 1185p. $50.00. LC 66-28797.

The final edition of the *General Armory*, first compiled in 1842, was published in 1884. Because of the needs of librarians and genealogists in the resurgence of family searching, it seems that there have never been enough copies available. It was reprinted in the 1960s and now, because it was once again out of print, it has again been reprinted. It is regarded as the foremost publication on British heraldry; while it is true that mistakes have been pointed out, there is nothing to take its place. There are approximately 70,000 descriptions of British coats-of-arms, sections on Royal heraldry and the British orders of knighthood, and finally a dictionary of terms, an illustrated glossary, and a list of mottoes. Unless already held, this is a must for every library of any size and for artists. [R: ARBA 77, p. 241]   P. William Filby

236.   Fox-Davies, Arthur Charles. **A Complete Guide to Heraldry.** Rev. and annotated by J. P. Brooke-Little. New York, Barnes & Noble, 1969. 513p. illus. color plates. $30.00. ISBN 0-389-01208-4.

First published in 1909, with a revised edition by C. A. H. Franklyn published in 1949. Fox-Davies died in 1928 and this edition is now revised by J. P. Brooke-Little, an authority on heraldry.

This comprehensive and authoritative work covers the history of armory, including such matters as regalia, seals, badges, cadency, the law of armorial bearings, etc., arranged in short chapter form. Most of the material has been updated, providing details of new rulings and developments in heraldry since the time the old edition was written. A new concluding chapter is concerned with such matters as coats-of-arms of the younger members of the Royal Family, corporate arms, Commonwealth heraldry, current fees, and a general guide to procedure for those who wish to apply for a coat-of-arms. Well illustrated. [R: ARBA 70, p. 76; Choice, July 70, p. 670; LJ, 1 Mar 70, p. 882]

237. Smith, Whitney. **Flags and Arms across the World.** New York, McGraw-Hill, 1980. 256p. illus. (col.). index. $9.95. LC 79-13271. ISBN 0-07-059094-X.

This is a popularly priced, up-to-date guide to the flags of the 174 nations of the world. Included are national flags, coats of arms, state and provincial flags, and presidential and ministerial banners. Nearly 1,000 full-color illustrations make this an attractive as well as an authoritative book, and the brief accompanying text explains the history and symbolism of each flag. The work is arranged alphabetically by country, and a useful index of countries and a flag index facilitate use of the volume. The author is a world authority on flags and serves as executive director of the Flag Research Center in Winchester, Massachusetts. Recommended for public, school, and academic libraries.

Robert F. Van Benthuysen

NAMES

238. Mackey, Mary Stuart, and Maryette Goodwin Mackey. **The Pronunciation of 10,000 Proper Names.** New York, Dodd, Meade, 1922; repr., Detroit, Gale, 1979. 329p. (A Firenze Book). $29.00. LC 70-167059. ISBN 0-8103-4137-9.

The reissue of this standard work is timely, since it has been long out of print and newer libraries had been unable to obtain a copy. This edition, with corrections and the addition of important words, making a total of 12,000 names, was published in 1922. Changes in pronunciation were few, so accurate had the authors been in their earlier edition. The proper names include famous geographical and biographical names, names of books and art, fictional characters, foreign titles, and all manner of other name forms. Although not intended for the scholar and linguist, but rather for the average reader, this work will be universally used simply because no one person can be the master of all languages. Each name has the pronunciation with stress symbols, and once the sounds and marks in giving pronunciation are mastered, there will be no difficulty in getting the pronunciation right. It is a most useful book to have on any reference shelf, and the many questions of pronunciation received by public library reference desks can be answered immediately.

Ed. note: Webster's Dictionary of Proper Names (1975), based on the British publication *Payton's Proper Names* but revised to meet the needs of American researchers, is another important work. A comprehensive and well-balanced listing of a wide variety of proper names. [R: ARBA 80, p. 217] P. William Filby

239. Mossman, Jennifer, ed. **Pseudonyms and Nicknames Dictionary: A Guide to Pseudonyms, Pen Names, Nicknames, Epithets, Stage Names, Cognomens, Aliases, and Sobriquets of Twentieth-Century Persons.** 1st ed. Detroit, Gale, 1980. 627p. $48.00. LC 80-13274. ISBN 0-8103-0549-6.

This directory of assumed names is drawn from 95 sources (biographical dictionaries, encyclopedias of sports, entertainment, music, literature, etc.), citing from one to three sources for each of its 17,129 real names, 55% of them entertainers and athletes, 40% authors, and 5% ranging from religious leaders to Spanish matadors. North Americans and Western Europeans are emphasized. Assumed and real names are in one alphabet, with "see" references from the assumed to the real name, under which are given birth and death dates, nationality, occupation, assumed name or names, and sources, with parts of names not used by persons shown in brackets. A few, such as Edward S[ylvester] Ellis, have a dozen pseudonyms, which brings the total to 21,443. Broad coverage, careful editing, emphasis on contemporary figures, and inclusion of brief biographical data distinguish this substantial addition not only to sources of assumed names but to biography indexes.   Frances Neel Cheney

240.   Smith, Elsdon C. **New Dictionary of American Family Names.** New York, Harper and Row, 1973. 572p. $15.00. LC 72-79693. ISBN 0-06-013933-1.

In 1956 Mr. Smith published a definitive study that included 10,000 American family names. It was hailed then as the most complete dictionary of American names, but in the intervening years Mr. Smith has found many more.

The present work is three times as large as the first edition, and if it is not as complete in explanations as some of the earlier attempts by British scholars, it will completely satisfy American users. The original edition was faulted for its lack of references, roots, etymological origins, and early forms of the words from which the surnames were derived. Perhaps so, but such a work would be too unwieldy and, therefore, these references are still omitted. However, explanations of surnames are emphasized as are "the meaning of the words and the manner in which they were used to evolve into hereditary family names, rather than the technical etymology of the words from which the names were derived." The result is a book that answers the question: "How did my surname originate?" It is a definitive study.

Mr. Smith, a recognized authority on the subject, is also author of *American Surnames* (Chilton, 1969), a reference book which offers a thorough examination of the roots and derivations of American surnames, including Jewish and black surnames and immigrant alterations.

Ed. note: See also George R. Stewart's *American Given Names: Their Origin and History in the Context of the English Language* (Oxford University Press, 1979. 264p. $14.95) for an engrossing explanation of the linguistic formation of given and traditional names traced from Anglo-Saxon times to the present. [R: ARBA 74, p. 141; BL, 15 Mar 73, p. 674; Choice, June 73, p. 603; WLB, Mar 73, p. 609]   P. William Filby

241.   Withycombe, E. G. **The Oxford Dictionary of English Christian Names.** 3rd ed. New York, Oxford University Press, 1977. 310p. $4.95pa. ISBN 0-19-869124-6.

The third edition of this classic on English Christian names merits inclusion in every library's collection. Each name is researched extensively, and the user is assured of finding definitive information. Also noteworthy in this area is P. H. Reaney's *Dictionary of British Surnames* (2nd ed. with corrections and additions by R. M. Wilson. Boston, Routledge and Kegan Paul, 1977. 398p. $38.00), long established as the standard work in the study of British surnames. [R: ARBA 78, p. 223; WLB, Dec 77, p. 345]

7   POLITICAL SCIENCE

GENERAL WORKS

242.   Robert, Henry M. **Robert's Rules of Order, Newly Revised.** A new and enl. ed., by Sarah Corbin Robert and others. Glenview, IL, Scott, Foresman, 1970. 594p. index. $9.95. LC 71-106451. ISBN 0-673-05714-3.

This revision (the first major revision since 1915) of the authoritative manual of parliamentary procedures is almost completely rewritten, especially the chapters on voting, mass meetings, and disciplinary procedures. There is a substantial revision in the second chapter on the "Conduct of Business in a Deliberate Assembly." *Robert's* is also available in paperback (Morrow, 1971. $2.95).

Deschler's Rules of Order (Prentice-Hall, 1976, 220p. $10.00), prepared by Lewis Deschler, parliamentarian of the U.S. House of Representatives for 46 years, does not differ significantly from *Robert's*, except that it provides historical background and offers valuable advice on forming a membership organization, incorporating, and finances. [R: ARBA 71, p. 145; LJ, 15 Mar 71, p. 2623; LJ, 15 Nov 71, p. 3724]

DICTIONARIES

243.   Laqueur, Walter, ed. **A Dictionary of Politics.** Rev. ed. New York, Free Press, 1974. 565p. $14.95. LC 74-9232.

The purpose of this rather comprehensive dictionary is to present information about important political events, changes in terminology, and the historical background of contemporary politics, including some biographical sketches of prominent politicians. This edition contains slightly fewer pages than the 1971 edition, but has about the same number of entries (3,000). Although most entries are identical in the two editions, appropriate revisions have been made: statistical information about countries has been updated, closing dates have been added for persons now dead, parts of entries have been revised, and, in some cases, wholly new entries have been added. Few standard political terms are defined or explained.

Major liabilities of the first edition remain: too much in too little space; lack of a pronunciation guide; rapid obsolescence; treatment which may be too advanced for the beginner, but too simplified for the expert; inadequate accessibility to some information in longer entries. However, the assets of the first edition also remain: succinct, objective political history; relatively complete coverage of the world; easily used format; one-volume convenience package; and the fact that the work was compiled under the direction of a distinguished scholar and commentator. [R: ARBA 75, p. 219; BL, 15 July 75, p. 1216; Choice, Jan 75, p. 1608; WLB, Dec 74, p. 314]   William C. Robinson

244.   Plano, Jack C., and others. **Political Science Dictionary.** New York, Holt, Rinehart & Winston, 1973. 418p. $10.95pa. LC 73-10501. ISBN 0-03-086191-8.

The *Dictionary's* approximately 2,000 key terms, "the working language of political science," are intended to meet the needs of the undergraduate political science student who needs concise, accurate definitions of basic vocabulary relating to these aspects of political science: important political philosophies and ideologies; landmark (political) historical events; major U.S. federal agencies, legislation, and Supreme Court decisions; approaches to the study of political behavior; political theories; political activities; forms, rules, and characteristics; U.S. political institutions and processes; major foreign political institutions and processes; major international organizations; and non-political science terms important to the political scientist.

Unlike Plano's *American Political Dictionary* (see entry 251) or *International Relations Dictionary* (see entry 267), this work is arranged in straight alphabetical sequence. Both "see" and "see also" references are frequently and appropriately given, although "The Passenger Cases" is found under "T" with no reference from "P." References are made both to main entries and to subjects treated within a main entry. Format is satisfactory, although a wide gutter would facilitate use.

Another major difference between this work and Plano's other works is that the significance statements, which provide an intellectual context for most definitions, have been deleted here. Thus, the *Political Science Dictionary* does *not* supersede these works, with their fuller definitions. Definitions in the *Political Science Dictionary* are likely to be more helpful to the student interested in terms of contemporary usage rather than of political history. [R: ARBA 75, p. 220]   William C. Robinson

245. Safire, William. **Safire's Political Dictionary: An Enlarged, Up-to-Date Edition of** *The New Language of Politics*. 1st ed. New York, Random House, 1978. 845p. index. $15.95. LC 78-57124. ISBN 0-394-50261-2.

It is quite possible that President Nixon and the Watergate situation made necessary this new edition of Safire's original work. William Safire, a well-known columnist, speechwriter, and Pulitzer Prize winner, could not leave words such as "plumber," "stonewalling," "enemies list," or "inoperative" out of his book. Henry Kissinger also added to the list with "shuttle diplomacy." And while "Gerald Ford's presidency was unique in this century for not producing a single memorable phrase," President Carter is carrying on with "ethnic purity" and "lust in my heart."

Containing 450,000 words, with 1,600 terms defined in about 1,200 entries, the *Dictionary* is arranged alphabetically with a number of "see" and "see also" references. Each entry includes a definition of the word or phrase, a short etymology, and a history of the way it was used politically and by whom. The bibliography and personal name index are very complete and very useful. The introductions from all three editions are included. From them, one can see how political language has changed in just 10 years. This is not a language-of-government dictionary, for words such as "diplomat," "amendment," and "president" are not included; rather it seeks to describe words that have gained popular usage through the political arena. The author states that the "prime purpose of this book is to make readily available the words that worked for politicians." *Safire's Political Dictionary* is a most enjoyable book in which to browse. One is reminded of great, sad, and bitter moments in history. The quotations from politicians are always apt and informative, and Safire's style of writing is excellent and very non-partisan. [R: ARBA 80, p. 220; BL, 1 Jan 79, p. 735; Choice, Mar 79, p. 60; LJ, 1 Oct 78, p. 1970; WLB, Feb 79, p. 472]

                                                                       Maggie Johnson

HANDBOOKS

246. Herman, Valentine. **Parliaments of the World: A Reference Compendium.** With the collaboration of Françoise Mendel. New York, Walter de Gruyter, 1976. 985p. bibliog. index. $99.00. LC 76-17574. ISBN 3-11-006975-X.

This work, three years in the making, is a continuation of *Parliament*, which was last published in 1966. Inquiries were sent to all parliaments of the world to collect and update information — 56 different parliamentary governments are described in this study. The 70 tables given here cover all facets (composition, organization and operation, legislative functions, finance, executive control, and judicial) that affect parliamentary procedures.

Subject matter in each table is presented in a text format, and the data are summarized at the completion of the table. This allows the reader a quick overview of the statistics. These notes give the "particulars" for each parliament and are extremely helpful for ready reference information. There are also supplemental tables with many of the 70 base tables. A general bibliography, followed by a country-by-country approach as to where information was obtained, concludes this worthwhile study. [R: ARBA 77, p. 245; BL, 15 July 77, p. 1749; Choice, Mar 77, p. 43; C&RL, Jan 77, p. 51; LJ, 1 Feb 77, P. 369; RQ, Summer 77, p. 346]   Thomas Bauhs

247.   **Rulers and Governments of the World: Volume 1, Earliest Times to 1491.** Martha Ross, comp. New York, R. R. Bowker, 1978. 735p. bibliog. index. $49.50. LC 77-72342. ISBN 0-85935-021-5.

248.   **Rulers and Governments of the World: Volume 2, 1492-1929.** By Bertold Spuler. New York, R. R. Bowker, 1977. 779p. index. $49.50. LC 77-70294. ISBN 0-85935-009-6.

249.   **Rulers and Governments of the World: Volume 3, 1930-1975.** Bertold Spuler, C. G. Allen, and Neil Saunders, comps. New York, R. R. Bowker, 1977. 688p. index. $49.50; $135.00/set. LC 77-72339. ISBN 0-85935-056-8; 0-85935-051-7/set(3 volumes).

Volumes 2 and 3 of this work are an English translation of the comprehensive German guide to world leaders, *Regenten und Regierungen der Welt*, by Bertold Spuler. Arranged alphabetically by country or political territory, and chronologically within the country, they list heads of states and principal government ministers (including the papacy), providing place and date of birth, tenure in office, and political party affiliation (if any). Complete lists of cabinets for 18 major European countries and for Australia, Canada, South Africa, and the United States are also included. In some cases, a brief note explaining the origins of the state is provided.

The accuracy, meticulous editing, and, for major countries, the comprehensiveness of the works are remarkable. Since these volumes are a translation, one must be aware that Germanic name forms (e.g., Ludwig for Ludvik in Norwegian) are used; hence, the reader cannot automatically cite this as a name authority according to contemporary standards of scholarship. Coverage of minor countries is not extensive: in volume 3, Norway is allocated two pages and only its prime ministers and foreign ministers are identified. (In comparison, Italy has 20 pages and includes all officials through the level of the minister of tourism.)

Volume 1 is an entirely new compilation, which supplements volumes 2 and 3 by listing territories not covered by these volumes beyond 1491, and by featuring full lists of indigenous African rulers up to the end of the colonial era. Included are more than 300 lists of emperors, kings, dukes and counts, caliphs and popes, and archbishops and bishops throughout the world from the earliest times to 1491. Within the overall scheme of alphabetical arrangement according to territory and dynasty, each ruler is listed chronologically with date of accession, nomination, date of birth, nature of kinship with preceding ruler, date of election or usurpation, and date of death. The value of this volume is enhanced by the inclusion of such features as a table of first or given names in various languages, an index of territories, dynasties, sees, and herds, and a bibliography. This volume is extremely valuable, since no other reference work provides such comprehensive coverage of rulers of the countries of the world for the earlier period.

All three of the volumes contain exceptionally detailed indexes, which provide quick access to the information. The set as a whole is irreplaceable, and it is enthusiastically recommended to college and university libraries and large public libraries.

Ed. note: An excellent ready reference source for information on leaders of governments and states in the modern world is Alan R. Langville's *Modern World Rulers: A*

Chronology (Scarecrow, 1979. 362p. $18.50). This useful handbook provides a chronological listing of heads of state and government for all nations independent for at least 20 years since 1800—a total of 180 countries. An index lists all names (over 6,000) appearing in the chronological tables, with birth and death dates as well as country and period of office. [R: ARBA 80, p. 223; Choice, June 79, p. 512; LJ, 1 May 79, p. 1043; WLB, June 79, p. 726; ARBA 78, p. 229; Choice, Apr 78, p. 212; LJ, 15 Oct 77, p. 2150; RQ, Fall 78, p. 104; WLB, Dec 77, p. 344; ARBA 79, p. 253; BL, 15 May 79, p. 1456; Choice, Sept 78, p. 844; LJ, Aug 78, p. 1498; WLB, June 78, p. 810]   Sharad Karkhanis
Erwin K. Welsch

U.S. GOVERNMENT

DICTIONARIES AND ENCYCLOPEDIAS

250.   DeConde, Alexander, ed. **Encyclopedia of American Foreign Policy: Studies of the Principal Movements and Ideas.** New York, Scribner's, 1978. 3v. index. $130.00/set. LC 78-5453. ISBN 0-684-155036-6.

The *Encyclopedia* is a collection of 95 commissioned essays that analyze the development, application, and meaning of basic concepts in foreign policy. The essays, which average 10 pages in length, deal with broad concepts ("Isolationism," "National Self-Determination"); specific policies ("Monroe Doctrine," "Marshall Plan"); and historiography ("Revisionism," "Behavioral Approach to Diplomatic History"). Although there are no biographical notes on the contributors, most are American historians who are authorities in their fields, and many are included in *Directory of American Scholars*.

The *Encyclopedia* is not a substitute for a single-volume reference work containing short entries on a large number of specific topics, such as John Findling's *Dictionary of American Diplomatic History*, nor does it replace conventional texts that cover the history of foreign relations chronologically. The selective conceptual approach, properly chosen for an encyclopedia, does involve some factual overlapping, while other topics (e.g., Mobile Act, Rapidan Conference) are not covered. The U.S. occupation of Vera Cruz in 1914 is discussed in three articles: "Missionary Diplomacy," "Recognition Policy," and "The Constitution and Foreign Policy." The index entry for "Vera Cruz Intervention" includes two of these references and the third can be located under "Mexico-U.S. Interventions."

A number of essays apparently cover the same ground as the *International Encyclopedia of the Social Sciences*, published 10 years earlier (see articles on "Containment," "Balance of Power," "National Security," and others). However, close comparison reveals that each work is quite distinctive: whereas the *International Encyclopedia* is true to its title in treating these topics, the work under review is equally consistent in its emphasis on American diplomatic history. There are cross references and a bibliographical essay at the end of each article. A separate biographical section in volume 3, much of it reprinted from the *Concise Dictionary of American Biography* or condensed from *DAB* supplements, includes both living and dead contributors to the development of foreign policy.

Written for both scholars and laymen, this *Encyclopedia* is a unique compilation that admirably complements other types of reference works in the field of American foreign policy. [R: BL, 1 Apr 79, p. 1238; Choice, July 79, p. 351; Choice, Dec 78, p. 1346; LJ, 1 Nov 78, p. 2228; LJ, 15 Apr 79, p. 886; WLB, Dec 78, p. 347]   Elliot S. Palais

251.   Plano, Jack C., and Milton Greenberg. **The American Political Dictionary.** 5th ed. New York, Holt, Rinehart and Winston, 1979. 488p. index. $15.95; $9.95pa. LC 78-12223. ISBN 0-03-047601-1; 0-03-045096-9pa.

The fifth edition of this popular reference work consists of about 1,200 statutes, court cases, terms, and government agencies. Each item is defined, and its significance in American government is explained. The definitions are concise, and there are frequent cross references. The book is arranged by 18 major topics, such as "The Legislative Process," "Finance and Taxation," or "State and Local Governments," so that a reader may become familiar with the jargon in a certain area by reading a specific chapter. The index refers one to a specific word or phrase. New terms such as "health maintenance organizations" and old phrases such as "divine right" are included. While this book does not have the wit and style of *Safire's Political Dictionary* (see entry 245), perhaps it is a more practical purchase for most libraries. [R: ARBA 80, p. 229; LJ, 1 May 79, p. 1044; WLB, Sept 79, p. 69]   Maggie Johnson

FEDERAL GOVERNMENT

252. **Congress and the Nation, Volume IV, 1973-1976: A Review of Government and Politics.** Washington, Congressional Quarterly, 1977. 1217p. index. $62.00. LC 65-22351. ISBN 0-87187-112-2.

This volume continues Congressional Quarterly's fine reference series begun in 1965 reviewing American politics and government. Volume 1 covered the 20 years following World War II (1945-1964). Subsequent volumes have conformed to four-year presidential terms: volume 2, 1965-1968; volume 3, 1969-1972; and the present volume, 1973-1976. Based largely on information gathered in the preparation of CQ's widely read *Weekly Report, Congress and the Nation* has become a highly respected, authoritative source of information on executive, legislative, and political activities for the years indicated in each volume's title.

Volume 4 follows the format established for earlier volumes. It contains chapters for each major area of governmental and political activity and interest such as "Politics and National Issues," "Economic Policy," "National Security Policy," "Energy and Environment," "Health, Education and Welfare," etc. Important events relating to these topics are summarized chronologically. Charts, graphs, and background information inserts are placed at appropriate points in the text. An appendix includes such information as key congressional votes, controversial presidential nominations, presidential vetoes, and State of the Union messages. A detailed table of contents and an adequate index provide good access to this wealth of information.

Volume 4 of *Congress and the Nation* is especially noteworthy because of the momentous events that occurred during the years it covers. As the introduction states, "during the four years covered by this book, the Constitution survived the tests of a major White House scandal, a congressional move to impeach the President and the first presidential resignation in United States history. Congress moved to reassert itself in its relations with the executive branch. . . . And, while these events captured national and frequently world attention, the everyday legislative process went on." Certainly, any library that must provide reference services relating to recent American government and political history will want to have *Congress and the Nation, Volume IV* on hand. [R: ARBA 79, p. 258; Choice, May 78, p. 371]   Walter L. Newsome

253. **Congressional Quarterly's Guide to Congress.** 2nd ed. Washington, Congressional Quarterly, 1976. 1v. (various paging). illus. index. $62.00. LC 78-167743. ISBN 0-87187-100-9.

Five years after the initial *Guide to Congress*, the Congressional Quarterly issued this revised, expanded version of their original comprehensive volume. As befits a reference work emanating from the publishers of the *CQ Weekly Report* and the *CQ Almanac*, this new volume provides clear, accurate, disinterested information as to the history, structure, powers, and workings of the Congress. At the same time, it informs the reader as to the basic sources for each topic discussed should further research be necessary.

The primary divisions of the book (each with subchapters) are: "Origins and Development of Congress," "Powers of Congress," "Congressional Procedures," "Housing and Support of Congress," "Congress and the Electorate," "Pressures on Congress," and "Qualifications and Conduct of Members." Given the changes in congressional structure since 1971, when the first edition was published, we can reasonably expect the new guide to cover such things as Watergate and impeachment, war powers legislation, Congress's new budgeting procedures, intelligence agency activities and investigations thereof, new campaign financing legislation, and ethics investigations, and the volume does this. Additionally, it covers reforms and changes in the internal structure of Congress, all of which have ramifications for legislation passing through that body. Rounding out the volume are the appendices, including the texts of the Declaration of Independence, the Articles of Confederation, the Constitution, and essential pre-Constitutional documents. Also discussed are congressional rules, congressional facts, impeachment (including the articles of impeachment against Andrew Johnson and those proposed against Richard Nixon), judicial review, lobbying, and both congressional reform movements of this decade (1970 and 1974). The least useful appendix is the "Biographical Index of Members of Congress, 1789-1976," since it provides only party affiliation, dates of service, birth and death dates, and district represented. However, the fact that all the information is gathered into one volume and that the volume guides the reader to other sources at the end of each chapter makes it almost indispensable as a convenient, authoritative source for anyone seeking to understand the workings of a body of over 500 people whose actions shape our lives. [R: ARBA 77, p. 253; BL, 1 July 77, p. 1675; Choice, May 77, p. 344; WLB, Apr 77, p. 684]

254.   Johnson, Donald Bruce, comp. **National Party Platforms.** Rev. ed. Urbana, University of Illinois Press, 1978. 2v. index. $35.00/set. LC 78-17373. ISBN 0-252-00692-5.

Included in this first revised edition of *National Party Platforms* are copies of the platforms of all major political parties and principal minor parties from 1840-1976. It is sometimes difficult to determine what constitutes a national political party; therefore, in selecting the parties to include in this volume, the compiler has considered the size of any group that purported to be a national party, the relative permanence of the party, and its historical significance. The reprinted platforms are arranged chronologically. A brief discussion of the parties involved, as well as the election returns and electoral count for each candidate, prefaces the chapters. The volumes each include a subject index and index of names. References in the subject index are to page numbers, but also note political party and year, which makes the index even more useful. According to the publishers, only the second volume will be updated in future years, making it unnecessary for purchasers to buy the first volume (platforms through 1956) of later editions.

Ed. note: Libraries owning Johnson's work will want to purchase Edward W. Chester's *Guide to Political Platforms* (Archon Books, 1977. 373p. $20.00), which presents complete analyses of all American political party platforms from 1832 through 1976. Each election is analyzed in terms of party platforms, resulting in a text that reveals ideological differences, significant shifts in party tradition, and campaign methods. The bibliographical section is very good, and annotations are provided for most of the items. A well-written and factual companion to *National Party Platforms.* [R: ARBA 79, p. 256; Choice, May 79, p. 445; LJ, 1 Apr 79, p. 816; RQ, Summer 79, p. 404]   Roberta R. Palen

255.   **National Party Conventions 1831-1976.** Washington, Congressional Quarterly, 1979. 227p. illus. index. $6.95pa. LC 79-20005. ISBN 0-87187-189-0.

Congressional Quarterly's new edition of its highly praised *National Party Conventions* is little more than a reprinting of the first edition (1976), updated to include information on the 1976 conventions and candidates. Nonetheless, a fascinating and very readable blend of history and statistics is presented here. Political selection prior to the introduction of conventions (1789-1828) is briefly discussed, followed by an essay on "The National Nominating Convention" and a concise list of convention highlights from 1831 (a gathering of the Anti-Masonic Party) to 1976. The longest and most interesting section of the book is the Convention Chronology. A brief narrative account of each convention is given, with excerpts from the party platforms. Small photos of the major presidential candidates are included. Most years rate about three pages of analysis, though recent conventions (1960-1976) are examined in greater detail (for example, nine pages are devoted to the 1976 conventions).

Other useful sections include: the results of key convention ballots (the presidential voting as well as any other issues vital to the convention); historical profiles of the political parties; a listing of the presidential and vice-presidential nominees for all major and minor parties; a biographical directory of those candidates receiving electoral votes; and a list of presidents and vice-presidents of the United States, from Washington through Carter. Bibliographies are appended to the narrative sections of the book, and these have been updated to include recently published books and articles. There is also a detailed index.

This is an essential purchase for all libraries lacking the first edition. For those libraries with the 1831-1972 compilation, the price of this new edition is so reasonable that it should be given serious consideration (thereby allowing the earlier volume to be switched from reference into the general library collection). [R: ARBA 80, p. 227]   Thomas A. Karel

256. Schlesinger, Arthur M., Jr., ed. **History of American Presidential Elections, 1789-1968.** New York, published in association with Chelsea House by McGraw-Hill, 1971. 4v. bibliog. index. $175.00/set. LC 70-139269. ISBN 0-07-079786-2.

Forty-five eminent scholars undertake to describe and analyze the circumstances and effects of all presidential elections held in the United States from 1789 through 1968. The format for the coverage of each election is essentially the same: an original descriptive and analytical essay followed by a selection of significant documents relating to the election. The documents have been selected to illustrate the key issues or events of the elections. Among items typically included are party platforms, acceptance speeches or other public statements, and a breakdown of electoral and popular voting results.

The essays are readable and historically accurate synopses of the events before, during, and after each election. When considered as a whole, they provide a rather impressive history of American presidential politics. Reference access to information about each election is facilitated by a good subject index. This publication is useful for gaining rather quickly the flavor and substance of any presidential election. [R: ARBA 72, p. 132; Choice, Feb 72, p. 1638; LJ, 15 Sept 71, p. 2757; LJ, 15 Apr 72, p. 1386]   Gary R. Purcell

STATE GOVERNMENT

257. Glashan, Roy R., comp. **American Governors and Gubernatorial Elections, 1775-1978.** Westport, CT, Meckler Books, a division of Microform Review, 1979. 370p. bibliog. $45.00. LC 79-15021. ISBN 0-930466-17-9.

American Governors and Gubernatorial Elections, 1775-1978 is an updated edition of a work that first appeared in 1975. Arranged alphabetically by name of state, the book contains brief biographical data on governors of states and territories, including date of birth, birth place, residence, occupation, party affiliation, date and age at death, and date and age on assuming office. A second set of tables for each state includes election statistics by party for all gubernatorial elections. Rather than relying heavily upon state manuals, Glashan has compiled the data from a wide variety of standard primary and secondary sources; an extensive bibliography lists both general works and references for each state.

An additional feature of the book is the inclusion of excerpts from the speeches and writings of the governors. The quotations are interspersed with the tables and identified in a separate listing of sources. Unfortunately, there is no author or subject index to the material, so that what might have proved a useful addition seems instead an afterthought.

This book is the only recent one-volume reference work on the subject. It updates Gateley's *Register of the Governors of the States of the United States of America*, covering the period 1776-1974, and Solomon's *The Governors of the States*, covering the period 1900-1974. An alternative source is Kallenbach and Kallenbach, *American State Governors 1776-1976* (Oceana). The Kallenbachs' book is a three-volume set that includes election statistics and biographical sketches, although the latter are in narrative rather than tabular format. [R: ARBA 80, p. 235]   Jane A. Benson

LOCAL GOVERNMENT

258. **Municipal Government Reference Sources: Publications and Collections.** Ed. for the American Library Association Government Documents Round Table by Peter Hernon, and others. New York, R. R. Bowker, 1978. 341p. index. $21.75. LC 78-17619. ISBN 0-8352-1003-0.

This is a cooperative effort of the Task Force on Local Documents of the American Library Association's Government Documents Round Table to identify municipal reference sources on a large scale. Organized by state, and within states, alphabetically by city, this guide includes over 2,000 publications from 167 cities with populations of over 100,000. Several municipal collections national in scope appear in the first section, "United States." In most cases, a state section begins with general publications, which cover several cities. Thereafter, each city is usually divided into two categories: "Publications" and "Collections." An overview of a city's publications is given where information is available. Publications listed may be published by the city government, regional councils of government, chambers of commerce, or other private groups. Local newspaper indexes are noted, based on the assumption that some of the best information on municipal activities is reported in local newspapers. The following types of sources were to be emphasized: checklists and bibliographies listing city publications, manuals and handbooks, directories, and the municipal code if it had a directory of city officials, an organization chart, or other reference material. Basic bibliographic information is given for each publication, as is an annotation in most cases. The "Collections" section for each city identifies libraries or public agencies with municipal collections. Citations to data bases available for public access appear under the respective city. A cross-reference list from county name to city is included as an appendix to the book. Entries are indexed by subject.

This book will be very valuable to general reference departments and to government documents departments, not only as a reference book for identifying sources of data, but as an acquisitions tool to develop a solid collection of current information on municipalities. The only drawback is the missing data from 33 cities with populations over 100,000 due to difficulty in locating individuals to collect the data. [R: ARBA 79, p. 264; Choice, Mar 79, p. 56; C&RL, Jan 79, p. 48; LJ, 15 Sept 78, p. 1730; WLB, Nov 78, p. 282]   Louise Stwalley

BIOGRAPHY

259. **Biographical Directory of the United States Executive Branch, 1774-1977.** Robert Sobel, ed.-in-chief. 2nd rev. ed. Westport, CT, Greenwood Press, 1977. 503p. index. $29.95. LC 77-84. ISBN 0-8371-9527-6.

The first edition of this work, published in 1971, provided some 500 biographical sketches of presidents and vice-presidents of the United States, and presidents of the Continental Congress, covering the period 1774 up to Nixon's second administration. Included in the second edition are 516 career biographies for the period 1774 through the Carter administration's original appointments; among these are some 50 new or revised sketches. This volume is similar in format to the *Biographical Directory of the American Congress, 1774-1971* and was apparently designed to complement and supplement this work.

The biographical sketches are arranged alphabetically by biographees' surnames and include birth and death dates, religious affiliation, and information on career and service before and after election or appointment to office. Many of the sketches also supply information on the biographee's publications, memberships in organizations, and major accomplishments associated with his or her political career. References to primary and secondary works are cited in brief bibliographies at the end of each sketch. The indexes (125 pages) include a list of presidential administrations and separate sections on presidents, vice-presidents, and cabinet officers. [R: ARBA 78, p. 237; BL, 1 Apr 78, p. 1275; Choice, Apr 78, p. 194; WLB, Dec 77, p. 344]

COMMUNISM

260. Kernig, C. D., ed. **Marxism, Communism and Western Society: A Comparative Encyclopedia.** New York, Herder and Herder; distr., New York, McGraw-Hill, 1973. 8v. $40.00/v.; $320.00/set. LC 79-176368. ISBN 0-07-073526-3(set).

This work attempts a comparative analysis between Western thought and that of Marxism and communism in various forms. Redefining the differences between communist and non-communist concepts and doctrines is the essential purpose of the more than 400 articles, written by eminent scholars, covering the humanities, sciences, and social sciences.

For the most part, articles have identical structure, consisting of three parts: Western aspects, Soviet and Marxist aspects, and a critical comparison. Cross references to related material are included within the articles, except for those that are brief, in which case the cross references are appended to the articles. At the end of each article, the author provides a rather comprehensive bibliography, international in scope. Titles in Western languages are not translated, but Russian titles and those of other less familiar languages are transliterated, followed by English translation. There is no general index, but there is a list of "Contents and Cross-References" at the beginning of each volume and an Index of Articles is to appear at the end of volume 8.

Individuals of major importance rate extensive biographical articles, whereas those of somewhat lesser significance are an integral part of articles about the ideas and movements with which they were associated.

This unique encyclopedia conforms to the highest standards of scholarly research in its successful non-partisan attempt to present and compare interpretations of communist and non-communist thought spanning the spectrum of knowledge. It is one of the most important works of reference undertaken in recent years by a team of competent scholars. [R: ARBA 73, p. 208; Choice, Mar 73, p. 62; LJ, 1 May 73, p. 1471; WLB, Feb 73, p. 517]

Bohdan S. Wynar

261. Lazitch, Branko, in collaboration with Milorad M. Drachkovitch. **Biographical Dictionary of the Comintern.** Stanford, CA, Hoover Institution Press, 1973. 458p. (Hoover Institution Publications, No. 121). $25.00(microfilm). LC 72-187265. ISBN 0-8179-1211-8.

The Communist International (1919-1943) played an important role in the communist movement until its liquidation by Stalin. The present work, the only biographical dictionary of its leaders, contains 716 biographical sketches of members of the executive committee, speakers at the Comintern congresses, important delegates to congresses, and other members of the Comintern apparatus. The execution of a biographical dictionary of this scope and magnitude required the use of many sources; in general, the work seems to be remarkably well balanced.

The few shortcomings noted are minor. For example, in the article on Mykola Skrypnyk (probably not Nikolai Skrypnik, since this prominent Ukrainian Communist seldom used the Russian spelling of his name), one might expect to find more than the simple statement that he committed suicide in July 1933. An explanation of why he committed suicide is in order. Another example: although Shumsky's fate is rather well known, the author states that in 1927 "he completely disappeared, most probably a victim of political police." These minor points certainly do not detract from the excellence of this work. Among other things, this dictionary helps to decode some 350 pseudonyms used by Comintern leaders in their activities. It should be noted that the volume is out of print but available on microfilm for $25.00. [R: ARBA 74, p. 162; BL, 15 July 74, p. 1214; Choice, Feb 74, p. 1847]

Bohdan S. Wynar

262. Seidman, Joel, ed. **Communism in the United States: A Bibliography.** Ithaca, NY, Cornell University Press, 1969. 526p. index. $27.50. LC 69-12427. ISBN 0-8014-0514-9.

An earlier work, *Bibliography on the Communist Problem in the United States* (Fund of the Republic, 1955), contains some 5,000 books, pamphlets, and magazine articles on the subject. Seidman's comprehensive bibliography updates this work, and for materials listed in the older work provides more descriptive annotations. All entries are arranged in a single alphabet, with a detailed subject index at the end of the volume. This is by far the most comprehensive and well-selected bibliography on this subject, and hopefully it can be used as a helpful model for other scholarly works of this nature. [R: ARBA 71, p. 146; Choice, Apr 70, p. 219; C&RL, July 70, p. 277; LJ, 15 Feb 70, p. 652]   Bohdan S. Wynar

263. Sworakowski, Witold S., ed. **World Communism: A Handbook 1918-1965.** Stanford, CA, Hoover Institution Press, 1973. 576p. index. $25.00. LC 70-149798. ISBN 0-8179-1081-3.

Since 1967 the Hoover Institution has published, on an annual basis, the well-known *Yearbook on International Communist Affairs*, probably the most authoritative one-volume work on the subject. The present handbook offers a more concise treatment of communist affairs from 1918 to 1965.

Organized alphabetically by country, it contains an article on each of the 116 countries in which a communist party was active. Most of the articles include a brief history, plus information on organization and membership, party press organs and records, and congresses; each also has a selective bibliography. These short encyclopedic essays are written by a number of well-known specialists in their respective areas—e.g., John Reshetar, Jr. (Ukraine and the Soviet Union), Walter Kendall (Great Britain), Theodore Draper (Cuba), etc. Witold Sworakowski is Professor Emeritus of Stanford University and for many years served as director of the Hoover Institution Library. Thanks to him and to the skillfully selected contributors, this handbook is one of the best one-stop sources on the subject. [R: ARBA 74, p. 163; BL, 15 Jan 74, p. 501; Choice, Feb 74, p. 1851]   Bohdan S. Wynar

FASCISM

264. Laqueur, Walter, ed. **Fascism: A Reader's Guide; Analysis, Interpretations, Bibliography.** Berkeley, University of California Press, 1976. 500p. illus. index. $27.50; $6.95pa. LC 75-13158. ISBN 0-520-03033-8; 0-520-03642-5pa.

Laqueur's *Dictionary of Politics* (Free Press, 1974. 565p.) must be known to most reference librarians and students of political science. It is a very competent work on the topic. His volume on fascism is equally sound. Prepared in collaboration with a dozen well-known scholars, it offers an interpretive guide to all aspects of this political movement—political, social, economic, and even intellectual. The six main parts cover the following topics: historical perspective; Italy and Germany; local fascisms; ideology; fascism and the economy; and interpretations. The sources listed in the notes at the end of each essay will provide guidance for further research. This comprehensive study should be on the shelves of most libraries. [R: ARBA 77, p. 246; BL, 1 Apr 77, p. 1128; LJ, 1 Oct 76, p. 2070]

INTERNATIONAL RELATIONS

265. Grenville, John Ashley Soames. **The Major International Treaties 1914-1973: A History and Guide with Texts.** New York, Stein & Day, 1974. 575p. illus. maps. bibliog. index. $25.00. LC 75-163352. ISBN 0-8128-1654-4.

The author states his intention to provide a "usable collection of such [international] treaties in one volume . . . for students and the general reader concerned with international affairs," and he expresses the hope that this work will fill a gap in the literature where only specialized collections can so far be found. His material is organized both chronologically and regionally; edited texts of the treaties are preceded by historical summaries of the events that led up to them, and, where it was deemed pertinent, partial texts of letters and statements of governments or government officials have also been included. The section on "source references" at the end of the book provides information as to where one may locate the full texts of the various treaties described. There is a detailed subject index.

The author has defined the term "international treaty" broadly, and has used the widest possible latitude in including materials. The *Atlantic Charter*, primarily a declaration of principles, has been included, as has the *Charter of the Organization of American States.*

While the introduction provides a definition of the term and an explanation of the form, structure, and manner of drafting treaties, it also includes a section on treaty vocabulary. Lifting this section out and replacing it with a longer glossary of terms as one of the appendixes would make the work more useful for the general reader and the beginning student. We are given an explanation of such terms as "casus foederis" and "procès-verbal," but it would also be useful to have explanations of such terms as "protocol," "minute," "joint declaration," "statute," and "charter" in the context of international treaties.

All aspects of the international scene have been covered, and it is to be hoped that this extremely useful work will be followed by supplements. [R: ARBA 75, p. 244; Choice, Nov 74, p. 1284; LJ, 15 Feb 74, p. 473; LJ, 15 Apr 75, p. 733]   Margaret Anderson

266. Hajnal, Peter I. **Guide to United Nations Organization, Documentation, & Publishing for Students, Researchers, Librarians.** Dobbs Ferry, NY, Oceana Publications, 1978. 450p. bibliog. index. $35.00. LC 78-2223. ISBN 0-379-20257-8.

This guide is intended to aid researchers, students, librarians, and others who need to know about United Nations activities and use United Nations publications. It is a much-needed successor to Brimmer's *Guide to the Use of United Nations Documents* (1962). The first section describes the structure, organization, functions, and evolution of the United Nations and its relation to other organizations. This is followed by an explanation of UN publications and other documentation, and a practical guide to their use, acquisition, and organization. A selected and annotated bibliography of primary and secondary literature as well as the texts of selected important UN documents are also included. Finally, there is a brief survey of international intergovernmental organizations related to the UN. The index to the bibliography is buried in the middle of the volume, following the bibliography; and the general index is rather short and must be used in conjunction with the table of contents and the index to the bibliography. The table of contents entry for the general index has been inserted in the wrong sequence, and no page reference is given for it. The whole volume would have been much easier to read if the publisher had reduced the size of the type font, but this will prove to be a useful reference book and is a valuable addition to the field. [R: ARBA 79, p. 273; BL, 1 May 79, p. 1389; Choice, Jan 79, p. 1498; LJ, Aug 78, p. 1496; RQ, Winter 78, p. 204] Gail M. Nichols

267. Plano, Jack C., and Roy Olton. **The International Relations Dictionary.** New York, Holt, 1969. 337p. LC 69-17657.

Topics are arranged within 12 subject matter chapters; thus, terms relating to regional arrangements like NATO or the Arab League can be found in the chapter titled "International Organizations: The United Nations and Regional Organizations." In addition, the index provides an alphabetical approach.

The terms and concepts are clearly defined in simple language suitable for undergraduate students. Most entries offer little historical background, instead emphasizing contemporary meanings. In some cases such an approach has its limitations, such as the entry for "Wars of National Liberation." According to this dictionary the term is synonymous with a recent communist tactical doctrine calling for anti-Western or anti-capitalistic uprisings in the developing countries. Historically speaking, such an interpretation is not complete, since the term was widely used in political literature of the nineteenth century and later by both Lenin and Stalin. Unlike *Dictionary of the Social Sciences*, this dictionary does not provide references to pertinent literature; nevertheless, it will be useful for beginning students of international relations as a manageable starting point. Its distillation of a large spectrum of material is valuable. [R: ARBA 70, p. 92; LJ, 15 Apr 70, p. 1441; RQ, Spring 70, p. 279]

8 LAW

GENERAL WORKS

268. **Congressional Quarterly's Guide to the U.S. Supreme Court.** Elder Witt, ed. Washington, Congressional Quarterly, 1979. 1022p. illus. index. $65.00. LC 79-20210. ISBN 0-87187-184-X.

Congressional Quarterly's Guide is an encyclopedic treatment of the high court's origins, procedures, members, and decisions. While other works, including the more scholarly, multivolume *History of the Supreme Court of the United States* (Paul Freund, gen. ed. New York: Macmillan, 1971-), are already available, this single-volume reference tool can be distinguished because of its comprehensive coverage of both historical and current matter, its simple style, and its objectivity.

The *Guide* first provides a brief history of the origins and development of the Supreme Court. The editors next examine the Supreme Court's constitutional powers in relationship to those powers of Congress, the presidency, the states, and other lower federal courts. Another section scrutinizes the Court's role in defining individual rights and freedoms, with many references to the Constitution and landmark Court decisions. The *Guide* also contains biographies and pictures of all the justices who have served on the Court through mid-1979, and another important section summarizes in chronological order the Court's key decisions from 1790-1979. More thorough discussion of these decisions is contained in other parts of the *Guide* and can be located by using the case index, which provides complete legal citations. Footnotes and selected bibliographies provide bases for further, more intensive research, while the appendix contains the Declaration of Independence, the Articles of Confederation, the Constitution, and other useful judicial material. [R: ARBA 80, p. 242] Susan Beverly Kuklin

BIBLIOGRAPHIES

269. Fisher, Mary L., ed. **Guide to State Legislative Materials.** Littleton, CO, published for the American Association of Law Libraries by Fred B. Rothman, 1979. 1v. (unpaged). (AALL Publication Series, No. 15). $28.50(looseleaf). LC 79-21870. ISBN 0-8377-0113-9.

This compendium provides valuable information on the publication and availability of state legislative and selected administrative materials. The kinds of state materials examined include bills, hearings, debates, reports, journals and proceedings, slip laws, session laws, attorney general opinions, administrative regulations, and other state documents. In most cases, the editor obtained her information by circulating questionnaires to state libraries across the United States. Therefore, completeness of the format varies from state to state. The basic format of the guide is similar to a checklist; no textual analysis or commentary is provided, except in a brief notations section following some of the states. Instead, short statements indicate the availability, format, frequency of issue, cost, etc., of the particular state materials surveyed. Addresses and telephone numbers are also provided for major government agencies and some commercial publishers that deal with state legislative publications. The looseleaf binding will allow for corrections and supplementation.

No other comprehensive, state-by-state compilation exists. The *Guide* provides a quick way to access needed reference information and reduces considerably the necessity of scanning individual state publications such as legislative research manuals or blue books in order to find the answer to ready reference questions. This should be a most welcome addition to general reference, documents, and law collections.   Susan Beverly Kuklin

270. Johnson, Nancy P., comp. **Sources of Compiled Legislative Histories: A Bibliography of Government Documents, Periodical Articles, and Books, 1st Congress—94th Congress.** Littleton, CO, published for the American Association of Law Libraries by Fred B. Rothman, 1979. 1v. (various paging). (AALL Publication Series, No. 14). $22.50(looseleaf). LC 79-51869. ISBN 0-8377-0112-0.

This volume, number 14 in the American Association of Law Libraries series, is an excellent presentation of the bibliographic information for the available compiled legislative histories of federal statutes. These legislative histories have long been viewed by legal researchers as one of the most difficult of bibliographic enterprises. They are used with increasing frequency by the courts, however, as guides to interpreting complex and ambiguous law and are thus becoming persistent challenges for researchers. Locating a previously compiled history thus can save significant time and travail for the researcher. The information here is arranged both by official citation of the statute and by publisher, and brings together for the first time in one place access to all previously compiled legislative histories. This is a most welcome addition to the literature. The AALL Publication Series has been a consistent source of excellent bibliographic tools, and in this looseleaf volume, Ms. Johnson continues the tradition. It is a recommended purchase for any academic, law, or public library where legislative research is being done. One hopes that the looseleaf format means that the volume will be supplemented.

Robert C. Berring, Jr.

DICTIONARIES

271. Black, Henry Campbell. **Black's Law Dictionary: Definitions of the Terms and Phrases of American and English Jurisprudence, Ancient and Modern.** Joseph R. Nolan, and M. J. Connolly, contributing authors. 5th ed. St. Paul, MN, West Publishing, 1979. 1511p. $16.95; $35.00/deluxe ed. LC 79-12547. ISBN 0-8299-2041-2; 0-8299-2045-5(deluxe).

Black's has long been the standard law dictionary for ready reference. The fifth edition is the first revision since 1968 and includes over 10,000 new or revised entries. All areas of the law are covered: taxes, accounting, commercial transactions, civil procedure, criminal procedure, federal court rules, evidence, finance, insurance, labor relations, estate planning, federal agencies, restatements of the law, and uniform and model laws.

More than simple definitions are provided by *Black's*. In instances where a term has been affected by legislation, court rules, or court decisions, these developments are reflected, and appropriate citations are supplied. Case citations have been updated whenever possible. Internal cross references lead to related terms. Several useful appendices appear in the volume: a table of abbreviations; the U.S. Constitution; a time chart of the members of the U.S. Supreme Court; an organizational chart of the U.S. government; and a table of British regnal years (listed improperly in the table of contents as a second table of abbreviations). Both the standard and deluxe editions of *Black's* are thumb-indexed; the deluxe edition has a padded leather cover stamped in gold. Most libraries will want to acquire this standard reference tool.

Ed. note: Lawrence Deems Egbert's *Multilingual Law Dictionary* (Oceana, 1978. 551p. $50.00; $37.00pa.) is an excellent listing of equivalent legal terms in English, French, German, and Spanish in a vertical list format. [R: ARBA 80, p. 245]   Janet H. Littlefield

272.   Gamboa, Melquiades J. **A Dictionary of International Law and Diplomacy.** Quezon City, Philippines, Central Lawbook Publishing Co.; distr., Dobbs Ferry, NY, Oceana, 1974. 351p. $18.00. LC 73-20396. ISBN 0-379-00219-1.

The value of adequate dictionaries in any scholarly field is readily apparent. As Oliver Wendell Holmes noted in the 1925 Supreme Court decision, *Towne v. Eisner*, "A word is not a crystal, transparent and unchanged, it is the skin of a living thought and may vary greatly in color and content according to the circumstances in which it is used." The dictionary will, however, help to establish some degree of uniformity in the application of words. In few scholarly areas is this need more evident than in international law and international relations.

Gamboa, a former ambassador for the Philippines to Great Britain, India, Sweden, Norway, Denmark, and the United Nations, as well as professor of law at the University of the Philippines, is admirably well qualified to correct this situation. The dictionary is, in effect, a revision of the author's earlier work, *Elements of Diplomatic and Consular Practice: A Glossary.* There are three appendixes: the Charter of the United Nations, the statutory base of the International Court of Justice, and the Vienna Convention on the Law of Treaties. [R: ARBA 75, p. 253]   Jerry E. Stephens

SOURCES AND DOCUMENTS

273.   Schwartz, Bernard. **The Bill of Rights: A Documentary History.** New York, Chelsea House in association with McGraw-Hill, 1971. 2v. index. $75.00. LC 71-150209. ISBN 0-07-079613-0.

Professor Bernard Schwartz contends that it is impossible to study the American Bill of Rights in a vacuum. A thorough knowledge of the English and American precedents which shaped the thinking of James Madison and his colleagues is essential. Consequently Schwartz has attempted to present the extensive history of the Bill of Rights in documentary form. His choice of material is naturally subjective, but Schwartz, a distinguished professor of law and author of many works in legal history, is qualified to make the choice. The documents are arranged chronologically in the following categories: English antecedents since the Magna Carta; the colonial period; the revolutionary declarations and constitutions; developments under the Articles of Confederation; the state ratifying conventions; the legislative history of the federal Bill of Rights; and the ratification by the states. Each of the divisions is preceded by a brief but helpful introduction, as are most of the documents themselves. These brief explanations, placing the sources in historical perspective, are invaluable for the student, and the excellent index makes individual items easy to find.

Professor Schwartz has provided a fine reference tool for the study of constitutional, legal, and general American history. This work is absolutely essential for all public, school, and college libraries, an invaluable reference aid for all students of history. [R: ARBA 72, p. 179; Choice, Apr 72, p. 276; LJ, 1 Feb 72, p. 498]   Nancy G. Boles

274.   Schwartz, Bernard et al., ed. **Statutory History of the United States.** New York, Chelsea House in association with McGraw-Hill, 1970. 4v. in 3. index. $80.00(v.1); $50.00(v.2); $50.00(v.3); $135.00/set. LC 79-78410. ISBN 0-07-055681-4(v.1); 0-07-055682-2(v.2); 0-07-055683-0(v.3).

This work constitutes a comprehensive survey of the statutory history of the United States in three areas: *Civil Rights* (two volumes), *Labor Relations*, and *Income Security.* The first two volumes cover the history of civil rights legislation from the ratification of the Thirteenth Amendment to the Constitution through the Civil Rights Act of 1968. Volume I includes all constitutional amendments and enactments through the Repeal Act of 1894;

volume II deals with those laws which have been passed since 1900. Edited legislative source material for each enactment considered is included.

The study of labor relations contains the important federal statutes relative to labor organization dating from the enactment of the Railway Labor Act in 1926 through the Landrum Griffin Act of 1959. Presidential messages, committee reports, excerpts from the debates on the floor of the Congress, and pertinent court decisions are included, in addition to reproductions of the statutes themselves. Each statutory discussion is preceded by editorial commentary.

The final volume in this series concentrates in depth on the federal statutes pertaining to income security, defined as "cash benefits." The Social Security Act and its numerous amendments receive major consideration in this chronological presentation, which includes an introductory survey of the pre-New Deal developments.

This work is a valuable source of basic legislative background material, used either as a complete set or as separate volumes. [R: ARBA 72, p. 180; WLB, May 71, p. 883]

Helen M. Burns

BIOGRAPHY

275.   Friedman, Leon, ed. **The Justices of the United States Supreme Court, Their Lives and Major Opinions: Volume V, The Burger Court, 1969-1978.** New York, Chelsea House Publishers in association with R. R. Bowker, 1978. 510p. index. $49.00. LC 69-13699. ISBN 0-8352-0141-3.

After a 10-year hiatus, a fifth volume has been added to *The Justices of the United States Supreme Court, 1789-1969, Their Lives and Major Opinions.* Spanning 1969-1978, the added volume does more than chart the continuing careers of Justices Stewart, White, and Brennan. It provides an opportunity for a more deep evaluation of Chief Justice Warren Burger and Justice Thurgood Marshall than was possible 10 years ago when they were relatively new to the Supreme Court. The resignations of Justices Douglas, Harlan, and Black during this period made it possible for this volume to summarize their work, and to bid farewell to the era of the Warren Court. The new direction of the Burger Court may be detected most strongly from the section on Chief Justice Burger. However, the pieces on the Nixon and Ford appointees to the Court, Blackmun, Powell, Rehnquist, and Stevens, are enlightening in this regard also. The format remains the same as in earlier volumes. Pieces on particular justices are written by different authors, most of whom are professors of law or practicing attorneys. The writing styles differ, and so does the content, to some degree. Each piece is structured around a section devoted to personal and professional biographical information, and a section of representative opinions. It is a good combination for a reader anxious to know individual contributions of justices to constitutional development.

Although an attempt is made to be even-handed in evaluating each justice, the authors are more critical of the newer justices and the chief justice. Connections between the earlier volumes and this one are not consistently made. There are excellent references from the new section on Douglas to the earlier section, but many pages are wasted in the new piece on Marshall, repeating biographical information contained in the earlier volume. The index is for the most part quite good; it links justices with topics and also lists major topics handled by each justice separately. Each case is also indexed by name of plaintiff. Additional biographical references at the end of each article allow readers the option of pursuing research beyond the scope of this work.

This volume can stand alone, but it really should be considered an addition to the earlier four-volume set. Any general reference collection would benefit from this handy, concise source of biographical information for justices of the Supreme Court. [R: ARBA 80, p. 256]

Barbara Van Deventer

276. **Who's Who in American Law.** 2nd ed. Chicago, Marquis Who's Who, 1979. 1007p. $57.50. LC 77-79896. ISBN 0-8379-3502-4.

This second edition provides biographical information on about 34,000 lawyers, judges, and educators. The first edition of this directory, published in 1977, offered similar information on only 18,000 biographees. The greatly increased number of biographees makes this edition of the directory all the more valuable. Included in both editions are United States attorneys, key members of bar associations, general counsel to large U.S. corporations, and partners in major law firms. Many judges from federal, state, and local courts are also listed, as are deans and prominent professors from leading law schools. Generally, the same high quality of the first edition is maintained in the second edition. Data such as name, vital statistics, education, career history, writings, address, and office phone are provided. [R: LJ, 1 Mar 80, p. 602]   Susan Beverly Kuklin

9 GEOGRAPHY

ATLASES

WORLD

277. **The Earth and Man: A Rand McNally World Atlas.** Chicago, Rand McNally, 1972. 439p. illus. (col.). maps. index. $35.00. LC 70-654432. ISBN 0-528-83050-3.

This handsome atlas is divided into three main parts. The first section is a potpourri of information, describing the earth in space, its structure, life on earth, resources, and man on earth. The colorful pictures of man's life on earth are beautifully executed and would be of interest to anyone. But no matter how attractive this part of the publication is, a map librarian might question the necessity of including this type of information in an atlas. A good handbook or encyclopedia can provide this information; an atlas should include maps and closely related information.

The second part consists of 150 pages of maps. It is a pleasure to look up information on these maps; they are vivid, uncluttered and easy to read. The clear printing makes it easy to find rivers, mountains, roads, railroads, localities, and other geographical information. One objectionable feature, however, is that different scales are used for various states and regions of the same continent.

Another poor feature is the way the atlas is indexed. The subject index, while well developed concerning cities and small localities, is very difficult to use to find information on a country. For instance, if someone tries to find a map of Austria, he cannot find "Austria" in the table of contents because it is included in the entry: Europe—Central Europe. The subject index entry for Austria directs the user to the map of Europe, where the map of Austria is rather small, instead of giving the page number of the previously mentioned map of Central Europe, where the map of Austria is quite adequate. Also, the "Index Map" provided is not very clear and is hidden on pages 146-47.

The third part of the atlas deals with geographical facts, figures, and information about the world and the United States. This kind of information is welcome in any atlas.

Since the format is not too large, the *Atlas* is easy to handle. The binding is sturdy and the paper is fine. [R: ARBA 73, p. 220; LJ, 1 Dec 72, p. 3890]   Louis Kiraldi

278. Espenshade, Edward B., Jr., ed. **Goode's World Atlas.** Joel L. Morrison, associate ed. 15th ed. Chicago, Rand McNally, 1978. 372p. illus. (col.) maps. index. $13.95; $10.95pa. LC 73-21108. ISBN 0-528-83061-9; 0-528-63004-0pa.

Goode's World Atlas was specifically designed to provide the kind of general and thematic maps, map content, and other current data required by students in economics, geography, and other related courses. Most college and university libraries will probably want to have recent editions of the best school atlases currently in print, and this volume continues the established tradition of being the leading American school atlas and much more. Rand McNally's policy of producing new editions to respond to the need for contemporary material and to keep abreast of cartographic innovation makes this atlas compare most favorably with all of the available school atlases.

Edward Espenshade, Jr. (Northwestern University) and Joel L. Morrison (University of Wisconsin) have made every effort to assemble the latest and most authentic source material to produce these clear, easily read maps and text. Each section now has a separate introduction with a chart of map symbols. The first is a physical, political, and economic atlas with worldwide information. The United States metropolitan area section of the fourteenth edition has been upgraded into a new 19-page section of maps of worldwide urbanized areas. A separate index to this section has been placed at the back just prior to the general index, but this placement may cause some initial confusion with new users.

The major portion of the atlas, the regional section, contains maps arranged sequentially by continent and regions within the continents—North and South America, Europe, Asia, Australia, Africa, and the ocean floor. In this fifteenth edition, the editors have added two new larger scale maps of Western and Central Africa. With all of the current interest in Southern Africa, it is unfortunate that a new map of this area was not included. Additions or improvements include five world thematic maps. A cartogram shows each country at a size proportional to population. A new two-page soil groups map has been added to reflect advances in soils classification. This map is considerably more complex than the older map and has additional text to guide the user. There are also new manufacturing, steel production, and natural and man-made fibers maps. The latter map, long overdue, reflects changes in textiles technology. For depicting land and ocean transportation, a new projection (the Robinson Projection, named in honor of Arthur H. Robinson of Wisconsin) has been introduced as a refreshing change to replace the old ocean and surface transportation maps. The last section contains the geographic tables, indexes, glossary of foreign and geographical terms, and pronouncing index. Unfortunately, the main index has been dropped from 35,000 to 32,000 entries. A conversion table has been added as a new feature.

The introduction has been tightened up and shortened, but the invaluable explanation of map projections has been maintained. This and the naming of projections used on each full-page map are important indications that this remains a quality cartographic product. Accurate depiction of an area on the surface of the earth requires that the projection vary from map to map and that the "right" projection be used for a particular country, continent, or region. Sources are indicated for the data and those maps that did not originate with the publisher. The *Atlas* retains the beautifully executed maps of Erwin Raisz and A. W. Küchler, and this edition contains an expanded and improved language map of Europe by Bogdon Zaborski, one of the other distinguished cooperating experts. The printing and typography have been improved; this book is designed for extensive use and is sturdily bound in impregnated cloth or "imitation leather." The fifteenth edition of *Goode's World Atlas* continues the original editor's convention of cartographic excellence and is recommended as an important initial purchase for a library's reference or geographic reference collection. [R: ARBA 79, p. 288]   Edward J. Hall, Jr.

279. **Hammond Citation World Atlas.** Maplewood, NJ, Hammond, 1978. 352p. illus. (part col.). maps. index. $14.95; $12.95pa. LC 78-16611. ISBN 0-8437-1233-3; 0-8437-1232-5pa.

Consistent with the Hammond style, this atlas has large detailed political maps without roads or railroads and smaller separate maps for topography and for agriculture, industry, and natural resources. Each continent is introduced by maps for population distribution, vegetation, temperature, rainfall, and topography, and historical maps appear appropriately throughout the atlas. Population and geographical features are listed adjacent to the maps. All national flags are illustrated, and each country has listed its area, population, capital, largest city, highest point, monetary unit, major languages, and major religions. The index lists places and geographical features. The strength of this atlas is in the clear political divisions indicated for all countries, including internal political subdivisions.

An augmented version of this atlas, the *Hammond Medallion World Atlas* (1977, $39.95), incorporates additional material in the form of over 600 well-executed maps which provide more physical, political, and thematic data on every nation and each state within the United States. This expanded work is a superior general atlas that provides easy access to basic geographical, demographic, and historical information.

Another in the Hammond series, the *Hammond Ambassador World Atlas* (1977, $24.95), contains some 320 pages of full-color maps, 40% of which are devoted to the United States. Included are insets indicating generalized topography, dominant land use, and major mineral occurrences. Other entry data provided are administrative designations, population totals, and ZIP codes for U.S. communities. Appendixes contain map projections and foreign geographical terminology. Textual material is minimal; however, marginal information listing areal size, total population, capital, highest point, monetary unit, major language(s), and principal religion is included with maps of each nation. The *Hammond International World Atlas* (1977, $10.95) is also an excellent reference work. The emphasis here is on regions outside the United States, arranged by continent. [R: ARBA 80, p. 258]

Lawrence E. Spellman
Lee Steinberg

280. **The New Oxford Atlas.** Prepared by the Cartographic Department. rev. ed. New York, Oxford University Press, 1978. 202p. illus. (col.). maps. index. $24.00. ISBN 0-19-211572-3.

This is a revised edition of the *New Oxford Atlas* first published in 1975, which in turn was a second edition of the *Oxford Atlas*, newly compiled and published in 1951. It includes 80 pages of large-format general reference physical maps of the continents and regions of the world. These are characterized by clarity and accuracy. In addition, it contains 28 pages of special maps: world maps of climate, land use, and population; continental maps of the physical environment; and special detailed maps for the United Kingdom of population, geology, vegetation, climate, and land use. The gazetteer and index includes 50,000 entries. In the category of moderately priced general reference and student atlases, this is a very well established publication. [R: ARBA 80, p. 259; LJ, 1 Jan 79, p. 95]

Chauncy D. Harris

281. **The Rand McNally Atlas of the Oceans.** New York, Rand McNally, 1977. 208p. illus. (part col.). index. $29.95. LC 77-73772. ISBN 0-528-83082-1.

Despite the title, this is much more than an atlas; it is virtually an encyclopedia of the world's oceans. A large format (10¾x14½ inches) provides for double-page spreads that lay flat to reveal beautifully drawn bathymetric maps of each of the oceans and the principal seas (i.e., the North, Mediterranean, Red, and Caribbean). Additional maps of mineral and living resources, and wind and water circulation are also provided. Although the maps are excellent, the interpretive drawings are particularly impressive (e.g., vulcanism along the tectonic plate margins, the successive deltas of the Mississippi River, sulfur mining methods, a cutaway of a stern trawler, deep sea drilling by the *Glomar Challenger*, whales and dolphins, early navigation instruments, and several hundred more). Full-color photographs abound, including many made by satellites, deep sea research vessels, and microphotographic and sonographic techniques. A 15-page section systematically examines life in the sea class by class. Very timely information is included on pollution and power generation. There is an excellent summary of the principal resolutions and the remaining conflicting national interests identified in the 1976 Law of the Sea Conference.

A brief glossary and an extensive index are provided. This is recommended as a key work on an increasingly vital resource. It is a suitable, indeed, highly desirable work for all secondary school, public, and academic libraries. [R: ARBA 78, p. 271; Choice, May 78, p. 379; LJ, 1 Feb 78, p. 355; LJ, 15 Apr 78, p. 818; LJ, 1 May 78, p. 930; WLB, Mar 78, p. 585]

Charles William Conaway

282. **Rand McNally Concise Atlas of the Earth.** New York, Rand McNally, 1976. 240p. illus. (col.). maps. index. $19.95. LC 76-3070.

A geographic reference work, international in scope, with over 130 physical and political maps, all in color. These range up to 13½ inches by 20 inches, and the majority are scaled at 1:3 million (1 inch equals 47 miles) or 1:6 million (1 inch equals 95 miles). Terrain is displayed by shaded relief rather than hypsometric means. Data include major highways, railroads, and canals. Four dozen maps concentrate on the largest metropolitan areas. The gazetteer lists 36,000 natural and man-made features, with map locations based on geographical coordinates to the nearest minute. No text accompanies the maps, but a 42-page prefatory section delineates geological and biological factors influencing man's habitation of Earth and emphasizes his ecological options. Tabular information includes areal extent, population, form of government, capital, and predominant languages spoken for every nation as of January 1976. Summation: the *Atlas* is competent, up to date, and well arranged, incorporating excellent, albeit small-scale, maps. [R: ARBA 77, p. 269; BL, 1 Sept 77, p. 63; WLB, Feb 77, p. 540] Lawrence E. Spellman

283. **The Times Atlas of the World: Comprehensive Edition.** New York, Quadrangle/The New York Times Book Co., 1975. 1v. (various paging). illus. (col.). maps. index. $79.50. LC 75-5875. ISBN 0-8129-0562-8.

A thoroughly revised edition of the standard atlas. The Times of London has been a publisher of atlases since 1895, and this, the fourth *Times Atlas of the World: Comprehensive Edition*, is now in its fifth edition. The comprehensive edition is based on the cartography of the previous five-volume Mid-Century Edition (1955-59, 5v.; the maps in this edition carry the copyright dates 1967 and 1968). The new material in this edition includes sections on the moon and artificial satellites as well as a series of highly detailed thematic maps of the world's food, mineral, and energy resources.

The justification for frequently revised editions is the fact that the world itself and our cartographic understanding of it are changing rapidly. Some of the changes since 1972 are realigned frontiers (particularly in Africa), new settlements, new states. In addition, plans of many more cities have been included. The introductory plates on world physiography and oceanography have been completely revised to record the latest findings of geological science.

Ed. note: The *New York Times Atlas of the World: Concise Edition* ($39.95), published in 1978, includes over 250 full-color maps and map insets; tables indicating map symbols, abbreviations, and geographical comparison; a section of textual material dealing with the human environment, navigation techniques, and outer space; and an index listing cultural as well as major physical features. Both editions (comprehensive and concise) are extremely useful atlases characterized by well-drawn and easily read maps. A sixth edition of the *Comprehensive* was published in 1980, but was unavailable for review at the time of this writing. [R: ARBA 76, p. 277; BL, 15 July 76, p. 1632; Choice, May 76, p. 344; WLB, Apr 76, p. 652] Richard A. Gray

UNITED STATES

284. **Photo-Atlas of the United States: A Complete Photographic Atlas of the U.S.A. Using Satellite Photography.** Pasadena, CA, Ward Ritchie Press, 1975. 127p. illus. (part col.). $7.95pa. LC 75-18099. ISBN 0-0378-04692-6.

The first of its type in commercial publishing, this work contains over 70 duotone and full-color photomaps of the United States obtained variously by Landsat, Skylab, U-2, and RB57 flights. These range up to 12 inches by 15 inches with an approximate scale of 1:1,250,000 (1 inch on the photomap equals 18 miles on the ground), and each covers about

60,000 square miles or the equivalent of the state of Georgia. All are oriented with the top margin at true (i.e., geographic meridional) north.

Annotations identify major administrative boundaries, mountain ranges, drainage systems, and great metropolitan complexes. Each photomap is accompanied by brief marginal notes treating geographic, geological, and historic highlights of the region portrayed. Arrangement is north to south and west to east, with a double-page index map providing location information. Coverage includes Alaska and Hawaii but does not extend to Puerto Rico, the U.S. Virgin Islands, Guam, or American Samoa. Technical data on the photography/imagery recording means and techniques utilized are excluded.

The basic thrust of the volume is popular and, in this respect, a gazetteer and a reading list would seem appropriate. Clarity is fair to good on the duotone reproductions, excellent on the multi-color enlargements of 10 selected larger city areas to include New York, Los Angeles, Chicago, and San Francisco. This is a regional photo-atlas with high visual appeal, incorporating much useful and precise information on relative shape, size, and location of natural and cultural features in the 50 states. [R: ARBA 76, p. 279]

Lawrence E. Spellman

285. U.S. Geological Survey. **The National Atlas of the United States.** Washington, Geological Survey, 1970. 417p. illus. index. $100.00.

Prepared by the Geological Survey with the cooperation of more than 80 federal agencies, this atlas is designed to be of "practical use to decision makers in government and business, planners, research scholars and others needing to visualize country-wide distributional patterns and relationships between environmental phenomena and human activities."

It was the most significant reference work published by the United States government in 1970. Adding to its significance is the fact that it was the first national atlas of the United States. It contains 756 maps of various scales under the following headings: general reference, physical, historical, economic, socio-cultural, administrative, mapping and charting, and the world. Of particular interest to those in business who are engaged in international commerce are maps showing foreign service and U.S. foreign trade areas. The economic maps include many that are comparable to those found in the *Rand McNally Commercial Atlas and Marketing Guide*, which has long been unique in this area. The section entitled "Administrative Maps" shows the changing face of regional administration of the federal government as well as public lands such as national parks, forests, and wilderness areas. A detailed subject index is included at the beginning of the atlas, with an index of 41,000 place names at the end. [R: ARBA 71, p. 175; BL, 15 Mar 71, p. 587; LJ, 15 Apr 71, p. 1327; LJ, 1 May 71, p. 1599]

Sally Wynkoop

AFRICA

286. Chi-Bonnardel, Regine Van. **The Atlas of Africa.** New York, Free Press, 1973. 335p. illus. (col.). maps. index. $90.00. LC 73-17932.

A geographical, social, and economic overview of Africa and its nations – first of its kind in two decades – prepared primarily by faculty members of the University of Paris and published originally in French by Editions Jeune Afrique with Unesco assistance.

The backbone of the work consists of close to 200 multicolored maps/map insets compiled by L'Institut Géographique National de Paris. These range up to 9x12-inches in size, with scales from 1:1,000,000 (1 inch is approximately 16 miles) to 1:10,000,000 (1 inch is about 158 miles). All maps are thus relatively small scale, but they are accurate, cleanly drawn, and easy to interpret. Types include topographic and thematic (population, agriculture, mineral resources, industries, etc.). The unusually extensive, unpedantic text emphasizes those geographic, climatic, historical, and economic factors considered critically influential in the cultural and political development of Africa and its peoples from both a regional and a national standpoint. The alphanumeric index is a facile location finder, but, with fewer than 6,000 entries, it is rather skeletal. A multilingual glossary of geographic terms will prove helpful to readers of English; the absence of metric conversion tables is regrettable. This is a timely, vitally essential reference work characterized by a high order of scholarship and cartographic portrayal. [R: ARBA 75, p. 263; BL, 15 Nov 74, p. 348; Choice, June 74, p. 578; LJ, July 74, p. 1792; WLB, May 74, p. 764]

Lawrence E. Spellman

CANADA

287. **The National Atlas of Canada.** 4th ed. Toronto, Macmillan Company of Canada, in association with the Department of Energy, Mines and Resources, and Information, Canada; distr., New York, Books Canada, 1974. 254p. illus. bibliog. $67.50. ISBN 0-7705-1243-7.

This standard atlas of Canada has a long publishing history. The first edition, which appeared in 1906, was published by the Federal Ministry of Interior; the third edition appeared in 1957, and a French edition in 1959. The present fourth edition, published simultaneously in English and French, is considerably updated. This is the most comprehensive atlas of our northern neighbor, with an emphasis on physical and economic geography and demography. [R: ARBA 76, p. 280; BL, Apr 75, p. 200; Choice, Apr 75, p. 200]

CENTRAL AMERICA

288. Arbingast, Stanley A., and others. **Atlas of Central America.** Austin, University of Texas, Bureau of Business Research, 1979. 62p. illus. maps. $18.00pa. LC 78-64336. ISBN 0-87755-262-2.

One of the most misunderstood regions of the Americas has always been the Central American area. While there is no shortage of scholarly studies or tourist information about the region, no single volume has emerged that would give the reader an accurate picture of the economy, population, and geography of the region. This atlas offers libraries such a volume.

Central America, located in the 1,200 miles of territory between the southern border of Mexico and the northern border of Colombia, contains the seven nations of Guatemala, Belize, El Salvador, Honduras, Nicaragua, Costa Rica, and Panama. There are seven sections of the *Atlas*, one for each nation, containing an economic and social profile as well as extremely well prepared and presented maps of the administrative areas, population, economic activity, transportation, and surface geology. Although the *Atlas* was published in 1979, its latest data is for the year 1974. This is unfortunate, but by using the sources of information given with each map or chart, it is possible to update the data with ease. Libraries with any interest in the region or with collections of atlases should not overlook the opportunity to acquire this well-organized and scholarly atlas. Information of this quality for the Central American region is simply not available elsewhere in such a convenient format. [R: ARBA 80, p. 261]

Roger A. Jones

CHINA

289. **The Times Atlas of China.** P. J. M. Geelan and D. C. Twitchett, eds. New York, Quadrangle/The New York Times Book Co., 1974. 144 + 27p. illus. (col.). maps. index. ISBN 0-7230-0118-9.

This work contains over 125 colored maps/map insets up to 13½ inches by 20½ inches in size, employing scales that average 1:2,000,000 (1 inch equals approximately 30 miles). Types include topographic, historical, and thematic (demography, climate, resources, etc.). Scale is defined in miles/kilometers, major elevations in meters. A special section shows plans of 36 significant urban areas. Every map is crisply drawn, eminently legible, and attractively tinted. Maps are arranged by province and autonomous region. A 75,000-word text describes these from the standpoint of geographical characteristics, agriculture, commerce, and modes of transportation. The essays are hardly definitive, but each does furnish an excellent overall picture of the land, its inhabitants, and their style of life. Alphanumeric locator indexes are printed in both Chinese characters and English. The main index lists 20,000 entries on populated places and natural features. A brief bilingual glossary is appended, accompanied by helpful notes on transcription based on the Wade-Giles system. This is an unusually comprehensive general atlas of the Chinese People's Republic, with a large number of high-quality maps.

Ed. note: Another excellent source of material on China's land and society is Chaio-min Hsieh's *Atlas of China* (ed. by Christopher L. Salter. McGraw-Hill, 1973. $19.95), which contains a variety of physical, cultural, regional, and historical maps complemented by a well-written text. [R: ARBA 76, p. 280; Choice, May 75, p. 376; LJ, 15 May 75, p. 570]   Lawrence E. Spellman

BIBLIOGRAPHIES

290.   Alexander, Gerald L. **Guide to Atlases: World, Regional, National Thematic; An International Listing of Atlases Published since 1950.** Metuchen, NJ, Scarecrow, 1971. 671p. index. $21.50. ISBN 0-8108-0414-X.

This checklist of published atlases is quite comprehensive, listing some 5,500 entries. There are several sections. World atlases have been arranged chronologically by date and, within each year, alphabetically by publisher. Regional atlases are usually listed within each continent alphabetically by name of publisher. National atlases are listed under their respective regions; thematic atlases are divided first alphabetically by subject (e.g., economy, geology, etc.), then alphabetically by publisher within each category. Atlases are listed more than once if they cover more than one area or subject. In terms of languages represented, this checklist covers only 33 languages, and some languages (e.g., Slovak, Korean, and Japanese) are rather poorly represented. Appended are an index of publishers, an alphabetical language index, and an index of authors, cartographers, and editors. The *Guide to Atlases Supplement* (Scarecrow, 1977. 362p. $15.50) extends coverage through 1975. [R: ARBA 72, p. 190; BL, 15 Sept 72, p. 49; Choice, June 72, p. 489; LJ, 15 Jan 72, p. 184; LJ, 15 Apr 72, p. 1385; RQ, Summer 72, p. 376; WLB, Jan 72, p. 449]   Bohdan S. Wynar

291.   Harris, Chauncy D. **Bibliography of Geography: Part I, Introduction to General Aids.** Chicago, Department of Geography, University of Chicago, 1976. 276p. index. (Research Paper, No. 179). $8.00pa. LC 76-1910. ISBN 0-89065-086-1.

Finally, after Wright and Platt's *Aids to Geographical Research*, published in 1947, we have a competent work by a well-known author. His *Annotated World List of Selected Current Geographical Serials* (4th ed., 1980) and his larger work—namely, Harris and Fellmann's *International List of Geographical Serials* (3rd ed., 1980; see entry 292)—are important contributions in this field.

The present work is divided into 16 chapters. The first 4 chapters are concerned with bibliographies of bibliographies, with comprehensive bibliographies of geography, both current and retrospective, and with certain specialized bibliographies or bibliographic series. The following 11 chapters cover specialized types of material: books, gazetteers, dictionaries (two chapters), encyclopedias, statistical sources, and methodology in geography. All entries are annotated and provide full bibliographic descriptions. With its well-balanced international coverage, this is a must purchase for even the smallest libraries. [R: ARBA 77, p. 270]   Bohdan S. Wynar

292.   Harris, Chauncy D., and Jerome D. Fellmann. **International List of Geographical Serials**. 3rd ed. Chicago, University of Chicago, Department of Geography, 1980. 457p. (Research Paper No. 193). $8.00; $6.00 series subscription. LC 80-16392. ISBN 0-89065-100-0.

The first edition of this standard directory, published in 1960, contained 1,651 entries; the 1971 second edition, 2,415 entries. The present edition, substantially revised and enlarged, adds 1,000 new titles for a total of 3,445 entries from over 100 countries. Some 70 scholars cooperated in the preparation of this edition, with the purpose of providing "a comprehensive inventory of all known geographical serials, both those currently being published and those no longer active (closed)."

As in previous editions, the material is arranged by country, with adequate bibliographical description of titles listed. For current serials, the compilers provided additional information if known (e.g., frequency of publication, languages used in articles, tables of contents or abstracts, and address of publication). The form of the titles is generally that used in the *Union List of Serials*. Occasionally, the compilers have problems with some foreign titles, primarily in the area of transliteration, but such errors (some typographical) are minor in nature and are often unavoidable in a work of this type.

Bohdan S. Wynar

293.   Heise, Jon O., and others, eds. **Travel Guidebooks in Review**. 3rd ed., rev. Syracuse, NY, Gaylord Professional Publications, 1978. 187p. $9.95pa. LC 78-16930. ISBN 0-915794-25-X.

Many so-called guidebooks are practically useless to the average traveler, since they specialize only in recommending excellent restaurants and hotels as well as stores for purchasing souvenirs; they do little in the way of guiding tourists through the sights of the various countries. *Travel Guidebooks in Review* seeks to aid both the traveler and the librarian who is asked to recommend a guidebook. The editor, Jon O. Heise, director of the International Center at the University of Michigan, is very well qualified to edit such a reference work.

The guidebook is divided into five parts covering Europe, Asia, Africa, South America, and "Worldwide." All types of guidebooks are included, from books for young people on bicycling or hiking tours to those guides for affluent Americans who wish to travel deluxe. Appendixes list all travel books in English, names and addresses of publishers of the travel books reviewed, guidebooks published in series, a basic travel library, a basic study-abroad library, and basic international employment sources. As one would expect, the guide is most helpful in the evaluation for student and low-cost travelers, less so for the more affluent travelers. For example, the *Blue Guides*, the *Michelin Green Guides*, and *Nagel's Encyclopedia-Guides* are rather slighted in their descriptions, yet these guides are perhaps the most valuable ones for adults traveling abroad. This criticism, however, is minor. [R: ARBA 79, p. 294; RQ, Fall 79, p. 92; WLB, Mar 79, p. 527]

William C. Young

294.   Mickwitz, Ann-Mari, and Leena Miekkavaara, comps. **The A. E. Nordenskiöld Collection in the Helsinki University Library: Annotated Catalogue of Maps Made up to**

1800, Vol. 1, Atlases A-J. Helsinki, Finland, Helsinki University Library; distr., Atlantic Highlands, NJ, Humanities Press, 1979. 250p. illus. (part col.). maps. $77.50. ISBN 0-391-01393-9.

This superb cartobibliography will be a classic reference work in libraries supporting undergraduate and graduate degrees in geography, and in historical libraries interested in pre-1800 maps. Nordenskiöld's landmark collection in geography and cartography, which began when he decided to assemble as complete a collection as possible of geographic and cartographic literature appearing before 1570, is so good that only three or four of the world's great national libraries had as complete and valuable a collection as did he in the late nineteenth century—and perhaps not many more now have better collections. He began collecting maps seriously in 1883 and died in 1901.

Altogether, there are about 24,000 pre-nineteenth century maps in this mind-boggling collection, most of which are contained in the library's approximately 500 atlases. Attempts to catalog the collection were made off and on after 1901, but not started seriously until 1968, when the decision was made to catalog each map in each atlas individually, in sufficient detail to permit some measure of comparative work from the catalog alone. The catalog, when completed, will list all pre-nineteenth century maps in the collection, whether contained in atlases or books, or as loose sheets, whether facsimiles or originals. Atlases and general geographic accounts will be cataloged in volumes 1 and 2, indexes in volumes 4 and 5. The maps are in alphabetical order by author or publisher, and within those categories by chronological order; the maps are listed by title if there is no author, and under "Collections" if there is no title. First atlases are listed, and each given a unique number; then maps in each individual atlas are described.

The volume is illustrated with small, clear, black-and-white map motifs, and large, beautifully printed and selected color facsimiles of relatively unusual maps. A floating page in the back of the work gives full cites for the literature in the cartobibliographic cites; a final bibliography, covering the whole work, is to be published in volume 3. In the individual cites the notes are perhaps the most interesting feature, constituting as they do mini-lectures on historical cartography. A must purchase for collections with any pretensions at all to keeping historical cartography works.   Mary Larsgaard

295.   Wheat, James Clements, and Christian Brun. **Bibliography of Maps and Charts Published in America before 1800.** New Haven, CT, Yale University Press, 1969. 215p. maps. index. LC 69-15464.

Providing a valuable tool for the historian and cartographer, this comprehensive and annotated bibliography of 915 maps represents the first attempt to describe the entire known cartographical contribution of the American press prior to 1800. Included are not only maps and charts published separately, but also those used as illustrations in books and pamphlets and from other sources such as atlases, gazetteers, almanacs, and magazines. Most of the items included pertain to the area that became the United States, but there are also entries covering parts of Latin America, Europe, Africa, the West Indies, and Asia.

Arranged chronologically by region, entries include date of publication, description, size and scale, the publication in which the map first appeared, and the location of existing copies. Included are reproductions of 18 rare maps of the period, as well as a 20-page list of books referred to in this pioneering study. [R: ARBA 70, p. 96; LJ, 15 Sept 69, p. 3041; RQ, Winter 69, p. 181]

296.   Winch, Kenneth L., ed. **International Maps and Atlases in Print.** 2nd ed. New York, R. R. Bowker, 1976. 866p. maps. index. $55.00. LC 73-13336. ISBN 0-85935-036-3.

The first edition, published in 1974, was noted for its essential usefulness, although it was somewhat marred by excessive typographical errors. The second edition includes more than 15,000 maps and atlases produced by about 1,000 commercial and official governmental map publishers throughout the world. Almost 400 index maps record coverage of multi-sheet series. This compilation is valuable for its relative comprehensiveness in listing available maps and atlases, arranged in an ordered regional sequence, and within each region or country by type of map and thematic coverage. Appropriate bibliographical details are provided. An alphabetical index lists geographical names (mainly countries).

The second edition includes new maps and atlases issued since the first edition. The text has been reset for greater clarity, particularly by use of boldface headings. Accents have been added for those foreign languages using diacritics. An examination of the entries for the Soviet Union reveals a marked reduction in the number of typographical errors, though they are still at a rather high level. The volume provides an incomparable assemblage of information on the corpus of available maps and atlases. It is a major bibliographical tool and checklist, valuable for any library making substantial acquisitions of atlases or maps, and particularly for the specialized map library or map purchaser. [R: ARBA 78, p. 269; BL, 1 Oct 77, p. 325; LJ, 1 Apr 77, p. 789; WLB, May 77, p. 782]

Chauncy D. Harris

DICTIONARIES

297. Monkhouse, F. J., and John Small. **A Dictionary of the Natural Environment.** New York, John Wiley, 1978. 320p. illus. (A Halsted Press Book). $28.95; $7.95pa. LC 77-21069. ISBN 0-470-99333-2; 0-470-99334-0pa.

This new, expanded version of F. J. Monkhouse's 1965 edition of *A Dictionary of Geography* presents the physical definitions collected by Monkhouse before his death in 1975, supplemented by material gathered by the author, John Small. It is intended as a reference book for geography and the environmental sciences. Although the bulk of material on nonphysical geography (such as statistical methods and human geography) has been omitted in an attempt to keep the book a manageable size, 465 new definitions, 18 new diagrams, and a new offering of photographs have been added to the original book. A list of abbreviations appears at the beginning of the alphabetically arranged, paragraph-length definitions. [R: ARBA 80, p. 263]

Judith G. Gerber

298. Tooley, Ronald Vere, comp. **Tooley's Dictionary of Mapmakers.** New York, Alan R. Liss; Amsterdam, Meridian Publishing, 1979. 684p. illus. maps. bibliog. $120.00. LC 79-1936. ISBN 0-8451-1701-7.

What a beautifully produced, substantial work! It is easy to believe that this work is a reflection of the author's decades of work in the field of cartography. The aim of the publication is to give in the most compact form information on persons associated with the production of maps from the earliest times to 1900, and the aim is true. The reader might make minor quibbles with the author concerning the information in some of the cites, but, in the main, this classic reference work is excellent. Approximately one-half of the information first appeared in *Map Collector's Circle* (now discontinued), but even that has been revised and enlarged, thus making this a good purchase even for those libraries that have copies of the *Circle*. There are illustrations to break up the alphabetical entries; sad to say, some of the maps are poorly reproduced and blurry. A good extra touch is the inclusion of signatures of major mapmakers. The only aid this volume lacks is a geographic index, and it is so massive as is, that it seems picky to insist on that point. For all academic libraries that support degrees in geography, this will be a basic reference work in cartography. [R: ARBA 80, p. 263]

Mary Larsgaard

DIRECTORIES

299.   Carrington, David K., and Richard W. Stephenson, comps. **Map Collections in the United States and Canada: A Directory.** 3rd ed. New York, Geography and Map Division, Special Libraries Association, 1978. 230p. index. $19.75pa. LC 77-26685. ISBN 0-87111-243-4.

The long-awaited and definitely overdue third edition of this work has finally arrived, and even though the information in it was three years old at date of publication, it is an invaluable tool for all map librarians and general reference sections. There is a considerable increase in coverage (745 map collections covered, a 23% increase over the 1970 edition, the introduction informs us), matched by what must be a considerable increase in price: $19.75 does seem an outrageous price for a 230-page paperback book. Not only are more map libraries included, but more information has been garnered for each. Staff, number of maps, books and other materials, annual accessions, area, subject and chronological specializations, special cartographic collections, cataloging and classification, depositories, public served, reproduction facilities, when established, interlibrary loan, name of map librarian, and telephone number are included when available. Information is presented alphabetically by state, and within states, alphabetically by city. Expensive, well presented and put together, this is irreplaceable. A detailed index is included. [R: ARBA 79, p. 117]

Mary Larsgaard

PLACE NAMES

300.   Kane, Joseph Nathan, and Gerard L. Alexander. **Nicknames and Sobriquets of U.S. Cities, States, and Counties.** 3rd ed. Metuchen, NJ, Scarecrow, 1979. 429p. index. $17.50. LC 79-20193. ISBN 0-8108-1255-X.

Nicknames continues to improve and to fill the void in reference books identified by Joseph N. Kane in his 1938 book and by Gerard L. Alexander in his 1951 publication. The friendship of Kane and Alexander has resulted in this third edition of their collaborative effort. Kane and Alexander was selected as an outstanding reference book in 1965, and with the addition of the nicknames of counties, this continues to be a standard tool in libraries of all types. The addition of county nicknames is a logical and important addition as cities continue to expand outward and their outlying regions become more significant. As a reference, this book provides specific answers to the direct questions from all types of patrons.

Kane and Alexander provide an introductory essay which describes the origins and peculiarities of these nicknames. The major part of the edition is six separate indexes arranged by state and alphabetically by name of city. These provide access by cities, counties, and states and by nicknames. The addition of 2,300 nicknames brings the total in this third edition to approximately 12,500 names, in an improved format. The listing of All-American cities found in earlier editions has become outdated and has been dropped, although it is still available in these older editions.

Nicknames remains a "fun" book, providing much enjoyment for those wishing to look up the nicknames of cities in which they have lived and giving "clues" to researchers about some aspect of the past of a certain city, county, or state. This latter aspect of the volume could be improved by the addition of some comments about places like Waltham, Massachusetts — the precision city (for its production of watches and other timing devices). Laconic notes of this type would help the user in separating the public relations "fluff" from the "familiar epithets naturally ascribed."

The authors acknowledge that this is merely a "record" of impartially listed names and nicknames and is not intended as a scholarly work. This book has a wealth of information for the trivia fan as well as some interest for the casual browser. No successor to Shankle's *American Nicknames* or Stewart's *American Place Names* has yet been published. Until a more scholarly and comprehensive work appears, this reference book is a must for all reference libraries—both large and small. [R: WLB, May 80, p. 590]   Edward J. Hall, Jr.

301.   Stewart, George R. **American Place Names: A Concise and Selective Dictionary for the Continental United States of America.** New York, Oxford University Press, 1970. 550p. $19.95. LC 72-83018.

This volume contains about 12,000 entries for United States place names, arranged alphabetically, dictionary fashion, in one sequence. Each entry mentions the states in which the place name occurs, followed by a concise explanation as to the origin of the name. Indian names (e.g., Milwaukee) are included. The work is judiciously selective, emphasizing names that people might be expected to question, such as well-known place names, names often repeated, or unusual names. "Obviously obvious" names were eliminated, as were Hawaiian names (Hawaii not being part of the continental United States).

American Place Names is particularly valuable as a reference source because it is concise, usefully arranged in dictionary fashion, intended for the general reader, free of technical terms, and it has an excellent bibliography. This volume is a happy combination of sound scholarship, general usefulness, and a pleasing format, making it the standard work on place names in the United States.

C. M. Matthews' *Place Names of the English-Speaking World* (New York, Scribner's, 1972) traces the origins and changes of place names from the early history of the English-speaking areas of the world, with emphasis on Britain and North America. While the social and historical significance of place names is discussed in considerable depth, the author has produced a history that is vivid and very readable. The book is factual and extremely accurate; standard etymological sources have been well chosen, and there is much original research. Appendixes include a chronological table of events that have influenced place names, and there is a select bibliography. [R: ARBA 71, p. 144; LJ, 1 Nov 70, p. 3762; LJ, 15 Apr 71, p. 1327; WLB, Mar 71, p. 689]   Donald Empson
P. William Filby

10 EDUCATION

BIBLIOGRAPHIES

302. Buros, Oscar Krisen, ed. **English Tests and Reviews: A Monograph Consisting of the English Sections of the Seven Mental Measurements Yearbooks (1938-72) and Tests in Print II (1974).** Highland Park, NJ, Gryphon Press, 1975. 395p. index. (An MMY Monograph). $25.00. LC 75-8109. ISBN 0-910674-15-9.

303. Buros, Oscar Krisen, ed. **Foreign Language Tests and Reviews: A Monograph Consisting of the Foreign Language Sections of the Seven Mental Measurements Yearbooks (1938-72) and Tests in Print II (1974).** Highland Park, NJ, Gryphon Press, 1975. 312p. index. (An MMY Monograph). $23.00. LC 75-8110. ISBN 0-910674-16-7.

304. Buros, Oscar Krisen, ed. **Intelligence Tests and Reviews: A Monograph Consisting of the Intelligence Sections of the Seven Mental Measurements Yearbooks (1938-72) and Tests in Print II (1974).** Highland Park, NJ, Gryphon Press, 1975. 1129p. index. (An MMY Monograph). $55.00. LC 75-8112. ISBN 0-910674-17-5.

305. Buros, Oscar Krisen, ed. **Mathematics Tests and Reviews: A Monograph Consisting of the Mathematics Sections of the Seven Mental Measurements Yearbooks (1938-72) and Tests in Print II (1974).** Highland Park, NJ, Gryphon Press, 1975. 435p. index. (An MMY Monograph). $25.00. LC 75-8113. ISBN 0-910674-18-3.

306. Buros, Oscar Krisen, ed. **Personality Tests and Reviews II: A Monograph Consisting of the Personality Sections of the Seventh Mental Measurements Yearbook (1972) and Tests in Print II (1974).** Highland Park, NJ, Gryphon Press, 1975. 841p. index. (An MMY Monograph). $45.00. LC 74-13192. ISBN 0-910674-19-1.

307. Buros, Oscar Krisen, ed. **Reading Tests and Reviews II: A Monograph Consisting of the Reading Sections of the Seventh Mental Measurements Yearbook (1972) and Tests in Print II (1974).** Highland Park, NJ, Gryphon Press, 1975. 257p. index. (An MMY Monograph). $20.00. LC 70-13495. ISBN 0-910674-20-5.

308. Buros, Oscar Krisen, ed. **Science Tests and Reviews: A Monograph Consisting of the Science Sections of the Seven Mental Measurements Yearbooks (1938-72) and Tests in Print II (1974).** Highland Park, NJ, Gryphon Press, 1975. 296p. index. (An MMY Monograph). $22.00. LC 75-8114. ISBN 0-910674-21-3.

309. Buros, Oscar Krisen, ed. **Social Studies Tests and Reviews: A Monograph Consisting of the Social Studies Sections of the Seven Mental Measurements Yearbooks (1938-72) and Tests in Print II (1974).** Highland Park, NJ, Gryphon Press, 1975. 227p. index. (An MMY Monograph). $20.00. LC 75-8115. ISBN 0-910674-22-1.

310. Buros, Oscar Krisen, ed. **Vocational Tests and Reviews: A Monograph Consisting of the Vocational Sections of the Seven Mental Measurements Yearbook (1938-72) and Tests in Print II (1974).** Highland Park, NJ, Gryphon Press, 1975. 1087p. index. (An MMY Monograph). $55.00. LC 75-8116. ISBN 0-910674-23-X.

Oscar K. Buros has been producing outstanding reference tools for test users in education, industry, and psychology for over 40 years. His major contribution, *The Mental Measurements Yearbook* (*MMY*), has been published since 1938.

In 1975, Buros' Gryphon Press issued nine monographs, each dealing with published examinations in one of the following fields: 1) English language and literature; 2) foreign languages; 3) intelligence; 4) mathematics; 5) personality; 6) reading; 7) science; 8) social studies; and 9) vocational counseling. These books consist essentially of reprints, as their subtitles indicate. In addition to extensive test information from *Tests in Print II* (*TIP II*) and scholarly reviews of examinations from volumes of MMY, each of the monographs contains the following: 1) a list of reviewers; 2) a brief preface; 3) an introduction describing in detail the scope of the book and how it may be used; 4) a classified subject index, reprinted from *TIP II*, referring to examinations in various fields, including those not covered by the book; 5) a directory of test publishers and a publisher index; 6) a title index; 7) a name index; and 8) a classified subject index limited to material in the book.

These volumes are international in scope, treating examinations available in English-speaking countries throughout the world. All citations in the indexes and cross references are to numbered test entries, not to pages. Running heads and feet are provided in the test and review sections to assist the reader in locating desired material.

Two of the nine books, those in the areas of personality and reading, supplement monographs issued in 1970 and 1968, respectively, and contain material from only the seventh edition of *MMY*. Therefore, they have to be used with the previously published monographs. Buros' other 1975 publications, however, include reprints from the first seven issues of *MMY* and may, consequently, be used independently of his earlier works. It should be noted, however, that none of the pertinent book reviews in *MMY* have been reprinted in these volumes.

These monographs have been prepared especially for those examiners in specialized fields who lack access to *MMY* and *TIP II*. Although they provide not a bit of additional information, the spin-offs are convenient to use, authoritative, and relatively inexpensive (at $20.00 to $55.00 per copy). Purchased individually, the books from which each of these monographs (except for those dealing with personality and reading tests) is derived would cost the reader $312.50. The material in the 1975 publications is supplemented and updated by *The Eighth Mental Measurements Yearbook* (2v. 1978. $120.00/set). [R: ARBA 76, p. 291; Choice, May 75, p. 367; Choice, Dec 75, pp. 1286-88; LJ, 1 Nov 75, p. 2058]

Leonard Grundt

311. Buros, Oscar Krisen, ed. **Tests in Print II: An Index to Tests, Test Reviews, and the Literature on Specific Tests.** Highland Park, NJ, Gryphon Press, 1974. 1107p. index. $70.00. ISBN 0-910674-14-0.

The first edition of *Tests in Print* (*TIP*) was published in 1961. This present edition contains: 1) a comprehensive bibliography of all tests in print as of early 1974 that were published for use with English-speaking subjects, together with over 16,000 references to articles and reviews on the construction, use, and validity of specific tests; 2) a directory of 493 test publishers with complete listings of their tests; 3) a title index listing both in-print and out-of-print tests; 4) a cumulative author index to approximately 70,000 items (tests, reviews, etc.) in *TIP II*, to the first seven issues of *Mental Measurements Yearbook*, to *Personality Tests and Reviews*, and to *Reading Tests and Reviews*; 5) a reprinting of *Standards for Educational and Psychological Tests*; and 6) a "scanning" index for quickly locating tests designed for a particular population. A valuable complement to the *Mental Measurements Yearbook*. [R: ARBA 75, p. 727; Choice, May 75, p. 367; WLB, Mar 75, p. 528]

312. Cordasco, Francesco, and David N. Alloway. **Sociology of Education: A Guide to Information Sources.** Detroit, Gale, 1979. 266p. index. (Education Information Guide Series, Vol. 2; Gale Information Guide Library). $28.00. LC 78-10725. ISBN 0-8103-1436-3.

Francesco Cordasco was an outstanding choice on the part of the publishers to be selected to undertake the task of bringing together in one volume the plethora of informational materials dealing with the sociology of education. Professor of education at Montclair State College in New Jersey, Cordasco is a person of prodigious scholarly energies, a trait that has facilitated his authorship or editorship of many important works in the fields of education, ethnicity, urban affairs, and minority studies. His already strong sociological bent, unusual among educationalists, is further emphasized in this work through his collaboration with David N. Alloway, a sociologist at Montclair State.

Like other volumes issued in this series of guides by Gale, the present tome seeks to include in summary form listings of the most noteworthy books, pamphlets, reports, and articles dealing with the subject at hand, in this instance, the sociology of education. Given the numerous themes that constitute this area of concentration, the coauthors have done an exemplary job in covering the subject matter, including the most important materials illuminating the sociology of the school, levels of education, and special aspects of education. These general categories are preceded by an introductory section indicating important reference, bibliographical, and textual materials of a general nature necessary to understand the more specialized documents listed later. Each of the major sections is in turn divided into specific classifications of information—e.g., the school includes sections dealing with teaching and teaching personnel, educational administration, and guidance and counseling.

The entries in the text are numbered and total 1,508 separate listings. Each entry contains the name of the author, the title in caps, place of publication and publisher, date of publication, and number of pages. Given the fairly recent definition of sociology of education as a field of investigation, it is not surprising to find that most of the entries date from the 1960s and 1970s. Separate author, title, and subject indexes conclude the work. [R: ARBA 80, p. 279]   Norman Lederer

313. Laubenfels, Jean. **The Gifted Student: An Annotated Bibliography.** Westport, CT, Greenwood Press, 1977. 220p. index. (Contemporary Problems of Childhood, No. 1). $15.00. LC 77-82696. ISBN 0-8371-9760-0.

Interest in the problems of childhood seems to fluctuate with the social and political tenor of the times. The Russians' successful launching of Sputnik, for example, stimulated an instantaneous concern for the gifted, whose talents in mathematics and science were seen as vital elements in the nation's program of national defense. Later, attention was turned to the culturally deprived and disadvantaged, whose needs were to be satisfied with such programs as compensatory education. This bibliography on "giftedness" represents a return to attention on students of superior ability or achievement. Its appearance at this stage in the spontaneous growth of the literature makes it an invaluable reference tool.

The Gifted Student is an annotated bibliography containing some 1,300 references selected from the literature published since 1961. Coverage includes journal articles, books, conference reports, government documents, pamphlets, and dissertations. The entries are grouped according to major categories, such as "characteristics of the gifted," "identification techniques," and "longitudinal studies." Because there is much overlapping of subjects, it is necessary to consult the Selective Key Word Index for specific descriptors. Full citations are given for each listing, including either the presence of a bibliography or, in the case of a journal article, usually the number of references to be found.

Five appendices form an essential and unique part of this extraordinary bibliography. They include a list of individuals and organizations concerned with the gifted; a list of instruments most often used in assessing the gifted; audiovisual materials and media aids for teachers; as well as lists of major manual and computerized reference tools. There are three components in the indices. The author index includes the personal names of individuals cited as author, joint author, or compiler. The Selective Key Word Subject Index lists important words in entry titles. In general, only unique terms are given. The list of journal abbreviations alphabetically lists all journals cited in the text.

If this title is an example of forthcoming works in the Contemporary Problems of Childhood series, then the future of literature control in this area is in excellent hands. Both the editor of the series and the compiler of this bibliography are to be commended for their excellent work. [R: ARBA 79, p. 307; BL, 15 June 78, p. 1635; Choice, May 78, p. 376; LJ, 1 Mar 78, p. 554; WLB, May 78, p. 729]   Lorraine Mathies

314.   U.S. Office of Education. **Bibliography of Research Studies in Education, 1926-1940.** Detroit, Gale, 1974. 4v. index. $165.00. LC 74-1124. ISBN 0-8103-0975-0.

The *Bibliography of Research Studies in Education* was a serial publication issued by the United States Office of Education in its Bulletin series from 1928 to 1941, covering the school years from 1926 to 1940. The 14 annual issues have been reprinted by Gale and bound together in four large hardcover volumes. In all, the set includes 47,866 entries, many of them annotated, covering a wide range of subjects.

Each issue contains from 3,000 to 4,000 entries, arranged in a classified listing that includes such subjects as educational history, biography, educational psychology and sociology, tests and measurements, educational theory and practice, international aspects of education, methods of instruction, special curricular areas and subjects, teacher training, salaries and professional status of teachers, education on the several levels, buildings and equipment, vocational education, education of special groups, educational extension, and libraries and reading. Within each category, entries are arranged alphabetically by author. Each entry gives author, title, imprint information, date, and number of pages. Unpublished materials are indicated by the abbreviation "ms." Materials available on loan from the Office of Education library are identified by an asterisk. Some of the annotations were prepared by staff members at the library, others by the person who submitted the report.

This is a very comprehensive bibliography on educational research, without parallel for the years covered. The scope is so broad that it will provide references for scholars in many fields related to education. The coverage of materials on libraries and reading will be of special interest to librarians. [R: ARBA 75, p. 292; Choice, Apr 75, p. 202]
Shirley L. Hopkinson

315.   Weber, J. Sherwood, ed. **Good Reading: A Guide for Serious Readers.** 21st ed. New York, R. R. Bowker, 1978. 313p. index. $17.95. LC 78-2424. ISBN 0-8352-1063-4.

A reading list should inform potential users both of the range of materials available and of the depth that one might find in those materials eventually recommended. *Good Reading*, now in its twenty-first edition, attempts to cover the entire field of knowledge, and while the coverage is broad, it does lack depth in the annotations. Thus, a budding reader should apparently take the listing here as a recommendation rather than look for comments of any particular insight. "Sketchily descriptive" might adequately convey this reviewer's impression of the annotations. Also, subject arrangement is slightly peculiar. The first section deals with both "historical and regional" cultures—e.g., Greece (ancient), the eighteenth century (only in Europe, with very little on the Americas), and Latin America (all periods). The second concerns literary forms—the novel (vigorously subdivided), the short story, poetry, drama, biography, and essays, letters, criticism, and magazines. The third major section covers the humanities, social sciences, and sciences. The slant is away from the hard sciences in all areas, which is to be regretted in an age so dependent upon them. A short final section lists reference books of use to a general reader. A combined author, title, subject index concludes the book.

This list is not so academically oriented as that in Parker and Hawes' *College on Your Own* (Bantam Books, 1978), so it might better serve the reader seeking general self-improvement. Overlap might also be observed between this and Clifton Fadiman's *Lifetime Reading Plan* (Thomas Y. Crowell, 1978), but the two do complement one another to a degree. However, any library with a decision to make between the two is advised to choose *Good Reading*, as it seems the most balanced in terms of classic works and important works on contemporary issues. [R: ARBA 79, p. 337; LJ, 1 Jan 79, p. 95]

Koert C. Loomis, Jr.

316. Woodbury, Marda. **A Guide to Sources of Educational Information.** Washington, Information Resources Press, 1976. 371p. index. $25.00. LC 75-37116. ISBN 0-87815-015-3.

Although several guides have been published on this subject in the last 10 years, Marda Woodbury's guide is not only the most current but also the most comprehensive. It has high professional standards, and is a worthy successor to Arvid J. Burke's classic *Documentation in Education* (1967).

Some 700 titles are listed here, organized into 19 chapters that cover basic tools for effective research, printed research tools, special subjects, and nonprint sources. The introductory bibliographical essay provided for each chapter identifies key sources or offers some methodological advice. Bibliographical citations are complete except for pagination for monographs and LC numbers or ISBNs; whenever possible, price is also given. The emphasis is on current sources, and for the most part, imprints are exclusively American. Annotations are brief but descriptive. As the author states in the preface, she tried in her annotations "to convey the scopes, uses, strengths, and weaknesses of these selections for educators, policy-setters, parents, researchers, and librarians" (p. xi).

A few minor flaws do not overshadow the overall professional execution of this excellent work. It is hoped that the next edition can be somewhat enlarged. In the meantime, one can safely say that Woodbury's work is by far the best sourcebook for educational information; the educational community will find it very useful. [R: ARBA 77, p. 285; Choice, Nov 76, p. 1122, C&RL, Jan 77, p. 71; RQ, Spring 77, p. 262; WLB, Nov 76, p. 264]

Bohdan S. Wynar

DICTIONARIES AND ENCYCLOPEDIAS

317. **The Encyclopedia of Education.** Lee C. Deighton, ed.-in-chief. New York, Macmillan and Free Press, 1971. 10v. bibliog. index. $199.00. LC 70-133143.

This comprehensive work summarizes the achievements in education not only in this country but also, to some extent, internationally. *The Encyclopedia of Education* is well edited and well balanced in the treatment of most subject areas. The preface clearly states the scope of this major undertaking, indicating that "in more than 1,000 articles, if offers a view of the institutions and people, of the processes and products, found in educational practice. The articles deal with history, theory, research, and philosophy, as well as with the structure and fabric of education." The most important topics are treated in depth. As an example, the 45-page article on child development is subdivided into nine different aspects, starting with overview, effects of infant care, infant-mother attachment, maternal deprivation, etc. Under "Maternal deprivation," such problems as institutionalization, sensory stimulation, long-term effects of deprivation, intervention studies, and disadvantaged environments are discussed. Most longer articles contain bibliographies; thus, the article on child development contains nine bibliographies, one after each subheading, totaling 264 references for further reading. The encyclopedia contains many good articles in the area of comparative education; most major countries and their educational systems are represented. There are also several articles pertaining to library education.

In general this is a well-prepared and authoritative encyclopedia covering a wide range of pertinent topics. It does exclude biographical sketches of leading educators – an understandable editorial policy in view of the fact that we now have a number of good sources for biographical information. Excluded also are articles on individual universities, again an understandable fact; this information can be found with ease elsewhere. Most articles have good bibliographies, and the last volume contains a directory of contributors as well as an excellent index with all necessary cross references. [R: ARBA 72, p. 223; C&RL, Jan 72, p. 44; LJ, 15 Apr 72, p. 1384; WLB, Dec 71, p. 363]   Bohdan S. Wynar

318.   **Encyclopedia of Educational Research.** 4th ed. New York, Macmillan, 1969. 1522p. $38.95. LC 75-4932.

This fourth edition of a standard reference work is essentially a new work, rather than a revision of the third edition. The subject content has been designated and the structure designed with the advice of a distinguished board of editors appointed by the American Educational Research Association. As in previous editions, contributions are signed and are written by specialists in their respective fields. Many of these contributors are new in this edition, but even repeat articles have been completely rewritten. The lists of selected references for each topic, which formed so valuable a feature of the third edition, have been continued, although the substitution of APA-style name-date citations for the old numbered system of Walter S. Monroe has reduced ease of use for rapid reference work. The latest items cited appear to be 1966, and the *Review of Educational Research* must be used for later material.

As with the previous edition, a subject index on yellow stock is inserted in the middle of the book, but it is now a concept rather than a specific entry index, which somewhat reduces its usefulness for reference work. The format includes a content outline with lists of articles in each area, a list of contributors with their articles in each area, an alphabetical list of articles, and a list of abbreviations used. [R: ARBA 71, p. 208; LJ, 15 Apr 70, p. 1438]   John Morgan

319.   Good, Carter V., ed. **Dictionary of Education.** 3rd ed. Prep. under the auspices of Phi Delta Kappa. New York, McGraw-Hill, 1973. 681p. $30.00. LC 73-4784. ISBN 0-07-023720-4.

The first edition of this work was published in 1945, the second in 1959. According to the preface, the dictionary is "concerned with technical and professional terms and concepts in the entire area of education. As a general policy, it has excluded names of persons, institutions, school systems, organizations, places, and titles of publications and journals, except where a movement, method, or plan is represented" (p. ix). Foreign terms are no longer listed. Since the present edition adds some 8,000 entries (to make a total of around 33,000), it represents a substantial updating of this well-known dictionary.

Page and Thomas' *International Dictionary of Education* (Nichols, 1977. 381p. $22.50) is a worthwhile tool for any library, and an excellent supplement to Good's *Dictionary*. Though it has only about one-third as many entries, it includes more recent terms, foreign terms, and British usage not covered by Good, and provides well-rounded coverage of American terminology as well. A well laid out book, with good typography, and easy to use, it is organized as a phrase book rather than a noun dictionary (with "positive relationship" under "positive" rather than under "relationship"). Its clear definitions facilitate use of extensive cross references by italicizing words or noting phrases discussed elsewhere. Illustrations, though few, are used judiciously to represent concepts best portrayed pictorially. As an international dictionary, it includes descriptions and addresses of major international and national educational associations and government agencies within its main text, with a separate list of abbreviations (acronyms) in an appendix. Overall, this is a convenient, well-selected, comprehensive (but not exhaustive) dictionary, particularly valuable for its international aspects. [R: ARBA 74, p. 206; Choice, Oct 73, p. 1162; WLB, Sept 73, p. 83]

Marda Woodbury
Bohdan S. Wynar

320. **The International Encyclopedia of Higher Education.** Ed.-in-chief, Asa S. Knowles. 1st ed. San Francisco, Jossey-Bass Publishers, 1977. 10v. index. $475.00/set. LC 77-73647. ISBN 0-87589-323-6/set.

A noteworthy trend in higher education in recent years has been a growing internationalism and interdependency among colleges and universities worldwide. In accordance with these developments, the *International Encyclopedia of Higher Education* attempts to present information from a global perspective on: national systems; academic fields of study; educational associations; research centers, institutes, and documentation centers; academic and administrative policies and procedures; current issues and trends in education. It is the editor's view that administrative practices should be treated as thoroughly as academic concerns are, and that presentation of information should reflect a well-defined national, international, or comparative approach. The *Encyclopedia* aims to give both the lay person and the specialist a broad overview of international aspects of higher education, rather than in-depth coverage of selected topics.

The *Encyclopedia* is well edited and remarkably consistent in its international treatment of most subject areas. The editorial precision is evident in the preface, where it is stated that the *Encyclopedia* contains 1,300 entries, by 588 authors in 69 countries throughout the world representing 211 colleges, universities, and academic institutions. In addition to an alphabetical listing of entries and a classification of entries, volume 1 includes an excellent multilingual glossary, and the foreign terms in the glossary are preferred where appropriate in the succeeding articles. Other features of the *Encyclopedia* are, following the articles, an "International Directory of Documentation and Information Centers" (with 201 entries), name, and subject indexes.

It is stated in its preface that the *International Encyclopedia of Higher Education* is intended to "supplement, rather than duplicate, established and highly regarded existing references in the field." In this, it succeeds admirably. Its international approach generates much new information, and provides a new and stimulating perspective on higher education around the world. [R: ARBA 79, p. 312]

Deborah Jane Brewer

321. Monroe, Paul. **A Cyclopedia of Education.** With a new introductory essay by William W. Brickman. Detroit, Gale, 1968. 5v. illus. $220.00/set. LC 68-56361.

This work was originally published by Macmillan from 1911 to 1913. It seems likely that while other works will (and must) supplement it, this uniquely comprehensive work will never be totally replaced. The early 1900s was a time of great change in education, and many of the contributors gave direction to that change. The *Cyclopedia* was important in that it stabilized terminology and established a base for further educational development. A book of ideas and not merely of facts, it is strong on theory and the exploration of relationships. Browsing through the volumes, one notes foreshadowings or precursors of such movements as the library-college, or the university-without-walls.

With comprehensiveness as a goal, the *Cyclopedia* covered philosophy of education, history of education, educational biography, institutions, elementary and secondary education, curriculum, administration, home and foreign school systems, methodology, educational psychology, hygiene, and school architecture. Every subject taught in school was considered in detail. Topics are connected by cross references (a number of which are of the "wild goose chase" variety), and many of the articles are furnished with bibliographies. Although it is arranged alphabetically, the analytical index (end of v. 5) allows the encyclopedia to be used as an exhaustive treatise on a particular aspect of education.

To produce the work, a qualified (and sometimes distinguished) editor was responsible for each of the 15 major areas. John Dewey, for example, was the general editor of the philosophy of education material; he himself wrote 115 articles, some of which are over 6,000 words in length. Altogether, more than 1,000 scholars are numbered among the contributors. Monroe, the director, was a member of the Columbia University faculty for 41 years (1898-1938); he was a noted scholar, published numerous writings on the history of education, held many offices, and was most influential in the roster of students whom he trained.

For this reprint, Brickman contributes a new introduction, which gives both a general description of this work and also a bibliographic survey of other educational encyclopedias. Although the quality of the reprint is good, the binding is not especially sturdy, and there are no guide letters on the spines of the five volumes. [R: ARBA 71, p. 206]

Joseph W. Sprug

322.   Unwin, Derick, and Ray McAleese. **The Encyclopaedia of Educational Media Communications and Technology.** Westport, CT, Greenwood Press, 1978. 800p. illus. $59.95. LC 78-26988. ISBN 0-313-20921-9.

The *Encyclopaedia*'s editors, contributors, consultants, and advisors come primarily from Commonwealth countries, with a handful from the United States and some European countries. As a result, the orientation, sources cited in footnotes, and spelling are British. Nevertheless, media professionals in this country will find it a valuable reference.

Entries range from simple definitions to signed articles of 10 or more pages, complete with footnotes. In scope, they encompass the ancillary disciplines of information science and education, as a random sample of the titles of major articles indicates: "Artificial Intelligence," "Audio Instruction," "Computers in Education," "Economics of Media," "Individualisation of Instruction," "Laser Holography," "Simulation and Games," "Telephone Seminars," "UNESCO." These and about 40 others provide state-of-the-art overviews, research summaries, and evaluations. Several are illustrated with charts, tables, or line drawings. A random sample of the dictionary-type entries is equally wide-ranging: "Conditioning," "Erase Head," "Matrix," "Microfilming," "Motor Skills," "Risk Analysis," "Thesaurus."

It may be a reflection of British usage that there are no entries starting with "instructional," though there are several under "educational." A few inaccuracies in alphabetizing were noted ("mechanical copyright" follows "media classification"), as well as some misplaced running heads (" media recording" at the head of pages carrying the article on "media classification"). The review copy had some loose pages. These imperfections, of course, do not seriously interfere with the volume's usefulness.

The nearest thing published in this country is *Educational Technology: Definition and Glossary of Terms* (Washington, Association for Educational Communications and Technology). Even at its high price, the *Encyclopaedia* is a better buy and could prove more useful than a number of separate monographs or serial subscriptions aggregating the same amount. [R: ARBA 80, p. 283; WLB, Nov 79, p. 194]   Mary R. Sive

DIRECTORIES

323. **Barron's Guide to the Two-Year Colleges: Volume II, Occupational Program Selector.** Comp. and ed. by the College Division of Barron's Educational Series. Completely rev. and updated. Woodbury, NY, Barron's Educational Series, 1979. 106p. index. $11.95; $4.50pa. LC 78-8611. ISBN 0-8120-5295-1; 0-8120-0778-6pa.

The *Occupational Program Selector* displays in chart form 157 specialized programs of study offered by over 1,400 junior colleges, community colleges, technical-vocational institutes, business schools, and four-year colleges and universities with two-year programs. The information in this edition has been updated, and a number of new occupational fields are included.

Part 1 of the *Selector* gives data arranged under major categories: agriculture, applied arts, business and commercial, media, ecology, medical health support, public services, and a miscellaneous category called "Special." Each category is subdivided into several specific programs such as ceramics, hotel/motel management, library assistant, pollution technology, or inhalation therapy. Part 2 is devoted to a tenth category, trade and technical, and lists 44 programs. In both parts, the institutions are grouped first by state, then listed alphabetically by name. Symbols classify each institution's program as transfer, terminal, or either. A supplement lists the institutions with their addresses. No attempt is made to evaluate the programs of study. The *Selector* is intended only to be a method of finding quickly where particular programs are offered. The student can then turn to volume 1 for detailed descriptions of the institutions being considered. The *Selector* also provides a profile of programs offered by a particular institution.   Shirley L. Hopkinson

324. Cass, James, and Max Birnbaum. **Comparative Guide to American Colleges.** 9th ed. New York, Harper and Row, 1979. 850p. index. $24.95. $9.95pa. LC 79-1657. ISBN 0-06-010643-3; 0-06-090739-8pa.

Since its first publication in 1964, this guide has acquired the reputation of being one of the better reference tools for general data on every accredited four-year college and undergraduate program in the United States. The present edition has a similar structure to that found in earlier volumes, and contains revised and updated information on admission requirements, costs and tuition, faculty, special programs, curriculum, loans, and intellectual, social, and cultural environment. Information is provided on careers pursued by graduates of the various institutions. The four indexes — state index, selectivity index, religious index, and index of institutions conferring the largest number of baccalaureate degrees in selected fields — will prove to be useful for the college-bound student. The data in this guide is comprehensive and quite reliable.

A useful companion volume is Cass and Birnbaum's *Comparative Guide to Two Year Colleges and Career Programs* (Harper and Row, 1976. 549p. $19.95; $6.95pa.), which focuses on career programs below the baccalaureate level, ranging in time from a few weeks to more than two years, and, in degree of sophistication, from training for semi-skilled work to the semi-professional, technician level. Descriptions are provided of some 1,740 institutions: community and junior colleges, technical schools and institutes, and four-year colleges offering shorter career-oriented programs. A field of study selectivity index and a religious affiliation index are included.   Shirley L. Hopkinson
Anna T. Wynar

325. **The College Blue Book.** 17th ed. Vol. 1, **U.S. Colleges: Narrative Descriptions.** Vol. 2, **U.S. Colleges: Tabular Data.** Vol. 3, **Degrees Offered by Colleges and Subjects.** Supplemental vol., **Occupational Education.** New York, Macmillan, 1979. 4v. $117.50/set. ISBN 0-02-695180-0.

The first volume (narrative description) offers information on colleges that includes address, description, entrance requirements, admission procedure, costs, and collegiate and community environment. A map for each state locates each institution. Arrangement is by state and then by the name of institution. The second volume also lists colleges by state, then presents the information in tabular form. The third volume consists of two parts. In the first, under the name of each college (listed alphabetically by state), appears the list of the subject areas for which degrees are offered. Part 2 includes an alphabetical listing of subject areas for which degrees are granted by one or more institution of higher learning. The supplemental volume lists institutions alphabetically by city under state headings. Brief information provided includes name, type of school, contact, accreditation, entrance requirements, and curricula. A large section lists schools by curricula and programs of instruction, while smaller sections list schools by broad area (e.g., medical and dental technology, nursing), give information on financial aid, and list sources of additional information.

The *College Blue Book* offers a great deal of statistical information – probably more than other directories of this type. There is only one serious drawback: because statistical information becomes rapidly obsolete, many directories are now published annually, with the result that some of them are more up to date than this comprehensive work. The *College Blue Book* enjoys a fine professional reputation.   Bohdan S. Wynar

326.   Lovejoy, Clarence E. **Lovejoy's College Guide: A Complete Reference Book to Some 3,600 American Colleges and Universities.** 14th ed. New York, Simon & Schuster, 1979. 386p. index. (Lovejoy's Educational Guides). $10.95; $5.95pa. ISBN 0-671-22221-X; 0-671-22222-8pa.

This directory brings up to date the information on American colleges provided in previous editions (the thirteenth edition was published in 1976). The format and coverage remain the same. Schools are described in terms of enrollment, cost, admission requirements, accreditation, and degrees offered. The institutions themselves have provided these facts. The compilers have relisted the colleges in various categories, such as the availability of professional curricula or career programs, and the provision of special facilities. Lovejoy's also covers all aspects of applying for and choosing a college, as well as obtaining financial assistance. However, colleges are rated in broad categories only, and little attempt is made to convey the flavor or intangible aspects of college life. For such descriptions, users will prefer *Barron's Profiles of American Colleges.* A monthly update, *Lovejoy's Guidance Digest*, is available. [R: SLJ, Sept 79, p. 172]   Margaret Norden

INDEXES

327.   **Comprehensive Dissertation Index, 1861-1972.** Ann Arbor, MI, Xerox University Microfilms, 1973. 37v. $2495.00; $1995.00 microfiche; $100.00 individual vols. LC 73-89046.

This comprehensive inventory of doctoral dissertations, with a total of 417,000 entries, provides a nearly complete listing of the impressive output of graduate schools in the United States, plus some foreign universities. It is an expanded version of its predecessor, *Dissertation Abstracts International Retrospective Index*, published by University Microfilms in 1970. Other sources were consulted as well – namely, *American Doctoral Dissertations, Index to American Doctoral Dissertations, Dissertation Abstracts International, Dissertation Abstracts*, and *Microfilm Abstracts*. In addition to these Xerox University Microfilms sources, other reference tools were used, especially the Library of Congress' *List of American Doctoral Dissertations Printed in 1912-1932* and H. W. Wilson's *Doctoral Dissertations Accepted by American Universities 1933/34-1954/55*. The

Index also contains listings of doctoral dissertations from some 70 universities not completely covered by any of the above-mentioned works.

The first 32 volumes of the set present subject coverage for 22 individual disciplines, and a five-volume author index concludes the set. Five volumes are devoted to education, four to chemistry, three to engineering, three to the biological sciences, two each to psychology, business and economics, language and literature, and astronomy and physics. The following subjects are covered in single volumes: mathematics and statistics, health and environmental sciences, agriculture, geography and geology, social sciences, law and political science, history, communications and the arts, and philosophy and religion. Each volume of the set starts with a 21-page introduction (identical in all volumes), including a complete table of contents, instructions for use, a list of schools covered, a bibliography of sources consulted, instructions for obtaining dissertation copies, etc. The subject index is a computer-produced keyword title index. Each dissertation is assigned to one specific subject area; within that area dissertations are listed by keyword (an average of six separate keyword entries for each, according to the publisher). Individual dissertations are listed under the keyword in their titles, first by date (beginning with the most recent), then alphabetically by school, and finally alphabetically by author. Each keyword entry and each entry in the author section provides full information: title, author, degree, date, institution, number of pages, reference to the source from which the citation was obtained, and the order number for dissertations that can be acquired from Xerox University Microfilms.

The use of keyword instead of a traditional subject approach presents several problems. For example, 35 pages (three columns to a page) are devoted to the keyword "economic," 58 pages to "elementary," etc. Even the publishers will admit that the search will be somewhat time-consuming here. In addition, many dissertation titles avoid describing the actual subject matter in simple terms, offering instead a great deal of "sophistication," which quite frequently obscures the real topic under investigation.

In addition to the difficulty of finding a dissertation through one of its keywords, the user must be aware that initial assignment of a dissertation to a discipline is also open to question. As a matter of editorial policy, a given dissertation was placed in only one subject group. Once a dissertation has been placed in the wrong subject group, it is irretrievable except through the author. The introduction provided in each volume indicates that cross references at the beginning of subject sections should help the user locate dissertations on related subjects and disciplines. The cross references can be helpful, however, only if the dissertations have been placed in proper subject categories.

In spite of its deficiencies, *Comprehensive Dissertation Index* is a monumental undertaking. Xerox University Microfilms has published a five-year cumulation for the years 1973-1977 in 19 volumes, and coverage is extended through annual supplements. [R: ARBA 75, p. 309; BL, 1 July 74, p. 1164; Choice, July 74, p. 734; C&RL, July 74, p. 245; LJ, Aug 74, p. 1915; RQ, Fall 74, p. 61]   Bohdan S. Wynar

BIOGRAPHY

328. **Directory of American Scholars.** Ed. by Jaques Cattell Press. 7th ed. New York, R. R. Bowker, 1978. 4v. index. $175.00/set; $48.00/vol. LC 57-9125. ISBN 0-8352-1073-1(v.1); 0-8352-1075-8(v.2); 0-8352-1076-6(v.3); 0-8352-1077-4(v.4). ISSN 0070-5105.

In the seventh edition of this work, more than 39,000 scholars are listed, including almost 5,000 persons listed for the first time. Volume 1 lists about 12,000 scholars in art history, musicology, and classical archaeology. Another 12,000-plus persons in the fields of English, speech, drama, communications, cinema and film studies, and English as a second language are in volume 2. Scholars in foreign languages, linguistics, comparative literature, classics, and philology are found in volume 3. The last volume lists persons in philosophy, religion, and law, and it also contains an alphabetical index of all persons included in the full set. Each volume has its own geographical index, which provides both state and city access. Information is presented in typical *Who's Who* style: name, birthplace and date; citizenship; marriage date and children; discipline; education; honorary degrees; professional experience; concurrent appointments, honors, and awards; current professional memberships; chief research interests; publications (maximum of eight listed here); and mailing address.

Coverage is somewhat spotty; nevertheless, the set does provide a good first-choice source for locating reasonably current information about scholars in the fields covered.

Ed. note: Leaders in Education 1974 (Jaques Cattell Press, ed. R. R. Bowker, 1974. 1309p. $52.50) serves as a companion to the *Directory of American Scholars*. Consisting of 17,000 biographical sketches included on the basis of such criteria as professional achievement, research activities, and professional positions held, this edition is a valuable and carefully edited reference source. [R: ARBA 79, p. 337]   G. Edward Evans

329.   Ohles, John F., ed. **Biographical Dictionary of American Educators.** Westport, CT, Greenwood Press, 1978. 3v. index. $95.00/set. LC 77-84750. ISBN 0-8371-9893-3.

The *Biographical Dictionary of American Educators* recognizes 1,665 teachers, reformers, theorists, and administrators, from colonial times to 1976. Many state and regional educators are included along with the more widely known national figures. Biographical format includes a brief description of the person's education, professional accomplishments, contribution to the educational movement, and personal data. In many instances, references for further study are given. Readers are referred to such reliable sources as the *Dictionary of American Biography*, the *National Cyclopaedia of American Biography*, and *Notable American Women*.

Five appendixes include groupings according to place of birth, state of major service, and field of work; a chronology of birth years; and important dates in American education. A general index provides further access to the information contained in the 1,665 entries. Unfortunately, the contents of each of the three volumes is not indicated alphabetically on the spines. Also, this information is not provided in the table of contents. This three-volume set would be useful in academic libraries. Since inclusion required that a person had reached the age of 60, had retired, or had died by January 1, 1975, it serves as a good complement to *Who's Who in Education* and the *National Faculty Directory*.

Peggy Clossey Boone

INSTRUCTIONAL MATERIALS

330.   Belch, Jean, comp. **Contemporary Games: A Directory and Bibliography Covering Games and Play Situations or Simulations Used for Instruction and Training by Schools, Colleges and Universities, Government, Business and Management.** Detroit, Gale, 1973-74. 2v. index. $64.00(v.1); $58.00(v.2). LC 72-6353. ISBN 0-8103-0968-8(v.1); 0-8103-0969-6(v.2).

Volume 1, the directory, lists over 900 "decision-making or problem-solving exercises" that the author finds suitable for educational purposes in schools, colleges and universities, government, or business. Excluded are traditional games like chess, checkers (Monopoly is included), card games, games primarily of chance or skill, and athletic sports. Only a few war games and a representative sampling of business and management games are included, but readers are referred to other sources for more comprehensive reviews.

Games are listed alphabetically, and the following information is given for each: subject, age or grade, playing time, mode (manual or computer), date originated, designer, producer, source, price, bibliographic citations for articles or books that describe or evaluate the game, and a brief description. Also included are a subject index, age and grade-level index, and a designers' and producers' index with addresses. All are adequately cross-indexed.

Volume 2, the bibliography, lists 2,375 citations to books, articles, scholarly papers, proceedings, directories, and bibliographies relating to games and simulations used in education, government, and business. Classic writings are included, but most of the items were published between 1957 and 1973. Both published and unpublished materials are included. Secondary references lead to sources where items have been reprinted in collections or in other books on the subject. Many of the entries contain annotations that the compiler prepared after personal examination of the materials.

Entries are grouped in five general categories: general information, games in the classroom, business games and management simulations, conflict resolutions, and land use and resource allocation. A sixth section lists reports on research employing or evaluating games and simulations, and a seventh contains entries for directories, bibliographies, and lists on the subject. Classroom games are further classified by subject areas. Within each section or subsection, entries are arranged alphabetically by author. Each entry has been assigned a consecutive item number that is used as a locator device in the indexes. Author, institution, game, and supplementary subject indexes are provided. [R: ARBA 74, p. 246; BL, 1 Dec 73, p. 357; Choice, Mar 74, p. 56; LJ, 1 May 74, p. 1290; RQ, Winter 73, p. 168; WLB, Nov 73, p. 263; ARBA 75, p. 314; Choice, Apr 75, p. 195; RQ, Spring 75, p. 254; WLB, Feb 75, p. 460]

Charles Farley
Shirley L. Hopkinson

331. Rosenberg, Kenyon C., and John S. Doskey. **Media Equipment: A Guide and Dictionary.** Littleton, CO, Libraries Unlimited, 1976. 190p. illus. bibliog. $17.50. LC 76-25554. ISBN 0-87287-155-X.

Anyone involved in the field of educational media must possess at least a minimum knowledge of the principles, terminology, and operation of basic types of audiovisual equipment. As teachers, librarians, and media specialists become involved in the testing, evaluation, and selection of equipment, they are likely to experience problems of communication and to realize that they need to be more knowledgeable and precise in their use of the technical vocabulary. *Media Equipment: A Guide and Dictionary* is designed to aid in the resolution of such problems and needs.

The "Guide" chapters (pp. 15-59) discuss general and specific criteria for media equipment selection. A general checklist for the purchase of AV equipment and 13 checklists for evaluation of types of equipment are included. The various types of equipment are described, with references to the dictionary entries provided for special terminology. Tips on the use and evaluation of specific equipment are included. These two chapters offer a basic introduction of the process of AV equipment evaluation.

The "Dictionary" (pp. 61-188) contains definitions for over 400 technical media equipment terms likely to be encountered in manufacturers' statements and claims with respect to AV equipment they offer. Also included are names of organizations (public and private), with statements of their functions and activities, and their addresses. These organizations are suggested as sources of additional information.

The entries were selected and written with the intent of providing the reader with a basic vocabulary, including those terms most often required in definitions of terms, equipment selection data, and information sources. The dictionary is arranged alphabetically letter-by-letter. An important innovation of this dictionary is its inclusion of minimum requirements (or specifications) in those definitions which warrant them. The dictionary is illustrated with 40 line drawings which amplify definitions of terms. A selected bibliography of additional AV information sources is appended. [R: ARBA 77, p. 319; Choice, Apr 77, p. 183; C&RL, Mar 77, p. 170; JAL, Nov 77, p. 302; JAL, Sept 78, p. 241; RQ, Summer 77, p. 359]

332. Woodbury, Marda. **Selecting Materials for Instruction: Issues and Policies.** Littleton, CO, Libraries Unlimited, 1979. 382p. illus. index. $22.50. LC 79-18400. ISBN 0-87287-197-5.

333. Woodbury, Marda. **Selecting Materials for Instruction: Media and the Curriculum.** Littleton, CO, Libraries Unlimited, 1980. 245p. index. $22.50. LC 79-18400. ISBN 0-87287-212-2.

334. Woodbury, Marda. **Selecting Materials for Instruction: Subject Areas and Implementation.** Littleton, CO, Libraries Unlimited, 1980. 335p. index. $22.50. LC 79-18400. ISBN 0-87287-213-0.

Choosing instructional materials can be an awesome responsibility. Materials must meet a variety of requirements: curriculum guidelines, programs for exceptional children, individualized instruction, community standards – not to mention budgets. In these three handbooks, Woodbury presents an outstanding guide, both theoretical and practical, for educators and all others involved in the selection of instructional materials.

Issues and Policies lays the foundation for further sections on the establishment of effective selection criteria. Numerous examples of actual policy guidelines, materials evaluation forms, and checklists have been carefully chosen and reprinted here. Individual chapters treat topics such as fairness and bias, parent and community involvement, individualization, special education, gifted children, and young children.

Media and the Curriculum covers the selection of specific print and nonprint materials, sources from which they may be obtained, and ways in which they may be integrated into the curriculum. Included are government publications, photographs, films, games, television programs, recyclables, free materials, toys, and the like.

Subject Areas and Implementation is subject specific, describing sources and criteria for selecting materials to be used in teaching science, math, environmental studies, language arts, social studies, sex education, and a variety of other special subjects.

While these handbooks are aimed primarily at elementary and secondary school educators, anyone involved in the educational process, from parents to administrators, will find a virtual resource library in these three volumes. [R: BL, 15 Apr 80, p. 1212; C&RL, July 80, p. 382; JAL, May 80, p. 113; SLJ, Sept 80, p. 45]

11 RECREATION AND SPORTS

BIBLIOGRAPHIES

335.   Nunn, Marshall E. **Sports**. Littleton, CO, Libraries Unlimited, 1976. 224p. index. (Spare Time Guides, No. 10). $11.50. LC 75-33869. ISBN 0-87287-124-X.

Information on 649 books on major U.S. sports, covering all aspects of a given sport (reference titles, how-to-play books, biographies and autobiographies of players and coaches, histories, and collections of anecdotes and articles), is provided in this guide to popular sports literature. In addition to complete bibliographic information (including pagination, price, and LC card number), descriptive annotations are given for all titles. Entries are arranged in subject chapters, subdivided into reference and non-reference sections and arranged alphabetically within these subdivisions. Following the main chapters of the book is an annotated listing of 93 sports periodicals, arranged by subject. Associations and organizations are described in a separate listing, and a directory of publishers (with addresses) and a complete author-title index conclude the book.

The popularity of professional spectator sports in the United States today is paralleled by an increasing interest in participatory sports – and the result has been a prodigious production of books in both areas. The present volume provides librarians, sportsmen, and sports fans with guidance through the multitude of available sports books. [R: ARBA 77, p. 324; BL, 15 June 77, p. 1596; Choice, Oct 76, p. 960; LJ, 1 Apr 77, p. 788; WLB, Sept 76, p. 90]

DICTIONARIES AND ENCYCLOPEDIAS

336.   Menke, Frank G. **The Encyclopedia of Sports**. 6th rev. ed. Revisions by Pete Palmer. London, Thomas Yoseloff; Cranbury, NJ, A. S. Barnes, 1978 (c1977). 1132p. illus. index. $30.00. LC 76-58581. ISBN 0-498-02114-9.

Menke's *Encyclopedia of Sports* is by now a familiar title on the sports reference book shelf. Since the publication of its fifth edition in 1975 (with coverage through 1972), many important events have taken place in the sports world. The book's format remains the same as in previous editions: arrangement is alphabetical by name of sport, and each entry includes the history of the sport, the names of champions and record holders, scores, rules, and diagrams and dimensions of playing areas. Coverage also remains extremely broad and includes all of the well-known sports as well as such off-beat ones as Gaelic football and hurling. Menke's work remains an essential purchase for all types of libraries; it is a valuable one-volume compendium of sports information and is noted for its accuracy, wide coverage, wealth of detail, and up-to-date information. [R: ARBA 79, p. 339; WLB, Dec 78, p. 346]   Marshall E. Nunn

337.   Sparano, Vin T. **Complete Outdoors Encyclopedia**. New York, Harper and Row, 1973. 622p. illus. (part col.). index. (An Outdoor Life Book). $18.95. LC 72-90934. ISBN 0-06-013955-2.

This compilation, nicely illustrated, devotes almost a third of the text to fishing – equipment, techniques, and the fish themselves, many shown in the color plates. Shooting, hunting, and game animals together are allotted almost the same amount of space with details of types of firearms, habits of wildlife, etc. Considerably less attention is given to camping, boating, archery, hunting dogs, and first aid. There are also lists of sources of information (fish and game departments, state travel agencies, and shooting preserves), plus a fairly good bibliography of recent books on the subjects covered. Quite a few specific brand name products are mentioned, probably because of the availability of good photographs of them.

Some of the older books of this sort, although outdated in many ways, are still quite good and should not be discarded. *The Hunter's Encyclopedia*, edited by Raymond Camp (Stackpole, o.p.) is a favorite for answering a variety of reference questions (such as methods of tanning hides). Other titles include *The Outdoor Encyclopedia* (A. S. Barnes, 1957, o.p.) and the *Outdoor Life Cyclopedia* (Grosset & Dunlap, 1942, o.p.), which are quite valuable for their articles by many of the "greats" in the old outdoor writing field: Townsend Whelen, Jack O'Connor, Ellsworth Jaeger, etc.

Ed. note: A second edition of the *Complete Outdoors Encyclopedia* was published in 1980, but was unavailable for review at the time of this writing. [R: ARBA 74, p. 228; LJ, 15 Apr 73, p. 1304; LJ, 15 Apr 74, p. 1100; WLB, June 73, p. 869]   R. G. Schipf

338. **Webster's Sports Dictionary.** Springfield, MA, G. & C. Merriam, 1976. 503p. illus. $8.95. LC 75-42076. ISBN 0-87779-067-1.

Webster's Sports Dictionary is the standard and authoritative reference book in its field. Its coverage, treatment, and scope mark it as an outstanding source. It defines terms used in widely popular spectator sports, in international games (cricket, rugby, Australian football), and in recreational activities (hunting, fishing, scuba diving, mountain climbing). It is designed mainly for use by the casual fan, but the more knowledgeable sports buff will turn to it for explanations of peculiarities in rules and for specifications of playing fields and equipment. The definitions themselves, presented in a standard A-Z format, include quotations from prominent athletes and sportswriters showing how words are used in context; they are exceptionally well done. More than 200 drawings and diagrams depict playing fields, techniques, and equipment. A winner all the way. [R: ARBA 77, p. 326; BL, 1 Nov 76, p. 420; LJ, July 76, p. 1515; LJ, 15 Apr 77, p. 875; WLB, Sept 76, p. 90]   Marshall E. Nunn

BASEBALL

339. **Official Encyclopedia of Baseball.** 10th ed. by Hy Turkin and S. C. Thompson. Ed. by Pete Palmer. Cranbury, NJ, A. S. Barnes, 1979. 650p. illus. $17.95. LC 78-68004. ISBN 0-498-02374-5.

Although Turkin's work lacks the distinctive depth of *The Baseball Encyclopedia* (see following entry), it still is a valuable reference book in its own right. It has fact-packed chapters on baseball history, the World Series, best lifetime marks of all kinds, Baseball Hall of Fame, umpires' register, official rules, and a special features section. If your library does not have *The Baseball Encyclopedia*, you should buy this work for your sports reference section.   Marshall E. Nunn

340. Reichler, Joseph L., ed. **The Baseball Encyclopedia: The Complete and Official Record of Major League Baseball.** 4th ed., rev. and expanded. New York, Macmillan Publishing; London, Collier Macmillan Publishers, 1979. 2245p. $29.95. LC 73-21291. ISBN 0-02-578970-8.

This is the most complete compilation of baseball statistics available. Major sections include: all-time single season and lifetime batting, pitching, and fielding records; year-by-year records of each team and its players (order of finish, lineups, team statistics, etc.); manager register, including complete record of each; player register (most pitchers *excluded* for the first time); pitcher register; world series and championship playoffs (line scores, pitchers, home runs, highlights, composite box scores, world series lifetime batting and pitching leaders); and all-star games (line scores, pitchers, home runs, highlights). There is explanatory material on the background of baseball and on the research and editing done on pre-1920 records.

This edition has new compilations: no-hit, no-run pitchers; consecutive games played; Hall of Fame roster; triple-crown, MVP, Cy Young, and rookie-of-the-year award winners; and lifetime major league team rosters. One feature dropped, and missed, from this edition is the listing of injuries/illnesses with each individual player's record: an apparent dropoff in performance or a gap in the record was often explained by this notation. Errors seem more numerous in this edition, although mistakes are somewhat understandable considering the mass of data involved. In the "manager register," there are numerous conflicting rankings (a manager's rank in the top 10 in games managed, games won, etc., is indicated in his record, as appropriate).

Mistakes notwithstanding, this is an invaluable reference tool and a feast for the baseball figure filbert. Binding, paper, and typography are excellent.

Ed. note: David Neft's *Sports Encyclopedia: Baseball* (Grosset and Dunlap, 1979. $12.95pa.) serves as a useful and unusual supplement to *The Baseball Encyclopedia* by arranging its information in chapters according to certain time periods. The editors summarize major league baseball action in each time period and then provide summaries of individual seasons and detailed team rosters and statistics for each season. [R: ARBA 80, p. 314; LJ, 1 Sept 79, p. 1685]   Jerry Cao

BASKETBALL

341. Hollander, Zander, ed. **The Modern Encyclopedia of Basketball.** 2nd rev. ed. New York, Doubleday, 1979. 624p. illus. bibliog. index. (An Associated Features Book; Dolphin Books). $12.50pa. LC 78-22636. ISBN 0-385-14381-8.

First published in 1969 and now presented in its second revision, Hollander's work is comprehensive, thorough, and accurate. It devotes almost equal attention to the colleges and the pros; emphasis in both sections is on the modern years. The yearly round-ups for college play begin with the 1937-38 season and include all scores in the NCAA and NIT champion games; the rest of the college section includes all-time major college records, profiles of the greatest players and coaches, and year-by-year records of the major colleges from 1938. The pro section has the same type of information, with one important addition: the NBA and ABA all-time register of every player who has appeared in league competition since 1956. Miscellaneous sections at the end of the book include players and teams elected to the Hall of Fame, and official amateur rules.

The editors have added two new but very brief chapters to the college section: one on collegiate women's basketball and one on junior college competition. And they have brought the information in all the other chapters up to date. Please note that this new edition appears in paperback and is issued by a different publisher. It remains the one indispensable source on this subject for sports fans and libraries alike. [R: ARBA 80, p. 315; LJ, 1 Oct 79, p. 2085]   Marshall E. Nunn

FOOTBALL AND SOCCER

342. Henshaw, Richard. **The Encyclopedia of World Soccer.** Washington, New Republic Books, 1979. 828p. illus. bibliog. $25.00. LC 78-26570. ISBN 0-915220-34-2.

Soccer, the most popular game in the world today, is making great strides in popularity in the United States and Canada. The North American Soccer League (NASL), fully discussed in this book, has grown to 24 teams since its beginning in 1968. The growing number of players, notably among the young, augurs well for the future of the game here and implies a need for this hefty volume in libraries.

Among the attractive features in the *Encyclopedia of World Soccer* are: the history and statistics of soccer in countries and territories of the world, from Afghanistan to Zambia; origins and development of the famous soccer clubs of the world; biographies of 80 players; and meanings of 140 technical and colloquial terms.

Facts and figures that should be useful to the reference desk in helping to settle bets include complete game-by-game statistics of the World Cup, year-by-year records of the NASL, and rules of the game. Among the sidelights herein are entries for women's soccer, great disasters, and origins of the game. College soccer in the United States, perhaps because it is little noticed, is a notable omission.

The author, Richard Henshaw, an American, is a former university soccer player who has contributed to periodicals and film encyclopedias. He spent seven years in writing this book. It is an obvious labor of love, written for the enthusiast. Carefully laid out and cross-referenced, it contains balck-and-white photographs, judiciously used. The extensive bibliography is divided into five parts: general reference, yearbooks, origins and early history of games, general books, and World Cup.

As an aficionado of the game who first watched exhibition games between the Vancouver (British Columbia) All-Stars and visiting international sides, including the Moscow Dynamo, the Glasgow Rangers, and Tottemham Hotspur in the 1950s, I find the book to be comprehensive, well organized, and interestingly written. It should be an invaluable help in reference wherever there is interest in soccer. A true feeling for the game is evident here.   Randy Rafferty

343.   Treat, Roger. **The Encyclopedia of Football.** 16th rev. ed. Ed. by Pete Palmer. Cranbury, NJ, A. S. Barnes, 1979. 738p. illus. $17.95. LC 79-63272. ISBN 0-498-02421-0.

The sixteenth revised edition of *The Encyclopedia of Football* is still an excellent authority on what happened when in professional football. Within the book's chapters, one finds the complete National Football League, American Football League, and the All-American Football Conference records, team rosters, some basic data on every player who ever wore a professional football team's uniform, draft choices, a year-by-year history of professional football from 1919 to the present, Hall of Fame members, listings of individual and team champions, and a rundown on other leagues that existed at some time. There are stadium diagrams and small head shots of some of the better-known players. A list of retirements and deaths for each year is a useful feature. Brief descriptions of the playoff games and the Superbowls will settle many arguments.   Susan Ebershoff-Coles

GAMES

344.   Brace, Edward R. **An Illustrated Dictionary of Chess.** 1st American ed. New York, David McKay, 1977. 320p. illus. $14.95. LC 77-77542. ISBN 0-679-50814-7.

This up-to-date, comprehensive volume provides the chess enthusiast with an alphabetical listing of a wide variety of game-related information. Included within its scope are biographies of leading players, definitions of terms, standard openings and endings, defenses (and variations), and a selective list of books about chess and chess players. Valuable cross references direct the reader from one entry to another. Biographies are given of current players rated International Master or International Grandmaster, as well as for other outstanding players. Entries include dates of titles held, details of tournaments, and, for living players, their Elo rating. Sources of biographical information are not cited.

Descriptions for standard openings and endings include identifying moves and, often, historical background. Characteristic or defining moves are noted in italics in the text of entries for many openings, defenses, and variations. Illustrations of board positions also accompany the more notable moves. Selected book titles on chess and chess players are included within the alphabetical sequence. However, readers searching for a complete bibliography of chess works should consult Betts' *Chess: An Annotated Bibliography of Works Published in the English Language, 1850-1968* (G. K. Hall, 1974. $35.00). Likewise, those interested in the organization of chess in various countries, or in chess and its relationship to fields such as drama or psychology, would find such information in Anne Sunnucks' *Encyclopaedia of Chess* (St. Martin's Press, 1977. $17.95). As a source for quickly locating concise information on chess and its players, though, Brace's work is a thorough and very useful compilation. [R: ARBA 79, p. 347]   Susan F. Sudduth

345. Frey, Richard L., ed.-in-chief. **The Official Encyclopedia of Bridge.** 3rd ed., new, rev., and expanded. Authorized by the American Contract Bridge League and prepared with the assistance of its staff. New York, Crown, 1976. 858p. bibliog. $15.95. LC 76-17053. ISBN 0-517-52724-3.

This encyclopedia is the definitive guide to contract bridge, as well as an instruction manual, and player's guide. Representing a complete revision of the 1970 second edition, it provides up-to-date information, including the 1975 change in the laws of duplicate bridge. All North American and most important international tournament winners are covered through 1974. The principal sections include general information, biographies, tournament results, and bibliography. *The Official Encyclopedia of Bridge* is designed to interest every bridge player from beginner to professional. It gives definitions for every term, including slang, along with illustrated descriptions of every standard bid, recognized convention, and type of play. There are long essays on the history of bridge, as well as the history of playing cards, bridge etiquette and ethics, tournament direction, and bridge clubs and their management. Every bridge-playing country is represented, although the foreign-language glossary of the earlier edition is not included. The term "official" is quite accurate for this work. [R: ARBA 78, p. 322]   James R. Crawford

346. Morehead, Albert H., and Geoffrey Mott-Smith, eds. **Hoyle Up-To-Date.** Newly rev. New York, Grosset & Dunlap, 1970. 279p. illus. glossary. $2.95.

Edmund Hoyle (1672-1769) published his first work on card games in 1742. Early titles concerned themselves with individual games such as whist, piquet, quadrille, and others, and it was not until later editions that many games were combined into one volume. Hoyle was widely recognized as an authority on the rules and strategy of cards, and he gave lessons in London. Although his name is carried on in the many editions since his death, many games are included now that were unheard of during his lifetime.

Like the other editions, this volume presents the rules, strategy, purpose, and, at times, the mathematical probabilities of achieving certain goals or hands during play. Line drawings and diagrams are included for clarification. A comparison of the present volume with other editions, such as Frey, reveals relatively few significant differences. Rules change in minor points as common usage dictates, or upon the decision of organizations devoted to promoting national and international play, and games are added, or dropped, from one edition to another as popularity waxes or wanes. This is a good edition, but it differs little from relatively recent editions of Hoyle.

Ed. note: Another comprehensive volume on games is *Scarne's Encyclopedia of Games* (Harper and Row, 1973. 628p. $20.00), which organizes instructions for over 1,000 games of chance under 28 chapters. There are a glossary of game terms and a detailed index. Clearly written and more readable than Hoyle, Scarne includes games for all ages and covers more than just card games. [R: ARBA 72, p. 258]   Cecil F. Clotfelter

GOLF

347.   Ross, John M., ed. **Golf Magazine's Encyclopedia of Golf.** updated and rev. New York, Harper & Row, Publishers, 1979. 439p. illus. index. $19.95. LC 77-11818. ISBN 0-06-011552-1.

One of the primary references for the sport of golf, this work has had a major overhauling since its original 1970 edition. So major is the revision that the book carries a new copyright date. Everything under the sun and on the green that has to do with the game, past and present, bounces between the pages like the proverbial white ball that aficionados pursue. We are treated to a history of golf, and to its personalities, rules, equipment, fundamentals, championship courses, and worldwide tournaments. The interested can find statistics, records, and all sorts of lesser-known facts and fancies. Information seekers are aided by a detailed table of contents and index, and an appropriate glossary, all of which afford the user quick access to the right answer. A generous portion of black-and-white photographs and drawings illustrates the text. If you think a shotgun tournament is played with live ammunition and hunting dogs, then you definitely need this book. Old caddies never die, they just become golf professionals and followers of the game. [R: ARBA 80, p. 322]   Steve Rybicki

348.   Ward-Thomas, Pat, and others. **The World Atlas of Golf.** New York, Random House, 1976. 280p. illus. (part col.). index. $25.00. LC 76-10297. ISBN 0-394-40814-4.

If you are not one of the approximately 16 million golfers in the United States and Britain, for whom this book will be a constant temptation until purchased, the book may just persuade you to join the ranks. Gorgeously illustrated, the book describes and provides drawings (full color) and photographs (full color also) of 70 of the "world's greatest" golf courses. Reading through the book also provides a desultory history of the game, with photographs of the great players interspersed with pictures of specific holes on specific courses, and sometimes the two in conjunction. The authors have concentrated, however, on golf architecture, the creation of the courses themselves, and they have done an admirable job. Too, they describe the evolution of courses and equipment, which may provide some surprises (and sighs for having missed some of the early fun). For golfers who plan to play the courses described some day, the authors have also given precise descriptions of yardage for each hole, the greens, and possible difficult spots (complete with advice as to how to play them). Alistair Cooke's introduction provides the perfect tone for appreciating the text, but it is merely frosting on the cake. [R: ARBA 77, p. 335; BL, 1 Sept 77, p. 74; LJ, 15 Feb 77, p. 509]   Koert C. Loomis, Jr.

HOCKEY

349.   Hollander, Zander, and Hal Bock, eds. **The Complete Encyclopedia of Ice Hockey.** Rev. ed. Englewood Cliffs, NJ, Prentice-Hall, 1974. 702p. illus. index. LC 73-15019. ISBN 0-13-149913-5.

A good indication of the scope of this volume is to be found in its subtitle, "The Heroes, Teams, Great Moments, and Records of the National Hockey League." One of the most readable books on the subject, this edition covers the activities of the National Hockey League from its founding in 1917 through the 1973/74 season. It also includes, for the first time, complete records of the World Hockey Association.

The *Pro and Amateur Hockey Guide* (St. Louis, Sporting News. $3.00pa.) provides annual updates on leagues, teams, records, and playoff games. [R: ARBA 76, p. 363; Choice, Apr 75, p. 198; LJ, 1 Jan 75, p. 44; RQ, Summer 75, p. 356]

HUNTING AND FISHING

350. Clotfelter, Cecil F. **Hunting and Fishing.** Littleton, CO, Libraries Unlimited, 1974. 118p. index. (Spare Time Guides, No. 2). $7.50. LC 73-90569. ISBN 0-87287-079-0.

Individual sportsmen, as well as librarians, will find this volume of the Spare Time Guides series to be a useful source of information. Mr. Clotfelter has provided a list of 168 books and 26 large-circulation periodicals, with annotations that describe the kinds of information each book or periodical contains. Listed in separate sections are various national organizations concerned with aspects of hunting and fishing, the publishers of the books included in the bibliography (with addresses), and the names and addresses of manufacturers and suppliers of hunting and fishing equipment. In this one volume, then, is a wealth of information about hunting and fishing, whether the reader wants a general overview of the subject or something very specific. The complete author-title-subject index facilitates use of the guide.

Anyone interested in hunting, archery, firearms, or fishing will be interested in this book. Not a how-to book, this guide provides information on where to find information. Whether the subject is hunting dogs, trout fishing, fly-tying, hand-loading ammunition, or bow-hunting for deer, Mr. Clotfelter's guide tells one where to look. [R: ARBA 75, p. 324; Choice, Oct 74, p. 1106; LJ, 1 Sept 74, p. 2054; RQ, Fall 74, p. 70; WLB, June 74, p. 852]

351. McClane, Albert Jules, ed. **McClane's New Standard Fishing Encyclopedia and International Angling Guide.** Enl. and rev. ed. New York, Holt, Rinehart & Winston, 1974. 1156p. illus. bibliog. $50.00. LC 74-6108. ISBN 0-03-060325-0.

While it is nice to have a large selection of books and magazines about fishing close at hand, for quick reference there is no substitute for an excellent encyclopedic reference work. This revised and updated edition is the one to have.

There are 1,156 pages (99 more than in the first edition) with hundreds of line drawings, color photos, and black-and-white photos. Entries are arranged alphabetically from Aawa, a fish of Hawaiian waters, to Zooplankton. Within the alphabetical arrangement are common terms, technical terms, biographies of persons important to fishing, states and their fishing offerings, both freshwater and saltwater fish, and much more. Fishing in other nations of the world is included, and one can find the names of the famous rivers and lakes listed under the country in which they are located. Definitions and articles vary in length from a few words to many pages, depending on the subject. All articles are written by people well qualified in the subject field; the list of contributors and their qualifications fills six pages. There is also a 19-page bibliography of sources.

All in all, this encyclopedia is undoubtedly the most complete and up-to-date reference work on fishing that can be found. It includes material of value to the biologist as well as to the sportsman. [R: ARBA 75, p. 338; BL, 15 July 75, p. 1207; Choice, Apr 75, p. 198; WLB, Jan 75, p. 358]   Cecil F. Clotfelter

MOTOR SPORTS

352. Ebershoff-Coles, Susan, and Charla Ann Leibenguth. **Motorsports: A Guide to Information Sources.** Detroit, Gale, 1979. 193p. index. (Sports, Games, and Pastimes Information Guide Series, Vol. 5; Gale Information Guide Library). $28.00. LC 79-13736. ISBN 0-8103-1446-0.

This is the only work of its kind and is so well done that, although periodic updating will be needed, it is unlikely to be superseded. The bibliography is comprehensive, covering all forms of motorsport; it lists English-language materials published since 1965, though some important older works are included. Periodicals are listed by title only; specific articles are not indexed. Every item is annotated, sometimes extensively, and there are author, title, and subject indexes.

There are two especially valuable features of this bibliography. The first is its inclusion of much important material that is peripheral to the literature: sources for racing films; a list of race drivers' schools; museums and libraries with collections of motorsport materials and literature; and a directory of about 130 racing organizations. All except the last are annotated.

The second special feature is easily overlooked at first glance—the authors provide addresses for every school, museum, film source, library, organization, and periodical. A separate list gives addresses for every publisher of a work in the bibliography, including those privately printed (many of these publications are from small, relatively obscure presses). Since the user may not have access to a library with extensive holdings in motorsport literature, and since many of these works are still in print, the addresses are a useful, thoughtful addition to the book. [R: ARBA 80, p. 325]   Philip R. Rider

353.   Georgano, G. N., ed. **The Encyclopedia of Motor Sport.** New York, Viking, 1971. 656p. illus. (A Studio Book). LC 73-162664. ISBN 0-670-29405-5.

Twenty-five writers have contributed to this book, which is divided into four major parts. Part 1, a general introduction, includes information about racing formulas, American racing clubs, and racing specialties. Part 2 describes 161 racing events. Part 3 contains the biographies of more than 350 racing car drivers. Part 4 describes all makes of all car sizes. The extent of coverage of the sport is quite good; there are 1,700 photographs (including 62 excellent color plates), a glossary, and an index. [R: ARBA 73, p. 279; LJ, 15 Jan 72, p. 184]

SAILING

354.   **Encyclopedia of Sailing.** Rev. and updated by the eds. of *Yacht Racing/Cruising*, with Robert Scharff and Richard Henderson. New York, Harper and Row, 1978. 468p. illus. $24.95. LC 76-26233. ISBN 0-06-013292-2.

Armchair sailors, day trippers, and racing enthusiasts will find a detailed, clear orderly presentation of numerous aspects of sailing in this revised *Encyclopedia*. Unfortunately, it has no index, and it is arranged not alphabetically but by topic. The table of contents is detailed, but specific information was difficult to locate. For someone willing to sit down and read through the book, it provides well-written chapters on racing tactics and rules, the history of pleasure sailing, and detailed sections on day sailing and cruising. Of particular interest is the catalog of class boats, with photographs of each type as well as all the specifications for several hundred one-design and offshore cruising or racing boats. This *Encyclopedia* will be useful as a reference or circulating book. [R: ARBA 79, p. 352]
                Margery Read

SKIING

355.   Needham, Richard, ed. **Ski Magazine's Encyclopedia of Skiing.** Rev. and updated. New York, Harper & Row, Publishers, 1979. 452p. illus. index. $25.00. LC 77-11803. ISBN 0-06-014006-2.

The arrangement of this volume is the same as in earlier editions, in six sections: "The History of Skiing," "Ski Equipment," "Principles of Skiing," "Ski Competition," "Where to Ski," a glossary, lexicon, and directory of ski associations, and an index, which was lacking in the first edition. The longest sections are those on principles of skiing and ski competition. Information on cross-country skiing has been greatly expanded in both the equipment and principles sections. The competition section is up to date through the 1976 Winter Olympics and includes other statistics as recent as 1978. Information given on ski areas is also very current. The volume is well illustrated with more than 250 photographs and drawings that are clear and relevant to the text. Questions such as "what Alpine skiers have won three Olympic gold medals?" and "how effective are waxless cross-country skis?" can easily be answered by this encyclopedia. It is a useful reference book and is also enjoyable for browsing. [R: ARBA 80, p. 327]   David W. Brunton

SWIMMING

356.   Besford, Pat, comp. **Encyclopaedia of Swimming**. 2nd ed. London, Robert Hale; distr., New York, St. Martin's Press, 1976. 302p. illus. index. $10.00. LC 76-16687. ISBN 0-7091-5063-6.

When the first edition of this book was published in 1971, it quickly established itself as the single most comprehensive and authoritative reference work on competitive swimming. The second edition enhances this reputation. The author continues the format and emphasis that he used so successfully in the first edition: arrangement of entries is alphabetical and the work contains many concise and well-done biographical sketches as well as lists of various champions and records. There are also two sections of black-and-white action photographs. [R: ARBA 78, p. 328; LJ, 1 Feb 77, p. 372; WLB, May 77, p. 779]   Marshall E. Nunn

TENNIS

357.   Shannon, Bill, ed. **United States Tennis Association Official Encyclopedia of Tennis**. Rev. and updated. New York, Harper and Row, 1979. 497p. illus. index. $20.00. LC 77-3777. ISBN 0-06-014478-5.

The *Official Encyclopedia of Tennis*, written under the aegis of the United States Tennis Association, remains the most comprehensive work on this subject. Well illustrated with hundreds of photos and drawings, the *Encyclopedia* covers nearly every aspect of the game—its history, equipment, rules, major championship and tournament results, the Tennis Hall of Fame, playing techniques—and includes a glossary of tennis terms. Numerous tables present a comprehensive record of tennis competition results through 1977. The biographical section provides sketches of Hall of Fame members, with brief entries for foreign players and American tennis greats who were not elected to the Hall of Fame.

Unfortunately, the major weakness of the *Encyclopedia* has not been corrected in this revised edition. Location of the information is often difficult, since the table of contents is in run-on paragraph style, listing only the first page number of each section. For example, the section on major tournaments and championships gives the first page in that section and then lists two pages of headings with no page numbers. Also, none of the names in the biographical section are listed in the index. Consequently, one must look through the entire section to trace a particular player's career. Nevertheless, this is the most complete and authoritative book on the game of tennis. [R: LJ, 1 Oct 79, p. 2086]   Susan C. Holte

12 SOCIOLOGY

BIBLIOGRAPHIES

358. Mark, Charles. **Sociology of America: A Guide to Information Sources.** Detroit, Gale, 1976. 454p. index. (American Studies Information Guide Series, Volume 1). $28.00. LC 73-17560. ISBN 0-8103-1267-0.

This selective bibliography contains 1,861 numbered entries, almost 80% of which are annotated. Included are primarily scholarly publications focusing on American society in general and specific aspects of American life and culture in particular. While studies by American sociologists published after 1960 comprise the bulk of this volume, classics published earlier and important books on American society by non-Americans are listed, too. The material has been carefully selected on the basis of several criteria designed to yield the most significant, most frequently cited or consulted works. Intentionally omitted are many titles dealing with theoretical and applied sociology.

Organized into 24 chapters, this guide begins with three chapters on bibliographic resources, general reference tools, and periodical literature. The remaining chapters enumerate monographs and research reports in four major areas of sociological specialization: 1) American society as a whole, the population, and its spatial distribution in regions and in rural and urban communities; 2) principal segments of a socially stratified system and its division by race, religion, national origin, and social class; 3) the private sphere of life, including socialization, education, and recreation; and 4) the structure of power relations in society. Some theoretical works dealing with American sociology are listed in the final chapter.

Author, title, and subject indexes complete this useful bibliographic tool. Unlike some less substantial volumes in the Gale Information Guide Library, this one is certainly worth its price. [R: ARBA 77, p. 339; BL, 1 Apr 77, p. 1198; Choice, Dec 76, p. 1274; WLB, Oct 76, p. 189]   Leonard Grundt

DIRECTORIES

359. Romanofsky, Peter, ed.-in-chief. **Social Service Organizations.** Westport, CT, Greenwood Press, 1978. 2v. index. (The Greenwood Encyclopedia of American Institutions). $59.50. LC 77-84754. ISBN 0-8371-9829-1/set.

This compilation contains historical sketches of nearly 200 voluntary agencies whose primary function is to provide social services. Organizations included are representative of major fields of social work (child welfare, health, migrants, family services, etc.), and were selected because of their historical significance, longevity, size, influence, or, in some cases, the activity of nationally prominent individuals. The editor, a specialist in the history of social and child welfare, wrote most of the articles; the remaining 33 were composed by other specialists and are signed. Each agency biography not only chronicles its founding, leaders, structural changes, mergers, and highlights of activity, but also analyzes its position in relation to other agencies and its historical period. Each article also cites the best sources of information for further study. In the four appendices are: a list of church-related agencies, a list of agencies by function, a chronology of founding dates, and organization genealogies. The complete table of contents, with cross references, appears in both volumes; a detailed index completes the set. This important reference tool contains much more information than other directories currently available covering similar fields; it will frequently be the first place to look for material on such voluntary organizations. [R: ARBA 79, p. 355; BL, 1 Apr 79, p. 1243; Choice, Nov 78, p. 1191; LJ, 15 June 78, p. 1259; LJ, 15 Apr 79, p. 886; WLB, Oct 78, p. 188]   Laura H. McGuire

ENCYCLOPEDIAS

360.   **Encyclopedia of Social Work. Seventeenth Issue.** John B. Turner, ed.-in-chief. Washington, National Association of Social Workers, 1977. 2v. index. $40.00/set. LC 30-30948. ISBN 0-87101-074-7.

The *Encyclopedia* is without reservation an indispensable source for information and data on every aspect of the social work craft, as well as on salient facets of the fields of sociology, anthropology, public affairs, social welfare history, human organization, and urban and regional planning. Well printed in easy-to-read type with an excellent binding, the two-volume set encompasses a cornucopia of informational materials that can be put to immediate use by social work practitioners or employed as background information by workers in the field of behavioral science. The cost of the set constitutes an excellent bargain, given the high quality of the contents and the immensity of information contained within the 1,700 double-columned pages of print. The present edition builds upon earlier versions of the *Encyclopedia* in retaining a dual classification system that incorporates the categories of social work and social welfare within a single alphabetical sequence. In addition, biographies of prominent deceased social work and social welfare personalities are included, as well as a separate section of pertinent national statistical trends. The entries are written not only by specialists in social work and social welfare but also by prominent sociologists, anthropologists, psychologists, and a scattering of social historians. The entries are arranged in alphabetical order according to topic, with cross references and bibliographical aids appended to many of them. A comprehensive index and a serviceable table of contents act as finding aids. Twenty-one context articles dealing with major topics are included to illustrate the manner in which social work and social welfare relate to major societal themes. [R: ARBA 78, p. 336; Choice, Jan 78, p. 1478]   Norman Lederer

361.   **Encyclopedia of Sociology.** Guilford, CT, Dushkin, 1974. 330p. illus. bibliog. $5.95pa. LC 73-87072. ISBN 0-87967-055-X.

Sociology has produced an extensive interdisciplinary literature and vocabulary, and ready reference sources have not always kept pace with the expanding literature. There is a particular need for high-quality, current dictionaries like the *Encyclopedia of Sociology*.

This work provides 1,300 concise articles, arranged alphabetically, covering "the language of sociology, the full range of its theories, the institutions of sociology, and the leading figures in both historical and contemporary sociology." Prepared by scholars in the field, the articles treat sociology as an interdisciplinary subject and touch upon psychology, economics, anthropology, political science, education, and history. The value of this source is enhanced by "see" and "see also" references, photographs, suggestions for further readings, and a bibliography. Subject maps throughout the volume outline coverage of 15 major subject areas; these include, among others, methodology and statistics, race and ethnic relations, urban sociology, and social theory. [R: ARBA 75, p. 351; BL, 15 Sept 74, p. 105; Choice, July 74, p. 734]   Peter Hernon

AGING

362.   Norback, Craig, and Peter Norback. **The Older American's Handbook: Practical Information and Help on Medical and Nursing Care, Housing, Recreation, Legal Services, Employment, In-Home Services, Food, Associations and Organizations, Transportation,**

Mental Health and Counseling for Older and Retired Americans. New York, Van Nostrand Reinhold, 1977. 311p. $8.95pa. LC 77-11945. ISBN 0-442-26062-8.

This book is basically a compilation of lists of various agencies, associations, publications, government programs, etc., that are likely to be of use to the older American. Arrangement is alphabetical by the title given to a particular list. The emphasis is on governmental programs (especially federal), but private programs are also included. A partial listing of contents includes area agencies on aging, housing (which covers United States housing developments for the elderly), legal services, mental health centers, shows and conventions. The title is inexact; the book is more useful for those working with organized programs for the older American than for the average individual older American. It can be used both for an overview of programs available for the aged and for quick directory-type information (the lack of an index makes the latter use dependent on finding the correct list through the table of contents).

In the last few years, a number of subject compilations of information have become available in other directories. In comparison to some of these other compilations (for example, *Educational Marketplace* by the same authors), the *Older American's Handbook* is one of the most useful. In comparison to a publication on the same subject, *Sourcebook on Aging* (Marquis, 1979. $39.50), the *Handbook* is better for addresses and explanations of government programs. The *Sourcebook* is better for statistics and for lists of sources, and it does have an index. Arranged in 10 sections — Aging in General, Health, Economic Status, Housing, Employment, Education, Transportation, Leisure and Retirement, Special Concerns and Problems, and Government Programs — the *Sourcebook* is invaluable for anyone planning services or writing proposals relating to the aging. Carefully documented statistics are provided for each topic. [R: ARBA 79, p. 357; BL, 15 Feb 78, p. 979; LJ, 1 Feb 78, p. 378; WLB, Apr 78, p. 650]   Genevieve M. Casey
Janet Sheets

MARRIAGE AND THE FAMILY

363.   Bernstein, Joanne E. **Books to Help Children Cope with Separation and Loss.** New York, R. R. Bowker, 1977. 255p. index. $16.25. LC 77-23970. ISBN 0-8352-0837-0.

"Long after I was a man grown I read a confession by Samuel Butler that he had never loved his father; before that I had supposed I was the only such wretch that ever lived." So wrote E. W. Howe in his autobiography 50 years ago. The recognition that he was not unique in his experience was important but too late to have saved him the agonies of guilt he carried throughout his life. Joanne Bernstein's fine book provides 438 annotated entries for books dealing with the traumas of separation and loss (Howe's father had deserted his family) for young people between the ages of 3 and 16, books that, when accompanied by the personal guidance of caring adults, can help a child realize that others, too, grieve, feel guilt, know disruption.

The introductory section, "Using Books to Help Children Cope with Separation and Loss," is a model of clarity and conciseness. Criteria for the selection of titles are thorough and the compiler set herself the task of reading every book she listed after she had searched the review media. Bernstein also includes "certain books that enjoy considerable popularity and wide circulation . . . even though, [in her opinion], they are poorly written and may be of questionable therapeutic value" (p. 5).

Bernstein's chapters on "Separation and Loss" and "Bibliotherapy" are jargon-free, constructive, cautious, and provide excellent summations of grief therapy, thanatology, and bibliotherapy. She reminds the reader that in our culture, "death and other separations have come to be looked upon as unnatural events, perhaps even sins" (p. 15). She also issues a vital caveat: no one should "begin to believe, even for a moment, that reading will magically solve problems or that insight gained from reading and discussion will replace the active work that is necessary to overcome personal difficulties" (p. 37).

This work will be useful beyond its stated topic. The annotations and thoughtful arrangement of entries not only provide the necessary bibliographical information (including the availability of the book in paperback), but also reading and interest levels. Several thorough indices are appended, as is a section on "Selected Reading for Adult Guides." Although I disagree with some of the titles the compiler has included, readily acknowledging the subjectivity of choice, this is such an excellent guide that I would like to see yearly supplements that would include the newest books, of which there are many, on the topics that Bernstein has discussed so well. [R: ARBA 79, p. 361; BL, 15 Mar 78, p. 1217; JAL, Jan 78, p. 356; SLJ, Mar 78, p. 104; WLB, Feb 78, p. 507]   Ruth I. Gordon

364.   Sell, Kenneth D., and Betty H. Sell. **Divorce in the United States, Canada, and Great Britain: A Guide to Information Sources.** Detroit, Gale, 1978. 298p. index. (Social Issues and Social Problems Information Guide Series, Vol. 1; Gale Information Guide Library). $28.00. LC 78-15894. ISBN 0-8103-1396-0.

This is a well-planned and carefully researched work consisting of 13 chapters, an addendum, and three indexes. As indicated in the title, this book is a guide to information sources on divorce. It is a research guide and is not a subject bibliography on the topic.

Chapters 1, 2, 4, and 5 contain information on using bibliographical sources. The authors discuss the use of bibliographies to locate specific bibliographies, books and articles, dissertations and theses, and unpublished materials. Chapters 3, 6, and 7 provide guidance for locating divorce information in basic reference books and statistical sources. Chapters 8 through 13 deal with finding divorce information in such places as the legal literature, and the news and nonprint media.

Although "divorce" is the theme subject of this guide, this reviewer feels that a more appropriate title for this work would be "Research Sources in the Social Sciences, as Applied to the Topic of Divorce." However, this is a valuable guide for people who are interested in learning how to do research. The authors have organized the materials in the same way that a knowledgeable librarian would, and the search strategies they describe are those which experienced researchers would perform. With some imagination, any researcher, graduate student, or library science student could use this work as a model for learning how to do indepth research in the social sciences.   Priscilla C. Geahigan

PRISONS

365.   Williams, Vergil L. **Dictionary of American Penology: An Introductory Guide.** Westport, CT, Greenwood Press, 1979. 530p. bibliog. index. $29.95. LC 77-94751. ISBN 0-313-20327-X.

This encyclopedic dictionary is especially geared to college students, citizens concerned with prison reform, and career correction personnel. Over half of the volume is devoted to appendices, including over 200 pages of U.S. government statistics taken mostly from the *Sourcebook of Criminal Justice Statistics, 1977*. It is unfortunate that no list of the 77 tables included was provided, as this makes it difficult to quickly locate specific information from this section. Other appendices give addresses of organizations, agencies, and prison systems.

Over one-half of the main text focuses on the ideological disputes among penologists during the last two decades: the increasing emphasis on rehabilitation, community-based corrections, and work release programs, among others. The remaining entries cover federal and state prisons and prison systems, and describe their administrative structures, geographical locations, capacities, and special problems. Important individual prisons, such as Attica, are also detailed. Some of the topics covered include the Attica uprising, disparity of sentences, homosexuality, political prisoners, recidivism, and Synanon. Numerous cross references, full bibliographic citations, and a thorough index contribute to the book's overall reference usefulness.   Gary D. Barber

13 WOMEN'S STUDIES

GENERAL WORKS

366. Hinding, Andrea, ed. **Women's History Sources: A Guide to Archives and Manuscript Collections in the United States.** Ames Sheldon Bower, associate ed.; Clarke A. Chambers, consulting ed. New York, R. R. Bowker, 1979. 2v. index. $175.00/set. LC 78-15634. ISBN 0-8352-1103-7.

Though Bowker hailed the advent of Hinding's monumental effort at ALA in the summer of 1978 with a gala champagne party, many of us in libraries, archives, women's studies, American studies, and in social history began wondering what had happened to this long-awaited source which did not surface until the fall of 1979. To say that this guide to more than 18,000 women-related collections housed in approximately 1,600 repositories throughout the United States could not be birthed hurriedly understates its scope and significance. The extensive verification of maiden and married names and of birth and death dates may have delayed the process, but this care will render invaluable assistance to researchers for decades to come.

Anyone who has ever dealt with archival materials related to women knows that as a rule women's papers have literally been buried in the collections listed under the name of a male relative, usually the husband. Unless a researcher knows a repository well, or happens upon a particularly knowledgeable archivist in a given repository, or makes a serindipitous discovery, she probably has been handicapped in doing women's history.

The survey method used to locate women's papers for *WHS* began with a "grand manuscript search" in the early 1970s led by such luminaries of women's history as Gerda Lerner, Carl Degler, Clarke Chambers, Anne Firor Scott, and Janet Wilson James. Funding of the project to the tune of $600,000 came from the National Endowment for the Humanities and the University of Minnesota (Hinding's affiliation).

Since the Women's History Sources Survey, from which *WHS* was generated, hinged upon the responses provided by over 7,000 repositories, supplemented only by the efforts of 20 fieldworkers during 1976 and 1977, the editors themselves are painfully aware of the "limitations and inconsistencies" that exist in *WHS* due to misinterpretations and/or carelessness on the part of responding institutions. Understaffed, underfunded and lacking name authority files to verify their holdings in many cases, many repositories' reports required extensive verification. This is why one who relies totally on *WHS* is likely to go astray. With regard to a book I am writing on political women, I sent out more than 300 letters to libraries and archives, and received replies from many institutions about materials not listed in *WHS*. On the other hand, I have found a great deal of "buried" material from locations that might never have occurred to me to query by using the splendid index volume of *WHS* with its personal, variant, and corporate name access. More excellent leads came my way when I checked the geographical areas.

A look at the full-page entry no. 9647 for the oral history holdings of the Minnesota Historical Society's Audio Visual Library demonstrates the precision of a *WHS* entry at its best – this particular entry, however, is in Editor Hinding's own geographical backyard.

No one knows better the problems of *Women's History Sources* than the editors themselves and the archivists and historians of women's history who assisted with this tremendous project. Anyone who seeks to find written and taped records generated by the notable and the not-so-notable women of American society – the poets and politicians, the nuns and novelists, the prostitutes and the paleobotanists – will laud this unparalleled source, surely the most significant contribution to women's history since *Notable American Women* (Belknap Press of Harvard University Press, 1971). [R: LJ, 15 Apr 80, p. 971; WLB, May 80, p. 589]   Esther F. Stineman

367. Partnow, Elaine, comp. and ed. **The Quotable Woman 1800-1975.** Los Angeles, Corwin Books, 1977. 539p. index. $20.00. LC 77-76016. ISBN 0-89474-006-7.

Most astounding of all when one considers this book of insights, perceptions, epigrams, musings, commentaries, exclamations, tributes, and lyrics all authored by women, is that no one thought of undertaking the project before this. The enormity of the task may have discouraged even those who saw the need, for from the outset, this was clearly a labor of retrieving women's buried and lost thoughts. The author's preface notes that 0.5% of the total number of quotations in *Bartlett's Familiar Quotations* and only 1% in the *Oxford Book* can be attributed to women.

Assuredly it cannot be that women have had nothing worthwhile to say. Partnow's sifting, selecting, and ordering of over 8,000 quotations, authored by some 1,300 women from Bernice Abbott to Clara Zetkin, prove that much has been said well both aloud and in print by women, later to be mislaid, minimized, and forgotten. Chronologically arranged by author's birth date from 1800 on (didn't any women before the nineteenth century utter a pithy phrase?), these quotations span a dazzling subject array from abandonment to Zionism, with predictable clusters at such terms as aging, children, freedom, love, marriage, motherhood, men, sexuality, war, work, and, of course, women.

The carefully wrought author index alone qualifies this book as an essential reference tool: each entry gives the author's full name (including married name), dates, nationality, relationships to other notables, profession, outstanding contributions, and honors. Partnow has handled the selection of most quotable lines with great skill when one considers the editorial problems of choosing lines from writers as eloquent and prolific as Simone de Beauvoir, Virginia Woolf, and George Eliot, or as obscure as Olive Custance and Katherine Hanky. Partnow has chosen well. Though some may fault the emphasis on contemporary women, or lament the omission of this or that scholar or writer, *The Quotable Woman* is a splendid achievement.

McPhee and FitzGerald's *Feminist Quotations: Voices of Rebels, Reformers, and Visionaries* (Thomas Y. Crowell, 1979. 271p. $12.95), though neither as international in scope nor as large as *The Quotable Woman* (its 271 pages and 1,500 "succinct statements" are dwarfed by *QW*'s 540 pages and 8,000 quotations), is nonetheless a unique source with a more specific mission. Its purpose is to order and make available relevant quotes from the work of feminists *only*; this *Feminist Quotations* does by way of a topical arrangement, with such headings as "Creatures of Man"; "Figures of Fantasy"; "The Business of Marriage"; "Leaders"; "Sisterhood"; and "Liberation of the Body." There is little overlap between the two works. Though both tend to pick up on the standard bearers of feminism from the first and second waves, Elizabeth Cady Stanton, the Pankhursts, Gloria Steinem, Charlotte Perkins Gilman, and Germaine Greer being notable examples, one is more likely to encounter the utterances of literati (Lillian Hellman, Doris Lessing, Gertrude Stein) and actresses (Elizabeth Taylor, Lily Tomlin) in *Quotable Woman. Feminist Quotations*, on the other hand, is quite strong on nineteenth-century feminist writers and theorists (Lillie Devreux Blake, Frances Power Cobbe, Virginia Penny).

Without *Feminist Quotations*, Lillie Devreux Blake's buried quip might have remained forever inaccessible for most of us—"'Adam was first formed, then Eve.' What does that prove? Either nothing, or that man is inferior to the fishes." This and other gems found in *Feminist Quotations* suggest that it deserves its place alongside *The Quotable Woman* and *Bartlett's* (actually "The Quotable Man") on most reference shelves. [R: ARBA 79, p. 373; BL, 1 July 78, p. 1700; Choice, June 78, p. 528; LJ, 15 Mar 78, p. 653; LJ, 15 Apr 78, p. 816; WLB, Sept 78, p. 89]   Esther F. Stineman

BIBLIOGRAPHIES

368. Harrison, Cynthia E., ed. **Women in American History: A Bibliography.** Pamela R. Byrne, managing ed. Santa Barbara, CA, ABC-Clio Press, 1979. 374p. index. (Clio Bibliography Series, No. 5). $78.00. LC 78-26194. ISBN 0-87436-260-1.

The idea behind the excellent tool *Women in American History*, edited and introduced by social historians who have written extensively about American women, is so good that it is surprising that no one thought of doing it until now. Searching volumes 1 through 14 of the American Bibliographical Center's *America: History and Life*, a major historical abstracting service, yielded nearly 3,400 relevant abstracts from a pool of 64,000. Historian Anne Firor Scott writes that this search "brought in every article even remotely touching upon the subjects of family or sex . . . from dozens of fields: sociology, anthropology, literature, demography, religion, economics, statistics, comparative studies, medicine, psychology, politics — to list a few."

Without a doubt, this is *the* source for scholarly periodical literature about women with a historical and interdisciplinary emphasis. The abstracts, in the main, are meaty, the index a pleasure to use. Browsing the index one finds references to every aspect of women-related scholarship: the American Revolution, actresses, clothing, communes, eugenics, labor unions, polygamy, travel accounts — in a word, the scope of social history. Personal names surface readily, and the subject index is particularly fine in locating materials state by state. In the 25 or so entries under "Colorado," one finds the range from suffrage to "Baby Doe" Tabor of silver mining fame. Because the abstracts are substantial, users will have a fair idea of whether an article is useful or not, certainly a help for people requiring interlibrary loan assistance in getting the actual articles.

Scholarly periodical literature about women has posed a particular access problem for women's studies students and scholars, and for social historians. *Women in American History* provides the best coverage to date of the academic journals, and one looks for periodic updates of this landmark project. Esther F. Stineman

369. Hughes, Marija Matich. **The Sexual Barrier: Legal, Medical, Economic and Social Aspects of Sex Discrimination.** Washington, Hughes Press, 1977. 843p. index. $50.00. LC 77-83214. ISBN 0-912560-04-5.

This is absolutely essential for any reference desk. Buy it and use it! An enlarged, revised edition of the original 1970 version and the 1971 and 1972 supplements, it includes a staggering 8,000 items arranged alphabetically in 17 chapters. It covers books, pamphlets, articles, government documents, and United Nations' documents published between 1960 and 1975 in the United States and in other countries. There is a pamphlet from Peking on women in the communes and a thick volume from Delhi on marriage and working women in India. There is a book on abortion published by Catholics United for the Faith and another issued by Planned Parenthood of New York City. Most of the materials are carefully annotated. There is a table of cases, listing which items refer to specific law cases. If you can't find what you need here on legal, medical, economic sex discrimination, it probably does not exist. Wouldn't it be nice if such a book were not necessary? But it is, and we should all be grateful to Marija Matich Hughes. The book received the Joseph L. Andrews bibliographic award by the American Association of Law Librarians as the outstanding reference work of 1977. [R: ARBA 79, p. 368; BL, 1 June 78, p. 1572; Choice, Apr 78, p. 208; LJ, 15 Feb 78, p. 449; WLB, Sept 78, p. 90] Fay M. Blake

370. Stineman, Esther. **Women's Studies: A Recommended Core Bibliography.** With the assistance of Catherine Loeb. Littleton, CO, Libraries Unlimited, 1979. 672p. index. $35.00. LC 79-13679. ISBN 0-87287-196-7.

Women's Studies identifies an annotated core collection of 1,763 woman-related books and periodicals that will support a women's studies program comprising courses with predominantly undergraduate enrollment. The books are grouped into 21 subject areas, including anthropology, business, fine arts, law, literature, medicine, religion, and sports. A separate reference section concentrates on 156 major reference books and bibliographies considered essential for such a core collection. Periodicals are covered in a separate section. Entries are indexed by author, title, and subject.

Each book or periodical was examined for inclusion in the bibliography. The lengthy annotations (averaging 250 words each) have been written to give full bibliographic information and a firm idea of what can be expected from the books in terms of content. Much thought has been given to assisting librarians, especially reference librarians, in recommending titles to patrons and in building their collections. All libraries need to think in terms of reshaping their existing collection policies to reflect the reality that the selection and purchase of woman-related materials will improve the total collection. [R: ARBA 80, p. 341; LJ, 1 Nov 79, p. 2333; Choice, Apr 80, p. 206; C&RL, Jan 80, p. 90; JAL, Jan 80, p. 362; RQ, Winter 79, p. 185; SLJ, Nov 79, p. 21]

BIOGRAPHY

371. Mainiero, Lina, ed. **American Women Writers: A Critical Reference Guide from Colonial Times to the Present. Volumes 1 and 2.** New York, Frederick Ungar Publishing, 1979-1980. 2v. $45.00/vol. LC 78-20945. ISBN 0-8044-3151-5(v.1); 0-8044-3152-3(v.2).

It is good to finally have available a reference source on women writers of the caliber of *American Women Writers*. Though *Notable American Women* (Edward T. James, Janet Wilson James, and Paul S. Boyer, eds., 1951) provides some overlap, *AWW* is a substantially different source because it concentrates exclusively on writers—"those who are known and read, and those who have been generally neglected or undervalued because they were women." Each critical biography meticulously assesses the writer's contribution; provides the basic biographical information, including married and maiden names, pseudonyms, and aliases that often elude even diligent searchers; and lists complete bibliographies (the first such compilations for many of the women included). Every biography is signed by a scholar or editor working in the fields of literature, women's studies, or American studies, which may account for the excellent overall quality of the entries. The range of writers represented is considerable—from little-known names to the contemporary literary luminaries. Elizabeth Bishop, Harriette Arnow, and Louisa May Alcott are, not surprisingly, here, but so are the newer names—Olga Broumas, E. M. Broner, and Rita Mae Brown. Nor is this work confined to poets and fiction writers. Diarists, journalists, anthropologists, historians, and academicians figure into the unparalleled resource, too.

Volumes 3 and 4 are due for publication in 1980, with the final volume including a comprehensive index of names and subjects. The four-volume set will cover over 1,000 writers in all fields. Libraries of all types will look forward to the appearance of the two companion volumes. [R: ARBA 80, p. 563; LJ, Aug 79, p. 1551]   Esther F. Stineman

14 ANTHROPOLOGY AND ETHNOLOGY

ATLASES

372. Hawkes, Jacquetta. **The Atlas of Early Man.** New York, St. Martin's Press, 1976. 255p. illus. (part col.). maps. index. $20.00. LC 75-43424.

Archaeologist Jacquetta Hawkes examines the period between 35,000 B.C. and A.D. 500 in a series of eight time steps. For each of these steps she discusses art, architecture, technology, and general history on a global basis. The later steps cover shorter time spans, since cultures were developing more rapidly and since more precise information is available for the later periods. The eight steps are 35,000-8000 B.C., 8000-5000 B.C., 5000-3000 B.C., 3000-2000 B.C., 2000-1000 B.C., 1000-500 B.C., 500 B.C.-A.D. 1, and A.D. 1-500. The most useful feature of this particular work is that it shows concurrent developments across the ancient world in each separate time period, thus answering the question "what happened at the same time as what?" The book is lavishly illustrated with both color and black-and-white photographs as well as drawings, charts, maps, and graphs. The photos chosen are an excellent mix of unfamiliar objects and universally known artifacts. The summary charts are particularly useful. Hawkes provides a summary chart for each period by region showing various aspects of the economy, centers of society, events and developments of major importance, people, religion, technology and inventions, architecture, and art. Archaeological site maps locate the sites referred to in the text. A gazetteer refers to page numbers and map grids. Very well written and organized, it can be used for general reading as well as a reference tool. It is an excellent supplement to the study of early man and the growth of civilization. [R: ARBA 78, p. 177; BL, 1 Feb 77, p. 801; Choice, Mar 77, p. 43; LJ, 15 Apr 77, p. 916; WLB, Feb 77, p. 24]   Susan Ebershoff-Coles

BIBLIOGRAPHIES

373. **Ethnographic Bibliography of North America.** 4th ed. By George Peter Murdock and Timothy J. O'Leary. New Haven, CT, Human Relations Area Files Press, 1975. 5v. illus. index. (Behavior Science Bibliographies). $175.00/set; $35.00/v. LC 75-17091. ISBN 0-87536-205-2(v.1); 0-87536-207-9(v.2); 0-87536-209-5(v.3); 0-87536-211-7(v.4); 0-87536-213-3(v.5).

In order to meet an increasing research demand, there has been a proliferation of bibliographies on Native Americans. Many of these reflect the holdings of particular libraries. The fourth edition of this bibliography, which originated in 1941, is divided into five volumes: "General North America," "Arctic and Subarctic," "Far West and Pacific Coast," "Eastern United States," and "Plains and Southwest." It covers extensively nonfiction books and articles, primarily in the English language, on the cultures and lifestyles of Eskimos and Indians. Other subjects, such as linguistics, archaeology, history, and medicine, are covered selectively. The approximately 40,000 entries span the years from the nineteenth century through 1972. Additional references are provided for those interested in government publications, theses and dissertations, manuscript collections, nonprint materials, and maps. For convenience of use, there is an index of the names of ethnic groups.

This computerized bibliography is based on a variation of the Human Relations Area Files Automated Bibliographic System (HABS). Computer output microfilm (COM) could be generated and inserted in pocket parts so that recent information would be available before future editions are printed. The bottoms of several pages are closely trimmed, but the print is legible. At any rate, this bibliography offers a good starting point for research on the topic.   Peter Hernon

ENCYCLOPEDIAS

374. Hunter, David E., and Phillip Whitten, eds. **Encyclopedia of Anthropology**. New York, Harper and Row, 1976. 411p. illus. bibliog. $9.95pa. LC 75-41386. ISBN 0-06-047094-1.

In terms of dictionaries or encyclopedias, the field of anthropology is much neglected. There are few dictionaries, and most of them are inadequate. The editors of this first encyclopedic work in English are attempting to fill the need for a "compact, comprehensive, accessible reference work" in the field (preface). With the assistance of almost 100 contributors (from sociology, psychology, biology, and genetics as well as from anthropology), they have provided a professionally designed encyclopedia of some 1,400 articles, which range in length from 25 to 3,000 words, depending on the relative importance of a subject. All but the shortest articles include bibliographic references. Cross references are liberally provided. Besides covering the terminology of the field, the encyclopedia provides articles on theories and trends, biographical articles, and articles on concepts from related fields. The text contains many maps, diagrams, photographs, and statistical tables. It is a pioneering work that should serve the profession well as an authoritative source of information on major aspects of anthropology. [R: ARBA 77, p. 360; Choice, Sept 76, p. 796; RQ, Summer 77, p. 348]   Bohdan S. Wynar

375. **The Illustrated Encyclopedia of Mankind.** New York, Marshall Cavendish, 1978. 20v. illus. (col.). maps. bibliog. index. $299.00/set. LC 77-93622. ISBN 0-85685-455-7/set.

Cultural anthropology is defined as a study of the new behavior within human societies. It consists of ethnography, ethnology, social anthropology, and linguistics. The present *Illustrated Encyclopedia of Mankind* constitutes the most comprehensive reference publication, covering more than 500 peoples and culture groups in the twentieth century. According to Richard Carlisle, the executive editor, "this encyclopedia seeks the broadest possible comprehensiveness to illustrate the range of social, cultural and economic forms that today characterize societies throughout the world" (preface, p. iii). It is a unique product of collective undertaking by over 100 specialists in various fields of cultural anthropology in terms of its subject coverage and typographical execution. This encyclopedic set may be divided into two major parts. The first 15 volumes alphabetically cover individual peoples and cultures of mankind as well as urban behavior in major world cities. The last five volumes (16-20) "go into topics, concepts and issues facing people of the world in our time" (p. v) and cover such topics as architecture, costume, music, dance, and communications, the life cycle, social organization, law, conflict, the beliefs of man, human art, and culture contact. The last volume also includes a brief bibliography ("Further Reading," pp. 2670-74), and a comprehensive name and subject index.

First, let's examine the encyclopedic articles pertaining to individual peoples and cultures covered in the first 15 volumes. The entries include basic information pertaining to geography, history, ethnography, economy, sociology, and customs of all listed ethnic entities. For each culture group a colored map is included which relates the specific geographical location to a larger geographic area. An outstanding feature of the *Encyclopedia of Mankind* is the inclusion of colored illustrations depicting ritual practices, the environment, housing, dress, and social activities of the various cultures. This reviewer agrees with Professor von Fürer-Haimensdorf's statement that many of the illustrations "provide an ethnographic record of considerable documentary value" (foreword, p. iv).

For those students interested in a cross-cultural approach to the important aspects of society's structure among various peoples, a wealth of information is contained in the remaining five volumes of the set, which provide analytical articles on man's cultural, social, and economic organization. These volumes have a cross-cultural and inter-disciplinary perspective and supplement the first 15 volumes. Such topics as racial conflicts, patterns of war, forms of religion, conquest and colonialism, design for living, population control, systems of domination, and many others permit the student to use a conceptual approach in studying world cultures on a comparative basis.

The physical features of *IEM* are outstanding: the binding is sturdy, the paper is of high quality, and the 10-point typesetting in the main text facilitates the easy use of this reference tool. The *Encyclopedia* is well structured and up to date and constitutes an essential reference compendium for school and college students as well as adult readers interested in present-day cultures and ethnic groups.

Several critical comments may be raised in regard to a few areas of *IEM*'s content and reference features. It was found that some important ethnic groups and cultures are not covered. For instance, there is no entry for Byelorussians – the third largest nation in the Soviet Union. Also, such groups as Azerbaijani, Tatars, Bashkirs, Karaimes, Kalmyks, Bats, and Bezhitas are not listed in the table of contents or index. The historical account of Russians (vol. 13, p. 1647) is rather questionable. The author confused several major terms – "Kievan Rus" and "Russian State" – and states that "the capital of Rus was moved to Vladimir," following the outdated pre-1917 periodization and terminology of East European history. On the other hand, the article on "Ukrainians" (vol. 14, p. 1815) contains the more appropriate term "Medieval Kievan State," which relates to Ukrainian medieval history. It is very important to clarify all major historical concepts in an encyclopedic or any other reference publication.

This reviewer also noticed a lack of necessary cross references. For instance, in the table of contents one does not find a separate entry for Estonians, Latvians, or Lithuanians; these people are listed under "Baltic People" (vol. 2). The "see" reference from Lithuanians, Latvians, and Estonians to "Baltic People" is needed. The same observation is valid in regard to "Yugoslavs" (vol. 14). This reviewer did not find a separate entry in the table of contents for Croats, Serbs, or Slovenes. They are listed under "Yugoslavs," and no necessary cross references are provided in the table of contents or the main text. It is interesting to note that the author of the "Yugoslavs" entry correctly states that the word "Yugoslavs" is "a misnomer: ethnically speaking, there is not and there never has been any such thing as a Yugoslav nation" (p. 1908). Why "Yugoslavs" is used in this *anthropological* encyclopedia as a main entry instead of individual Yugoslavian ethnic groups or nations is an enigma, especially since the individual cultures and the people constitute the major research unit of anthropological analysis. The problem should be solved in the next edition of *IEM*.

In regard to the above-mentioned brief bibliography (vol. 20), it is highly selective and does not provide a regular bibliographic description (the place of publication and publishers are not listed). This reviewer strongly recommends that the bibliographic section be expanded and that it be more representative and current. There are two indexes: the first subject-name index covers the first 15 volumes and is located in volume 15; the second index covers all volumes and follows the same pattern as the previous one (vol. 20). Again, the necessary "see" and "see also" references are needed for better usage of individual topics and ethnic groups presented in this work. Final recommendations pertain to individual contributions and authorship. It seems that in such a comprehensive encyclopedic work, all articles should be signed by individual contributors or editors.

These critical comments are presented in the context of a positive criticism, with the hope that some of the recommendations will be incorporated in the second revised edition of this important work. This reviewer considers *IEM* to be an important pioneering anthropological encyclopedia, which will be appreciated by students, librarians, and educators. The editorial staff and contributors should be complimented on the execution of an outstanding anthropological reference publication. It is recommended for school, public, and academic libraries. [R: ARBA 80, p. 345]   Lubomyr R. Wynar

HANDBOOKS

376. **Handbook of American Indians: North of Mexico.** Ed. by Frederick Webb Hodge. Washington, GPO, 1907-10; repr., New York, Rowman and Littlefield; distr., St. Clair Shores, MI, Scholarly Press, 1971. 2v. (U.S. Bureau of American Ethnology, Bulletin 30). $95.00.

This handbook is by far one of the most important publications on this subject. Originally published by the GPO, it was reissued by the Smithsonian Institution in 1912 and again reprinted in 1959 by Pageant Books.

This newest reprint, on durable paper with good binding, covers all the tribes north of Mexico, including the Eskimo, and those tribes south of the boundary that are more or less affiliated with those in the United States. Entries provide a brief description of every linguistic stock, confederacy, tribe, subtribe or tribal division, and settlement known in historical sources (or even according to tradition), as well as the origin and derivation of every name represented. Cross references to many forms of names and synonyms, arranged in alphabetical order, are found in the second volume. Under the tribal descriptions, one finds a brief account of the ethnic relations of the tribe, its history, its location at various periods, statistics of population, etc. Accompanying each synonym (the earliest date is usually given), the reader will find a reference to an authoritative source, which thus provides a bibliography of writings pertaining to a particular tribe.

The monumental project of which this handbook is an outgrowth was begun as early as 1873 by Professor Otis T. Mason, and the introduction provides a rather detailed account of its history. All in all, this is an essential sourcebook on the subject. [R: ARBA 72, p. 295]   Bohdan S. Wynar

377. **A Handbook of Method in Cultural Anthropology.** Ed. by Raoul Naroll and Ronald Cohen. New York, Columbia University Press, 1973. 1017p. illus. bibliog. index. $45.00; $17.00pa. LC 72-12762. ISBN 0-231-03731-7; 0-231-03749-Xpa.

Though termed a "Handbook of Method," concern with theory is abundantly evident in this impressive volume, and concern for basic pholosophical issues continually enters many of the presentations. When 72 first-class scientists contribute to a work such as this, there must necessarily be considerable overlap and, surprisingly sometimes, notable shortcomings. Among the latter would seem to be "a model of role analysis" which still treats the concept as it was handled in sociology and psychology over 20 years ago. No distinction is made between status and position, and the concepts of role expectations, perceptions, and enactments either are not distinguished or are badly confounded. Another weakness is the lack of attention afforded communication, especially of the nonverbal type. Kinesics and proxemics, neither of which appears in the index, are summarily treated in a few lines in the body of one article. Linguistic analysis is essentially ignored. This reviewer soon learned that there was much more in the various articles than was made evident by the index.

Despite these considerations, there can be little doubt that this notable work will remain a central reference source on both method and theory for many years to come.

Bernard Spilka

378. **Handbook of Middle American Indians. Vol. 9, Physical Anthropology.** Ed. by
T. Dale Stewart. **Vols. 14 and 15, Guide to Ethnohistorical Sources, Parts Three and Four.**
Ed. by Howard F. Cline. Austin, University of Texas Press, 1970, 1975. 3v. illus. $20.00
(v.9); $44.95(v.14 and 15). LC 64-10316. ISBN 0-292-70014-8(v.9); 0-292-70154-3(v.14 and
15/set).

The 15 articles contained in the ninth volume of this set describe the human biology of
Middle America using both primary and secondary source material. The authors are
recognized authorities in their respective fields, e.g., Juan Comas, Arturo Romano, San-
tiago Genoves T., Javier Romero, Eusebio Davalos Hurtado, Johanna Faulhaber,
G. Albin Matson, Marshall Newman, T. D. Stewart, Mildred Trotter, Oliver Duggins,
Nevin Scrimshaw, and Carlos Tejada. Articles are arranged chronologically from
prehistoric to contemporary times and contain important material on Middle American
Indians, on prehistoric human remains, anthropometry, osteopathology, blood groups,
physiological studies, physical plasticity and adaptation, psychobiometry and an excellent
section related to skin, hair, and eyes.

One of the problems relating to multi-volume publication is the unevenness resulting
from the different times at which the various articles were submitted and the references
used. A scan of the 36-page reference section reveals that most of the notations are
pre-1960, which emphasizes the historical and more traditional rather than the "new"
physical anthropology with its heavy emphasis on the breakthroughs in genetics; e.g., the
latest reference in the article on psychobiometry is 1961, and the latest reference in the article on blood groups is 1966.

Nonetheless there is a wealth of material (thoroughly indexed) on the physical anthropology of Middle America in this volume. Large numbers of foldouts, tables, charts, maps,
and graphs make immense amounts of data available for observation and analysis,
although the binding procedure used makes it difficult to read some of the data of the inner
margins. (There is a slip inserted in the volume containing these "difficult to read" lines.)
This volume, as well as others earlier published in this series, is an excellent and scholarly
reference work and a welcome companion to the *Handbook of South American Indians*
earlier edited by Julian Steward.

Volumes 14 and 15 of the *Handbook of Middle American Indians* constitute parts 3
and 4 of the *Guide to Ethnohistorical Sources*. The *Handbook*, under the general editorship of Robert Wauchope, was published under the sponsorship of the National Research
Council Committee on Latin American Anthropology, in cooperation with the Middle
American Research Institute at Tulane University. Both volumes 14 and 15 deal with
sources in the native traditions. Geography and ethnogeography were covered in volume
12, and sources in the European tradition comprise volume 13.

Volume 14 contains the following studies: "A Survey of Native Middle American Pic-
torial Manuscripts," by John Glass; "A Census of Native Middle American Pictorial
Manuscripts," also by Glass in collaboration with Donald Robertson; "Techialoyan
Manuscripts and Paintings, with a Catalog," by Robertson; "A Census of Middle
American Testerian Manuscripts," and "A Catalog of Falsified Middle American Pictorial
Manuscripts," both by John Glass.

Volume 15, also devoted to sources in the native tradition, has the following studies:
"Prose Sources in the Native Historical Tradition — (a) A Survey of Middle American Prose
Manuscripts" (by Charles Gibson), "(b) A Census of Middle American Prose Manuscripts"
(by Gibson and Glass); "A Checklist of Institutional Holdings of Middle American
Manuscripts in the Native Historical Tradition," by Glass; "The Boturini Collection," by
Glass; "Middle American Ethnohistory: An Overview," by H. B. Nicholson; "Index of

Authors, Titles, and Synonyms," by Glass; and "Annotated References," by Glass. The last section of this volume contains illustrations and figures. [R: ARBA 71, p. 262; ARBA 76, p. 389]

Robert H. Amundson
Anna T. Wynar

379.   **Handbook of North American Indians: Volume 8, California.** Robert F. Heizer, ed. Washington, Smithsonian Institution; distr., Washington, GPO, 1978. 800p. illus. bibliog. index. $13.50. LC 77-17162. S/N 047-000-00347-4.

Monumental is a word applied to too many works that do not deserve such praise. In the case of the *Handbook of North American Indians*, monumental will be an inadequate accolade when the last of the 20 volumes is published. The *California* volume is the first of the projected series of volumes. If the first volume is representative of what will be in the other 19 volumes, the editors will have no difficulty in achieving their "encyclopedic summary of what is known about the pre-history, history, and cultures of the aboriginal peoples of North America who lived north of the urban civilizations of central Mexico." The only problem in this volume is the frequent reference to material in forthcoming volumes.

Kroeber's *Handbook of California Indians* was and is a classic review of the material that was available on California Indians as of 1925. Today, no one person is capable of adequately covering all of the new material that has been accumulated. Therefore, in this volume, the 44 articles were written by the 33 leading specialists on the native peoples of California. Naturally, the authors drew on all the data available, so much of the material will seem reminiscent of Kroeber's book. It is important to note that the "California" of this book is not the *state* of California. Most of the tribes that lived east of the Sierra Madres are not included in this volume; they will be covered in volumes 9, 11, and 12. The Tipai are covered, although a major portion of their lands are now in Mexico. Also, the Tolowa, Karok, and Shasta lands extended beyond the present state boundaries, but they are included. In addition to individual tribal chapters, there are 25 chapters on archaeology, linguistics, social patterns, economic activities, and the contemporary situation. Each article is signed and concludes with a section on sources; however, there is only one comprehensive bibliography at the end of the volume. The bibliography appears to be a slightly condensed version of Heizer and Elsasser's *Bibliography of California Indians*.

This volume is *the* definitive and comprehensive review of California Indians. In fact, it is doubtful if there will ever be another work as comprehensive in coverage—the task will be too great. The final bonus of this volume is its amazingly low price.

Ed. note: Volumes 9 (*Southwest*) and 15(*Northeast*) were published in 1979 and 1978, respectively, and both will be reviewed in *American Reference Books Annual 1981*. [R: ARBA 79, p. 384; Choice, Dec 78, p. 1348; C&RL, Jan 79, p. 53; LJ, 15 Apr 79, p. 884]

G. Edward Evans

15 STATISTICS AND DEMOGRAPHY

GENERAL WORKS

380. Showers, Victor. **World Facts and Figures.** New York, John Wiley, 1979. 757p. illus. bibliog. index. (A Wiley-Interscience Publication). $22.95. LC 78-14041. ISBN 0-471-04941-7.

This is a revised, updated, and renamed edition of *The World in Figures* (Wiley, 1973), expanded from 585 to 757 pages. Added features include "Current Trends in World Facts and Figures," with highlights such as new names of countries or new data on the size of holdings of major libraries of the world on a more comparable basis, and with headings for the major sections: the world in summary, the physical base, country comparisons, city comparisons, outstanding works by man, country gazetteer (by continent), city gazetteer (by continent and country), and selected bibliography. Comparable data are provided for 222 individual countries, 2,000 cities, and more than 2,500 other geographic and cultural features. A valuable and up-to-date reference book with much data not easily located in other sources. [R: ARBA 80, p. 353; LJ, 1 June 79, p. 1244]   Chauncy D. Harris

381. U.S. Bureau of the Census. **Historical Statistics of the United States: Colonial Times to 1970.** Washington, GPO, 1976. 1200p. index. $26.00. LC 75-38832. S/N 003-024-00120-9.

This compilation is the third in a historical series that supplements the annual *Statistical Abstract of the United States.* It supersedes the second edition, published in 1960, which covered the period through 1957, and a continuation to 1962, which was published in 1965. The first edition, published in 1949, covered the period from 1789 to 1945 and was continued to 1952 by a 1954 supplement.

This third edition brings together over 12,500 time series of wide general interest — 50% more than the second edition — mostly at the national level. Data for regions, states, or smaller localities are given only where such presentation is essential for correct interpretation of the data. Annual data are given preference, but certain series are presented only for years of a national census, or for scattered years when limited data are available. The latest year covered is 1970, and series are extended back as far as usable data are available. Data are presented in chapters under the following topics: population; vital statistics, health, and medical care; migration; labor; prices and price indexes; national income and wealth; consumer income and expenditures; social statistics; land, water, and climate; agriculture; forestry and fisheries; minerals; construction and housing; manufactures; transportation; communications; energy; distribution and services; international transactions and foreign commerce; business enterprise; productivity and technological development; financial markets and institutions; government; colonial and pre-federal statistics. The introduction to each chapter presents the sources of the data, often defines the concepts and terms used, and provides sufficient methodological and historical information to permit intelligent use of the data. [R: ARBA 77, p. 364; Choice, Oct 76, p. 964; LJ, 1 June 76, p. 1276]   LeRoy C. Schwarzkopf

DICTIONARIES AND ENCYCLOPEDIAS

382. Kruskal, William H., and Judith M. Tanur, eds. **International Encyclopedia of Statistics.** New York, Free Press, a division of Macmillan Publishing, 1978. 2v. index. $100.00. LC 78-17324. ISBN 0-02-917960-2.

This work is based on articles reprinted from the *International Encyclopedia of Social Sciences* (*IESS*). Owners of *IESS* should not, however, dismiss the *Encyclopedia of Statistics*, since the articles are updated, revised, and expanded to cover the years since the publication of *IESS* in 1968. The two volumes contain 75 articles on statistics, 42 articles on social science topics with a special reference to statistics, and 57 biographies. Authors of the original articles in *IESS* were asked to update their work, and given the choice of rewriting the article, amending it, or adding a postscript, so that the format is not entirely consistent. This is no problem since all begin with a general summary and proceed to a thorough discussion of the topic. Bibliographies follow each article. A very detailed index concludes the set. The *International Encyclopedia of Statistics* will be useful to a wide variety of students and researchers. [R: ARBA 80, p. 349; Choice, May 79, p. 364; C&RL, July 79, p. 350; LJ, 1 May 79, p. 1044; WLB, Oct 79, p. 136]

383.   Webb, Augustus D. **The New Dictionary of Statistics: A Complement to the Fourth Edition of Mulhall's "Dictionary of Statistics."** London, George Routledge and Sons, Ltd.; New York, E. P. Dutton and Co., 1911; repr., Detroit, Gale, 1974. 682p. bibliog. index. $38.00. LC 74-2349. ISBN 0-8103-3988-9.

Mulhall's *Dictionary of Statistics* (4th rev. ed., covering the period up to November 1898) was originally published by Routledge in 1899 and reprinted by Gale in 1969. It is one of the best older dictionaries of historical statistics.

Webb's dictionary, supplement to Mulhall's, concentrates on economic and social statistics. The 130 subject-oriented chapters are arranged alphabetically—e.g., Accidents, Agricultural Holdings, Agriculture and Live Stock, Alcohol, Aliens. Most of the statistical tables attempt to cover several countries, but some cover only Great Britain (e.g., Aliens). In most cases, sources are provided, with reference to the 325-item bibliography at the end of the volume. Ample cross references and an excellent index facilitate use of the great body of statistical material. All in all, it is a useful reference book for locating historical statistical information that is not readily available in other sources. [R: ARBA 75, p. 387]

Bohdan S. Wynar

16 ECONOMICS AND BUSINESS

ATLASES

384. **Oxford Economic Atlas of the World.** Prep. by the Cartographic Dept. of the Clarendon Press. Advisory ed., D. B. Jones. 4th ed. New York, Oxford University Press, 1972. 239p. illus. charts. maps. bibliog. index. $29.95; $9.95pa. ISBN 0-19-894106-4; 0-19-894107-2pa.

World maps (90 pages of them) in modified Gall projections are grouped in 13 sections, and the Statistical Supplement is alphabetically arranged by country. The maps provide a world distribution view of eight commodity groups—crops, livestock, forestry and fishing, fibers and textiles, energy (gas, oil, coal, electricity, nuclear), minerals and metals, transport industries, and manufacturing industries. An introductory section of physical geography includes maps of political units, of the environment (temperature, ocean currents, winds), frost incidence, precipitation, seasonal climates, relief, soils, land use, and economic geology (mineral deposits—nature and origin). Four sections provide information on demography, disease, social and political factors, and communications.

Most maps are based on the period from 1963 to 1965, with comparative figures from 1953 to 1955. International boundaries are those that existed in 1965. Maps also show production/yield of commodities, with tables that indicate information for selected countries.

The Statistical Supplement, including a gazetteer of over 8,000 populated places, specific sites (dams, mines), physical features, and administrative divisions, gives statistics for each country. In addition, it shows the relative importance of any commodity in the country's economic profile. Statistics were obtained from international bodies for maximum comparability; where this was impossible, they were obtained from national associations, private companies, and individuals.

Ed. note: Also recommended are the *Oxford Regional Economic Atlas: Western Europe* (1971. 96p. $15.00; $6.95pa.) and the *Oxford Regional Economic Atlas: The United States and Canada*, 2nd ed. (1975. 128p. $8.95pa.). [R: ARBA 74, p. 296; BL, 15 Mar 73, p. 653; Choice, Sept 72, p. 792]   Albert C. Vara

BIBLIOGRAPHIES

385. Daniells, Lorna M. **Business Information Sources.** Berkeley, University of California Press, 1976. 439p. index. $16.95. LC 74-30517. ISBN 0-520-02946-1.

This guide is designed to serve as a revision of Edwin T. Coman's *Sources of Business Information* (2nd ed.; University of California Press, 1964). Lorna Daniells, head of the reference department at Baker Library, Harvard University, points out in the preface that "no one could hope to write the same sort of book Mr. Coman did, with his interesting discussions about each topic and his insightful annotations" (p. xiii). The current work, then, is "a selected, annotated list of business books and reference sources, with an emphasis on recent material in the English language."

The first chapter, "Methods of Locating Facts," contains rather pedestrian discussions of such topics as business services of public libraries (not quite one page), company libraries, university libraries, etc. All of the information presented here lacks the depth that one would expect to find in the "successor" to Coman.

The first chapters, "Basic Time-Saving Sources" (about bibliographies, indexes, etc.) and "Locating Information on Companies, Organizations and Individuals" (primarily listing directories of all kinds) describe the more general business sources, in varying degrees of comprehensiveness. A second grouping of chapters covers aspects of management and marketing. There are some six or seven entries per page. Entries provide the usual bibliographical data (but they give no pagination for monographs and they omit the first year of publication for serials); the brief annotations are occasionally too brief to be meaningful.

Under "Business Dictionaries" (p. 25) one finds only two entries: *Dictionary of Management* (International Publications Service, 1975) and *International Dictionary of Management* (Houghton Mifflin, 1975). Both should be in the section under management, since other specialized dictionaries included in the guide are listed under the specialized heading (e.g., accounting, finance, data processing, marketing, etc.). What should be listed here instead are such works as *Economics 73/74 Encyclopedia* (Dushkin, 1973). We looked further in the section on "Economics Literature," since a note pointed out that "of special interest are the several excellent economics dictionaries listed in Chapter 8" (p. 25). Indeed, here we found Hanson, *McGraw-Hill Dictionary of Modern Economics*, Nemmers' *Dictionary of Economics and Business* (a rather poor beginner's dictionary of 5,000 terms), Sloan and Zurcher's *Dictionary of Economics*, and finally *Dictionary of Economic and Statistical Terms* (2nd ed.; GPO, 1972). This is not a representative selection.

The following annotation is provided for Peter Wyckoff's *The Language of Wall Street* (Hopkinson and Blake, 1973): "A glossary of standard financial and investment terms, compiled by a financial writer" (p. 120). The reader would never know from this annotation that Wyckoff's glossary contains 1,500 definitions and is probably one of the most comprehensive of its kind.

In conclusion, and in all fairness to Ms. Daniells, one must say that her bibliography indeed includes many entries and is more comprehensive than some of the other recently published guides. Unfortunately, a replacement for Coman's work it is not. We still have to wait for it a little longer. [R: ARBA 77, p. 371; BL, 1 July 77, p. 1674; Choice, Mar 77, p. 42; C&RL, July 77, p. 359; LJ, 15 Feb 77, p. 474; LJ, 1 Mar 77, p. 556; RQ, Summer 77, p. 342; WLB, Feb 77, p. 539] Bohdan S. Wynar

386. Wasserman, Paul. **Encyclopedia of Business Information Sources.** 4th ed. Charlotte Georgi and James Woy, associate eds. Detroit, Gale, 1980. 778p. $72.00. LC 79-24771. ISBN 0-8103-0368-X.

The third edition of this work appeared in 1976. The present volume, fully revised and updated, includes material as current as fall 1979, and is 111 pages longer than the previous edition. Designed to lead business executives to sources of information on specific topics, this extensive bibliography now covers commercially available on-line data bases as well as the same types of publications and organizations found in earlier issues.

The new *Encyclopedia of Business Information Sources* contains about 20,000 entries, primarily for American sources. They are arranged under more than 1,200 subject headings (from "Abbreviations" to "Zoological Gardens"), and, within each subject, sources of information are organized by type—e.g., encyclopedias and dictionaries, handbooks and manuals, almanacs and yearbooks, directories, periodicals, statistics sources, trade associations and professional societies. Each entry includes, at the very least, a name and address to which users may write for additional data. There are cross references to subjects in an alphabetical table of contents and in the body of this work, but there are no indexes.

Anyone can quite easily detect a few errors and omissions in this big book. It is, nevertheless, an extremely useful tool that deserves to be found in every library serving the business community.

Ed. note: Paul Wasserman's *Encyclopedia of Geographic Information Sources* (Gale, 1978. 167p. $42.00) serves as a companion to *Business Information Sources*, listing business reference works for some 390 countries, regions, states, and cities.

Leonard Grundt

DICTIONARIES AND ENCYCLOPEDIAS

387. International Labour Office. **Encyclopaedia of Occupational Health and Safety.** New York, McGraw-Hill, 1972. 2v. illus. index. $89.95/set. LC 74-39329. ISBN 0-07-079555-X.

The first edition of this encyclopedia, entitled *Occupation and Health*, was published between 1930 and 1934 in accordance with the resolution adopted by the First Session of the International Labour Conference in 1919, the year this organization was founded. It contained 416 articles by 95 contributors from 16 different countries. By 1944, six supplements had been issued, containing 52 additional articles.

The present edition is practically a new work; it contains 900 articles prepared by 700 specialists from 70 different countries. All articles are arranged in one alphabet (with cross references), and they are usually accompanied by additional bibliographical references. They vary in length depending on the relative importance of a given subject. For example, the article on antibiotics is two-and-a-half pages long, the same length as the one on asphalt, but the article on the automobile industry has five pages, subdivided by such specific topics as hazards and their prevention, automobiles — safe design, etc. Most articles are accompanied by technical data and some illustrations.

This is an indispensable reference work for all those concerned with occupational safety and health, since it provides competent practical information in a form that is not too technical even for those with no specialized technical or medical knowledge. The encyclopedia covers all major aspects of the subject, emphasizing industrial hygiene, accident prevention, occupational and social medicine, toxicology, etc., as related to specific subjects. The treatment of a given topic usually has international dimensions. A most authoritative work. [R: ARBA 73, p. 316; Choice, Apr 73, p. 264]   Bohdan S. Wynar

388. **The McGraw-Hill Dictionary of Modern Economics: A Handbook of Terms and Organizations.** 2nd ed. By Douglas Greenwald and others. New York, McGraw-Hill, 1973. 792p. illus. $32.50. LC 72-11813. ISBN 0-07-024369-7.

All in all, this is one of the best one-volume dictionaries on economic terminology. It contains brief but concise definitions of some 1,400 frequently used terms in economic theory and applied economics, plus a description of approximately 225 private, public, and nonprofit agencies active in the general field of economics and business, including marketing.

An especially helpful feature of this dictionary is the use of appended references to both current and original sources of information that can provide more detailed information on a given term. Incorporated in the text are numerous charts and statistical tables, which help clarify the definitions. The McGraw-Hill dictionary provides more in-depth information than Sloan and Zurcher's *Dictionary of Economics*, 5th ed. (Barnes & Noble, 1970). Compare, for example, the definitions of fringe benefits or peril points in the two dictionaries. Because the McGraw-Hill dictionary does presume a background in economics, some may prefer Donald Moffat's *Economics Dictionary* (Elsevier, 1976. 301p. $17.00; $10.95pa.), which provides simple, clear, and generally shorter definitions. [R: ARBA 74, pp. 292-93; Choice, Oct 73, p. 1168; WLB, Sept 73, p. 84]   Bohdan S. Wynar

389. Palgrave, Robert Harry Inglis, ed. **Dictionary of Political Economy.** London, Macmillan, 1910; repr., Detroit, Gale, 1976. 3v. illus. index. $110.00/set. LC 74-31358. ISBN 0-8103-4210-3.

Although this magisterial dictionary — really an encyclopedia — is now nearly 70 years old, it remains filled with virtue, for the Edwardians comprehended more within the term "political economy" than we do today in the term "economics." The reader can accordingly expect to find not only economic but also business and legal terms such as "earnest money" and "flotsam and jetsam," and medieval and classical terms such as "jurande" and "latifundium." It also contains numerous biographical entries, for worthies as diverse as Samuel Johnson and Pietro Verri, as well as the full entries one would expect on more narrowly economic matters such as "free trade" and "interest."

The problems with a work such as this are implicit in its venerable age; relatively recent terms such as "multiplier" and "Cobb-Douglas function" will obviously not be found, and others, which are to be found, mean quite different things to us than they did to Palgrave and his collaborators. Still, for any sort of historical research, this is an advantage because it provides contemporary definitions and in general preserves the conventional wisdom of its day. The articles are a real pleasure to read. In short, an interesting and useful work, well worth reprinting yet again. [R: ARBA 77, p. 376]   John G. Williamson

390.   Rosenberg, Jerry M. **Dictionary of Business and Management.** New York, John Wiley, 1978. 564p. (A Wiley-Interscience Publication). $25.95. LC 78-7796. ISBN 0-471-01681-0.

Current meanings of more than 8,000 terms used in various business fields, ranging from accounting through warehousing, are clarified in this work. Alternate usage in different applications is clearly indicated; for instance, *margin* as it is used in finance, in securities, and in accounting, and *load* in its shipping, computer, and securities senses. This is an example of responsible dictionary making, filling a noticeable gap that has grown as organization change accelerates and the "profusion of new words and numerous reinterpretations of old ones" grow. Fuzzy areas have fuzzy distinctions, as with the differentiation between *operations research, systems analysis*, and *MAPS*. There is a little bit of inconsistency, as terms are sometimes entered in their complete form and at other times as abbreviations; for instance, PPBS is listed at "Planning, programming, budgeting" (PPB) with a cross reference from PPBS, but "Management by objectives" is at MBO, and MIS is at "Management information system." A valuable accumulation of tables and other useful information appears as appendixes A through M.

Ed. note: The *Dictionary of Business and Economics* (Free Press, 1977. 461p. $19.95), by Christine Ammer and Dean Ammer, is an excellent ready-reference tool for business and economic terms. This clear, concise, and remarkably complete dictionary contains over 3,000 entries covering a great variety of terms, along with charts, tables, and diagrams. [R: ARBA 80, p. 356; Choice, May 79, p. 564; JAL, May 79, p. 112; WLB, May 79, p. 657]   Doris H. Banks

DIRECTORIES

391.   Crowley, Ellen T. **Trade Names Dictionary: A Guide to Consumer-Oriented Trade Names, Brand Names, Product Names, Coined Names, Model Names, and Design Names, with Addresses of their Manufacturers, Importers, Marketers, or Distributors.** 2nd ed. Detroit, Gale, 1979. 2v. $110.00/set. LC 79-12685. ISBN 0-8103-0694-8.

392.   Crowley, Ellen T., ed. **Trade Names Dictionary: Company Index; A Companion Volume to Trade Names Dictionary, with Each Company Entry Followed by an Alphabetical Listing of Its Brands and with a Special Section Giving Addresses of the Companies.** 2nd ed. Detroit, Gale, 1979. 897p. $125.00. LC 79-19239. ISBN 0-8103-0695-6.

Reference librarians who welcomed the first edition of this dictionary (1976) will be delighted with the publication of an updated and expanded version. In compiling the second edition, 61 directories were consulted, as contrasted to 37 for the previous edition.

The current edition contains over 130,000 entries, as opposed to 106,000 in the earlier set. Not only have thousands of new entries been added, but changes have been made, as well, in some 8,000 first-edition entries.

While the *Dictionary* has been revised and enlarged, the purpose and editorial policies remain the same. The emphasis continues to be on products and services of interest to the general public, rather than on those that meet commercial or industrial needs. As in the initial list, consideration is given to the past as well as the present. There are entries for some historically interesting items that are no longer in production, as well as for trade names that have evolved into generic terms. An innovation in the second edition is the use of boldface type for trade names, which makes it easier to find desired entries quickly.

In the pattern established by the first edition, the *Dictionary* contains two basic types of entries: one for the trade name itself and one for the company that manufactures, imports, markets, or distributes the item. A typical trade name entry includes a brief description of the product, the name of the company associated with it, and a code identifying the directory from which the listing was taken. A typical company entry consists of the name and address of the firm, along with a code indicating the source of the information. Cross references are used to reflect corporate name changes and affiliations. Both trade name and company entries are incorporated in a single alphabetical arrangement. While entries beginning with numbers are included in the body of the *Dictionary*, they are also repeated in a special numerical appendix at the end of the set.

The publisher is careful to warn users that the *Trade Names Dictionary* is not meant to serve as a source of legal authority. This will be of little concern to most librarians, since they will be employing the *Dictionary* to trace products for consumers rather than to establish legal rights.

The price of the two-volume set is substantial. However, many librarians will decide that the investment is justified because of savings in staff time and increased patron satisfaction. Few libraries have direct access to all of the sources surveyed for this set. Even libraries with major holdings will find this dictionary to be a timesaver, since it assembles widely scattered information in one alphabetical arrangement. To maintain currency between editions, Gale Research Company issues a supplement, *New Trade Names*. A subscription to the 1980 and 1981 supplements is available for $65.

The *Company Index* was developed to provide a means for quickly determining the types of products or services offered by specific companies, and for pinpointing various trade names used by a single firm. As in the *Trade Names Dictionary*, companies which manufacture, distribute, import, or otherwise market products of interest to the general public are emphasized, although some commercial and industrial items are included. Nearly 30,000 firms are represented. It should be pointed out that the trade names in the *Company Index* have been selected from available published sources and do not necessarily represent all products of a particular company.

The *Company Index* is organized alphabetically by company name. Under each company entry in the main portion of the book there is an alphabetical list of the trade names associated with the firm. Trade names are followed by brief descriptions of the products or services they represent. A code identifies the source of information for each trade name. Company addresses are given in a separate section at the back of the book. Here also, a code designation indicates the source from which each entry was taken.

There are some inconsistencies in the book, and alphabetization in the main body of the book does not always match that in the address section. Nevertheless, the *Company Index* adds a new dimension to the information in the basic volumes of the *Trade Names Dictionary*, and business libraries, academic libraries serving students in business courses, and larger public libraries will want to consider adding it to their collections as a supplement to the *Trade Names Dictionary*. [R: ARBA 80, pp. 357-59; LJ, 1 Nov 79, p. 2334]

Shirley Miller

393. Wasserman, Paul, managing ed. **Training and Development Organizations Directory: A Reference Work Describing Firms, Institutes, and Other Agencies Offering Training Programs for Business, Industry, and Government.** Marlene A. Palmer, associate ed. Detroit, Gale, 1978. 614p. index. $72.00. LC 77-276. ISBN 0-8103-0313-2.

The editors of this work have created a major new reference tool responding to a growing need in business and industrial enterprises and in government agencies for reliable information on regularly offered seminars, institutes, workshops, non-credit short courses, and other training opportunities by which staff competencies and skills can be upgraded. Nearly 1,000 academic, commercial, and professional consulting service organizations are censused and described here in considerable detail. The majority of these organizations deal with management, production, human relations, administrative, and supervisory problem areas. Typical entries provide essential facts about the organizations: name, address, phone number, principals, full- and part-time staff, areas of special course emphasis, target audience, and year founded. Most entries also include a detailed description of each organization's chief concerns, the programs and titles of courses and workshops, and fees.

A sampling of the areas of specialization shows that training services have proliferated in such subject fields as computer applications, communication, personnel administration, all management areas, employee motivation, human relations, interpersonal relations, leadership, marketing, motivation, problem-solving, supervision, taxation, and time management. On the other hand, relatively few organizations seem to specialize in forecasting, grants and proposals, indexing, industrial engineering, labor law, land use, leisure, building maintenance, merchandising, mergers, noise control, performance measurement, pricing, sex roles, technical writing, warehousing, and zero-based budgeting. About one-half of the book is taken up by four indexes that provide alternative approaches to the content of the directory. The geographic index enables users to locate training and development organizations by city and state. Two subject indexes are provided: one, a broad subject index subdivided by geographic location; the other, an index with highly specialized headings. Finally, the alphabetical index of individuals lists all persons mentioned in the main part of the directory. The data were gathered by means of questionnaires. Because of the pervasive need, this directory will appeal to a wide range of libraries as well as to the entire corporate clientele. [R: ARBA 79, p. 398; BL, 15 Feb 79, p. 952; LJ, 15 Sept 78, p. 1731; WLB, Oct 78, p. 188]

Michael Keresztesi

394. Wasserman, Paul, and Janice McLean, eds. **Consultants and Consulting Organizations Directory: A Reference Guide to Concerns and Individuals Engaged in Consultation for Business and Industry.** 4th ed. Detroit, Gale, 1979. 1120p. index. $120.00. LC 79-4573. ISBN 0-8103-0353-1.

Wasserman's *Consultants and Consulting Organizations Directory*, now in the fourth edition, remains the definitive guide to these organizations. The current edition includes information on more than 6,000 public and private firms, almost 1,000 more than in the 1976 edition. Other major changes in this edition are organization (the work is now arranged geographically, alleviating the difficult-to-use geographical index found in the earlier editions) and a revised list of consulting fields. Each citation includes address and phone information, principals, branch offices, and a narrative description of the firm. All areas of consulting are included in the *Directory*, and a numerical index is provided to assist the user in locating firms in specific fields. Recommended for all libraries serving the professions.

Ed. note: The *Directory* is updated by *New Consultants: A Periodic Supplement* (Gale, 1979. 79p. $85.00/inter-edition subscription), which lists firms newly founded since the publication of the basic volume. Issues are published every six months (June and December). [R: ARBA 80, p. 361; LJ, 1 Nov 79, p. 2335]   Ronald F. Dow

ACCOUNTING

395. **Encyclopedia of Accounting Systems.** Jerome K. Pescow, ed. Englewood Cliffs, NJ, Prentice-Hall, 1976. 3v. illus. $79.50/set. LC 75-5607. ISBN 0-13-275214-X.

This outstanding, important work illustrates, describes, and explains accounting systems for some 70 different industries, businesses, professions, and nonprofit organizations. They are as diverse as airports, bakers, churches, dentists, furniture stores, labor unions, shoe manufacturers, and women's apparel chains. For each specialty, the chapter treats: 1) the industry in brief; 2) the accounting system; 3) account classification and books of account; 4) data processing procedures; 5) cost system; 6) time and payroll system; 7) plant and equipment records and depreciation; 8) the reporting system; 9) data processing applications; 10) time-saving techniques for small, medium-sized, and large businesses.

This is a must book for accountants who are faced with the accounting problems of a business or enterprise that is unfamiliar to them. It can aid in improving the current system; be valuable for setting up new books of record; help solve troublesome problems; and give an overview and understanding that would be difficult to get from any other source.

The chapters, each on one specific accounting system, range between 20 and 60 pages. The typeface is clear, clean, and easy to read. The authors, including Mr. Pescow, the editor, are outstanding authorities. In every case, the author has had considerable experience and expertise in this specialized field. For example, the chapter on clubs is authored by a partner of the leading accountancy firm doing club accounting: Harris, Kerr, Forster and Company.

The detail work is impressive. Forms are reproduced in their entirety, complex charts of accounts are listed, and a wide range of practical suggestions are made. The special features are very helpful. For instance, under "Department Stores" there is a glossary of several hundred specialized terms. The charts showing the interrelationship of the various records and departments are valuable. And organization charts, specific examples, principles and objectives all add to the authoritative tone of the work. [R: ARBA 77, p. 385]
Stanley J. Slote

396. Kohler, Eric L. **A Dictionary for Accountants.** 5th ed. Englewood Cliffs, NJ, Prentice-Hall, 1975. 497p. illus. $26.00. LC 74-1393C. ISBN 0-13-209783-4.

Since its first edition in 1952, this standard dictionary's ease of use and clear dependable definitions have captured for it a large and enthusiastic audience. Now its fifth edition defines over 3,000 terms and concepts in the fields of accounting theory, methods, and practice, and in related areas of management, law, and finance. Definitions for terms included in earlier editions have, in many cases, been expanded here to present new facets of meaning, and over 200 new terms have been added. It defines phrases as well as single words and abbreviations; illustrations, tables, and charts aid in clarifying concepts and terms. While many definitions are short, explanations of some terms fill several pages. The many cross references make it easy to use. A practical, authoritative source, it gives precise meanings in clear language and is useful for the layperson as well as the expert. [R: ARBA 76, p. 405]
Winifred F. Dean

ADVERTISING

397. Urdang, Laurence, ed. **Dictionary of Advertising Terms.** Chicago, Crain Books, 1979. 209p. illus. $14.95pa. LC 76-45506. ISBN 0-87251-042-5.

A compilation of some 4,000 terms used in advertising and marketing. Arranged alphabetically letter by letter, giving no pronunciations, the dictionary presents brief definitions of terms and abbreviations used in the industry; included are "special meanings of ordinary words, words unique to a single specialty, specialized terms, names of devices, services, and organizations, and extensive cross-references for abbreviations, acronyms, and synonyms." Some terms are illustrated by line drawings for further clarification. Definitions are much shorter than those found in Graham's *Encyclopedia of Advertising*, 2nd ed. (New York, Fairchild, 1969. $20.00), but this includes almost four times as many terms. The *Ayer Glossary of Advertising and Related Terms* (Ayer Press, 1977. $11.95) also defines terms briefly, but contains a smaller number than does this volume. Its comprehensiveness and cross references make this an excellent source for finding short, precise definitions of advertising terminology. [R: ARBA 78, p. 380; BL, 1 Sept 78, p. 72; LJ, 1 Sept 77, p. 1748]   Winifred F. Dean

FINANCE AND BANKING

398. Munn, Glenn G. **Encyclopedia of Banking and Finance.** 7th ed. Rev. and enl. by F. L. Garcia. Boston, Bankers Publishing Co., 1973. 953p. $49.75. LC 73-83395. ISBN 0-87267-019-8.

The first edition of this standard work was published in 1924, the sixth in 1962. The present edition, substantially enlarged, is some 200 pages longer than the sixth edition, with a total of 4,000 entries arranged alphabetically. Like the previous editions, it contains brief definitions of terms—e.g., checque, cheap money, etc.—and a number of encyclopedic articles on money, credit, banking practices, pertinent business laws and federal regulations, investment, insurance, brokerage, and other topics that require in-depth coverage. Professor F. L. Garcia of Fordham University was in charge of this editorial revision. He should be credited with achieving an excellent balance between the more traditional topics.

The clear presentation and the readability of articles are exemplified in the article on the cost of living index. The one-page, double-column article starts with a definition in terms of popular conception of the expression, followed by a technical presentation of its composition and computation, statistical data, and comparisons to other indexes. Bibliographies and cross references are appended to many of the longer articles. Munn's work furnishes authoritative and readable information on the whole spectrum of banking and related subjects. [R: ARBA 74, p. 293; Choice, June 74, p. 580]   Bohdan S. Wynar

399. Walmsley, Julian. **A Dictionary of International Finance.** Westport, CT, Greenwood Press, 1979. 270p. $27.50. LC 79-17753. ISBN 0-313-20974-X.

A Dictionary of International Finance has as its purpose to bring together terminology from a variety of fields that relate to international finance. Over 1,200 entries are assembled in order to explain terms used by dealers in such areas as securities, money markets, currencies, and commodities as well as the business vocabulary employed by bankers, exporters, importers, and economics.

This work has two strong points in its favor. First, it provides definitions for a variety of new terms and "buzz words" that are rapidly becoming a fundamental part of the language of business and finance. For example, what is "Pot Protection," a "Roly Poly CD," a "snake," or a "Samurai Bond"? Increasingly used abbreviations such as ECU, GDP, M3, OECD, and SWIFT are also included with brief but clear definitions. Second, the author has gone to the effort of providing specific citations to the books and articles from which selected terms were defined and explained, providing the reader with a source for obtaining additional background information. This title is an excellent, up-to-date effort that definitely is not merely a repeat of other standard economic dictionaries. Strongly recommended for all types of libraries.   Frank Wm. Goudy

INSURANCE

400.   Davids, Lewis E. **Dictionary of Insurance.** Totowa, NJ, Littlefield, Adams, 1977. 291p. (A Littlefield, Adams Quality Paperback, No. 62). $4.95pa. LC 77-5860. ISBN 0-8226-0062-5.

This is the fifth edition of a standard work initially published in 1959. It includes about 3,000 entries providing succinct explanations of the meanings of terms in the fields of life, health, property, liability, marine, pension, surety, and social insurance. The present edition has been enlarged with definitions prepared by the Commission of Insurance Terminology of the American Risk and Insurance Association, and with entries relating to Canadian insurance practices and institutions. This dictionary also identifies major court decisions which have a bearing on insurance. It has broadened its coverage of organizations and associations in the field. A list of state commissioners of insurance, with their addresses, and a directory of organizations, also with names and addresses, are added to the work.

While calling it a specialized dictionary for practitioners, students, and educators in the insurance business, the compiler has expropriated a large body of terms and abbreviations from law, business, and finance as well. As a rule, the entries are brief. Technical terminology, however, is amply described and defined, and often illustrated with mathematical formulae. Treatment of organizations amounts to merely spelling out their acronyms, and the lack of descriptive notes on their functions and contributions diminishes the dictionary's reference value. A spot check of the legal terms and entries dealing with insurance-related legislative acts and court decisions revealed that they are inadequately described and do not include dates and sources. The articles "Lincoln National Life vs. Commissioner of Insurance-Oklahoma" (on page 155), "Miller Dual Bond Act" (on page 168), and "McCarran-Wiler Bill (S.1508)" (on page 165) are typical examples of this irritating practice. Traces of superficial treatment can be found in other places as well, e.g., the entry "Citation," where U2DLR(2D)489 is given as illustration with no hint as to what these symbols mean.

For strictly technical terminology, abbreviations, and acronyms, this dictionary is adequate. Its sole competitor, Robert W. Osler and John S. Bickley's *Glossary of Insurance Terms* (Merritt, 1972), is both older and more modest in scope. [R: ARBA 79, p. 414]

Michael Keresztesi

LABOR

401.   **Dictionary of Occupational Titles.** 4th ed. Washington, Employment and Training Administration, U.S. Employment Service; distr., Washington, GPO, 1978. 1371p. index. $12.00pa. S/N 029-013-00079-9.

The *DOT* has been a basic resource for workers in the field of occupations and vocational education ever since its first appearance in 1939. The incorporation into this volume of thousands of job titles and descriptions provides a solid basis on which employment planning can be carried out, as well as denotes those jobs recognized as "legitimate" by the federal government and therefore possibly worthy of funding and support. Just about every conceivable type of legal job is included in the *DOT*, including as examples such modes of employment as casting room operator, fence manufacture supervisor, sanitary napkin machine tender, and deep submergence vehicle operator.

The fourth edition of this absolutely essential library acquisition has been purged of references to sex- and/or age-related occupational groupings and also contains a greatly increased number of job descriptions over those included in the third edition. The volume is divided into sections providing valuable introductory information on using the *DOT*, followed by a glossary, term titles and definitions, occupational group arrangements, and the two main portions of the text—an alphabetical index of occupational titles and a section on occupational titles arranged by industry designation. An industry index and an appendix explaining data, people, and things conclude the volume. Each entry in the occupational title section includes an occupational classificatory number of nine digits (explained in the introduction), the occupational title, a job description, and cross references. Many fairly general occupational titles are further divided into more specific descriptions of specialties within the general description. No general public or school library can afford to be without this volume. [R: ARBA 79, p. 417; BL, 15 Apr 78, p. 1335]

Norman Lederer

MANAGEMENT

402. Bakewell, K. G. B. **Management Principles and Practices: A Guide to Information Sources.** Detroit, Gale, 1977. 519p. index. (Management Information Guide, No. 32). $28.00. LC 76-16127. ISBN 0-8103-0832-0.

As stated in the introduction, "management is a vast subject," yet the author has managed to focus on the more substantial material in this field. The result is a selective, and at the same time, complete guide to the literature. Arrangement is in 21 sections covering such topics as general management, organizational structure, managers, social responsibility of business, financial management, and communication. Each section begins by briefly explaining the topics and giving reference to more specific sections or items. Within each section is a further breakdown by specialized topic or by type of publication. Full bibliographic information is provided. Annotations are brief but succinct. In addition to major reference works and books and periodicals, there are citations to organizations, films, and other audiovisual materials. While coverage is international in scope, concentration is on materials written between the early 1900s to mid-1970s and published in the United States and England. Appendices include three directories—of organizations, of periodicals, and of publishers. Further access to the guide is by proper name, title, and subject indexes. At present, this would appear to be one of the definitive works on the subject, very helpful to librarians and management alike. [R: ARBA 79, p. 423; Choice, June 78, p. 523; LJ, 15 Apr 78, p. 858; WLB, May 78, p. 731]

Joy Hastings

REAL ESTATE

403. Arnold, Alvin L., and Jack Kusnet. **The Arnold Encyclopedia of Real Estate.** Boston, Warren, Gorham & Lamont, 1978. 901p. $47.50. LC 78-67783. ISBN 0-88262-239-0.

The *Encyclopedia* is intended to be a "comprehensive one-volume real estate library." To achieve that end, the authors have basically given us a two-part publication. Section 1 is an encyclopedic dictionary of real estate terms, alphabetically arranged, with definitions varying in length from a single sentence to several pages. Legal and legislative aspects of the topic, with the accompanying jargon, are more carefully and thoroughly covered than the construction and architectural terms, while useful cross references aid the user in assuring comprehensive definitions.

Section 2 (the appendix) contains charts and tables covering the economics and demographics of the construction and real estate industries. This section is of more limited use than the first because of the dating of the statistics, but will be useful to those who have limited access to the government statistics from which this data was reproduced. The publication will be a useful addition to any library seeking a single-volume reference collection in the real estate area, or to those wishing to supplement a basic reference collection with a more legalistic approach to the topic. [R: ARBA 80, p. 377; WLB, May 79, p. 657]

Ronald F. Dow

17 FINE ARTS

BIBLIOGRAPHIES

404. **Art Books, 1950-1979: Including an International Directory of Museum Permanent Collection Catalogs.** New York, R. R. Bowker, 1979. 1500p. $75.00. ISBN 0-8352-1189-4; ISSN 0000-0418.

Main entries for approximately 37,000 books dealing with various aspects of art are arranged under 14,000 subject headings in this guide. Bibliographic information provided in each citation includes: title, author, Dewey and LC classification, edition, series, notes, ISBN, publisher, date, and subject tracings. This straightforward listing makes accessibility to art publications of 1950-1978 (there is a gap in 1979 publications) a simple process and further indicates which of the volumes listed are still in print.

Aside from its bibliographic function, the compilation contains a unique element: an index incorporating permanent collection catalogs of museums. International in scope, this index supplies complete citations (including prices) for publications by the museum on their respective collections. Such a tool should greatly facilitate the work of researchers. Other assets of the book are a geographic guide to museums of the world, a subject area directory based on LC with cross references, and a directory of publishers and distributors.

Lamia Doumato

405. Ehresmann, Donald L. **Fine Arts: A Bibliographic Guide to Basic Reference Works, Histories, and Handbooks.** 2nd ed. Littleton, CO, Libraries Unlimited, 1979. 349p. index. $25.00. LC 79-9051. ISBN 0-87287-201-7.

The second edition of *Fine Arts* is a comprehensive, classified, and annotated bibliography of over 1,675 reference works, histories, and handbooks on the history of world art published in Western European languages from 1830 to 1978. The first edition, published in 1975, depended on Mary Chamberlin's *Guide to Art Reference Works* for coverage of pre-1958 titles. In this second edition, all titles in Chamberlin that correspond to the scope of this new edition of *Fine Arts* have been reexamined, and all but the most ephemeral have been incorporated, together with 322 pre-1958 titles overlooked by Chamberlin. Finally, the addition of 147 books published since 1973 brings the coverage forward some five years. These changes and enlargements increase the number of titles by more than 50% over the number appearing in the first edition.

To be included in *Fine Arts*, a work must treat two or more of the major media: architecture, sculpture, and painting. The reference works covered in part I, arranged by publication type, include periodical articles and books published after 1830. The general histories and handbooks in part II are books published after 1875; they are arranged by period and geographical area. The annotations are intended to be descriptive, and, where warranted, critical comments appear. The entries are indexed by author, main entry title, series title, and subject. [R: ARBA 80, p. 382; Choice, July 80, p. 652; C&RL, July 80, p. 361; JAL, Mar 80, p. 55; LJ, 1 Mar 80, p. 602; WLB, Mar 80, p. 461]

406. Karpel, Bernard, ed. **Arts in America: A Bibliography.** Washington, DC, Smithsonian Institution Press, 1979. 4v. index. $190.00. LC 79-15321. ISBN 0-87474-578-0.

For so long, there has been a great need for a comprehensive bibliography on the fine arts in the United States. When, several years ago, the prospectus for this multivolume work described it as the fruit of a cooperative effort by many specialist bibliographers who were working under the editorship of Bernard Karpel (former librarian of the Museum of

Modern Art) and as being under the auspices of the Smithsonian Institution, American studies scholars and art historians began to develop high hopes for it. The criticism expressed below notwithstanding, *Arts in America: A Bibliography* is a success, and it will remain the chief bibliographic tool for American art for many years to come.

It consists of four volumes, three containing 21 separate bibliographies dedicated to aspects of the chief media of the visual arts, plus theatre, dance, and music, and three special sections dealing with serials and publications, dissertations and theses, and visual resources in relation to the visual arts in America. There are 20,498 entries in all. The fourth volume is a comprehensive index to the work. This impressive compilation puts the United States in the bibliographic class of such countries as Sweden and Denmark, both of which have excellent comprehensive national art bibliographies. (To remain in this illustrious company, it will be necessary for the United States to establish a serial bibliography that will update the present work.)

The editorial policy of having the individual compilers determine the scope and form of their bibliographies must be criticized. It has resulted in considerable disparity of the information conveyed in the various sections. Some, such as the bibliography on the art of Native Americans, are almost completely unannotated. Others, like the section devoted to the decorative arts, are introduced with a good essay that gives an overview of the state of the literature. Other very important sections, such as that on architecture, do not provide this important insight. Similarly, there are inconsistencies in the coverage. Although most of the sections follow a similar classification system — beginning with general reference works and concluding with specialized works on individual subjects — the general sections differ considerably from bibliography to bibliography. In the bibliography of architecture, the two-volume bibliography covering American architects from the Civil War to the present, by Lawrence Wodehouse, is conspicuously absent, even though the more general work by Dennis Sharp is included. In similar fashion, it is difficult to discern why Theodore Bestermann's *A World Bibliography of Bibliographies* is listed under bibliographies in the section on twentieth-century design, while other, more specific bibliographies on the fine arts, such as those by Mary Walls Chamberlin, E. Louise Lucas, and Donald L. Ehresmann, are not. With the possible exception of the section on painting, all the bibliographies could have benefited from a more thorough evaluation of general reference works as they apply to the study of American art. The failure to state inclusive dates of coverage is particularly inexcusable.

Words of special praise are due two excellent sections. William J. Dane has compiled a model list of serials and periodicals. His annotations to 253 titles give a good idea of the history, scope, and importance of a varietous collection. Equally informative is the survey of pictorial materials on Americana available for study and purchase in institutions in the United States, compiled under the coordination of Judith A. Hoffberg.

Donald L. Ehresmann

DICTIONARIES

407. McGraw-Hill Dictionary of Art. Edited by Bernard S. Myers; Assistant Editor, Shirley D. Myers. New York, McGraw-Hill, 1969. 5v. illus. (part col.). bibliog. LC 68-26314.

This is not an abridgment of the monumental 15-volume *Encyclopedia of World Art*, also published by McGraw-Hill, but an independent work. As one might expect, the dictionary treatment of material is more popular.

This dictionary contains approximately 15,000 entries in alphabetical arrangement, covering all important countries and periods and all major areas of architecture, painting, sculpture, and decorative and graphic arts. There is a wide range of entries, including biographies, definitions, concepts, schools and trends, and description of the major monuments and museums and individual works of art. Depending on the topic, these articles vary in length from 25 to 2,000 words; they were written by a total of 125 contributors. Entries are extensively cross-referenced. For example, biographies are cross-referenced to stylistic articles, and general period articles are cross-referenced to individual artists, monuments, and definitions of terms. The text is accompanied by numerous illustrations—1,700 halftones, 400 full-color photographs, and 200 line drawings. [R: ARBA 70, p. 2; LJ, 1 Nov 69; WLB, Oct 69]

408. Myers, Bernard S., and Shirley D. Myers, eds. **Dictionary of 20th Century Art.** New York, McGraw-Hill, 1974. 440p. illus. bibliog. index. $9.95. LC 74-4200. ISBN 0-07-044220-7.

This compact reference work on the art of our century is prepared for students, general readers, and those wanting the basic facts on a modern artist or movement. As clearly stated in the preface, the co-editors carefully selected most of the entries from their earlier work, the five-volume *McGraw-Hill Dictionary of Art* (see previous entry). A few new entries were prepared, but most were previously published in the larger work, frequently with a fuller entry. However, the concentration on art history from about 1905 to the contemporary scene is welcome. The editors bring a wealth of expertise to the project, which emphasizes biography. The dates and locations of art works mentioned in the biographic entries appear in parentheses after each title. While not for the specialist or advanced student, this dictionary should be useful in general reference collections in addition to branch and art school libraries. [R: ARBA 75, p. 438; BL, 15 Apr 75, p. 877; WLB, Feb 75, p. 459]

William J. Dane

409. **Phaidon Dictionary of Twentieth-Century Art.** 2nd ed. Oxford, Phaidon Press; distr., New York, E. P. Dutton, 1977. 420p. LC 77-81957. ISBN 0-7148-1822-4.

In this first-class reference tool, major movements and artists of the past 75 years are described, along with hundreds of lesser-known artists and terms, all on a truly international scale. Bibliographies are brief and there are no illustrations; but this dictionary has much to recommend it, and the entries generally travel fast and light—no wasted words. Contemporary developments such as shaped canvas, hard edge, and minimal art are described along with biographies of such current artists as Marisol, Agam, Stella, and Hockney. Expert writing and editing coupled with a solid format make this a highly recommended acquisition for humanities and art collections. [R: ARBA 79, p. 430]

William J. Dane

ENCYCLOPEDIAS

410. **The Britannica Encyclopedia of American Art.** Chicago, Encyclopaedia Britannica Educational Corp.; distr., New York, Simon and Schuster, 1974. 669p. illus. (part col.). bibliog. (A Chanticleer Press Edition). $36.50. LC 73-6527. ISBN 0-671-21616-3.

This is the first major encyclopedic work devoted solely to American art. Its broad definition of art includes photography, landscape architecture, handcrafts, industrial design, and even circus wagons, in addition to the usual genres of painting, sculpture, architecture, etc. The *Encyclopedia* is beautifully laid out with many well-chosen illustrations (both color and black and white). Topical entries, in alphabetical order, include persons, periods, movements, etc., and range in length from several pages to brief paragraphs.

Most entries are signed with the initials of the contributors, who are listed at the front of the book.

The main criticism of this encyclopedia stems from its selection of topics for inclusion. The editors' disclaimer in the foreword ("informed readers will note omissions, especially of the work of younger artists whose reputations have yet to stand the test of time") does not excuse many of the omissions. For instance, try to find American Indian art, or any Wyeth other than Andrew. Coverage of artistic styles or movements is also uneven. Romanticism and surrealism are here, but realism and the New Realism (or California School of Realism) are not. Museums and other notable collections of art are included in an appended directory entitled "Guide to Museums and Public Collections."

The lack of an index is a major handicap in using this encyclopedia, but numerous cross references are provided in two ways: 1) within entries, where an asterisk follows a name that is an entry itself; and 2) directly, as in "New York School, see Abstract Expressionism." However, many articles include significant mentions of people or events that do not have entries of their own, and without an index there is no way to locate this material.

Supplementary materials in the *Britannica Encyclopedia of American Art* are a glossary, a guide to entries by arts, a guide to museums and public collections, and a bibliography. The bibliography is in two sections — general works (by subject), and then a bibliography according to entries. This encyclopedia is an important item because of the wealth of material here that is not in other sources. [R: ARBA 75, p. 436; BL, 1 Dec 74, p. 389; Choice, Mar 74, p. 56]   Sally Wynkoop

411. **Praeger Encyclopedia of Art.** New York, Praeger, 1971. 5v. illus. (some col.). bibliog. index. LC 75-122093. ISBN 0-275-47490-9.

This five-volume encyclopedia is based on the French encyclopedia *Dictionnaire universel de l'art et des artistes*, published in three volumes by Fernand Hazan in Paris in 1967. This English edition is copyrighted by Pall Mall Press in London. According to the preface, "the purpose of this encyclopedia is to provide, within reasonable limitations of space, a comprehensive and authoritative reference guide for both student and general reader — as well as a lively appreciation of the history of world art." There are some 4,000 alphabetically arranged entries (including some 1,000 survey articles) covering periods, styles, schools, and movements. There are 3,000 articles on individual artists from all nations and periods. The text is well integrated with the excellent illustrations (1,700 in color), and there are about 1,000 pictures per volume. Liberal cross references and a general index are included.

Some comparison with the *McGraw-Hill Dictionary of Art* (see entry 407) might be in order. The McGraw-Hill work includes 15,000 entries with 2,500 longer articles. The text in the Praeger encyclopedia is arranged in four columns and has about 300,000 fewer words than the McGraw-Hill work. In terms of contributors, the present work seems somewhat better balanced (100 contributors of various nationality backgrounds with many French, as opposed to 125 American and British contributors in McGraw-Hill's dictionary). The emphasis in the two works is on slightly different types of material. For example, it seems that certain topics (e.g., Swedish art or Baroque art) are better documented here; on the other hand, the McGraw-Hill dictionary offers a number of brief articles on art centers or about art techniques not represented in Praeger. In other words, the two works complement and supplement each other. They are not designed for the specialist but contain a wealth of information for the layperson. (A one-volume condensation of the Praeger encyclopedia, *Phaidon Encyclopedia of Art and Artists* (E. P. Dutton), was published in 1978.) [R: ARBA 72, p. 352; BL, 1 Nov 71, p. 209; Choice, Mar 71, p. 40; LJ, July 71, p. 2296; WLB, May 71, p. 883]

412.   Quick, John. **Artists' and Illustrators' Encyclopedia.** 2nd ed. New York, McGraw-Hill, 1977. 327p. illus. bibliog. index. $18.95. LC 77-6700. ISBN 0-07-051063-6.

The original edition published in 1969 was intended as a ready reference for professionals in commercial and fine art, photography, the graphic arts, and printing. Some 800 new entries have been added, but the basic objective is the same. There are numerous illustrations of objects and of examples of forms and techniques, as well as an extensive index that provides access to terms not used as entry words. In covering such a vast field, the compiler has necessarily had to be highly selective, and in a few cases the number of terms is not fully adequate (e.g., barely 50 under "bookbinding"). On the other hand, students will find numerous definitions of words used infrequently in this field. Thus, anyone interested in the history of printing and book illustration (including specialists) will find here definitions of terms encountered only occasionally. A special value of the work is its careful attention to terms used for the graphics of television and motion pictures. [R: ARBA 78, p. 409; Choice, Apr 78, p. 212]   Lawrence S. Thompson

INDEXES

413.   Havlice, Patricia Pate. **Index to Artistic Biography.** Metuchen, NJ, Scarecrow, 1973. 2v. $40.00/set. LC 72-6412. ISBN 0-8108-0540-5.

This massive reference guide to biographic information covers 70,000 artists. The compiler used 64 art publications as sources for the listing of international artists active from antiquity to contemporary times. The source books were published between 1902 and 1970 in 10 different languages. The listing is truly international; it includes artists from Iceland, Israel, Norway, Scotland, Japan, Australia, Poland, Argentina, and Brazil, in addition to the more standard entries for European, British, and American artists. Cross references are used for alternate names and for variant spellings, while the information for each artist includes dates, nationality, media, and pseudonyms.

A random checking of a cross section of contemporary and nineteenth-century artists proved successful, although a number of the death dates that are omitted could have been found with further research. There are 90 entries under the name of Jones, and well over 200 Smiths listed. Since we are living in a time of aggressive art collecting by institutions and individuals, there is a real need for this type of art research tool; this index immediately takes a place of prominence in the realm of art biography. [R: ARBA 74, p. 332; Choice, Nov 73, p. 1356; LJ, 1 Sept 73, p. 2423; WLB, Oct 73, p. 168]   William J. Dane

BIOGRAPHY

414.   **Contemporary Artists.** Ed. by Colin Naylor and Genesis P-Orridge. London, St. James Press; New York, St. Martin's Press, 1977. 1077p. illus. $50.00. LC 76-54627. ISBN 0-333-22672-0.

St. Martin's Press has produced another important volume in their series on contemporary fine artists. Although there are other guides to living artists, nothing quite compares to this volume. International in scope (with strong emphasis on Europe and the United States and a fairly impressive listing of Japanese artists), it covers all forms of visual arts. Earthworks, performance art, video, conceptual, body art, and environments are among the newer art forms that have been included. The editors enlisted a panel of 20 advisors to help in the selection of artists to be included. This panel consisted of several well-known art critics—e.g., Paul Cummings, Lucy Lippard, Thomas Messer, and K. G. Pontus-Hulten. The selection criteria were broad: an artist must have been an artist for at least five years; had several one-person shows and have been included in two or more large survey shows; been represented in the permanent collections of major museums; and finally, attracted "serious critical attention." Using these and other criteria, the editors included almost 1,300 artists.

Each entry consists of the standard biographical data used in St. Martin's contemporary fine art series (*Dramatists, Novelists,* and *Poets*). In addition, the work contains lists of one-man shows, primary art dealers, collections of the artist's work, and a bibliography of printed works by and about the artist. A large percentage of the entries also have a brief statement by the artist and/or a signed critical analysis of the individual's art. Most of the critical analyses were written by regular critics for such publications as *Arts Magazine* and *Art International.* Although the volume is contemporary in orientation, some early twentieth-century artists such as Picasso, Chagall, and Matisse are included. The inclusion of deceased artists was justified on the basis of "continuing influence" on contemporary artists. This is an important addition to any library collection that serves art programs. [R: ARBA 79, p. 443; BL, 15 Oct 78, p. 402; Choice, Apr 78, p. 207; LJ, 15 Feb 78, p. 449]   G. Edward Evans

415. **Creative Canada: A Biographical Dictionary of Twentieth-Century Creative and Performing Artists.** Comp. by Reference Division, McPherson Library, University of Victoria. Buffalo, NY, University of Toronto Press, 1971-72. 2v. index. $20.00/v. LC 72-151387. ISBN 0-8020-3262-1(v.1); 0-8020-3285-0(v.2).

As indicated in the first volume of this series, the purpose of the work is to cover those "creative and performing artists who have contributed as individuals to the culture of Canada in the twentieth century, and who have had this individual contribution recognized in print. The amount of critical acclaim in print has been a guide to the compilers, since it is inconceivable in this era of the media and the message that any artist will be of significance if he has not received critical acclaim in books, journal articles, or newspapers."

According to the stated objectives, authors of "works of the imagination" are included, such as "artists and sculptors, musicians, and performing artists in the fields of ballet, modern dance, radio, theatre, television, and motion pictures; directors, designers, and producers in theatre, cinema, radio and television, and the dance." Excluded are architects, commercial artists, creators of handicraft and patrons of the arts, as well as journalists, historians, etc., "unless they have an established reputation as individual artists in one of the categories listed above."

Each volume contains about 500 entries listed in one alphabetical arrangement. The length of the biographical sketches varies from a few lines to several pages. As stated in the preface to the second volume, "an artist of some stature producing very little actual material will not have as lengthy an entry as another of equal or lesser importance who has produced a great deal." It is not enough simply to provide inventory-type information and put it into proper perspective. Although this is an interesting work and provides a great deal of detail that will not be found elsewhere, it is out of balance in terms of editorial attention. In addition, an index by profession is an essential ingredient in works of this type. In spite of its deficiencies, this is a unique work. [R: ARBA 72, p. 353; ARBA 73, p. 357; Choice, June 72, p. 489; Choice, Apr 73, p. 262]

416. Cummings, Paul. **Dictionary of Contemporary American Artists.** 3rd ed. New York, St. Martin's Press, 1977. 545p. $35.00. LC 76-10548. ISBN 0-312-20090-0.

The second edition of Cummings' *Dictionary* was recognized as a well-balanced work that would serve as an important source book on twentieth-century American artists. The third edition is thoroughly updated to the beginning of 1976 and adds 85 new artists (for a total of 872). Included are artists, both American-born and those who later became U.S. residents, whose works have been exhibited in at least one important show.

The information supplied follows the pattern of the previous editions—the artist's education, teaching career, address; the artist's dealer and address; complete lists of exhibitions, collections, special commissions, awards; notes on the artist's specialty; and a bibliography of books about the artist. Death dates and obituaries are also given. Accompanying the biographical entries are 100 newly selected black-and-white illustrations of representative works. Additional features are an index to artists (with pronunciation given for difficult names), a key to museums around the world, and a list of all American galleries mentioned in the biographies.

Cummings is inevitably compared to Bowker's *Who's Who in American Art*, which is much broader in scope but lacks the detail of Cummings. The 1978 edition of Bowker's *Who's Who* contains over 10,000 entries covering art educators, critics, dealers, museum directors, printmakers, etc., as well as artists from the United States, Mexico, and Canada. Cummings is a valuable reference, especially for very well known artists and those in the New York area. A useful supplement to Cummings for the western United States is Samuels' *Illustrated Biographical Encyclopedia of Artists of the American West* (Doubleday, 1976. $30.00). [R: ARBA 78, p. 424; BL, 15 Dec 77, p. 703; WLB, Oct 77, p. 187]

Christine Gehrt Wynar

ARCHITECTURE

417. Pevsner, Nikolaus, John Fleming, and Hugh Honour. **A Dictionary of Architecture.** Rev. and enl. Woodstock, NY, Overlook Press, 1976. 556p. illus. $17.95. LC 75-27325. ISBN 0-87951-040-4.

With some 2,400 entries and over 1,000 illustrations, this edition of a British standard work is much expanded from the original 1966 volume. Pevsner himself, a recognized authority on the history of art and architecture, was responsible for the medieval and nineteenth- and twentieth-century sections and a couple of the "national" entries.

Entries are often brief, but the ones on a country (e.g., Italian architecture) are longer; most are critical as well as descriptive, and are often quite lively and opinionated. While the work is of British origin, it seems reasonably reflective of American architectural history and practice. Biographical articles are present but are limited to the most important figures. These, the national entries, and some others usually have at least one reference for further study. Recommended for any library with subject interest. [R: ARBA 77, p. 421; LJ, Aug 76, p. 1618]

Walter C. Allen

418. **Who's Who in Architecture from 1400 to the Present.** Ed. by J. M. Richards. New York, Holt, Rinehart, and Winston, 1977. 368p. illus. (part col.). $19.95. LC 76-44323. ISBN 0-03-017381-7.

The author of this invaluable reference work is an architectural writer, critic, and historian of distinction. For English and American readers interested in architects and their buildings, he provides over 600 alphabetically arranged entries for architects, engineers, town planners, and landscape architects who have made a significant contribution to the development of architecture. About 50 of the entries constitute fairly substantial, informative, and stimulating essays written by specialists on individuals or periods. The geographical scope is the Western world, plus those other parts of the world whose culture is derived from the West.

Sixteen color pages and 250 black-and-white illustrations are included. Books on individual architects, when they exist in English, are given at the end of each biographical entry. A classified list of other recommended books for further reading is given, along with acknowledgments and a select list of buildings by country.

Kathleen J. Voigt

GRAPHIC ARTS

419. Beall, Karen F., comp. **American Prints in the Library of Congress: A Catalogue of the Collection.** Baltimore, published for the Library of Congress by Johns Hopkins Press, 1970. 568p. illus. index. $40.00. LC 73-106134. ISBN 0-8108-1077-9.

This is an outstanding reference book in the field of graphic art. It documents the work of 1,250 artists, listing about 12,000 American prints stretching from colonial times to 1970. Over 1,600 illustrations are reproduced in this complete catalog of a great print collection specializing in American graphic art. The informative entries, arranged alphabetically by artists, are followed by lists of the artists' prints owned by the Library of Congress. For each print title is given the date of execution, place of publication, printer, date of publication (if different from execution date), and medium. Print measurements are given in centimeters, followed by analytical notes of considerable research value. The extensive listings for Arms, Pennell, Sloan, and Whistler are nearly catalogues raisonnés for these prolific artists. Indexes for geographic iconography, names, and series, a list of print societies and clubs, and a select bibliography are welcome additions to this outstanding title, which immediately takes a place of major importance in the bibliography of American art history. [R: ARBA 71, p. 332]   William J. Dane

420. Kingman, Lee, Grace Allen Hogarth, and Harriet Quimby, comps. **Illustrators of Children's Books, 1967-1976.** Boston, Horn Book, 1978. 290p. illus. bibliog. index. $32.50. LC 78-13759. ISBN 0-87675-018-8.

Reference books identifying children's book authors and illustrators are in danger of becoming a deluge, but this well-known series is a standard source with a distinguished record. The Horn Book entries offer the usual biographical information and personal comments by the artist about his or her work or philosophy of art; length of entries varies greatly. The main contribution lies in the selectivity of the entries; 478 artists were chosen as the best or most representative of those active in children's book illustration during 1967-1976. A selective bibliography of illustrators, identifying the best of an artist's work, is also included as a separate section.

The most valuable part of the book may be the essays that survey the development of children's book illustration during the past decade and offer some analysis of illustration in different parts of the world. Walter Lorraine raises the issue of whether illustration is an integral or independent part of a picture book; Brian Alderson writes about Europe's contribution; Teiji Seta and Momoko Ishii examine the Japanese picture book; and T. P. Bicknell surveys the trends in illustration on both sides of the Atlantic. The illustrations chosen for the essays are eloquent statements of the many paths that illustrators have followed the past 10 years. The appendix is an especially helpful aid, containing bibliographical notes to the essays; a list of artists represented by the illustrations; an index to all parts of the essays, biographies, and bibliographies; and a cumulative index to biographies and bibliographies in all four volumes of the series. The volume is an essential reference for any collection supporting the study of children's books. [R: ARBA 79, p. 438; BL, 1 Feb 79, p. 871; Choice, June 79, p. 524; WLB, Mar 79, p. 522]

Christine Gehrt Wynar

421. Stevenson, George A. **Graphic Arts Encyclopedia.** 2nd ed. New York, McGraw-Hill, 1979. 483p. illus. bibliog. index. $26.95. LC 78-7298. ISBN 0-07-061288-9.

Employing a user-oriented visual approach, this alphabetical encyclopedia defines and describes the terms and techniques used in copy preparation, art reproduction, copying, and printing. Revised, updated, and expanded from the first edition (1968), this practical encyclopedia covers the newest machinery and processes, including electronic word processing, covered in entries on keyboarding equipment; video display terminals; photographic and composition typesetters; and all their peripheral equipment. Advanced printing presses, microfilm equipment, process cameras, and copying machines (including color copiers) are all discussed in simple, straightforward language that can be easily understood by nonspecialists. Nearly 300 crisp black-and-white illustrations clarify and highlight the text.

Keywords are presented in boldface type for easy identification, and include many cross references to equipment and processes. Although many descriptions are brief, some topics are actually covered in short essays. For example, the entry "Offset Printing Press" is five pages long and includes eight photographs of various types of presses. Included also are tables and charts showing metric equivalents, standard paper sizes and weights, paper cutting requirements, and symbols for use when selecting and proofing type. A well-selected bibliography, product and manufacturer information, and an index conclude this recommended ready reference for all artists, designers, and students of the graphic arts. [R: ARBA 80, p. 394; WLB, Nov 79, p. 194]   Judy Gay Caraghar

PAINTING

422. Foskett, Daphne. **A Dictionary of British Miniature Painters.** 2v. New York, Praeger, 1972. illus. (part col.). $145.00/set. LC 72-112634.

A solid and enduring piece of scholarship, this is also a luxurious production in terms of illustration. To Basil Long's *British Miniaturists* (1929), Foskett has added over 2,000 miniaturists and has extended the period covered by Long to 1910. Volume 1 lists almost 4,500 names or initials of miniaturists who were native to or worked in Great Britain and Ireland. Biographical and stylistic information in the entries is sufficient and succinct. One hundred fine color illustrations are interspersed in the 600 pages of the first volume, which also contains a brief discussion of miniature materials and techniques, as well as a selective but discriminating bibliography. Volume 2 is devoted to monochrome illustrations—967 of them. The illustration list for volume 2 has thoughtfully been included in both volumes. For collectors, dealers, and scholars, this will be a mandatory acquisition. [R: ARBA 73, p. 362; Choice, July 72, p. 634; LJ, 15 June 72, p. 2171]   Julia M. Ehresmann

423. **An Illustrated Inventory of Famous Dismembered Works of Art with a Section on Dismembered Tombs in France: European Painting.** Paris, Unesco; distr., New York, Unipub, 1974. 221p. illus. $23.10. ISBN 92-3-101040-9.

Throughout world history, works of art have been displaced or dismembered by private owners in the course of inheritance disputes, by conquering armies, and by disreputable dealers and collectors. In an effort to find a solution to this problem of dispersal and dismemberment, Unesco commissioned eight renowned art historians to make a study of the situation in each of their countries, and thus to focus world attention on the gravity of the worldwide dispersal, through fragmentation, of some of the greatest works of art.

About 70 of these dismembered masterpieces are illustrated in black and white and discussed in this extremely important pilot study. All of the participants in the project employed a similar format for the presentation of their conclusions. A narrative description of the circumstances leading to the dismemberments is followed by discussions of specific works of art, each including artist, original location, shape, dimensions, paint layer, support, subject, previous history, locations of fragments, suggested reconstitutions, and bibliography. Italian, Flemish, French, Spanish, German, and Russian paintings form the core of the text, but two chapters are also included on European manuscripts and French sculpture. Although it is doubtful that the Unesco study will sway nations into sacrificing prized possessions to permit permanent reconstitution of paintings, the study nevertheless is of vital importance to scholars. It is hoped that it will lead to further concentration on this extremely complex area of study. [R: ARBA 76, p. 448; Choice, July/Aug 75, p. 672]

Jacqueline D. Sisson

424.　Muehsam, Gerd, ed. **French Painters and Paintings from the Fourteenth Century to Post-Impressionism.** New York, Ungar, 1970. 646p. illus. (A Library of Art Criticism Series). $30.00. LC 70-98344. ISBN 0-8044-3210-4.

In contrast to other publications dealing with sources and documents, Gerd Muehsam's impressive book is solely concerned with art criticism. A concise, lucid introduction provides background on the history of art academies and the development of art criticism in France.

The entries, arranged chronologically by artist, consist of brief biographical resumes followed by examples of art criticism pertaining to a specific work of art and, in some cases, general criticisms of the artist's total oeuvre. Frequently the selections include statements by the artist and his contemporaries as well as selections from twentieth-century critics and art historians. For example, the criticisms of Poussin's paintings are from works by Bellori, Félibien, Voltaire, Reynolds, Stendhal, Ingres, Delacroix, Ruskin, Cézanne, Magne, Gide, Friedlaender, and De Tolnay. Regrettably, illustrations are not always included. The entries covering the work of anonymous painters, such as the Master of Aix and the Master of Moulins, are especially successful in illustrating the variety of approaches art historians use to establish or attempt to establish attributions. The task of selecting the materials must have been monumental. Although specialists consulting this valuable reference book will not always agree with all the selections made, there is no doubt that Gerd Muehsam has a scholarly knowledge of the field and its bibliography. The only serious omissions are the small number of negative criticisms, incomplete textual and bibliographic information on Charles Sterling's attribution to Quarton of the School of Avignon *Piéta*, and the omission of K. E. Maison's denial of a Daumier attribution for the final painting of *L'Émeute*.

This sizable book, an important American art reference tool, is consulted by scholars and students in all fields of the humanities. The impressive selected bibliography is an excellent checklist for libraries. [R: ARBA 71, p. 330; LJ, July 70, p. 2455]

Jacqueline D. Sisson

425.　New York Historical Society. **Catalogue of American Portraits.** Comp. by Wendy J. Shadwell and Robert Strunsky. New Haven, Yale University Press, 1974. 2v. illus. $65.00/set. LC 74-79974. ISBN 0-300-01477-5.

Meticulously researched, this catalog of the New York Historical Society portrait collection of or by Americans is a vital reference tool for research on portraiture and costuming as well as on numerous facets of American cultural, economic, and political history. Executed in various media, the portraits range in artistic quality from the height of portraiture to primitive works whose naivete and unintended humor are totally captivating. Except for a separate section devoted to unidentified portraits, the 2,420 catalog entries and 1,000 illustrations are alphabetically arranged by the sitters' names. Extensive cross-referencing is employed for the portraits of women. The entries are listed according to the person's name at the time the portrait was made with, whenever possible, cross references from maiden names or married names (depending on the marital status at the time the portrait was executed). The sitters and artists are not limited to famous persons nor to New York residents. Portraits of North American Indians are included only if it was possible to determine that the work is an authentic portrait and if the sitter can be identified.

Each entry includes a biography of the sitter, attribution of the work, date, measurements, medium, inscriptions, stylistic analysis, and description. A bibliography usually accompanies each entry. The provenance of the portraits is not as fully developed as one could wish. A sizable bibliography and an artist index complete this catalog of one of the richest collections of American portraiture. The authors are to be commended for their careful planning, which has resulted in an unusually user-oriented format. [R: ARBA 76, p. 436; Choice, Feb 75, p. 1756; LJ, 15 Jan 75, p. 114]   Jacqueline D. Sisson

426.   Norman, Geraldine. **Nineteenth-Century Painters and Painting: A Dictionary.** Berkeley, University of California Press, 1977. 240p. illus. (part col.). bibliog. index. $38.50. LC 76-24594. ISBN 0-520-03328-0.

In recent years, several fine one-volume English-language dictionaries of modern (i.e., principally twentieth century) art and artists have appeared, but none covering the entire range of nineteenth-century painting. Norman's *Dictionary*, which includes information on "major figures of all the national schools" in Europe and the United States and their interaction with each other, does much to fill this gap in the reference literature. The dictionary proper is prefaced by brief descriptions of major types and styles of nineteenth-century painting, these illustrated by color reproductions. Of the 700 or more dictionary entries, most are biographies of individual painters, but also included are entries on artistic movements, techniques, and institutions. The articles are brief, but reliable, and more readable than many drier dictionary accounts. Short bibliographies are appended in most instances; these include primarily monographs and range from studies done in the nineteenth century to recent scholarly publications. The citations are not duplicated in the bibliography at the end of the book, which provides additional references to dictionaries and studies of nineteenth-century art, academies, individual countries, and movements.

The format is roughly similar to the *Britannica Encyclopedia of American Art*. Small monochrome illustrations run alongside the text. These are identified by painter, title, and date with further information (medium, size, location, and photo source) supplied in a list arranged alphabetically by painter following the bibliography. Norman's book will be useful in all types of libraries. It provides the most up-to-date dictionary coverage of many painters and gives locations for their *oeuvres* in cities and museums throughout Europe and the United States. [R: ARBA 79, p. 442; Choice, Sept 78, p. 843; LJ, 15 May 78, p. 1051]
Carole Franklin

427.   Ormond, Richard, and Malcolm Rogers, eds. **Dictionary of British Portraiture, in Four Volumes: Volumes 1 & 2.** New York, Oxford University Press, 1979. 2v. $45.00(v.1); $49.50(v.2). LC 79-22598. ISBN 0-19-520180-9(v.1); 0-19-520181-7(v.2).

Catalogs of the National Portrait Gallery, the British Museum, and other sources have been used in compiling this dictionary of famous figures from the Middle Ages to 1900. Chosen from the *Dictionary of National Biography*, with omission of minor names and a few additions, are men and women whose portraits are in galleries, institutions, or other collections open to the public. A few are found outside Britain, e.g., the Ellesmere Chaucer at the Huntington Library. The first two volumes, covering the Middle Ages to 1700 and 1700 to 1800, are alphabetically arranged, giving the following information for each entry: name of sitter, birth and death dates, profession or occupation, genre (painting, drawing, sculpture, photograph, etc.), name of artist, date of portrait, size (i.e., half length, full length), other distinguishing features, medium, and location. Illustrations would have enlivened the volumes but would have made them prohibitively large and expensive. The concise information found in these volumes will be very useful for identification, especially since this is the first comprehensive handbook of its kind.   Frances Neel Cheney

428.   Waterhouse, Ellis. **Roman Baroque Painting: A List of the Principal Painters and Their Works in and around Rome.** Oxford, England, Phaidon Press; distr., New York, Abner Schram, 1976. 163p. illus. index. $45.00. ISBN 0-7148-1701-5.

This classic source book by a noted British art historian has been unavailable for decades. Professor Waterhouse has now written an updated historical survey running to 38 pages, followed by a list of works by 60 major baroque painters, which are to be found in and around Rome. The listings are annotated and recent changes in attribution are mentioned. The bibliographic entries have been updated and 81 crisply reproduced black and white illustrations add to the book's reference value. A topographical index lists the locations of the paintings in the basic listing, with the majority of the works to be found in churches and palaces in Rome. Considering that the book is less than average length, has no color plates, and has good but not notable production values, it is overpriced—at least through the American distributor. However, because of its specialized topic and period covered, this is an important art reference title of considerable value to research libraries and essential to institutions holding baroque paintings. [R: ARBA 77, p. 426; Choice, July 76, p. 655]   William J. Dane

SCULPTURE

429.   Clapp, Jane. **Sculpture Index.** Metuchen, NJ, Scarecrow, 1970-71. 2v. $35.00(v.1); $40.00(v.2). LC 79-9538. ISBN 0-8108-0249-X(v.1); 0-8108-0311-9(v.2).

This work indexes about 950 sources, including art histories, museum catalogs, and art reference books. Except for a few European museum catalogs, all are in English. Periodical articles and monographs on individual artists are excluded. Locations of original sculptures are indicated, and there is a very impressive 157-page list of public and private collections arranged by country and city. The shorter list (four pages) of names of collections without location may present problems for the searcher.

Although emphasis is placed on work since 1900, sculpture from all periods is included. Volume 1 covers Europe and the contemporary Middle East; volume 2 covers the Americas, the Orient, Africa, the Pacific area, and the classical world.

The index is alphabetically arranged under names of sculptures, by titles and subjects. Nationality and dates are given for sculptors; for their works, the original and present location(s), material used, dimensions in inches, museum identification number, and the sources where illustrations are found. Types of sculpture include portraits, architectural elements, church accessories, and a variety of decorative objects such as masks, jewelry, fountains, and musical instruments. Major subjects include countries, by century (extensively covered) and by major art periods (unevenly covered). Minor subjects cover a very impressive range of people, deities, animals, battles, games, sports, coins, buildings, and themes.

This is a well-made, much-needed reference book that will serve both as a source for illustrations of sculpture and as a general illustration index. [R: ARBA 72, p. 365; LJ, 1 June 70, p. 2132; LJ, 15 Apr 71, p. 1352; RQ, Winter 71, p. 173]   Paul Breed

430.   Maillard, Robert, ed. **New Dictionary of Modern Sculpture.** Trans. from the French by Bettina Wadia. New York, Tudor, 1971. 328p. illus. $12.50. LC 70-153118. ISBN 0-8148-0479-9.

A translation of *Nouveau dictionnaire de la sculpture moderne* (first published in 1960 under the title *Dictionnaire de la sculpture moderne*, which appeared under the English title *Dictionary of Modern Sculpture*; New York, Tudor, 1960). The first edition of this work had biographical and critical sketches of 412 modern sculptors (beginning with Rodin), with 453 illustrations of their works. This revision has about 200 additional artists and an equal number of new illustrations. Articles are initialed by the 34 contributors, a distinguished list including Robert Cogniat, Carola Giedion-Welcker, and Nello Ponente. Biographical information is minimal; emphasis is placed on a sculptor's artistic career, medium, style, and characteristics of work. Important exhibitions are mentioned, along with a few of an artist's best-known works. Usually one or two illustrations appear for each sculptor, but for a few there are none. The brief, succinct descriptions of the salient features of sculptors' works are very well done, but the small space allotted for articles results in truncation (from half a column to three columns), and no bibliographical references are provided.

The dictionary is strictly biographical—there are no articles on movements, countries, or other subjects, and there is no index of subjects or of illustrations. Nevertheless, modern sculptors from all parts of the world are well represented. [R: ARBA 73, p. 364; Choice, July 72, p. 626; LJ, 15 Feb 72, p. 672; WLB, Feb 72, p. 543]   Paul Breed

431.   Richter, Gisela M. A. **The Sculpture and Sculptors of the Greeks.** 4th ed. rev. New Haven, CT, Yale University Press, 1970. 317p. illus. index. $42.50. LC 70-99838. ISBN 0-300-01281-0.

In the fourth edition of this firmly established reference book (the first edition appeared in 1929), Ms. Richter, curator of classical art at the Metropolitan Museum before her retirement, combines knowledge, enthusiasm, and skillful writing in the presentation of her material.

The book is divided into two major sections. Part 1 discusses the sculpture through a chronological survey, followed by chapters on general characteristics, the human figure, the head, drapery, composition, animals, and technique. Part 2 covers individual sculptors and their followers in chronological order from the archaic period through the first century B.C. Of special reference value are a 12-page chronology of outstanding sculptures, an excellent bibliography, an extensive index to the text, an index to the illustrations, and a list of illustrations indicating the material of the sculptures and their location. The more than 800 illustrations referred to in the main body of the text are gathered at the end of the volume, a very satisfactory working arrangement.

Richter states that she has been able to make many additions and corrections in the text in the light of new discoveries and acquisitions. There also have been additions and improvements in the section of illustrations. Although the discussion is technical and the analysis detailed, one never loses sight of the broad transitional pattern of the five centuries of sculptural development that are covered. The book is of value to both the general reader and the serious student. [R: ARBA 71, p. 335; Choice, May 71, p. 376]   Joan E. Burns

18 APPLIED ARTS

GENERAL WORKS

432. Ehresmann, Donald L. **Applied and Decorative Arts: A Bibliographic Guide to Basic Reference Works, Histories, and Handbooks.** Littleton, CO, Libraries Unlimited, 1977. 232p. index. $22.50. LC 76-55416. ISBN 0-87287-136-3.

This work, a companion volume to Ehresmann's *Fine Arts* (see entry 405), is the first classified and annotated bibliography of books on the history of the applied and decorative arts. For the purposes of this bibliography the meaning of applied and decorative arts combines the narrow definition that concentrates on the so-called minor arts of ceramics, enamels, furniture, glass, ivory, leather, metalwork, and textiles, with the broader definition that takes in the more applied mixed media of arms and armor, clocks and watches, costume, jewelry, lacquer, medals and seals, musical instruments, and toys. Objects of pure technology or craft are excluded. So are those that are essentially adjuncts of the major arts, such as drawing, graphic arts, mosaic, etc.

Included are 1,240 annotated entries for books written in Western European languages, published between 1875 and 1975. Pamphlets, periodical articles, and exhibition catalogs are excluded. [R: ARBA 78, p. 426; Choice, Sept 77, p. 828; LJ, 15 May 77, p. 1169; WLB, May 77, p. 775]

433. Osborne, Harold, ed. **The Oxford Companion to the Decorative Arts.** New York, Oxford University Press, 1975. 865p. illus. bibliog. $49.50. ISBN 0-19-866113-4.

The Oxford Companions are well known. This particular volume is similar in structure to its predecessors. It covers a wide variety of subjects—e.g., costume, furniture, jewelry, etc. The coverage is supposed to be international, but not all countries are equally represented, and the emphasis is still on Great Britain, the United States, and the Western European countries. Countries in Asia, including India and China, are mentioned only occasionally, as is also true of the Soviet Union and other countries in Eastern Europe. As always, the material is well documented. [R: ARBA 76, p. 450; BL, 15 June 76, p. 1486; LJ, 15 Nov 75, p. 2133; WLB, Feb 76, p. 493]

DICTIONARIES AND ENCYCLOPEDIAS

434. Fleming, John, and Hugh Honour. **Dictionary of the Decorative Arts.** New York, Harper and Row, 1977. 896p. illus. $29.95. LC 76-50163. ISBN 0-06-011936-5.

Previously published in Great Britain under the title *Penguin Dictionary of Decorative Arts*, this latest addition to the growing list of similar dictionaries is intended as a companion volume to the excellent *Penguin Dictionary of Architecture* (Penguin, 1973. $3.95pa.). The 4,000 entries and approximately 1,000 illustrations are limited to European and North American furniture and furnishings, beginning with the medieval period for the former and the colonial period for the latter and continuing up to the present. Those Near and Far Eastern decorative arts having an influence on European and North American styles are included, but personal adornments are excluded. Written by two internationally recognized art historians, the entries (which include the names of factories, definitions, biographies, materials and processes) are precise, scholarly, and frequently provide brief but well selected bibliographies. There are also separate sections illustrating the most common ceramic, silver, and pewter marks and monograms.

There is no doubt that this dictionary is one of the finest to date, and due to the inclusion of bibliographies, it will be a valuable, in fact, indispensable addition to the growing list of reference tools on this subject even though some criticisms of specific areas are discussed further in this review. An item-by-item comparison with other dictionaries predictably reveals that no one reference tool is complete unto itself. Fleming and Honour have included entries not found in other dictionaries, but the same is true of, for example, the *Studio Dictionary of Design and Decoration* (Viking, 1973. $28.50), which has far more comprehensive coverage of American furniture and furnishings. In their foreword, Fleming and Honour specifically mention the importance of the MacQuoid and Edwards *Dictionary of English Furniture*, but they do not list Wallace Nutting's equally important *Treasury of American Furniture*. This may explain why, for example, the American versions of Chippendale and Sheraton are ignored in their text. While there are entries such as Shaker Furniture, Paul Revere, and Rookwood Pottery, no reference is made to Amish work even in the quilt entry. On the other hand, there is an illustrated entry for early Norwegian tapestry, and commendably, there is even a listing under Albrecht Altdorfer due to the influence of his engravings on European furniture design.

The omission from this dictionary, and most others claiming to include North America, of references to, if not full-scale entries on, Indian pottery, basketry, weaving, and bead work is difficult to understand. Even Maria Martinez, the well-known creator of Pueblo black-on-black pottery, is not listed. The inclusion of such entries is long overdue, since the artistic qualities of the decorative arts of our Native Americans have recently had an important, international impact on collecting and decorating. Art historians should have been the first to recognize that this sophisticated art form can no longer be classed simply as primitive art unless, of course, dictionaries are simply intended to include only mass-produced or manufactured items.

As stated earlier, the above specific criticisms do not negate the overall importance of especially the European coverage of this dictionary. [R: ARBA 78, p. 426; BL, 1 Mar 78, p. 1135; Choice, Feb 78, p. 1622; LJ, 15 Sept 77, p. 1833; WLB, Dec 77, p. 346]

Jacqueline D. Sisson

435. Garner, Philippe, ed. **The Encyclopedia of Decorative Arts 1890-1940.** New York, Van Nostrand Reinhold, 1978. 320p. illus. (part col.). bibliog. index. (A Quarto Book). $35.00. LC 78-7479. ISBN 0-442-22577-6.

This work is a welcome addition to the growing list of much-needed reference works on the history of the applied and decorative arts. Although the *Oxford Companion to the Decorative Arts* (see entry 433) and the *Penguin Dictionary of Decorative Arts* (Penguin, 1977) give excellent coverage to the main topics of modern decorative arts, for more specific information on the late nineteenth and early twentieth centuries, one has had to rely on *The Random House Collector's Encyclopedia: Victoriana to Art Deco* (Random House, 1974), which is directed toward the average collector and slights the higher manifestations of modern decorative arts.

Garner's work aims at presenting the general reader with the best of these arts through three groups of well-illustrated essays written by leading European curators and critics. The first group sketches the development of style from art nouveau to the surrealism of the 1930s, supplemented with chapters on revivalism and industrial design. These are followed by more detailed chapters on the development of the decorative arts in Europe and the United States, each conveniently subdivided by media. Part 3 presents a series of essays on the background to the history of modern decorative arts. These briefly touch on such subjects as the great exhibitions that set so many of the stylistic directions, photography and the cinema, and the relationship between painting and the decorative arts. A list of the major craftsmen and designers (unfortunately with only limited information), a good classified bibliography of books in all languages, a glossary of terms, and an index round out this useful, popular reference work. The literate and informative text and the high

quality of the works illustrated (some with exceptionally fine color plates) make a real contribution toward dispelling the dilettantism that has surrounded most of the popular
literature on modern decorative arts. [R: ARBA 80, p. 398; LJ, 15 May 79, p. 1132; WLB,
Sept 79, p. 68]
Donald L. Ehresmann

COLLECTING

ANTIQUES

436.   Bond, Harold Lewis. **An Encyclopedia of Antiques.** Detroit, Gale, 1975 (c1945).
389p. bibliog. illus. $26.00. LC 74-31297. ISBN 0-8103-4206-5.

A reprint of the valuable 1945 edition. Divided into five parts (Furniture, Pottery and
Porcelain, Glass, Textiles, and Metals), the *Encyclopedia* is a combination textbook, dictionary, and handbook to the field. It is a useful compendium of essential information on
such terms as: acanthus, Lancashire chair, lignum vitae, gallipot, insufflated galloon, and
pinchbeck. While some terms can undoubtedly be found elsewhere, few other guides to the
nomenclature of antiques are as handy as this one. Bond has also included two useful
appendices—biographical information on important figures, and bibliographical
references on specific aspects in the field. The volume is a "must" for the antique collector.
While it is not a "how to" or even a guide to collecting, it does contain most of the essential
information in the field for collectors, dealers, and researchers. Many photographs and
line drawings illustrate points of interest in the text. While the work is now over 30 years
old, and it contains no citations to research past the 1930s, it is still a highly useful classic in
the field. [R: ARBA 77, p. 432]
Ralph L. Scott

437.   **The Complete Color Encyclopedia of Antiques.** Rev. and expanded ed. Comp. by
The Connoisseur, London. Ed. by L. G. G. Ramsey. New York, Hawthorn Books, 1975.
704p. illus. (part col.). bibliog. index. $37.50. LC 74-7888. ISBN 0-8015-1538-6.

Handsomely illustrated with color plates, this edition has, in some areas, been greatly
revised and in many others, not at all. Sections on the Aesthetic Movement, the Arts and
Crafts Movement, Art Nouveau, Art Deco, Antiquities, and Ethnographies are totally
new. The text of other sections (Arms and Armour; Barometers, Clocks and Watches;
Carpets; Coins and Medals; Furniture; Glass; Jewelry; Metalwork; Mirrors; Needlework
and Embroidery; Pottery and Porcelain; Prints; Scientific Instruments; and Silver) remains
nearly verbatim, except for the commendable addition of descriptions of Far Eastern furniture, glass, and metalwork.

Each section's format consists of historical resumes, including, in some cases, lists of
craftsmen, arranged alphabetically by country. Each section has its own glossary. There
are some inconsistencies in the methods used to compile terms and names for inclusion in
the glossaries, and the quality of indexing varies greatly section by section. Another type of
inconsistency is found in the needlework section, where the resumes of national work (such
as Chinese and Greek) are found in the glossary and not in the main text. It is essential that
the glossaries and indexes of encyclopedias be inclusive and extremely meticulous. That is
not the case in this publication. Also, while the coverage of American and British antiques
is good throughout the publication, that of other countries varies greatly and there are
some glaring omissions. The sections in the 1962 edition pertaining to books and book
binding, painting, drawing, and sculpture have been deleted from the 1975 edition, but the
section on prints has been left intact. Again, the coverage concentrates on American and
British prints and a total of only four pages is devoted to the Continent.

The list of museums, arranged by types of antiques, continues to be a convenient
reference tool. Here again, however, there are serious oversights: the world-renowned glass

collection in the Toledo Museum of Art is not mentioned, and no U.S. museums are listed under the category "Japanese Prints." The selected bibliography has been reorganized in a more efficient manner and will be a useful basic checklist for libraries. Except for very narrow gutters, the appearance of the new edition has been much improved and, as mentioned above, the revised edition includes new material as well as new illustrations. Even though the text is, in most instances, unchanged, this edition must not be thought of as superseding the 1962 edition, which contains a far greater variety of examples of each type of object. [R: ARBA 76, p. 455; LJ, 1 Nov 75, p. 2038; WLB, Dec 75, p. 326]

Jacqueline D. Sisson

438. Savage, George. **Dictionary of 19th Century Antiques and Later Objets d'Art.** New York, G. P. Putnam's, 1978. 401p. illus. (part col.). bibliog. $22.50. LC 78-53435. ISBN 0-399-12209-5.

This beautiful and comprehensive work covers antique furniture, glass, ceramics, and metalwork of the nineteenth century as well as later objets d'art up to and including art nouveau and art deco. It has 1,500 entries, cross referenced, in dictionary format, and 500 photographs, 32 in color. George Savage is, of course, widely known and respected for his many books on the decorative arts, including *The Antique Collector's Handbook*, and his contributions to art and antiques journals.

This volume invites comparison with Collins' *Encyclopedia of Antiques* and *The Collector's Encyclopedia: Victoriana to Art Deco* (Wm. Collins, 1974; published in the U.S. as *The Random House Collector's Encyclopedia: Victoriana to Art Deco*, Random House, 1974) and is very similar to the latter in its dictionary format and extremely high quality of text and illustration, as well as in its parallel coverage (both include the art deco period). Using Ruskin Pottery and Charles Schneider as tests, Savage has an entry under Ruskin, with a "see" reference to Bernard Moore, while the Collins work refers the reader to an entry under Edward Taylor. Both cover Schneider under his own name. Collins has illustrations of each; Savage does not. Savage has fewer color plates, but often they are of entire rooms, giving the proper context and setting for the objects displayed. Otherwise, the choice between these two reference works is difficult, unless one can afford specialized volumes on each period, e.g., Laver's *Victoriana* (James Laver, Pyne, 1975), the various collector's books of art nouveau, Battersby's *Decorative Twenties* (Walker, 1969) and *Decorative Thirties* (Walker, 1971), or Lesieutre's *The Spirit and Splendor of Art Deco* (Paddington, 1974). The prices of the two are similar, but the emphasis is slightly different, so one should purchase both for maximum coverage. [R: ARBA 80, p. 401; LJ, Aug 79, p. 1554]

Ann Skene-Melvin

439. Voss, Thomas M. **Antique American Country Furniture: A Field Guide.** Philadelphia, J. B. Lippincott, 1978. 383p. illus. bibliog, index. $9.95; $6.95pa. LC 77-15898. ISBN 0-397-01219-5; 0-397-01267-5pa.

The author, himself a collector, has provided in this well-organized work an extremely useful guide to the collection of American country antiques, which he generally defines as "furniture made by hand away from urban centers in America before 1840." The book is meant to be toted and is, therefore, organized so that pertinent information is readily accessible. Chapters 1-5 give general information on country furniture: where and how to buy, what to look for in determining authenticity, a brief introduction to periods and styles of American furniture, and some factors involved in pricing. Chapters 6-13 describe specific types of furniture—chairs; Windsor and Windsor-derived chairs; settles, settees, and benches; tables and stands; chests and chests of drawers; desks; cupboards; and beds. Each of these chapters details construction, gives a checklist of things to look for, and then describes and illustrates with line drawings specific pieces, giving dates, provenance, availability, and price. A glossary of terms used by dealers and collectors, with cross references to the figures in chapters 6-13, follows. The picture index, which facilitates finding any piece described in the book is a recapitulation of all the individual figures in chapters 6-13 by number. A subject index references the various styles discussed in the text. The work is completed with a briefly annotated bibliography for further reading. The author claims that 99% of the pieces described have been recently offered on the open market. This is an extremely useful visual tool for the collector. [R: ARBA 79, p. 450; BL, 15 May 78, p. 1468; LJ, 1 Apr 78, p. 740]

Carol Jean Carlson

440. Wills, Geoffrey. **A Concise Encyclopedia of Antiques.** New York, Van Nostrand Reinhold, 1975. 304p. illus. (part col.). index. $15.00. LC 75-22082. ISBN 0-442-29488-3.

A guide to English decorative arts, this small encyclopedia is divided into two parts. Part I (81 pages) identifies and summarizes nine separate periods: Tudor, 1500-1600; Early Stuart, 1600-1660; Late Stuart, 1660-1714; Early Georgian, 1715-1750; Mid-Georgian, 1750-1765; Late Georgian, 1765-1810; Regency and George IV, 1810-1830; William IV and Early Victorian, 1830-1860; and Later Victorian, 1860-1890. The summaries include subsections on the principal architects, sculptors, painters, etc., of each period. In part II (205 pages), craftsmen, factories, basic terms, etc., are listed alphabetically under five headings: furniture; pottery and porcelain; glass; silver; and copper, bronze, pewter, and other metals. The subsections are further divided. For example, under furniture are separate alphabetical listings for woods, ornamentation and styles, articles of furniture, etc.; under pottery: methods, materials, factories, etc. A general index makes this complicated subsection arrangement manageable.

The material selected for illustration is, for the most part, appropriate. However, there are too few illustrations, many are poorly reproduced ("The Saloon, Saltram, Devon," p. 54), and many are too small to be of real value ("The Five Roman Orders of Architecture," p. 8). A handy general reference, this volume contains definitions of technical terms and factory listings not included in other standard encyclopedias of the decorative arts. [R: ARBA 78, p. 433; BL, 1 June 77, p. 1520; WLB, Sept 76, p. 89]

Romaine S. Somerville

COINS AND CURRENCY

441. Breen, Walter. **Walter Breen's Encyclopedia of U.S. and Colonial Proof Coins 1722-1977.** Albertson, NY, F.C.I. Press, 1977. 324p. illus. LC 77-79912. ISBN 0-930076-01-X.

This is a definitive encyclopedia, catalog, and guide to all known United States proof coins and presentation pieces. Proof coins are specially prepared, specially struck specimen coins that have been made in nearly every year since 1816 and are considered to be the caviar of American coinage. Presentation pieces and foreign-made pre-1816 colonial proofs are also covered.

It is difficult to describe this work in terms other than superlatives. Until its publication, U.S. proofs were poorly treated, if at all, in existing works, and pre-1858 proofs received no coverage whatever, save in a previous shorter work by Breen. In this work, all proofs are grouped under their dates, i.e., all coins from one-half cent to $20 gold of 1853 are listed under 1853. Breen's exhaustively detailed coverage of each date gives: varieties, pedigrees of existing specimens of rarities, detailed die characteristics, striking and surface traits, grades/appearances of known specimens of rarities, (occasionally) auction prices realized, frequent black-and-white photos, mintages (whether established or problematical), data on year sets, correlation to die variety catalogs, occasions for striking, market histories and speculations and hoards, (often) exact dates of striking, official authorizations, (occasionally) chronological order of striking of certain die varieties/combinations, and even such historical exotica as the name/sailing date of the boat that carried the planchets to America! All photos are identified as to variety (if applicable) and pedigree/specific piece. Breen also provides a brief history of proofs and various proofing processes, an excellent glossary, a price guide/catalog (based on auction records), and a brief overview of proofs as investments. There is also a listing of books and auction catalogs (mostly the latter) used in the text, together with relevant abbreviations.

This reviewer can, in a manner of speaking, authenticate the work's accuracy through personal knowledge of Breen's status as the individual currently having greater knowledge than anyone else of not only U.S. proof coins but of all U.S. coins. Likewise, Breen's capabilities as an authenticator of proofs have on two occasions (once in 1957, once in 1975) saved this reviewer from making ill-advised purchases.

No work is without fault, of course. This book lacks an index, which is especially needed because of Breen's habit of inserting important and generally applicable commentary (as on cleaning, rounded lips of certain proofs, shenanigans of mint officials, etc.) in the midst of data on specific dates and pieces. The work needs also an introductory explanation of how to best comprehend the entries and styles therein, with explicated sample entries. Last but not least, the binding is substandard, with many groups of pages insufficiently sewn in.

It would be folly to term this work necessary for beginning to low-intermediate collectors. But for advanced collectors and serious students of U.S. numismatics, it is an absolute necessity. And for numismatic scholarship, it is in the topmost rank with works by the likes of Eric Newman and William H. Sheldon. Most particularly, it is recommended for the sheer joy of browsing within it, even for collectors/numismatists unable to afford any but the most recent of the pieces covered. [R: ARBA 79, p. 448]   Richard H. Rosichan

442.   Bruce, Colin R., II, ed. **Standard Catalog of World Coins, 1981 Edition.** 7th ed. Iola, WI, Krause Publications, 1980. 2000p. illus. index. $29.50pa. LC 79-640940. ISBN 0-87341-054-8.

This treasury of data covers coins issued by 1,300 authorized governments from 1760 to the present. The compilers, who authored previous editions of the *Catalog* as well as other tools for coin collectors, are recognized experts on numismatics. The seventh edition has been enlarged to cover a greater number of issues, update mintage statistics and average prices (which are given for four coin grades), and to include a greater number of black-and-white illustrations. The introductory material is similar to that found in earlier editions, such as a guide to typical coin issues, a chart of standard international numerical systems, diagrams of coin sizes, and a list of coin denominations. There are also general information on coin collecting (how to identify mint marks, determine values, identify fakes, etc.) and an index by country. There are two types of material added to the 1981 *Catalog*. An introductory chart provides values for silver and gold bullion, and many coin descriptions include actual silver or gold weights. This information enables the user to compute the intrinsic value of coins. In its size, paper quality, topography, and binding, this reference work resembles a telephone book. Although this format is not permanent or attractive, it is suitable to the book's purpose and allows the publisher to offer a vast amount of information at a low price. Specialists in a particular country will need supplementary material on non-legal tender and medallic issues.   Margaret Norden

443.   Friedberg, Robert. **Paper Money of the United States: A Complete Illustrated Guide with Valuations.** 9th ed., with revisions by Arthur L. Friedberg and Ira S. Friedberg. Iola, WI, Krause Publications, 1978. 251p. illus. $17.50. LC 78-66813. ISBN 0-87184-509-1.

In this detailed catalog for intermediate and advanced collectors, most notes are evaluated in three grades, including Unc. Federal reserve notes are cataloged by city as well as signature combination, and national currency is cataloged for each state/territory under each type/denomination. Issuance figures are given for notes when known (each note is numbered). Major and intermediate varieties are cataloged. Suffice it to say that all paper money produced by the U.S. government from the 1861 "demand notes" to the date of publication is cataloged, including fractionals. Encased postage stamps are also covered. Almost every type is largely and clearly photo-illustrated, obverse and reverse. Supplements include a complete list of national banks in the United States that issued currency, arranged by charter number, and a list of treasury officials with tenures, dates, etc., arranged to show concurrent terms of office for all officeholders. There is an introductory section dealing with collecting, counterfeiting, etc., and a short bibliography. The catalog doesn't cover Confederate or private-issue banknotes.

The serious student of U.S. paper money needs to have either this work or Gene Hessler's *Comprehensive Catalog of U.S. Paper Money* (BNR Press). [R: ARBA 80, p. 403]   Richard H. Rosichan

444.   Rosichan, Richard H. **Stamps and Coins.** Littleton, CO, Libraries Unlimited, 1974. 404p. index. (Spare Time Guides: Information Sources for Hobbies and Recreation, No. 5). $13.50. LC 73-90498. ISBN 0-87287-071-5.

Stamps and Coins includes more than 1,100 entries on numismatics and over 500 entries on philately. Author, title, place and date of publication, publisher, pagination, price, LC card number, and ISBN are provided for most entries. The detailed annotations will help the user distinguish between similar works. Subsidiary or related works are listed under the heading "Other Works Include" within specific subdivisions. Titles listed, regardless of the date of publication, are generally in print and/or readily available from distributors, from coin or stamp dealers, or from most dealers in numismatic or philatelic books.

The final chapters provide separate coverage of the periodicals, organizations, and libraries of the two fields. A publishers' directory lists all publishers whose works were included in the guide, with their addresses. Three indexes — title, author, and subject — complete the work. [R: ARBA 75, p. 459; Choice, Mar 75, p. 51; LJ, 1 Feb 75, p. 280; WLB, Jan 75, p. 358]

445.   Schön, Günter. **Simon and Schuster World Coin Catalogue 1979-1980: Twentieth Century.** Rev. and expanded ed. New York, Simon and Schuster, 1978. 1290p. illus. $16.50; $9.95pa. ISBN 0-671-24638-0; 0-671-23639-9pa.

Coins officially minted throughout the world from 1900 to 1978 are cataloged in this comprehensive guide. The revised edition, like the previous one, was originally published in German. However, the English translation of the last edition was delayed for several years, while this one has been made available promptly. The compilation is similar in format to the standard guides by Reinfeld and Hobson, and Krause, and gives much of the same information. Over 300 countries are covered alphabetically, with the coinage of each arranged by denomination and by chronology. There are brief historical notes, clear black-and-white illustrations, and recent prices (fine or uncirculated condition) for most coins. Although references to additional works appear in the introduction, there is no formal bibliography. Miscellaneous prefatory information on grading, evaluations, and purchasing is provided. This excellent overview is a handy guide, particularly for the identification of new issues. For the price, it is a bargain. [R: ARBA 80, p. 404]   Margaret Norden

FIREARMS

446.   Chapel, Charles E. **The Gun Collector's Handbook of Values.** 13th rev. ed. New York, Coward, McCann and Geoghegan, 1979. illus. bibliog. index. $16.95. $8.95pa. LC 79-16182. ISBN 0-698-11011-0; 0-698-11010-2pa.

This is one of the standard references to the monetary values of most of the firearms commonly collected by Americans. The original edition was privately published in 1940; it quickly went out of print and is itself a collector's item. The first extensive revision was issued in 1963 (sixth edition) and the present edition is essentially an "update" of that one, with the suggested values more in line with today's prices. Chapel died in 1967, so the editions since that time are the work of his widow, Dorothy.

Aside from the introductory material, which every collector or gun buff should read, most of the text is devoted to descriptions of the many kinds of firearms usually encountered in the trade. As the occasion demands, these descriptions will include such information as dates of manufacture, type of wood/metal used, barrel length, caliber, model number, other distinguishing features, etc. A large number of photographs illustrate many of the described guns. About two-thirds of the book is concerned with handguns, the remainder is about rifles and muskets. With the illustrations and descriptions, the book is intended to serve the needs of beginning and moderately advanced collectors, but it could also serve as a fairly simple identifying device for people who happen to acquire an old firearm. For this latter group, the book may serve a useful function in the reference collection. I have fairly often been asked to identify old guns or bayonets and realize that every possible source of data will help. The present book has the advantage of being available through regular trade channels; many pertinent books are never listed in *Books in Print*. Recommended for appropriate reference collections.   R. G. Schipf

447.   Hogg, Ian V. **The Complete Illustrated Encyclopedia of the World's Firearms.** New York, A & W Publishers, 1978. 320p. illus. (part col.). (A Quarto Book). $24.95. LC 78-56305. ISBN 0-89479-031-5.

This handsomely illustrated reference work is divided into three parts. The first part presents a brief history of firearms from around 1350 to the present, with separate sections on the matchlock, wheel-lock, flintlock, revolver, pistol, machine gun, automatic pistol, and automatic rifle and submachine gun. The second and major part is an alphabetically arranged encyclopedia of makes and makers of firearms from 1830 to the present. The year 1830 was adopted as a cutoff date, since it was around this time that Forsyth's revolutionary percussion principle was entering common use, and that development had begun on the bolt-action rifle and pin-fire cartridge. The third part is a short glossary of technical terms with line drawing illustrations.

The alphabetical encyclopedia contains about 750 entries of significant weapons from throughout the world, with descriptions of their development and operation; significant designers, inventors, and gunsmiths such as Samuel Colt and John Browning (including biographical information and their contributions to firearms development); and significant firearms firms. The book contains over 500 illustrations, most of which present exterior views. However, an adequate number of exploded or interior views and line drawings are presented for the general reader. The author does not claim comprehensive treatment, except in the title. However, he has made a judicious selection of weapons that "deserve mention by their innovation, their effect on firearms history and design, their wide use in war and recreation, and their outright fame." Gun buffs may wish coverage of more weapons, more technical data and description, and more schematic drawings. However, the work will answer most questions by the general reader about the history and development of firearms, and will provide a useful addition to a general reference collection. [R: ARBA 80, p. 407; WLB, June 79, p. 726]   LeRoy C. Schwarzkopf

GLASS

448. McKearin, Helen, and Kenneth M. Wilson. **American Bottles & Flasks and Their Ancestry.** New York, Crown Publishers, 1978. 779p. illus. (part col.). bibliog. index. $29.95. LC 78-18520. ISBN 0-517-53147-X.

This is unquestionably *the* book for libraries, as well as for collectors, on American bottles and flasks. Too often books on American antiques and collectibles are marked by historical inaccuracies because they are based on speculation rather than historical research; that is not the case here. The authors have done a meticulous and outstanding job of using the techniques of scholarship to produce a book that will stand as a landmark in the field for years to come.

First, there is an excellent, brief introductory section that deals with the names of bottles, the composition of glass, and the techniques of glassblowing. Next there is a strong historical section, which, after providing a good, short summary history of glass through the ages, concentrates on seventeenth- to nineteenth-century American production. That section includes brief historical sketches of 79 individual American glasshouses, giving information about the owners, locations, date of operation, types of products, etc. Then the various kinds of bottles (wine, spirits and beverage, utilitarian and commercial, medicine and bitters, pattern molded bottles, flasks, and jugs, smelling scent and cologne, and figured flasks and calabash bottles) are described in detail. McKearin's father's listing of historical flasks is reproduced from his *American Glass* (1941) with only minor additions and modifications. Finally, there is a brief section by Wilson on twentieth-century figured bottles and flasks, including reproductions. The written material is accompanied by an outstanding selection of illustrations and photographs (both color and black and white) that complement the text and illustrate particular points and facts. It is difficult to find any fault with this book, which clearly deserves to be the basis for any collection of works on American glass. [R: ARBA 80, p. 413; WLB, June 79, p. 728]   Norman D. Stevens

449. Newman, Harold. **An Illustrated Dictionary of Glass.** New York, Thames and Hudson; distr., New York, W. W. Norton, 1977. 351p. illus. (part col.). $24.95. ISBN 0-500-23262-8.

Newman's handsome and useful dictionary belongs in all—large or small, public or personal—libraries. The 2,442 entries are primarily concerned with the methods of production and decoration of glassworks, but individuals are by no means neglected. Furthermore, Newman has attempted to rectify what he calls misnomers, and it could well be that if other specialists agree with him, this dictionary will serve as an authority file for the establishment of universal terminology. In all such cases of misnomers, the author provides explanatory cross references. The dictionary is heavily illustrated, and the excellent plates tend to be adjacent to the entries. No bibliography is included, but references to specific titles are frequently included within the individual entries.

Only a glass specialist can address himself to the total accuracy of the entries, and, while this reviewer does not claim expertise in this field, some lack of specificity was noted at times, such as the omission of dates for factories. The entry for Legras & Cie. is one example, as no date is given for the founding of this company. In addition, no mention is made of signed pieces by Legras, who was a follower of Gallé. The above is a small factor in comparison to the valuable assistance that the majority of the entries will give in providing answers to quick reference questions. To date, there have been few English-language dictionaries for this popular field of collecting, and of those still listed in *Books in Print*, Newman's is by far the most comprehensive and useful for all phases of worldwide glassmaking, from ancient to modern times. [R: ARBA 79, p. 451; Choice, Sept 78, p. 843; LJ, 15 Apr 78, p. 862]   Jacqueline D. Sisson

OTHER COLLECTIBLES

450. Cabeen, Richard McP. **Standard Handbook of Stamp Collecting.** New rev. ed. New York, Thomas Y. Crowell, 1979. 630p. illus. index. $13.95. LC 78-3297. ISBN 0-690-01773-1.

Richard McP. Cabeen was, for many years, the stamp editor for the *Chicago Tribune*, and this work, which first appeared in 1957, is a distillation of his knowledge in the field. It is a comprehensive handbook of philatelic information that will be of interest and help to even the expert collector of postage stamps, but a veritable gold mine of information to the beginning collector.

The *Handbook* is divided into five parts. Of most value to the neophyte is part 5, "Classification and Identification," which will prove of great help in identifying the country of origin, particularly for those stamps which do not carry a country name. There is also a table of stamps giving a historical background for the first publication of stamps, as well as name changes for countries. Other sections cover "An Introduction to Stamp Collecting"; "Postal History and Cover Collecting"; and miscellaneous subjects such as unusual uses for stamps and technical matters (e.g., paper, gum, perforations, and errors).

It is my belief that the one who will benefit most will be the beginning collector, but it is a book that even the noncollector or expert could enjoy browsing through for the odd bits of information provided. It is a book recommended for any public library.

James M. Hillard

451. Miller, Robert W. **Wallace-Homestead Price Guide to Dolls.** 2nd ed. Des Moines, IA, Wallace-Homestead Book, 1979. 216p. illus. (part col.). $9.95pa. LC 79-63081. ISBN 0-87069-269-0.

To many, collecting dolls has been an enjoyable hobby, whether their collections represent a style or a sampling from many periods of time. Often the monetary value of these collections is unknown, or the buyer has questions regarding the price of a prospective purchase. In this second edition of *Wallace-Homestead Price Guide to Dolls*, Robert W. Miller has provided an excellent pictorial dictionary representing more than 1,000 dolls from all over the world (most of them available to collectors) covering a wide range of time. The photographs are clear, large enough for details to be evident, and accompanied by brief and well-written descriptions.

Prices for each doll (considered in excellent condition) were established by experts as the accepted retail values at the time of publication. Auction prices may vary depending on demand and physical condition. Added attractions in the guide include a seven-page color section, a six-page glossary of doll terms (with the note that more terms will appear in the next edition), and a brief outline of what determines prices. The basic chronology presented at the beginning of the book relates to the doll examples in the guide, whereby a reader can approximate a date of production, the author stating that some companies may have produced a certain doll style for a number of years, thus making it "nearly impossible to precisely date a doll." In spite of this statement, it would have been helpful to list a circa date with each doll picture/description even when a precise date could not be established.

This is a handsome book, well researched, and well worth purchasing by a collector or a library.

Patricia C. Harpole

CRAFTS

BIBLIOGRAPHIES

452.   Harwell, Rolly M., and Ann J. Harwell. **Crafts for Today: Ceramics, Glasscrafting, Leatherworking, Candlemaking, and Other Popular Crafts.** Littleton, CO, Libraries Unlimited, 1974. 211p. index. (Spare Time Guides: Information Sources for Hobbies and Recreation, No. 4). $9.50. LC 73-92979. ISBN 0-87287-067-7.

This book is intended for, and includes material for, all craftsmen regardless of experience, skill, or talent. After an initial section that lists books concerned with general crafts, the arrangement of the bibliography is alphabetical by craft. The crafts represented are beads, candles, decoupage, egg decorating, glass, jewelry, leather, metal and wire, mobile and collages, mosaics, paper, pebbles and shells, plastics, pottery and ceramics, toys, and woodworking and carving. There are 474 numbered entries in all. An emphasis was placed on recent books, although older classic titles available in many libraries were also included when they contained valuable material. A section on crafts periodicals lists the major national periodicals, and the volume concludes with a list of crafts organizations, a directory of publishers whose books are listed, and an author-title-subject index. This selective bibliography, with its lengthy annotations, will provide guidance to craftsmen and librarians, directing them to the most valuable books in the areas covered. [R: ARBA 75, p. 454; LJ, 15 Nov 74, p. 2954; WLB, Oct 74, p. 185]

ENCYCLOPEDIAS

453.   Scott, Michael. **The Crafts Business Encyclopedia: Marketing, Management, and Money.** New York, Harcourt Brace Jovanovich, 1977. 286p. LC 76-54209. ISBN 0-15-122752-7.

Michael Scott has written a highly useful book about all that is involved in realizing a profit from crafts. The book should become a standard reference in both crafts workshops and libraries. The arrangement of topics in an alphabetic sequence provides a comprehensive source of business information. The subjects range from management; financial management; insurance; labor and employees; and safety, to accounting and bookkeeping; credit; pricing; taxes; sales promotion and publicity; selling and marketing; and professional crafts organizations. Questions – such as how to price; how to get a patent or a trademark; how to keep records for tax purposes; how to sell at crafts shows, galleries, one's own shop, or through the mail; and what federal regulations govern retail selling and labeling – are readily answered by looking up the particular topic.

The book is easy to use. There are approximately 375 entries, some of which are a few paragraphs long and many, several pages in length. Cross references are often made to related topics, and, occasionally, books and pamphlets are suggested for additional reading. Michael Scott knows the crafts business well. He is the publisher of *The Crafts Report*, a monthly newsletter, and has been a professional writer and editor for over 25 years and president of the International Guild of Craft Journalists, Authors, and Photographers. [R: ARBA 79, p. 458; BL, 15 Apr 77, p. 1235; LJ, 1 Apr 77, p. 788]

Amity Doering

454.   Torbet, Laura, ed. **The Encyclopedia of Crafts.** New York, Scribner's, 1980. 3v. illus. $80.00. LC 80-13431. ISBN 0-684-16409-4/set.

As a reference tool, the *Encyclopedia of Crafts* proposes to "fulfill a long-standing need for a single source reference" as an adjunct to single-craft books for the contemporary craftsperson. An "A to Z Guide" to 50 crafts with over 12,000 entries, these three volumes are profusely illustrated by Gary Tong with 2,500 well-detailed illustrations. Descriptions, detailed instructions, and explanations are provided by 15 contributors specializing in basketry, woodworking, candlemaking, kites, mosaics, tincraft, beadwork, block printing, découpage, fabric printing, leather, papercraft, papier mâché, stenciling, jewelry, stained glass, ceramics, metalworking, plastics, enameling, gem cutting, batik and tie dye, quilts, stitchery, toys (including dollmaking), crochet, knitting, macramé, general art and design, silk screen, bookbinding, amber, bone, coral, horn, ivory, jet, shell carving, lacemaking, tatting, crewelwork, embroidery, needlepoint, rugmaking, spinning and dyeing, and weaving. Articles are of varying lengths, from eight pages to short paragraphs. A complicated "Guide to the Use of the Encyclopedia" is provided in the form of entry word or phrase; craft classification; synonyms, variations, and abbreviations; the entry (text); cross-reference system; and illustrations.

This three-volume encyclopedia is designed to be a basic tool for both the "professional and amateur craftsperson." It contains information not usually found in traditional "how-to" books, including historical and background information, detailed treatment of tools and materials, facts on care and restoration, obscure patterns, and general design terms. The cross-reference system provides access to information that permits applications of an idea from one craft to another. Illustrations provide clarification for the articles. Some of the "see" references provided (e.g., "yellow colorant . . . see pigment oxide"; "yellow rouge . . . see buffing compound," etc.) are terms that would be familiar to the professional, but not necessarily to the amateur craftsperson. An excellent source book, this reference tool provides extensive information, but it would be difficult to develop any expertise in an individual craft through its use. No index is provided.   Donald D. Foos

CERAMICS

455. Boger, Louise Ade. **The Dictionary of World Pottery and Porcelain, from Prehistoric Times to the Present.** New York, Scribner's, 1971. 533p. illus. (part col.). LC 72-123829.

This volume has 2,200 entries, which cover basic information about a variety of potteries, styles, and techniques. There are numerous cross references and plenty of illustrations—drawings of makers' marks, characteristic shapes and designs, and color plates that give an idea of the differences in color and glazing. A section of black-and-white photographs at the end of the volume is a visual overview of the development of world ceramics. This section is followed by succinct but informative notes on these illustrations. The bibliography is divided into the same general categories as these photographs.

Louise Boger is known for earlier books, as well as for answering queries in *House and Garden*. She compiled this book as a "comprehensive and concise guide for the collector and student as well as the general reader." [R: ARBA 72, p. 379; BL, 15 May 72, p. 777; LJ, 1 Jan 72, p. 58; LJ, 15 Apr 72, p. 1384; RQ, Spring 72, p. 278; WLB, Feb 72, p. 543]
                                                                    Julia Sabine

456. Savage, George, and Harold Newman. **An Illustrated Dictionary of Ceramics: Defining 3,054 Terms Relating to Wares, Materials, Processes, Styles, Patterns, and Shapes from Antiquity to the Present Day.** New York, Van Nostrand Reinhold, 1974. 320p. illus. (part col.). $24.95. LC 73-17999. ISBN 0-442-27364-9.

Except for a list of European factories and their marks, prepared by John Cushion of the Victoria and Albert Museum, this dictionary, unlike most, is totally concerned with the physical piece: its material, pattern, decoration, type, and glaze. The artist and/or manufacturer are identified in the definitions but are not listed by name in the dictionary. Numerous cross references serve two purposes: they avoid duplication and they guide the reader to further pertinent references. General terms such as lid, cover, handle, and spout, not commonly included in dictionaries, have been deliberately listed by the authors, who are respected specialists, in order to establish once and for all a definitive terminology. It is their hope that by so doing they will prevent future misuse of the terms. Cross references from major European terms to their English equivalents are provided throughout this book, which encompasses European, Middle and Far Eastern wares, including figurines, from ancient to contemporary times. Although some American ceramics are listed, coverage of them is not and was not intended to be extensive. Even the briefest perusal of this dictionary reveals solutions for terms that previously required extensive reference work. Even though the authors claim that this publication is not intended for the specialist, it is by far one of the most comprehensive and lucid dictionaries in its field. In addition to its excellent coverage of 3,054 terms, the book's typography, layout, and excellent and copious illustrations, some of which are in color, are models of clarity. [R: ARBA 75, p. 456; Choice, Sept 74, p. 918; LJ, 1 June 74, p. 1534; LJ, 15 Apr 75, p. 733; WLB, Sept 74, p. 93]

Jacqueline D. Sisson

NEEDLEWORK

457. Clabburn, Pamela. **The Needleworker's Dictionary.** New York, William Morrow, 1976. 296p. illus. (part col.). bibliog. $19.95. LC 75-45517. ISBN 0-688-03054-8.

This is a fascinating compendium of information on needlework—i.e., embroidery and needlepoint. Alphabetically arranged entries (nearly 2,000 of them) cover all aspects of needlework except dressmaking, tailoring, shoemaking, sailmaking, and leatherwork. The clear and easy-to-read definitions are often amplified with the author's personal comments. Each page has two, three, or more illustrations—either detailed line drawings or black-and-white photographs exemplifying types of needlework. In addition, there are about 40 full-page color photographs of needlework items (a Yugoslavian waistcoat, a firescreen worked by Mrs. Theodore Roosevelt, Jr., a detail of a hanging from Kathiawar, etc.).

There are entries for stitches, motifs, countries, types of thread and yarn, design terminology, organizations and associations, types of embroidery, and people. The bibliography (some 300 items) gives author, title, date, place of publication, and publisher for most entries. This is followed by a "select list of museums and collections where textiles can be seen," subdivided by Great Britain, North America, and "other museums." Information provided here is simply city, then name of museum or collection, with no attempt to describe the extent of a particular institution's collection; institutions that have a separate entry in the dictionary are starred, so the user can locate additional information for many of them. In all, this dictionary provides excellent coverage of the craft of needlework. [R: ARBA 77, p. 429]

Ann J. Harwell

458. Gioello, Debbie Ann, and Beverly Berke. **Fashion Production Terms.** New York, Fairchild Publications, 1979. 340p. illus. bibliog. index. (Language of Fashion Series). $22.50. LC 78-62284. ISBN 0-87005-200-4.

For those interested in commercial fashion design, home economics, or even home sewing, this generously illustrated cyclopedia of fashion production terms offers clear definitions and photographs or sketches for more than 600 terms. The 39 chapters focus on drafting and draping, fabrics, cutting equipment, needles and threads (with their characteristics), hems, facings, pressing techniques, and equipment. Each chapter has a table of contents, and there is an overall index and bibliography. Tables compare zippers, threads, needles, and trims. A very clear, informative presentation. [R: ARBA 80, p. 414; Choice, Sept 79, p. 798; LJ, 1 Mar 79, p. 629]

Margery Read

459. **Reader's Digest Complete Guide to Needlework.** Virginia Colton, ed. Pleasantville, NY, Reader's Digest Association, 1979. 504p. illus. (part col.). $18.95. LC 78-71704. ISBN 0-89577-059-8.

Once again, the Reader's Digest Association has produced an authoritative, comprehensive "how to" guide. The *Complete Guide to Needlework* has 2,600 photographs and illustrations (mostly full-color) and covers 10 major needlework fields (embroidery, needlepoint, applique, patchwork, quilting, knitting, crochet, lacework, macrame, and rugmaking). Not only are the basics for each field covered, but also tools and supplies needed (with photographs), more advanced techniques, cross references, and several projects complete with instructions. Every stitch, pattern, technique, or project has fully illustrated step-by-step directions, as well as an accompanying photograph of the finished product. Instructions for lefthanders—a real boon—are also included.

The guide is useful for both beginners and more advanced craftsworkers. Such topics as how color can affect a patchwork design (p. 217), measuring a bed for a quilt (p. 245), and instructions for different types of knitted necklines, sleeves, borders, buttonholes, hems, pockets, etc. (pp. 332-42) are provided. The emphasis is on equipping an individual with techniques necessary for the creative, original use of needlework, rather than on merely providing the skills necessary for following patterns. The *Complete Guide to Needlework* is the best guide of its kind published to date; it is obviously superior to the Doubleday *Complete Encyclopedia of Stitchery* and Running Press' *Complete Encyclopedia of Needlework*. [R: ARBA 80, p. 416; LJ, 1 Nov 79, p. 2336]   Deborah S. Lueck

TEXTILES

460. Axford, Lavonne Brady. **Weaving, Spinning, and Dyeing.** Littleton, CO, Libraries Unlimited, 1975. 148p. index. (Spare Time Guides: Information Sources for Hobbies and Recreation, No. 7). $11.50. LC 75-16436. ISBN 0-87287-080-4.

This work includes annotations for 389 books, alphabetically arranged under handweaving (which includes general books on textiles), spinning, dyeing and resist dyeing (batik and tie-dye), and related crafts (baskets, bobbin lace and sprang, macramé, and rug hooking). In addition, it includes a list of periodicals in the field, a directory of organizations, a directory of supply sources, and a directory of publishers. Books at many different levels are included, though no "play books" are listed. A complete index aids the user and increases the utility of the publication. Annotations are complete, include bibliographical information, and are critical enough to allow the user to select the item needed. [R: ARBA 76, p. 450; Choice, Feb 76, p. 1547; LJ, 15 Dec 75, p. 2314; RQ, Spring 76, p. 263; WLB, Dec 75, p. 328]   Rosemary Henderson

461. Wingate, Isabel B. **Fairchild's Dictionary of Textiles.** 6th ed. New York, Fairchild Publications, 1979. 691p. illus. $40.00. LC 78-73964. ISBN 0-87005-198-9.

Fairchild's defines terms relating to fibers, fabrics, yarns, finishes, textile processes and machinery, finished products (including needlework, embroidery, and carpets and rugs), and standard laboratory tests. This edition updates the fifth edition, published in 1967, and reflects the latest developments, such as the ban on the flame retardant Tris due to its suspected link to cancer. The scope also encompasses acronyms, standards, foreign and historical terms, important inventors and developers, and trade names. The 14,000 definitions are cross referenced and include textile characteristics and uses; some show the term's derivations. The trademark definitions state company ownership. Although *Fairchild's* includes over 150 illustrations, they are too few for a subject that lends itself to extensive graphic treatment. Moreover, the existing illustrations are often small and unclear. Pronunciation guides are not provided and would be helpful for terms like "durreeaee." The appendix listing major textile trade associations does not include addresses and telephone numbers. This is a useful tool for professional textile workers, home economics students and instructors, and serious hobbyists. Its detailed coverage and limited audience make it an appropriate choice for reference collections in large libraries. [R: ARBA 80, p. 421; Choice, July 79, p. 646; LJ, 15 May 79, p. 1131; WLB, Nov 79, p. 196]   Linda Schallan

WOODWORKING

462.   Salaman, R. A. **Dictionary of Tools Used in the Woodworking and Allied Trades, c1700-1970.** New York, Scribner's, 1976 (c1975). 545p. illus. bibliog. $47.50. LC 75-35059. ISBN 0-684-14535-9.

Tool collectors, museum curators, and historians who formerly had to rely on such books as Eric Sloane's *A Museum of Early American Tools* or old tool company catalogs for their research will be ecstatic over this "dictionary." It has been the author's goal to attempt to describe every tool used in the woodworking trades from about 1700 to the present time, and to explain its purpose. R. A. Salaman comes well qualified, having been a scholar and collector concerned with tools for most of his life. The organization of the book, the illustrations, and his comments will contribute much to the study of industrial archaeology. The tools are grouped by their generic name and arranged alphabetically, with cross references from alternative or local names. The parts of the tool are described first, and pictures and descriptions of use and of variations of the tool follow. Of particular value are the numerous entries that cover various woodworking and allied trades, describing the principal operations and tools used. A nine-page bibliography of books, journals, pamphlets, and catalogs adds much to the value of the work. Although the price is high, curators and researchers will find it worth every penny. [R: ARBA 77, p. 430; BL, 15 Nov 76, p. 499; LJ, 1 Dec 76, p. 2471]   Robert J. Havlik

PHOTOGRAPHY

463.   **Encyclopedia of Practical Photography.** Ed. by and published for Eastman Kodak. New York, Amphoto; distr., New York, Scribner's, 1977-78. 14v. illus. (part col.). $15.95/vol.; $159.95/set (trade ed.); $223.30/set (library ed.). LC 77-22562. ISBN 0-8174-3050-4/set (trade ed.); 0-8174-3200-0/set (library ed.).

This comprehensive 14-volume set is beautifully done, and may prove to be the definitive photography encyclopedia. Every conceivable topic seems to be covered: biographies of photographers, advertising photography, architectural photography, astrophotography, cameras, color theory, etc. All are illustrated with charts, graphs, and photographs. The library edition is bound in a brown plastic, which gives the appearance of leather and seems to be able to withstand heavy use. The coverage of some topics may seem cursory to a professional photographer, who will still prefer the *Photo Lab Index* (Morgan, $44.95), but the amateur and general photographer will be pleased with the very ambitious coverage of material. The reader should always be aware, however, that most products discussed are Kodak products, naturally. A cumulative index forms the last volume.   Gil McNamee

464.   Parry, Pamela Jeffcott, comp. **Photography Index: A Guide to Reproductions.** Westport, CT, Greenwood Press, 1979. 372p. $25.00. LC 78-26897. ISBN 0-313-20700-3.

This work should prove valuable to any reference librarian or library user who attempts to locate photographs of either a variety of subjects or those by a specific photographer. Ms. Parry has indexed the photographs to be found in more than 80 volumes, all of which are heavily illustrated, and most of which are recent. Most large and medium public and academic libraries should already own the bulk of these volumes, and this index provides the needed access.

The work is arranged into three major sections: a chronological index to anonymous photographs; an index by photographer; and a subject and title index. In the photographer index, the artist's birth and death years plus nationality are provided when known. The greater part of the indices, by means of which one can find illustrations by subject, is primarily devoted to either reproductions of paintings or to specific titles (e.g., Jane Clapp's *Art in "Life,"* Scarecrow, 1959; Supplement, 1965; Patricia Havlice's *Art in "Time,"* Scarecrow, 1970). Jessie Ellis' *Index to Illustrations* (Faxon, 1966) does include photographs, but is keyed to fewer titles and is almost 15 years old. At least for the present, then, Ms. Parry's work is *hors concours*. [R: ARBA 80, p. 419; Choice, Oct 79, p. 998; LJ, 15 Apr 79, p. 940; WLB, Sept 79, pp. 68-69]   Kenyon C. Rosenberg

465. Spencer, D. A. **The Focal Dictionary of Photographic Technologies.** Englewood Cliffs, NJ, Prentice-Hall, 1973. 725p. illus. bibliog. $39.95. LC 72-97893. ISBN 0-13-322719-7.

With its distinctly British flavor, this photographic dictionary makes an excellent addition to any reference shelf and complements nicely another worthwhile Focal Press publication: *The Focal Encyclopedia of Photography* (McGraw-Hill). The two volumes, side by side, fairly exhaust all possible questions on any given photographic term or technique.

The Focal Dictionary is especially handy for quick, lucid, and concise definitions of terminology, with marginal line drawings and diagrams expanding upon the textual explanations. Appendixes include the EMR spectrum, symbols and abbreviations, photographic effects, nomograms, standards, and a bibliography. [R: ARBA 74, p. 370]

Steve Rybicki

19 MUSIC

GENERAL WORKS

466.   Scholes, Percy A. **The Oxford Companion to Music.** 10th ed., rev. and reset. Edited by John Owen Ward. New York, Oxford University Press, 1970. 1189p. music. plates. $35.00. ISBN 0-19-311306-6.

Though it is not without faults, the *Oxford Companion to Music* has long been recognized as a standard reference work in music, particularly for home use. The ninth edition was reprinted five times, with revisions, and this tenth edition is basically a consolidation and resetting of the final text of the ninth edition. It contains 91 new articles, 76 of which are biographical. The basic defect of the work results from Scholes' original approach, which consisted of writing a series of small treatises on various aspects of music and then cutting them up into shorter articles for alphabetical arrangement, with a minimum of editing. Biographical articles and foreign terms are included in the alphabetical arrangement. Paper and typography are excellent.

The popular *Oxford Junior Companion to Music* (Oxford University Press, 1979. 353p. $25.00) is now available in its second edition. A beautifully produced volume, well illustrated, presenting a balanced treatment of jazz, pop, and the European classics for young people. [R: ARBA 71, p. 370; BL, 15 July 70, p. 1384; BL, 15 Nov 71, p. 250; LJ, July 70, p. 2451; WLB, Sept 70, p. 89]

BIBLIOGRAPHIES

467.   Duckles, Vincent, comp. **Music Reference and Research Materials: An Annotated Bibliography.** 3rd ed. New York, Free Press, 1974. 526p. index. $12.95. LC 73-10697. ISBN 0-02-907700-1.

No serious research in music or any of its affiliated areas in traditional academic studies should be attempted without this exceptionally fine volume, in this edition. (If you have the second edition, from 1967, donate it to a smaller college or public library.) It will also save reference librarians quite a bit of time if their patrons know about "Duckles 3," which is 551 entries richer and 141 pages longer than the second edition.

The citations are complete, and the analytic annotations are objective (locations for major reviews are offered for some titles). The entries are then not always of publications equal in value to their companions, but scholars of any age will be sensitive to this and *ipso facto* it might be well to mark both desk and public copies with local call numbers. The former copy then serves as an aid in acquisitions (some jobbers list Duckles numbers almost as an *imprimatur*). If there are no citations in particular fields, this may be an indication that a book or article on the subject has not yet been prepared for research or reference needs. Highly recommended for all serious music collections. [R: ARBA 75, p. 488; BL, 1 Dec 74, p. 384; Choice, Oct 74, p. 1108; WLB, Sept 74, p. 87]

Dominique-René de Lerma

468.   Farish, Margaret K., ed. **Orchestral Music in Print.** 1st ed. Philadelphia, Musicdata, 1979. 1029p. index. $70.00. LC 79-24460. ISBN 0-88478-010-4; ISSN 0146-7883.

This is the fifth volume in a series that is designed to survey, on an international basis, all appropriate works currently available for purchase or rent. More than 44,000 titles are offered, with citation of composer, title, instrumentation, price, duration, and other data as available. This work, a lavishly virtuosic display of bibliographic research and the skills of computer technology, will prove of great value to all who have need for this information. Any work as extensive as this will certainly have shortcomings, however. The absence of diacriticals is an initial concern relating to the computer, and there seems not to be an editorial policy regarding capitals. Arias and choral works are included, but the availability of piano-vocal scores is not indicated. Also, a sample check shows that the Peer-Southern catalog is not fully represented (e.g., Saint-Georges, whose only entry is from Germany). The cross references include title entries. A publisher and agent directory is offered, as well as a special section on education materials. Important for all serious music collections.   Dominique-René de Lerma

469.   Lowens, Irving. **A Bibliography of Songsters Printed in America before 1821.** Worcester, MA, American Antiquarian Society, 1976. 229p. index. $16.00. LC 75-5021. ISBN 0-912296-05-4.

For the purposes of this bibliography, the author defines a songster as "a collection of three or more secular poems intended to be sung" (p. ix). Although songsters are primarily collections of lyrics, without musical notation, they do sometimes refer to the names of tunes the compiler had in mind when choosing the lyrics.

This bibliography lists 649 songsters published before 1821. Arrangement is chronological by title, then alphabetical within years. If there is an extant copy of a particular songster, with title page, then original spelling and punctuation are given and line endings are indicated. Pagination and contents are noted, as is previous mention in an earlier bibliography. Location is given when known, and the author indicates the exact number of songs in each extant songster. Earlier and later editions are listed.

A key to symbols and list of bibliographies cited (with the abbreviations used) are at the front of the book. The bibliography of songsters is followed by a geographical directory of printers, publishers, etc., an index of compilers and authors, a table that correlates years and item numbers, and a title index.

This is a carefully compiled bibliography that will be of value to anyone interested in early American secular music. [R: ARBA 77, p. 460]

470.   Marco, Guy A. **Information on Music: A Handbook of Reference Sources in European Languages; Volume I, Basic and Universal Sources.** With the assistance of Sharon Paugh Ferris. Littleton, CO, Libraries Unlimited, 1975. 164p. $17.50. LC 74-32132. ISBN 0-87287-096-0.

471.   Marco, Guy A., Ann M. Garfield, and Sharon Paugh Ferris. **Information on Music: A Handbook of Reference Sources in European Languages; Volume II, The Americas.** Littleton, CO, Libraries Unlimited, 1977. 296p. $22.50. LC 74-32132. ISBN 0-87287-141-X.

Volume I, *Basic and Universal Sources*, goes beyond the scope of traditional guides to music reference books and bibliography in that it includes nonmusic bibliographies where these are essential to a total understanding of music bibliography. Thus, the standard periodical indexes are included, but they are discussed from the point of view of their musical significance. Also, this book is correlated with the third edition of Duckles' *Music Reference and Research Materials* (see entry 467). The work includes 503 carefully selected books arranged under the following six chapter headings: The Language of Music; Direct Information Sources; Universal Biographical Sources; Guides to Other Sources of Information in General Categories; Lists of Music; and General Discographies.

Volume II, *The Americas*, annotates over 800 reference sources concerning music in the Western Hemisphere. A special feature of this volume is the cumulative author-title and subject indexes, covering both volumes.

The handbooks provide complete bibliographical information and clear and precise annotations for each entry. Citations to entry numbers in Duckles, Chase, Jackson, *American Reference Books Annual*, Winchell, and Sheehy are especially handy features. [R: ARBA 76, p. 472; Choice, Oct 75, p. 982; Choice, May 76, p. 322; C&RL, July 77, p. 326; LJ, 15 June 75, p. 1203; RQ, Fall 75, p. 76; Choice, Apr 78, pp. 210, 212; JAL, Mar 78, p. 49; LJ, 1 Mar 78, p. 554]

DICTIONARIES AND ENCYCLOPEDIAS

472.   Apel, Willi. **Harvard Dictionary of Music.** 2nd ed., rev. and enl. Cambridge, MA, The Belknap Press of Harvard University Press, 1969. 935p. illus. plates, music. $25.00; $2.75pa. LC 68-21970. ISBN 0-674-37501-7; 0-671-78142-1pa.

The second edition of this standard and authoritative dictionary was thoroughly revised, updated, and substantially enlarged. As in the first edition, the emphasis is on the historical point of view; biographical articles are omitted. The definitions cover a wide range of topics: music history, forms, instruments, notation, performance, theory, etc. The second edition gives special attention to compositional techniques, including electronic music and serial music. Individual compositions, representative of every type from every era, are described. Bibliographies follow each article. There are numerous illustrations, including drawings of instruments, music examples, diagrams, and charts. Additional features include a list of music libraries and their holdings; the section on historical editions now lists 53 collections of music and briefly describes each volume within each collection.

A condensed version of this authoritative one-volume dictionary is the *Harvard Concise Dictionary of Music*, compiled by Don Michael Randel (Belknap Press of Harvard University Press, 1978. 577p. $15.00; $6.95pa.). Although the emphasis is on Western concert music, there are some entries relating to non-Western music and Western music outside of the classical tradition. Current popular music is not included. Biographical information for over 2,000 composers is provided, as well as entries for terms, genres, and instruments. Randel has succeeded in condensing Apel's more comprehensive work into a convenient dictionary suitable for the student. [R: ARBA 70, p. 23; BL, 1 May 70, p. 1055; LJ, 15 Apr 70, p. 1440]

473.   Grove, Sir George. **Grove's Dictionary of Music and Musicians.** 5th ed. Ed. by Eric Blom. New York, St. Martin's, 1970 (c1954). 10v. illus. ports. music. Originally published in 9 vols. in 1954. Suppl. vol. (v.10) published in 1961. $200.00/set; $79.50/set(pa.). LC 54-11819rev.2. ISBN 0-312-20160-5; 0-312-20125-7pa.

Grove's Dictionary of Music and Musicians was first published in 1879-1889 in four volumes. This reprint includes all nine volumes of the fifth edition, plus the supplementary volume published in 1961. *Grove's* has long been the standard English-language encyclopedia of music. Special emphasis is given to English subjects, but the encyclopedia covers the whole field of music from 1450 and includes musical history, theory, practice, terminology, biography, songs, operas, etc. It does not give opera plots. Articles are signed by specialists. In this edition, periodical articles have been added to the bibliographies. The sixth edition, *The New Grove Dictionary of Music & Musicians* (Washington, Grove's Dictionaries of Music. 20v. $1,900.00), was published in late 1980 but was unavailable for review at the time of this writing. [R: ARBA 71, p. 368]

474.   Scholes, Percy A. **The Concise Oxford Dictionary of Music.** 2nd ed. Ed. by John Owen Ward. New York, Oxford University Press, 1969 (c1964). 636p. illus. $12.95; $5.50pa. LC 64-5946. ISBN 0-19-311307-3; 0-19-311302-3pa.

Musical reference works of broad scope and modest size are usually aimed at penurious students and at individual amateurs wanting a concise home reference source. Anyone with more serious needs or intentions will, whenever possible, consult *Grove's Dictionary*, the *Harvard Dictionary of Music*, or *Baker's Biographical Dictionary of Musicians* (see entries 473, 472, and 490).

The work at hand is, in a sense, a cut-down version of the author's *Oxford Companion to Music* (see entry 466), providing information on the historical, esthetic, and technical phases of music, in addition to defining terms and identifying persons. However, it does this in short articles and with much broader coverage of composers, performers, and conductors than its progenitor. It also escapes most of the idiosyncracies of the former work. In nearly every way, even in price, it is superficially comparable with J. A. Westrup and F. Ll. Harrison's *New College Encyclopedia of Music* (see entry 475), but the two are very often complementary in detail, particularly in the biographical articles. Scholes seems to be more accurate in his dates, but Westrup and Harrison give more of them. Although both originated in Britain (Westrup and Harrison as the *Collins Encyclopedia of Music*; London, Collins, 1959), the British emphasis is much more evident in the present work, again making the two complementary. Westrup and Harrison provide exact dates of birth and death, pronunciations, and musical examples, none of which are in Scholes. On the whole, however, anyone wishing to own this sort of reference work should acquire both. [R: ARBA 71, p. 370] Dennis North

475. Westrup, J. A., and F. Ll. Harrison. **The New College Encyclopedia of Music.** Rev. by Conrad Wilson. New York, W. W. Norton, 1976. 608p. illus. $19.95. LC 76-22891. ISBN 0-393-02191-2.

This is a revision of the *Collins Encyclopedia of Music*, originally published in 1959. The original work was a reliable student encyclopedia of music, with a sometimes idiosyncratic character and with a British bias. In undertaking the revision, Conrad Wilson has attempted to retain the "original flavour" of the book, "while at the same time trying to ensure that it reflects current tastes and attitudes and answers the questions that a listener in the 1970s and 80s is likely to ask" (preface to the revised edition).

The present edition contains over 6,000 entries for composers, performers, terms, genres, instruments, operas, etc. The information provided in the readable definitions is made even clearer by the use of numerous illustrations (musical examples, paintings of instruments, portraits of composers). Brief bibliographies are often provided (e.g., four references are listed under "Fauxbourdon").

A pronunciation key is included at the beginning of the book, in order not to "interrupt the flow of articles with pronunciation guides for every different entry" (ibid.). The key is less helpful than one might wish, however, partly because of this separate placement and partly because the symbols and spellings used will be confusing to anyone who knows IPA.

Coverage of American musicians and composers is not comprehensive. Jazz musicians Armstrong, Ellington, Bessie Smith, Kid Ory, and Jack Teagarden are all included; however, Brubeck, Kenton, Ella Fitzgerald, and Scott Joplin are not. William Billings is omitted. Though there is an entry for Douglas Moore, there are no separate entries for *The Devil and Daniel Webster* or *The Ballad of Baby Doe*.

The explanations for terms are more than sufficient for student or amateur use, and the selected bibliographies provide guidance for the first steps toward further study. Overall, this is a competent work at a reasonable price. Recommended for high school and public libraries. [R: ARBA 77, p. 465; Choice, Sept 77, p. 837] Ann J. Harwell

INDEXES

476. Havlice, Patricia Pate. **Popular Song Index, First Supplement.** Metuchen, NJ, Scarecrow, 1978. 386p. bibliog. $16.50. LC 77-25219. ISBN 0-8108-1099-9.

Popular Song Index (Scarecrow, 1975) indexed 301 anthologized song books (words and music) published between 1940 and 1972. It complemented *Song Index* and *Songs in Collection*; its scope is "popular" in the sense of "non-classical" (*Folk Songs from Newfoundland* can hardly be classed popular in a demand sense)—folk songs, hymns, popular music, children's songs, etc. The *Supplement* adds 72 anthologies, mainly published during 1970-1975 (but with one-half dozen from 1959-1966). The index is by title, by first line of verse, and by first line of chorus—all coded to the numbered anthologies. Another index lists the composers and lyricists. This would be a good book to have, especially since future supplements are promised. [R: ARBA 79, p. 477; BL, 1 Apr 79, p. 1243; LJ, July 78, p. 1386; WLB, Sept 78, p. 89]   Dean Tudor

INSTRUMENTS

477. Barrett, Henry. **The Viola: Complete Guide for Teachers and Students.** 2nd ed., rev. and enl. University, University of Alabama Press, 1978. 218p. illus. $17.95. LC 77-12759. ISBN 0-8173-6402-1.

When Barrett's *Guide* first appeared in 1972, it was hailed—and unjustifiably so—as an outstanding book for string teachers and performers. The second edition retains many useful features from the first edition ("Representative Programs for Advanced Players," "Foreign Terms Used in Viola Music," discussions of technique, practice, music reading, switching from violin to viola, learning problems, etc.), but it adds significant new material as well. A new chapter examines the relationship of good bodily functioning to successful performance. Correct breathing and posture, means of relaxing, "refinement of motion," and Zen as a means of mastering one's self are discussed, and a few exercises are given. Also presented are practice techniques for learning études and a brief discussion of left-hand articulation. Other additions include short bibliographies of "Source Books for Solo Viola Literature" (in chapter 1) and "Books Analyzing Bowing Problems" (in chapter 2). Lists of study material, transcriptions, and other repertoire and graded lists of studies and solos are revised and made current.

The extensive appendix (89 pages), "Viola Music in Print," is also revised and updated, and the section listing duets for viola and one other instrument is greatly expanded. A comparison with comparable lists in Margaret K. Farish's *String Music in Print* (2nd ed., Musicdata, 1980. $60.00) reveals a number of items listed only in Barrett. This is a must for violists and libraries lacking the first edition, and it is recommended as well for others who already own the earlier edition. [R: ARBA 79, p. 482]   Carole Franklin

478. The Diagram Group. **Musical Instruments of the World: An Illustrated Encyclopedia.** New York, Paddington Press/Two Continents, 1976. 320p. illus. (part col.). bibliog. index. $17.95. LC 76-21722. ISBN 0-8467-0134-0.

Perhaps a better subtitle for this excellent work would be: "A Visual Encyclopedia." The illustrations virtually *are* the work, and in this it surpasses all its rivals since the sixteenth century in coverage and extent. Apart from short introductory paragraphs to each section and subsection, the text consists of captions to the illustrations. These were meticulously drawn from authentic sources—monographs, manufacturers' catalogs, actual instruments, pictures of items in major collections—by members of The Diagram Group.

These drawings, more than 4,000 of them, picture instruments of every type: ancient and modern, ethnic and folk, primitive and electronic, popular and classical. The work endeavors to be comprehensive; it uses the system of Erich von Hornbostel and Curt Sachs as the basis of its arrangement. The major sections are: aerophones (vibrating air instruments), idiophones (self-vibrating instruments), membrophones (vibrating membrane instruments), chordophones (vibrating string instruments), and mechanical and electric instruments. Three further sections function as visual subject indexes (by geographical areas, by time periods, and by instrumental ensembles) to the instruments already pictured. A final section contains illustrated biographical entries on 23 persons and 7 family groups important in instrumental history as makers, virtuosos, and writers. There is a short-title bibliography of 122 entries, which lists publishers. A 71-item list of museums and a five-page name-subject index complete the work. Besides the appearance of the instruments, the book conveys an understanding of their structure, physical-acoustical functioning, history and development, terminology, and mode of performance, all through the illustrations.

Ed. note: A paperback edition of this work is available from Bantam Books (1978. $9.95pa.). [R: ARBA 77, p. 464; LJ, 1 Jan 77, p. 90; RQ, Summer 77, p. 354; WLB, Jan 77, p. 440]   Dennis North

479. Hinson, Maurice. **The Piano in Chamber Ensemble: An Annotated Guide.** Bloomington, Indiana University Press, 1978. 570p. index. $19.50. LC 77-9862. ISBN 0-253-34493-X.

In the preface to the volume, Maurice Hinson, one of the leading authorities on piano literature, carefully stakes out the areas to be covered and what to look for in each listing. Clear and precise examples are supplied. The author has included an abbreviation section and (a bonus) a list of American publishers and agents and the publications they handle.

The book is organized to cover first those works for a solo instrument and piano, which takes up over one-half the book and includes some of the more unusual instruments. Many contemporary works are included. By page 299, we have music for piano and two other instruments, and so on, up to and including piano and seven other instruments. An annotated bibliography and an index of composers conclude this volume. Most of the listings in the various categories have a concise musical analysis, an annotation that affords the user valuable insight into each ensemble's musical virtues.

This work is a worthwhile source for discerning the available repertory for various instruments in combination with the piano. Those searching for ensemble pieces that include their favorite instrument will find here a wealth of materials. Superior scholarship on the part of Hinson has produced a well-organized and easy-to-use reference tool. Any musician will find it difficult to put aside once (s)he starts to examine the contents. [R: ARBA 79, p. 483; Choice, Dec 78, p. 1349; LJ, 15 Mar 78, p. 666]   Joseph J. Chouinard

OPERA

480. Loewenberg, Alfred, comp. **Annals of Opera, 1597-1940.** 3rd ed., rev. and corrected. Totowa, NJ, Rowman and Littlefield, 1978. 1v. (unpaged). index. $49.50. ISBN 0-87471-851-1.

Loewenberg's *Annals of Opera* has been one of the truly indispensable tools for operatic research ever since its first appearance in 1943. Its familiar virtues really need no elaboration. Its format, organization, and reliability have proven that the original work was well planned and well executed. The revised second edition (1955) was in two volumes (the indexes being relegated to a separate volume), with disadvantages for busy music libraries, which can run into difficulties trying to keep volumes together. The 1970 reprint put all back together in one volume, and, happily, this third revised edition is also in one.

This latest edition is by Harold Rosenthal (editor of the British *Opera* magazine). Revisions have been made, and some additional material has been added. Mr. Rosenthal is preparing a supplementary volume, which will cover 1941 to 1978. Asterisks have been added after the titles in the basic volume, which will have entries in the new volume. (This will prove to be a valuable feature when the new volume appears.) An introduction for this revised volume by Mr. Rosenthal, giving details of his revisions, would seem to be an essential part of this edition, but none was included. A brief mention at the end of the basic introduction and some notes on the back of the dust jacket are all that he gets. For such a basic reference tool, any and all revisions are of prime importance, and librarians of specialized music collections cannot fail to note the need to replace copies of earlier editions with this new one. [R: ARBA 80, p. 438; Choice, Oct 79, p. 996; WLB, Oct 79, p. 129]

George Louis Mayer

481. **New Kobbé's Complete Opera Book.** Ed. and rev. by The Earl of Harewood. New York, G. P. Putnam's, 1976. 1694p. illus. index. $25.00. LC 76-12106. ISBN 0-399-11633-8.

The widening of the opera repertory so evident during the 1950s and 1960s is clearly reflected in the latest edition of this great standard in the literature of music reference. This updated and extensively revised edition tells in detail the stories of more than 300 operas and also describes the music. First published in 1922 and revised four times, this classic compilation is arranged by century and subdivided by country. The 1972 edition covered 237 operas, so the new edition is clearly far more inclusive. Harewood writes with enthusiasm, and his expertise is evident throughout. His personal favorites are probably revealed by the fact that the works of three composers are assigned nearly a quarter of the total text. These golden three are Verdi, with over 150 pages; Wagner, with nearly 150 pages; and Benjamin Britten, covered in over 100 pages. In summary, this is a highly successful updating and expansion of a classic survey. [R: ARBA 77, p. 466; Choice, Apr 77, p. 180; LJ, 1 Nov 76, p. 2268]

William J. Dane

482. Rosenthal, Harold, and John Warrack. **The Concise Oxford Dictionary of Opera.** 2nd ed. New York, Oxford University Press, 1979. 561p. $19.95. ISBN 0-19-311318-X.

The original 1964 version of this dictionary (with corrected 1966 and 1972 printings) proved itself a useful and reliable reference tool. This new edition has been completely revised, every entry having been reconsidered, many of them rewritten, and a few old entries of marginal importance dropped. Expansion has been considerable. Entries for countries and cities are more numerous and fuller; literary references (operas on the subject of *Faust*, etc.) have been increased; singers who have come into prominence since the first edition, such as Teresa Zylis-Gara, Frederica von Stade, and Shirley Verrett, have been added, and the number of entries for singers of the past, especially from France and Russia, has been increased. Birthdates have been changed for Jennie Tourel, Carmela Ponselle, and others.

The editors can take pride in their choice of material and on their accuracy. One error spotted, however, is the continued listing of 1949 rather than 1959 as the date of the Met debut of Giulietta Simionato. Although generously international in scope and coverage, the *Dictionary* is basically British and includes and excludes entries that would have been weighed somewhat differently in America. An American book, for example, surely would have included the up-and-coming operatic composers Thomas Pasatieri and Dominick Argento. This is the best of the concise dictionaries on the subject and is very reasonably priced, considering its value as a well-executed reference resource. [R: ARBA 80, p. 439; LJ, 1 Sept 79, p. 1686; WLB, Oct 79, p. 129]

George Louis Mayer

POPULAR MUSIC

483. The Illustrated Encyclopedia of Country Music. Fred Dellar, Roy Thompson, and Douglas B. Green. New York, Harmony Books, a division of Crown, 1977. 256p. illus. (part col.). index. (A Salamander Book). $17.95; $8.95pa. LC 77-087125. ISBN 0-517-53155-0; 0-517-53156-9pa.

The caption to a half-page photo in the middle of this rather cluttered, but personality-packed, popular encyclopedia reads: "Gimme a middle C'. Nashville's most overworked vocal group, the Jordannaires, lending a helping eight hands to the studio piano tuner." The "piano tuner" is Elvis Presley. This type of humor and familiarity pervades the text, and it, plus the hundreds of album cover and publicity photographs sprinkled throughout, gives the book a charming readability and a country sentiment. About 450 performers and groups who represent the mainstream of country music, country rock, rockabilly, blue grass, and country gospel are given loose biographical sketches of about 200 words. Each sketch mentions facts and observations about the career, musical characteristics, hit recordings, and current prominence of the musical personality. A few terms, such as "dobro" and "Grand Ole Opry," are described in chatty essays. Unfortunately, the informality of the text sometimes gets out of hand, leading to malapropisms, tangled allusions, and downright inaccurate statements. The generous color and black-and-white pictures, large (8½x11-inches) format, and extensive coverage distinguish this work from Melvin Shestack's *Country Music Encyclopedia* (Crowell, 1974. $15.95; $7.95pa.), the current standard reference source, which offers fewer but much more comprehensive and better-written entries. A brief selected list of representative LP albums follows each entry in the Thompson and Green book, and an index conveniently coordinates names that appear in several entries. [R: ARBA 78, p. 468; BL, 15 Oct 78, p. 406; Choice, June 78, p. 558]
Stephen M. Fry

484. The Illustrated Encyclopedia of Rock. Comp. by Nick Logan and Bob Woffinden. New York, Harmony Books, a division of Crown, 1977. 255p. illus. (part col.). index. (A Salamander Book). $17.95; $8.95pa. LC 76-40219. ISBN 0-517-52852-5; 0-517-52853-3pa.

Rock music is an unstable field in which it is not uncommon for performers to appear as solo artists and as members of various groups, often simultaneously. Similarly, groups may change members almost completely over a period of time. Logan and Woffinden, editor and associate editor of Britain's rock weekly, *New Musical Express*, have provided a densely packed encyclopedic guide to this world from its beginnings to the cut-off date of May 1976. Coverage is primarily of individual performers and groups (some not widely known), but important producers, executives, and even places which have had an impact on rock are also included. The authors admit, however, that it was difficult to decide whom to include, and there are some curious omissions. The Four Tops and The Impressions have individual entries, but The Supremes are mentioned only as one group which recorded for Tamla Motown. Diana Ross is given a cross reference to Tamla Motown, although the index does reveal several passing references to her name in other articles. Other groups and individuals are treated in much the same manner, yet several admittedly peripheral groups are granted full entries. This is, in fact, a strength of the encyclopedia, since such information is often very difficult to find, but it also means that other sources must be consulted to get complete coverage.

The articles themselves vary in length from a few sentences to a page or more. The style is journalistic and is usually quite opinionated, but the career and biographical information provided is extremely valuable. Most of the illustrations are reproductions of record jackets and standard publicity shots. There are cross references within the text, but the index should be consulted for most effective use. This would be an important addition to any collection serving a public with an interest in rock music. [R: ARBA 78, p. 468; BL, 1 July 77, p. 1678; LJ, 15 Apr 77, p. 903; SLJ, May 77, p. 85; WLB, May 77, p. 776]

Barbara E. Kemp

485.   Rust, Brian. **Jazz Records 1897-1942: Fourth Revised and Enlarged Edition.** New Rochelle, NY, Arlington House Publishers, 1978. 2v. index. $60.00/set. LC 78-1693. ISBN 0-87000-404-2.

One of the bibles of the jazz disc collector has returned – updated, corrected, and extended (by virtue of data from 10 new record labels and international correspondence by the compiler). The first edition contained 1,872 pages of discographic matter; this fourth edition of 1,753 pages of discography is smaller, but that is because certain artists have been shifted to Rust's *Complete Entertainment Discography* and *American Dance Band Discography* (both also published by Arlington House, 1973 and 1976, respectively). Basically, 30,000 jazz recordings from the pre-1943 period are listed (being drawn from 239 labels) in what is now standard discographic form: entered by name of artist, with subentry by group (if a variant), followed by personnel and instrumentation (along with changes in the personnel), and chronologically arranged by session and place. The titles are listed in order of matrix number as recorded (including takes and false starts), and then completed by the label and catalog issue number (and 78rpm reissue number, if such was the case). Vocals are also indicated. The catalog issue data is still limited to 78rpm numbers (plus all known long-playing issues of performances *never* issued on 78rpm, all known "rejected" titles, air checks, sound tracks, test pressings, etc.). It would have been useful to indicate what was on long-playing records as reissues, but for that one has to see the periodical *Micrography*, published in Holland.

New to the fourth edition are the 250 pages devoted to a song index (16,000 titles) and the artist index (10,000 band leaders, musicians, singers, and arrangers). Through the song index, one can quickly locate 49 versions of "I Got Rhythm" and 135 versions of "St. Louis Blues." At last I had a chance to check out – quite extensively – the entries in an index. For the past eight years, I've maintained a title index for personal use. I traced all of my pre-1943 titles (about 4,000) against Rust and found not one error. Personal name cross references abound in both the text and the artist index, a feature especially useful for identifying pseudonyms. [R: ARBA 79, p. 488; Choice, Nov 78, p. 1196; LJ, 1 Oct 78, p. 1970]

Dean Tudor

486.   Stambler, Irwin. **Encyclopedia of Pop, Rock, and Soul.** Rev. ed. New York, St. Martin's Press, 1976. 609p. $6.95pa. LC 73-87393.

This work updates, but does not replace, the author's *Encyclopedia of Popular Music* (St. Martin's Press, 1965). *Pop, Rock, and Soul* was originally published in a hardcover edition in 1975 ($19.95). This paperback edition is a reprint of the 1975 work (which is still available), adding a 4-page section on "British Pop and Rock since the Beatles" and 17 pages of addendum for persons and groups active in the mid-1970s. This work is far more comprehensive than Roxon's *Rock Encyclopedia* (Grosset and Dunlap, 1971) or Norm Nite's *Rock On* (Popular Libraries, 1977). Most libraries and individuals should take advantage of the low price and add this title to their collections. [R: ARBA 78, p. 469; WLB, Mar 77, p. 602]

487.   Tudor, Dean, and Nancy Tudor. **Contemporary Popular Music.** Littleton, CO, Libraries Unlimited, 1979. 313p. index. (American Popular Music on Elpee). $22.50. LC 78-32124. ISBN 0-87287-191-6.

Covering both mainstream popular music and rock music, *Contemporary Popular Music* surveys and evaluates some 750 records chosen from those available at the time of writing. The mainstream section covers general popular music, vocal stylists (male, female, groups), instrumental ensembles, novelty/humor, big bands, and stage and film music. The rock section surveys rockabilly, rock 'n' roll, blues rock, country/folk rock, hard rock, and notable experimentation. Less specialized than its companion volumes (*Black Music*, see entry 217; *Grass Roots Music*, see entry 488; and *Jazz*, see entry 489), this handbook will be used by reference and acquisitions librarians, and by patrons seeking familiar favorites or new sounds. The 19-page introductory survey material outlines a suggested order of collection building tailored to various needs and budgets. The format of *Contemporary Popular Music* follows that of the Tudors' *Black Music*, identifying first purchase items, giving ordering information, and providing directories of labels and specialized record stores. Also included are a bibliography of books and periodicals on each music style, and an artists index to each main section. [R: ARBA 80, p. 443; RQ, Winter 79, p. 177; WLB, Oct 79, p. 130]

488. Tudor, Dean, and Nancy Tudor. **Grass Roots Music.** Littleton, CO, Libraries Unlimited, 1979. 367p. index. (American Popular Music on Elpee). $25.00. LC 78-31686. ISBN 0-87287-133-9.

Dean Tudor and Nancy Tudor survey the development of the different types of folk music that are part of our American heritage. Annotations of some 1,700 currently available records provide coverage of ethnic offerings, the British and American folk traditions, the American folk revival, old time music, bluegrass, country music, sacred music, and contemporary troubadors. Following the format established by the authors' *Black Music* (see entry 217), an introductory survey outlines a suggested order of purchasing for various needs and budgets, directories of labels and specialized record stores are provided, and an index gives access to artists and recordings included in this volume. [R: ARBA 80, p. 443; Choice, Nov 79, p. 1156; WLB, Oct 79, p. 130]

489. Tudor, Dean, and Nancy Tudor. **Jazz.** Littleton, CO, Libraries Unlimited, 1979. 302p. index. (American Popular Music on Elpee). $22.50. LC 78-11737. ISBN 0-87287-148-7.

Jazz is a buying guide for both individual collectors and libraries. Following the format established in *Black Music* (see entry 217), the authors have selected and evaluated approximately 1,300 recordings on the basis of musical development, popularity, the artistic merit of the record, and extra-musical developments affecting those recordings. The authors utilized citation analysis over an 11-year period, which revealed that certain artists and tunes keep appearing; hence, any important record is so by virtue of its historical worth, influence, best-selling or trendsetting nature.

Arrangement is by musical style — New Orleans, Dixieland, ragtime, instrumental blues, swing, modern — and subdivided into anthologies, innovators, and standards. The introductory survey, bibliography, directories, and author index provided in each of the companion volumes to *Jazz* (*Black Music, Contemporary Popular Music,* and *Grass Roots Music*) are replicated in this volume. An added feature of *Jazz* is the provision of sound quality evaluations, averaging 300 words, of both old and new recordings. This is especially useful to collectors trying to select older recordings; a disc that received rave reviews a decade ago might be consigned to the wastebasket today. [R: ARBA 80, p. 444; Choice, July 79, p. 651; LJ, 15 Apr 79, p. 940; WLB, May 79, p. 655]

BIOGRAPHY

490. Baker, Theodore. **Baker's Biographical Dictionary of Musicians.** Completely rev. by Nicolas Slonimsky. 6th ed. New York, Schirmer Books, a division of Macmillan Publishing, 1978. 1955p. $75.00. LC 78-3205. ISBN 0-02-870240-9.

This standard work, first published in 1900, is now in its sixth edition. Slonimsky edited two supplements (1965, 1971) to the fifth edition (1958). This new edition brings together the additions and revisions of the supplements, and adds new entries for musicians who have recently become prominent. Revision of the fifth edition is complete: entries for deceased and retired musicians have been corrected, and entries for "forgotten" musicians of the past have been shortened (but none eliminated). Coverage is very wide, including not only composers and performers, but teachers, musicologists, critics, instrument makers, publishers, and patrons. *Baker's* is strongest for composers, and better for deceased than living musicians. The researcher may have to consult other sources for information about living artists. However, no other one-volume reference work provides as much biographical information. Entries include lists of works and bibliographies when appropriate. *Baker's* remains an essential item for all music library collections. [R: ARBA 80, p. 447; Choice, June 79, p. 505; LJ, 1 Mar 79, p. 618; WLB, Oct 79, p. 130]

Janet H. Littlefield

491. Ewen, David, comp. and ed. **Musicians since 1900: Performers in Concert and Opera.** New York, H. W. Wilson, 1978. 974p. $35.00. LC 78-12727. ISBN 0-8242-0565-0.

David Ewen has been one of the most prolific writers on music, generally addressing the lay audience on subjects of broad appeal: Gershwin, popular music, musical theater, and the like. Within these areas, he is quite sober and scholarly. Such is the case with this work, which in fact is designed to supersede his 1940 *Living Musicians* and its 1957 supplementary volume. Libraries that have acquired the sixth edition of *Baker's Biographical Dictionary of Musicians* (see the previous entry) might wonder if the Ewen volume would be a redundant purchase. If *Baker's* has any shortcoming, it is exactly in the area of Ewen's coverage, and even entries that are duplicated are worth it.

Ewen includes a vast amount of information, from repertoire to marriages and divorces, which will appeal even to the casual reader. He does not avoid reference to scandal, to personality conflicts, or to political and social factors, thus often providing insights which other references might ignore. This is a reference book of quality, which will be most helpful to the librarian, the music student, the radio broadcaster, and, in fact, almost anyone interested in contemporary biography. [R: ARBA 80, p. 447; Choice, June 79, p. 507; LJ, 1 Mar 79, p. 616; RQ, Fall 79, p. 89; WLB, May 79, p. 655]

Dominique-René de Lerma

492. Harris, Sheldon. **Blues Who's Who: A Biographical Dictionary of Blues Singers.** New Rochelle, NY, Arlington House, 1979. 775p. illus. bibliog. index. $35.00. LC 78-27073. ISBN 0-87000-425-5.

The names Chester Burnett, McKinley Morganfield, Riley King, and Peter Chatman may not ring any bells of recognition for blues enthusiasts until it is realized that these performers usually are billed under the names Howlin' Wolf, Muddy Waters, B. B. King, and Memphis Slim. The entries in this colossal work are the real names of the singers, who seem more often than not to adopt a clever alias or to acquire another name from earlier days. What is important in this regard is that there are copious references from all of these variations to the correct names.

The scope of *Blues Who's Who* goes beyond the above-mentioned singers. Dinah Washington, Ethel Waters, Richie Havens, Janis Joplin, Jimi Hendrix, Woody Guthrie, Jimmie Rodgers, Ray Charles, and the more popular blues stylists Joe Williams, Joe Turner, Lou Rawls, plus Paul Butterfield and Little Richard are all here. Curiously, Billie Holiday and Mahalia Jackson are missing from such a broad cross-section of blues performers. Most of the performers treated here, however, are the local city and rural singers who gained national and international recognition.

For each performer the book gives brief biographical information: his or her birth date and place, marriages, children, instruments played, songs composed, influences, reference sources, and critical quotations describing their music and careers. The bulk of each entry comprises a substantially complete accounting of all professional performances in concerts, television and radio shows, films, and other media; for such prolific performers as Sonny Terry and Brownie McGhee, these lists cover many pages. Appendices include a selected bibliography, film, radio, TV, and theater indices, a name and place index, and an incredibly comprehensive song index. This is the most substantial and complete source for blues performers available. [R: ARBA 80, p. 447; LJ, July 79, p. 1441]

Stephen M. Fry

493. York, William, comp. and ed. **Who's Who in Rock Music.** Seattle, WA, Atomic Press, 1978. 260p. $6.95pa. (retail); $5.55 (library).

The 6,000-plus name (personal and group) listings here comprise all of the major and most of the minor figures of rock, although the intensity of coverage varies considerably. Generous cross references facilitate tracing relationships among musicians, which is never easy anyway but is at least recognized here as a potential problem. Entries sometimes include all of the following information (but certainly not always): name, specialty (vocal/instrument—if group entry, this is broken down member by member), descriptor, notes as to session work (if any—and there's a lot of it), and notes as to albums (if any) and dates of release. Thus, this is not standard biographical fare, but strictly music-related information, most of it taken, according to the compiler, from album jackets and albums themselves. Descriptors are sometimes judgmental, but primarily they present capsule histories of careers (and usually the declines thereof). For more standard biographical fare, Irwin Stambler's *Encyclopedia of Pop, Rock, and Soul* (see entry 486), combined with Norm Nite's two volumes of *Rock On* (Popular Libraries, 1977), will yield better results.

Nothing of a truly standard nature has been done in popular music biography, as most are chatty histories providing spotty coverage and lists of records. This *Who's Who* has more sheer facts in it than any other such item covering rock from its beginnings to the present (1977, in this case). The only thing to watch is a tendency to avoid giving cross-over artists complete coverage: for example, Emmy Lou Harris' session work for Bob Dylan, Johnathan Edwards, John Sebastian, and Neil Young is noted, but not the Gram Parsons album on which she received co-billing. Nor is her solo album *Luxury Liner* (1977) here. So, you don't get *everything* here, but for sheer data on rock music, and at this price, no person or library seriously interested in the field can afford to pass this up. [R: ARBA 79, p. 490; WLB, Dec 78, p. 343]

Koert C. Loomis, Jr.

20 THEATRE

GENERAL WORKS

494. Anderson, Michael, and others. **Crowell's Handbook of Contemporary Drama.** New York, T. Y. Crowell, 1971. 505p. $10.00. LC 79-158714. ISBN 0-690-22643-8.

A convenient one-volume guide to "developments in the drama in Europe and the Americas since the Second World War—or, in the case of Spain, since the Civil War. The emphasis is entirely on written drama, not on theater." It includes: 1) surveys of modern drama in various countries in fairly long overview studies; 2) biographical sketches and critical appraisal of the career and work of many playwrights; 3) descriptive and critical evaluation of the more important and representative plays, and 4) brief presentation of theorists, directors, movements, and companies that have had an influence on dramatic form.

Fourteen authorities have contributed material on the drama and dramatists of Czechoslovakia, Scandinavia, Finland, France, Germany, Austria and Switzerland, Great Britain, Hungary, Italy, Latin America, Poland, Spain and Portugal, and the United States. Entries are arranged alphabetically in unsigned articles. In some entries, bibliographical information is given for additional sources, but this is not a strong point in this work. Emphasis is on the overview of the drama in various countries, and on the biographical information. An authoritative and useful source for critical appraisal of present-day drama and dramatists, reflecting "the central importance of social criticism and political ideology in the drama of many nations today." [R: ARBA 72, p. 489; Choice, July 72, p. 663]   Paul A. Winckler

495. Geisinger, Marion. **Plays, Players and Playwrights: An Illustrated History of the Theatre.** New York, Hart, 1971. 768p. illus. index. $20.00. LC 77-162054. ISBN 0-8055-1091-5.

A copiously illustrated chronological history of the theatre beginning with ancient Greece and Rome. Not as detailed as the *Oxford Companion*, but it provides basic information accompanied by luscious illustrations of actors, stage settings, theatres, and even playbills.

It is chronologically arranged, with an accent on the English-speaking theatre, although background information on ancient Greece and Rome and the Commedia dell' Arte is provided.

Unfortunately, some of the entries are tantalizing in their brevity. For example, a five-line paragraph on Tennessee Williams precedes far more lengthy discussion of his plays but gives no biographical information on him, discussing only the plays themselves. This defect is offset by two chapters on Russian theatre and American musical comedy, neither of which is handled as well or as extensively anywhere else. [R: ARBA 72, p. 420; Choice, Mar 72, p. 74; LJ, 15 Feb 72, p. 697]   Judith Rosenberg

496. Hartnoll, Phyllis, ed. **The Concise Oxford Companion to the Theatre.** New York, Oxford University Press, 1972. 640p. bibliog. $8.95pa. ISBN 0-19-281102-9.

This paperback edition is based on the third edition of *The Oxford Companion to the Theatre*. Notable changes in this edition are the omission of long articles on individual countries and on technical aspects of the theatre, and the lack of illustrations. The editor states that "every article, however short, has been reconsidered and, in most cases, recast and rewritten in miniature in such a way as to retain the essential facts and still leave room, where necessary, for new material" (preface). The new material is certainly kept to a minimum; it is mostly reflected in the addition of a date here and there (e.g., Tallulah Bankhead's and John Steinbeck's deaths in 1968, Noel Coward's 1970 knighting, and a sentence on two new Neil Simon plays presented in 1969 and 1970). The extensive bibliography reflects more updating and includes many books with 1967 to 1970 imprints. In sum, this is a useful, accurate, well-organized condensation of the original encyclopedic work. [R: ARBA 74, p. 414; Choice, Mar 73, p. 60]

BIBLIOGRAPHIES

497. Eddleman, Floyd Eugene, comp. **American Drama Criticism: Interpretations, 1890-1977.** 2nd ed. Hamden, CT, Shoe String Press, 1979. 488p. index. $27.50. LC 78-31346. ISBN 0-208-01713-5.

This volume updates Helen H. Palmer and Jane Anne Dyson's first edition (1967) and first supplement (1970), as well as Eddleman's second supplement (1976). Listed are critiques and reviews of American plays appearing in some 200 books and monographs and in more than 400 periodicals. Published primarily between 1890 and 1977, these items are arranged by playwright and then by play title. No attempt has been made to evaluate the quality of the materials. Excluded from this edition are interviews, biographies, author bibliographies, listings on non-American dramatists, nondramatic works of playwrights, and newspaper references. Added, usefully, for musicals are the names of all authors: of the book, lyrics, and music. Also new to this volume are an index of critics and an index of adapted authors and works. Other indexes retained list books and journals covered, play titles, and playwrights (this one is expendable).

Eddleman's work remains the most comprehensive listing available for "interpretations" of American plays, although for some playwrights, more critiques can oe found in Paul F. Breed and Florence M. Sniderman's *Dramatic Criticism Index* (see entry 506) and more reviews in James M. Salem's *Guide to Critical Reviews: Part I: American Drama, 1909-1969,* 2nd ed. (Scarecrow, 1973. $19.00). [R: ARBA 80, p. 451]   Richard J. Kelly

498. Stratman, Carl J. **Bibliography of Medieval Drama.** 2nd ed., rev. and enl. New York, Ungar, 1972. 2v. index. $35.00. LC 78-163141. ISBN 0-8044-3272-3.

This updating of the 1954 edition is arranged in 10 sections (General Studies, Festschriften, Liturgical Latin Drama, English Drama, Byzantine Drama, French Drama, German Drama, Italian Drama, Low Countries' Drama, Spanish Drama) plus addenda and a general index of subjects and authors of works listed. Within sections, the entries are arranged chronologically instead of alphabetically, as they were in the first edition. This is helpful for historical research, but it puts a greater responsibility on the index.

The work has been planned as an aid to students of English drama and does not supplant bibliographies exclusively concerned with medieval drama in any of the countries represented. According to the preface, 5,000 entries have been added since the 1954 edition. Each entry includes full author, complete title, place, publisher, date, pagination, indication of any significant bibliographies included, and symbol of library location (including that of manuscripts). Although there are no annotations, the items considered most important by the editor are asterisked.

The bibliography is an important, but quite special, reference tool that should be available to all students of the history of European drama. [R: ARBA 73, p. 481; Choice, Apr 73, p. 270]   Richard M. Buck

DICTIONARIES AND ENCYCLOPEDIAS

499. The Encyclopedia of World Theater: With 420 Illustrations and an Index of Play Titles. New York, Scribner's, 1977. 320p. illus. index. $25.00. LC 76-19741. ISBN 0-684-14834-X.

Martin Esslin, theatre critic and author of books about theatre, has prepared a one-volume encyclopedia based on the German *Friedrichs Theaterlexikon* (1969). Completely updated and revised by Esslin, the work now includes many new entries extending from playwrights to designers. Covering both historical and current aspects of theatre, the *Encyclopedia* brings together information that should be useful to lay theatre buffs, students, and historians alike. The 400 black-and-white illustrations depict scenes from plays, theatres, directors, etc.; they add appeal and complement the varied entries. A guide to the use of the work provides explanations of abbreviations, cross references (2,000), dates, play titles (5,000), and bibliographical references. The brief alphabetical entries are easy to understand and contain language references. This is an excellent tool, either for browsing or for looking up a given entry. An index of play titles and illustration credits concludes the work. [R: ARBA 78, p. 476; BL, 15 Feb 78, p. 979; Choice, May 78, p. 372; LJ, 15 Oct 77, p. 2148; RQ, Fall 78, p. 93; WLB, Jan 78, p. 423]   Carolyn J. Henderson

500. Gassner, John, and Edward Quinn, eds. **The Reader's Encyclopedia of World Drama.** New York, Thomas Y. Crowell, 1969. 1029p. illus. bibliog. $15.00. LC 69-11830. ISBN 0-690-67483-X.

Designed as a ready-reference book, this one-volume encyclopedia concentrates on drama "as literature, not as theater." Entries focus primarily on plays, their authors, and their literary characteristics.

Entries fall into four categories. One of these is national drama, where under the name of each country, there is a historical survey of the development of that nation's drama from its origins to its contemporary forms. In most cases, a brief bibliography is appended, with works primarily in the English language. Another category covers the significant playwrights from the standpoint of either literary merit or importance to national drama. Playwrights are treated in separate entries, which provide biographical sketches, list important works, and give some critical evaluations. Entries in the third category, covering plays, generally include a precis of the main action and critical commentary. And, finally, all the major dramatic modes and many minor ones are discussed in articles of varying length, depending on the relative importance of the topic. All articles are initialed; there are some 95 contributors.

An appendix includes basic documents in dramatic theory but, unfortunately, there is no index. This work is quite readable and has well-balanced international coverage. It is intended for a general audience. [R: ARBA 70, p. 65; BL, 1 Jan 70, p. 537; C&RL, July 70, p. 275; LJ, 15 Feb 70, p. 651; LJ, 15 Apr 70, p. 1440]

501. Koegler, Horst. **The Concise Oxford Dictionary of Ballet.** New York, Oxford University Press, 1977. 583p. $14.95. ISBN 0-19-311314-7.

Based on *Friedrichs Ballettlexikon von A-Z* (1972), *The Concise Oxford Dictionary of Ballet* offers some 5,000 alphabetically arranged entries on all aspects of this subject—e.g., the history of ballet, theatres, dancers, choreographers, composers, schools and companies, and basic definitions. Entries vary in length from a few lines to three columns. In comparison to the German work, there is a significant change in emphasis, with much material added to meet the demands of a new audience.

The best source on this subject is still Chujoy and Manchester's *Dance Encyclopedia* (rev. ed. Simon and Schuster, 1967. 992p.), which contains some 5,000 entries. However,

Koegler's work is more comprehensive than Wilson's *Dictionary of Ballet* (3rd ed. Theatre Arts, 1974), which limits itself primarily to Great Britain, France, Germany, and the United States. The inclusion of bibliographical sources for many subjects is a valuable feature of Koegler's work. In spite of its somewhat dry style, this dictionary will be of substantial assistance to libraries of all types. [R: ARBA 78, p. 476; BL, 1 Sept 77, p. 66; Choice, July 77, p. 658; LJ, 1 Mar 77, p. 593; WLB, Apr 77, p. 681]

502. **McGraw-Hill Encyclopedia of World Drama: An International Reference Work in Four Volumes.** New York, McGraw-Hill, 1972. 4v. $139.50. LC 70-37382. ISBN 0-07-079567-3.

This is the first specialized encyclopedia on this subject in the English language. Its coverage of biographical materials far exceeds that of such one-volume works as, for example, *The Reader's Encyclopedia of World Drama*, by Gassner and Quinn (see entry 500). The *McGraw-Hill Encyclopedia of World Drama* is a major achievement. According to the introduction, the objective of this work is to bring "into focus the accomplishments of the world's major dramatists. It also touches on many of the lesser figures. . . ." In general, the two types of dramatists covered in this work can be roughly classified as "major" and "lesser." Each article about a major dramatist is divided into several sections—factual discussion of the author's life, short synopses of several if not all of the author's plays, comprehensive listings of the entire body of work, and bibliographical information. Scattered among the biographical entries in the text are about 100 abbreviated non-biographical entries—dramatic terms, theatre movements and styles, anonymous plays—which serve as useful collateral material. The entries for 300 "major" dramatists provide, in addition to the information mentioned above, a complete chronology of the writer's scripts, describing types of plays, the earliest publication, and date and place of the first production. There are listings of some 600 "minor" playwrights with less extensive information. Thus, there are some 900-plus "author" entries, and 100 articles providing definitions of terms. Some 2,000 photographs, many full page or half page, are integrated in the text. The length of the "author articles" varies from about 12 or 13 pages to one or two paragraphs. An index to play titles is appended in the fourth volume.

It should be pointed out that this encyclopedia covers what we may call "dramatic literature." Its main objective is to cover individual plays and playwrights rather than to dwell on the relationships between drama as literature and drama as theatre. Michael Kirby, who provided a long review for this encyclopedia in the *New York Times Book Review*, indicated that in this encyclopedia " 'drama' means only 'dramatic literature.' 'Encyclopedia of Plays and Playwrights' would have been a much more accurate title. . . . This mirrors the literary approach to drama that still dominates our schools and colleges." We think, on the contrary, that the objectives of this work are clearly defined and that the editors have a right to concentrate on drama as dramatic literature, especially since there are many other reference works covering such topics as staging, directors, actors, etc. Nevertheless, it might have been unwise to limit this work to individual playwrights. What disturbed this reviewer is the lack of survey-type articles on trends in dramatic writing and on the historical development of drama in individual countries. Gassner and Quinn, in the work mentioned above, rightly point out that drama as a universal phenomenon is deeply rooted in the culture of the community (we would add "and of a particular nation") as well as in the experience of the individual. The latter aspect is covered well in the McGraw-Hill work. The synthetic approach, defining drama in terms of its historical and cultural milieu, is missing. Missing also are extremely important playwrights from Eastern cultures—from such countries as China, Japan, etc. Western playwrights are well represented, even including playwrights from such countries as Russia, Poland, and the rest of Eastern Europe (with the exceptions of Rumania, Ukraine, Bulgaria, and, to our surprise, even some of the Scandinavian playwrights).

For all practical purposes, this comprehensive and well-executed work is primarily concerned with the European tradition. [R: ARBA 73, p. 479; BL, 15 Oct 73, p. 184; Choice, Mar 73, p. 62; LJ, 15 Apr 73, p. 1242; WLB, Jan 73, p. 447]   Bohdan S. Wynar

503.   Matlaw, Myron. **Modern World Drama: An Encyclopedia.** New York, Dutton, 1972. 960p. illus. index. LC 71-185032. ISBN 0-525-15902-9.

This comprehensive work on twentieth-century drama is apparently the sole responsibility of the author, save for the research sources and specialists mentioned in the preface, in which Matlaw also notes that the contents reflect "my own tastes and attitudes." In scope, entries cover geographical areas, biographies of playwrights (no producers, directors, or actors), names of plays (some with full plot outlines, many without), and modern technical terms such as "absurd." The articles are well cross referenced, except that the small-caps indication for cross referencing is used only the first time the word is used in any particular article. In addition to the main A-Z entries, there are a character index and a general index. In the general index, where the playwright's name in parentheses follows the play title, small caps are not used to show which playwrights have their own entries, although the play titles are so differentiated.

From a rather careful examination of selected entries, it seems that new European playwrights fare better than American, but the emphasis is essentially on the standard moderns from Ibsen to O'Neill and even here the decisions as to whether to provide full or brief coverage seem peculiarly arbitrary. Of the Europeans, Ionesco rightly has a major entry, and *Amédée, Rhinoceros*, and *The Killer* have full plot summaries, but *Exit the King* and *The Pedestrian in the Air* do not; Gombrowicz has an entry, but Handke is mentioned only under Austria; Pinget has an entry, but his plays do not have separate entries. Most of the major avant-garde playwrights have entries, but they are not treated as fully as the naturalists. Of the Americans, both Kopit and *O, Dad, Poor Dad . . .* have entries, but there are no entries for Rochelle Owens, Israel Horovitz, or Sam Shepard, or for any of their plays — all these and many others must be traced through the general index to the "United States" article. Musicals are slighted even more — there are entries for very few American musicals except *My Fair Lady*. Hardly any musical playwrights are separately listed, and no composers that I could find.

Matlaw's choice of which plays to plot in full is consistently arbitrary, with no indication in the general index as to which plays have been given the full plot treatment. Despite the limitations, this is the only reference work of its kind. It should be valuable for library reference, especially as a supplement to the *McGraw-Hill Encyclopedia of World Drama* (see entry 502), which is easier to use because all main entries are under the playwright. [R: ARBA 73, p. 478; BL, 1 Oct 72, p. 123; BL, 15 Oct 72, p. 190; Choice, Mar 73, p. 62; C&RL, Jan 73, p. 65; LJ, 15 Apr 73, p. 1242; WLB, Sept 72, p. 89]   Richard M. Buck

DIRECTORIES

504.   Salem, James M. **Drury's Guide to Best Plays.** 3rd ed. Metuchen, NJ, Scarecrow, 1978. 421p. index. $18.00. LC 77-18139. ISBN 0-8108-1097-2.

Last published in 1969, this standard source continues to be a reliable guide to non-musical plays in English (including translations) generally available for performance. Plays range from the Greek and Roman classics to recent On/Off Broadway hits. Entries contain author, title, date of first production or publication, publisher or anthology found in, royalty fee, a concise plot synopsis, and notes as to the number of acts, sets, and actors for each. Cast, broad subject, and title indexes are retained, as are lists of popular, prize-winning, and recommended plays. A list of long-running plays on the New York stage has been added. The index of co-authors, original authors, and adapters has been dropped in favor of cross references—a good decision. Set in smaller typeface than the other editions, this third edition has fewer pages but seemingly more plays than the last one. Some older plays were eliminated, but many more have been added, while those of such current playwrights as Tom Stoppard and Alan Ayckbourn appear for the first time. [R: ARBA 79, p. 499; WLB, June 78, p. 808]   Richard J. Kelly

505.   Young, William C. **American Theatrical Arts: A Guide to Manuscripts and Special Collections in the United States and Canada.** Chicago, American Library Association, 1972. 166p. index. $9.95. LC 78-161234. ISBN 0-8389-0104-2.

An extremely important publication for locating primary source material of American and Canadian theatrical personalities including actors, directors, authors, designers, choreographers, composers, critics, dancers, and other performers of opera, film, and the circus. Also included are listings of American and Canadian collections containing playbills, theatre history, promptbooks, and posters.

The guide lists the collections of 138 institutions, most of them in the United States. Many of these collections have not been cataloged and do not appear in the Library of Congress Union List of Manuscripts. The guide is arranged alphabetically by state and then by institution. Most entries indicate the number of pieces in the collection and give a brief description of it. A very good name and subject index facilitates the use of the tool.

Mr. Young's outstanding effort will certainly assist in the documenting of American theatrical history. [R: ARBA 73, p. 411; Choice, July 72, p. 630; LJ, 15 Apr 72, p. 1420; RQ, Summer 72, p. 391; WLB, Apr 72, p. 745]   Judith Armstrong

INDEXES

506.   Breed, Paul F., and Florence M. Sniderman, comps. and eds. **Dramatic Criticism Index: A Bibliography of Commentaries on Playwrights from Ibsen to the Avant-Garde.** Detroit, Gale, 1972. 1022p. $36.00. LC 79-127598. ISBN 0-8103-1090-2.

According to the preface, this selective index is a result of the examination of "approximately 630 books and over 200 periodicals." There are "nearly 12,000 entries in English on 300 or more American and foreign playwrights, the majority of them from the twentieth century." Entries are arranged alphabetically by playwright, with a general section followed by an alphabetical listing of works. The commentaries cited under each heading range from major articles and chapters of books to one or two pages from a longer work. Few play reviews are included, unless no other comment was found for the particular work. There are three supplementary indexes: play titles, critics (which lists play title and playwright criticized), and books indexed (which is the only place where full citation of the books is given). Although no cut-off date for inclusion is noted, the latest date found for either books or periodicals indexed was 1969.

The index is admittedly selective, but it seems to be the best bibliography of its kind available. Only *Modern Drama: A Checklist of Critical Literature on 20th Century Plays* (Adelman and Dworkin, Scarecrow, 1967) is comparable to it. The 1967 index is less extensive, though it does include articles in languages other than English and is certainly not superseded by this work. The *Dramatic Criticism Index* is a helpful reference tool for libraries that hold even a few of the books and periodicals indexed. [R: ARBA 73, p. 477; Choice, Mar 73, p. 58; C&RL, Jan 73, p. 64; LJ, 15 Apr 73, p. 1242; WLB, Dec 72, p. 361]
                Richard M. Buck

507. Connor, John M., and Billie M. Connor. **Ottemiller's Index to Plays in Collections: An Author and Title Index to Plays Appearing in Collections Published between 1900 and Early 1975.** 6th ed., rev. and enl. Metuchen, NJ, Scarecrow, 1976. 523p. $19.50. LC 71-166073. ISBN 0-8103-0919-2.

Ottemiller's Index to Plays in Collections is a mandatory purchase for ready reference collections because it provides immediate solutions for library patrons who need a certain play but find that the single copy of that play is charged, missing, stolen, snagged, or lost. Ottemiller comes to the rescue, providing the handiest bibliographic citation to "10,351 copies of 3,686 different plays by 1,937 different authors." To achieve access to all these full-length plays, 1,237 collections were analyzed (190 new collections since the fifth edition).

The index begins with an author index (pp. 1-203), where one can look up an author (e.g., Ben Jonson) and find his birth and death dates, name of play, first production date, and an acronym representing the collection in which the play is to be found. The "List of Collections Analyzed and Key to Symbols" (pp. 205-432) gives full bibliographic information on the collections, which should be studied by librarians charged with collection development (since patrons will be asking for the indexed books). The index concludes with a title index (pp. 433-523).

The adjective that best describes this index is useful. Editions of Ottemiller are cited in Sheehy's *Guide to Reference Books* (9th ed. BD 175) and in *Books for College Libraries* (1975). [R: ARBA 77, p. 480; Choice, Oct 77, p. 1026; LJ, 15 Sept 76, p. 1845; WLB, Feb 77, p. 536]   Richard R. Centing

508. Fidell, Estelle A., ed. **Play Index 1973-1977: An Index to 3,878 Plays.** New York, H. W. Wilson, 1978. 457p. $28.00. LC 64-1054. ISSN 0554-3037.

This, the fifth issue of the Wilson Company's popular and highly regarded indexing service for published plays of all types, remains virtually unchanged in format since the previous volume (1973. 403p. $20.00), which also covered a five-year period, 1968-1972.

Like the preceding volumes, it can be adapted to a variety of uses, due to its great breadth and broad scope, covering nearly 4,000 plays ranging from puppet plays to classical drama, published either separately or as part of collections. Those plays designed for children or young people are designated as such by use of symbols *C* or *Y*.

Part I is the main section, an index of authors, titles, and subjects, with the fullest bibliographic description appearing under the author (title, publisher, date, pagination, title of anthology if part of a collection). Also found under the author entry is a brief descriptive note of the plot and cast. An especially important standard feature is part II, "Cast Analysis," designed to identify plays by the number and sex of cast members needed (men, women, boys, girls), and organized under six categories, including "Variable Cast" (indicating that the parts may be held by either sex).

Part III lists the indexed collections by author and title, providing full bibliographic information under the author. A new feature here is the inclusion of ISBN designations and LC card numbers when readily available. Part IV is as usual the "Directory of Publishers and Distributors," in which full addresses are provided for all publishers whose works have been indexed. The *Play Index* continues to be an indispensable source of information for access to published drama. [R: ARBA 80, p. 455]   Ron Blazek

509. Keller, Dean H. **Index to Plays in Periodicals.** Rev. and expanded ed. Metuchen, NJ, Scarecrow, 1979. 824p. $35.00. LC 92-962. ISBN 0-8108-1208-8.

This revised and expanded edition of the *Index to Plays in Periodicals* (1971) and its *Supplement* (1973) consists of 9,562 entries culled from 267 periodicals running through 1976. All types of plays in various languages are included. The book is arranged in such a way as to make location of a play quite simple. There are two parts. The first part lists entries according to author and contains clear and adequate information for locating the play, including the author's full names and dates, title of the play, brief description, number of acts, and volume and date of the periodical. The second part of the book contains titles, which are numbered to correspond with entries in the author section. There are cross references for joint authors, translators, adapters, editors, and pseudonyms. It is a well-designed and easy-to-use book, and would be an asset to most general collections and a necessity for theatre collections. [R: ARBA 80, p. 456; LJ, 1 Dec 79, p. 2560]

Richard P. Halgin

510. La Beau, Dennis, ed. **Theatre, Film and Television Biographies Master Index.** 1st ed. Detroit, Gale, 1979. 477p. (Gale Biographical Index Series, No. 5). $48.00. LC 77-2470. ISBN 0-8103-1081-3.

The subtitle of this detailed index tells the user much more: "A consolidated guide to over 100,000 biographical sketches of persons living and dead, as they appear in over 40 of the principal biographical dictionaries devoted to the theatre, film and television." The reference works indexed range from the *Celebrity Register* to both editions of *Who's Who in the American Theatre*; the second (*Notable Names in the American Theatre*) was published in 1976 (see entry 512), as was David Thomson's *Biographical Dictionary of Film*, also used as a source. The earliest source is *Who's Who on the Stage* (1906 and 1908 editions). This reviewer cannot cite any major sources for American performers that have been overlooked; the major English source, *Who's Who in the Theatre*, is represented by the Gale retrospective multivolume set and the 1977 16th edition. Those invaluable series *Theatre World, Theatre World Annual* (London), and *Screen World* are not represented, but so many volumes are out of print that only major research collections would have the earlier ones. "The books cited in the *TF & T* are readily available and widely held in most reference collections" (introduction, p. vi).

The introduction also claims over 100,000 entries, including a "no listing" entry if none exists in the sources used. The usage suggestions in the introduction are helpful and should be read before pushing into the 477 pages of entries. A valuable reference work for any collection holding a good number of the sources. [R: ARBA 80, p. 456; Choice, Nov 79, p. 1152; LJ, 1 Oct 79, p. 2084; WLB, Nov 79, p. 192]

Richard M. Buck

BIOGRAPHY

511. Herbert, Ian. **Who's Who in the Theatre: A Biographical Record of the Contemporary Stage.** 16th ed. Detroit, Gale, 1977. 1389p. $68.00. ISBN 0-8103-0233-0.

This standard work, once called by Kenneth Tynan the "portable memory of the British Theatre in the twentieth century," remains invaluable, though this latest edition shows some disturbing signs of amnesia. Dropped since the last edition (1972), owing to economic and space considerations, are the General Index to London Playbills as well as the sections on Centres for Theatre Research, Honours in the Theatre, the Arts Council of Great Britain, the British Council, the Repertory Movement in Great Britain, the National Theatre, and the Royal Shakespeare Company in London. Nonetheless, the chief elements of the work remain and flourish in a new and more readable typeface: the up-to-date biographical sketches of actors, dramatists, directors, designers, and producers of the English stage are, of course, here—and this edition places greater emphasis than did past ones on recent developments in Australian theatre. Also retained and updated are the London and New York playbills, lists of long runs in both cities, data on London and New York theatres, references to names in previous editions, and obituaries for 1971-1976. The "memory loss" evidenced in the present edition of *WWT* makes it important to keep earlier volumes at hand. [R: ARBA 78, p. 481; BL, 1 July 78, p. 1700; LJ, 1 Apr 77, p. 789]

Richard J. Kelly

512. **Notable Names in the American Theatre.** Clifton, NJ, James T. White, 1976. 1250p. $69.00. LC 76-27356. ISBN 0-88371-018-8.

This large volume is the "second edition" of the *Biographical Encyclopedia and Who's Who of the American Theatre* published by James H. Heineman (1966). The object was to do a 10-year update as well as to augment and "continue the availability of a one-volume reference work containing the answers to the professional and casual researchers' and the students' basic queries about the theatre in this country" (p. vii). The cut-off date for most of the information is the end of the 1974 New York theatre season (May 31), but some of the lists include 1975 and 1976 information.

The work is divided into nine sections. "New York Productions" (those that opened between 1900 and the cut-off date) includes name of play, type of production, name of theatre, opening date, and length of run. Names of playwrights are not given. "Premieres in America" lists, as completely as available sources allowed, the title, author, premiere date, producing group, and theatre of all such first performances from 1968 to the cut-off date, with an author index. "Premieres of American Plays Abroad" lists the same type of information as given in the American premieres section for the first professional performances of plays by U.S. playwrights that occurred in foreign countries (including Canada) *before* the plays had a U.S. premiere. The section covers December 1948 to April 1974 chronologically, with no index. "Theatre Group Biographies," a catch-all section, has entries of varying length on active and important defunct performing groups, as well as on theatrical unions, professional organizations, acting schools (in New York only) and a good summary article on "Stage Periodicals." "Theatre Building Biographies" covers New York theatres only, often listing the architect, past and present owners, name changes, and opening production, and, if demolished, the demolition date. The "Awards" section includes the Oscars, Tonys, and Obies; "Best play" listings; the Derwent, Donaldson, Margo Jones, George Jean Nathan, and Drama Critics Circle Awards; Pulitzer Prizes for Drama; and many lesser-known awards (listed from the beginning of each, with the cut-off date for most being 1975, for some, 1976). "Biographical Bibliography" lists books by and about significant personalities of the theatre, but not critical discussions of a person's work. There are 900 names and 2,900 titles. "Necrology" is a list, as complete as possible, of U.S. stage personalities, from the colonial period to the present, who died before the volume went to press.

"Notable Names in the American Theatre" is the final, longest, and, of course, most important and useful section. Many of the biographies from the earlier edition have been updated by the biographees and by research. Persons covered include performers, producers, playwrights, directors, designers, choreographers, composers, lyricists, conductors, casting directors, teachers, critics, educators, authors, historians, archivists, administrators, representatives (agents), and publicists. A basic criterion was that they all be individuals of achievement who have made an important contribution to the American stage. "Who's who" facts are given—profession, birth date (if available) and place, education, marital status, professional memberships, at least professional address and sometimes phone number—followed by the career listing, which covers, as appropriate: Pre-Theatre, Theatre, Concerts, Films and Television, Radio, Other Activities, Discography, Published Works, Awards, and Recreation.

There is so much here that the volume is invaluable, indeed indispensable, for any kind of basic research on the theatre in the United States. The information included in the individual biographical entries is carefully organized and apparently well researched. Spot checking indicates that very little significant information about anyone listed has been omitted, and, in many cases, the detail is quite amazing. Also amazing is that the list price of $69.00 is $13.50 less than that of the earlier edition.

The editor(s) should make some more explicit explanations in the next edition about criteria for inclusion, and place the introduction to each section with that section. Perhaps one or two sections need complete revision and rethinking in regard to usefulness for reference. In any case, the volume is highly recommended to all libraries of any size and to individuals who work in, go to, or just love the theatre. [R: ARBA 78, p. 482; Choice, Nov 77, p. 1194; LJ, 15 June 77, p. 1365]   Richard M. Buck

513. Vinson, James, ed. **Contemporary Dramatists**. 2nd ed. New York, St. Martin's Press, 1977. 1088p. index. $35.00. LC 76-54628. ISBN 0-900997-86-9.

Vinson's first edition (1973) was received with considerable acclaim by reviewers and was considered a valuable reference source on contemporary dramatists. As in the first edition, this work contains biographical entries for some 300 living dramatists writing in English together with signed critical essays about each and bibliographies of each one's published works. Supplementary material includes essays on contemporary theatre forms, and useful lists of and information about screenwriters, librettists, and radio/TV writers. Among the several critical comments about the first edition was the observation that the book would need almost immediate updating to maintain its usefulness as a source of contemporary writers. While the new edition has taken four years to appear, it has increased considerably in size (926p. versus 1088p.). Much of the increase is due to the addition of new works and updating of biographical information. The most notable new feature is a nearly 70-page title index to all plays listed in the text. A necrology of playwrights who died since the mid-1950s is appended. The second edition contains a wealth of otherwise elusive information and is an essential reference for theatre collections. [R: ARBA 78, p. 484; BL, 15 Apr 79, p. 1313; Choice, Oct 77, p. 1028]

514. **Who Was Who in the Theatre: 1912-1976: A Biographical Dictionary of Actors, Actresses, Directors, Playwrights, and Producers of the English-Speaking Theatre.** Detroit, Gale, 1978. 4v. (Gale Composite Biographical Dictionary Series, No. 3; An Omnigraphics Book). $190.00/set. LC 78-9634. ISBN 0-8103-0406-6.

Gale's *Who Was Who . . .* series has not fared well at the hands of this reviewer up to this point, primarily for sloppiness of execution and what appeared to be a total lack of editorial principle. It is, then, a pleasure to be able to give this set from Gale much higher marks in all areas than were given the similar volumes that preceded it. This set has one source— *Who's Who in the Theatre*, 1912-1972—and that source appears to have been well edited to begin with. The single alphabet listings include everyone listed in that source unless still active at the time of publication; some 4,100 persons in all are included.

Entries include a person's original name, birth facts, education, marital career, credits, favorite parts, extra-theatrical activities and interests, and last address known. The disparities among typefaces are not nearly so noticeable as in the previous Gale efforts along this "composite book" line, and this set has even been edited to include death dates up to 1976 when they were not part of the original entry. The entries are *not* a mine of information, but they appear reasonably informative about the famous as well as the obscure. Not the stuff from which great dissertations are made, this set still could be useful to the student of theatre, even though no bibliographical information is included on the entrants. In sum, this could be valuable for minor theatrical figures more than for the major ones on whom book-length individual studies have appeared. [R: ARBA 80, p. 458; Choice, June 79, p. 514; WLB, June 79, p. 720]   Koert C. Loomis, Jr.

21 FILMS

GENERAL WORKS

515. Allen, Nancy. **Film Study Collections: A Guide to Their Development and Use.** New York, Frederick Ungar Publishing, 1979. 194p. index. (Ungar Film Library). $14.00. LC 78-20935. ISBN 0-8044-2001-7.

As interest in and respect for film have grown in the last decade, so has the quantity of film materials. As a result, pressure to develop collections for the study of film has increased dramatically. Nancy Allen has provided those charged with collection development and maintenance with a practical and specific guide. The book includes an annotated bibliography of the monograph series that dominated the field of film studies until the last few years; annotated lists of bibliographies to aid in collection development and maintenance; and lists of periodicals, including mention of where each is indexed and thereby an indication of its value to the majority of researchers. Allen also devotes a chapter to evaluation criteria for published materials, and provides a one-chapter course in the role of nonprint media in film studies and the relation of that material to the copyright law. In addition, she lists 1) sources for scripts, books, and memorabilia, 2) major film archives in the United States, and 3) print and on-line reference resources—all fully annotated. Finally, in case this handbook still appears incomplete, the work includes a chapter on cataloging and classifying all these film study materials, which was written by Michael Gorman, coeditor of *Anglo-American Cataloguing Rules*, 2nd ed.

Amazingly, there is even more to this little book, including a brief discussion of the instruction users of the collection may require and a review of the resources to be found in over 100 film study libraries. All this information is clearly written and well presented. In fact, each chapter has a different format in order to best arrange the information it includes, and it is all indexed by topic, by work, even by film study collection. This guide is clearly a valuable resource. [R: ARBA 80, p. 459; BL, 15 Oct 79, p. 327; JAL, Nov 79, p. 299; LJ, 1 Sept 79, p. 1634]   F. W. Ramey

516. Bawden, Liz-Anne, ed. **The Oxford Companion to Film.** New York, Oxford University Press, 1976. 767p. illus. $29.95. LC 76-1463. ISBN 0-19-211541-3.

The *Oxford Companion* is, as expected, beautifully constructed and well designed; but the content belies the promise of its setting. In the preface we read that the aim is "to answer any query which may occur to the amateur in the course of reading or film-going and lead him on to topics of related interest" (p. vii). Since there are very few bibliographical appendages to articles, the main place one is led is deeper into this peculiar volume.

First, the facts: one alphabet, with cross references; entries ranging from individuals to all kinds of technical terms; small caps indicating the word is an entry; cut-off date at the end of 1974; illustrations from stills reproduced in correct aspect ratio. "Individual films have been selected for entry on grounds of their artistic, historical, or sociological interest" (p. vii).

Herein begins to lie the rub. Selected by whom? The list of contributors is impressive, but none of the articles are signed: a five-page essay on "propaganda," many subjective comments about hundreds of films, value judgments on performers—and all anonymous. For a real hatchet-job review, see *The New York Review of Books* (Sept. 16, 1976, pp. 38-40), where Mark Crispin Miller compares the *Companion* very unfavorably to the fourth edition of Leslie Halliwell's *The Filmgoer's Companion* (see entry 517). Miller is not always correct; we have checked some of the supposed factual errors and found him wrong and the *Companion* right. However, there are glaring omissions from the entries — Films: *Darling, King and Country, The Last Picture Show, Mickey One, An American in Paris, The Great Ziegfeld.* Performers: Mischa Auer, Lili Darvis, Geraldine Fitzgerald, Keir Dullea. Sources: *The Napoleon of Broadway* not cited as source of *Twentieth Century.* There is the aggravating policy of not using standard English variants for the titles of French films (did all the contributors speak French?). Reading the adjectival comments on the film entries ("most affecting," "brilliant," "sensual," "pungent," "outstanding," "incisive," "thoughtful and authoritative") gives one the nagging feeling that the anonymous contributor was writing ad copy. Thomson's eccentricities in his *Biographical Dictionary of Film* (see entry 521) or the American Film Institute Catalog's straightforward (but sometimes unintentionally humorous) plot summaries are much preferable.

Some worthwhile points: The film entries list the major credits, including screenwriter and cinematographer (but giving the running time to the nearest quarter-hour will certainly put off the purist). Real names of performers are given, and birth/death dates. The country and technical entries are mainly well done and not too obscure for the layperson. There is great emphasis on Middle and Eastern European films and film-makers; the contributors have a great affinity for these areas. When I read that Jancsó's *The Round-Up*, with "its cold beauty and accomplished craftsmanship" (676), confirmed him "for foreign audiences as the major figure of the post-fifties Hungarian cinema" (676), all I could think was, "So what else is new?" He is the *only* figure (with the possible exception of Szabó) for foreign audiences of the post-fifties Hungarian cinema, and to most of these foreign audiences his films are tedious to the point of deadliness. But, of course, that too is opinion, and the *OCF* contributors are entitled to theirs, minority though it may be.

Thus, in many ways the *Oxford Companion to Film* is as arbitrary as Thomson while pretending to objectivity. However, it is valuable and useful if approached with discretion and an understanding of its deficiencies and subjectivity. We still need Halliwell and the AFI catalog volumes. By them all else will be measured. Meanwhile, in the second edition of *OCF*, let us hope for signed articles, objectivity, and translation from the French. [R: ARBA 77, p. 481; BL, 15 Sept 77, p. 227; Choice, Apr 77, p. 182; LJ, 15 Apr 77, p. 875; LJ, 1 May 77, p. 1004; WLB, Sept 76, p. 86]   Richard M. Buck

517. Halliwell, Leslie. **Halliwell's Filmgoer's Companion.** 7th ed. New York, Scribner's, 1980. 745p. illus. bibliog. index. $39.50. LC 80-50651. ISBN 0-684-16660-7.

This encyclopedic dictionary, which first appeared in 1966, contains over 11,000 entries, including the names of directors, actors, and producers, and gives dates of birth, film debut, and films participated in. Halliwell has italicized the subject's most significant films (best performance, most commercially successful, etc.). The volume includes 1,000 more entries than the sixth edition, and by the author's count, over 6,000 minor corrections, extensions, and emendations.

Although in general this volume is reasonably comprehensive, there are some shortcomings. As in earlier editions, cast and production credits are not included. The user might refer to *Halliwell's Film Guide* (Scribner's, 1980. 1018p. $36.00) for such credits. The *Film Guide* is recommended as a complement to the *Filmgoer's Companion.*

Each film entry contains an evaluative annotation, but the evaluative part of the entry does in some cases impinge on the description of the work. The same personal taste that has colored other editions has dictated what films receive their own entries here. For instance, while in the entry for Robert Altman, Halliwell designates *Nashville* as the director's greatest work, the only Altman film with its own entry is *M*A*S*H.* And the author's bias in favor of the glorious days of Hollywood abounds in his choice of films, his annotations, and his nominees for "Halliwell's Hall of Fame." As he boldly remarks: "Today's filmmakers lack even the skill to imitate satisfactorily."

A subject index would have been helpful both in locating films and pulling together references to others handling similar themes. The short articles on themes are not well done because of their brevity; for example, the article on abortion attempts to cover the subject in only 151 words. Halliwell should have either created a separate section wherein he could deal with the themes adequately or else eliminated them completely.

Despite the weaknesses noted above, this edition is more comprehensive and up to date than the sixth, and should prove useful to any library patron with either a scholarly or casual interest in cinema.

Norman Frankel
F. W. Ramey

DICTIONARIES AND ENCYCLOPEDIAS

518. Sadoul, Georges. **Dictionary of Films.** Trans., ed., and updated by Peter Morris. Berkeley, University of California Press, 1972. 432p. $21.50; $6.95pa. LC 74-136027. ISBN 0-520-01864-8; 0-520-02152-5pa.

519. Sadoul, Georges. **Dictionary of Film Makers.** Trans., ed., and updated by Peter Morris. Berkeley, University of California Press, 1972. 288p. $20.00; $5.95pa. LC 78-136028. ISBN 0-520-01862-1; 0-520-02151-7pa.

These complementary volumes were originally published in France in 1965; this is their first appearance in English.

Films includes about 1,200 entries (in the original languages with cross references from English) that attempt "to give a panorama of world cinema since its origins" (preface). Each entry includes credit list, running time, short plot summary, and a critical note. For the English edition, Morris has corrected and added to the original entries, and contributed new entries and critical comments of his own – in all cases these changes and additions are indicated. The changing and adding holds true for both dictionaries, each of which is expanded by "some fifteen percent" (introduction).

Film Makers includes over "a thousand entries devoted to directors, scriptwriters, cinematographers, art directors, composers, producers, inventors," but "no technicians, . . . exhibitors, distributors or exporters" (preface). The directors' filmographies are the key – each director's entry includes his own filmography (not always complete, although Morris has expanded the originals) and a critical appraisal. The works included in *Films* are not evaluated here, but their inclusion in *Films* is noted by an asterisk. For this reason – and also because neither work has a separate index and each must act as an index to the other – both should be available to gain full value from either.

The one great lack for English-speaking monolinguists is that titles in *Film Makers* are in French. German and Italian have not been translated when the English release title is a simple translation. For example, if one is using the Jean Renoir entry in *Film Makers* to find the listing for a specific Renoir film in the other volume, he must know it by its French title. In *Films*, although the English release titles are cross referenced to the original language entry, this presupposes that one knows the release title, which is not always the case.

A sampling of the entries in both dictionaries indicated that there are critical comments in most cases, usually the expected ones, to only a few of which one could take exception. Some landmark films such as *Greed* (three columns) and *Intolerance* (two columns) are covered very thoroughly; other entries seem arbitrary: Disney's *Snow White* gets two columns to one for *Wild Strawberries*; *2001* gets one and one-half to one for *The Silence*.

Despite any shortcomings, omissions, errors, or critical misjudgments, these dictionaries are valuable reference tools. They supplement any other bibliographies available in English, including the multivolume catalog produced under the aegis of the American Film Institute. [R: ARBA 73, p. 422; Choice, Mar 73, p. 65; LJ, 1 Oct 72, p. 3138]

Richard M. Buck

520. Spottiswoode, Raymond, gen. ed. **The Focal Encyclopedia of Film and Television Techniques.** New York, Hastings, 1969. $45.00. 1100p. ISBN 0-8038-2268-5.

While calling itself an encyclopedia, this large volume will be most appreciated as a technical manual. Organized in dictionary fashion (1,600 entries) with a visual code to indicate whether the term pertains to film, TV, or both, the book includes the work of the producer, director, cameraman, and editor, and describes technical processes. The text is well illustrated throughout. Added to the main body of the text is a general overview, with cross references to the specifics found in the main text. The book is well indexed, and suggestions for further readings are given with individual entries.

Under a general editorial board, approximately 90 highly competent people (almost all British) have made contributions in special areas. The overall competence of the book is clear, and nothing quite like it exists—certainly not in such a compact form. The writing is clear, and remains very readable without losing its scientific stress, so that readers other than technicians can use the book. In criticism, it must be said that, while all differences between U.S. and U.K. systems are noted, apparently there was no U.S. general consultantship. There are national differences and even national prejudices. Further U.S. editorial involvement would be reassuring to technicians on this side of the Atlantic. [R: ARBA 71, p. 391; LJ, 15 Jan 69; LJ, 15 Apr 70, p. 1440]

Irving Wortis

521. Thomson, David. **A Biographical Dictionary of Film.** New York, William Morrow, 1976. 629p. $9.95pa. LC 75-20044. ISBN 0-688-07974-1.

Thomson's monument to his own critical eccentricities will be a joy to some, a bore to some, and a cause of anger to others. He is fed up with dictionaries that "strive toward objectivity, freedom from bias and elimination of opinion" (p. vii). Therefore, he has compiled "a Personal, Opinionated and Obsessive Biographical Dictionary of the Cinema" (p. viii), and the entries include "the sharp expression of personal taste; jokes; digressions; insults and eulogies" (p. viii). He points out that he has attempted to present useful and stimulating accounts of significant individuals for the perusal of the student, critic, buff, or anyone who believes that cinema contributes to our makeshift culture. For me, he has eminently succeeded; this is the kind of dictionary one really wants to read from cover to cover—it is so much fun to deal with a witty and literate mind that reflects many of one's own cinema tastes. Those who love *The Sound of Music* and other pablum will find little comfort here: "Thus the reassurance that the film, and Julie Andrews, projected seem to me depressing indications of the present middle class capacity for dissociation. Such crass comfort only indicates appalling insecurity" (p. 10).

The factual parts of the entries include the *first* release date of films, original title and English-language variants under the director entry, and English variants *only* under the entry of any actor or actress in the film, complete film lists under the directors, important films only under the performers. Real names of individuals are listed in parentheses after the entry name, followed by birth/death dates and place of birth. All the director entries start with the complete film list, but Thomson doesn't always tell about the career before the person became a director. Performers' and producers' careers are discussed pretty much chronologically.

Although there are some serious omissions in all categories (Leland Hayward, Dustin Hoffman, Al Pacino, Dorothy Arzner, Adolph Zukor), there are beautiful long essays that make one forgive most of the lapses. Thomson gives us three appreciative columns on Pasolini, a thoughtful critical essay on Hitchcock, two-and-a-half pages on Andy Warhol that could not be bettered, and a revealing piece on Max Ophuls in which Thomson expresses his great joy in "discovering" a great director. For these, I can forgive, also, his intense dislike of Stanley Kubrick and Mike Nichols, and his overenthusiasm for Jacques Rivette: *Celine and Julie Go Boating* "I take to be the most important film made since Citizen Kane" (p. 483).

This dictionary is really for anyone who has strong opinions about films and their creators—it makes one want to sit down and do Thomson one better, something that surely has *not* been done by the *Oxford Companion to Film*. Neither can be used as a totally reliable film reference; both must be supplemented by other confirming sources for many facts, but Thomson is more enjoyable and less pretentiously fatuous than the *OCF*. [R: ARBA 77, p. 491; BL, 1 Jan 77, p. 684]   Richard M. Buck

FILMOGRAPHIES

522. **The American Film Institute Catalog of Motion Pictures: Feature Films 1961-1970.** Comp. by The American Film Institute. Richard P. Krafsun, executive ed. New York, R. R. Bowker, 1976. 2v. index. $98.00/set. LC 79-128587. ISBN 0-8352-0453-7.

This massive set (2,240 pages in the two volumes) is the second of the AFI catalog series to be published. As the Bowker press release for this set aptly puts it, "*Feature Films 1921-1930* is a 2-volume work already established as the basic standard reference in the field." The grandiose AFI plan is to produce periodically volumes covering features, shorts, and newsreels from the "beginnings" (1893) to at least 1970. Surely the plans for the 1971-1980 volumes are already underway.

The first volume of the present set includes the alphabetical listing, and this time all foreign releases of any significance that have been shown in the United States are included. For foreign films, the original release date outside the United States is relegated to a note. Under the main entry is found just about all the basic information a researcher needs on a film, although the *complete* credit list has not been transcribed verbatim from the film itself. Copyright, U.S. release date (and usually place), length, color processes, and all other documentable information that could be found is included. Cast lists are complete almost down to the extras, and there is a synopsis, often extensive. This plot summary is usually dry, always objective, quite valuable, and sometimes unconsciously amusing. Needless to say, the synopses take up the greatest amount of space in the volume. There are no critical comments. The notes include varied kinds of information, such as shooting locations, foreign titles, title changes, other productions of the same title, changes in running time, etc.

The second volume of the set is the various indexes—Credit, Literary and Dramatic Source, Subject, and National Production (including U.S.-foreign co-productions). They are extensive, but *not* analytical. The Credit Index gives only name, film, and locating number in the other volume. It would have been more helpful had the name been followed by the kind of credit (actor, director, screenwriter, etc.). The same comment applies to the Literary and Dramatic Source Index, which also lists only name, film, and locating number. The Subject Index seems quite complete, but the method of arranging the subjects after the synopsis of each film in volume I (a "schematic grouping of terms into twelve classes") seems an arbitrary pedantic methodology that smacks of Adler's "101 Great Ideas of Western Man" and makes just about as much sense.

But any carping against this set is like beating an elephant with a fly swatter. It is the second step in a monument to film research that will remain, for the foreseeable future, the definitive source for films released in the United States, and a key to every other source of information on the films. A must for any library where film research is done. (For a good summary of the history and background of the AFI cataloging project, see the article by Phyllis Zucker in *Performing Arts Resources*, Vol. I, 1974, pp. 147-52. [R: ARBA 77, p. 485; BL, 15 Feb 77, p. 920; LJ, July 76, p. 1511; WLB, Oct 76, p. 183]   Richard M. Buck

523.   Emmens, Carol A. **Short Stories on Film.** Littleton, CO, Libraries Unlimited, 1978. 345p. index. $25.00. LC 78-13488. ISBN 0-87287-146-0.

Emmens identifies those films produced between 1920 and 1976 that were based on short stories by American authors or by outstanding international authors who were well known in America. The over 1,300 entries are arranged alphabetically by short story author and subdivided by an alphabetical list of the story titles; therefore, all the films based on a single story are listed in one place. Each entry contains the film title, a source material note, technical information, production credits, cast credits, and an annotation, with a note if applicable. Access to an entry by short story or film title is assured by the title indexes. These follow the directory of distributors, which lists current distributors of prints of the films, not the original theatrical distributors. [R: ARBA 79, p. 509]

524.   **Films on Art: A Source Book.** Comp. and ed. by The Canadian Centre for Films on Art for the American Federation of Arts. New York, published by Watson-Guptill Publications in association with The Canadian Film Institute, 1977. 220p. index. $17.95. LC 77-21339. ISBN 0-8230-1780-X.

This unique, meticulous, and indispensable reference tool is a qualitative list of over 450 films (including some produced for television) pertaining to painting, drawing, prints, sculpture, architecture, photography, and archaeology. Instructions for ordering the films and concise descriptions of the methodology employed in the selection of the films and the compilation of the entries and indexes are followed by the actual list, which is alphabetically arranged by title. Included are: duration; color; gauge; sound; country of origin; date; producer; credits (including director, writer, narrator, photographer, participants); chief consultants; composer; summary description of the contents; and finally distribution (both sales and rentals). Separate subject and artist indexes provide a variety of retrieval accesses as does the alphabetical index, which includes, when applicable, cross references from the titles of individual films to their appropriate series title. Commendably, the compilers have chosen to be selective. All of the films were viewed and evaluated by a highly qualified group of experts; therefore this book, unlike earlier and far less comprehensive publications, includes only films of merit. Unique to this publication is the inclusion of independent filmmakers and small distributors whose films have been judged to be artistically excellent as well as accurate in content. The latter is a critical factor since a large number of superb "art" films have sacrificed factual accuracy in the pursuit of creativity. [R: ARBA 79, p. 509; BL, 1 May 78, p. 1574; LJ, 1 Mar 78, p. 553]   Jacqueline D. Sisson

525.   Hochman, Stanley, comp. and ed. **American Film Directors: With Filmographies and Index of Critics and Films.** New York, Ungar, 1974. 590p. index. (A Library of Film Criticism). $27.50. LC 73-92923. ISBN 0-8044-3120-5.

The first volume of a proposed series on film criticism, this work includes criticism of the films of 65 outstanding American directors, including most of the films of such luminaries as Alfred Hitchcock, Frank Capra, William Wyler, and Stanley Kubrick. For the most part, the reviews are contemporary with the films, but, in some cases, reviews by later critics are included as well. While most of the reviews show perception of the film as art, some that do not are included, as the author states, "to show what an intelligent director was up against."

The entries are arranged chronologically by review date and alphabetically by director, so that occasionally reviews of the same film are not consecutive. Many of the entries are excerpted, so that only pertinent critical portions remain. At the end of each is the reviewer's name and the source of the piece. A list of directors is included, as well as filmographies of the directors and an author-title index. Several directors whose work is divided between the United States and another country (such as Josef von Sternberg and Fritz Lang) are included, but only their American works are discussed.

This tool will provide ready access to criticism that would otherwise be hard to locate, unless one had access to NYPL's fine collection. [R: ARBA 75, p. 532; BL, 1 Apr 75, p. 821; C&RL, Jan 75, p. 65]   Judith Rosenberg

526. Klotman, Phyllis Rauch. **Frame by Frame: A Black Filmography.** Bloomington, Indiana University Press, 1979. 700p. bibliog. index. $25.00. LC 78-20403. ISBN 0-253-16423-0.

If Klotman's filmography is not exhaustive, it is close enough. The sourcebook she has provided for students of black films and for blacks in film is invaluable. Her goal was to list those films to which black Americans, black Latin Americans, black Africans, or blacks from the Afro-Caribbean had made contributions in bit parts or major roles or as directors, writers, or producers. To this end she has provided all available information on approximately 3,000 films.

Each film is categorized by type (feature, comedy short, documentary, etc.), fully described, and annotated. Descriptions include alternative titles or series; the names of narrators, cast, writers, director, and producer; technical information; date; country; and distributor. The annotations are generally non-judgmental, although occasionally an editorial tone does arise in the treatment of those films that are the most racist and simplistic ("Louise Beavers plays her maid's role"). Separate indexes of black performers, authors, scenarists, producers, and directors are well-considered additions to an already ambitious work.

Works like Sampson's sourcebook, *Blacks in Black and White* (Scarecrow, 1977), have treated "race films," and Powers' *Blacks in American Movies* (Scarecrow, 1974) provided lists of feature films. Cyr's *Filmography of the Third World* (Scarecrow, 1976) and Ohrm and Riley's *Africa from Real to Reel* (African Studies Association, 1976) focus on contributions to film made by black peoples from other parts of the world, and Meeker's *Jazz in the Movies* (Arlington House, 1978) includes treatment of black musicians in the cinema. But Klotman has spanned the field. She has brought together a great amount of information in an impressive, inclusive reference source. [R: ARBA 80, p. 464; SLJ, Dec 79, p. 2639]   F. W. Ramey

527. Lee, Walt, comp. **Reference Guide to Fantastic Films: Science Fiction, Fantasy, and Horror.** Los Angeles, Chelsea-Lee Books, 1972-74. 3v. illus. $47.85/set. LC 72-88775. ISBN 0-913974-04-8(set).

Walt Lee has compiled a three-volume work that attempts exhaustive worldwide coverage of fantastic films, identifying some 20,000 films produced over a period of 75 years. Fifteen years in the making, his *Reference Guide* might be compared in bibliographic significance to work done in the literature of fantasy and science fiction by Blieler, Day, Tuck, the New England Science Fiction Association, Clareson, and Hal Hall.

For purposes of his *Guide*, Lee defines fantastic films as "motion pictures depicting exceptions to man's natural conception of reality" as explained by common sense or scientific opinion. The films included are listed alphabetically under theatrical release title, television title, original title if different from the above, and translation of original title. The last three are cross referenced to main listing, as are sequels, other versions of the same story, and closely related titles. Thus, it is possible to locate a film regardless of the name by which it might be known to the researcher. Information following each entry includes some or all of the following: variant title, date of release, country of production, length, cast, credits, character designations, classification, brief content note, and references to reviews. This bibliographical work is accurate, unique in its tremendous scope, and obviously a labor of love. [R: ARBA 75, p. 524; Choice, Feb 74, p. 1847; LJ, 15 Nov 72, p. 3697; RQ, Fall 74, p. 65]   Mary Jo Walker

528.   Weaver, Kathleen, ed. **Film Programmer's Guide to 16mm Rentals.** 3rd ed. Richard Prelinger, associate ed. Albany, CA, Reel Research, 1980. 318p. index. $20.00pa. LC 79-66526. ISBN 0-934456-02-X.

Improved format and increased coverage highlight this third edition from Reel Research. The editor is quick to praise the several grant sources that helped fund the project, and rightly so. The resulting computerization of the data compilation enabled the editors to double the number of distributors listed compared to the last edition, and the film titles have been increased to 14,000. Fortunately, the computer's activity didn't intrude upon the handsome format, an eye-appealing mix of boldface type for the titles and regular type for the remaining data, making the text easy to read despite the small letters.

Feature Films on 8mm, 16mm, and Videotape, 6th ed. (Bowker, 1979. $26.25), by James Limbacher, is the other major source used to identify distributors of feature films. Limbacher lists 6,000 more film titles than Reel Research, and he includes the familiar Swank Company's films, which for some reason Swank would not allow Reel Research to include. Furthermore, Limbacher includes 8mm films and videotape, absent from Reel Research. On the other hand, the *Film Programmer's Guide* lists short films (absent from Limbacher). The *Guide* has an advertising section, while Limbacher does not, though this kind of window dressing seems marginally useful. More important is the *Guide*'s inclusion of the rental cost charged by each distributor of a given film, permitting the film booker an easy side-by-side comparison of costs. For example, the 12 distributors of *The Days of Wine and Roses* range from $35 to $65. Though this cost information may not be entirely current, due to the different publication dates of the distributors' catalogs and subsequent price changes, nevertheless cost comparison of this kind will be increasingly valuable for the economy-minded 1980s.

Like Limbacher, the *Film Programmer's Guide* has a fine index by film director, useful for cinema classes emphasizing a particular director's work. The very prominent large type abbreviations of the distributors' names make for very easy use. However, the paperback, glued-in-pages format may prove inadequate for the heavy usage which this excellent sourcebook is likely to enjoy.

Since both the Limbacher and the *Film Programmer's Guide* have their own unique features, and since each lists distributors not included by the other, both books should be on the desk of anyone responsible for booking feature films.   Richard W. Grefrath

22 RELIGION

GENERAL WORKS

529.   Adams, Charles J., ed. **A Reader's Guide to the Great Religions.** 2nd ed. New York, Free Press, a division of Macmillan, 1977. 521p. index. $17.95. LC 76-10496. ISBN 0-02-900240-0.

When the first edition of this collection of bibliographical essays appeared in 1965, it was quickly hailed as the most authoritative available guide for the study of the world's great religions. We are fortunate in having a second edition that not only sustains this reputation by careful updating but also by substantial (about 50%) expansion. New books and periodical articles through 1975 are appropriately interspersed by topic (not tacked on to the ends of sections). The first edition had eight chapters: primitive religion; religions of China; Hinduism; Buddhism; religions of Japan; Judaism; Christianity; and Islam. The second edition divides Judaism into two chapters and adds the following new ones: the ancient world; religions of Mexico and of Central and South America; the Sikhs; the Jainas; and an appendix entitled "The History of the History of Religions." Each chapter is by a different specialist. The general editor, who is professor and director of the Institute of Islamic Studies, McGill University, also contributes the chapter on Islam.

Each essay contains a good, brief introduction and illuminating comments concerning specialized topics, as well as authoritative evaluations of the many works cited. Most of the items reviewed are in English, with some from European and Oriental languages. Several chapters have bonus features like appendices on major reference books and periodicals. There are an index of authors, compilers, translators, and editors (pp. 477-93) and an index of subjects (pp. 494-521). Both appear to be comprehensive and thorough. It is hard to fault such an excellent work. One does wonder, however, whether sufficient attention has been paid to the religions of Africa (apart from Islam and Christianity). The appearance of Harold Turner's *Bibliography of New Religious Movements in Primal Societies: Volume I: Black Africa* (Boston, G. K. Hall, 1977) would suggest that this may have been an area of comparative neglect. High school, college, university, and medium-to-large public libraries would benefit by the addition of this volume to their reference collections. [R: ARBA 78, p. 496; Choice, Oct 77, p. 1021; LJ, 1 Jan 77, p. 92; WLB, June 77, p. 818]

A. Robert Rogers

ATLASES

530.   Gaustad, Edwin Scott. **Historical Atlas of Religion in America.** Rev. ed. New York, Harper and Row, 1976. 189p. illus. maps. index. $22.50. LC 76-25947. ISBN 0-06-063089-2.

In the preface to the first edition of this survey, Gaustad cites religious statistics as the prime example of the deceptions, ambiguities, and non-sequiturs inherent in statistics in general. In spite of those apparent limitations, that edition was hailed as a milestone in charting religious growth in the United States. The present edition carries the same warning concerning the statistics, since, the author notes, many denominations provide their own statistics (sometimes only estimates), many others refuse to report any statistics, and the federal government has not surveyed religious bodies for over 40 years. All that not-withstanding, Gaustad has made substantial improvements in this new edition, chief among them the use of maps which show denominational strength by counties rather than simply by states, as in the old book. New maps and charts have been added, and the line graphs have been updated. Two maps inserted in a sleeve (in the back) show, in vivid colors, denominational distribution throughout the country as of 1970 and the Protestant-Catholic dominance county-by-county for that same year.

Part 1 covers the period 1650-1800, part 2 covers colonial and large non-colonial denominations for the years 1800-1975, and part 3 surveys non-colonial bodies for that same span, 1800-1975. Part 4 covers special aspects of American religion, such as Indians, Judaism, blacks, Alaska, and Hawaii. Appendices detail the numbers and denominations of churches in 1650, 1750, 1850, and 1950. Within the primary sections, Gaustad provides a capsule history of each denomination, with appropriate maps and charts to illustrate its growth. The style in the text is sometimes mildly irritating (rhetorical questions get old fast, and some flourishes, such as the description of the Methodist bishop Francis Asbury, whose circuit "sowed Methodist seed in unbelievably good soil," may be a bit strong), but it is not boring and does not sacrifice sense or information to verbal effect. This reviewer also had some trouble with the maps showing each particular denomination's strength by county in 1950. For instance, the map of Roman Catholic distribution barely indicates that Denver, Colorado, was the headquarters of a diocese, since it is only a tiny black dot in the center of a primarily white (meaing 1-2 churches per county) state. The statistics for the 1950 maps were taken from studies by the National Council of Churches, and scholars should perhaps study those statistics in their original form rather than rely solely on these maps. Indexes are to authors and titles, places, religious bodies, and names and subjects.

However, for anyone, scholar of layperson, interested in the general progress of religion in America or simply in the progress of one particular denomination (13 major bodies and numerous minor ones), this revised study will be indispensable. Perhaps in the long run, the stylistic excesses are not so objectionable, since they contrast so much with the graphs, maps, and charts that the volume considered as a whole emerges as rarely dull and constantly enlightening. [R: ARBA 77, p. 493; Choice, Oct 77, p. 1023]

Koert C. Loomis, Jr.

531. **Historical Atlas of the Religions of the World.** Isma'il Ragi al Faruqi, ed. David E. Sopher, map ed. New York, Macmillan, 1974. 346p. illus. maps. index. $21.95. LC 73-16583. ISBN 0-02-336400-9.

This book is far more than a collection of maps. There are 20 chapters (prepared by 13 scholars from various parts of the world) that give historical background, illustrated by 65 maps and well over 100 black-and-white photographs. The chapters, which are signed, vary in length from 4 to 5 pages to over 30 pages. The major divisions of the atlas are as follows: religions of the past (Mesopotamia, Egypt, Canaan-Phoenicia, greater Syria, ancient Greece and Rome, Shamanism, Amerindian religions); ethnic religions of the present (traditional religions of Africa, Hinduism, Jainism, Sikhism, Confucianism and Taoism, Shinto, Zoroastrianism, Judaism); universal religions of the present (Theravada Buddhism, Mahayana Buddhism, Christianity, Islam).

The work is well organized for reference purposes. The preface concludes with a short bibliography. The list of contributors and their credentials is followed by the table of contents and a list of maps. Each article contains a select bibliography. There are helpful chronologies for religions of the past and the present. The subject index is reasonably detailed, and there is an extensive index of proper names. The maps (especially for African and Far Eastern religions) break new ground in the field of religious cartography. [R: ARBA 76, p. 522; BL, 15 Dec 75, p. 592]

A. Robert Rogers

BIBLIOGRAPHIES

532. McCabe, James Patrick. **Critical Guide to Catholic Reference Books.** 2nd ed. Littleton, CO, Libraries Unlimited, 1980. 282p. bibliog. index. (Research Studies in Library Science). $22.50. LC 80-16209. ISBN 0-87287-203-3.

The most comprehensive annotated guide to reference works relating to Catholicism has been updated and revised to include new works and new editions, bringing the total to over 1,100 entries. The annotations are evaluative and contain quotes from and references to reviews. While the main emphasis is on works in English, foreign-language titles have been freely included if they are widely known, comprehensive in scope, and scholarly; if there is no English-language equivalent; or if they are more up to date than similar English-language works or translations.

The reference works are grouped into five chapters: general reference works, theology, humanities, social sciences, and history. The books listed fall into two classes: 1) those dealing with topics peculiar to the Church, such as liturgy and other theological disciplines; and 2) those dealing with the social sciences, literature, the arts, and similar subjects to which Catholics have traditionally contributed a unique perspective. An extensive author/title/subject index concludes the work. A valuable and scholarly basic guide in Catholic studies as well as a useful aid for ecumenical researchers. [R: ARBA 81; Choice, Dec 80; LJ, 1 Nov 80]

533. Rowe, Kenneth E., ed. **Methodist Union Catalog: Pre-1976 Imprints, Volume IV: Do-Fy.** Metuchen, NJ, Scarecrow, 1979. 436p. $22.50. LC 75-33190. ISBN 0-8108-1225-8.

The fourth volume in this set, for which 20 volumes plus indexes are planned, continues the impeccable bibliographic standards adhered to in the first 3 volumes. Without question, this work will be the standard bibliography on Methodism and the writings of Methodists, some of which have nothing to do with religion (e.g., William Preston Few's Harvard Ph.D. dissertation on aspects of Middle English syntax, p. 285).

This reviewer does want to register one very mild complaint about the apparent omission of anything related to Methodism not in print form. The scope is clearly limited to "imprints," and, of course, it is unfair to wish this set were something it does not claim to be. And yet any serious research into contemporary Methodism has to include films and other teaching media, such as flannel graphs produced by church boards and publishing houses as well as tapes of religious radio broadcasts. Could the editor, the highly respected Methodist librarian at Drew University and editor for the American Theological Library Association, be persuaded, perhaps, to do a nonprint addendum?   Joseph McDonald

DICTIONARIES

534. Brauer, Jerald C., ed. **The Westminster Dictionary of Church History.** Philadelphia, Westminster Press, 1971. 887p. $19.95. LC 79-11071. ISBN 0-664-21285-9.

In the light of Brauer's comment that coverage emphasizes the modern period, with particularly heavy concentration on the church in the United States, this reviewer found a surprisingly wide range of people and topics from all periods and countries in the generally brief (10 to 30 lines) articles. (There are a few longer articles on major topics with brief bibliographies appended.) Arrangement is alphabetical. There are a few "see" references. Over 140 contributors from various parts of the United States wrote articles which were edited by specialists in early church history, the medieval period, the Reformation, and modern times. Proportionality and factual accuracy appear to be well maintained. The relatively small number of Roman Catholic contributors led this reviewer to examine several articles (including Council of Trent, Ignatius of Loyola, Teresa of Avila, Vatican I and II) for evidence of bias. The impression which emerges is not one of polemic or deliberate distortion, but simply that the compilers are more at home in a liberal and ecumenical Protestant perspective. Vatican II does receive more cordial treatment than Vatican I, but fairness and factuality usually prevail. Church and seminary librarians will find this book indispensable, while reference librarians servicing religion collections in college, university, and medium-to-large public libraries should also find it very useful. [R: ARBA 72, p. 437; BL, 15 Jan 72, p. 401]   A. Robert Rogers

535. Davies, J. G., ed. **The Westminster Dictionary of Worship.** Philadelphia, Westminster Press, 1979. 385p. illus. $12.50. LC 78-25582. ISBN 0-664-21373-1.

Originally published in 1972 (Macmillan) as *A Dictionary of Liturgy and Worship* and now reprinted under a new title, this excellent ecumenical work concentrates mainly on Christian worship, with some attention to other religions. Signed articles by the 65 contributors contain not only definitions, but historical accounts and, where substantial differences exist, subsections on the viewpoints of the various denominations. Some entries include brief bibliographies. The 43 black-and-white photographs and 27 sketches are particularly useful for illustrating church architecture and ecclesiastical vestments. There is no index, but the cross references, though insufficient in number, are useful. Another valuable source is Gerhard Podhradsky's *New Dictionary of the Liturgy* (Alba House, 1967).   A. Robert Rogers

536. **Dictionary of Comparative Religions.** S. G. F. Brandon, general ed. New York, Scribner's, 1970. 704p. bibliog. $27.50. LC 76-111390. ISBN 0-684-31009-0.

This concise dictionary covers iconography, philosophy, anthropology, and the psychology of primitive, ancient, Asian, and Western religions. There are articles about the religion of specific groups, such as the Hittites, as well as on practices and philosophies, such as ancestor worship and existentialism. Many entries contain cross references, and short bibliographies are appended to major articles. There is a list of terminology relevant to each major religion. A comprehensive general index guides the reader to subjects that do not have independent entries but that are treated in related articles. [R: ARBA 71, p. 396; Choice, Jan 71, p. 1490; C&RL, Jan 71, p. 39; LJ, 1 Oct 70, p. 3263; RQ, Spring 71, p. 264; WLB, Jan 71, p. 499]

537. Douglas, J. D., general ed. **The New International Dictionary of the Christian Church.** Rev. ed. Grand Rapids, MI, Zondervan Publishing House, 1978. 1074p. $24.95. LC 74-8999. ISBN 0-310-23830-7.

Like the *Oxford Dictionary of the Christian Church* (see entry 541), this work is international and ecumenical, with coverage of all denominations and periods of church history. Among the 4,800 articles are numerous biographies, some definitions of theological terms, descriptions of movements, short accounts of Christianity in various countries, and articles on other religions that have interacted with Christianity. A list of the 150 contributors with their credentials is given, and all articles are signed. Scholars from Australia, Canada, South Africa, and a few other countries have contributed; but most authors are from the United Kingdom or the United States and tend to represent a conservative Protestant viewpoint. A deliberate sampling of controversial topics ("Abortion," "World Council of Churches," "Fosdick, Harry Emerson") revealed a high degree of fairness. The claims on the dust jacket about extensive revisions since the first edition in 1974 are more sweeping than the modest statement by the editor in the preface. The only bibliography in the sample of articles examined with an imprint later than 1974 was the one with the article on "Women in the Church." (Most articles do not have bibliographies.) This is a good reference book, especially for public libraries; but those with the first edition may not need the second. [R: ARBA 79, p. 517]   A. Robert Rogers

538.   Henry, Carl F. H., ed. **Baker's Dictionary of Christian Ethics.** Paperback ed. Grand Rapids, MI, Baker Book House, 1978. 726p. $11.95pa. LC 74-83488. ISBN 0-8010-4199-6.

Non-evangelicals may take exception to the use of the word "Christian" in the title of this dictionary, since it definitely represents evangelical perspectives only. Apart from the title, though, there is certainly no attempt to disguise this orientation.

This paperback edition reproduces without any alteration the original hardcover published in 1973. It is somewhat dated, yet still useful as a compilation of representative (but not necessarily definitive) evangelical viewpoints, and as a source of factual information on specific thinkers, schools, and positions. There is more diversity among evangelicals than some of the articles would suggest, and that diversity is probably even greater now than in 1973, particularly on such issues as abortion, homosexuality, and the status of women. A revision, particularly with updated bibliographies, would have been preferable to this reprinting. Lacking that, and with nothing better available that would be similar in coverage, this dictionary can still be recommended for libraries where there is interest in Christian ethics. The paperback binding may not take well to extremely heavy use but should be adequate under normal conditions. [R: ARBA 74, p. 432; ARBA 80, p. 473; WLB, Feb 74, p. 504]   Hans E. Bynagle

539.   Hughes, Thomas Patrick. **A Dictionary of Islam, Being a Cyclopaedia of the Doctrines, Rites, Ceremonies, and Customs, together with the Technical and Theological Terms of the Muhammadan Religion.** London, 1885; repr., Delhi, India, Oriental Publishers; distr., Columbia, MO, South Asia Books, 1973. 750p. illus. bibliog. index. $32.00.

This antique has a wealth of information on the sciences of Islam: the Koran (it serves as a dictionary of its terms, has a synopsis of the entire book, and is, in effect, a subject index of Koranic verses because most articles are larded with relevant quotations from the Koran as well as Hadiths, the oral traditions of the Prophet); Hadith terminology; philosophy and theology; Islamic law; festivals; and popular Islam. Other aspects of Arab-Islamic civilization are also included, such as a 12-page illustrated history of the Arabic script; Arabic dictionaries; Muslim houses; and dozens of brief biographies.

Aimed at Hughes' fellow Christian missionaries, and at British officials who were ignorant of Islam but had to deal with it on a daily basis in India, it provides complete, careful explanations and definitions that presuppose no previous knowledge. Indeed, many of Hughes' articles, which generally range from 5 to 100 lines of this double-columned tome (sometimes more), are much more comprehensible than the often technical and confusing, albeit highly useful, scholarship of the *Shorter Encyclopedia of Islam* (Leiden, Brill, 1961), next to which it should be shelved. Heading terms are either in English for the Christian who would look up religious subjects in Christian terminology, or in romanized Arabic, with cross references from the unused form. There is a separate index of the terms in Arabic script that accompany each article. There are innumerable cross references between articles. Despite evident Christian bias, Hughes made an honest effort to provide all the facts, utilizing the latest Western and Eastern works as well as classical Arabic sources, many of which are cited in the articles. This Indian edition, it should be noted, is complete, in contrast to the 1965 Pakistani reprint (Lahore, 1965), which excised many of Hughes' statements that are offensive to Orthodox Islam.

Hughes' work and the *Shorter Encyclopedia* as yet have not been equalled, let alone surpassed in usefulness. [R: ARBA 74, p. 432; Choice, Sept 73, p. 944]

David W. Littlefield

540.   Neill, Stephen Charles, Gerald H. Anderson, and John Goodwin, eds. **Concise Dictionary of the Christian World Mission.** Nashville, Abingdon Press, 1971. 682p. (World Christian Books). $10.50. LC 76-21888. ISBN 0-687-09371-6.

This carefully edited work appears to be more comprehensive than *The Encyclopedia of Modern Christian Missions: The Agencies* (Thomas Nelson, 1967), which is the only modern book even remotely comparable. The entire period of Christian expansion from 1492 to the present is covered. The editorial viewpoint may be described as international, ecumenical, and liberal. Over 200 contributors from all over the world have written signed articles (most with bibliographies).

Countries, leaders, and subjects are treated in concise, yet comprehensive, articles arranged in one alphabet with three types of cross references: from headings not used to those that are used; from small topics without separate articles to larger topics that include the smaller; and from words in the text that are themselves subjects of separate articles (such words being indicated by asterisks). A random check of 10 words revealed no blind references. Large and small countries alike are included. Treatment in the samples examined was proportional to each country's importance (e.g., five pages for China and nine lines for Portuguese Guinea). Entries normally include basic facts (area, population, brief history, major religions) as well as matters specifically pertaining to Christian missionary activity. Leaders still alive are not included. Nor are leaders (e.g., Niebuhr, Tillich) without strong missionary identification. There are entries for Carey, Grenfell, Martyn, Mott, Latourette, Ricci, Scudder, and Xavier. Treatment of Vatican II is brief and confined to the missionary aspects. Similar consistency applied to other subjects sampled. [R: ARBA 72, p. 438; Choice, June 71, p. 534; LJ, July 71, p. 2296; WLB, Feb 72, p. 543]

A. Robert Rogers

541. **The Oxford Dictionary of the Christian Church.** 2nd ed. Ed. by F. L. Cross and E. A. Livingstone. New York, Oxford University Press, 1974. 1518p. $48.00. LC 74-163871. ISBN 0-19-211545-6.

Soon after its initial publication in 1957, the *ODCC* was recognized as one of the most indispensable one-volume reference works covering the broad spectrum of Christianity. It contained approximately 6,000 entries ranging from just a few lines to about 2,500 words, and nearly 4,500 brief bibliographies. Minor corrections and additions were incorporated in several reprintings, but in many ways this second edition is an entirely new work. The volume has been increased in size by one-tenth through the addition of 200 new articles and over 50 additional "see" references. The number of contributors was enlarged from 94 to 247, and the dictionary has been completely reset. Minor, often subtle, changes have been incorporated in many of the articles, and a great many of the bibliographies have been expanded and updated (through 1972). New features include a memoir to Frank Leslie Cross (d. 1968) and a Chronological List of Popes and Antipopes. (Still absent, however, are companion lists of archbishops of Canterbury and patriarchs of Constantinople.)

Some of the notable new entries are: Aggiornamento; Coventry; Ecumenical Movement; "Honest to God"; Humanae Vitae; North India, Church of; Orthodox Church; Pacem in Terris; Process Theology, Taize Community; and Vatican Council, The Second. Among the over 60 new biographies are ones on Athenagoras (1886-1972), O. Cullmann, El Greco, G. F. Fisher, M. Heidegger, John XXIII, Martin Luther King, H. R. Niebuhr, M. Noth, Paul VI, A. M. Ramsey, Teilhard de Chardin, and Ralph Vaughn Williams. Coverage of the Eastern Orthodox Church, particularly in its liturgical terminology, has been considerably enlarged, and the inclusion of abbeys and monasteries has been increased, although neither term, per se, is defined. One continuing serious deficiency is the poor coverage of American Christianity. Because 25 entries have been either shortened or deleted, there may be some value in having both editions readily available. [R: ARBA 75, p. 537; BL, 1 Dec 74, p. 384; Choice, July 74, p. 741; WLB, Nov 74, p. 246]

Glenn R. Wittig

542. Parrinder, Geoffrey. **Dictionary of Non-Christian Religions.** Philadelphia, Westminster Press, 1973 (c1971). 320p. illus. $10.95. LC 73-4781. ISBN 0-664-20981-5.

This one-volume dictionary contains a large number of brief entries dealing with deities, cults, sacred objects, names and places, philosophies and philosophers, and other terms associated with non-Christian religions throughout history. The stress seems to be on Hinduism, Buddhism, and Islam. There are 242 small drawings that are clear and very well done. The 94 black-and-white photographs are helpful, but some are dark and lacking in clarity. Three listings of dynasties and a short bibliography are appended.

The entries tend to be short and factual, with a considerable number of cross references added. The language is usually simple and easy to understand, which adds to the ready reference value of the work. The *Dictionary of Comparative Religions* (see entry 536) has some of the terms and names, with more information. However, the present work includes many items not found in that dictionary. In addition, its entries are certainly easier to read and therefore will probably be more useful for the layperson. Since reference works in religion have tended to include less information on non-Christian religions, this work serves a very useful purpose. [R: ARBA 74, p. 433; BL, 1 June 74, p. 1070; LJ, 1 Sept 73, p. 2424; WLB, Jan 74, p. 419]

Dennis Thomison

543. Penrice, John. **A Dictionary and Glossary of the Koran; with Copious Grammatical References and Explanations of the Text.** London, Curzon Press; distr., Totowa, NJ, Rowman and Littlefield, 1976. 166p. $12.50.

This work, a reprint of the 1873 edition, is still the only reliable and practical glossary of the *Qur'ān* available to English speakers starting on the pursuit of Islamic studies. Because Penrice provides extensive explanations of both textual references and the Arabic grammar of the *Qur'ān*, the beginning student can proceed into this work without encountering the jungle of a large classical Arabic dictionary and without becoming discouraged by failing to find classical terms and references in a dictionary of modern literary Arabic.

Penrice based his work on the 1834 edition of the *Qur'ān*, edited by Fluegel and printed at Leipzig. This edition is still available in reprint and would be a logical reference source along with Penrice. The present edition of Penrice has included, in addition to his original preface, a new introduction to Professor Serjeant of Cambridge, suggesting more current reference tools than were available to Penrice, including Arberry's translation of the *Qur'ān*, and other works in English.

The Arab world, predominantly Muslim in religion, is moving closer to center stage on the world scene. In this world, the *Qur'ān* is not simply a religious text but is considered to be the literal word of God. Quotations from it appear almost daily in the speeches and writing of Arabs from all walks of life, and those in the West who would truly understand Arab society in order to negotiate with it on any level, need some understanding of its religious base. For any serious introductory study of the text of the *Qur'ān*, Penrice has provided an indispensable tool for speakers of English. [R: ARBA 78, p. 502]

Margaret Anderson

544. Stutley, Margaret, and James Stutley. **Harper's Dictionary of Hinduism: Its Mythology, Folklore, Philosophy, Literature, and History.** New York, Harper and Row, 1977. 372p. bibliog. $35.00. LC 76-9999. ISBN 0-06-067763-5.

In the past, when one sought a competent reference book on Hinduism, (s)he was faced with Dowson's *Classical Dictionary of Hindu Mythology and Religion*, characterized as a "little fraud" in one review, Walker's *Hindu World* (1968), which the *Times Literary Supplement* termed hostile to Hinduism and "a miserable performance," or Farquhar's *Outline of the Religious Literature of India*, which, although published in 1920, still served as a provisional encyclopedia of Hinduism. This incredible lacuna has been marvelously overcome by the Stutleys' dictionary.

The 2,500 entries include most aspects of religion, philosophy, and mythology and also key personal and geographical names. The definitions are rigorously thorough and objective; virtually all of them provide historical as well as philosophical and religious analysis. Information is drawn from both the Hindu texts and scholarly works, and entries have explanatory and bibliographic footnotes. Scholars will find the use of Monier-Williams' *Sanskrit-English Dictionary* transliterations a major plus, although student users will occasionally be baffled when commonly used spellings do not match the formal transliterations. A bibliography of approximately 1,000 items is appended, as is a list of 200 or so common English terms and their Sanskrit equivalents.

Students of Hinduism finally have a tool to match the recent dictionaries and encyclopedias of Buddhism. This outstanding work will be a standard reference tool in libraries for many years to come. [R: ARBA 78, p. 503; Choice, May 78, p. 380; LJ, 15 Nov 77, p. 2335; LJ, 15 Apr 78, p. 817; WLB, May 78, p. 729]   Leon J. Stout

ENCYCLOPEDIAS

545. **The Catholic Encyclopedia.** By Robert C. Broderick. Nashville, Thomas Nelson, 1976. 612p. illus. (part col.). $24.95. LC 76-10976. ISBN 0-8407-5096-X.

This encyclopedic dictionary includes about 4,000 entries intended to cover new terms and provide a reassessment of older ones; entries also cover books and notable persons of the Bible and descriptions of denominations and religions other than Catholic. Currently used abbreviations for Catholic organizations are listed, honors and awards are briefly described, and the more familiar hymns and prayers are included, often with their words in English. The volume bears the imprimatur.

Most of the entries relate directly to Catholic beliefs and practices. Entries are arranged in one alphabet, word by word, and range in length from 20 to about 2,500 words (the latter for only a few entries—e.g., Vatican II and heresies). A number reflect recent developments: parish council, marriage encounter, and new order of the Mass. "See" references are adequate in most cases. Pertinent biblical texts are freely cited, as well as documents of Vatican II, the latter often quoted in part. There are no appended bibliographies. On the whole, the articles are readable and well selected for a work intended for home and school use. It is in no sense a scholarly theological dictionary.

Virginia Broderick, illustrator of many Catholic books, has done 150 attractive black-and-white drawings that accompany the text. These are more useful than the three separate sections giving 51 colored and black-and-white photographs, chiefly of religious art and architecture and eminent persons. Robert Broderick, the editor, is a freelance writer and author of the *Concise Catholic Dictionary*.

This work is not comparable with the multi-volumed *New Catholic Encyclopedia* (see entry 546), which covers many more subjects and in much greater detail. However, it is similar in purpose to *The Maryknoll Catholic Dictionary*, compiled and edited by Albert J. Nevins (Grosset and Dunlap, 1965). Its 10,000 entries, on the whole more succinctly treated, include many hymns, terms, and place and personal names not found in *The Catholic Encyclopedia*, which in turn contains many newer terms not found in the dictionary. The dictionary usually gives pronunciation and derivation.

The Catholic Encyclopedia does not replace *The Maryknoll Dictionary*, but it serves as a very useful supplement for home and school use. [R: ARBA 77, p. 501; BL, 15 Feb 77, p. 924; Choice, Mar 77, p. 40; LJ, 1 Nov 76, p. 2264; WLB, Dec 76, p. 366]

Frances Neel Cheney

546. **New Catholic Encyclopedia.** Prepared by an editorial staff at the Catholic University of America. Washington, Publishers Guild, in association with McGraw-Hill, 1967-1979. 17v. illus. $450.00/set. LC 66-22292.

Not a revision of *The Catholic Encyclopedia* (see entry 545) but an entirely new work, *The New Catholic Encyclopedia* emphasizes Catholic topics and the Catholic Church in the English-speaking world, although topics of a more general nature are discussed. Some 4,800 scholars, Catholic and non-Catholic, contributed signed articles with appended bibliographies. There are 17,000 articles accompanied by over 300 maps and 7,500 excellent illustrations. Biographies do not include living persons.

Current issues receive detailed treatment here, while the original *Catholic Encyclopedia* gives greater emphasis to historical articles.

An extensive bibliography and an index form volume 15 of the set. Volumes 16 and 17 (published in 1974 and 1979, respectively) are supplements to the basic set. The acquisition of the supplements is mandatory for any library possessing the main volumes of the *Encyclopedia*. [R: ARBA 76, p. 519; BL, 1 Sept 75, p. 67; Choice, Sept 75, p. 818; ARBA 80, p. 476]

BIBLE STUDIES

547. Botterweck, G. Johannes, and Helmer Ringgren. **Theological Dictionary of the Old Testament, Volumes I-III.** Grand Rapids, MI, William B. Eerdmans Publishing, 1974-1978. 3v. $18.50/vol. LC 73-76170. ISBN 0-8028-2325-4(v.1); 0-8028-2326-2(v.2); 0-8028-2327-0(v.3); 0-8028-2338-6/set.

The quantity and quality of works dealing with Sacred Scripture have grown over recent decades. An already acclaimed addition to that body of biblical interpretation is this *Theological Dictionary of the Old Testament*, a monumental work by international scholars, which is being translated into English in a projected 12 volumes. Volumes 1 and 2 were well received, and volume 3, which covers *gillulîm-hāras*, likewise contains much useful information. Arrangement in this work is alphabetical by Hebrew or Aramaic word, with emphasis on Hebrew terminology and biblical usage. Each article treats both the etymological and the biblical usage of the words, as well as historical-critical interpretation. Related terms and words with similar roots are discussed. Usage of this important reference work requires at least an elementary preparation in Hebrew, and its audience is definitely the student and scholar. Generous bibliographical footnotes and the many references accompanying each article provide ample opportunity for follow-up and further research. A welcome addition to biblical scholarship. [R: ARBA 76, p. 524; Choice, Jan 75, p. 509; ARBA 80, p. 481]   Harry S. Otterson

548. **The Broadman Bible Commentary.** Clifton J. Allen, general ed. Nashville, Broadman, 1969. 12v. $8.00/v. LC 78-93918.

The purpose of this 12-volume commentary is to make the Bible known and understood in the context of modern life. The scholars contributing to this effort are primarily from the Southern Baptist Convention. For each book of the Bible there is an introduction and an outline; a paragraph-by-paragraph interpretation and exposition of the text (the Revised Standard Version is used) is developed within that framework. The introductions deal with questions of purpose, date, authorship, and setting.

A sampling indicates that the work achieves its aim of avoiding extremes in interpretation. Volume 1 contains general articles on the Bible, translations, interpretation, geography, archaeology, the canon, history of Israel, theology of the Old Testament, and contemporary approaches to Old Testament study; it also contains the introductions and commentaries on Genesis and Exodus. In volume 8 there are general articles on the background, canon, theology, and contemporary study of the New Testament, plus introduction and commentary on Matthew and Mark; volume 9 is concerned with the gospels of Luke and John. In addition to bibliographical footnotes in the text, there is a select bibliography at the end of each introduction. No index is included in individual volumes. [R: ARBA 71, p. 400; Choice, May 70, p. 363; Choice, June 70, p. 523; Choice, Feb 71, p. 1643; Choice, Oct 71, p. 992; LJ, 1 Feb 70, p. 500]   Joseph W. Sprug

549.   **The Cambridge History of the Bible.** Ed. by P. R. Ackroyd and C. F. Evans. New York, Cambridge University Press, 1963-70, 1975pa. 3v. illus. bibliog. index. $45.00/v.; $120.00/set; $14.95pa./v.; $37.50pa./set. LC 63-24435. ISBN 0-521-07418-5(v.1); 0-521-04255-0(v.2); 0-521-29016-3(v.3); 0-521-08778-3(set); 0-521-09973-0(pa. set).

Contents: Volume 1: *From the Beginnings to Jerome*, edited by P. R. Ackroyd (1970); Volume 2: *The West, from the Fathers to the Reformation*, edited by G. W. H. Lampe (1969); Volume 3: *The West, from the Reformation to the Present Day*, edited by S. L. Greenslade (1963).

This history does not deal directly with the contents of the Bible nor with the science of biblical scholarship. Rather, it is "an account of the text and versions of the Bible used in the West, of its multiplication in manuscript and print and its circulation; of attitudes toward its authority and exegesis; and of its place in the life of the Western Church." Volume 1 deals with the origin of the text of the Christian Bible, the development of the canon, and the place of the Bible in the early Church. Volumes 2 and 3 concern themselves with the place of the Bible in the Church during the periods indicated, and especially with the various translations, revisions, and printings of the text.

Approximately 50 scholars from all denominations contributed the essays of which each volume is composed. Some articles are highly technical, while others are written in lively narrative fashion with touches of humor. A few articles assume knowledge of Hebrew, Greek, Latin, French, or German, incorporating foreign words or phrases in the text and appending multilingual bibliographies. Also, each volume includes a detailed table of contents, an extensive general index, an index of biblical references, and from 25 to 50 black-and-white plates. Volume 3 also contains appendixes on commentaries and other aids to Bible study. There are no table of contents or index for the set as a whole. Recent versions of the Bible (e.g., the *Living Bible* and the *New English Bible*) appeared after this work went into production and therefore do not appear in it. [R: ARBA 72, p. 442; Choice, Mar 71, p. 82; LJ, July 70, p. 2483; LJ, 15 Apr 71, p. 1328; ARBA 76, p. 525]
James P. McCabe
A. Robert Rogers

550.   Davis, John D. **Davis Dictionary of the Bible.** 4th rev. ed. Philadelphia, Westminster Press, 1924; repr., Grand Rapids, MI, Baker Book House, 1972. 888p. illus. ISBN 0-8010-2805-1.

First published in 1898, this important Bible dictionary was revised by its original compiler in 1903, 1911, and 1924. In 1944, a revision by Henry Snyder Gehman was published under the title *The Westminster Dictionary of the Bible*. In 1954, Baker Book House reprinted Davis' original work with permission of the former publishers. Some 18 reprintings were issued.

The present version (the nineteenth) incorporates several changes — almost 50 pages of photographs and 26 full-color maps. Meanwhile, Gehman revised and expanded his version (*New Westminster Dictionary of the Bible*, see entry 551), thus widening the differences without eliminating important similarities. The article on "Aaron" is almost word-for-word the same. However, Davis called the etymology "doubtful," whereas Gehman says "probably of Egyptian origin." Gehman gives a phonetic pronunciation. The same scripture references are cited, and the same cross references to other articles are given.

However, Davis quoted from the Authorized Version and the Revised Version, whereas Gehman uses the Revised Standard Version. Two areas of striking difference are the inclusion of new articles in the text and the use of photographs and maps. Davis has no textual entries for "Dead Sea Scrolls" or "Qumran," while Gehman devotes about two pages to each. The photographs and maps appear to be totally different. Both books are well bound. The typography and layout of Gehman are superior. [R: ARBA 73, p. 430]

A. Robert Rogers

551.   Gehman, Henry Snyder, ed. **The New Westminster Dictionary of the Bible.** Rev. ed. Philadelphia, Westminster Press, 1970. 1027p. illus. maps (part col.). (Westminster Aids to the Study of the Scriptures). $16.95. LC 69-10000. ISBN 0-664-21277-8.

Although somewhat narrow in viewpoint, this revision of the author's 1944 work is a useful source of detailed information on over 5,000 biblical persons, places, and things. Hundreds of photographs, maps, and charts illustrate the articles, which are of moderate length and which contain an abundance of etymological, historical, political, and geographical detail. Pronunciation is given for each word, but bibliographies are not supplied. References to scriptural passages and occasionally to some major authorities are provided. Frequent cross references and an appended selection of "Historical Maps of Bible Lands" add to the book's reference value.

The main value of the work probably lies in its readily available factual content and not in its interpretations, which are the work of one man and which reflect traditional Protestant viewpoints more extensively than Jewish or Catholic veiwpoints. Information is lacking on some of the more current scriptural developments in such areas as hermeneutics, for which there is no article; eschatology, for which there are six lines; hope, which is not included (although faith and charity are); and immortality and the resurrection, which receive sketchy treatment. However, Gehman does consider relevant archaeological discoveries of the recent past and includes information about such topics as the Dead Sea Scrolls and Qumran. On the whole, this revision represents a considerable improvement over the previous text. The book is well bound and typography and layout are superior. [R: ARBA 71, p. 401; Choice, Feb 71, p. 1643; LJ, 1 Sept 70; RQ, Spring 71, p. 268]

James P. McCabe

552.   **The International Standard Bible Encyclopedia, Volume 1: A-D.** Geoffrey W. Bromiley, general ed. Rev. ed. Grand Rapids, MI, William B. Eerdmans Publishing, 1979. 1006p. illus. (part col.). maps. index. $29.95. LC 79-12280. ISBN 0-8028-8161-0(v.1); 0-8028-8160-2(set).

Originally published in 1915 and revised in 1929, this classic work has undergone extensive revision over the past 15 years by an international (mainly American and British) and ecumenical (mainly Protestant) team of scholars, headed by Geoffrey W. Bromiley, professor of church history and historical theology, Fuller Theological Seminary, Pasadena, California. Intended for scholars, pastors, and laypersons, it includes articles on all persons and places mentioned in the Bible and also treats theological and ethical topics. In addition, there are articles on such matters as the Canon of the Old Testament, the Canon of the New Testament, and tools for Bible study (commentaries, concordances, etc.).

Articles typically provide pronunciation, etymology (transliterated), and evolution of meaning through the Old Testament and the New. Some carry the discussion through church history to the present. All of the longer articles are signed, and the contributors (with information about their positions) are listed in the front. Authors of articles from the original edition are asterisked. There are numerous cross references, black-and-white photographs, line drawings, and maps, in convenient proximity to the text. At the end of volume 1, there are 26 color maps with an index to the maps. Articles are entered under words used in the Revised Standard Version, with references to comparable terms in the King James Version, the American Standard Version, and the New English Bible. Detailed information about arrangement and instructions for use are given in the front.

A sampling of articles (e.g., "Authority," "Baptism," "Divorce") indicates a scholarly, conservative approach to biblical interpretation, but with some recognition of different viewpoints. Planned for completion in four volumes, this new edition is recommended for church and seminary libraries and for those public and academic libraries that need well-rounded collections in religion to answer inquiries from their users. [R: ARBA 80, p. 473; LJ, 15 Nov 79, p. 2446] A. Robert Rogers

553. Kittel, Gerhard, and Gerhard Friedrich, eds. **Theological Dictionary of the New Testament.** Geoffrey W. Bromiley, translator and editor. Grand Rapids, MI, Eerdmans, 1964-1976. 10v. $255.00/set. LC 64-15136. ISBN 0-8028-2323-8.

With the translation of the tenth, index volume, the *Theologisches Wörterbuch zum Neuen Testament* was fully translated into English for the first time. The intent of the editors of the entire work has been to provide lexicographical links with theology, utilizing words (including meaningful prepositions and numbers) of theological significance. This is an important publication for the understanding of the Bible, and an indispensable starting point for serious study of the ideas of the New Testament. Since the first fascicle appeared (in German, 1932), this work has been regarded as a classic, as one of the best products of Protestant scholarship of this or any century. There has been praise for the accuracy of translation and quotation in Bromiley's rendition.

Articles vary in length: one or two pages for less significant terms; booklet length for such words as *agape* or *hamartia*. The longer articles, packed with information and bibliographical leads, are preceded by a contents note.

The index volume renders the information in the entire work easily accessible. This volume consists of indexes of English keywords, Greek keywords, Hebrew and Aramaic keywords, and most extensive, biblical references (subdivided according to Old Testament, the Apocrypha, and the New Testament). Following notes on contributors and co-workers, a detailed "Pre-history of the *Theological Dictionary of the New Testament*" is presented, covering the Complutensian Polyglot translation/commentary and all other commentaries up through Cremer and Deissmann.

In conjunction with the *Theological Dictionary of the Old Testament* (see entry 547), this set will provide scholar and minister alike with incomparable entry into biblical theology. [R: RBA 71, p. 402; ARBA 77, p. 506; Choice, June 70, p. 526; Choice, Mar 73, p. 62] Joseph W. Sprug
Bohdan S. Wynar

554. Laymon, Charles M., ed. **The Interpreter's One-Volume Commentary on the Bible.** Nashville, Abingdon Press, 1971. 1386p. illus. maps. (part col.). index. $22.95; $27.95 (thumb-indexed ed.).

This commentary, based on the Revised Standard Version of the Bible, includes the books of the Apocrypha. It is the result of many years of research and the work of 70 Bible scholars from the United States, Canada, and Great Britain. Designed for use by laypersons, ministers, librarians, and anyone studying the Bible, it includes commentary on historical background, scope, and significance of each book of the Bible; many general articles; full-color maps; and many sketch maps, drawings, and photographs. Two indexes (to scripture references and to subjects) further enhance the usefulness of this valuable work.

Another essential title by Abingdon Press is *The Interpreter's Dictionary of the Bible: An Illustrated Encyclopedia* (5v. 1976. $84.95), one of the most authoritative sources of modern biblical studies. Based on the King James Version and the Revised Standard Version, the *IDB* contains several thousand entries contributed by scholars from many countries, accompanied by excellent illustrations. [R: ARBA 72, p. 443; C&RL, July 72, p. 322; LJ, 15 Apr 72, p. 1387; WLB, Oct 71, p. 193]

555. Léon-Dufour, Xavier, ed. **Dictionary of Biblical Theology.** 2nd ed., rev. and enl. New York, Seabury, 1973. 712p. (A Crossroad Book). $22.50. LC 73-6437. ISBN 0-8164-1146-8.

This dictionary is a preeminent one for biblical theology. The French original — *Vocabulaire de théologie biblique*, which was published in 1962 and enlarged in 1968 — has been highly praised. The English translations followed in 1967 and 1973, and the dictionary has been or is being translated into 11 other languages as well.

The differences between the two editions are considerable. Among the 40 new articles are those on adultery, anguish, city, conscience, dreams, farewell speeches, perfume, responsibility, salt, and violence, as well as one on Jesus Christ (a topic strangely missing from the first edition). Most of the original articles have been revised and/or corrected by their respective authors. Fuller and more detailed cross references have been added at the end of each article. The index (or more precisely, the reading guide) that has been added arranges a large number of the articles under three major theological divisions. The new work is almost 100 pages longer.

Due to an editorial mix-up, the analytic table of all terms discussed in the dictionary still appears separately at the back of the volume, instead of being interspersed alphabetically as announced in the foreword (and as is actually done throughout the first 10 pages). Uncommon abbreviations are used for the books of the Bible. [R: ARBA 75, p. 542; Choice, Mar 74, pp. 62, 64]   Glenn R. Wittig

556. Morrison, Clinton. **An Analytical Concordance to the Revised Standard Version of the New Testament.** Philadelphia, Westminster Press, 1979. 770p. illus. maps. $45.00. LC 77-26210. ISBN 0-664-20773-1.

Among concordances to the English Bible, the most famous is that of Cruden's, first published in 1737. Two others — more complete and including analytical information — were compiled by Robert Young and James Strong, but they, too, are based on the KJV and its unreliable Greek text. Too many advances in scholarship have occurred within this century for these works to suffice any longer. While there are available good, modern English concordances (one for the superior RSV was computer-produced within months following the publication of that translation), Morrison's work is the first truly modern analytical concordance. As such, it is a landmark contribution. It analyzes the English of the RSV New Testament (2nd ed., 1971) and the original Greek words being translated, yet requires no knowledge of the Greek to use. It is handsomely formatted on 2-column 7½x10½-inch pages, typographically clean and clear, and as convenient and easy to use as a dictionary. The introductory "Explanatory Notes" is superior to anything else ever seen, and cross references are minimally yet fruitfully employed. This is an important new tool of superb quality.

Ths work is divided into two major sections: the concordance proper and an index-lexicon. In the concordance, every entry begins with the English word presented in boldface capital letters. A subtitle line comprised of three elements — definition, the Greek word, and an English transliteration of the Greek word — follows. Then every Scripture passage containing the English word is cited, reference first, followed by a line of context material. "Idiomatic" and "contextual" renderings are also identified. The order of presentation of the index-lexicon is as follows: the transliterated Greek word in boldface capital letters, followed by the ancient Greek spelling, appears on the title line, and the English word(s) used by the RSV to translate the Greek word appears indented underneath, together with the frequency of occurrence in parentheses. This section also serves as an index to the concordance. Two appendices ("Notes on the Analysis of the RSV New Testament" and "Former Readings of the RSV New Testament") and two maps complete the work. [R: ARBA 80, p. 483; Choice, Oct 79, pp. 996-98; LJ, Aug 79, p. 1551]

Glenn R. Wittig

557. The New International Dictionary of New Testament Theology. Colin Brown, general ed. Translated, with additions and revisions, from the German *Theologisches Begriffslexikon zum Neuen Testament*. Grand Rapids, MI, Zondervan Publishing House, 1975-1978. 3v. index. $27.95ea. (v.1 & 2); $39.95(v.3); $90.00(set). LC 75-38895. ISBN 0-310-21890-X(v.1); 0-310-21900-0(v.2); 0-310-21910-8(v.3); 0-310-21928-0(set).

The *New International Dictionary of New Testament Theology* is a translation of the German *Theologisches Begriffslexikon zum Neuen Testament*, published from 1967 to 1971. The *Dictionary* is limited to terms that are considered to be of "theological relevance," thus excluding historical, geographical, and archaeological terms one would normally expect to find in a general Bible dictionary. Its purpose is "to provide an introduction and the tools to enable the reader to make his own way into the field of study." This work actually goes beyond a mere translation, as Brown and the contributors have revised and expanded the original German articles to include more recent literature and scholarly research. The useful bibliographies at the end of the articles have also been enlarged, and now provide English works in addition to the titles listed in the German edition.

Entries are arranged alphabetically by the English terms. Each entry contains the following: discussion of the term in secular Greek (including references to classical literature, inscriptions, and papyri); treatment of the word and related terms in the Old Testament; and discussion of the word and related terms in the New Testament (noting statistical occurrences, usage in relation to background, and specific emphases of individual writers and writings).

Volume 1 provides a lengthy list of abbreviations and a key to the transliteration of Hebrew, Greek, and Arabic words, as well as a "Glossary of Technical Terms." The third volume contains a combined index to all three volumes, providing access by Hebrew and Aramaic words, Greek words, and by subject.

The *Dictionary* is a thorough, scholarly work, which reflects extensive research and high standards. This authoritative source will be invaluable to ministers, students, teachers, and others involved in biblical studies. [R: ARBA 77, p. 504; ARBA 78, p. 509; ARBA 80, p. 1060]

Susan C. Holte

558. Owens, John Joseph. **Genesis.** 1st ed. New York, Harper and Row, Publishers, 1978. 306p. (Analytical Key to the Old Testament). $5.95pa. LC 77-7852. ISBN 0-06-066406.

Some 30 years ago, when the study of the biblical languages was considered more important to the ministry than the pursuit of sociological problems, there was an adage among Catholic seminarians that "Hebrew is the language of heaven; purgatory consists in learning it." Unfortunately, such welcome aids as the book under consideration generally were not available then. Just imagine—a complete, word-by-word, columnar listing of the text of Genesis in Hebrew, with translation and exhaustive grammatical analysis! The analysis also includes the root verb and page number of the Brown-Driver-Briggs lexicon, where each word can be found and further studied. Chapter and verse numbers are centered over the analysis of each verse for those who are not completely confident in their reading knowledge of Hebrew. The text is that of Kittel's seventh edition, but textual variants are also treated in the analysis. In a quick glance over the contents, the only "mistakes" that the reviewer could detect were probably the result either of the photo-printing or of an unevenly registered copy of the Hebrew text used for the printing; e.g., in 1:1 (p. 1) *hashshamiim* appears for *hashshamaim*, where *pathakh* has become *khirik* by default. But the user of this work undoubtedly would have his Kittel at hand, so that there would be no dire consequences. The work is very carefully and clearly compiled, and it should prove to be a great help to biblical students (at $5.95, a real bargain). [R: ARBA 79, p. 524]

Francis J. Witty

559. The Encyclopedia of Philosophy. Paul Edwards, ed.-in-chief. New York, Macmillan, 1967; repr., New York, Macmillan, 1973. 8v. in 4. index. $125.00. LC 67-10059. ISBN 0-02-894950-1.

A four-volume reprint of the eight-volume original, which was published in 1967. Approximately 1,500 articles attempt to cover philosophy in its entirety—both Eastern and Western—including relevance to other disciplines. Some articles are of such length that they could constitute small books, and most have prodigious bibliographies. More than 500 philosophers from throughout the world have contributed to this work, and their names, brief credentials, and major publications are provided.

Biographical coverage of ancient, medieval, and early modern philosophers is generally good. That of contemporary philosophers is better for Western Europe, North America, and India than it is for the Soviet bloc and the People's Republic of China. There are excellent articles on philosophical movements, major ideas, the philosophies of various disciplines, and the history of philosophy in various countries. Articles of particular interest include those on philosophical bibliographies, dictionaries, encyclopedias, and journals.

The integrated approach has been preferred to a series of short articles, and subtopics can be located by use of the detailed index in volume 8. Although the type size has been reduced, the print is still very easily read. This is a valuable, definitive encyclopedia. [R: ARBA 75, p. 546; BL, 1 Nov 73, p. 253; WLB, Dec 73, p. 276]

560. Flew, Antony, ed. consultant. A Dictionary of Philosophy. New York, St. Martin's Press, 1979. 351p. $20.00. ISBN 0-312-20921-5.

This is a good work of its kind—concise, single volume, easy to use, providing explanations of terms as well as brief articles on key thinkers, movements, ideas, and subdivisions of the field. Useful for both students and professionals (some articles presuppose more background than others), it is generally clear and well organized.

There are two comparable works, each likewise titled *Dictionary of Philosophy*, currently in print. One, edited by D. D. Runes (several editions), has not been significantly updated since its first edition in 1942 (when, incidentally, it was repudiated by 13 of its contributors). It remains somewhat useful, especially for oriental philosophy (scantily covered by Flew) and historical figures presently considered minor. The other, by A. R. Lacey (Routledge & Kegan Paul, 1976. $14.95), is a more serious competitor. Flew has many more entries, including many for shorthand designations or nicknames for concepts, ideas, or theories—e.g., "boo-hooray theory," "Buridan's ass," "chain of being," "Hume's fork"—not found in Lacey. Flew's biographical articles are longer (up to 4,000 words for major figures) and more useful than Lacey's. On the other hand, Lacey has a few entries not found in Flew, and some articles are much better or more expansive than their counterparts in Flew (e.g., those on "Categories" and "Thinking"). Flew gives some coverage to non-Western thought (mainly through survey articles), Lacey none. Both emphasize Anglo-American philosophy and epistemological and logical topics. Lacey's chief advantage is his bibliographies, sometimes surprisingly extensive. Flew has no bibliographies. In sum, the three philosophical dictionaries do not simply duplicate each other; many libraries could use all three. For general usefulness, I would rank Flew first, Lacey second.

Though this work bears Flew's name, a well-recognized one in Anglo-American philosophy, it is unclear how much responsibility he bears for its contents. The title page identifies him as "editorial consultant." A later page lists a different name as editor, along with an assistant editor and 33 contributors, including Flew. [R: ARBA 80, p. 489]

Hans E. Bynagle

561. Guerry, Herbert, ed. and comp. **A Bibliography of Philosophical Bibliographies.** Westport, CT, Greenwood Press, 1977. 332p. index. $25.00. LC 77-71862. ISBN 0-8371-9542-X.

Surveys in the past have shown that most reference questions in philosophy are bibliographical in nature. Although bibliographies abound, bibliographies of bibliographies in philosophy are scarce. This work fills a real gap. The compiler has attempted international coverage for the period since the invention of printing (c.1450) through 1974. Scope is confined to separately published bibliographies and those appearing in journals, with only a few major bibliographies that appeared as appendices to monographs. There are 2,353 entries, numbered consecutively. The first part (1-1,395) is arranged alphabetically by individual philosophers and schools bearing their names. The second part is arranged alphabetically by topic. There is a name index (pp. 313-32), which refers to entry numbers, and there are cross references. Some items are annotated, though most are not.

Generally, the bibliography is easy to use, and its scope and arrangement are clearly explained in the introduction. Coverage is international, though mainly in Western languages. Non-Roman alphabets (e.g., Russian) are transliterated. Titles in oriental languages are both transliterated and translated, with note of the original language. There is no entry or cross reference for "Confucianism" in the subject portion, though relevant items may be found under "Chinese philosophy." On the other hand, there is a cross reference "Hinduism. See Indian philosophy and Hinduism." There is only one entry under "African philosophy," but this may reflect level of publication; much that is relevant may be found under "Islamic or Arabian philosophy." In the samples checked, cross references and index references to item numbers were found to be accurate. On the other hand, a few minor typos were noticed — e.g., "Enggus" instead of "Engels" in the cross reference under "Communist philosophy," and the difference between "Rodi, Fritjof" in the index and "Rodi, Fritjob" in the entry under the item number. Generally, however, the level of accuracy appears to be reasonably high. Recommended for college, university, and large public libraries. [R: ARBA 78, p. 512; BL, 1 Oct 78, p. 321; Choice, May 78, p. 374; LJ, 15 Dec 77, p. 2492; RQ, Summer 78, p. 349]

A. Robert Rogers

562. Reich, Warren T., ed.-in-chief. **Encyclopedia of Bioethics.** New York, Free Press, a division of Macmillan Publishing, 1978. 4v. index. $200.00. LC 78-8821. ISBN 0-02-926060-4.

The *Encyclopedia of Bioethics* is a comprehensive source of information on ethical and social issues in the life sciences, medicine, health care, and the health professions. Bioethics as a recognized discipline did not exist 10 years ago, but modern technological advances have produced new ethical problems — prolongation of life, euthanasia, abortion, amniocentesis, gene therapy, behavior control, the definition of death — all questions of basic human values and rights. The *Encyclopedia* was designed to "synthesize, analyze, and compare the positions taken on the problems of bioethics, in the past as well as in the present, to indicate which issues require further exploring, and to point to anticipated developments in the ethics of the life sciences." Designed not only to aid students and researchers, the *Encyclopedia* may aid professionals in decision making, developing policy, and further research.

The editors recognize that the material can quickly become outdated. The *Encyclopedia* is not a definitive statement of fixed categories, but intends to summarize and analyze the historical development and current state of a topic to facilitate understanding of current and future thought. Topics are viewed at various levels: the range of concrete ethical problems; the basic concepts and principles that define the problem; the ethical theories that guide conduct in the area; the religious traditions involved; the history of medical ethics applied to the problem; and the various disciplines bearing on bioethics. Bioethics includes medical ethics but also involves other social science disciplines as well. So, while the bulk of the editorial advisors and the authors of articles are health-care professionals and philosophers, specialists in law, religion, racism, civil disobedience, advertising, etc., are represented. The editorial board, which has some "big names," like the late Margaret Mead and Elisabeth Kübler-Ross, was chosen to represent not only the American point of view, but the non-American and non-Western as well. The 285 contributors represent 15 countries.

Entries are arranged alphabetically, ranging from "abortion" to "women and biomedicine." Since many entries require an interdisciplinary examination, an entry may be composed of several articles by different authors. Technical language has been avoided. Articles are geared to an educated person who may not be a specialist in the subject. Each article is signed by its author and followed by a selective bibliography. If an article refers to another work, it is cited in the text and listed in the bibliography. Cross references are supplied when appropriate, and the work has a comprehensive index. Future research will make portions of this work obsolete, but occasional supplements can remedy the problem. The *Encyclopedia of Bioethics* addresses topics of current popular interest and will be a valuable acquisition in many academic and public libraries. [R: ARBA 80, p. 490; Choice, Nov 79, p. 1150; LJ, 1 Mar 79, p. 616; WLB, Sept 79, p. 66]   Janet H. Littlefield

563. Wiener, Philip P., ed.-in-chief. **Dictionary of the History of Ideas: Studies of Selected Pivotal Ideas.** New York, Scribner's, 1973-74. 5v. illus. index. $255.00/set. LC 72-7943. ISBN 0-684-13293-1(set).

In view of the interdisciplinary character of the curriculum in academia, this interesting work seems to be timely and long overdue. Its major emphasis is on intellectual history. Over 300 articles included in the five-volume compendium describe significant ideas in Western thought, demonstrating the interrelationships of intellectual concepts in different disciplines. The reader will find, generally speaking, three types of articles: cross-cultural studies limited to a given century or period; studies that trace the origin of certain thoughts from antiquity to the present time; and finally, studies that trace the evolution of an idea in the writings of its leading proponents. Each article is signed (contributors are well-known authors from various countries), and each concludes with a bibliography that lists not only the works referred to in the text but also some standard titles pertaining to a given topic. At the end of each article are a number of helpful cross references that direct the reader to related material. There is a separate index volume.

As indicated above, the interdisciplinary character of this work emphasizes intellectual history. Thus, a number of articles deal with literature and the arts, philosophy, history, religion, science, mathematics, and the broad spectrum of social sciences. There are many articles of particularly contemporary significance—academic freedom, civil disobedience, and social attitudes toward women, to name only a few. As Philip P. Wiener indicates in the preface, "the purpose of these studies of the historical interrelationships of ideas is to help establish some sense of the unity of human thought and its cultural manifestations in the midst of a world of ever-increasing specialization and alienation. These cumulative acquisitions of centuries of work in the arts and sciences constitute our best insurance against intellectual and cultural bankruptcy. Taking stock of the ideas that have created our cultural heritage is a prerequisite of the future growth and flourishing of the human spirit" (vol. 1, p. vii). We think that these objectives have been achieved in this work. [R: ARBA 74, p. 442; BL, 1 Oct 74, p. 189; BL, 1 Feb 75, p. 581; Choice, Oct 73, p. 1173; LJ, 1 Nov 73, p. 3250; WLB, Sept 73, p. 83; WLB, Jan 75, p. 359]   Bohdan S. Wynar

MYTHOLOGY AND FOLKLORE

564. **Brewer's Dictionary of Phrase and Fable.** Centenary Edition. Rev. by Ivor H. Evans. New York, Harper & Row, 1971. 1175p. $22.95. LC 79-107024. ISBN 0-06-010466-X.

This British work has a long history, the first edition having been published in 1870. Three more recent editions were published in 1959, 1963, and 1970 by Cassell and Company in Great Britain and Harper & Row in this country.

The present edition is based on that of 1963, but the editor, as he explains in the preface, "sought to return more closely to Dr. Brewer's original conception by discarding entries, e.g., Artesian Wells, which seemed to have little claim to be in a dictionary of Phrase and Fable. Words which have no particular 'tale to tell' have also been deleted, as well as numerous words and technical expressions, etc., for an explanation of which the average reader would naturally turn to the household dictionary, general encyclopedia, or specialized reference book." Thus, this dictionary includes primarily colloquial and proverbial phrases in a wide range of subjects (archaeology, history, religion, the arts, the sciences, etc.), as well as biographical and mythological references, fictitious characters, and other hard-to-find information. In this edition, there are many more Americanisms, and repetitions have been largely eliminated by comprehensive cross referencing. Nevertheless, we would recommend that libraries also keep the old edition, since some of the material that was dropped in this new edition may occasionally be useful. [R: ARBA 72, p. 455]

565. Briggs, Katharine M. **A Dictionary of British Folk-Tales in the English Language, Incorporating the F. J. Norton Collection. Part A, Folk Narratives. Part B, Folk Legends.** Bloomington, Indiana University Press, 1970-71. 4v. bibliog. indexes. LC 70-97241.

In the British Isles, the study of folklore developed slowly. The latter part of the nineteenth century saw collections of local legends of some north and west counties, but these were mostly amateurish rather than scholarly projects. Not until the appearance of *A Dictionary of British Folk-Tales* has the British material been brought together in any kind of organized fashion. Dr. Briggs, who is recognized as the outstanding student of the British folk-tale today, has previously published, with Ruth L. Tongue, *Folktales of England*. This was a selection of surviving tales drawn from oral sources along with scholarly apparatus.

The work reviewed here is an ambitious collection of British folk-tales from various printed and manuscript sources. Many have been found in obscure county collections, in general periodicals like *Notes and Queries*, and in other sources where they have lain buried. Among the unpublished sources have been the manuscript and tape collections of F. J. Norton, Ruth L. Tongue, the School of Scottish Studies, and the Irish Folk-Life Commission. Part A consists of folk narratives, or tales told primarily for entertainment. They are presented full-length or in summary, with reference to the immediate, original, and parallel sources. Arrangement is by type, following the universally used Aarne-Thompson system: fables, fairy tales, jocular tales, novelle, and nursery tales. Legends comprise the two volumes of part B; unlike the narratives, these are tales that were believed and told as true by the folk narrator. Their arrangement is by subject: black dogs, bogies, devils, dragons, fairies, ghosts, and giants. Legendary material cannot be fitted into the Aarne-Thompson scheme. The legend, being a supposedly true account, is not embellished in the telling, as the narrative frequently is, and Dr. Briggs has tried to restrict part B to those tales that reported what was actually believed. In order to hold the collection to a manageable and publishable length, she has excluded those tales of the British Isles in the Celtic, Gaelic, Irish, and Welsh languages, admitting only those handed down in English. Tales differing only in slight detail have also been omitted. About 850 narratives are included in part A, and over 1,200 legends in part B. Whether given in their original form or in summary, they are written well, are authoritative, and are fully documented. Each of the two parts includes a bibliography, a motif or classified index, and an index of story titles. The most complete collection of the British folk-tale yet published. [R: ARBA 72, p. 456; Choice, Dec 70, p. 1353; C&RL, Jan 71, p. 43; LJ, 1 Oct 70; LJ, Aug 71, p. 2480; LJ, 15 Apr 72, p. 1386; WLB, Jan 7, p. 499]   Rolland E. Stevens

566. Briggs, Katharine. **An Encyclopedia of Fairies: Hobgoblins, Brownies, Bogies, and Other Supernatural Creatures.** New York, Pantheon Books, 1977 (c1976). 481p. bibliog. illus. index. $12.95. LC 76-12939. ISBN 0-394-40918-3.
     Material to "enthrall and horrify" has been collected here. And that it does. Briggs, somewhat legendary among folklorists herself, has collected material on "that whole area of the supernatural which is not claimed by angels, devils or ghosts" in Britain over the last 10 centuries. It is arranged alphabetically, and generously cross referenced by use of words and names in solid capitals. There are illustrations (Rackham, Fuseli, J. Simmons, and others), but they surely should have been in color (the only cavil that this reviewer has concerning the book). A list of those works most cited (that bear further investigation by the reader) has been appended, as have been type and motif indexes based on Stith Thompson's *Folk-Motif Index.* (Even the indexes are interesting!)
     Fairy morality. Impetigo. Changeling. Phouka (*pooka*). Trooping fairies. Solitary fairies. Dependence of fairies upon mortals. Banshee. Meg Mullach. Selkies. Keightley, Thomas. Dress and appearance of the fairies. Dragons. Mermaids. Wish hounds. These and many others. Briggs' prose is as pithy as it ought to be, and she quotes generously and well from her sources. Each entry is also noted as to when types or motifs are pertinent, an indication of how much knowledge has gone into this work. Every collection needs something with "a wild fairy air" about it, and this is *the* work. (R: ARBA 78, p. 518; BL, 1 Feb 77, p. 751; Choice, July/Aug 77, p. 652; LJ, 1 Dec 76, pp. 2468-70; RQ, Fall 77, p. 71; WLB, May 77, p. 778]   Koert C. Loomis, Jr.

567. Cotterell, Arthur. **A Dictionary of World Mythology.** 1st American ed. New York, G. P. Putnam's, 1980. 256p. illus. maps. bibliog. index. $12.95. LC 79-54889. ISBN 0-399-12464-0.
     Arthur Cotterell, a British writer whose previous works have been studies of Chinese history, has now written a concise guide to diverse mythologies. As many reference librarians will testify, information about Western mythologies, especially regarding the Greek, Roman, and Norse gods, is much more accessible than information about more exotic mythological figures. The strength of Cotterell's book is that it includes all areas of Asia, the Americas, Africa, and Oceania as well as Europe. Each section begins with an overview of the historical development of myth and religion in the area. The remainder of each section is an alphabetical listing of the major deities, place names, and mythological terms. This arrangement makes it possible to use the book either as a general introduction to a mythology or as a reference to specific names or terms. Entries vary in length from 35 words to a page or more. All are concise, clear, and written in a lively, personal style.

Supplementary material includes a four-page listing of books suggested for further reading. Many of the books are standard works, and the list will be useful to many readers, although the citations include only the place and date of first publication. Black-and-white photographs throughout the book break up the text and give some examples of the way in which mythological themes have influenced art, but the poor reproduction of many of the pictures makes them less useful than they otherwise would have been.

Both academic and public libraries will find this inexpensive book useful, especially as a source of information about the mythologies of non-Western cultures.   Adele M. Fasick

568.   Ireland, Norma Olin. **Index to Fairy Tales, 1949-1972: Including Folklore, Legends & Myths in Collections.** Westwood, MA, Faxon, 1973. 741p. (Useful Reference Series, No. 101). $18.00. LC 26-11491. ISBN 0-87305-101-7.

Compiled as a continuation of Mary Huse Eastman's *Index to Fairy Tales, Myths and Legends* (Boston, Faxon, 1926. Supps. 1937, 1952), this work begins where Eastman's second supplement stops. Some 406 collections have been indexed, under titles and subjects. Included are all the fairy tales, folklore, legends, and myths of all countries that appear in these collections. Authors have been included only when specifically mentioned in the collections being indexed. Main entries are under titles. Comprehensive subject headings have been chosen with the needs of children's librarians in mind. The ALA filing rules are followed in arrangement of entries. The extensive subject indexing is an innovation and a major improvement over Eastman. Cross references (both "see" and "see also") enhance the usefulness of the book, which should be an immense timesaver for busy reference and children's librarians. [R: ARBA 74, p. 445; BL, 15 Feb 74, p. 607; Choice, Feb 74, p. 1847; Choice, Nov 74, p. 1273; LJ, 1 Dec 73, p. 3544; LJ, 15 Apr 74, p. 1099; WLB, Dec 73, p. 340]   A. Robert Rogers

569.   Leach, Maria, ed. **Funk & Wagnalls Standard Dictionary of Folklore, Mythology, and Legend.** New York, Funk & Wagnalls; distr., New York, T. Y. Crowell, 1972. 1236p. index. $22.95. LC 72-78268. ISBN 0-308-40090-9.

This is a one-volume, but complete and uncut version of *Funk & Wagnalls Standard Dictionary of Folklore, Mythology, and Legend*, published in two volumes in 1949-50. The significant feature of this edition is a key to the 2,405 countries, regions, cultures, areas, people, tribes, and ethnic groups presented or discussed in the book. As is well known, this dictionary offers comprehensive coverage of customs, beliefs, songs, tales, heroes, dances, games, etc., for the various cultures of the world, including survey articles with bibliographies on individual regions and on special topics. [R: ARBA 73, p. 437; BL, 1 Nov 73, p. 253; LJ, 15 Mar 73, p. 858; RQ, Spring 73, p. 318]

570.   **The New Century Handbook of Greek Mythology and Legend.** Ed. by Catherine B. Avery. New York, Appleton-Century-Crofts, 1972. 565p. illus. LC 75-183796. ISBN 0-13-611996-4.

This encyclopedic dictionary of figures from ancient Greek mythology has been extracted from a larger work, *The New Century Classical Handbook*. The text is very readable and is intended to entertain as well as instruct. Some of the articles have been prepared by the late Jotham Johnson and by professors Abraham Holtz and Philip Mayerson. The book contains approximately 900 entries; those on the principal 14 gods and heroes, such as Apollo, Athena, Heracles, or Zeus, are long and detailed, with 400 or more lines each. Attractive, small illustrations are reproduced from authentic vase paintings. Each page is provided with a guide to pronunciation. In the final analysis, this is a popular compilation: no bibliography, few references to sources, and little or no critical analysis of the subject material. The book should be particularly useful for school assignments, but its value for serious students is limited. [R: ARBA 73, p. 438; Choice, Oct 72, p. 954]

Theodore M. Avery, Jr.

571. Tripp, Edward. **Crowell's Handbook of Classical Mythology.** New York, Thomas Y. Crowell, 1970. 631p. illus. $16.95. LC 74-127614. ISBN 0-690-22608-X.

Original sources used in the compilation of this handbook have included most of the major writers of classical antiquity, usually in versions most familiar to modern readers. Citations refer to editions in the Loeb Classical Library. Coverage, though less complete than in monumental works such as Roscher's *Ausführliches Lexikon der griechischen und römischen Mythologie*, appears to be more comprehensive than in Oswalt's *Concise Encyclopedia of Greek and Roman Mythology* (Follett, 1969) or the Greek and Roman sections of *Larousse Encyclopedia of Mythology* (Prometheus, 1959).

The arrangement is alphabetical by specific subjects. Cross references are fairly plentiful. Complete information is given under the main entry, with shorter accounts under other headings. It is easier to use than Larousse. There are maps and family trees, but no other illustrations, in marked contrast to Oswalt (which must average almost one per page) and Larousse (which even has a few color plates). Pronunciations are given in a separate "Pronouncing Index" (pp. 611-31). Though not glamorous in appearance, this volume is sturdily bound, generously leaded, and printed in very readable type on good quality paper. [R: ARBA 71, p. 412; BL, 1 May 71, p. 716; LJ, 1 Dec 70, p. 4159; LJ, 15 Apr 71, p. 1328; WLB, Jan 71, p. 499]

A. Robert Rogers

POPULAR CUSTOMS

572. Gregory, Ruth W. **Anniversaries and Holidays.** 3rd ed. A revision of the work by Mary Emogene Hazeltine. Chicago, American Library Association, 1975. 246p. bibliog. index. $12.50. LC 74-23163. ISBN 0-8389-0200-6.

The precursor of this work was Mary Hazeltine's *Anniversaries and Holidays*, 2nd ed. (Chicago, ALA, 1944). For many years librarians have regretted that Hazeltine's very useful book was completely obsolete. Indeed, the need for a complete revision was urgent. The world today is a completely different place from what it was in the 1940s. Most of the nation states existing today did not exist then, and each of today's nation states has its own anniversaries and holidays, to cite only one reason for a revision.

The revision by Ruth Gregory follows the organization of her model. Like the earlier work, the revision is divided into three parts: the "Calendar of Fixed Dates," arranged calendrically (January through December); the "Calendars of Movable Days," subdivided according to the Christian, Islamic, and Jewish calendars and the festivals of the Eastern and Western worlds; and a bibliography of books about anniversaries and holidays.

The Calendar of Fixed Dates constitutes the body of the book (146p.). Set forth month by month and day by day, the entries very briefly describe the reason why each day is special to someone, somewhere. Example: "July 3—Idaho Admission Day. Idaho became the 43rd state on July 3, 1890."

Part II (Movable Days) is theoretically more complicated. For example, the differences in calendrical systems (Julian, Gregorian, Jewish, Islamic) are important, and their implications for dating have to be explained. The explanations are good as far as they go, but in many instances they should go further. The great Christian movable feast, Easter, is not, as it should be, elucidated in terms of how Easter Sunday is fixed each year. The bibliography is a sound, workable, and thoroughly updated tool containing complete citations. The index is sufficiently detailed to provide access by all pertinent points of reference—people, places, political units, etc. [R: ARBA 76, p. 533; BL, 15 Nov 76, p. 497; Choice, May 76, p. 348; RQ, Summer 76, p. 355; WLB, Mar 76, p. 556]   Richard A. Gray

573.   Hatch, Jane M., comp. and ed. **The American Book of Days.** 3rd ed. New York, H. W. Wilson, 1978. 1214p. index. $50.00. LC 78-16239. ISBN 0-8242-0593-6.

The appearance of the third edition of the *American Book of Days* is itself a welcome occasion. While Douglas' work has been a reference staple since the late 1930s, it has been sadly out of date for several decades (the second edition was published in 1948). The new editor, Jane Hatch, preserved the purpose and style of the first two editions, but pruned some material no longer pertinent to users of the 1980s and added much new material as well as updating and revising the whole.

Emphasis is given to historical events relative to the founding and development of the United States and to major religious and public holidays. Dates of admission to the Union for all the states are recorded in separate articles. Topics such as Native American and women's rights are expanded. In addition, some 240 new articles were added plus 56 new biographies. In addition to the contents (a full listing of articles arranged chronologically from January 1 to December 31), the index also aids in accessing topics, key people, and events contained in the lengthy articles. Not all names and events cited in articles are found in the index, but it is a great improvement over the second edition. The third edition of the *American Book of Days* provides a wealth of data on historic events of the American nation. [R: ARBA 80, p. 495; BL, 1 Dec 79, p. 571; Choice, July 79, p. 648; LJ, 1 Mar 79, p. 619; WLB, Apr 79, p. 590]   Christine Gehrt Wynar

574.   Inge, M. Thomas, ed. **Handbook of American Popular Culture: Volume 1.** Westport, CT, Greenwood Press, 1978. 404p. index. $25.00. LC 77-95357. ISBN 0-313-20325-3.

With the increase of courses and the establishment of programs devoted to the study of popular culture within our universities, this work has appeared at an opportune time. The *Handbook* represents a serious effort to incorporate into one volume bibliographic data important to the study of 15 major areas of popular culture. Included are the following: animation, automobile, children's literature, comic art, detective and mystery novels, film, gothic novels, popular music, pulps, radio, science fiction, sports, stage entertainment, television, and westerns. A separate chapter, prepared by an authority within the field, is devoted to each of the above topics and provides the user with a concise history of the medium; a critical essay on the standard bibliographies, histories, journals, reference works, and critical studies; an excellent description of various research centers as well as collections of primary and secondary source materials; and a bibliography to the cited books, articles, and periodicals. A proper name index completes this volume.

A second volume, published in 1980, includes those areas of popular culture not covered within this handbook. In general, for those interested in popular culture, this work will prove to be quite a valuable resource. Recommended for large public and academic libraries. [R: ARBA 80, p. 496; LJ, 15 Jan 79, p. 204; WLB, Sept 79, p. 68]

Anna T. Wynar

575.   Post, Elizabeth L. **The New Emily Post's Etiquette.** 14th ed. New York, Funk & Wagnalls, 1975. 978p. illus. index. $11.95; $12.95(thumb-indexed). LC 74-14667. ISBN 0-308-10167-7; 0-308-10168-5(thumb-indexed).

Revised to meet modern-day needs, this edition of the classic etiquette book now discusses such topics as obscene phone calls, doggy bags, and what to do about unmarried couples as weekend guests. A useful, unstodgy, and up-to-date approach to etiquette. As is pointed out in the preface, Emily Post's 1922 definition of etiquette is still valid today: its purpose is "to make the world a pleasanter place to live in, and you a more pleasant person to live with" (p. vii). [R: ARBA 76, p. 533; BL, 1 Apr 75, p. 781; WLB, June 75, p. 757]

576.   Vanderbilt, Amy. **The Amy Vanderbilt Complete Book of Etiquette: A Guide to Contemporary Living.** Rev. and expanded by Letitia Baldrige. New York, Doubleday, 1978. 879p. illus. index. $10.95; $11.95(thumb-indexed). LC 77-16896. ISBN 0-385-13375-8; 0-385-14238-2(thumb-indexed).

Books of etiquette are indispensable to reference work, and the *Amy Vanderbilt Complete Book of Etiquette* is one of the better such books. The author, Letitia Baldrige, has worked as a social secretary to such distinguished Americans as Ambassador Clare Boothe Luce and Jacqueline Kennedy during her years in the White House. She heads her own public relations firm in New York City, is the author of several books, and contributes to magazines and newspapers. Qualified to carry on in the high traditions established by her forebear, Amy Vanderbilt, that arbiter of manners and mores whose first edition of this book was published in 1952, Letitia Baldrige has given us a book that is well organized and smoothly written.

The volume is divided into nine parts. Part 1, "The Importance of Family and Home," includes chapters on such topics as family relationships and manners in the family. The second part, "Ceremonies of Life," offers comprehensive instructions and advice on weddings and funerals. Other major and no less complete parts of the book cover in detail entertaining, manners in business for men and women, stationery, how to present one's self in public life (but without the "get yours" attitude of many recent books), gift giving, and the etiquette of travel. The emphasis, where appropriate, is on handling the sometimes difficult and awkward situations that arise as a result of changing attitudes toward marriage, divorce, living together, sex, and feminism. For example, the book explicitly addresses problems of drugs, alcohol, and tobacco, calling marijuana use marginally socially acceptable, and declaring that parents need to educate their children on drinking. A chapter is devoted to options available to the growing number of single persons. Yet the book is equally strong in the critical traditional areas of concern, such as correct forms of address.

Ms. Baldrige believes manners ought to be based on "a superb trait of character called kindness" (p. xi), but she also adopts a flexible, unstodgy view of modern manners, as did the original author, which befits the range of options in behavior open to most people today. Her book complements the valuable *New Emily Post's Etiquette* (see entry 575). It is informed, easy to use, has a fine index, gives authoritative advice, and is written with verve, style, and panache. It will prove to be a trusted source of information and advice in any library. [R: ARBA 80, p. 496; BL, 1 Feb 79, p. 852; LJ, 1 Jan 79, p. 108]

Randy Rafferty

25   LINGUISTICS

BIBLIOGRAPHIES

577.   Walford, A. J., and J. E. O. Screen, eds. **A Guide to Foreign Language Courses and Dictionaries.** 3rd ed., rev. and enl. Westport, CT, Greenwood Press, 1977. 343p. index. $19.95. LC 77-26283. ISBN 0-313-20100-5.

The first edition of this work was published in 1964 under the title *A Guide to Foreign Language Grammars and Dictionaries*. The second edition was published by the Library Association in 1967 and covered Chinese, Dutch, Finnish, Italian, Spanish, Portuguese, German, Russian, and Scandinavian languages. This substantially enlarged edition (by some 100 pages) includes such additional languages as Greek, Japanese, Arabic, Ukrainian, Byelorussian, Bulgarian, Macedonian, Serbo-Croat, Slovene, Czech, Slovak, Polish, Rumanian, and Hungarian. The material is presented in bibliographic essay form, with a selected list of courses and dictionaries fully described. In comparison to the second edition, the audiovisual aid sections have been expanded, but monographs on several aspects of grammar and of etymological and historical dictionaries have been generally excluded, together with dictionaries of synonyms and slang. The chapter on Finnish was written by co-author J. E. O. Screen; chapters on French, Spanish, and Portuguese by Walford; and the rest of the chapters by invited subject specialists.

We have examined the chapter on Ukrainian language prepared by Victor Swoboda. The coverage is obviously highly selective, but the author is familiar with his subject and on eight pages provides a well-balanced coverage of representative textbooks, courses, grammars, and dictionaries for Ukrainian. The only important omission is G. N. Duravetz's *Ukrainian: Conversational and Grammatical* (Level I, 1973; Level II, 1976; published by Ontario Modern Language Teachers' Association) – in our judgment, the best book in its category. One may find omissions of a similar nature in other sections, primarily in the area of American and Canadian imprints. British and European imprints are covered rather well. Indeed, this is a substantial improvement over the second edition, of interest to smaller libraries that would like to have one conveniently arranged volume covering 24 languages. [R: ARBA 79, p. 536; WLB, Nov 78, p. 284]   Bohdan S. Wynar

ENGLISH LANGUAGE DICTIONARIES

GENERAL WORKS

578.   Kister, Kenneth F. **Dictionary Buying Guide: A Consumer Guide to General English-Language Wordbooks in Print.** New York, R. R. Bowker, 1977. 358p. bibliog. index. $19.25. LC 77-15010. ISBN 0-8352-1038-3.

The worst thing that can be said about this book is that it probably will receive neither the attention nor the use that it deserves. Those fortunate enough to know about it, though, will have every reason to be grateful to Kister for presenting us with such a thorough, well-informed, nicely written guide to the purchase of wordbooks. Kister also compiled the *Encyclopedia Buying Guide* (see entry 42). Following the general information section, "A Word about Dictionaries" provides a succinct view of the past and present states of the lexicographer's art. "Choosing the Right Dictionary" performs a valuable service in that its format duplicates that for the entries while, at the same time, it indicates Kister's criteria for evaluation under each category. Comparative charts for the adult and children's dictionaries are an aid, but not a substitute for the actual descriptions.

The book is divided into sections concerned first with general dictionaries for adults (unabridged, semi-unabridged, abridged, and pocket) and children (secondary, middle, elementary, and pre-school, and English as a foreign language). Other sections concern special purpose works under such categories as new words; etymology and history of words; usage and idioms; style manuals; secretarial handbooks; slang and dialect; synonyms, antonyms, and homonyms; word games; rhymes; spelling and syllabication; pronunciation; abbreviations and acronyms; signs and symbols; and foreign words and phrases. The three appendixes contain a list of recently discontinued dictionaries, a dictionary bibliography (review sources and notable books and articles), and a directory of U.S. publishers and distributors.

Evaluations are most lengthy for the unabridged adult works, and these include comments under the headings of purpose and scope, authority, vocabulary treatment, encyclopedic features, graphics, physical format, summary (of the proceeding), and other critical opinions (reviews noted from *ARBA, Booklist, Basic Information Sources, LJ*, Sheehy, and other sources). The annotations shorten as the dictionaries become progressively more simple, and comments then are often subsumed under a general heading. Kister's judicious use of "Consumer Note" headings serves to alert prospective buyers to such things as duplicate works under different titles for different prices.

Libraries should make a point of alerting patrons to the existence of this book. Kister provides even-handed treatment of the prescriptive/descriptive debate (especially over *Webster's Third*, the most obvious case), allowing the reader to decide his or her own preference. In an area in which all the items available for consideration seem to blur into a gigantic Webster-descended mass, Kister maintains clarity. He cross references (by title) similar works, his work is current as of the 1977 crop, and he provides the widest, deepest, and most genuinely informative survey of dictionaries and other wordbooks currently available. [R: ARBA 78, p. 527; BL, 15 Apr 78, p. 1328; BL, 1 Sept 78, p. 72; Choice, July 78, p. 670; C&RL, July 78, p. 308; LJ, 15 Apr 78, p. 816; LJ, 1 June 78, p. 1149; WLB, Apr 78, p. 649]   Koert C. Loomis, Jr.

COMPREHENSIVE

579.   **The American Heritage Dictionary of the English Language.** Ed. by William Morris. Boston, Houghton Mifflin and American Heritage, 1973. 1550p. illus. $16.95(thumb-indexed). LC 76-86995. ISBN 0-395-09066-0.

"First published in the fall of 1969, and continuously revised since then," this much-touted dictionary has continuously revised its dust jacket blurb, but not much else, naturally. It has also changed in binding from blue to red, and the editors have added some illustrations on a few pages that had none — total illustrations number about 4,000. All well and good, for it is a fine dictionary.

The editors can be faulted, however, for not correcting a few minor errors in the 1969 edition. Also, there is an individual entry for *founder* (to become disabled), but *founder* (one who casts metals) and *founder* (one who establishes) must be located under the definitions for the various meanings of *found*. Introductory, prefatory, and appended material remains virtually unaltered, except for a change in major offices in the American Heritage Publishing Company. Dates of death are not included for Harry Truman or Lyndon Johnson, though less recent events, such as the resignation of Harold Wilson as British Prime Minister and the establishment of Bangladesh have been noted. United States population statistics are those for 1970, but foreign population is further off. [R: ARBA 74, p. 451]   Frances Neel Cheney

580. **Funk & Wagnalls Comprehensive Standard International Dictionary: Bicentennial Edition.** Chicago, J. G. Ferguson Publishing Co., 1973; distr., New York, Thomas Y. Crowell, 1974. 1929p. illus. (part col.). $49.95. LC 74-150152. ISBN 0-308-10109-X.

The editor of this dictionary is Sidney I. Landau, and the chairman of the editorial advisory board is Allen Walker Read. The consulting editors and members of the editorial staff, listed on pages ii and iii, include a number of distinguished scholars and lexicographers as well as representatives from business and industry.

In terms of its scope, this dictionary belongs to the family of comprehensive abridged dictionaries, with a vocabulary range of approximately 175,000 entries. Entries include not only colloquialisms, slang, synonyms and antonyms, etc., but also personal and place names, scientific and technical vocabulary (on a selective basis), and, to warrant the use of "international" in the title, a selected number of foreign-language terms in general use, as well as British, Canadian, Australian, and Scottish terms. In word treatment the American spelling is stressed, with British variations noted. The etymologies present a very concise history of the word with reference to origin, form changes, and semantic development. Greek roots are given in the Roman alphabet. The dictionary also contains a number of small black-and-white illustrations, and there are several plates and numerous illustrations in the "Encyclopedic Supplement." This supplementary material (420 pages) covers a wide variety of linguistic subjects — e.g., grammar and usage, quotations, almanac-type information on the United States and other countries, and even a section on writing business letters. Most of this information can be readily found in other sources.

An evaluation of this dictionary should stress, first, that its vocabulary is well selected, with clear definitions and the minimum etymology necessary for home or school use. Like most other abridged dictionaries, this work is not prescriptive but descriptive, reflecting standard usage. The format is handy, and the volume is thumb-indexed for easy use. Consequently, this abridged dictionary will be of substantial assistance in homes and to the general reader. [R: ARBA 75, p. 552; BL, 15 Jan 75, p. 511; WLB, Sept 74, p. 93]

Bohdan S. Wynar

581. **6,000 Words: A Supplement to Webster's Third New International Dictionary.** Springfield, MA, G. & C. Merriam, 1976. 240p. $8.50. LC 75-45056. ISBN 0-87779-007-8.

Words that have come into established use in the language over the past 15 years are the principal subject of this dictionary: over 6,000 words, according to the publisher's blurb. Many of the words would be considered by some to be slang and unconventional. No such discrimination is made, however, between the treatments of *cyborg, make out* (sexual connotation), and *AC/DC* (also sexual); they are given equal time, apparently because they have appeared in publications. Among the 6,000 are words that antedate the year 1960, but they have been included because they were omitted from the *Third International.* Examples are often given from published literature, especially for the "slangy" (reviewer's opinion) expressions. Typeface and arrangement are practically and tastefully chosen. Binding is sturdy. This is a work the users of the *Third New International* have been long awaiting, and it will undoubtedly be gladly welcomed by them. [R: ARBA 77, p. 518]

Francis J. Witty

SCHOOL AND COLLEGE

582. **Children's Dictionary.** Boston, Houghton Mifflin, 1979. 816p. illus. (part col.). $10.95. (An American Heritage Dictionary). LC 78-27636. ISBN 0-395-27512-1.

Houghton has produced a completely new children's dictionary to join the highly successful *American Heritage Dictionary of the English Language* and the useful *American Heritage School Dictionary.* The size (816 pages) and format of the *Children's Dictionary* are similar to other competing dictionaries for grades 3-8, such as *Webster's New World Dictionary for Young Readers* (see entry 587). Houghton's philosophy is to take "language seriously while it makes learning fun" (publisher's descriptive material). While this is hardly a new concept, one expects, and finds, more emphasis on illustrations (quantity, relevance, and quality of reproduction), and design that opens up the pages and emphasizes simplicity. The 1,500 illustrations include 804 four-color drawings. Colored tabs and blocks are used effectively throughout the text to identify pronunciation keys, word histories, and alphabet letter guides. A major design innovation in *Children's Dictionary* is the adoption of a single-column text page, using large, clear type. The outer edge portion of the page is reserved for illustrations.

The over 30,000 entries are listed under some 13,000 entry words. Large bold type makes the entry words easy to locate. Syllabification is indicated as well as pronunciation. The part of speech is written out in full and not abbreviated as in many other dictionaries. Several meanings are given for most entry words, accompanied by sample phrases and sentences. A diamond marks sound-alike words. Brief word histories are scattered throughout the dictionary. A pronunciation key is printed on every two-page spread. Idioms are highlighted in bold type and usually are illustrated by sentences. Every United States state and Canadian province is listed, but other political entities or geographical names are included on a highly selective basis. Curiously, France and Germany are listed, but Iran, Jordan, Saudi Arabia, Yugoslavia, and others are missing.

The tendency to simplify that is demonstrated in *Children's Dictionary* at times can be somewhat misleading or result in unclear definitions. But in general, the definitions are adequate for young readers. No maps are included in the dictionary, and, with the exception of the introductory article by Stephen Krensky, "The History of the English Language" (pp. x-xiii), no additional materials are incorporated. A brief but clearly written and illustrated "Guide to the Dictionary" illustrates use of and access to all the types of information in the dictionary.

Students who are ready to move up from beginning dictionaries such as *The Charlie Brown Dictionary* will find the *Children's Dictionary* a practical, easy-to-read, and attractive reference book. Better readers in the 8-12 year range may find it too limiting and will soon move to more complete dictionaries, such as *Webster's New World Dictionary for Young Readers* (46,000 entries) or *The American Heritage School Dictionary* (35,000 main entries, or 50,000 entry forms). [R: ARBA 80, p. 504; SLJ, Oct 79, p. 148]

Christine Gehrt Wynar

583. Ehrlich, Eugene, and others. **Oxford American Dictionary.** New York, Oxford University Press, 1980. 816p. $14.95. LC 80-16510. ISBN 0-19-502795-7.

Following in the tradition of the Oxford dictionaries started by Sir James Murray with the *Oxford English Dictionary*, this new abridged dictionary is thoroughly up to date, thoroughly American. Strictly a dictionary with no pretense of serving as a one-volume reference library, the *Oxford American Dictionary* was designed to give its users a standard for correct American usage of the English language.

The lexicographers and editors are Americans. Those names appearing on the title page are: Eugene Uhrlich, senior lecturer of English and comparative literature at Columbia University; Stuart Berg Flexner, a widely quoted lexicographer and author of *I Hear America Talking* and the *Dictionary of American Slang*; and Gorton Carruth, former editor-in-chief of Funk & Wagnalls, editor of *Roget's International Thesaurus, The New York Times Crossword Puzzle*, and numerous other reference books. Also, working with these scholars was Joyce M. Hawkins of the Oxford dictionary staff in England. Hawkins served as an editor of the *Supplements* to the *Oxford English Dictionary*, the *Concise*

Oxford Dictionary, the *Oxford Illustrated Dictionary*, and was the compiler of the *Oxford Paperback Dictionary*.

The *Oxford American Dictionary* is not intended to be comprehensive. Synonyms are given only when they can distinguish shades of meaning; definitions are clear, precise, and limited to current meanings. No etymologies are included. The pronunciation system employed gives the syllable that is to be stressed in boldfaced type, eliminating elaborate explanations and obscure symbols. The spelling is completely American. The user will find such words as "theater," "check," and "color" but not "theatre," "cheque," and "colour." Syllabication is indicated with a center dot. Plurals of nouns and comparatives and superlatives of adjectives are given; inflected forms of verbs are included when they are irregular or when there may be a question about their spelling; and symbols are to designate usage notes. Also included are useful comments on meanings of words and phrases that are often confused.

A welcome feature of the *Oxford American Dictionary* is the prescriptive assistance given in determining correct American usage, which in some ways makes it an updating of *Webster's New International Dictionary of the English Language*. Some examples: "You-all" is used in the southern United States and is informal; "different than" is sometimes correct but "different from" is always correct; if you are not well or are upset, say "I feel bad" not "I feel badly"; and instead of using "contact" as a verb use "write," "call," or "visit."

The *Oxford American Dictionary* is an attractive work. Bound in the traditional navy blue used by Oxford, it is most readable. Its introduction on how to use the dictionary is lucid; and the "Publisher's Note" gives valuable biographical material on Sir James Murray and the work that brought the *Oxford English Dictionary* into being. The *Oxford American Dictionary* will be most useful to individuals in the home and in schools and universities and will merit consideration with such abridged dictionaries as *Webster's New Collegiate Dictionary, Webster's New Collegiate Dictionary of the American Language*, 2nd college ed., and the *American Heritage Dictionary of the English Language*, and will find a place in all reference collections alongside Sir William A. Craigie and James R. Hulbert's *Dictionary of American English on Historical Principles*; Mitford McLeod Mathews' *Dictionary of Americanisms on Historical Principles*; and, of course, Sir James Augustus Henry Murray's *Oxford English Dictionary*. [R: ARBA 81; LJ, 1 Nov 80, p. 2318]   Jefferson D. Caskey

584. **Macmillan Dictionary for Children.** William D. Halsey, editorial director; Christopher G. Morris, ed. New York, Macmillan, 1975. 724p. illus. (part col.). $10.95. LC 74-24661.

This large-size volume for the early intermediate grades through junior high contains about 30,000 entries printed in large type with many small, clear, color illustrations. Entry words are written as children ordinarily see them—no diacritical marks or syllable division—thus making them easy to identify and locate. Plurals that are spelled differently (*elves*) are entered separately as well as being noted under the singular (*elf*). Names of places (countries, states, planets) are included, as are organizations. Contractions (*don't, we'll*) and common phrases (*double-cross, comic-strip, navy blue*) are also listed separately. Definitions, parts of speech, plurals, pronunciations, and sample sentences are given. There are also "language notes" for many words that give background or usage. The relatively simple pronunciation key appears on alternate pages for easy reference. The introductory material is particularly good; it is simply worded and clearly explains what a dictionary is and how to use one. [R: ARBA 76, p. 541; BL, 1 Oct 75, p. 261; SLJ, Sept 75, p. 103]   Eleanor Elving Schwartz

585. Thorndike, E. L., and Clarence L. Barnhart. **Scott, Foresman Advanced Dictionary.** Doubleday ed. New York, Doubleday, 1979. 1186p. illus. $14.95. ISBN 0-385-14852-6.

The *Advanced Dictionary*, designed for junior and senior high school students, is a revision of the *Thorndike-Barnhart Advanced Dictionary* and the *Thorndike-Barnhart High School Dictionary*. The *Dictionary* contains over 95,000 entries for ordinary words, biographical names, geographical names, abbreviations, and foreign words and phrases, arranged in a single alphabet. Some 900 synonym studies and usage notes provide additional information on syntax, spelling, and shades of meaning. Also included are some 16,000 etymologies.

The parts of the dictionary entry number up to 13 elements, including: entry word, in boldface; homograph number; pronunciation; part of speech label; inflected forms, in small boldface; restrictive label; definition; illustrated sentence, in italics; idiom, in small boldface; etymology, in brackets; run-on entry; a synonym study; and a usage note. An extensive guide to the use of the *Dictionary* (with exercises) discusses all the parts of the dictionary entry and how to become familiar with their meaning and correct use. Dictionary entries are printed in fairly small but readable type in three-column pages. A pronunciation key is printed on each double-page layout. The 1,300 small black-and-white drawings and spotmaps are clearly printed and informative, as are the several full-page illustrations (geological time, language tree, periodic table of elements, etc.). Entries include numerous up-to-date inclusions of interest to teenagers (e.g., skateboards), although some recently coined terms are not found (e.g., microcomputers). In general, the selection of entries is adequate, and their definitions are concise and appear accurate as compared to similar school dictionaries.

The *Advanced Dictionary* may be compared to *The Macmillan Dictionary* in terms of intended readership, content, and physical appearance. Both dictionaries are concerned with vocabulary requirements of secondary school age readers. The *Macmillan Dictionary* contains 90,000 main entry words (about 120,000 definitions), a slightly smaller number than in the *Advanced Dictionary*. The format, typeface, and illustrations in *Macmillan* produce a more readable and attractive book, but the *Advanced Dictionary* is also well suited to teenage readers and can be recommended.

Ed. note: The *Scott, Foresman Intermediate Dictionary* (Doubleday, 1979. 1066p. $12.95), a 57,000-word dictionary, provides excellent coverage, introductory material, and instructional games for students (grades 6-10 and above). [R: ARBA 80, p. 503]

Christine Gehrt Wynar

586. **Webster's New Collegiate Dictionary.** Springfield, MA, G. & C. Merriam, 1979. 1536p. $11.95; $12.95(thumb-indexed). LC 72-10966. ISBN 0-87779-358-1; 0-87779-359-X(thumb-indexed).

The origins of this desk dictionary date back to 1898. From 1963 to 1972 the dictionary was titled *Webster's Seventh New Collegiate Dictionary*. This edition, based on *Webster's Third New International Dictionary* and numerous Merriam-Webster citation files, contains 152,337 entries plus separate sections for 6,051 biographical and 12,485 geographical entries, 566 foreign words and phrases, a list of colleges and universities, signs and symbols, and a handbook of style. A handy index at the end of the dictionary quickly reveals the location of such items as a table of Easter dates or a table of metric measures and English equivalents. Introductory matter includes explanatory notes on the use of the dictionary and an essay by W. Nelson Francis, "The English Language and Its History."

The page format is condensed, but the type, in double columns, is clear and legible; 892 small line drawings are fitted into the text. Each entry word is printed in boldface, followed by pronunciation, functional labels, inflected forms, etymology, usage, and sense division. Some 24,000 phrases, including 3,093 quotations from authors, are added to show how certain words are used. The editors state that 1,875 synonyms and antonyms are provided for words believed to be of interest to dictionary users. *Webster's New Collegiate Dictionary* is a well-edited desk dictionary. [R: ARBA 74, p. 452; BL, 1 Nov 73, p. 251; Choice, Sept 73, p. 952; WLB, June 73, p. 866]   Christine Gehrt Wynar

587. **Webster's New World Dictionary for Young Readers.** David B. Guralnik, ed.-in-chief. Cleveland, OH, William Collins Publishers, 1979. 880p. illus. (part col.). maps. $9.95. LC 78-59178. ISBN 0-529-05625-9.

The *New World Dictionary for Young Readers* (also published as *Basic School Edition* by Prentice-Hall) was first published in 1961 and was updated in 1966, 1971, and 1979. This edition, attractively printed in easy-to-read type set in two columns, contains some 46,000 entry words, 800 synonyms, and 2,800 idiomatic phrases for children in grades 4-8. The text is illustrated by 1,900 color and black-and-white photos, spot maps, and drawings. Color is used to highlight guide words, pronunciation keys on each double-page spread, word histories, and synonyms. Entries include, in addition to ordinary words, abbreviations, prefixes, and geographical and biographical entries. Entries include up to 20 elements, such as syllable division, pronunciation, parts of speech, definition and sentence, mark for an Americanism, variant terms, usage note, synonyms, cross reference, idiom. Definitions are clearly written in simple language and compare favorably with those in *Children's Dictionary* (see entry 582). A handy reference appendix contains nine full-color tables, charts, and maps: solar system, firsts in space, weather and cloud patterns, geological time chart, chronology of American events, metric conversion table, and three maps. The end sheets give brief histories of state names. Introductory material in the dictionary is in two parts: "A Story of Some American Words" (illustrated in color) and a guide to locating words in the dictionary, with exercises.

Webster's is an attractive and well-compiled dictionary. Students who are beyond the beginning picture dictionaries and need more than can be provided in dictionaries such as *Macmillan Dictionary for Children* will find challenge here. It will be valuable for children to learn to use along with, for example, *Children's Dictionary*, which employs different pronunciation symbols. [R: ARBA 80, p. 505]   Christine Gehrt Wynar

588. **Webster's New World Dictionary of the American Language.** David B. Guralnik, general ed. 2nd concise ed. Cleveland, OH, Collins + World, 1979. 882p. illus. $9.95. LC 79-50954. ISBN 0-529-05267-9.

One of the additions to the burgeoning family of Webster's New World dictionaries, this large-print volume has many pleasing features. With a word stock of over 105,000 entries—compared with about one-half that number in other concise or large print dictionaries—it provides a comprehensive, up-to-date vocabulary with precise, succinct definitions aimed at business or professional people, office workers, high school students, crossword puzzle addicts, students of English as a second language, and those who simply want a good dictionary in large type.

Entries have been selected on the basis of their frequency of occurrence in general interest publications. While avoiding colloquial, faddish, esoteric, or ephemeral words, the *Dictionary* does include special terms in the arts, sciences, and business, along with some new slang or informal language. Users will find abbreviations, foreign terms, and personal and geographical names in one alphabetical order without having to search through several appendices. All main entries appear in boldface type, usually in lower case, unless the word ordinarily begins with a capital letter. Pronunciations, parts-of-speech labels, irregular inflections, and brief etymologies immediately follow entry words and precede definitions. When a term has more than one meaning, the various senses are arranged in such a way as to show development from earliest meanings (given first) to current use. Usage notes, field labels for specialized areas of knowledge, and idiomatic phrases follow definitions whenever appropriate. More than 600 small drawings are set into the text. Several charts — including a table of chemical elements, a geologic time chart, and a list of international monetary units — are scattered throughout. Endpapers feature a metrical conversion table, a table of alphabets, a key to pronunciation, and a map showing United States time zones. A table of weights and measures and a lengthy "Guide to the Mechanics of Writing" comprise the two appendices. A complete index to the supplementary materials would have been a helpful addition.

The main body of the dictionary is thumb-indexed. Varying typefaces within each entry enable users to scan for information quickly. The clear, well-defined print has been set by computer in the largest practicable size: any larger would have resulted in an extremely cumbersome volume. This one has a sturdy binding, opens easily, and lies flat. Older people, who make up a large proportion of those needing large print, may find it too heavy to handle easily. Others who want extensive etymologies, lengthy definitions, rare or technical terms will doubtlessly prefer a collegiate or unabridged edition. This attractive volume nevertheless offers a larger word stock, fuller definitions, and more "extras" than any other existing large-print dictionary. [R: ARBA 79, p. 541]   Mary Jo Walker

HISTORICAL

589.   The Compact Edition of the Oxford English Dictionary: Complete Text Reproduced Micrographically. New York, Oxford University Press, 1971. 2v. $125.00/set. LC 72-177361. ISBN 0-19-861117-X.

The publisher has micrographically reduced the $595, 13-volume *OED* to a compact, two-volume form, with four pages of the original fitted onto one new page. A rectangular magnifying glass is supplied with this edition. The quality of reproduction is excellent. [R: ARBA 73, p. 448; LJ, 15 Mar 72, p. 1002]

590.   Morris, William, and Mary Morris. Dictionary of Word and Phrase Origins. New York, Harper & Row, 1962-1971. 3v. LC 62-10842. ISBN 0-06-111260-7(v.1); 0-06-111201-1(v.2); 0-06-013068-7(v.3).

Designed to supplement the *American Heritage Dictionary of the English Language*, this standard, widely popular reference book is a treasury of hard-to-find information. It provides little-known stories about everyday words and expressions. Arranged in convenient alphabetical order, these capsule accounts range from the earliest years of our language to current teen-age slang. Entries vary in length depending on the popularity of the expression and on the background material assembled by the compilers. Quite frequently, definitions are selected for wit (e.g., Churchill's definition of a fanatic: "one who can't change his mind and won't change the subject"). [R: ARBA 70, v.2, p. 50; ARBA 72, p. 468; Choice, Dec 68; LJ, 15 June 71, p. 2139]

591.   The Shorter Oxford English Dictionary on Historical Principles. Prep. by William Little, H. W. Fowler, and Jessie Coulson. 3rd ed. Rev. and ed. by C. T. Onions. New York, Oxford University Press, 1973. 2v. $99.50; $110.00(thumb-indexed). ISBN 0-19-861126-9; 0-19-861127-7(thumb-indexed).

This is an authorized abridgment of the *Oxford English Dictionary*. The first edition was published in 1933, the second in 1936, and the third in 1944. This third edition has been reprinted 13 times with some corrections and revisions, most recently in 1972. The present edition, according to the publisher's note, incorporates two new features: "The etymologies of all words in the body of the Dictionary have been revised by Dr. G. W. S. Freidrichsen, former colleague of the late Dr. C. T. Onions; this major undertaking represents more than eight years' work by Dr. Friedrichsen. The second main feature is the inclusion of a fresh set of Addenda, drawn chiefly from the material assembled for the new Supplement to the *O.E.D.* (the first volume of which was published in the autumn of 1972), and presenting notable accessions to the English language in the period since *O.E.D.* appeared. The entries in the main text of the Dictionary remain essentially as they were, pending the completion of the Supplement to the *O.E.D.* towards the end of the present decade." Thus, the new material is based primarily on the first volume of the Supplement (letters A-G) plus the card files for letters H-P and Q-Z.

The introduction's claim that "the etymologies of all words have been revised and for the most part rewritten, ultimately on the basis of the material presented in the *Oxford Dictionary of English Etymology* (1966), which embodies recent research on the etymologies of English and of the other languages concerned" (p. xii) is not necessarily true for all cases. A comparison of etymologies in the 1970 printing with those in the 1973 printing shows that many, but not all, have been revised. Also, many of these revisions are only of a remedial or supplementary nature. Secondly, an updated addenda list (pp. 2598-2672) indeed has many new words; it has almost twice as many pages as the 1970 printing. But the larger type size for the 1973 printing probably accounts for a substantial part of this increase.

The excellent quality of typography and paper makes the *SOED* very easy to use. The fact is that it provides a larger amount of information about the history of the word than any other dictionary of comparable size (163,000 words, combinations, and idiomatic phrases), and it contains some material not in the *OED*. Many libraries probably already have purchased *The Compact Edition of the Oxford English Dictionary*, a micrographically reproduced complete set in two volumes, published in 1971. This abridgment is a valuable reference work either by itself in smaller libraries, or in conjunction with the micrographically reproduced *OED* for libraries that do not have an original set. [R: ARBA 75, p. 553; BL, 1 Nov 74, p. 298; Choice, July 74, p. 740; RQ, Summer 74, p. 364; WLB, Feb 74, p. 508]   Bohdan S. Wynar

592.   **A Supplement to the Oxford English Dictionary. Volume II, H-N.** Ed. by R. W. Burchfield. New York, Oxford University Press, 1976. 1282p. $65.00. ISBN 0-19-861123-4.

The editors of the *Oxford English Dictionary* and its supplements have taken as their goal the formation of a "permanent record of the language of our time, the useful and the neutral, those [words] that are decorous and well-formed, beside those that are controversial, tasteless, or worse." Volume I of the Supplement, published in 1972, covered the letters A-G, and the plan was for two more volumes to complete it. However, the editors found that their quotation and word files had expanded so rapidly that it was necessary to plan for four, rather than three, volumes. Thus, O-S was due some time in 1980 and T-Z (with a bibliography of works cited throughout the Supplement), in 1985. In the interim, they have given us a wealth of material with this volume, H-N.

The present volume contains approximately 13,000 main words, divided into some 22,000 senses. Defined combinations number about 8,000, while the undefined combinations number about 5,000. The illustrative quotations, drawn from American and Canadian magazines and newspapers as well as British (including Scottish and West Indian) sources, number 125,000. The editors state that they do not necessarily approve of some words listed, but in the interests of complete historical accuracy, they felt compelled to include every usage for which they had a record. Thus, they have made a conscious effort to update religious or racial terms which have, in the past, been used as slurs, but they have never excluded a word because a particular group might find it offensive. They have, in sum, brought the dictionary up to date with the language, as much as is possible in the never-ending job of the lexicographer.

After you purchase the first volume, buy the present volume; use and cherish it. Wait anxiously for the next two. No library can claim to be complete without the original and its supplements. [R: ARBA 77, p. 520; BL, 15 May 77, p. 1455; LJ, 15 Dec 76, p. 2559]

Koert C. Loomis, Jr.

593.   Sykes, J. B., ed. **The Concise Oxford Dictionary of Current English: Based on the "Oxford English Dictionary" and Its Supplements.** 6th ed. New York, Oxford University Press, 1976. 1368p. $16.95; $19.95(thumb-indexed). ISBN 0-19-861121-8; 0-19-861122-6 (thumb-indexed).

The fifth edition of the *Concise Oxford Dictionary* was first published in 1964, and American users often found it to be heavily slanted toward British Isle usage, both in definitions and in word choices. The editor of this edition notes that a substantial effort has been made to remedy this provincialism, primarily through the use of the published sections of the second Supplement and the card files for the unpublished volumes. Additionally, this edition incorporates the previously separate abbreviations section into the main word list, systematizes interrelated terms, and incorporates many new technical terms and meanings. The introduction has been substantially changed, and the editor advises the reader to consult it prior to using this volume.

Entries in this present volume number 74,000 (with nearly 40,000 headwords, the remainder of the entries comprised of derivatives, compounds, and abbreviations). All entries are arranged (as in the *OED*) historically, with the most current meaning listed last. Unlike the parent volumes, this edition omits the illustrative quotations. The editor notes that a change in typography was introduced in this edition to "allow greater ease of use," but the change from 10-point to 8-point type for headwords does not appear to have been entirely successful. Nevertheless, this edition can be recommended to libraries and individuals for both its thoroughness and its currency. The dictionary does reflect the language as it is used, and it is invaluable as a quick reference. [R: ARBA 77, p. 521; Choice, Feb 77, p. 1570; LJ, 15 Oct 76, p. 2161; WLB, Jan 77, p. 439]   Koert C. Loomis, Jr.

SLANG

594.   Cowie, A. P., and R. Mackin. **Oxford Dictionary of Current Idiomatic English. Volume 1, Verbs with Prepositions and Particles.** New York, Oxford University Press, 1975. 396p. $13.50. ISBN 0-19-431145-7.

Contains some 20,000 idiomatic expressions, with entries arranged by verbal elements. The coverage of this first volume is limited to merged verbs and phrasal verbs. The introductory section (80p.) serves as a thorough study of such verbs. Each entry provides a definition and commented citations taken from post-war British materials — literary works, media broadcasts, and a few periodicals and magazines. Many of the entries provide alternative forms, which is a useful feature for this reviewer, whose mother tongue is not English. The definitions provided and the illustrative quotations are carefully prepared in the Oxford tradition, but, as one might expect, this work relies heavily on British usage; Americanisms and idioms used in other parts of the English-speaking world are, for the most part, ignored. This is clearly reflected by the sources used in preparing this unique work, and one must regret such a serious shortcoming in this otherwise monumental undertaking. An index of nouns, adjectives, and adverbs used in the text is appended to the end of the volume.

In closing, we again stress the excellence of this dictionary for British usage of idiomatic phrases. Nevertheless, we feel the dictionary would only gain in importance if its editors were to use criteria similar to those used for *The Barnhart Dictionary of New English since 1963* (Harper and Row, 1973). The two dictionaries serve different purposes, of course, but the 5,000 entries in the Barnhart work were chosen from half a billion words published not only in British sources but also in American, Canadian, etc., during the time period covered. [R: ARBA 77, p. 519; Choice, July 76, p. 647; RQ, Summer 76, p. 352]

Bohdan S. Wynar

595. Wentworth, Harold, and Stuart Berg Flexner, comps. and eds. **Dictionary of American Slang.** 2nd supplemented ed. New York, Thomas Y. Crowell, 1975. 766p. bibliog. $12.95. LC 75-8644. ISBN 0-690-00670-5.

In 1960 the first edition of this work was published. In 1967, the publisher issued a revised edition consisting of the original Wentworth/Flexner vocabulary in one alphabetic sequence, followed by a 48-page supplement prepared by Flexner alone. The present "second supplemented edition" consists of the original 1960 dictionary in one sequence, and the 1969 Flexner supplement that has, in turn, been augmented by insertion of new slang terms coming into vogue in the late 1960s and early 1970s. The supplement that was 48 pages in length in 1967 is now 88 pages. Ergo, the new matter in this edition is exactly 40 pages.

An examination of the newly augmented supplement shows that it does indeed record some recent coinages. An example: "Barbie Doll," to designate a typical all-American WASP conformist of either sex. This slang phrase is dated by Flexner as 1972. Slang, as Flexner carefully points out, always appears first in oral discourse. Only later does it find its way into print. Therefore, all dated references to first uses in print are to be construed as only approximate indicators of the date of invention. [R: ARBA 76, p. 545; BL, 15 June 76, p. 1484; Choice, Apr 76, p. 208; LJ, Aug 75, p. 1404; WLB, Jan 76, p. 408]

Richard A. Gray

SYNONYMS AND ANTONYMS

596. **The Doubleday Roget's Thesaurus in Dictionary Form.** Sidney I. Landau, ed.-in-chief. Garden City, NY, Doubleday, 1977. 804p. $5.95; $7.95(thumb-indexed). LC 76-7696. ISBN 0-385-01236-5; 0-385-12479-5(thumb-indexed).

In spite of Roget's name in the title, the arrangement here is strictly alphabetical, with no subject or category classifications. Entries are based on those in *The Doubleday Dictionary* with greater emphasis on slang terms and words of recent origin or with recently acquired meanings than is found in many similar works. The editors claim a total of 250,000 synonyms and antonyms (not entries), with an average of 10 to 15 synonyms given per entry. The synonyms are listed in order of usage from the most to least common. Parts of speech are labelled, as are slang terms. Although the editors acknowledge that there are few exact synonyms in English, there is no attempt to guide the user in selecting the most appropriate term from the lengthy lists provided. For instance, there are important differences between a lecher and a flirt, yet both terms are given as synonyms for "philanderer." "Bankrupt" and "broke" are listed as synonyms for "needy." While special cases might allow the use of these words as synonyms, they are hardly synonymous in common usage.

The Doubleday thesaurus must be compared with the new *Webster's Collegiate Thesaurus* (see entry 598), which is very similar in scope and coverage. Webster's thesaurus does provide more guidelines on usage. The Doubleday work emphasizes current slang but ignores much of the currently popular vulgar and sexual slang and terms of the gay liberation movement. Again Webster's thesaurus seems to have the edge in both type and depth of coverage. Although *Webster's Collegiate Thesaurus* might be preferred for thes reasons, most libraries will still have use for the Doubleday thesaurus, which is reasonat priced and up to date. [R: ARBA 78, p. 535; Choice, May 77, p. 344; LJ, 1 May 77, p. 1002; WLB, Sept 77, p. 88]   Barbara E. Kemp

597. **Roget's International Thesaurus.** 4th ed. Revised by Robert L. Chapman. New York, Thomas Y. Crowell, 1977. 1317p. index. $10.50(plain); $11.95(thumb-indexed). LC 62-12806. ISBN 0-690-00010-3(plain); 0-690-00011-1(thumb-indexed).

An actual thesaurus, as opposed to a dictionary of synonyms, this work follows the original plan of Peter Mark Roget to present words by topical arrangement (updated, of course), this followed by an extensive alphabetical index of the words in that first section. Fifteen years have passed since the third edition (1962), so it was more than time for this volume, which does indeed include the vocabulary of the 1970s — clone, cyborg, gay, UFO — along with those words from *before* 1970 of which we all remain so fond. Typeface is clear and the format is very easy to work with. The most important or commonly used terms are indicated by the use of boldface type, and slang is noted as such. Beyond that, no fine distinctions are indicated, meaning that the writer in doubt must (gasp) go to a dictionary to discover them. Too bad. The thesaurus is intended to serve people who know words but need a memory jog or those who are interested enough in conveying clear thought to take the time to look them up; it is not intended to serve as a crutch for the lazy.

This volume contains more than 250,000 words, including foreign words and phrases. There is information on combining words, but in text entries, not a separate section. It *is* a thesaurus, and a good one. However, anyone desiring a simpler format — as, say, an alphabetically arranged synonym dictionary — would do well to consult something comprehensive like *Webster's Collegiate Thesaurus* (see entry 598). [R: ARBA 78, p. 535; WLB, Jan 78, p. 421]   Koert C. Loomis, Jr.

598. **Webster's Collegiate Thesaurus.** Springfield, MA, G. & C. Merriam, 1976. 944p. $10.95(thumb-indexed). LC 75-45167. ISBN 0-87779-069-8.

This is the first completely new thesaurus to appear since Roget, 120 years ago — though Roget has, of course, been supplemented and re-edited many times. The editors of the new *Webster's Collegiate Thesaurus* are generous in their praise of Roget, but they suggest that "it is far more often recommended by instructors than it is used by students," because of its complexity and elaborate structural plan. After many years of reference experience, I would not only agree, but would further suggest that Roget is probably far more often recommended by instructors than it is used by them.

The introductory directions and illustrative explanatory chart are clear and easily followed. The editors describe, with examples, classes of words or phrases presented: synonyms and antonyms, related and contrasted words, phrases and idiomatic equivalents (this last treating of word equivalents), glosses (which restate the meaning of words), and idioms.

A few observations following rather close inspection of the book: "gnome" as a noun is synonymously related to maxim, apothegm, aphorism, etc., but not to the little creature of fairyland; "lobster" is said to be synonymous with oaf, klutz, lump, palooka, etc., but in 60 years I have never seen or heard this pejorative; "loch" does not include "lake" among its synonyms, though that certainly is one. Nevertheless, there is no doubting the essentiality of this work for virtually any kind of library. [R: ARBA 77, p. 524; BL, 1 July 77, p. 1671; Choice, May 77, p. 344; LJ, July 76, p. 1516; LJ, 15 Apr 77, p. 876; WLB, Sept 76, p. 90]
                                                                D. Bernard Theall

599. **Webster's New Dictionary of Synonyms.** Springfield, MA, G. & C. Merriam, 1980. 942p. $10.95(thumb-indexed). ISBN 0-87779-241-0.

A revision of the work that first appeared in 1942, this work is an alphabetically arranged thesaurus of words with definitions, synonyms, antonyms, and closely related terms, which also includes quotations from respected authors to aid in correct usage. Every device is provided to make consultation easy: thumb-indexing, caption guides, explanations of symbols and abbreviations at the foot of each page, an abundance of clear cross references, and precise and authoritative definitions. However, care should be exercised in its use: a string of words after an entry does not necessarily consist of true synonyms—e.g., "biennial: *biannual, semiannual"; the word marked with the asterisk (complete entry with definitions, etc.) should be consulted. If we look under "biannual," we find that the three terms are "frequently confused" and that "semiannual" is "unequivocal, since it means half-yearly." The typography is tastefully chosen both for aesthetics and for clarity, and the binding is serviceable. The introduction on the history of English synonymy is substantially the same as in the former editions, but it is recommended reading for the reference librarian who has not yet perused it.   Francis J. Witty

600. **Webster's Students Thesaurus.** Springfield, MA, G. & C. Merriam, 1978. 499p. (A Merriam-Webster). $7.95. LC 78-585. ISBN 0-87779-078-7.

Webster's Students Thesaurus is planned to be both "easy to use and sufficiently inclusive to provide real help in vocabulary building and word selection . . . a reference book that is close to being an adult tool." It offers an alternative to the complexity of the topical arrangement of Chapman's *Roget's International Thesaurus* and closely follows the plan of the innovative *Webster's Collegiate Thesaurus*. The thesaurus contains 43,000 synonyms, antonyms, and related and contrasted words, arranged alphabetically by entry word. Explanatory notes fully illustrate the content and ordering of the main entries and secondary entries.

The main entry is made up of several elements, e.g., boldface headword, part of speech label, sense number, a meaning core with a short verbal illustration, and a short list of synonyms, followed by related words, idiomatic phrases, contrasted words, and antonyms. Secondary entries contain the boldface headword and part of speech label plus a synonym cross reference directing the reader to the appropriate main entry, in which the secondary entry appears as a synonym. Thus, the cross references aid in reducing the number of duplicate listings. The editors have imposed strict control over the listing of synonyms. The "one arbitrary rule" followed is: "no word may appear in more than one list at any single sense of a main or secondary entry" (p. 11a). Secondary entries also list related words, idiomatic phrases, contrasted words, and antonyms.

The thesaurus proves to be a very handy and easy-to-use reference with one exception—the small type size discourages the casual reader and makes longer searches wearisome. *Webster's* is recommended for students who have mastered beginning thesauri such as Schiller's *In Other Words* (Lothrop, 1978) and *Junior Thesaurus* (Lothrop, 1978) and who need an adult-type reference book. [R: ARBA 80, p. 510; WLB, Sept 78, p. 85]

Christine Gehrt Wynar

FOREIGN TERMS

601. Carroll, David. **The Dictionary of Foreign Terms in the English Language.** New York, Hawthorn Books, 1973. 212p. $10.95. LC 70-39281.

Frequently used terms in French, German, Latin, Spanish, Japanese, Gaelic—approximately 7,000 terms from almost 30 languages—are listed in one alphabet and defined. Each word or phrase is succinctly defined, and, when necessary for clarification, the term is used in a sentence. Language of origin is indicated by an abbreviation, but no pronunciation is given. Words that have been assimilated into English are in roman type, rather than in the italics used for strictly foreign terms. Commonly used abbreviations of foreign terms are appended in a separate section. Those who need a quick definition (with no etymological background) of foreign terms used in English will find this to be a most helpful reference source. [R: ARBA 74, p. 450; BL, 1 Dec 73, p. 351; Choice, Dec 73, p. 1525; LJ, 15 Mar 73, p. 857; WLB, Oct 73, p. 163]

602. Mawson, C. O. Sylvester. **Dictionary of Foreign Terms.** 2nd ed. Rev. and updated by Charles Berlitz. New York, Thomas Y. Crowell, 1975. 368p. $9.95. LC 74-12492. ISBN 0-690-00171-1.

This dictionary contains some 15,000 words and phrases from more than 50 languages. It is a revision of the venerable *Dictionary of Foreign Terms Found in English and American Writings of Yesterday and Today*, which appeared in 1934. The new material included in this second edition should make it more useful to the current generation.

Much has happened to the English language, especially the American variety, in the last 40 years. This edition reflects the foreign influences upon American English that have resulted from the expansion of the language into all parts of the world since World War II. Additions include words and phrases from the Far East, especially Japan, and from African and American Indian languages.

Rather than relying principally on literature, the second edition reflects many areas of human endeavor, including cuisine, law, the military, business, the fine arts, and diplomacy. Nevertheless, it is fortunate that the material derived from classical and modern literature has been retained. Since the decline and virtual disappearance of liberal education, even the well-educated reader of today must turn to a reference of this type for the meanings of Greek, Latin, French, or German expressions that an earlier generation would have recognized.

Entries are arranged alphabetically letter-by-letter, including articles and prepositions. Except for Greek, all entries are in the Roman alphabet. [R: ARBA 76, p. 540; BL, 15 Jan 75, p. 476; Choice, Sept 75, p. 818; LJ, 15 Apr 75, p. 748; WLB, June 75, p. 753]

Stanley Joe McCord

GRAMMAR AND USAGE

603. Barnhart, Clarence L., Sol Steinmetz, and Robert K. Barnhart. **The Barnhart Dictionary of New English since 1963.** Bronxville, NY, Barnhart/Harper and Row, 1973. 512p. $14.95. LC 73-712. ISBN 0-06-010223-3.

This record of the English language from 1963 to 1972 consists of some 5,000 entries, selected from half a billion words printed in British, American, and Canadian books and periodicals during the time period. Technical dictionaries were not consulted, since the aim was to list those words that have entered the common vocabulary. Pronunciation is provided when necessary, following a pronunciation key based on the IPA. Concise definitions are given, along with part of speech and the single usage label "slang." Meanings for entries used in more than one sense are given in order of frequency (in the editors' judgment).

Quotations are used to show the word in an actual context, to supply additional details about the word's connotation, to point out the range of use in different times and places, and to indicate the type of writing in which the word appears. The source (including author) is indicated after each quotation; names of publications are spelled out and dates are given in full for the reader's convenience. This work is an essential source of information on the English language as it is now spoken and written. [R: ARBA 74, p. 457; BL, 15 May 74, p. 1011; Choice, July 74, p. 733; C&RL, Jan 74, p. 35; LJ, 15 Sept 73, p. 2536; LJ, 15 Apr 74, p. 1098]

604.   Follett, Wilson. **Modern American Usage.** Ed. and completed by Jacques Barzun, in collaboration with Carlos Baker and others. New York, Warner Paperback Library, 1974. 528p. $2.50pa. ISBN 0-446-78119-3.

Follett spent his life studying language and its usage, and, during his last years, he composed this work, which was then published post-humously. It consists mainly of a lexicon of American usage, the entries of which can easily be controlled through the "Inventory of Main Entries" in the introductory material; cross references are generously supplied throughout. Appendixes covering "shall/will, should/would" and punctuation complete the volume.

Mention should be made of the delightful introduction by Follett; it is probably the best *apologia*, to this reader's knowledge, of traditional grammatical concepts and of the attitude that there is a right way and a wrong way to express thoughts in one's native tongue. In an age when, on the one hand, information specialists are desperately trying to store data for retrieval under precise terms, and, on the other, we are faced with dictionary compilers who accept anything so long as it is used, it is exceedingly refreshing to peruse an author who has the courage to speak out against these lexicographical "Charlie Browns."
[R: ARBA 75, p. 569]   Francis J. Witty

FOREIGN LANGUAGE DICTIONARIES

ARABIC

605.   Wehr, Hans. **A Dictionary of Modern Written Arabic.** 3rd ed. Ithaca, NY, Spoken Language Services, 1976. 1110p. LC 75-24236. ISBN 0-87950-001-8.

This is an enlarged and improved translation of Hans Wehr's original *Arabisches Worterbuch für die Schriftsprache der Gegenwart*, published in 1952. The dictionary, according to the author, presents the vocabulary and phraseology of modern written Arabic, the language used in the Arab mass media. This English edition includes all the material contained in the German edition of the dictionary and in the *Supplement*, plus a number of additions and corrections, the need for which became obvious only after the publication of the *Supplement*. The second edition of *Webster's New International Dictionary* was used as a standard reference for spelling and for certain definitions.

Arabic words are arranged according to Arabic roots. Foreign words are listed alphabetically. Arabicized loan words, if they clearly fit under the roots, are entered both ways, often with the root entry giving a reference to the alphabetical listing. Synonyms and usage are given for many terms. The dictionary fails to give a table for standard transliteration. The author relied to a large extent on Arab students at the University of Munster for the approximately correct pronunciation.

On the whole, the dictionary is comprehensive and accurate; it is highly recommended. It will definitely be of great value for all students of modern standard Arabic and others who want to find the English meaning of words used by the Arab media.

Ed. note: A fourth edition of the *Dictionary* (1300p. $115.00) was to be published in 1980 but was unavailable for review. [R: ARBA 78, p. 539]   Mohammed M. Aman

CHINESE

606.   Yutang, Lin. **Chinese-English Dictionary of Modern Usage.** Hong Kong, Chinese University, 1972; distr., New York, McGraw-Hill, 1973. 1920p. index. $55.00. LC 72-3899. ISBN 0-07-099695-4.

Dr. Lin Yutang has summed up a lifetime of knowledge and experience in this monumental work. Its predecessors were two other notable works: *Chinese-English Dictionary,* by Herbert A. Giles (1892) and *Chinese-English Dictionary,* by R. H. Mathews (1932).

Among the features of the work are: 1) entries that relate the successive meanings of the words; 2) a convenient romanization system; 3) an index system that, among other things, reduces the 214 Kanghsi radicals to only 50; 4) the inclusion of levels of speech (e.g., "derogatory," "courteous," "facetious," etc.); 5) a list of characters from the regular to the simplified and from the simplified to the regular.

The basic principle of the work, according to the author, is contextual semantics — i.e., the imperceptible changes of meaning due to context. The influence of past usage on the present is pointed out, and there is an emphasis on the spoken language. Supplementary material includes directions for using the dictionary; a numerical index of characters; an explanation of cycles; lists of Chinese dynasties, geographical names, and common English and Chinese names; the 214 radicals; and an English index. [R: ARBA 75, p. 560; Choice, Sept 73, p. 948; LJ, July 73, p. 2069; WLB, Sept 73, p. 85]   Suzine Har Nicolescu

CZECHOSLOVAKIAN

607.   **Dictionary of the Czech Literary Language.** Slovnik Spisovneho Jazyka Ceskeho. Praga, Ceckoslovenske Akademie Ved, 1958-1966; distr., University, University of Alabama Press, 1971. 4v. $35.00/v. LC 66-16431. ISBN 0-8173-0850-4(v.1); 0-8173-0851-2(v.2); 0-8173-0852-0(v.3); 0-8173-0853-9(v.4).

This is by far the most comprehensive dictionary of Czech literary language, published by the Czechoslovak Academy of Science. No etymologies or complete historical definitions are given, but vocabulary is adequately explained in terms of contemporary use. In addition, the secondary definitions remind us somewhat of those provided in the *American Heritage Dictionary of the English Language.* (R: ARBA 72, p. 478]

EGYPTIAN HIEROGLYPHIC

608.   Budge, E. A. Wallis. **An Egyptian Hieroglyphic Dictionary.** London, John Murray, 1920; repr., New York, Dover Publications, 1978. 2v. index. $10.00/v. LC 77-90344. ISBN 0-486-23615-3.

Undoubtedly inspired by the recent mania for things Egyptian, this reprint of Budge's 1920 standard work will prove a bargain to libraries needing such an item. Listing some 28,000 words or terms from the period 3000 B.C. to 600 A.D., the work provides a transliteration, the hieroglyph, the English equivalent, and, quite often, a reference to a text wherein the word or term is used. A long introduction by Budge traces developments in hieroglyphic studies up to 1920. A list of hieroglyphic characters, and the Coptic, Semitic, and Persian cuneiform alphabets are provided. Following the dictionary proper are a list of kings' names; a list of countries, cities, and towns; an index of English words, an index of kings' names, and an index of geographical terms. A section details geographical names in Coptic, Greek, Hebrew, Assyrian, Syriac, and Arabic, while another provides the Coptic words quoted in the dictionary section. The final appendix (all of which occupies some 550 pages) lists non-Egyptian words quoted in the main section (Greek, Hebrew, etc.).

An addition to the reprint explains briefly the arrangement of words in the *Dictionary*, but this is the only new matter. Budge also prepared an edition of the *Book of the Dead* and a two-volume *Gods of the Egyptians*, both of which have been reprinted by Dover (among other of his works). Anyone working with those volumes will find this to be of inestimable help. Budge is still recommended by Sheehy and Walford, and Dover is to be commended for bringing out these volumes to round out their reprints of his works. [R: ARBA 79, p. 554]   Koert C. Loomis, Jr.

FRENCH

609.   Atkins, Beryl T., and others. **Collins-Robert French-English, English-French Dictionary.** Cleveland, OH, Collins + World, 1978. 1536p. $16.95; $17.95(thumb-indexed). ISBN 0-00-433478-7; 0-00-433479-5(thumb-indexed).

Two topnotch teams—one French under Paul Robert (of *Grand* and *Petit Robert* fame) and one British under Jan Collins (of *Collins Spanish Dictionary* renown)—labored for over 15 years to produce this masterpiece, emphasizing the current, living language of every day communication. Since the United States and England are separated by the same language (gas, gasoline versus petrol), labels specify usage on each side of the Atlantic, and also in French Canada, Ireland, and Scotland. Other labels further pinpoint meaning. Single daggers denote terms gone out of fashion ("teddy-boys," whose French equivalent, *blousons-noirs*, is still used), double ones signal obsolescent words still found in literary texts. Refreshingly up to date: the asterisks no longer *in* the four-letter words (*mots de cinq lettres*), but *after* them (three for no-nos, two for slang, one for colloquialisms). Modern terms like "jet lag" find their longer French equivalents: *les troubles dûs au décalage horaire*, or vice versa; "to get high" (on drugs): *se défoncer* (slang). "Bulldozer" is not yet *bulldozeur*, although already accepted. "Pipeline" remains *pipeline* (pajplajn), although some French say peepleen. We missed "turnpike" (U.S.) for toll road, and CB radio (citizen band car-to-car radio), while the translation of *trinquer* ("to clink glasses") cannot really satisfy the oenophile. Although 717 pages of French-English, 741 pages of English-French, and 200,000 words and phrases try to bridge the Anglo-French language gap with eloquence and precision (and *clear* typography and IPA pronunciation), all of those fluent in two or more languages know that basically translating is a "mission impossible." Even transliterating becomes exquisite torture when facing Baudelaire's verses or Shakespeare's drama. Vide the Collins-Robert experts' *lecteur* (p. xviii) while they mean "speaker," for which there is no good French equivalent here except *celui (celle) qui parle*. Good list of abbreviations, but what about word divisions, if only the advice "don't"? A good buy. [R: ARBA 79, p. 554]   Adriaan de Wit

610.   Mansion, J. E., ed. **Harrap's New Standard French and English Dictionary; Part One, French-English.** Rev. and ed. by R. P. L. Ledésert and Margaret Ledésert. New York, Scribner's, 1972. 2v. $32.50/v. LC 72-2297. ISBN 0-684-13006-8(v.1); 0-684-13045-9(v.2).

After 25 years of research, M. and Mme. Ledésert presented Part One (French-English, in two volumes) of *Harrap's New Standard French and English Dictionary*. Not only have all articles been revised to reflect current usage, but the *New Standard* contains 50 to 60% more material than the original. Terms that are the result of developments in science and technology are included, and there are also large numbers of idioms, slang expressions, and "franglais" words. The very readable preface gives detailed information on criteria, orthography (English versus American), and use of the dictionary. It also reveals, in an interesting sidelight, the perils of presenting handwritten copy to the typesetter.

Entries provide pronunciation, utilizing the International Phonetic Alphabet; part of speech; translation; variant meanings; and examples. In addition, specialized meanings (Bot., Nau., etc.) are so identified, as are archaic, obsolescent, and literary words, vulgar terms, and colloquialisms and slang expressions.

Part Two of the *New Standard* (the English-French part) is not yet available. Until it is published, Part Two (English-French) of *Harrap's Standard French and English Dictionary* must be used. [R: ARBA 73, p. 459; Choice, Apr 73, p. 266; LJ, 15 Feb 73, p. 524; WLB, Apr 73, p. 701]

GERMAN

611. Betteridge, Harold T. **Cassell's German-English, English-German Dictionary: Deutsch-Englisches, Englisch-Deutsches Wörterbuch.** Completely rev. ed. New York, Macmillan Publishing; London, Cassell, 1978. 1580p. $13.50; $14.95(thumb-indexed). LC 77-18452. ISBN 0-02-522920-6; 0-02-522930-3(thumb-indexed).

Only a long period of use can provide an adequate basis for review of a dictionary. This reviewer has used Cassell's bilingual Latin dictionary over a long period of classroom purposes and has found it thoroughly adequate, and the same report comes from colleagues in French, Spanish, and German who have used Cassell's corresponding dictionaries in their fields. Obviously, there are very high editorial standards.

This reviewer ordinarily uses the much larger and much more expensive Oxford-Harrap and Muret-Sanders bilingual German dictionaries, but he has also found that the older edition of Cassell's is quite satisfactory for ready reference and that there are no contradictions in definitions from these two larger and more authoritative works. Several hours spent with this new edition revealed no typos (there must be some; even the *OED* is not totally unblemished), no misleading definitions, no other obvious deficiency. This new edition has certain attractive features, viz., some 300 more pages than the previous one, phonetic transcriptions of German keywords and a key to German pronunciation, whether verbal prefixes are separable or not, a new bibliography of technical and specialist dictionaries, and proper names in the main text. All are worthwhile, but the Cassell dictionaries can be promoted on their established reputation alone. [R: ARBA 80, p. 514]

Lawrence S. Thompson

612. Messinger, Heinz. **Langenscheidt's Comprehensive English-German Dictionary.** Berlin, Langenscheidt; distr., New York, Optimum Book Marketing, 1972. 1104p. ISBN 0-88254-050-5.

The dust jacket tells us that there are 120,000 entries; but then it also states that there are 1,134 pages. The work is a large, well-bound quarto with three columns to a page; it is easy to consult, with its entry words in heavy roman, meanings in a clear, legible type, and eye-catching cross references. Altogether it represents a fine job of printing and proof-reading. The work is presented as "a new dictionary for the 1970s," with the statement that "great attention has been given to the exhaustive treatment of key words" which have "crowded into the vocabulary" in the 1960s. Its stated aim is to "take a middle course between Langenscheidt's *Muret-Sanders* and the *College English-German Dictionary*, profiting from the merits of both works."

The introductory explanations are set out in parallel columns in German and English. Appendixes cover abbreviations, names, numerals, temperature conversion, weights and measures, and irregular verbs. Like most English-foreign language dictionaries of the reviewer's acquaintance, this one sometimes is not mutually exhaustive in its treatment of synonyms; e.g., under "grave clothes" we find only *Totengewand*; under "shroud" we find *Leichentuch, Totenhemd*. But this is a difficult area to cover exhaustively, even with the aid of a computer. The stated "middle course" followed by the compiler makes the work practical in size without taking too much away from its comprehensiveness. On the whole, this dictionary is highly regarded. [R: ARBA 74, p. 465; LJ, 15 June 73, p. 1904]

Francis J. Witty

613. **The Oxford-Harrap Standard German-English Dictionary.** Ed. by Trevor Jones. New York, Oxford University Press, 1978. 3v. $49.00/v. ISBN 0-19-864129-X(v.1); 0-19-864130-3(v.2); 0-19-864131-1(v.3).

Typographical and linguistic accuracy is a hallmark of this great work, and its utility for scholars in any field is readily apparent. Pagination starts over with each letter of the alphabet, but there seems to be no real virtue in this policy, and some confusion could result when references are made to the work.

Comparison with the revised edition of *Langenscheidts enzyklopädisches Wörterbuch* (1974-1975, 2v.) is inevitable. Both have an abundance of examples from current and literary German and English usage. Despite the title of the German work, Oxford-Harrap tends to be somewhat more encyclopedic in terms of the number of names and technical terms included. On the other hand, Langenscheidt seems to have more German compounds. No scholar would make a mistake in investing in either work, and, if the funds are available, in both. [R: ARBA 79, p. 556]

Lawrence S. Thompson

INDONESIAN

614. Echols, John M., and Hassan Shadily. **An English-Indonesian Dictionary.** Ithaca, NY, Cornell University Press, 1975. 660p. $37.50; $20.00pa. LC 72-5638. ISBN 0-8014-0728-1; 0-8014-9859-7pa.

Indonesian is the national language and the only official language of the largest country in Southeast Asia and the most widely taught Southeast Asian language in American and Australian universities. Thus, the absence for so long of a good, basic, modern Indonesian-English dictionary is to be wondered at.

This dictionary is more specifically an American English-Indonesian dictionary, with American spelling and standard American pronunciation indicated. The new orthography jointly adopted by the governments of Indonesia and Malaysia has been employed throughout, and the major features of the new spelling system are briefly described in the introduction.

The dictionary has been prepared specifically for Indonesians, although the preface and introduction are in English. The abbreviations used to indicate parts of speech and special usages are mainly in Indonesian, although some English abbreviations are used. Sentences and colloquial phrases illustrating variant uses of English words are generously employed. The authors have, however, incorporated some devices to make the dictionary useful to English speakers; the dictionary will no doubt be the standard English-Indonesian dictionary for many years, and perhaps decades, to come. [R: ARBA 76, p. 554; LJ, July 75, p. 1306]

Charles R. Bryant

ITALIAN

615. Reynolds, Barbara, comp. **The Concise Cambridge Italian Dictionary.** New York, Cambridge University Press, 1975. 792p. $34.50. LC 74-77384. ISBN 0-521-07273-5.

This dictionary, as its title suggests, is a concise version of the well-regarded *Cambridge Italian Dictionary*. While primarily designed for the English speaker, it is equally proficient at rendering English into good, current Italian. Barbara Reynolds has made a sincere attempt to preserve the swing and syntax of modern Italian in translating from

English; the emphasis, however, is on British usage, and many Americanisms have been omitted. Little attempt is made at etymology in this shortened format, and pronunciation is supplied only in cases in which the person having reasonable acquaintance with Italian would feel some doubt. The three-column format compensates for the compact size of the volume, and the print, although small, is quite clear.

Syllabication is provided for all polysyllabic words. Parenthetical abbreviations (e.g., mil., mus., geo.) indicate the specialized uses to which certain words are put. Elements of dialect are found scattered throughout, including words peculiar to Tuscan or Sicilian usage. The compiler has a tendency to translate rather than to define, but a concise Italian reference grammar and several useful tables are appended as aids to comprehension. Overall, the *Concise Cambridge Italian Dictionary* is a very commendable reduction of a large, highly technical work into a convenient and portable volume. It provides an extremely competent rendering of colloquial (British) English into the *lingua parlata* of mainstream contemporary Italian. [R: ARBA 76, p. 555; Choice, Sept 75, p. 821; LJ, 15 Mar 75, p. 570; LJ, 15 Apr 75, p. 747; WLB, June 75, p. 754]   Bruce A. Shuman

LATIN

616.   Glare, P. G. W., ed. **Oxford Latin Dictionary.** Oxford, Clarendon Press, 1968- ; distr., New York, Oxford University Press, 1968- . 8fas. $36.50pa./fas. (fas.1, 2, & 5); $32.50pa./fas. (fas.3, 4, & 6). ISBN 0-19-864209-1(fas.1); 0-19-864215-6(fas.2); 0-19-864216-4(fas.3); 0-19-864217-2(fas.4); 0-19-864218-0(fas.5); 0-19-864219-9(fas.6). In progress.

Latin-English dictionaries previously have been largely translated or adapted from European dictionaries, which have themselves been in part derivative. This dictionary is independent of all other dictionaries, being the first on this scale and based on a fresh and thorough reading of all the available sources. The entire text of the thesaurus is, however, in Latin, restricting its use to the most exclusive of specialists.

The *Oxford Latin Dictionary* follows, generally speaking, the principles of the *Oxford English Dictionary*, and its formal layout of articles is similar. Within each section or subsection, quotations are arranged chronologically, the first example showing, where practicable, the earliest known instance of that particular definition or usage. The dictionary is designed to give a full account of the meaning and use of words occurring in Latin from the beginnings to about 200 A.D. Other features include both translational and explanatory English equivalents, phraseology and grammar, and concise but reliable etymological and derivational indications. This is a major work of scholarship that will support the interpretive studies of our classical heritage.

The work will be complete in eight fascicles. The first fascicle, "A—Calcitro," published in 1968, includes a list of references and other aids to the reader. Other fascicles include: Fascicle II: "Calcitro-Demitto" (1969); Fascicle III: "Demiurgus-Gorgoneus" (1971); Fascicle IV: "Gorgonia-Libero" (1973); Fascicle V: "Libero-Pactum" (1976); and Fascicle VI: "Pactum-Qualitercumque" (1977).

PERSIAN

617.   Steingass, F. **A Comprehensive Persian-English Dictionary: Including the Arabic Words and Phrases To Be Met with in Persian Literature, Being Johnson and Richardson's Persian, Arabic, and English Dictionary, Revised, Enlarged, and Entirely Reconstructed.** Boston, Routledge and Kegan Paul, 1892, 1977 printing. 1539p. $52.00. ISBN 0-7100-2152-6.

Given the scope of the Persian language, the subtleties and complexities of Arabic and Persian meaning, and the limits imposed in providing a comprehensive and useful tool in one volume, this dictionary represents the most useful, reliable, and up-to-date resource available to students of Persian. Each entry is translated with variable meanings, including idiomatic, colloquial, compound usage, and phrases. The transliteration used in exception to Persian script for all subentries is justified by way of reducing the size of the book, which is large anyway. Although this reviewer would prefer to have the Persian without transliteration, the romanization of Persian is only a small obstacle in exchange for increased entries with comprehensive translations. Arabic words common to Persian, technical and scientific terms, and words of other foreign origin are included according to their natural importance to contemporary Persian usage. Research resources used by the author range from Firdausi and Answari to major contemporary writers. Without access to the original Johnson and Richardson *Persian, Arabic, and English Dictionary*, from which this edition has been "revised, enlarged, and entirely reconstructed," this reviewer must defer to the work at hand and recommend this dictionary as a remarkably accurate, reasonably comprehensive, and useful tool for any student or scholar of Persian. [R: ARBA 79, p. 559]   Eugene L. Keyser

POLISH

618.   Bulas, Kazimierz, and Francis J. Whitfield. **The Kościuszko Foundation Dictionary. Vol. I, English-Polish. Vol. II, Polish-English.** The Hague, Mouton; distr., New York, Humanities Press, 1969. 2v.

The first volume of this dictionary was published in 1959 and the second in 1961; both were published in Poland's Millennium Series by the Foundation. This is the most comprehensive dictionary of this type on the market; it is already listed in all standard reference sources, including Walford. The most comprehensive dictionary of the Polish language is a Warsaw publication (planned in 12 volumes) by the Polish Academy of Sciences—*Slownik jezyka polskiego*, but it is still in progress. [R: ARBA 71, p. 426]

RUSSIAN

619.   Smirnitsky, A. I., and others, comps. **Russian-English Dictionary.** Newly rev. ed. New York, Dutton, 1973. 766p. $19.95. LC 58-5989. ISBN 0-525-19520-3.

"Smirnitsky" has long been accepted in this country as the best standard dictionary for college and school use. Now in its ninth edition, it still retains its usefulness as a general all-purpose dictionary, with a total vocabulary of some 50,000 words. This edition is the first completely reset version since the third edition (published in 1958), although it retains the same number of words.

In 1972 a new *Oxford Russian-English Dictionary* was published, edited by B. O. Unbegaun (918p. $39.95). The Oxford work contains about 70,000 entries, including colloquial vocabulary and idioms and a selected number of scientific terms. A comparison between the two dictionaries reveals that the *Oxford Russian-English Dictionary* gives more English equivalents for Russian words; also, it defines about 20,000 more words, and the grammatical information accompanying entries seems to be better structured. Nevertheless, both dictionaries are reliable, and both serve their stated purpose well. Choosing between them will be largely a matter of personal preference. [R: ARBA 75, p. 564; Choice, Feb 74, p. 1850]   Bohdan S. Wynar

SERBO-CROATIAN

620. Benson, Morton. **An English-Serbocroatian Dictionary.** Philadelphia, University of Pennsylvania Press, 1979. 669p. $35.00. LC 78-64520. ISBN 0-8122-7764-3.

A welcome addition to the world of dictionaries, this work will be found indispensable in any type of library: public, academic, and special. It serves as a companion volume to the compiler's *Serbocroatian-English Dictionary*, published by Prosveta, Belgrade (1971, 1974, and 1977) and the University of Pennsylvania Press (1971). The consultants to this work are outstanding scholars from Yugoslavia and the United States, all of whom speak Serbocroatian as their native language.

This volume should satisfy the acute need for an up-to-date English-Serbocroatian dictionary. It describes the lexicon of standard contemporary English. The norm described is the American variant of English as reflected in the speech of educated Americans and in the press. Essential Briticisms are also included. English words and expressions are glossed into their Eastern variant. If there is a "jekavian" form, this form is given. When the Zagreb standard uses a different word, this word is given after the designation "W" (meaning Western). A gloss may have both a "jekavian" form and a "W" lexical form. An example is given in the introduction — "for *bread* the basic gloss: *hleb - hljeb* (W: *kruh*)." Included are proverbial and idiomatic expressions, important scientific and technical terms, and frequently used abbreviations. A list of abbreviations used in this work is provided in both languages. In the introduction (given both in English and Serbocroatian), references to the extensive instructions in spelling, pronunciation, etc., will be found extremely useful. A random check revealed no errors in the spelling or the variants. Furthermore, the variants provided seem to represent, based on the reviewer's own knowledge of the language, a good representation of terms used throughout the country. [R: ARBA 80, p. 517]

Katherine Cveljo

SPANISH

621. **Simon and Schuster's International Dictionary: English/Spanish, Spanish/English.** Tana de Gámez, ed.-in-chief. New York, Simon and Schuster, 1973. 884 + 1605p. LC 71-180718. ISBN 0-671-21507-8; 0-671-21267-2(indexed).

Its 200,000-plus entries packed into a lightweight, readable, and inexpensive volume make this work a potential bargain for the individual and the institutional buyer alike. More fundamentally, the Simon and Schuster stands on its own special merits — namely, balance and insight. Both of these qualities stem from the makeup of the editorial staff and the list of contributors, which helps to assure that European and American English and Spanish receive balanced coverage. Not only is there sufficient attention to idioms and regionalisms, but also British pronunciation is distinguished from the American.

Pronunciation is indicated in the International Phonetic Alphabet. The editors have sought to reflect current usage regardless of the dictates of the Spanish Royal Academy or other bodies. This descriptive policy extends to vulgarisms and international terms of sophistication, such as "ciao" or "gemütlich." While they have done a creditable job of providing exact equivalents in most cases, the editors have attempted to "convey the spirit as well as the meanings of words." To this end, the dictionary focuses on literary and folk expressions, versatile terms (e.g., "get," "*poner*") and false cognates, and bolsters these with frequent examples of usage. Finally, the editors have reduced the introductory sections to a minimum, yet filled them with enough information on grammar, verbs, and pronunciation so as not to encumber the text with too many symbols or details. On the

strength of its format, balance, and depth, the Simon and Schuster deserves consideration by anyone in the market for a complete Spanish-English dictionary. [R: ARBA 75, p. 566; Choice, Dec 73, p. 1534; LJ, 1 May 73, p. 1472; LJ, 15 Apr 74, p. 1098; WLB, May 73, p. 794]
John Robert Wheat

622.   **The University of Chicago Spanish Dictionary.** 3rd ed., rev. and enl. Comp. by Carlos Castillo and Otto F. Bond. Chicago, University of Chicago Press, 1977. 488p. illus. $9.95; $3.95pa. LC 76-449. ISBN 0-226-09673-4; 0-226-09674-2pa.

This is an excellent, handy-sized dictionary designed for Spanish or English speakers who are interested in the other language. It could be used by travellers as well as students. Each entry consists of a key to the pronunciation, part of speech, one or more meanings, and occasional examples of usage. In addition to the dictionary entries, it includes a general guide to pronunciation, a concise grammar for both languages, and, for Spanish, a list of "Nations, Cities, and Adjectives of Nationality."

A major new feature of this third edition is "A Spanish-English List of 1000 Common Idioms and Proverbs, with Dialectal Variants." This is a very good list of common idioms and proverbs with English translations. It would be even more useful if the compilers had made references to the idioms and proverbs in this list from related word entries in the dictionary proper. The list itself has its own index, but entries are made only under the first word of the English translation, including articles, rather than under keywords.

This dictionary is a very good tool that will contribute to a greater understanding of the written and spoken language, whether Spanish or English. [R: ARBA 78, p. 547]
Rafael Catalá

YIDDISH

623.   Weinreich, Uriel. **Modern English-Yiddish, Yiddish-English Dictionary.** New York, Schocken Books, 1977. 789p. $15.95pa. LC 77-76038.

This is a genuine, serious dictionary of the Yiddish language, not to be confused with such a work as Leo Rosten's *Joys of Yiddish* (McGraw-Hill, 1968). Yiddish words are printed in the Hebrew alphabet as adapted to the language, and English words are sometimes used in parentheses to explain possible ambiguities. Some 40 pages of "Guidelines" present an excellent introduction to the dictionary and to the lexicographical and grammatical peculiarities of Yiddish. This prolegomenon will be of particular help to the reference librarian who does not know the language but does read the Hebrew alphabet and some German. The Yiddish-English section (reading from back to middle) has a briefer introduction in Yiddish. The purpose of the dictionary, as stated in the late author's preface, "is to furnish the advanced student of Yiddish with access to the language of modern cultivated usage." It is taken for granted that the user has a firm grounding in English, even though his command of Yiddish is still rudimentary. The work appears to be reasonably comprehensive and well printed although margins are almost nonexistent. [R: ARBA 79, p. 564]
Francis J. Witty

624.   Brown, Les. **The New York Times Encyclopedia of Television.** New York, Times Books, 1977. 492p. illus. bibliog. $20.00. LC 77-79022. ISBN 0-8129-0721-3.

Les Brown's *Encyclopedia of Television* represents a convenient reference source to television programs and prominent personalities associated with the television industry, as well as definitions of television terminology. Individual entries are between 100 and 200 words in length, arranged alphabetically with pages divided into two columns. The information included under each entry contains either a brief bibliographical description of the individual TV personality, or a brief history of a particular TV program with remarks on its background. The former group includes not only actors but also company executives, directors, producers, and writers. There are no indexes or special cross references. This book is in strict alphabetical order with a brief bibliography at the end. The author's deadline for revisions and updating was set for May 1, 1977. Prominence and reference value were the criteria set for including an entry in this work. Final decisions on entries to be included were based upon judgments made in consultation with a team of experts from the TV industry and various television-related fields.

There are other radio and television dictionaries, such as *Elsevier's Dictionary of Television and Video Recording* (Elsevier, 1975. $85.50) and *Dictionary of Radio and Television* by W. E. Pannelt (Philosophical Library, 1967). However, none of them are as current or as comprehensive as Les Brown's *New York Times Encyclopedia of Television*. Due to its organization and contents, this work will be a useful reference tool in any library. [R: ARBA 79, p. 575; BL, 15 Sept 78, p. 254; LJ, 1 Nov 77, p. 2251; LJ, 15 Apr 78, p. 818; WLB, May 78, p. 730]   George V. Hodowanec

625.   Diamant, Lincoln, ed. **The Broadcast Communications Dictionary.** Rev. and expanded ed. New York, Hastings House Publishers, 1978. 201p. (Communication Arts Books). $9.95. LC 77-19258. ISBN 0-8038-0788-0.

The original edition of this work appeared in 1974 and was rightly hailed as a solid contribution for those both within and about the communications industry. This edition adds 73 pages of new and expanded entries. Many of the new entries account for foreign broadcast organizations and agencies previously not listed or having developed since the earlier edition. It is the organization of the material that deserves special commendation. The definitions are concise and clear, with very effective and well thought-out "see" references. In addition, many "compare" references are offered for analogous or synonymous words and phrases: i.e., the entry for documentary reads "recorded presentation of actual, unrehearsed events. Compare: cinema verity, direct cinema, slice." (Incidentally, the entry under "slice" refers to the "Slice of Life" school of television advertising techniques.)

This work is recommended for its ready usability and style. It is more up to date than Frank Jefkins' *Dictionary of Marketing and Communications* (International Ideas, 1973. $10.95) and more relevant to those terms applying to television and radio broadcasting. It should be noted that in addition to those terms strictly peculiar to these industries, this work accounts for those words that have moved over from the stage and motion picture industry. Thus, this can be recommended to all library collections of any size, to members of the industry from secretaries to top executives, and to teachers and researchers in the field. [R: ARBA 79, p. 568; Choice, Apr 79, p. 202; WLB, Nov 78, p. 283]

Gerald R. Shields

626.   Dunning, John. **Tune in Yesterday: The Ultimate Encyclopedia of Old-Time Radio 1925-1976.** Englewood Cliffs, NJ, Prentice-Hall, 1976. 703p. illus. index. $17.95. LC 76-28369. ISBN 0-13-932616-2.

Here is a listing of all the great drama, comedy, and variety radio series of yesteryear. Programs are arranged alphabetically by title. Information includes sponsors, writers, typical plots, cast and format changes, opening and closing dates, and brief biographical facts about major performers. A detailed index provides cross references to players, characters, and variant titles. The compiler has done a thorough research job, using many primary and secondary sources as well as drawing upon his own background and interest in the subject. This specialized reference book will be useful in answering serious questions about old-time radio, nurturing the nostalgia craze, and documenting an era that brought Helen Trent, Jack Armstrong, Gabriel Heatter, and Fibber McGee into homes across the nation, poor and wealthy alike. A useful adjunct source to Frank Buxton and Bill Owen's *The Big Broadcast 1920-1950* (Viking, 1972). [R: ARBA 78, p. 553; Choice, Nov 77, pp. 1204-1206; LJ, 15 Jan 77, p. 187; RQ, Fall 77, p. 87; WLB, May 77, pp. 776-77]

Edward Mapp

27 LITERATURE

GENERAL WORKS

627.   **Contemporary Literary Criticism: Excerpts from Criticism of the Works of Today's Novelists, Poets, Playwrights, and Other Creative Writers, Volumes 1-15.** Ed. by Dedria Bryfonski and others. Detroit, Gale, 1973-1980. 15v. $54.00/v. LC 76-38938. ISBN 0-8103-0100-8(v.1).

With the appearance of the latest installments, *Contemporary Literary Criticism* has grown to 15 volumes; the sixteenth volume is in preparation. Only months pass between the publication of volumes, and the series has long since become indispensable. Each successive volume marks the growth of the critical view of authors "being currently discussed." This is not a matter of criticism being presented chronologically in a multivolume treatment, but of the editors' recreating mutable critical portraits of authors who have drawn considerable public and professional interest.

On the average, 150 creative writers are treated in each volume. These authors include those who either are now living or have died since January 1, 1960 (although the criticism included may have appeared somewhat earlier). Individual entries begin with brief biographical sketches and include references to other *CLC* volumes in which the subjects are treated and to the volumes of the companion *Contemporary Authors* in which more detailed biographical information can be found. The critical excerpts are generally well-balanced—some are general evaluations; others deal with individual titles. Altogether the editors estimate that 750 individual excerpts appear in each volume. In addition, the volumes now include cumulative indexes to authors and critics.

Volume 12 deserves special mention; it is the first in the series that is devoted to a special topic. It treats 65 contemporary writers of young adult literature. The definition of this literature is broad—it includes popular songs, the work of cartoonists and humorists, and the creations of screenwriters, scriptwriters, and playwrights—but the treatment is as thorough as that in the other volumes. This focus is to be repeated periodically in other volumes.

In all, the series is well worth the price. [R: ARBA 74, p. 478; Choice, Oct 73, p. 1162; LJ, Aug 73, p. 2264; WLB, Oct 73, p. 169; BL, 1 Oct 74, p. 189; C&RL, Jan 74, p. 38; LJ, 15 Apr 74, p. 1099; LJ, Aug 74, p. 1928; LJ, 1 Apr 75, p. 654; ARBA 76, pp. 572, 573; ARBA 77, p. 548; BL, 1 Sept 79, p. 62]   F. W. Ramey

628.   **Twentieth-Century Literary Criticism: Excerpts from Criticism of the Works of Novelists, Poets, Playwrights, Short Story Writers, and Other Creative Writers 1900-1960, Volumes I-III.** Dedria Bryfonski and Phyllis Carmel Mendelson, eds. Detroit, Gale, 1978-1980. 3v. index. $54.00/v. LC 76-46132. ISBN 0-8103-0175-X(v.1); 0-8103-0176-8 (v.2); 0-8103-0177-6(v.3).

Intended as a companion to Gale's *Contemporary Literary Criticism* (covering authors living from 1960 to the present; see entry 627), these volumes are the first of a series on writers who died between 1900 and 1960. In the list of about 300 writers who will be treated in early volumes, the majority have established literary reputations: Brecht, Colette, Conrad, Woolf, Yeats. A few, such as Raymond Chandler, James Whitcomb Riley, and Mary Roberts Rinehart, were evidently selected on the basis of popularity. Each volume in the series covers 35-40 authors, each being characterized in an opening paragraph, followed by a list of principal works and by generous excerpts from books and critical articles (arranged chronologically by date of publication). The appended indexes to critics include such well-known names as Conrad Aiken, W. H. Auden, Eric Bentley, Van Wyck Brooks, and Edmund Wilson. Excerpts from individual books and articles are longer than those in *A Library of Literary Criticism*, although the latter sometimes quotes critics not found in the *Twentieth-Century Literary Criticism* section on the same writer. The series promises to be a great time-saver for students and others interested in writers of the period. [R: ARBA 79, p. 579; BL, 15 Apr 79, p. 1314; LJ, 15 Nov 78, p. 2325; WLB, Oct 78, p. 183]

Frances Neel Cheney

BIBLIOGRAPHIES

629. Bateson, F. W., and Harrison T. Meserole. **A Guide to English and American Literature**. 3rd ed. New York, Gordian Press, 1976. 334p. index. $15.00. LC 76-19083. ISBN 0-582-48414-6.

Bateson is best known as editor of the original volumes of the *Cambridge Bibliography of English Literature* (1940) and its *Supplement* (1957). As such, he was in a unique position regarding the scholarship concerning English literature. He then published (1965) the first edition of this work, a version no less penetrating and caustic than this third edition. The form here is that of evaluative bibliographic essays divided into chapters, an approach ideally suited to Bateson's sharp pen. The fact that he is biased (and shows it) may lessen, for some, the value of the work; but for this reviewer, a clear demonstration of inevitable prejudices makes it easier to cope with them than does the futile attempt to deny what everyone knows must be present. And Bateson's views *are* those of an informed person.

The section on general works is followed by sections on Medieval, Renaissance, Augustan, Romantic, and Modern (to 1970) literatures. The format here is especially useful, since each period is covered in two chapters, the first an overview of each period's trends and characteristics, the second the actual bibliography (authors listed by year of birth). Entries have been updated, and the Shakespeare section is entirely new. The section on literary scholarship is far more instructive than most courses designed to inculcate those principles, although notes on the scope of the learned journals could have been useful.

The part that is meant to be a service, but that ends up looking like an afterthought, is the section on American literature, new to this edition. The idea is fine, but allotting less than 60 pages to the execution of it makes no sense. Little can be done in such space that could not be torn apart quite easily, and that is not the point here. Suffice it to say that something like Lewis Leary's *American Literature: A Study and Research Guide* (St. Martin's, 1976. $12.95; $4.95pa.) would be infinitely preferable. Indeed, the approach in the two items is somewhat similar, although Leary is less acid than Bateson.

Literary prejudices well expressed are often a delight to read, even if one does not share them with the author. That is the charm of this book. Its utility lies in its broad approach, the concentration on essential materials, and the remarkably stimulating "interchapters" on the various periods. Indeed, those essays are themselves worth the price of the book. For completeness, naturally, one turns to the successor volumes to Bateson's original work, now called the *New Cambridge Bibliography of English Literature* (see entry 692). Using this small work, though, would be a stimulating and helpful introduction to English (although *not* American) literature.

Ed. note: Three other works of value to students of English and American literature are Richard Daniel Altick and Andrew H. Wright's *Selective Bibliography for the Study of English and American Literature*, 6th ed. (Macmillan, 1978. 168p. $6.95pa.); *A Concise Bibliography for Students of English*, 5th ed., by Arthur G. Kennedy and Donald B. Sands (rev. by William E. Colburn. Stanford University Press, 1972. 300p. $10.00; $5.00pa.); and

Philip H. Vitale's *Basic Tools of Research: An Annotated Guide for Students of English*, 3rd ed. rev. and enl. (Barron's, 1975. 279p. $2.95pa.). [R: ARBA 78, p. 557; Choice, Sept 77, p. 825]

Koert C. Loomis, Jr.

630.   Magill, Frank N., ed. **Magill's Bibliography of Literary Criticism: Selected Sources for the Study of More than 2,500 Outstanding Works of Western Literature.** Stephen L. Hanson, and Patricia King Hanson, associate eds. Englewood Cliffs, NJ, Salem Press, 1979. 4v. index. $200.00/set. LC 79-63017. ISBN 0-89356-188-6.

"Bibliography is the latchkey to the knowledge bank in a given field," writes editor Frank Magill in the preface to *Bibliography of Literary Criticism*. Certainly this four-volume set appears to be a master key, opening scholarly doors to the world of Western literature. Its time span extends from approximately 2000 B.C. through A.D. 1978, with 36,137 citations to 2,546 works by 613 major world writers. Under Magill's direction, a staff of 20 experienced librarians holding graduate degrees in library science and literature culled these citations from thousands of sources, some never previously indexed. Selections were geared primarily to the needs of librarians, undergraduates, and generalists rather than specialists. References include essays in books, entire books, and periodical articles, with emphasis on material published in English during the last 20 years.

Paged consecutively throughout, the set has wide margins, clear print, and sturdy, attractive bindings. It is easy to use. The editors did not divide materials by genre or form, but followed a basic alphabetical scheme from Aeschylus through Zola. Sections are headed with the full names and dates of the writers covered. Subheadings consist of selected novels, plays, poems, and stories in a continual alphabetical flow, each followed by an average of 12 to 25 sources arranged by author. Entries follow standard bibliographical style, giving full publication data and page references. There are no abbreviations, therefore no need to search for an explanatory key. All volumes begin with a list of authors and titles. The last concludes with a comprehensive title index. Running heads at the tops of pages help locate information quickly. The set has some shortcomings. Surprisingly, it does not include cross references for pseudonyms. Furthermore, because of its arrangement, every citation pertains to a specific title, resulting in few clues to general critical or biographical studies. Under Shakespeare, for example, users will find no mention of the comprehensive books on imagery by Caroline Spurgeon and Wolfgang Clemen, or the important critical biography by A. L. Rowse. Malcolm Cowley's fine overview of Hemingway's work, first printed in the *Portable Hemingway*, does not appear, nor does Edmund Wilson's often reprinted essay on Hemingway's women or D. H. Lawrence's witty analysis of the Hemingway hero. Arthur Mizener's *The Far Side of Paradise* shows up in connection with several titles by F. Scott Fitzgerald, but Andrew Turnbull's biography does not. Oddly, *The Beautiful and Damned* is omitted, though Fitzgerald's four other novels are included along with several major short stories. Finally, a list of sources similar to those provided in the Wilson indexes would have been helpful as a holdings or acquisitions checklist. Adding materials such as these, however, would have increased the size and cost of an already expensive set.

As it stands, *Magill's Bibliography of Literary Criticism* is a remarkable reference work. Compiled by librarians for librarians, it will help them guide undergraduates to adequate resources for papers and give more sophisticated users suggestions for further delving. As a key to Western literary scholarship, it will supplement and possibly supersede other sources. According to the publishers, this is "the most comprehensive bibliography ever published. . . . A breakthrough in bibliographic control." They may be right. [R: ARBA 80, p. 534]

Mary Jo Walker

631. Patterson, Margaret C. **Literary Research Guide: An Evaluative, Annotated Bibliography of Important Reference Books and Periodicals on American and English Literature, of the Most Useful Sources for Research in Other National Literatures, and of More Than 300 Reference Books in Literature-Related Subject Areas.** Detroit, Gale, 1976. 385p. index. $24.00. LC 75-13925. ISBN 0-8103-1102-X.

Periodically, literary research guides appear which firmly establish themselves and go through edition after edition—Tom P. Cross, Kennedy and Sands, Altick and Wright. On the strength of this absolutely first-rate guide, Margaret Patterson should be able to take her place among the pantheon. Undergraduate majors, graduate students, professors engaged in literary research, and all academic and large public library reference departments should budget now to purchase this book. Expensive as it is, and there are grounds for arguing that it is overpriced, it should through the years pay for itself many times. Armed with it, the budding scholar especially can chart a sensibly planned path to many useful research sources. One good example is the entry devoted to the background of the Center for Editions of American Authors (CEAA).

Each of the 18 major sections (general guides, national literatures—basic guides and bibliographies, bibliographies of bibliographies, annual and monthly bibliographies, abstracting and indexing services, genre research, English, Irish, Scottish, Welsh, Commonwealth, American, Continental, comparative, and world literatures, and the reference section—problems and solutions) is appropriately subdivided for easy use.

The 1,560 entries, most of which have critical annotations, take up 327 of the small-print pages. Among the remaining pages are a section on the logic of the Dewey Decimal System, a brief explanation of the Library of Congress Classification, a concise glossary of bibliographical terms, and an excellent, multi-access index.

This is an outstanding work that deserves wide distribution and use. It should stand among the top specialized reference books of the 1970s. [R: ARBA 77, p. 1126; BL, 1 Sept 76, p. 57; LJ, 1 Apr 76, p. 880; WLB, Sept 76, p. 744]   Charles R. Andrews

632. **The Reader's Adviser: A Layman's Guide to Literature. Volume 1: The Best in American and British Fiction, Poetry, Essays, Literary Biography, Bibliography, and Reference.** 12th ed. Ed. by Sarah L. Prakken. New York, R. R. Bowker, 1974. 808p. index. $25.00. LC 57-13277. ISBN 0-8352-0781-1. ISSN 0094-5943.

633. **The Reader's Adviser: A Layman's Guide to Literature. Volume 2: The Best in American and British Drama and World Literature in English Translation.** 12th ed. Ed. by F. J. Sypher. New York, R. R. Bowker, 1977. 774p. index. $25.00. LC 57-13277. ISBN 0-8352-0852-4. ISSN 0094-5943.

634. **The Reader's Adviser: A Layman's Guide to Literature. Volume 3: The Best in the Reference Literature of the World.** 12th ed. Ed. by Jack A. Clarke. New York, R. R. Bowker, 1977. 1034p. index. $25.00. LC 57-13277. ISBN 0-8352-0853-2. ISSN 0094-5943.

The eleventh edition of *The Reader's Adviser*, published in 1968, was expanded at that time from one to two volumes. The twelfth edition was published in three volumes.

Volume 1 consists of 16 chapters. The first 4 cover general background, bibliography, reference books, and anthologies. Chapters 5 through 9 discuss British and American poetry, by period, and chapters 10 through 14 cover fiction. Another innovation in this twelfth edition was the selection of a number of subject specialists to be responsible for individual chapters. This has resulted in some unevenness in coverage, which is indirectly acknowledged in the preface: "Because each chapter was revised by a different person, small individual differences of approach may be detected from chapter to chapter" (p. xi). In all, there are 16 contributing editors.

A comparison of volume 1 of the eleventh and twelfth editions reveals that most of the material has been substantially updated and certain chapters (e.g., Modern American Poetry) also show considerable revision. The general structure of the volume remains the same, including some of the previous weaknesses of *The Reader's Adviser*. In spite of the claim that "in the general bibliographies at the head of each chapter and in the reading lists about an individual author our editors have been highly selective, choosing only *la crème de la crème*" (p. xviii), bibliographies and other reference books are traditionally rather poorly represented. As an example, Aliki Dick's *Student's Guide to British Literature: A Selective Bibliography of 4,128 Titles and Reference Sources from the Anglo-Saxon Period to the Present* was selected by ALA as one of the "Best Reference Books" of 1972; nevertheless, it somehow did not pass the editorial criteria for *The Reader's Adviser*. The section on rare book prices does not even mention Mandeville's *The Used Book Price Guide*, which lists 74,000 books. However, it does include *Bookman's Price Index*, which lists 32,000 titles, and *American Book Prices Current*, which lists 28,000. Because *The Reader's Adviser* is used by many bookstores and secondhand dealers, coverage of this subject should be more balanced. The selection of representative editions for individual writers is the strongest point of volume 1, being usually sound and well balanced.

The large volume of existing materials on literature prompted *The Reader's Adviser* to expand its coverage of the field into a companion volume, volume 2, comprising American and British drama and foreign literature in English translation. Thus, the chapters on American and British drama (1-5) show essentially the same structure as in previous editions, with obvious updating of bibliographical listings, new introductions, and several new biographical sketches. One can probably quarrel with the subtitle, "The Best in American and British Drama," because, as it is pointed out in the introduction, *The Reader's Adviser* lists only titles in print (with very few exceptions). Certainly these are not always the "best" when we talk about literary scholarship, since not all substantial works remain constantly in print.

In general, most sections are well executed. Unfortunately, for translations of foreign works in English, some editors failed to consult standard sources well known to librarians. The selection of authors in volume 2 is occasionally done at random, and there are many omissions under the major writers.

The third and final volume of the twelfth edition consists of 12 chapters and covers the same ground as the eleventh edition (second volume) published in 1969 and edited by Winifred Courtney. It is indicated in the preface that "in preparation of this edition every title from the previous volume was reviewed and either updated or replaced" (p. xi). Indeed, there are many revisions, some updating, and more pages, but our examination of the coverage of specific topics, particularly economics, resulted in less than optimistic conclusions. On the positive side, *Paperbound Books in Economics* and *Praeger Special Studies* have been removed from this edition. However, some classics, such as Schumpeter's works, have also been removed completely. In 1970, Samuelson received the Nobel Prize in economics, but he is not listed; nor are three other American economists who received the Nobel Prize in subsequent years. It makes little difference how many pages are devoted to a single author or discipline, but a careful selection of existing literature is a must. Hopefully, librarians will evaluate other sections of this volume with better results.

These critical comments do not, of course, detract from the overall usefulness of these volumes. Although deficiencies remain—omissions of the year of publication for certain titles, inconsistencies in prices, and no pagination for monographic works—they will not deter the user who is already familiar with the format of bibliographic citations in *The Reader's Adviser*. This edition constitutes a definite improvement in comparison with the eleventh edition, is more comprehensive, and, on the balance, can be recommended for many bookstores, smaller libraries, and individuals who have no access to more sophisticated tools. [R: ARBA 75, p. 583; WLB, Mar 75, p. 528; ARBA 78, pp. 2, 558; BL, 1 Mar 78, p. 1129; WLB, May 77, p. 778]

Bohdan S. Wynar

DICTIONARIES AND ENCYCLOPEDIAS

635.   **Cassell's Encyclopaedia of World Literature.** Rev. and enl. ed. General ed., John Buchanan-Brown. New York, William Morrow, 1973. 3v. $47.95. LC 73-10405. ISBN 0-688-00228-5.

Both the first edition of this title, published in 1953, and the revised and enlarged edition were rapidly acclaimed standard ready reference tools. The first volume of this edition, subtitled "Histories and General Articles," includes essays on the literatures of various lands and languages (e.g., Finnish literature, Basque literature), genres (morality play, essay, epigram, etc.), and literary terms. The two remaining volumes are devoted to biographies only. There is a galaxy of entries, from virtually all inhabited continents. One is pleased to encounter such moderns as Solzhenitsyn, Isak Dinesen, and Allen Ginsberg, as well as such oldsters as Huigh Groot and Su Shih.

Each entry gives place and date of birth, place and date of death (and place of burial, if different), and spouse. Following these details is a biographical essay that concludes with a catalog of works and a bibliography of biographical and/or critical works. Every essay and entry in all three volumes is signed by the contributor; all contributors are scholars, and most are British. [R: ARBA 75, p. 584; BL, 15 July 74, p. 1209; Choice, June 74, p. 577, C&RL, July 74, p. 250]

Kenyon C. Rosenberg

636.   Cuddon, J. A. **A Dictionary of Literary Terms.** Garden City, NY, Doubleday, 1977. 745p. $17.95. LC 76-47853. ISBN 0-385-12713-8.

This readable and often amusing literary dictionary contains more than 2,000 literary terms in international use. The whole dictionary is cross referenced so that the reader can move readily from one entry to another. The purpose of the book is to give the reader information—be it ordinary or abstruse.

The plan of the dictionary is alphabetical, from abecedarius to zeugma. Each term is ascribed a description or definition; indications of origin are added in brackets, followed by descriptions of etymology and what the term denotes. Resumés of origins, history, and development are included, as well as details of notable examples and distinguished practitioners. The 10 main categories of terms are: 1) technical terms; 2) forms; 3) genres or kinds; 4) technicalities; 5) groups, schools, and movements; 6) well-known phrases; 7) -isms (e.g., realism, naturalism, primitivism); 8) motifs or themes; 9) personalities; 10) modes, attitudes, and styles.

Intended for the general reader, the dictionary is useful and attractive as well as accurate. The style is clear and simple. Students, librarians, literary scholars, and the general reader will find this a useful and accurate tool. [R: ARBA 78, p. 563; LJ, 1 Oct 77, p. 2048; WLB, Nov 77, p. 264]

Norman E. Tanis

637.   **Encyclopedia of World Literature in the 20th Century.** Wolfgang Bernard Fleischmann, gen. ed. New York, Ungar, 1967-1971. 3v. illus. $40.00(v.1); $46.00(v.2); $50.00(v.3). LC 67-13615. ISBN 0-8044-3092-6(v.1); 0-8044-3093-4(v.2); 0-8044-3094-2 (v.3).

638.   **Encyclopedia of World Literature in the 20th Century: Volume 4, Supplement and Index.** Ed. by Frederick Ungar and Lina Mainiero. New York, Ungar, 1975. 462p. illus. index. $50.00. LC 67-13615. ISBN 0-8044-3091-8.

Based on the well-known German encyclopedia *Lexikon der Weltliteratur im 20. Jahrhundert* (Herder, 1960-61, 2v.), this encyclopedia will adequately meet the needs of the general public, especially in the area of European literature. In comparison to the German work, this encyclopedia is substantially enlarged and updated, contains brief bibliographies, and occasionally has new quotations of critical comments about major writers.

Arrangement of the 1,300 entries is alphabetical. In general, the well-written, readable articles on all aspects of contemporary literature are rather brief, with the exception of those on national literature, on literary movements, etc. Information presented is well documented with primary and secondary sources. For example, the article on Ukrainian literature, written by a specialist, Professor G. Luckyj of Toronto University, is a balanced presentation of this little-known branch of Slavic literature, including a sufficient bibliography of most of the important works on the subject. The same is true of biographical articles on lesser-known persons, such as the Polish poet Tuwim and the Nigerian novelist Amos Tutuola. There are some scattered black-and-white portraits.

The passage of four years brought to world prominence new writers who either were not included or were given insufficient attention in the basic three-volume set. These have occasioned the supplementary volume. In general, its articles maintain the same high standards. At the end of this volume is an index that covers all four volumes. [R: ARBA 71, p. 439; Choice, June 68, p. 463; C&RL, July 68, p. 328; LJ, 15 Jan 68, p. 175; ARBA 72, p. 489; ARBA 76, p. 571; BL, 15 July 76, p. 1615; LJ, 1 Mar 76, p. 702; WLB, Mar 76, p. 553]

639. Freeman, William. **Dictionary of Fictional Characters.** Rev. by Fred Urquhart. Boston, The Writer, Inc., 1973. 579p. index. $12.00. LC 73-18065. ISBN 0-87116-085-4.

Originally published in Great Britain in 1963, this revised edition indexes over 20,000 fictional characters from novels, short stories, poems, plays, and operas written in the English language during the last six centuries. These characters were gleaned from over 2,000 works by approximately 500 British and American authors. Practically all the works of Shakespeare, Dickens, Hardy, Kipling, Wells, Jane Austen, and the Brontës are accounted for. But there are some real oddities. For instance, a work of Fanny Hurst is included, but one finds no entry for Huxley's *After Many a Summer Dies the Swan,* nor for any of the operas of Benjamin Britten. There is no mention of Norman Mailer or Gertrude Stein or Edward Albee or Robert Ruark. But we do encounter Thomas Love Peacock, Nora Hoult, and M. Pickthall. Despite these and other lapses, this effort answers many questions.

The *Dictionary* is arranged in three parts. The main section is alphabetically arranged (by fictional character's name), indicating that character's relationships to the important personae of the work. Also given is the title of the work in which these characters appear, plus the author and first date of publication. The remaining two indexes are devoted to authors and titles, respectively. The first of these gives page citations to the works listed under the author's name, while the title index gives only the name of the author. [R: ARBA 75, p. 588; BL, 15 Nov 74, p. 350; LJ, July 74, p. 1795]   Kenyon C. Rosenberg

640. Myers, Robin, comp. and ed. **A Dictionary of Literature in the English Language from Chaucer to 1940.** New York, Pergamon, 1970, 1971. 2v. illus. index. $70.00/set. LC 68-18529. ISBN 0-08-012079-2(v.1); 0-08-016142-1(v.2); 0-08-016143-X(set).

According to the preface, "the aim of this work is to provide in a single volume, bibliographical and biographical details of some 3,500 authors who have used English as their medium . . . with reference to other bibliographical studies. . . . The definition of literature is a wide one. It includes not only great poets, dramatists and novelists, but also such writers as might be considered to form part of the literary history of their time, together with select examples of such semi-literary genres as the detective story and the romantic novel, too numerous and too ephemeral to be fully documented in a work of this nature. Certain nonliterary writers, too, scientists, historians, economists, lawyers and statesmen, who have much influenced the thought of their day, or who have written excellently, have an undoubted place in literary history and are included in the dictionary. The user will find a selection of these peripheral literary figures who are often the very ones that the librarian finds most in demand." We have quoted this long excerpt from the preface because it not only shows the scope of this work but may indirectly explain its usefulness as a handy reference book in this hard-to-define area.

All entries are arranged in one alphabet; each entry consists of full name and title, biographical note, and a list of biographical sources consulted or suggested for further study. Then follows a list of the first editions of separately published literary works in chronological order. When appropriate, important collected editions are also listed. The second volume serves as a complete title-author index. In examining certain listings for individual literary figures, it might be safe to assume that the author relied heavily in his selection on such standard works as *The Cambridge Bibliography of English Literature*. Other entries, such as the listing for the famous anthropologist James George Frazer or the economist John Keynes, had to be located in a number of different sources. Actually, it is in this area that the real value of this work lies. Obviously, the reader might be somewhat disappointed at not finding Percy Williams Bridgman, who was not only a brilliant physicist and author of many classic works on the philosophy of science, but who was also a newspaper correspondent and the author of books on public affairs. There are many other omissions of this nature. Nevertheless, it is almost an impossible task to provide complete coverage in this peripheral area, where so much must depend on interpretation. [R: ARBA 72, p. 514; C&RL, Jan 71, p. 41; WLB, Jan 71, p. 500; WLB, Jan 72, p. 449]

Bohdan S. Wynar

641. Shipley, Joseph T., ed. **Dictionary of World Literary Terms: Forms, Technique, Criticism.** Completely rev. and enl. ed. Boston, Writer, 1970. 466p. $13.95. LC 75-91879. ISBN 0-87116-012-9.

Earlier editions (1943, 1953) of this work had the title *Dictionary of World Literature*. Since its first appearance, this dictionary has been regarded as important, especially for its contributions to theoretical aspects of literary criticism. Many revisions were made in the 1953 edition, and many more are apparent in this latest publication, to which more than 260 authorities contributed.

The 1970 edition marks the first time that the book has been arranged in parts: part I (the major section) contains the treatment of terms, forms, types, definitions, techniques, and genres; part II contains critical surveys of American, English, French, German, Greek, Italian, Latin, medieval, Russian, and Spanish criticism; part III includes selected lists of critics and works from 25 additional countries. There has also been some shifting of material (e.g., "Voice and Address" has been reentered under "Narrator"). Many of the more obscure or archaic terms (aeolist; anacephaloeosis; etc.) have been removed. New terms (Absurd, Theatre of the; black humor; happening; pornography; science fiction; etc.) have been added. Rewriting is evident throughout, more cross references have been added, and the bibliographies have been updated. Style of writing is generally more abstractly refined than in, for example, *A Handbook to Literature* (Thrall and Hibbard). It is recommended that all three editions of this work be retained. [R: ARBA 71, p. 440; RQ, Winter 70, p. 172]

Joseph W. Sprug

INDEXES

642.   Bogart, Gary L., ed. **Short Story Index: Supplement 1974-1978: An Index to Stories in Collections and Periodicals.** New York, H. W. Wilson, 1979. 802p. index. $25.00. LC 75-649762. ISSN 0360-9774.

This is the sixth supplement to Cook and Monro's *Short Story Index* published in 1953. In 1975, Wilson began issuing annual indexes, and this volume is actually a five-year cumulation of those covering 1974-1978. Also beginning in 1974, the coverage was broadened to include short stories appearing in periodicals.

This supplement indexes about 17,000 short stories appearing in 71 periodicals and 930 collections. It is made up of an author, title, and subject index; a list of collections indexed, with complete bibliographic citation under author or editor, and references under title; a directory of publishers, and a directory of periodicals. The index proper follows the typical Wilson dictionary arrangement of author, title, and subject, with the author entry being the only complete one. Subject headings are given in boldface, while author and first word of the title are in smaller boldface. This helps while scanning, although the dictionary arrangement tends to be a bit confusing. There are many "see" references among the subject headings and a few references from pseudonyms, but no "see also" references. The subject headings have the typical Wilson flavor, some being out of date (e.g., Feeble-minded, Cripples, Children, abnormal and backward, Problem Children, Brigands and Robbers). There is no explanation of how the subject analysis was done except that "stories dealing in whole or part with a particular subject are listed under that subject." There is no separate list of subject headings.

In all, this is a worthwhile and apparently complete index to short stories, being made especially so now by the inclusion of periodicals.   A. Neil Yerkey

643.   **Comprehensive Index to English-Language Little Magazines 1890-1970, Series One.** Marion Sader, ed. New York, Kraus-Thomson, 1976. 8v. index. $590.00. LC 74-11742. ISBN 0-527-00370-0.

The editor states that these volumes bring "complete bibliographic control to the contents of one hundred little magazine titles." Impressive as the index is in many respects, this is not quite an accurate appraisal. The most serious objection to that claim is the lack of any subject indexing beyond the inclusion of people as subjects. Thus, while there is a section on Shakespeare, one cannot trace tragedy, comedy, imagism, or symbolism, except through practitioners or theorists already known. However, this objection noted, it must also be said that Sader, formerly in charge of the extensive Marvin Sukov collection of little magazines at the University of Wisconsin, is uniquely qualified in this area and has performed a large service, with a promise of more to come.

The index makes accessible, through a single-alphabet listing of authors and "subjects," the contents of 100 leading (primarily American or partially American) "little magazines" (with the notable, unexplained exception of the *Dial*), and provides the bibliographic histories of each. Entries under each name are divided into "works by" and "works about" sections, with reviews of an author's works being included in the "about" section, as well as under the reviewer's name. All entries are described as article, poem, review, etc. Sader defines "little magazines" as "undefineable," and only through inference does one apprehend his bias toward the literary as opposed to the political. Too, he tends to stretch his definitions by including *Germ*, originally published in 1850 but fitting within his time-frame by virtue of being reprinted in London 41 years later.

There are errors in the index, some amusing. For instance, Boniface the Eighth can be found only under "Boniface VII." Potentially more confusing is the "Dante" section, wherein reviews of several different translations of the *Commedia* are subsumed under

John Ciardi, though most of the translations are not his work, nor are any of the reviews. Too, there is the oddity of single-name entries (Hegemeyer, Fitzgerald, Loomis), but one must assume here that the fault lay with the magazine's credits rather than with the indexer.

On the whole, then, one must credit Sader with this impressive achievement, for certainly the contents of such magazines should be available to researchers, and the index performs that function. Of course, the serious scholar will also consult the volumes of Stephen Goode's *Index to American Little Magazines* and his *Index to Commonwealth Little Magazines*, as well as Evelyn Lauer's *Index to Little Magazines*. While there will be duplication, the combination of these references will open the field of little magazines to more thorough examination than was previously possible, and Sader is to be thanked for his contribution. [R: ARBA 77, p. 551; LJ, 15 Nov 76, p. 2358]   Koert C. Loomis, Jr.

644.   Havlice, Patricia Pate. **Index to Literary Biography.** Metuchen, NJ, Scarecrow, 1975. 2v. $42.50. LC 74-8315. ISBN 0-8108-0745-9.

An easy-to-use index to 50 biographical tools, including 13 foreign-language tools. "This work is intended as a quick reference tool for locating biographical information on approximately 68,000 authors from antiquity to the present. Each entry includes the author's real name, pseudonyms, dates of birth and death and nationality, type of writing engaged in . . . " (p. iii). Referral to cited sources is done by a letter code similar to that used in *Granger's Index to Poetry*, and a complete bibliography with code is included at the beginning of volume 1.

Most libraries will find that they own a number of the cited sources; they should consider purchase of this useful, easy-to-use tool. [R: ARBA 76, p. 574; Choice, Nov 75, p. 1143; LJ, 1 Sept 75, p. 1535; RQ, Fall 75, pp. 74-75; WLB, Oct 75, p. 118]
Barbara Marconi

BIOGRAPHY

645.   Borklund, Elmer. **Contemporary Literary Critics.** New York, St. Martin's Press; London, St. James Press, 1977. 550p. (Contemporary Writers of the English Language). $25.00. LC 77-88429. ISBN 0-333-22667-4.

Among the volumes in the Contemporary Writers of the English Language series, this stands out by virtue of an editorial feature. While the others contain entries by different persons, all of the entries here were written by one person, Elmer Borklund. And he has done an admirable job, combining crisp, judicious summaries of complex critical positions with well-chosen quotations (often extensive) from the critic in question. The survey approach allows cross currents to be traced, influences to be noted, and disagreements to be examined. The practicing critics examined are both British and American and number 115; most are alive or were at the time of the writing. Pure researchers and biographers are omitted, as are philosophers who make occasional literary forays. The entries include a biographical sketch, an extensive bibliography, a listing of studies of the biographee as a critic, and the summary essay by Borklund.

This reviewer has read the entire book, something not normally done with a reference book but something somehow appropriate here. The balance that Borklund maintains throughout is admirable; witness his discussion of the controversy surrounding Ezra Pound long after his death. The biographical information is presented in capsule form, but the essays themselves vary in length from two to five pages and are fully developed discussions of central issues. This is probably the most specialized of the series (which covers poets, novelists, and dramatists also), so its audience will probably be smaller. But it will serve them quite well and will be a basic source for some time to come. [R: ARBA 79, p. 591; BL, 1 Oct 78, p. 322; Choice, Sept 78, p. 835; LJ, July 78, p. 1384; WLB, May 78, p. 728]
Koert C. Loomis, Jr.

646. Seymour-Smith, Martin. **Who's Who in Twentieth Century Literature.** New York, Holt, Rinehart and Winston, 1976. 414p. index. $12.95. LC 75-21470. ISBN 0-03-013926-0.

Approximately 700 poets, dramatists, novelists, biographers, essayists, and philosophers are included in this comprehensive guide to twentieth-century writers. Arranged alphabetically by author, the selections are consciously "biased towards British and American authors" but also include "major foreign authors" and "some less well known writers" felt by Seymour-Smith to "have been undeservedly neglected." Writers of children's literature and authors of detective stories are excluded. The focus is primarily literary. Sigmund Freud, for example, is included because of "his influence on literature"; this is "not the place to discuss his theories." Mark Twain is listed as "a nineteenth-century figure who need be mentioned here only to draw attention to his importance to modern literature."

The inadequacy of the two-page index, the only unsatisfactory aspect of this highly praiseworthy reference guide, is partially overcome by numerous cross references in the text itself.

Although most of the selections follow the same format (professional status, biographical details, intellectual achievements, critical analysis, major themes, important influences and selected bibliography), these entries are by no means dull compendia of facts. By isolating, defining, and analyzing each author's universe and scope, whether it be the regionalism of John Steinbeck or the "electronic media" of Marshall McLuhan, by presenting varied critical opinions, tracing the writer's development, explaining significant movements, and summarizing key ideas, Seymour-Smith successfully appeals to a general audience as well as to students of literature. [R: ARBA 77, p. 572; BL, 15 Sept 76, p. 205; Choice, Oct 76, p. 962; LJ, 15 Apr 77, p. 874] Colby H. Kullman

647. Vinson, James, ed. **Contemporary Novelists.** 2nd ed. London, St. James Press; New York, St. Martin's Press, 1976. 1636p. $40.00. LC 75-189694. ISBN 0-900997-28-1.

This book consists of a listing of contemporary novelists. Two, three, sometimes four pages are devoted to each author. Short biographical sketches are given of the novelists, followed by a list of their works and critical studies about their works, as recommended by the entrant. Then come signed comments on the works by one or two of the contributors; sometimes comments by the authors themselves are included (more than half of the writers have made such statements). The second edition is practically the same as the first (St. Martin's Press, 1972). There are additional entries for new novelists, and a supplemental listing of those who have died since the publication of the first edition. All uncollected short stories published since an entrant's last collection have been added to the list of works for each novelist in the second edition.

The preface (the same in both editions) is written by Walter Allen, one of the novelists listed, who is also an advisor and contributor. The editor states that the selection of the writers included is based upon the recommendations of the advisors. Some novelists listed in the first edition are omitted in the second edition. The advisors and contributors are listed alphabetically at the beginning and again at the end, with notes on each. Although the second edition is very much the same as the first edition, the updating of the lists of works should be of value. The additional number of novelists included in the second edition is not substantial.

Ed. note: Vinson is also editor of *Contemporary Poets*, 2nd ed. (St. Martin's Press, 1975. 1849p. $35.00), which includes comprehensive information on 800 poets: a bibliography of the works of each poet, an autobiographical note about the poet's verse, and a short, signed critical article about the poet's work. [R: ARBA 77, p. 572; BL, 15 Oct 76, p. 344; Choice, Nov 76, p. 1120; LJ, 1 June 76, p. 1276; WLB, Sept 76, p. 84]

Ruth Dahlgren Hartman

648. Vinson, James, ed. **Dramatists**. D. L. Kirkpatrick, associate ed. New York, St. Martin's Press, 1979. 648p. (Great Writers of the English Language). $45.00. LC 78-78303. ISBN 0-312-34570-4.

649. Vinson, James, ed. **Novelists and Prose Writers**. D. L. Kirkpatrick, associate ed. New York, St. Martin's Press, 1979. 1367p. (Great Writers of the English Language). $45.00. LC 78-78302. ISBN 0-312-34624-7.

650. Vinson, James, ed. **Poets**. D. L. Kirkpatrick, associate ed. New York, St. Martin's Press, 1979. 1141p. (Great Writers of the English Language). $45.00. LC 78-78299. ISBN 0-312-34640-9.

"The selection of writers included in this book is based on the recommendations of the advisers listed on page ix." This is the only statement of criteria for this series, and it appears in each volume. It is as disconcerting here as it was in St. Martin's Contemporary Writers Series. But as in the earlier series, the boards of advisers for these volumes are composed of figures with a stature conducive to such recommendations—F. W. Bateson, Roy Harvey Pearce, Walter Allen, et al. There are omissions, but the authors listed here belong, although most may more accurately be called major figures than great writers.

The scope is international, and the alphabetized lists include representatives of a great many English-writing cultures. The format is much like that of Contemporary Writers. For each of the authors (about 500 novelists, an equal number of poets, and about 130 dramatists), the series provides a capsule biography, a more or less complete bibliography, a brief list of major critical works, and an evaluative essay. Approximately 200 contributors to *Novelists* and *Poets* (fewer than 100 for *Dramatists*) more often than not provide perceptive, well-informed evaluations of their subjects, although occasionally this is simply prorogation of critical dispute. Still, while rarely over two pages long, the essays approach the major aspects of the author's life and works—the issues and the style.

Dispute will arise about the names included in the lists of the great, but writers like Edgar Rice Burroughs, Monk Lewis, and Earl Stanley Gardner are at least significant figures in the development of literary genres, as is Ogden Nash. Even Paddy Chayefsky must be considered a significant representative of the unavoidable attempt of popular culture to equate the audiences of drama, film, and television. Others included here may be harder to defend.

Likely, dispute over omissions will center upon contemporary figures. Perhaps excluding John Gardner is at this time as fashionable as including Thomas Pynchon, but writers not appearing here were treated in the earlier series, and some judgments require a little distance. More troubling is the omission of figures like William James and John Dewey; in fact, one wonders why the *Novelists and Prose Writers* volume was not simply limited to fiction writers. Still, the contributors seem to have defended well the advisers' recommendations; perhaps their omissions are also justifiable. [R: ARBA 80, p. 554]

F. W. Ramey

651. Wakeman, John, ed. **World Authors, 1970-1975**. Stanley J. Kunitz, ed. consultant. New York, H. W. Wilson, 1980. 894p. illus. (Wilson Authors Series). $40.00. LC 79-21847. ISBN 0-8242-0641-X.

As the latest book in the Wilson Authors Series, which began with Kunitz and Haycraft's *British Authors of the Nineteenth Century* (1936) and includes among other titles *Twentieth Century Authors* (1942) and its supplement and *World Authors, 1950-1970* (1975), this publication does not update biographies of authors dealt with elsewhere in the series, but is called a "companion" rather than a supplement to the preceding volumes. Based on the general selection of subjects included in the volume, the general policies of the series were followed, in that the 348 authors biographically described are considered "imaginative" writers — poets, novelists, dramatists — of literary importance and/or of exceptional popularity. A number of philosophers, historians, biographers, critics, scientists, journalists, and others whose work seemed of "sufficiently wide interest, influence, or literary merit" are also included. The majority of these 348 writers came to prominence between 1970 and 1975. Several authors omitted from previous volumes in the series "because of lack of biographical information, or because their work was not familiar to readers of English" are also included. The editor of this work no longer considers this a very significant criterion, "thanks to the vast increase in translations from all languages."

Approximately one-fifth of the authors included have provided autobiographical articles which are reproduced without alteration, except those that have been translated from foreign languages. Included with some autobiographical material, the author provides a "philosophy" of writing, e.g., Erica Jong describes herself as "self-mythologying" rather than a "confessional" writer. The text includes a very brief synopsis of an author's major works, with excerpts from a variety of critical reviews for most works. These are well written, scholarly, and literary. The editorial notes were written by specialists in the literature concerned, and checked and updated by independent researchers. Critical comment is fuller than in the earlier volumes in the series, a condition of *World Authors, 1950-1970*, but the editor states that this is not "an independent appraisal but . . . a fair summation of representative critical response."

The lists of Principal Works are intended to include all of the author's published books in English, with dates of first publication. The lists of writings about authors and their work are selective. In the text, foreign titles are followed by an English version of the title and a date in parentheses. Each entry follows the pattern of names ("see" references are provided for pseudonyms), dates, brief biography with a possible quote from the writer, followed by a mixture of biography and criticism, each covering two to four pages per author, and in some cases a black-and-white photographic headshot of the author is included. A "Key to Pronunciation" is provided. Authors are listed alphabetically by last name. The book is not indexed. Some works published after 1975 are included. A title index would expand the usefulness of this book to the stated intended audience, that of "students and common readers." [R: ARBA 81; LJ, 1 May 80, p. 1071; RQ, Summer 80, pp. 400-401; WLB, May 80, pp. 592-93]   Donald D. Foos

CHILDREN'S LITERATURE

GENERAL WORKS

652. Fisher, Margery. **Who's Who in Children's Books: A Treasury of the Familiar Characters of Childhood.** New York, Holt, Rinehart and Winston, 1975. 399p. illus. (part col.). index. $22.95. LC 75-5463. ISBN 0-03-015091-4.

A delightful compendium of information on about 1,000 characters in children's books. Despite the noted author's disclaimer that this "is not intended primarily as a reference book," it can be used as such, if the compiler's own statements are kept in mind. This is not meant to be inclusive; nursery rhyme and fairy tale figures as well as real historical persons who appear in fiction are excluded. Few minor characters appear unless essential to the plot or famous on their own.

It might also be noted that there is some British bias. Many English series (e.g., Biggles) that are hardly known in the United States are included, while equally well-known American series (e.g., Miss Pickerell, Encyclopedia Brown) are not. There are also many scenes from BBC-TV programs not known abroad.

The entry arrangement is alphabetical, but by the first word of the name as it appears in the original work: Miss Eglantine Price under M, Laura Ingalls (no Wilder given) under L, Great-Aunt Dympha under G, and so on. When groups are presented under family names, relationships are carefully explained.

Good information is charmingly presented, ranging from the Bobbsey Twins and Little Lord Fauntleroy (Cedric Errol) to Little Pear and Bilbo Baggins. The volume has approximately 400 illustrations, 16 of them full-page and in color. Pictures are primarily reproductions of book illustrations, but they also include stills from motion picture and TV versions of the works, title pages, and authors. [R: ARBA 76, p. 577; BL, 1 Jan 76, p. 625; BL, 1 July 76, p. 1549; Choice, Mar 76, p. 43; LJ, 15 Dec 75, p. 2315; LJ, 15 Apr 76, p. 969; WLB, May 76, p. 675, 743]   Eleanor Elving Schwartz

653.   **Newbery and Caldecott Medal Books, 1966-1975.** Ed. by Lee Kingman. Boston, Horn Book, 1975. 321p. illus. (part col.). index. $15.00. LC 75-20167. ISBN 0-87675-003-X.

Following the same format as the *Newbery and Caldecott Medal Books, 1956-1965* (Horn Book, 1965. $15.00), this volume is divided into two sections, the first covering Newbery medalists, the second, Caldecott medalists. The winners are listed chronologically, and entries include a brief plot synopsis, an excerpt from the book, the author's (or illustrator's) acceptance speech, and a biographical sketch of the author or illustrator. All of these materials can be found in the annual awards issue of the *Horn Book Magazine*. Not to be found therein are the occasional author's, editor's or artist's note. John Rowe Townsend penned an essay on the Newbery and Barbara Bader discusses the winning picture book illustrations, while Elizabeth Johnson writes about the Honor Books (formerly runners-up). Samples of the awarded illustrations are reproduced in color.

This is a standard reference work that will be of use to librarians and teachers who work with children. [R: ARBA 77, p. 578; Choice, July 76, p. 656; SLJ, Apr 76, p. 46]
                                        Judith Rosenberg

BIBLIOGRAPHIES

654.   **Childhood in Poetry: A Catalogue, with Biographical and Critical Annotations, of the Books of English and American Poets Comprising the Shaw Childhood in Poetry Collection Library of the Florida State University . . . Second Supplement.** By John Mackay Shaw. Detroit, Gale, 1976. 2v. index. $115.00/set; $58.00(v.2). LC 67-28092. ISBN 0-8108-0477-5(set); 0-8103-0479-1(v.2).

This two-volume supplement (1949p.) provides bibliographic entries on 3,000 volumes added to Florida State University's Shaw Childhood in Poetry Collection since 1972, the publication date of the *First Supplement* (3v., 1734p., covering 8,000 books). The *Base Set* (5v., 3447p., covering 10,000 books), the original catalog of the Shaw collection, appeared in 1968.

The bibliographic entries (vol. 1) are arranged by author, editor, illustrator, or, occasionally, subject. Despite these inconsistent main entries, adequate cross references make the set easy to use. Each main entry provides full bibliographic data, critical notes with background, and, often, brief sample quotations from the work.

The index (vol. 2), which may be bought separately, covers the *Base Set* and both supplements. It includes a "Keyword Poem-Title List," and a "Book Title Index" for the entire work, as well as a "Short Title List and Key" for each set. However, the extensive and carefully prepared index does not include every poem in each anthology listed, but only those poems which Shaw chose to illustrate the quality of the volume in his notes and sample quotations. Therefore, it cannot be used like Brewton's basic *Index to Children's Poetry* (H. W. Wilson, 1942) and succeeding volumes, which index all poems in each collection listed (see entry 661).

As this shortcoming became apparent, a test problem uncovered other specific areas of minor difficulty. Arnold Adoff's anthology *Black Out Loud* is numbered T-3 (vol. 1, p. 6) in the bibliographic entry. The eight poems cited in his notations are numbered T-4 ("Color," vol. 2, p. 155; "Black All Day," vol. 2, p. 65, etc.) in his "Keyword Poem-Title List," the catalog number for another Adoff anthology, *It Is the Poem Singing into Your Eyes* (vol. 1, p. 6). The remaining 59 poems from *Black Out Loud*, unmentioned in Shaw's notes, are omitted from the index as well.

Although the flyer claims that birth dates are given, Adoff's is not (he is both poet and anthologist). Gale's *Something about the Author* (vol. 5, 1973) lists Adoff's birth date, so it was easily accessible before these volumes went to press. If the date is omitted because he is better known as an anthologist than as a poet, why is poet Nikki Giovanni's birth date omitted (vol. 1, p. 325) while editor Arthur Quiller-Couch's dates are included (vol. 1, p. 667)?

Further, and of greater importance, "poetry" is loosely defined here, to include a wide range of material from Munro Leaf's *The Story of Ferdinand* (vol. 1, p. 479) and Baum's *Tik-Tok of Oz* (vol. 1, p. 70) to a letter from Thomas Babington Macaulay to H. S. Randall of New York concerning his " . . . Distrust of Jeffersonian Democracy" (vol. 1, p. 521) and Katharine Morrison McClinton's *A Handbook of Popular Antiques* and *Antique Collecting for Everyone* (vol. 1, p. 523).

For small libraries and general public libraries, this is no substitute for the standard Brewton poetry indexes. The detailed physical description of rare volumes should make it useful to rare book, research, and large university libraries. [R: ARBA 77, p. 556; Choice, Nov 76, p. 1118; WLB, Nov 76, p. 268]   Helen Gregory

655. **Children's Books in the Rare Book Division of the Library of Congress.** Library of Congress. Rare Book Division. Totowa, NJ, Rowman and Littlefield, 1975. 2v. $115.00. LC 75-9605. ISBN 0-87471-579-2.

Since the establishment of the Library of Congress Rare Book Division in 1927, its acquisition of rare children's books has resulted in a fine collection of some 15,000 volumes. It is the preeminent collection of Americana in children's books. The printed catalog of the collection records temporary cards not available in other LC printed catalogs or printed cards and adds a selection of some 1,000 items housed in the Children's Book Section. The latter titles are representative of each year's books to 1973. Criteria for these titles, selected by Virginia Haviland, are importance of author and illustrator, quality of design, and significance of a title in representing trends in the children's book field.

The catalog is arranged in two sections: authors and chronological list. The complete catalog card, reduced in size, is reproduced three columns per page in the authors volume and all authors are listed in a single alphabet. The editor points out that the catalog thus acts as a supplement to the Library's rare children's book collection card file (and shelf arrangement), which separates "well-known" authors' cards from the author file and the chronological file. (Well-known authors' cards are filed in a separate file.) Most of the entries in the catalog are for American imprints, but some English titles are represented, as well as a small number of foreign-language books from other countries. The chronological volume omits the portion of the cards below the collation area, or below notes if those are important (e.g., "imperfect copy"). The chronological entries begin with updated items.

•

The first dated book is 1635, Edmund Coate's *The English Schoole-Master*. Entries for the twentieth century (about 2,300) represent only 76 of the 493 pages, with nearly two-thirds of that space devoted to the period 1900 to 1950.

The catalog will serve as an excellent finding list for eighteenth- and nineteenth-century Americana, but it is obviously not as complete from 1900 forward. [R: ARBA 76, p. 576; BL, 1 Sept 76, p. 52; Choice, May 76, p. 351; RQ, Spring 76, p. 268; WLB, Feb 76, p. 492]   Christine Gehrt Wynar

656.   **Die Besten der Besten/The Best of the Best.** 2nd enl. ed. Ed. by Walter Scherf. New York, R. R. Bowker, 1976. 342p. illus. index. (Catalogs of the International Youth Library, No. 3). $19.95. LC 77-142169. ISBN 3-7940-3253-5.

Some 4,000 children's books in 67 languages and sub-languages are included in this second, expanded edition of "bests." They were chosen by correspondents, unnamed, of the IYL according to established criteria: books of lasting value, books that are "adequate psychologically," and books that foster understanding between nations and groups. Listed by country, then by language and age group, titles are translated into both German and English. Author, title, place of publication, publisher, and date are entered for each work. No prices are given; no annotations; no information on the availability of translations; no index.

The editor's introduction provides ample evidence of the bibliographic labor involved in selecting children's publications internationally, and an examination of the catalog reveals the need for much more work, especially in refining procedures of selecting and evaluating books submitted. The selection of titles is far from even, with numerous correspondents applying poorly defined criteria to the varying number and quality of books in print in their respective countries. (The 112 books of lasting value from the United States include such disparate titles as *Dinky Hocker Shoots Smack, The Middle Moffat, Go Ask Alice*, and *Two Logs Crossing*.) Entries for some countries list several works by one author, while other national lists give only one, sometimes a questionable minor work. Some countries (China) and languages (Yiddish) are not included.

Despite its marked deficiencies, the second edition of the IYL catalog offers a greater quantity of titles than the first. And in the absence of any other international bibliography of children's books of equal scope, it should be a welcome selection aid for those libraries establishing multilanguage collections or purchasing foreign-language books for ethnic children in the community. [R: ARBA 77, p. 555; BL, 15 Sept 76, p. 183; Choice, Oct 76, p. 962]   Joan H. Worley

657.   Haviland, Virginia, comp. **Children's Literature: A Guide to Reference Sources, Second Supplement.** With the assistance of Margaret N. Coughlan. Washington, Library of Congress; distr., Washington, GPO, 1977. 413p. illus. index. $7.75. LC 66-62734. ISBN 0-8444-0215-X. S/N 030-001-00075-3.

Arranged as the previous two volumes in this ongoing series, selective journal articles and books have been annotated in a numbered order, from the general topic to the specific. This volume lists those pieces appearing from about 1970 through 1974. The eight categories from the first two volumes ("History and Criticism," "Authorship," "Illustration," "Bibliography," "Books and Children," "The Library and Children's Books," "International Studies," and "National Studies") have not changed. Of the major categories, "International Studies" has been expanded the most. Subdivisions of categories appearing for the first time are "Selection of Nonprint Materials" (in "The Library and Children's Books"), "Research in Children's Literature" (in "Books and Children"), "Translation" (in "International Studies"), and "French Canada" (in "National Studies"). There are a total of

929 annotations, as compared to 1,073 in the first volume and 746 in the second. The index covers only those numbered annotations in this volume, a pattern set with the first two books.

Highly selective in annotated material and directing themselves primarily toward librarians, Haviland and Coughlan do masterful work in pulling together scattered articles and other works from around the world and organizing them into a usable form. Allied fields of children's literature and research (reading studies, dissertations, English literature studies) are peripherally mentioned, if at all. Expansion of children's literature-related articles located in larger works and beyond the library field would be welcomed. For instance, John Tebbel's *History of Book Publishing in the United States* and its sections on children's book publishing are lacking, while a library-oriented book such as *Issues in Children's Book Selection* has been annotated and subdivided. As new volumes in the series are published, a comprehensive index including all previously published volumes would be an asset. This will be a necessary purchase for all who purchased the first two volumes. Institutions not owning these volumes would be wise to get them. This is the only source of material with this scope and depth on the subject in a readily available form. [R: ARBA 79, p. 116; BL, 15 July 78, p. 1739; WLB, Sept 78, p. 87]   Jim Roginski

658.   Rosenberg, Judith K. **Young People's Literature in Series: Fiction, Non-Fiction, and Publishers' Series, 1973-1975.** Littleton, CO, Libraries Unlimited, 1977. 234p. index. $17.50. LC 76-57963. ISBN 0-87287-140-1.

Judith Rosenberg's first two volumes of *Young People's Literature in Series* (Fiction [1972]; Publishers' and Non-Fiction Series [1973]) received recognition for their comprehensive coverage of the flood of fiction and informational books currently put out in series. Both volumes are updated by this bibliography, which describes 263 fiction titles published in series since 1972 and 2,614 nonfiction and publishers' series books issued since 1973. Fiction titles cover books for grades 3-9; nonfiction titles are for grades 3-12.

The bibliography is not intended as an uncritical listing of all books in series produced for children, but as a guide to series titles which meet generally accepted selection criteria of children's librarians. Inclusion is based on an assessment of plot, writing quality, characterization, format, and author's reputation (for fiction) or on author expertise and overall quality of writing (for nonfiction series).

Fiction titles are arranged under authors' names in one section; nonfiction and publishers' series are arranged under series titles in a second section. Annotations for fiction titles describe the characters and plots common to a series and incorporate brief evaluative comments on the style and quality of writing. Similarly structured annotations are provided for the nonfiction and publishers' series. Age level recommendations are given for each series; series considered appropriate for reluctant readers are marked.

This bibliography can be used independently of the two earlier volumes both as a selection and reference tool. The value of the bibliography is enhanced by letter-codes that refer the reader to entries for authors and series located in the two previous volumes. *Young People's Literature in Series . . . 1976-1978* is due for publication in 1981. [R: ARBA 78, p. 577; BL, 1 Oct 77, p. 303; JAL, July 77, p. 168; JAL, May 78, p. 113; WLB, Sept 77, p. 86]

659.   Sutherland, Zena, ed. **The Best in Children's Books: The University of Chicago Guide to Children's Literature, 1973-1978.** Chicago, University of Chicago Press, 1980. 547p. index. $17.50. LC 79-24331. ISBN 0-226-78059-7.

The *Bulletin of the Center for Children's Books*, edited by Zena Sutherland, is the source for this latest five-year selection of best children's books. The 1,400 titles represent the critical judgments of *BCCB*'s advisory committee; evaluations are concise yet impart a sense of each author's style, as well as plot and theme. Each entry includes a suggested reader age range. Six indexes (title, developmental values, curricular uses, reading level, subject, type of literature) provide multiple access to the author-arranged reviews. Most users of the guide will find satisfaction in the title and subject indexes. However, only the title index refers to the author entry; all others cite entry numbers, a practice resulting in scores of numbers for many of the index entries. Since the indexes represent considerable expenditure of time and effort in their preparation, it is unfortunate that no method has yet been found to make them easier to use. This difficulty aside, the guide continues to be a welcome and reliable selection of quality children's books and reviews. Children's collections in schools and public libraries will want this new volume for reference and collection development. [R: ARBA 81; BL, 15 July 80, p. 1680; JAL, Nov 80, p. 300]

Christine Gehrt Wynar

660. Welch, d'Alté A. **A Bibliography of American Children's Books Printed Prior to 1821.** Barre, MA, Barre Publishers, 1972. 516p. index. $45.00. LC 77-163898. ISBN 0-8271-7133-1.

This carefully compiled and comprehensive bibliography of American children's books prior to 1821 was first published in six parts in *Proceedings* (American Antiquarian Society, April 1963, October 1963, October 1964, October 1965, April 1967). The compiler prepared notes for revisions prior to his death in 1970, and the edited version published in 1972 contains the corrections and additions. Introductory matter consists of acknowledgments recognizing the distinguished gallery of book collectors associated with Welch's project. A chronological history of American children's books sketches the development of publishing, citing the earliest and most famous titles, authors, and publishers. The most important part of this section is the "Method of the Work," which describes the scope, explains the entry form, abbreviations, and method of collation, and lists the location of symbols used in the bibliography. Locations are cited for books in 18 private collections and 185 libraries, including two Canadian libraries and the British Museum.

"The bibliography is primarily concerned with narrative books written in English, designed for children under 15 years of age. They should be the type of book read at leisure for pleasure. . . . Books written about or by children, treatises on education or how to rear children are avoided. . . . Broadsides, sermons, books of advice, catechisms, primers, and school books are excluded" (introduction). Entries for books of poetry, jokes and riddles, natural history, games, as well as narrative books, are included in the bibliography.

Arrangement is by author (when known) with his works listed alphabetically. Books by anonymous or unknown authors are listed under title. Each book with a separate title is numbered. Books first published in England are listed citing the first English edition. Entries give author and his dates, title, edition, place and publisher or printer, year, collation, size, any signatures, a description of binding and any other outstanding features, plus notes on missing pages or mutilations. Location symbols are included. The bibliography records 1,478 separate titles. At the end is an index of printers, publishers (with their dates and city), and imprints. Book numbers are listed in chronological sequence under each name. Welch's work is a significant contribution to the study of the history of American children's books. [R: ARBA 73, p. 90; LJ, 15 Oct 73, p. 3130]   Christine Gehrt Wynar

INDEXES

661. Brewton, John E., G. Meredith Blackburn, III, and Lorraine A. Blackburn, comps. **Index to Poetry for Children and Young People 1970-1975: A Title, Subject, Author, and First Line Index to Poetry in Collections for Children and Young People.** New York, H. W. Wilson, 1978. 472p. $20.00. LC 77-26036. ISBN 0-8242-0621-5.

Supplementing three earlier volumes that date from 1942 this continues to be the standard index for children's poetry. In this volume, over 10,000 poems are indexed from 110 collections published between 1970-1975, with about 2,500 authors and 2,000 specific subjects included. The dictionary organization provides access by author, title, subject, and first line, with symbols indicating the anthology in which each poem is contained. Collections were selected from a predetermined list by 16 consulting librarians and teachers in various parts of the United States; these are identified by name and institution. A separate list, "Analysis of Books of Poetry Indexed," will be useful for librarians engaged in collection building. It gives anthologies under editor name, indicating author, title, imprint, grade level, number of poems and poets contained, categories of contents, illustrators, and information on introductory materials and bibliographic notes. Collections suitable for elementary schools predominate, with about 82 of these as compared with 49 rated as suitable for grades 7-12.

To ascertain some omissions, headings for poetry collections were compared with those in *Senior High School Library Catalog* (11th ed.), *Junior High School Library Catalog* (3rd ed.), and *Children's Catalog* (13th ed.). The *Index* omitted some titles representing cultural groups, such as American blacks, Puerto Ricans, Indians, Eskimos, Chinese, black Africans, and Spanish. Hopkins' *Girls Can Too*, Larrick's *I Heard a Scream in the Street* (an anthology containing poems by urban youth), as well as several Oxford anthologies are also omitted. More adult-level collections will be needed for senior high school libraries. Despite such omissions, overall coverage is well balanced, and this index will be valued by all desiring to locate poems for children and young adults, especially when preparing programs for special occasions. [R: ARBA 79, p. 582; BL, 1 Feb 79, p. 881; Choice, June 79, p. 496; WLB, Sept 78, p. 88]   Valmai Fenster

662.   Silverman, Judith. **Index to Young Readers' Collective Biographies: Elementary and Junior High School Level.** 2nd ed. New York, R. R. Bowker, 1975. 322p. index. $15.95. LC 75-834. ISBN 0-8352-0741-2.

In updating her earlier edition (R. R. Bowker, 1970), Ms. Silverman has followed the same format: alphabetical listing of biographees, followed by birth and death dates, nationality, occupation, and symbols for the works in which they are included. This new edition encompasses 249 newly indexed volumes (although no cut-off date for inclusion is mentioned), plus the 471 in the original work, thus swelling the total of biographees to 5,833.

Several improvements over the previous edition have been made, notably an index of the titles of the books included therein, with a list of their contents. This index should help the book selector choose new items whose coverage does not duplicate titles already in their collections. Out-of-print editions have been indicated. In the Subject Listing of Biographees, 20 new areas have been added. Also appended are a key to publishers and an index to the subject headings; the latter seems rather superfluous, since it simply repeats the headings in exactly the same order as they appear in the Subject Listing.

While this is a well-presented and well-researched project, a few bugs remain to be ironed out in the next edition. In the case of sports or entertainment figures most commonly known by a nickname, the nickname is used for the entry, followed by the full name in parentheses. But there is no "see" reference from the full name. Nevertheless, this is a tremendously worthwhile project. [R: ARBA 76, p. 578; Choice, Nov 75, p. 1122; RQ, Fall 75, p. 81; WLB, Sept 75, p. 76]   Judith K. Rosenberg

663.   Smith, Dorothy B. Frizzell, and Eva L. Andrews, comps. **Subject Index to Poetry for Children and Young People, 1957-1975.** Chicago, American Library Association, 1977. 1035p. $40.00. LC 77-3296. ISBN 0-8389-0242-1.

Smith and Andrews have added a necessary subject index to the reference shelves of children's libraries in the new *Subject Index to Poetry for Children and Young People* (perhaps a redundant title). The compilers have added 263 of the newer anthologies to those indexed in the 1957 issue of this reference volume. *Sears' List of Subject Headings, Readers' Guide to Periodical Literature*, Eakin's *Subject Index to Books for Intermediate Grades*, and other reference works are the major sources for the subject headings used in this updated reference book. Arrangement is convenient when one has mastered the clearly explained code at the front of the volume.

The compilers have been conscious of the "growing interest and pride in ethnic, cultural, and national origins" that "prompted the use of a wide-ranging selection of poetry of African and American Indian . . . tribal and language groups," and other material not indexed in the 1957 edition of the work. The work at hand "does not supersede the 1957 edition, as no anthologies indexed in that volume are included in the new one" (p. iii). The work is not unique, for many titles are indexed in Brewton (see entry 661) and other reference sources; but this will be an important reference book in work with children, their teachers, librarians, and poetry, especially if they wish to bring the earlier edition up to date with this supplement. Not an inspired work—a necessary one. [R: ARBA 79, p. 584; Choice, Apr 78, p. 212; LJ, 15 Feb 78, p. 450; WLB, Jan 78, p. 424]   Ruth I. Gordon

BIOGRAPHY

664. Commire, Anne. **Something about the Author: Facts and Pictures about Authors and Illustrators of Books for Young People, Volume 17.** Detroit, Gale, 1979. 319p. illus. index. $30.00. LC 72-27107. ISBN 0-8108-0098-2.

Commire's series is perhaps the most valuable biographical source on children's authors and illustrators available to students of children's literature and to young people. Starting with the fifteenth volume, *SATA*'s scope has been expanded to encompass writers and illustrators who died prior to 1961. Formerly, the cutoff date was 1960; earlier figures were covered in the publisher's *Yesterday's Authors of Books for Children*. Typical sketches for living biographees are usually one or two pages, including personal data, career highlights, a list of writings, and sidelights on the life and creative activity of the person, usually prepared by the individual. Photos of the biographees and illustrations from their works are well-known features of *SATA*. Sketches of writers from past times are considerably longer than those provided for living or recently deceased biographees. In volume 17, the biography for James Whitcomb Riley is 12 pages; the sketch for N. C. Wyeth is nearly twice that length. *SATA*, with its expanded scope, continues to be an important reference for school, public, and college libraries. [R: ARBA 81; JAL, Jan 80, p. 356; ARBA 77, p. 563; BL, 1 July 76, pp. 1529, 1548; BL, 15 Nov 76, p. 481; BL, 1 Jan 78, p. 752]   Christine Gehrt Wynar

665. **Fourth Book of Junior Authors & Illustrators.** Ed. by Doris de Montreville and Elizabeth D. Crawford. New York, H. W. Wilson, 1978. 370p. index. $17.00. LC 78-115. ISBN 0-8242-0568-5.

The *Fourth Book* takes its place alongside the *Junior Book of Authors* (1934, revised 1951), *More Junior Authors* (1963), and *Third Book of Junior Authors* (1972). Compatible in format and scope with the earlier editions, the fourth extends coverage to illustrators, whose sketches number approximately one-third of the 280 in the volume. A comprehensive index to the 1,300 authors and illustrators in all four books is appended.

Entries are arranged alphabetically by surname, with a short (300-500 words) autobiographical essay aimed at junior readers, additional biographical data by the editors, a selected bibliography of works, and references to other biographical/critical books and articles about the author or illustrator. When the series began, only the autobiographical essay was included, with a few titles; the *Third* and *Fourth* have more usefulness for general reference, with biographical material and references to other works. Complete bibliographies and addresses would increase the reference value still further.

Coverage is aimed at but not entirely limited to living authors and illustrators. An advisory committee of five librarians and/or book people made the selections of authors and illustrators; among those they omitted are Betty Greene, Ashley Bryan, Tomie de Paola, Jamake Highwater, and Katherine Paterson.

The Junior Authors series is a well-recognized, worthwhile purchase for most libraries. Librarians considering its purchase may wish to compare it with *Twentieth-Century Children's Writers* (see entry 666). [R: ARBA 80, p. 541; BL, 15 May 78, p. 1499; BL, 15 Oct 78, p. 404; Choice, Dec 78, p. 1346; WLB, June 78, p. 808]   Joan H. Worley

666.   Kirkpatrick, D. L., ed. **Twentieth-Century Children's Writers.** New York, St. Martin's Press, 1978. 1507p. $40.00. ISBN 0-312-82413-0.

Joining the growing list of biographical reference tools devoted to children's writers is St. Martin's Press' extensive work, which details information on more than 600 English-language authors of fiction, poetry, and drama for children. Selection of entrants was made by a board of 19 distinguished specialists in children's literature, including such well-known authorities as Marcus Crouch, Ethel L. Heins, Naomi Lewis (who also contributed a lengthy introduction), Irma McDonough, Zena Sutherland, and John Rowe Townsend. Over 160 equally competent contributors to the work include authors, reviewers, critics, and teachers of children's literature from both sides of the Atlantic. Identifying notes on advisors and contributors are appended as a final section of the book.

Quick acquaintance with the selected entrants is provided by a simple list of names preceding the biographical section. Each entry in the main part includes a brief biography of some 10 lines followed by separate lists of publications for children and adults. Publisher and year are given for most titles, and original British and United States editions of all books have been listed. Bibliographies and critical studies of the biographee's works are also noted. A signed critical essay of one-half to one page completes the entry. Appended to the main section are 23 entries for the late nineteenth-century writers who have been particularly influential on twentieth-century writers. Foreign-language writers whose works are available in English translation are surveyed in a supplementary essay.

While considerable overlap can be expected among the numerous biographical dictionaries of children's writers and illustrators that are currently available, this volume has the advantage of offering some new insights into the style of these people and their importance to children's literature. *Twentieth-Century Children's Writers* is recommended for all libraries as a primary reference tool about children's writers. [R: ARBA 80, p. 543; BL, 15 Oct 79, p. 374; Choice, Jan 79, p. 1502; LJ, 15 Mar 79, p. 719; WLB, Jan 79, p. 403]

Christine Gehrt Wynar

COMICS

667.   Horn, Maurice, ed. **The World Encyclopedia of Comics.** New York, Chelsea House, 1976. 790p. illus. bibliog. index. $30.00. LC 75-22322. ISBN 0-87754-030-6.

This work has over 1,200 entries, prepared by 14 international contributors. There are more than 700 black-and-white illustrations, plus 64 pages of full-color reproductions of some major comics. In addition to the entries, which are in dictionary arrangement, the *Encyclopedia* provides feature chronologies, a history of the comics, a glossary, indices, and a good bibliography.

Entries are both descriptive and critical. Occasionally, the editor was perhaps too lenient with the opinions of his contributors. For example, the entry for *Nancy* (U.S.) is a biased 600- to 700-word harangue on the "rubber stamp" quality of the art work, the generally low level of the humor, and the dullness of anybody who would enjoy reading it. It is insinuated that the strip's long run might be due to internal pressure on newspaper editors, who mostly despised it. Fortunately, such clear bias is the exception and most entries are on a high professional level.

There is a great deal of repetition in the entries. Often several detailed columns will be devoted to the cartoonist, and then under the entry on his major strips, the same information is repeated. Shorter entries with appropriate cross references might have served the purpose.

The user of this tool must understand its scope: comics and comic strips. One would not expect, for example, to find an entry on Herblock, since he is an *editorial* cartoonist.

This is an ambitious attempt to provide a much-needed work, and it comes off well. It is a comprehensive, scholarly work, valuable to both the connoisseur and the student of this universally popular art form. [R: ARBA 77, p. 566; BL, 15 Mar 77, p. 1122; Choice, Feb 77, p. 1578; LJ, 15 Sept 76, p. 1844; SLJ, Oct 76, p. 125; WLB, Dec 76, p. 359]

Donald B. Cleveland

MYSTERY AND CRIME FICTION

668. Hubin, Allen J. **The Bibliography of Crime Fiction, 1749-1975: Listing All Mystery, Detective, Suspense, Police, and Gothic Fiction in Book Form Published in the English Language.** San Diego, University Extension, University of California; Del Mar, CA, Publisher's Inc.; distr., Chicago, Encyclopaedia Britannica Educational, 1979. 697p. index. $60.95. LC 78-23929. ISBN 0-89163-048-1.

This work, despite its price, is a must for any person or institution interested in criminous literature. Collectors, dealers, and libraries will find it indispensable.

The main entries are alphabetical by author, with titles listed alphabetically thereunder. The author's dates are given. Publisher and date of first publication are given for each title, with the British preceding the American. Cross references are given between pseudonyms and real names. Where a character recurs in more than one of an author's works, such is identified by code letters at the start of the entry, and the appropriate titles are so distinguished. There are two indices: one a series index alphabetically listing all series and series characters identified, and the other a title index.

The *Bibliography* is not, as it claims, a list of *all* the adult crime fiction published anywhere in the world in English from 1749 to 1975, but it does manage to include the very large part of it. There are errors, but in a book of this size such are to be expected, particularly typographical ones. Somewhat more serious are the mistakes in dates of publication, in titles, in publishers, and in the non-recognition of pseudonyms; however, in processing a collection of 4,000 volumes against the work, the error rate was slightly less than 1% and that is quite acceptable in a compilation of this magnitude. Still, one should use this volume only as a checklist and not a cataloging source.

Despite this quibbling caveat, Hubin deserves immense credit for his checklist. It will long stand, with *Crime, Detective, Espionage, Mystery, and Thriller Fiction and Film: A Comprehensive Bibliography of Critical Writing through 1979* (Greenwood Press, 1980), as one of the two requisite foundation acquisitions for any mystery collection, either private or institutional.

David Skene-Melvin

669. Steinbrunner, Chris, and Otto Penzler, eds.-in-chief. **Encyclopedia of Mystery and Detection.** New York, McGraw-Hill, 1976. 436p. illus. $24.50. LC 75-31645. ISBN 0-07-061121-1.

Steinbrunner and his colleagues have attempted nothing less than a comprehensive study of what they call "the country's favorite literary genre," mystery fiction. In 600 articles, they deal with more than 500 mystery writers, most of them British and American, from Poe and Wilkie Collins to the most noted present-day practitioners. These articles include plot synopses of major works and, often, a brief critical appraisal of the author. Major fictional creations have their own biographies. Not only Holmes, Sherlock, and Maigret, Jules, but Drew, Nancy, and Tracy, Dick, can be found in their proper alphabetical sequence. The bibliographic information is formidable. Titles by an author are chronologically arranged, with both British and American titles given if they differ. Films, plays, and radio or television dramas based on a book or a detective are listed with the title, date, production company, director, leading players and a brief synopsis of the plot. Abundant cross references serve principally to lead from a pseudonym to a true name or vice versa. The book also includes a few articles on subjects like the "Had-I-But-Known" School, Collecting Detective Fiction, and Orientals, Sinister.

It is hard not to carp a bit at what seem like errors of omission or commission. Why include Jacques Barzun but leave out W. S. Baring-Gould, biographer of Nero Wolfe and editor of *The Annotated Sherlock Holmes*? Why bother with F. Scott Fitzgerald, whose only contribution to mystery fiction was a short story published when he was 13 in a school magazine? Why are only some pseudonyms cross referenced? But it is easy to pick at a book like this. Whatever the authors may have put in unnecessarily or left out, they have performed a major service by pulling together in an easily usable form the masses of information they have included. [R: ARBA 77, p. 570; BL, 15 Feb 77, p. 921; Choice, Oct 77, p. 1011; LJ, 1 Apr 76, p. 878; WLB, Sept 76, p. 84]   Ruth Diebold

POETRY

670. Preminger, Alex, ed. **Princeton Encyclopedia of Poetry and Poetics.** Enl. ed. Princeton, NJ, Princeton University Press, 1975. 992p. $40.00; $9.95pa. LC 63-7076. ISBN 0-691-06280-3; 0-691-01317-9pa.

The first edition of this standard book on the subject was published in 1965. It is an authoritative and scholarly encyclopedia, international in scope; its discussions of literary movements and genres deal exclusively with theory. Terms used in criticism are defined, including some used in prose and in the fine arts. Omitted are articles on individual poets or poems and allusions. The impressive total of the first edition was some 1,000 signed articles in 906 pages. This "enlarged edition" consists of a page-by-page reprint of the first edition, with a supplement of some 75,000 words. The supplement covers some new topics, such as "Computer Poetry," and provides information on subjects left out of the first edition, such as "Harlem Renaissance." All essays in the first edition as well as in the "enlargement" are written by prominent authorities on this subject. The *Princeton Encyclopedia* is certainly a landmark book; adding a supplement to the first edition was probably more economical than resetting the entire text. [R: ARBA 76, p. 585; BL, 15 Feb 76, p. 897; Choice, Oct 75, p. 983; WLB, Sept 75, p. 70]   Bohdan S. Wynar

671. Smith, William James, ed. **Granger's Index to Poetry, 1970-1977.** New York, Columbia University Press, 1978. 635p. $59.50. LC 78-4097. ISBN 0-231-04248-5.

The long history of this standard source is well known to most librarians. This volume of *Granger's Index to Poetry* departs from previous publishing practice by covering seven (1970-1977) instead of five years, thanks in part to computerized production. Some 120 new poetry anthologies were selected for inclusion; in the selection process, the editors were assisted by a panel whose membership included the poet Stanley Kunitz. Their choices reflect the current interest in poetry by women (nine anthologies of women's poems were selected), blacks, and American Indians, as well as poems for children. Over 25,000 poems are indexed in the present volume. *The Chicorel Index to Poetry in Anthologies and Collections in Print* (1974) contains 250,000 *entries*, but the number of *poems* indexed by Chicorel is not specified. *Granger's* subject headings, expanded in this volume, are generally better than Chicorel's and include, as appropriate, the names of persons. The standard title, first line, and author indexes have been retained without change. As a result of requests from librarians, eight anthologies have been marked in the Key to Symbols listing with two asterisks (**) for "first purchase," and an additional 27 works have a single asterisk (*) to designate their importance for later acquisition. [R: ARBA 79, p. 588; C&RL, Jan 79, p. 56; LJ, 1 Nov 78, p. 2229; WLB, Sept 78, p. 86]   Deborah Jane Brewer

SCIENCE FICTION AND FANTASY LITERATURE

BIBLIOGRAPHIES

672.   Barron, Neil. **Anatomy of Wonder: Science Fiction.** New York, R. R. Bowker, 1976. 471p. index. (Bibliographic Guides for Contemporary Collections). $17.50; $9.50pa. LC 76-10260. ISBN 0-8352-0884-2; 0-8352-0949-0pa.

This is an excellent critical guide to the genre of science fiction, from its classical beginnings with the Greeks (e.g., the utopian theme of Plato's *Republic*) to the modern contemporary authors such as Robert A. Heinlein and Ursula K. Le Guin. The work, which is more than a bibliography, is divided into two main parts that encompass the literature of and the research aids to the field. The first part divides the literature into four basic sections, plus an additional section devoted to juvenile works. Each section is prefaced by an excellent introduction describing the essence of the period being considered.

The first section covers "Science Fiction: From Its Beginning to 1870." Its introduction also delves into the matter of the definitions of this class of literature and describes its early beginnings. This is the period also of Edgar Allan Poe, Mary W. Shelley, and Jonathan Swift. The second section treats "The Emergence of the Scientific Romance, 1870-1926." Here are works by such as Edward Bellamy, Edgar Rice Burroughs, Jack London, Jules Verne, and H. G. Wells. The third period is "The Gernsback Era, 1926-1937." This is the time of the proliferation of science fiction pulp magazines and the development of "modern themes and techniques" in their stories. Such authors as John W. Campbell, Aldous Huxley, A. Merritt, and W. Olaf Stapledon helped influence the writing of the period. The fourth and largest section covers "The Modern Period, 1938-1975." Here lies the period of exciting growth of quality novels by quality authors. Among only a few are Isaac Asimov, Ray Bradbury, Arthur C. Clarke, Harlan Ellison, Robert Silverberg, and Kurt Vonnegut, Jr. The fifth and final section covers "Juvenile Science Fiction"; some of the books described here have won high awards in the field of juvenile literature.

Each annotation presents a succinct plot summary noting the principal themes and describing, as appropriate, the work's strengths and weaknesses. Comparable works are mentioned, and a key number system is used to refer to other annotations in this volume. Awards and award nominations are cited. Information on whether the work was also published in paperback is provided, along with a notation on the author's nationality. Coverage of titles is certainly more than reasonably comprehensive, and annotations seem to be provided for every work of major significance.

The second part of this very useful reference work includes chapters with annotated bibliographies on "History, Criticism, and Biography." "Bibliographies, Indexes, and

Teaching Aids," and "Magazine and Book Review Indexes." Further chapters cover science fiction "Periodicals," "Literary Awards," a "Core Collection Checklist," a well-annotated list of "Library Collections of Science Fiction and Fantasy," a handy "Directory of Publishers," and valuable author and title indexes.

All in all, one must applaud this highly significant and useful reference and research tool to the field of science fiction. Libraries should purchase both reference and circulation copies. [R: ARBA 77, p. 568; BL, 1 Dec 76, p. 527; Choice, Dec 76, p. 1267; LJ, 15 Apr 77, p. 875; LJ, 1 Nov 76, p. 2264; RQ, Summer 77, p. 336; WLB, Nov 76, p. 267; WLB, Feb 77, p. 487]

Hans H. Weber

673. Tymn, Marshall B., Kenneth J. Zahorski, and Robert H. Boyer. **Fantasy Literature: A Core Collection and Reference Guide.** New York, R. R. Bowker, 1979. 273p. bibliog. index. $14.95. LC 79-1533. ISBN 0-8352-1153-3.

Fantasy Literature serves as a true guide to high fantasy writing. Following a graceful foreword on the values and essence of fantasy by Lloyd Alexander, the reader is offered an extensive analysis of high fantasy literature by Robert H. Boyer and Kenneth J. Zahorski (English faculty of St. Norbert College, Wisconsin). Their definition and classification of fantasy are more fully developed and clearer than what Diana Waggoner has given us in *The Hills of Faraway: A Guide to Fantasy* (Atheneum, 1978. $16.95).

The core collection of 240 seminal works is limited to books for adults or for all ages; books written exclusively for children are excluded. All selections are works of "high-quality prose fiction, judged by the same critical norms applied to any piece of literature" (p. xi). With one exception (*Undine*), all selections belong to the period of modern high fantasy; no works published after 1978 were considered. The core collection, the main part of the guide, lists works by author and gives brief bibliographic data, including the publisher and year of the first English-language edition and the publisher and year of the current reprint edition. Variant titles are noted (a list of the titles currently available in the United Kingdom is printed in the last section of the book). The descriptions contain a brief synopsis, critical evaluation (including comments on character and delineation), thematic import, narrative structure, subgenre classification, and the influence of the work on other writers.

"Research Aids," part II of the guide (prepared by Marshall B. Tymn), lists writings of fantasy scholarship (history/criticism, author studies), periodicals, organization, awards, and library collections. A directory of publishers and an index to the introductory text and to authors and titles in the core collection conclude the work. Librarians in secondary schools and in public and college libraries will find this guide useful for collection development and reader guidance. [R: ARBA 80, p. 552; LJ, 1 Dec 79, p. 2559]

Christine Gehrt Wynar

ENCYCLOPEDIAS

674. Ash, Brian, ed. **The Visual Encyclopedia of Science Fiction.** New York, Harmony Books, a division of Crown Publishers, 1977. 352p. illus. (part col.). index. $17.95; $7.95pa. ISBN 0-517-53174-7; 0-517-53175-5pa.

This work transcends its fundamental reference function, combining enjoyable reading with a comprehensive guide to the genre of science fiction. As with the genre as a whole, this work is rather innovative in presenting its subject matter. Preceded by a chronology recording notable events in science fiction since the beginning of the nineteenth century (including works of distinction, an author's first publication, births and expirations of magazines), the main section is concerned with the various themes of science fiction and their development by both authors and illustrators.

Each thematic section is preceded by a short introduction by a science fiction author noted as an authority on that particular subject (e.g., Isaac Asimov on robots and androids; J. G. Ballard on cataclysms and dooms). Other sections include such areas as biologies and environments; lost and parallel worlds; cities and cultures; and telepathy, psionics and ESP. The sections and subsections consist of commentary on the relevant basic, representative works; illustrations (many in color) from magazines and books, also identifying the illustrator; and a bibliography of additional publications. The thrust of each section is to "describe ideas, rather than to comment on the skill, or lack of it, with which they have been conveyed." The thematic sections are followed by the third part of the work, which (in three separately authored sections) provides a longer analysis of the entire genre in a more philosophical vein. The fourth major part of this encyclopedia consists of sections that generally detail the contributions to the genre by: fandom; science fiction art, cinema, television, magazines, comics, and commentators; and fringe cults. An author and title index concludes the work.

This reviewer found the book to be of excellent quality: errors were minor in nature, the illustrations were of high quality, and the previously mentioned innovative approach make this a very useful and usable work. [R: ARBA 79, p. 588; BL, 1 May 78, p. 1406; Choice, Sept 78, p. 846; LJ, 1 Mar 78, p. 567; RQ, Summer 78, p. 352; SLJ, Apr 78, p. 102]   Hans H. Weber

675.   Nicholls, Peter, general ed. **The Science Fiction Encyclopedia.** John Clute, associate ed. 1st ed. New York, Doubleday, 1979. 672p. illus. (Dolphin Books). $24.95; $12.95pa. LC 77-15167. ISBN 0-385-13000-7; 0-385-14743-0pa.

Peter Nicholls edited the often iconoclastic British science fiction journal, *Foundation*, from 1972-77. In this present work he sets out to produce an up-to-date and exhaustive encyclopedia of science fiction, arranged alphabetically and contained within one moderately priced volume, that would be entertaining as well as informative and reach the general public as well as the reference librarian. Though the task turned out to be impossible (as he admits), the author has gone a surprisingly long way toward accomplishing the goal. A refusal to rely on secondary sources and a close personal knowledge of his subject, plus a willingness to be evaluative, make this a substantial contribution.

Over 2,800 signed entries by 34 contributors cover authors, editors, critics, illustrators, books, films, periodicals, anthologies, and TV series, as well as awards, fanzines, comics, science fiction in other countries, terminology, and themes. The 175 theme entries are excellent, giving an overview of the major concerns of science fiction when taken as a whole. Essays of 1,000-3,000 words cover the history and development of such themes as robots, lost worlds, and computers. Representative stories and related themes are cross indexed.

Readers may wish to compare this work with Brian Ash's *Visual Encyclopedia of Science Fiction* (see entry 674), which also takes a thematic approach but is not arranged alphabetically. Although no replacement for the *Encyclopedia of Science Fiction and Fantasy through 1968* (see entry 676), Nicholls' *Encyclopedia* is a good, up-to-date source for public and academic libraries. [R: ARBA 80, p. 551; LJ, 1 Dec 79, p. 2558]

Cleon Robert Nixon, III

676.   Tuck, Donald H., comp. **The Encyclopedia of Science Fiction and Fantasy through 1968: Volumes 1 and 2. Who's Who, A-Z.** Chicago, Advent, 1974, 1978. 2v. index. $27.50/v. LC 73-91828. ISBN 0-911682-20-1(v.1); 0-911682-22-8(v.2).

Compiled and edited by Australian bibliophile Donald Tuck, *The Encyclopedia of Science Fiction and Fantasy* presents a comprehensive compendium of information in the field of speculative and imaginative literature. In 1974, Advent issued the first volume, sub-titled *Who's Who and Works, A-L*. Originally scheduled for publication in 1976, volume 2, subtitled *Who's Who, M-Z*, continues the coverage and format of the first volume, with biobibliographical information on writers, anthologists, editors, and artists whose names fall alphabetically within its scope. Entries present a biographical sketch for each person included, followed by bibliographical descriptions of all published works, brief glosses of major works, information on editions, reprints and translations, series notes, and tables of contents for anthologies or collections. Information in both volumes is complete only through 1968. A title index for all works cited in these two volumes concludes volume 2.

In a work of such scope, it is perhaps inevitable that errors should occur. A survey of volume 2 revealed several, two of them occurring in the section on Jack Williamson alone. However, with the possible exception of the much briefer, one-volume *Visual Encyclopedia of Science Fiction* (see entry 674), edited by Brian Ash, this is the most comprehensive reference work so far attempted in the field and should be a standard source for many years to come. [R: ARBA 75, p. 591; RQ, Winter 74, p. 182; ARBA 79, p. 589; BL, 15 July 79, p. 1647]   Mary Jo Walker

INDEXES

677.   Hall, H. W., ed. **Science Fiction Book Review Index, 1923-1973.** Detroit, Gale, 1975. 438p. index. $64.00. LC 74-29085. ISBN 0-8103-1054-6.

This is a complete record of all books reviewed in science fiction magazines from 1923 to 1973. Beginning in 1970, coverage was extended to include reviews of science fiction in selected general magazines, library magazines, and amateur magazines (fanzines). The book is divided into five parts: the index of books reviewed (a few title entries are included), the directory of magazines indexed, a listing of indexes to science fiction magazines, an editor index, and a title index. In all, citations are given to about 14,500 reviews from 216 magazines. Each title is listed under its author, and a listing of all reviews and reviewers is given immediately below. Excerpts from the reviews are not included.

Since the first magazine devoted exclusively to science fiction, *Amazing Stories*, began publication in 1926, the period covered by this index comprises almost the entire history of science fiction as a separate literary genre. The usefulness of the work is thereby enhanced. The major practical limitation to the usefulness of this book undoubtedly lies in the fact that most libraries would be unlikely to own the magazines mentioned in the citations; many of them are collectors' items now, and at the time of their issue they were considered unworthy of shelf space.

Science fiction has been fortunate in having more than its share of indexes and bibliographers. This work is another indication of that fact. Anyone interested in serious science fiction scholarship should have access to this book.

Ed. note: Yearly updates (since 1974) of *Science Fiction Book Review Index* have been published by H. W. Hall. [R: ARBA 76, p. 581; Choice, Jan 76, p. 1424; LJ, 1 Sept 75, p. 1535; WLB, Nov 75, p. 267]   Martin Andrews

678.   Siemon, Frederick. **Science Fiction Story Index, 1950-1968.** Chicago, American Library Association, 1971. 274p. $5.00pa. LC 70-162470. ISBN 0-8389-0107-7.

Indexers of science fiction undoubtedly are plagued with more than the usual number of indexing problems and decisions. Besides the major questions of time and scope and format, they must decide how they will define science fiction. Wherever the lines are drawn, someone will be displeased.

In the present guide, Siemon indexes over 3,400 short stories, novellas, novels, and poems in 237 anthologies. Although such writers as Saki and H. P. Lovecraft are represented, Siemon has concentrated on anthologies of pure or hard-line science fiction, covering approximately 90% of those published in the United States and England from 1950 through 1968. Periodical fiction is not indexed here, and Siemon has also excluded volumes produced in limited editions and books not readily identifiable as anthologies.

The guide consists of three clearly defined and easy-to-use sections. The first lists stories alphabetically by author. The second, which can double as a buying aid, describes the anthologies indexed, giving complete bibliographical information for each, plus reading level. The third section, an alphabetical listing by titles, refers the user to the author section or directly to the anthology in which the story appeared. Comprehensive and definitive within its scope, *Science Fiction Story Index* may be used alone in general reference collections. Libraries serving science fiction fans, however, will need to supplement it with W. R. Cole's *A Checklist of Science Fiction Anthologies* (Arno, 1975. $21.00), which covers 1927 through 1963, Bradford M. Day's *Index to Science Fiction Magazines 1926-1950*, and *1951-1965*, as well as more recent indexes. [R: ARBA 72, p. 493; LJ, 15 Oct 71, p. 3314; RQ, Winter 71, p. 180; WLB, Oct 71, p. 190]   Mary Jo Walker

AMERICAN LITERATURE
GENERAL WORKS

679.   Burke, W. J., and Will D. Howe. **American Authors and Books, 1640 to the Present Day.** 3rd rev. ed. Rev. by Irving Weiss and Anne Weiss. New York, Crown, 1973. 719p. $12.50. LC 62-11815. ISBN 0-517-501392.

American Authors and Books, first published in 1943, has become a standard reference source for those interested in American *belles lettres*. This edition has been thoroughly updated and revised, a commendable job. Entries are very brief and not really biographical in the usual sense. Entries for persons provide birth (and, where applicable, death) dates, birthplace, occupation (e.g., anthropologist, author), and titles and years of publications. In addition to entries for authors, this guide provides information on illustrators, periodicals, publishing companies, editors, etc. Title entries sometimes give a synopsis of the work but often provide only authors' names; "see" references are provided from pseudonyms to real names.

It should be noted that this volume encompasses more than literary figures or literature per se—e.g., there are entries for Craig Claiborne, H. W. Wilson, William Langer, John Holt, and Louis Shores. There are omissions and errors (e.g., only 10 novels are listed under the entry for the Lanny Budd series, but the entry for Upton Sinclair lists the eleventh novel), but these are exceptions to the overall high quality of this work. In all, this compilation is the most thorough work of its kind. [R: ARBA 74, p. 488; LJ, 15 Mar 73, p. 858; WLB, Mar 73, p. 609]   Sally Wynkoop

680.   Curley, Dorothy Nyren, Maurice Kramer, and Elaine Fialka Kramer, eds. **Modern American Literature.** 4th rev. and enl. ed. New York, Ungar, 1969. 3v. index. (Library of Literary Criticism). $75.00. LC 76-76599. ISBN 0-8044-3046-2.

This has been much improved since it was first published in 1960, meagerly following in the opulent tradition of C. W. Moulton's *A Library of Literary Criticism*. The present edition covers some 300 authors from the early 1900s on, alphabetically arranged. For each entry there is a bibliography and selection of British and American criticism. This edition includes about 100 more new writers than the third edition (1964), and more recent excerpts have been added to the entries for some two-thirds of the authors. In addition, comprehensive bibliographies of the works of all authors are at the end of each volume.

A supplement to the fourth edition was published in 1976 (Ungar, 624p. $30.00), adding 51 new writers and updating the information for half of those writers who appeared in the fourth edition. Critical excerpts now represent additional scholarly and popular sources, and coverage is complete through 1975. This title deserves a place as a standard reference source. [R: ARBA 70, v. 2, p. 72; LJ, 15 Sept 69, p. 3039; Choice, Sept 69, p. 788]

681. Spiller, Robert E., and others, eds. **Literary History of the United States.** 4th ed., rev. New York, Macmillan, 1974. 2v. bibliog. index. $27.50. LC 73-14014.

It is no easy task to ascertain the true history of *Literary History of the United States*; the best single chronicle of its various editions appears in the preface to the second bibliographical supplement (page 1037 of the bibliography volume of the present edition). The fact that this preface and much of what follows appear intact is suggestive of one important overriding fact about *LHUS*, fourth edition; it is mainly a reprint. The only thing new in the bibliography volume, for example, is the index, and it is new only in the sense that the contents of the original bibliography volume (1948), Supplement I (1959), and Supplement II (1972) all appear in one index.

The history volume does include some new material – but not much. It reprints the third edition (which had reprinted most of previous editions) up through page 1391. Actual revision begins in the second part of "End of an Era," and begins to cut new ground with the section "Mid-Century and After," which includes the chapters "The New Consciousness," "Poetry," "Drama," and "Fiction" – about 60 pages in all. The reader's bibliography which follows has been revised, and the index incorporates the new and revised materials, excepting the bibliography.

LHUS still stands as the definitive literary history of this century, and its bibliography is still useful – though challenged by the rush of new bibliographical reviews and research and criticism. But it is well to remember that most new editions of *LHUS* have come more as updates than as actual revisions. [R: ARBA 75, p. 594; Choice, Feb 75, p. 1778]

Edwin S. Gleaves

BIBLIOGRAPHIES

682. Blanck, Jacob, comp. **Bibliography of American Literature.** Comp. for the Bibliographical Society of America. New Haven, CT, Yale University Press, 1954- . $35.00/v.(v.1-4); $45.00(v.5); $40.00(v.6). LC 54-5283. ISBN 0-300-00310-2(v.1); 0-300-00311-0(v.2); 0-300-00312-9(v.3); 0-300-00313-7(v.4); 0-300-01099-0(v.5); 0-300-01618-2(v.6).

Begun in 1954, this monumental work will be the standard bibliography on the subject when it is complete. The first five volumes were published over the years 1954 to 1969. The complete set of eight or nine volumes is expected to cover about 300 authors who died before 1930 and to contain approximately 35,000 numbered entries alphabetically arranged by author. For each author, all first editions, fully collated, are presented in chronological order; subsequent editions incorporating textual changes are briefly described; and a selected list of bibliographical, critical, and biographical works is included. The sixth volume of *Bibliography of American Literature* covers Augustus Baldwin Longstreet to Thomas William Parsons and includes 35 authors.

Blanck, a former bibliographer in Americana at the Library of Congress and author of many bibliographies, is preparing this title under the direction of the Bibliographical Society of America. [R: ARBA 70, v.2, p. 73; ARBA 75, p. 593; Choice, July 74, p. 733]

683. **First Printings of American Authors: Contributions toward Descriptive Checklists, Volumes 1-4.** Matthew J. Bruccoli, series ed. 1st ed. Detroit, Gale, 1977-1979. 4v. illus. index. (A Bruccoli Clark Book). $180.00/4v. set. LC 74-11756. ISBN 0-8103-0933-5.

This excellent "field guide" will greatly help scholars, collectors, dealers, and librarians identify first American and first English printings of American novelists, poets, playwrights, and essayists. Each of the 500 authors has had works listed chronologically, with place of publication, publisher, year of publication, and varying degrees of bibliographical description being noted. The major difference between this effort and other checklists is that this is illustrated, liberally, with reproductions of the title pages of many of the works in question, so that there can be little doubt as to what, say, a first of William Goyen's *House of Breath* looks like. This, then, will be of great use to bibliographers, book dealers, and anyone else concerned with firsts. An additional merit is the tasteful production of the volumes themselves. They lie flat easily, have generous white space, and are, all in all, a pleasure to look at and use in themselves. This fine effort is a tribute to American letters, and Mr. Bruccoli and associates are to be congratulated for superb execution of that tribute. [R: ARBA 80, p. 558; LJ, 1 Sept 79, p. 1684]

Koert C. Loomis, Jr.

684. Leary, Lewis, and John Auchard. **American Literature: A Study and Research Guide.** New York, St. Martin's Press, 1976. 185p. index. $12.95. LC 75-38017.

This is a volume whose relative slimness belies its actual value. Primarily, it is an evaluative bibliographic guide to American literature—its major authors, its roots, its various manifestations, and the types of criticism that deal with it. Leary has long been a distinguished name in American literary studies (see his *Articles on American Literature, 1900-1950, 1950-1967,* and *1968-1975*); this volume presents a distillation of his experience for the use of students and professionals alike.

The first chapter, a history of the study and teaching of American literature, informs on many points usually neglected. Then follow the various bibliographic essay chapters on literary histories, studies in genre, influences, the different critical schools, periodicals, bibliographical guides, biographical sources, major American writers, and the (inevitable) model research paper. The essays are well written, densely packed with citations (including LC call numbers), and remarkably high in the quality of material included. (Items in paperback as of the time of compilation are starred.) For the major American writers section, Leary polled a large group of scholar-teachers, who provided him with so many names that he expanded his original notion of 20 to include 23 individuals and a grouping of the Schoolroom Poets (total of 28 writers). Such lists, as Leary notes, are often subject to attack, but his seems as representative as such a brief one could be.

As to omissions, there are remarkably few, although giving students an "outsider's" view of the Modern Language Association might have been beneficial; it could have been done by citing Edmund Wilson's pamphlet, *The Fruits of the MLA.* Annotating periodicals as to scope would have been useful. Too, some information is slightly out of date. In general, though, material is current when necessary and, if dated, still of use enough to merit its inclusion. Even the sample research paper is not uninteresting! Leary's book would benefit anyone connected with the study or teaching of American literature, although something like Turabian's *Student's Guide for Writing College Papers* would be of more practical long-term use than Leary's small section on that topic. Also, this would be much preferable to the American section of F. W. Bateson's *Guide to English and American Literature.* [R: ARBA 78, p. 570; Choice, May 77, p. 347; LJ, 15 Jan 77, p. 188]

Koert C. Loomis, Jr.

685. Rubin, Louis D., Jr., ed. **A Bibliographical Guide to the Study of Southern Literature.** Baton Rouge, Louisiana State University Press, 1969. 368p. (Southern Library Studies Series). $20.00; $6.95pa. LC 69-17627. ISBN 0-8071-0302-0; 0-8071-0139-7pa.

This work is intended as a comprehensive guide to the study of Southern writers from the colonial period to 1970. The checklists, contributed by 100 specialists, were edited by Mr. Rubin, a professor of English at the University of North Carolina.

The guide is organized in two parts. Part I, general topics, includes 23 special bibliographies with introductory comments (e.g., general works on Southern literature, humorists of the old Southwest and twentieth-century drama). Part II, individual writers, provides a brief introductory note followed by a checklist of critical books and articles from each of 135 writers. An appendix contains materials on 68 additional writers of the Colonial South, by J. A. Leo Lemay. This comprehensive work supplements and extends the bibliographies in Jay B. Hubbell's *The South in American Literature, 1607-1900* (Duke, 1954. $24.75). [R: ARBA 70, v.2, p. 74; Choice, Mar 70, p. 52; C&RL, July 70, p. 274; LJ, 15 Nov 69, p. 4130; WLB, 7 Dec 69, p. 461]

FICTION

686. Dickinson, A. T., Jr. **American Historical Fiction.** 3rd ed. Metuchen, NJ, Scarecrow, 1971. 380p. $12.50. LC 78-146503. ISBN 0-8108-0370-4.

Originally published in 1956 and revised and enlarged in 1963, this title was again enlarged and improved in its third edition. The number of titles listed has risen from 1,224 to 2,440; the subject index, now separate from the author-title index, is more detailed; and the publication dates of titles included now extend from 1917 (as previously) to 1969. Noteworthy or significant novels pre-dating 1917 are selectively included (works by Cooper, Hawthorne, the early Dreiser, etc.).

The list, covering colonial times to the late 1960s, is arranged by historical period, and brief descriptive annotations point out the historical bearing. By using a broad definition of "historical novel" — a novel that centers upon an identifiable time, place, person, event, or other aspect of the cultural landscape — the compiler includes a number of titles set in times contemporary with the author (*The Great Gatsby, Of Mice and Men, The Naked and the Dead*). Despite this latitude, the field marked out by Coan and Lillard's *America in Fiction* — fiction of merit that reflects some aspect of American life — is not seriously infringed upon. The two titles complement each other; both are necessary for the study of American history and life. [R: ARBA 72, p. 502; LJ, 1 Nov 71, p. 3594; WLB, Oct 71, p. 189]

David Rosenbaum

687. Eichelberger, Clayton L., comp. **A Guide to Critical Reviews of United States Fiction, 1870-1910.** Metuchen, NJ, Scarecrow, 1971. 415p. index. $12.50. LC 77-149998. ISBN 0-8108-0380-1.

688. Eichelberger, Clayton L., comp. **A Guide to Critical Reviews of United States Fiction, 1870-1910, Volume II.** Metuchen, NJ, Scarecrow, 1974. 351p. index. $11.00. LC 77-149998. ISBN 0-8108-0701-7.

For the first work, 30 English, Canadian, and American periodicals were searched for evaluative reviews of American fiction for the period covered. Because of the regional character of some of the periodicals, many obscure works are listed, some of which do not appear in Wright's *American Fiction 1851-1875* and *1876-1900* or in Blanck's *Bibliography of American Fiction*. Arrangement is alphabetical by author with an index of titles and an appendix of anonymous and pseudonymous works.

Volume II, published under the same title as the original work, is supplementary to it. Authors are listed alphabetically with cross references for pseudonymous and anonymous works. Under the author's name, individual titles are listed, followed by bibliographical references to journals reviewing the book. Approximately 9,000 references to critical notices are included, which expands the listing for the two volumes to over 20,000 items. This is an admirable work in concept, organization, and inclusiveness. [R: ARBA 72, p. 503; LJ, 1 Jan 72, p. 59; ARBA 75, p. 596; LJ, Aug 74, p. 1926; WLB, Oct 74, p. 183]

Paul Z. DuBois
James P. McCabe

BIOGRAPHY

689. Bain, Robert, Joseph M. Flora, and Louis D. Rubin, Jr., eds. **Southern Writers: A Biographical Dictionary.** Baton Rouge, Louisiana State University Press, 1979. 515p. (Southern Literary Studies). $40.00; $7.95pa. LC 78-25899. ISBN 0-8071-0354-3; 0-8071-0390-Xpa.

Designed as a reference tool to be used in conjunction with *A Bibliographical Guide to the Study of Southern Literature* (Louisiana State University Press, 1969. $20.00; $6.95pa.), the updated *Southern Literary Culture* (University of Alabama Press, 1979. $22.50), and the annual checklist published in the spring issue of *Mississippi Quarterly*, the new biographical dictionary fills the need for ready information otherwise time-consuming to attain. Compiled Southern literature, biographical sketches of 379 authors, and a bibliography of the first U.S. editions of the authors' major works are presented. The concise sketches are well balanced between factual information and evaluative commentary, and are generally uniform in quality.

Apparently, considerable effort was made to arrive at a consensus of scholars and editors as to which authors were to be included, although the final list seems to slight scholars, critics, and historians and to disproportionately favor Afro-American writers. One wonders, for instance, why such significant writers as Randall Stewart, F. Van Woodward, Frank Owsley, and Douglas Southall Freeman were omitted? Perhaps the editors felt that information about such writers was readily available elsewhere. Perhaps, too, the editors felt that past neglect of Afro-American writers called for special compensation in the present volume. However much one may wish the list to be more complete and more representative of a broader range of Southern writers, the dictionary is an extremely valuable contribution to the study of Southern literature. [R: ARBA 80, p. 561; LJ, Aug 79, p. 1552]   Robert L. Welker

BRITISH LITERATURE

BIBLIOGRAPHIES

690. DeLaura, David J., ed. **Victorian Prose: A Guide to Research.** New York, Modern Language Association of America, 1973. 560p. index. $16.00. $7.50pa. LC 73-80586. ISBN 0-87352-250-8; 0-87352-251-6pa.

This is the third research guide in Victoriana sponsored (and in this case published as well) by the Modern Language Association. This volume, on nonfictional prose, is edited by David J. DeLaura, winner of the MLA award for his article on Arnold and Carlyle, and a specialist in the field of Victorian studies. The scope is wide-ranging and thorough: minor figures are covered more fully than in the preceding volumes, yet attention to major figures remains sound. A section each is devoted to Macaulay; the Carlyles, Thomas and Jane; Newman; Mill; Ruskin; Arnold; Pater. Minor literary critics of the period are covered separately. An extensive section on religious prose covers the Oxford Movement and Victorian churchmen; non-believers are discussed in the final chapter. All writers and movements are examined from the standpoint of biographical material, bibliography, criticism, ideas, and influence. The evaluations are conscientiously balanced and objective.

As in all monumental studies of this kind, there are some omissions. The most serious case is that of Thomas DeQuincey, whose major contribution is in his prose; he therefore belongs within the province of this volume, although he may as easily be linked with the Romantics in spirit as with the Victorians in chronology. Less serious, because the authors' main contributions lie in other fields, is the omission of Lewis Carroll's mathematical writings; George Bernard Shaw's art, drama, and music criticism; A. E. Housman's classical papers. In no case, however, can one complain of total neglect; hardly a writer of the period escapes some mention, insofar as he relates to discussions of the major figures.

The 12 scholars who have combined their learning in this distinguished contribution to scholarship continue the same tradition of excellence as the preceding guides to research. The index, meticulously accurate and thorough, covers persons but not titles; it enhances the book's value. [R: ARBA 75, p. 610; LJ, 1 Mar 74, p. 643]   Dorothy E. Litt

691.   Howard-Hill, T. H. **British Bibliography and Textual Criticism: A Bibliography.** New York, Oxford University Press, 1979. 2v. (Index to British Literary Bibliography, Vols. 4 and 5). $115.00/set. ISBN 0-19-818163-9.

The first volume of Howard-Hill's ambitious *Index to British Literary Bibliography* appeared in 1969; the second in 1971. The set was to be of three volumes, but the present work comprises volumes IV and V in what is now projected to be a seven-volume bibliography. Howard-Hill is increasingly ambitious; his work, increasingly valuable.

These volumes list those writings in English published between 1890 and 1969 which treat any aspect of the printing, publication, or distribution of works in Britain since 1475. Volume IV includes well over 8,000 titles in separate sections for Bibliography and Textual Criticism; General and Period Bibliography; Regional Bibliography; Book Production and Distribution; and Forms, Genres, and Subjects. Volume V includes over 6,000 additional items that treat the bibliographical history of the works of specific authors. The items in each subsection of each volume are arranged chronologically by date of publication. When necessary, information is provided in brackets to explain the relevance of an item to textual criticism or the study of book collecting or bibliography. Occasional annotations make note of facsimiles and illustrated texts, and list the contents of substantial works.

The information in these two volumes is of immeasurable value to textual critics, bibliographers, and other bibliophiles. Unfortunately, it is at this time rather inaccessible. The index to both volumes incorporates the indexes to the earlier volumes, but constitutes volume VI, which is still in preparation. [R: ARBA 80, p. 572; Choice, Nov 79, p. 1154; LJ, 1 May 79, p. 1043; RQ, Fall 79, p. 90; WLB, Oct 79, p. 130]   F. W. Ramey

692.   **The New Cambridge Bibliography of English Literature.** Ed. by George Watson and I. R. Willison; index (v.5) by J. D. Pickles. New York, Cambridge University Press, 1969-1977. 5v. $120.00(v.1); $98.00(v.2-4); $35.00(v.5); $380.00(set). LC 73-82455. ISBN 0-521-20004-0(v.1); 0-521-07934-9(v.2); 0-521-07255-7(v.3); 0-521-08535-7(v.4); 0-521-21310-X(v.5); 0-521-08761-9(set).

A revision and substantial expansion of *The Cambridge Bibliography of English Literature*, edited by F. W. Bateson (Cambridge University Press, 1940. 4v. and suppl.). This new five-volume set is comprised of: volume 1, 600-1660; volume 2, 1660-1800; volume 3, 1800-1900; volume 4, 1900-1950; volume 5, Index. This monumental work aims to list and classify the whole of English studies, as represented by the literature of the British Isles, analyzing both primary and secondary sources. The *New Cambridge Bibliography of English Literature* is confined to authors native to, or mainly resident in, the British Isles, but no nationality or language restrictions are imposed on secondary materials (mainly biography and criticism).

Each of the first four volumes represents a literary period, which is divided by form (drama, poetry, etc.); these form divisions are in turn subdivided by individual authors and special topics. The author subdivisions list bibliographies and collections, primary material, and secondary material. Excluded are unpublished doctoral dissertations, "ephemeral journalism, encyclopaedia articles, reviews of secondary works, brief notes of less than crucial interest to scholarship, and sections in general works such as literary histories." The most important contribution to English studies, second only to the *Oxford English Dictionary*. [R: ARBA 72, p. 512; ARBA 73, p. 503; WLB, Dec 74, p. 316; ARBA 75, p. 611; BL, 15 Jan 75, p. 516; Choice 75, p. 1609; LJ, 1 Jan 75, p. 45; ARBA 76, p. 607; Choice, Nov 77, p. 1194; WLB, Nov 77, p. 262; ARBA 78, p. 590]

HANDBOOKS

693. Ruoff, James E. **Crowell's Handbook of Elizabethan & Stuart Literature**. New York, Thomas Y. Crowell, 1975. 468p. $14.95. LC 73-22097. ISBN 0-690-22661-6.

Much of what one would want to discover about Renaissance (1560-1660) literature in England can be found in this alphabetically arranged handbook of over 500 detailed yet concise entries. Significant works from about the time of Sir Thomas More to that of Milton are introduced, as are lesser authors and works not found in one place elsewhere.

There are articles for particular subjects, literary movements, important genres, literary by-paths, and cultural topics of special relevance to literature. Cross references are very helpful. An author entry includes biographical details, artistic development, accomplishments, and influence, along with a selected bibliography. An article for a work discusses composition, dates, editions, genre, and sources. There is also a precis or synopsis of the work. The entry closes with a bibliographical selection of outstanding critical writing about it.

Bounded by *Foxe's Book of Martyrs* and *A Yorkshire Tragedy*, this is a mine of valuable information, pleasurable to read, about Elizabethan and Stuart literature. This volume is a necessary reference tool for libraries. [R: ARBA 76, p. 608; BL, 15 Apr 75, p. 843; LJ, 15 Mar 75, p. 570]

Edward A. Richter

FICTION

694. Dyson, A. E., ed. **The English Novel**. New York, Oxford University Press, 1974. 372p. (Select Bibliographical Guides). $19.50; $7.95pa. ISBN 0-19-871033-X; 0-19-871027-5pa.

With the help of an admirable list of British and American contributors, A. E. Dyson here covers all major British novelists from John Bunyan to James Joyce; the only serious complaint is the exclusion of Virginia Woolf. The guide is intended for the serious scholar of English literature, specifically the novel.

Each critic follows the same format in discussing his author: a citing of authoritative texts; a sampling of representative criticism found in published essays, journals, and books; the kinds of biographies to be found and how (or whether) they illumine the artist's fiction; the presence, if any, of the author's own record in letters and diaries and the quality of editions available; the bibliographies that will offer access to other, possibly unmentioned, critics; and finally, background readings that make historical and philosophical suggestions to augment literary understanding. Each essay concludes with a bibliography listing all sources mentioned in the essay.

As a guide, this reference work is helpful in several ways. First, the chapters are similar in format, enabling users to identify easily the kind of information they seek. Second, because the contributors are critics themselves, they attempt to discuss schools of critical thought as well as the specific persons who initiated the schools. Third, an attempt is made to define the artists and their milieu, as well as the critical reaction to their work. And fourth, as an unexpected asset, this guide gives suggestions for needed research and does not hesitate to cite gaps in knowledge (e.g., "no modern collection of Bunyan," "no adequate study of Defoe's religious thought," "need for a fully annotated, definitive edition of

Gulliver's Travels," "no entirely satisfactory edition of *Tom Jones,*" "no large-scale bibliography of Jane Austen," etc.).

The English Novel makes no pretense at being exhaustive. As the editor states, "the contributors to this book are concerned with mapping territory, pointing to landmarks, suggesting routes." For the serious student of the English novel, this is a practical, functional, and worthwhile guide. [R: ARBA 75, p. 612; LJ, July 74, p. 1792; WLB, Oct 74, p. 181]

Sharon S. Peterson

695. Ford, George H., ed. **Victorian Fiction: A Second Guide to Research.** New York, Modern Language Association of America, 1978. 401p. index. $17.50; $9.00pa. LC 77-083468. ISBN 0-87352-254-0; 0-87532-255-9pa.

This revised bibliography is of particular importance today because of a new kind of interest in the Victorian writers, partly, but not entirely, caused by television presentations of the novels of Dickens and Trollope, among others. The reasons for today's interest in such authors may be very much the same ones that Lionel Trilling discovered a few years ago, when 10 times the expected number of undergraduates at Columbia signed up for a course of his in Jane Austen and her world. The Victorian period, if you were not among the very poor (and, some would say, if you were not a Roman Catholic) was one of stability, order, and comfort — even of general prosperity. But it is chiefly that stability and order that do seem to be vanishing from today's world, in England as well as in other countries, and in the United States also.

Following Richard Altick's introductory compilation of "General Materials" (with its interesting statistical suggestion that 40,000 pieces of fiction make up the Victorian corpus) are bibliographies concerning 17 authors, major and minor, women as well as men. Users of this work will look first, of course, for the authors they are "teaching," or for their favorites; I looked, among other favorites, for Gissing, and was a bit disappointed to find no entry for *Ryecroft,* though I know one can make a case for its being nonfictional. On the other hand, there is a reference to new French analysis of that wonderful book. This is an essential bibliography for all literature collections. [R: ARBA 79, p. 604; Choice, Dec 78, p. 1353]

D. Bernard Theall

696. Palmer, Helen H., and Anne Jane Dyson, comps. **English Novel Explication: Criticisms to 1972.** Hamden, CT, Shoe String Press, 1973. 329p. index. $15.00. LC 73-410. ISBN 0-208-01322-9.

This work is a supplement to Bell and Baird's *The English Novel* (Swallow, 1959), which covered the subject through 1957; hence, this volume covers criticisms essentially from 1958 to 1972. A few items that were overlooked by Bell and Baird and that were published earlier than 1957 are included here.

The arrangement is alphabetical by author, then by title; under title, criticisms are arranged alphabetically by author. There are three appendixes: a list of the books indexed, a list of the journals indexed, and an author/title index. Unfortunately, the fact that there is no table of contents makes it difficult to find the appendixes. Another minor difficulty stems from the omission of the quotation marks that should set off journal article titles.

Still, insofar as Bell and Baird's work is generally considered indispensable, so will this supplement be necessary. [R: ARBA 74, p. 514; Choice, Dec 73, p. 1531; LJ, 1 Sept 73, p. 2424; WLB, Dec 73, p. 339]

Kenyon C. Rosenberg

BIOGRAPHY

697. **British Writers: Volumes I, II, and III, William Langland to the English Bible; Thomas Middleton to George Farquhar; Daniel Defoe to The Gothic Novel.** Ian Scott-Kilvert, general ed. New York, Scribner's, 1979-80. 3v. $55.00/vol. LC 78-23483. ISBN 0-684-15798-5(v.1); 0-684-16407-8(v.2); 0-584-16408-6(v.3).

The British Council has undertaken sponsorship of a projected seven volumes of biographical/critical articles on the major figures in British literature from the fourteenth century to the late twentieth century. If the first volumes are exemplary of the entire effort, this would be a valuable acquisition for a number of reasons. First, the essays are enthusiastic, but also meticulous about dealing with inconsistencies in an author's production—in a word, balanced. In volume I, the essay on Shakespeare is mercifully short—a problem noted in the introduction was "how to handle Shakespeare?"—but appended is a lengthy bibliography that will be of service to many a scholar. There also has been included an essay on the composition and development of the English Bible, which demonstrates the editorial clearheadedness with which the project has been carried out.

Contributors include Derek Pearsall, Kenneth Muir, Frank Kermode, Nevill Coghill, Stanley Wells, Sylvia Townsend Warner, and J. H. Plumb. Essays are subdivided for convenient reference, and each has a bibliography covering the major critical works (and texts, if that is an issue). Biographical information is usually comprehensive enough to provide a good sketch of the subjects, with the remainder of each essay devoted to a survey of the author's works. Authors manage to take definite stands without sounding polemical, which is pleasant. All in all, the volumes should prove a valuable addition to any library's basic literature collection, as well as to scholars who could afford them.   Koert C. Loomis, Jr.

CANADIAN LITERATURE

698. Toye, William, ed. **Supplement to the Oxford Companion to Canadian History and Literature.** New York, Oxford University Press, 1973. 318p. $21.00. ISBN 0-19-540205-7.

Although some biographical articles on major authors who died before 1967 (e.g., Frederick Philip Grove, E. J. Pratt) have been reprinted from Norah Story's *The Oxford Companion to Canadian History and Literature* (Oxford University Press, 1967), most of the information deals with the years 1967 thorugh 1972. It is, thus, a true supplement, and not a work that supersedes or that can stand alone on the reference shelves. Unlike the original, which was the work of one person, the supplement includes signed articles from 37 contributors, most of whom are on the faculties of major Canadian universities. One notable feature (missing in the original) is the attention given to children's books in both English and French. Literature in French generally receives proportionately greater emphasis. Both the original and the supplement contain articles of monographic length on topics like "Fiction in English," "Literary Magazines in French," "History Studies in English," "Political Writings in French," etc. Both have numerous cross references from the names of individuals to the appropriate sections of these monographic articles. Both the biographical and the topical articles are rich in bibliographical citations, often accompanied by critical comments. These two volumes are a goldmine of useful information for all reference librarians whose patrons are interested in Canadian history or literature. [R: ARBA 75, p. 630; Choice, Apr 74, p. 240; LJ, 1 Apr 74, p. 1020]   A. Robert Rogers

CARIBBEAN LITERATURE

699. Herdeck, Donald E., ed. **Caribbean Writers: A Bio-Bibliographical-Critical Encyclopedia.** Maurice A. Lubin and others, associate eds. Washington, Three Continents Press, 1979. 943p. illus. bibliog. $45.00. LC 77-3841. ISBN 0-914478-74-5.

This bio-bibliographical work contains biographical information on some 2,000 writers, and bibliographical data on more than 15,000 works. The majority of entries are in English, Dutch, French, and Spanish, but a few are in creole languages. Caribbean as used here also refers to Belize, Guyana, Surinam, and French Guiana. The encyclopedia contains four parts: Spanish (37%), French (30%), English (28%), and Dutch (5%) (only writers from the Dominican Republic, Puerto Rico, and Cuba are included in the Spanish section). Each section has a single A-Z listing of writers.

The entries include brief biographical data (some have a photo or drawing of the person), a list of writings, and for some authors, biographical and critical sources. Most entries are less than one column, but some extend to a page or two. Included with each section are essays on the literature of that language in each country or area, a list of writers arranged by country or island, bibliographies of critical studies, anthologies, and bibliographies of that particular literature. Containing many biographies of writers that could be difficult to locate in other sources, this work can be highly recommended for libraries desiring biographical and bibliographical information on writers from the Caribbean from colonial times to the present day. [R: ARBA 80, p. 588]   Donald J. Lehnus

CLASSICAL GREEK AND ROMAN LITERATURE

700. Grant, Michael. **Greek and Latin Authors, 800 B.C.-A.D. 1000.** New York, H. W. Wilson, 1980. 490p. illus. (Wilson Author Series). $25.00. LC 79-27446. ISBN 0-8242-0640-1.

Why another handbook of classical studies, this one containing information on authors only? Pauly-Wissowa is hardly practical for ready reference. *Der kleine Pauly* and the *Lexikon der alten Welt* are accessible only to the dwindling number of scholars who read German easily. The *Oxford Classical Dictionary* provides adequate biographies (and much else). Grant updates the *OCD* (2nd ed., 1970) bibliographies and provides more detail in the biographies. Most libraries need both Grant and the *OCD*.

There are several special values in Grant's book besides the longish biographies (not quite as long as the still useful ones in older editions of the *Britannica*). Most important, Grant goes to the millennium. The classical tradition did not peter out, only sputtered after the fall of the Empire and the rise of Christianity. Grant has carefully selected some 60-odd authors, 500-1000 A.D., the majority Western, for inclusion—in all about a fifth of the total. Other selections for inclusion have been judicious, particularly in view of Latin and Greek authors whom we know only by name or from a few fragments. Nearly all articles are in proportion with respect to length.

Like other Wilson author biographical dictionaries, this one is practical for readers on almost any level. It is also a practical desk tool for the non-classicist and even for librarians in research collections. [R: ARBA 81; BL, 1 Dec 80, p. 534; Choice, Oct 80, p. 222; LJ, Aug 80, p. 1621; RQ, Fall 80, p. 96]   Lawrence S. Thompson

701. **The Oxford Classical Dictionary.** 2nd ed. Ed. by N. G. L. Hammond and H. H. Scullard. New York, Oxford University Press, 1970. 1176p. index. $37.50. ISBN 0-19-869117-3.

The first edition of this standard work was published in 1949. The introduction to the first edition stated that "it is designed to cover the same ground, though on a different scale, as the well-known dictionaries by Sir William Smith on Greek and Roman antiquities and on Greek and Roman biography, mythology, and geography." The eighth edition (1914) of Lübker's *Reallexikon* was taken as a general model, but with certain modifications in principle and with certain differences in emphasis.

The present work is intended to be less purely factual than Lübker. It devotes more space to biography and literature, less to geography and bibliographical information, aiming, in this latter respect, at no more than referring the reader to the best works, in English and foreign languages, on the various subjects. A special feature is the inclusion of longer articles designed to give a comprehensive survey of the main subjects and to place minor characters, places and events, the choice of which has been necessarily selective, against their appropriate library or historical background.

The second edition follows the same format; there is a little more emphasis on the archaeological background, some longer articles have been abbreviated a little (to make room for new additions), and the later Roman empire receives more comprehensive treatment. As in the first edition, most articles are brief, contain bibliographical references (up to 1968), and provide well-balanced coverage of most aspects of Greek and Roman culture. There is no separate article on *Aeneid* and other important works of literature, but all writers and poets are represented.

Some readers may prefer *New Century Classical Handbook* (Appleton-Century-Crofts, 1962) and for a more detailed treatment, one still has to consult *Pauly's Real-Encyclopädie der classischen Altertumwissenschaft*. All in all, however, this is one of the best one-volume sources on the subject. [R: ARBA 71, p. 439; BL, 1 Oct 71, p. 113; LJ, 1 May 71, p. 1599; WLB, Dec 70, p. 409]   Bohdan S. Wynar

FRENCH LITERATURE

702. Brooks, Richard A., general ed. **A Critical Bibliography of French Literature, Volume VI: The Twentieth Century.** Ed. by Douglas W. Alden. Syracuse, NY, Syracuse University Press, 1980 (c1979). 3v. index. $150.00. LC 47-3282. ISBN 0-8156-2204-X(set).

This bibliography on twentieth-century French literature constitutes the sixth volume of the highly regarded *Critical Bibliography of French Literature*, which was originally edited by David Clark Cabeen. Designed for the specialist and advanced student of French literature, it is a selective bibliography of "significant items" (books and articles) chosen by well-known scholars in the field. The deadline date for inclusion in this bibliography was originally 1974, but some material as recent as 1977 can be found. For each entry there is a brief, usually critical annotation, which is sometimes followed by citations of other reviews. Often the contents of books of collected essays are analyzed, and most of the journals utilized have been located either in *Union List of Serials* or *New Serial Titles*. Although the annotations are written in English, the materials described encompass many publications in foreign languages.

Arranged into three sections, part I of the bibliography covers general subjects and the novel before 1940; part II covers poetry, theater, and criticism before 1940, as well as essay; and part III takes care of all genres since 1940. Entries for individual writers in each part are neatly arranged according to type. (For example, in the section on Georges Bernanos, citations are grouped under such headings as "Biography," "Correspondence," "Themes and Ideas," etc.) Close to 18,000 numbered entries are incorporated into the bibliography, and the index at the back refers to these citation numbers rather than to page numbers. Arranged alphabetically by name, the index covers all writers, as well as major contributors of the work's annotations.

This newest volume of *A Critical Bibliography of French Literature* is thoughtfully executed and should prove itself as valuable a contribution as its predecessors. Despite its rather high price, it belongs in every library with a serious interest in French literature.
                                                                      Deborah Pearson

703. **Modern French Literature.** Comp. and ed. by Debra Popkin and Michael Popkin. New York, Frederick Ungar, 1977. 2v. index. (A Library of Literary Criticism). $60.00/set. LC 76-15655. ISBN 0-8044-3256-2.

A decade ago, the Library of Literary Criticism series presented *Modern Romance Literatures* (Ungar, 1967), with criticism selected mainly from British and American sources for a basic group of French and other romance writers. *Modern French Literature*, compiled by scholars Debra Popkin and Michael Popkin, pertains entirely to writers of France and the French-speaking countries of the world. Chosen for inclusion were 168 prominent authors who had received the most substantial critical acclaim during the past 10 years. Critical excerpts of generous length were selected from English and romance monographs and periodicals, translations were prepared, and full references provided. For each author the critical selections are presented chronologically, from appraisals earlier in the century to recent criticism, often of the 1970s. The sequential arrangement heightens the impact of the criticism, particularly for controversial writers. Many French authors also appear as critics, for a phenomenon of French literature is the extensive involvement of writers in the criticism of their contemporaries. Notable British and American writers are also among the critics: Truman Capote, John Dos Passos, T. S. Eliot, Ernest Hemingway, Dylan Thomas, John Updike, Richard Wright, and others.

Special features are a bibliography by author of all works mentioned in the critical selections, with dates of original publications and English translations; the listing of authors by country; the listing of French authors who appear as critics; an index of critics and their selections; and a cross reference index for authors mentioned within entries other than their own. *Modern French Literature* not only presents the convenient overview for which the series is noted but recreates the exciting and lively response to a rich and vivid literature. [R: ARBA 78, p. 606; LJ, 16 July 71, p. 279; WLB, Sept 77, p. 86]

Joyce L. Barnum

704. Reid, Joyce M. H., ed. **The Concise Oxford Dictionary of French Literature.** New York, Oxford University Press, 1976. 669p. illus. $15.95. ISBN 0-19-866118-5.

This is a revised and abridged version of the *Oxford Companion to French Literature*, first published in 1959. The format and style remain the same, but many articles have been abridged. The abridgment has been accomplished by condensing but not omitting information. Most articles on French-Canadian literature have been dropped, since there is now an *Oxford Companion to Canadian History and Literature*. Some articles have been expanded and updated, and new articles have been added. This is especially important for anyone with an interest in new literary trends, such as the *nouveau roman*, and contemporary authors. As the update to the *Oxford Companion*, this work should be in any reference collection having the original volume. It stands on its own, however, and can also be recommended as an ideal reference work for a personal library. [R: ARBA 78, p. 606; BL, Oct 77, p. 323; Choice, May 77, p. 344; LJ, 15 Jan 77, p. 189; WLB, June 77, p. 817]

Barbara E. Kemp

GERMAN LITERATURE

705. Garland, Henry, and Mary Garland. **The Oxford Companion to German Literature.** Oxford, England, Clarendon Press; distr., New York, Oxford University Press, 1976. 977p. $35.00. ISBN 0-19-866115-0.

This latest addition to the series will need no introduction to those familiar with the Oxford Companions to English, American, and French literatures. As in these other works, entries include biographies, synopses of important works, literary terms and movements, historical events and figures, and various other entries relevant to the social and intellectual background of the literature. Unfortunately, the authors' original plan to include entries for major characters had to be abandoned for lack of space.

Entries are connected by cross references which "serve to draw attention to the interconnection between literature and all aspects of history" (p. v). In keeping with the precedent set by earlier companions, the language is precise but not abbreviated or telegraphic. The book is a pleasure to read and, at the same time, contains an impressive amount of information for a desk-sized volume. The work covers the period from about 800 A.D. to the early 1970s.

This work belongs in the reference collection of any academic library and will no doubt become an indispensable volume in many a private library. It should prove to be of equal value to the neophyte and to the advanced scholar of German literature. [R: ARBA 77, p. 614; BL, 15 Apr 77, p. 1292; Choice, Oct 76, p. 958; LJ, July 76, p. 1513; WLB, Sept 76, p. 86]   Stanley Joe McCord

HUNGARIAN LITERATURE

706.   Tezla, Albert. **Hungarian Authors: A Bibliographical Handbook.** Cambridge, Harvard University Press, 1970. 792p. index. $30.00. LC 74-88813. ISBN 0-674-42650-9.

This annotated bibliography of 4,646 items is a companion volume to Tezla's *Introductory Bibliography to the Study of Hungarian Literature* (Harvard, 1964. $15.00). It lists, with full bibliographical data, first and subsequent editions of works by 162 major Hungarian-born authors. The selection spans the period from 1450 to 1970 and basically reflects the consensus of Hungarian and foreign experts and literary critics. Of course, one always could argue for the inclusion or elimination of one or another author. Tezla's high reputation, earned by his earlier work, together with the acknowledged participation of such Hungarian scholars as T. Klaniczay, S. Kozocsa, S. Lukácsy, and K. Bor, lend the work an unusual authority.

The tome opens with a long list of abbreviations, symbols, and Hungarian bibliographical terms and phrases. The introduction indicates that the systematic review for the book of primary and secondary sources was concluded with August 1, 1965. The main body of the volume is divided into two parts: authors from 1450 to 1945, and authors from 1945 to 1970—a division apparently suggested by the sociopolitical and ideological changes that have taken place in Hungary since World War II. Sections for most authors include a concise biographical sketch, as well as entries describing first editions, subsequent editions, biographies, bibliographical sources, and criticism pertaining to the particular author. On-the-spot research and interlibrary loans are facilitated by the addition of the international library location symbols (Gardner system) for each entry. Five appendixes supply information concerning published studies on Hungarian literature (1960-1965); literary awards, societies, and serial publications mentioned in the biographical sketches of authors; scholarly and literary periodicals used as sources of information for the main entries; identification of authors by major literary periods and trends; and codes and full names, with addresses, of source libraries in the United States and Europe. A name index to authors, compilers, editors, etc., enhances the usefulness of this excellent research tool. [R: ARBA 71, p. 465; Choice, Jan 71, p. 1496]   Ivan L. Kaldor

ITALIAN LITERATURE

707.   Bondanella, Peter, and Julia Conaway Bondanella, eds. **Dictionary of Italian Literature.** Westport, CT, Greenwood Press, 1979. 621p. bibliog. index. $35.00. LC 78-4022. ISBN 0-313-20421-7.

Approaching this new dictionary, not as a specialist in Italian literature but as a reference librarian and teacher of reference work for nearly 30 years, I find it a most welcome addition to the humanities reference collection. There are 362 entries, arranged in one alphabet; approximately two-thirds of these are on individual authors, the remainder on genres, periods, movements, and related general topics.

Checking rather carefully about 20 entries on persons or general topics, I found only one slight error: the medieval hagiographer and author of the *Golden Legend*, Jacobus De Voragine, is said to have been canonized in the early nineteenth century; he was, in fact, beatified in 1816, the step immediately preceding canonization. I should have liked to have seen an entry for Gaetano Moroni (1802-1883), a barber by trade and a historical scholar in his off hours, whose very useful historical-ecclesiastical dictionary in more than 100 volumes I have always found good for minor European—not only Italian—figures; he ended his days as private secretary to Pope Gregory XVI. Not even Sheehy carries an entry for him, and I find no reference librarians of today who know about the stores of information that can be winkled out of his volumes.

The appendix includes a helpful chart, called the "Time Line," showing from 1091 to 1977 important occurrences in Italian literature, world literature, political theory, history and religion, and philosophy, science, and the arts. If the budget allows, I recommend the *Dictionary* heartily. [R: ARBA 80, p. 1302; Choice, Oct 79, p. 990; LJ, 1 Dec 78, p. 2406; WLB, Sept 79, p. 64]   D. Bernard Theall

LATIN AMERICAN LITERATURE

708.   Foster, David William, and Virginia Ramos Foster, comps. and eds. **Modern Latin American Literature.** New York, Frederick Ungar, 1975. 2v. index. (A Library of Literary Criticism). $60.00. LC 72-81713. ISBN 0-8044-3139-6.

Modern Latin American Literature proposes to present "twentieth-century Latin American writers through the eyes of leading critics in their own countries and abroad, with particular stress on their reception in the United States." This two-volume compilation of international critical commentary follows the style of other volumes in Ungar's Library of Literary Criticism series by including critical excerpts in English on 137 Latin American writers. The excerpts were extracted from monographs, encyclopedias, periodicals, and newspapers; about half are translations from Spanish and Portuguese sources and the remainder come mainly from English-language publications.

The main body of the work is arranged alphabetically by the author being reviewed. The criticisms for each author are then arranged chronologically. Each volume includes an alphabetical list of all the writers reviewed as well as a list of the authors by country of origin. Volume II concludes with a cross-reference index to authors and an index to critics.

This outstanding compilation fills a tremendous void in Latin American literary criticism. In the past, critical sources for contemporary Latin American literary figures have been extremely elusive for a variety of reasons: the scarcity of Latin American periodicals in the United States, the diffuseness of critical reviews in the world press, and the lack of indexing. These volumes, by providing translations into English of many previously unavailable reviews and by offering the user a selected bibliography of sources, should help alleviate the situation. As a unique synthesis of literary criticism in the field, *Modern Latin American Literature* will be a valuable reference and research tool. [R: ARBA 76, p. 627; Choice, Oct 75, p. 978; LJ, 1 Sept 75, p. 1534; WLB, Nov 75, p. 268]
Laura Gutiérrez-Witt

ORIENTAL LITERATURE

709. Prusek, Jaroslav, general ed. **Dictionary of Oriental Literatures.** New York, Basic Books, 1975. 3v. $48.50/set. LC 73-82742. ISBN 0-465-01649-9.

The *Dictionary of Oriental Literatures* gives a concise overview of Oriental literatures. It contains three volumes: vol. I, East Asia; vol. II, South and South-East Asia; and vol. III, West and North Africa. It does not cover the literatures of black Africa, except for those of the ancient civilizations of North Africa and Maghreb, yet is somewhat more comprehensive than David M. Lang's *A Guide to Eastern Literatures* (Praeger, 1971. $15.00).

"The dictionary is arranged primarily on the basis of items devoted to individual authors, to major anonymous works, to the most important literary forms and genres, and to important schools of writing and literary movement" (preface). Entries for authors include dates, biographical information, and a brief account of the writer's work and its literary value. Most entries in this dictionary end with a select bibliography of well-known translations and studies in Western languages; references to standard works on the subject are also provided. Although the information is not current, it has been updated to 1971. All articles included in this dictionary are signed. This publication is a welcome addition to any library collection; invaluable to undergraduate students and to laypersons. [R: ARBA 77, p. 619; BL, 1 July 75, p. 1131; Choice, Jan 76, p. 1422; LJ, 15 Apr 76, p. 969; WLB, June 75, p. 754]   Samuel T. Huang

SLAVIC LITERATURE

710. **Modern Slavic Literatures: A Library of Literary Criticism. Volume I: Russian Literature.** Vasa D. Mihailovich, ed. New York, Ungar, 1972. 424p. index. $27.50. LC 75-163143. ISBN 0-8044-3176-0.

711. **Modern Slavic Literatures: A Library of Literary Criticism. Volume II: Bulgarian, Czechoslovak, Polish, Ukrainian, and Yugoslav Literature.** Vasa D. Mihailovich, ed. New York, Ungar, 1976. 720p. $35.00; $60.00(set). LC 72-170319. ISBN 0-8044-3177-9; 0-8044-3175-2(set).

These two companion volumes on twentieth-century Slavic literatures follow the format of other volumes in the Library of Literary Criticism series (American, British, German, and romance literatures).

The preface to volume I points out that "the critical selections represented here were chosen mainly with the idea of giving a balanced perspective of the authors' achievements and, where appropriate, of including extended remarks on individual works—such as Pasternak's *Doctor Zhivago* and Sholokhov's *The Quiet Don*—as well as overviews of the writers' careers." The 69 Russian writers represented in this volume range from the internationally known Chekhov and Pasternak to such writers as Pogodin, Platonov, and Balmont. The selections of critical comments were chosen from a variety of sources (e.g., book reviews, introductions, full-length critical studies, etc.), with an emphasis on material published in English. Nevertheless, foreign journals are represented.

Volume II surveys the works of nearly 200 writers. For many of these authors nothing has been available in the English language until publication of this volume. Critical excerpts cover such writers as Čapek and Hašek of Czechoslovakia, Gombrowicz and Andrzejewski of Poland, Franko of Ukraine, and Andrić and Krleža of Yugoslavia. The selection is very well balanced.

Like the other volumes in this series, *Modern Slavic Literatures* will be helpful for students of the literature or for study of comparative literatures. [R: ARBA 73, p. 529; Choice, June 73, p. 600; LJ, 1 Feb 73, p. 410; ARBA 78, p. 612; Choice, Apr 77, p. 180; LJ, 1 Feb 77, p. 386; WLB, Jan 77, p. 441]   Bohdan S. Wynar

SPANISH LITERATURE

712.   Ward, Philip, ed. **The Oxford Companion to Spanish Literature.** New York, Oxford University Press, 1978. 628p. $29.95. ISBN 0-19-866114-2.

The *Companion* is a desk encyclopedia of Spanish letters, including criticism, history, religion, and philosophy, from Roman Spain and pre-Columbian America to 1977. Entries include authors (with critical comment), books (with plot summaries), journals, libraries, publishers series, and literary movements, groups, and forms. Basque, Catalan, and Galician literature is included; Portuguese is excluded. Some Spanish-oriented writers of other nationalities are entered, e.g., Hudson's *Green Mansions* (but not Hemingway), as are occasional names from the sciences (von Humboldt) and other art forms (Buñuel, Dali).

Philip Ward, a librarian and poet, is also the author of *Spanish Literary Appreciation* (University of London, 1969). He "checked original works wherever feasible, submitted entries to living writers . . . , and utilized the expertise of scholars in four continents," according to the preface. There is no bibliography (a listing "in such a massive work written over twelve years is quite impossible"), but related and supplementary works are noted in many of the entries.

Works of such size and detail inevitably have inconsistencies and omissions that affect the use of the book. *Comedias sueltas* is not entered. Names are entered in the Spanish form, with selected referrals from the second part; thus, one must usually know beforehand the complete compound to locate the entry. There are referrals from pseudonyms, but none linking Rubén Darío and Félix Rubén Garcia Sarmiento, or Elena Puerto to Mercedes Fórmica. Alphabetizing for subject and title entries does not follow the nothing-before-something form the author specifies for names. Despite these deficiencies, the *Oxford Companion* is enhanced by precise proofreading and a taut and readable writing style. [R: ARBA 80, p. 597; BL, 15 July 79, p. 1649; Choice, Dec 78, p. 1351; C&RL, July 79, p. 349; LJ, 15 Apr 79, p. 889; WLB, Dec 78, p. 345]

Kathleen McCullough

GENERAL WORKS

713. Thornton, John L., and R. I. J. Tully. **Scientific Books, Libraries, and Collectors: A Study of Bibliography and the Book Trade in Relation to Science.** 3rd ed., rev. London, Library Association; distr., Detroit, Gale, 1971. 508p. illus. index. $31.00. ISBN 0-85365-424-7.

Thornton's guide to scientific literature (first published in 1954 and revised in 1962) has become the classic bibliographical history of science. Twelve revised and updated chapters survey the production, distribution, and storage of scientific literature from the pre-Gutenburg era through the mid-twentieth century. Six of these chapters discuss scientific authors and their publications; the remainder of the volume provides introductory commentary on scientific societies, the periodical literature, scientific libraries – private and public – and scientific publishing and bookselling. In addition, chapter 9 is a useful survey of guides to the literature, current and retrospective bibliographies, and other control tools. There is, naturally, a tendency to emphasize the bibliography of Continental Europe and Britain. However, the authors give reasonable coverage to significant U.S. bibliographies, books, libraries, and publishers.

Each chapter is supplemented by extensive footnotes, and the volume as a whole is capped by an 85-page bibliography – much expanded from the second edition. A detailed index completes the organization structure. Considering the myriad details and the titles and dates incorporated in text and footnotes, the overall design has typographical clarity and readability. The authors suggest that "the professional historian of science will find little new in these pages." However, no other source supplies such a convenient compendium of scientific bibliography and associated data.

Ed. note: Scientific Books, Libraries and Collectors: Supplement to the Third Edition (London, Library Association; distr., Oryx Press. 171p. $15.50), published in 1978, covers the years 1969 to 1975. [R: ARBA 73, p. 532; LJ, July 72, p. 2360] Laurel Grotzinger

BIBLIOGRAPHIES

714. **ISIS Cumulative Bibliography: A Bibliography of the History of Science Formed from ISIS Critical Bibliographies 1-90, 1913-65.** Ed. by Magda Whitrow. London, Mansell, in conjunction with the History of Science Society, 1971-1976. 3v. $105.00(v.1 & 2); $73.50(v.3). LC 72-186272. ISBN 0-7201-0183-2(v.1 & 2); 0-7201-0296-0(v.3).

The aim of this project is to offer a complete index to George Sarton's *ISIS*, the unique quarterly devoted to the history of science. Between 1913 and 1965, *ISIS* printed 90 brilliant critical bibliographies of scientists. The cumulation and grouping of the entries of these bibliographies according to an ingenious system of subdivisions have resulted in a list of more than 40,000 titles relating to over 10,000 personalities and institutions. Volume 1, part I and volume 2, part I contain, in alphabetical sequence, entries describing publications (including reference works, monographs, pamphlets, and magazine articles) dealing with the life and work of an individual scientist (subject entries), and also new editions and reissues of works (author entries). Where the number of entries under one personality warrants, convenient subdivisions are applied (e.g., bibliographies, life and work, large scale works, forerunners, biography, portraits, texts, etc.). In volume 2, part II (Institutions) efforts have been made to use entry forms which comply with the *Anglo-American Cataloging Rules*. International organizations have been entered under the English form of the name, with references from other versions. Close adherence to LC rules of cataloging, filing, and transliteration makes the contents of these extremely well-organized volumes even more accessible. The third volume, *Subjects*, contains over 20,000 entries originally published in the ISIS Critical Bibliographies, Nos. 1-90 (1913-65). It includes all these entries that deal with the history of science or of individual sciences without reference to a particular period of civilization, those that refer to more than two centuries during the modern period, and those that deal with two or more civilizations but are not restricted to a particular period of history. In addition, it contains twentieth-century material and material covering the nineteenth and twentieth centuries together, a departure from the current ISIS scheme. The arrangement of subjects follows very closely that used in the current ISIS Critical Bibliographies. The coverage is obviously international. Bibliographical citations are complete; there are occasionally brief notes for monographs or references to published reviews.

In summary, the *ISIS Cumulative Bibliography* easily qualifies for the title of the most significant research tool in the area of the history of science; its importance can be paralleled only by that of the bibliographical treasurehouse George Sarton offers in his own works. [R: ARBA 73, p. 532; C&RL, July 72, p. 327]   Ivan L. Kaldor
Bohdan S. Wynar

715. Malinowsky, H. Robert, and Jeanne M. Richardson. **Science and Engineering Literature: A Guide to Reference Sources.** 3rd ed. Littleton, CO, Libraries Unlimited, 1980. 342p. index. (Library Science Text Series). $22.50; $14.50pa. LC 80-21290. ISBN 0-87287-230-0; 0-87287-245-9pa.

Consistently used since its first edition in 1967 as a text for courses covering information sources in science and technology, *Science and Engineering Literature* is now in a revised, reorganized, and contemporized third edition. Like its predecessors, the text is also addressed to the needs of general librarians seeking guidance in science sources, and to science librarian specialists needing sources outside their area of specialty.

The introductory materials preceding the annotated list of reference sources in specific disciplines have been completely rewritten. New to this edition are a section on environmental science, and an expanded coverage of computer science. For each particular science, the goal has been to display the range of sources which reflect its unique information needs and the degree of its subfield complexity. The annotations are designed to point out the scope of the selected reference work, the intended audience, and the special features of the work. Because an understanding of the distinction between primary and secondary scientific publications is essential to providing reference service in the sciences, the forms characteristic to these two divisions are emphasized. Recommended for use as a resource in studies dealing with scientific bibliography or the literature of science and technology.

716. Wolff, Kathryn, and Jill Storey, comps. and eds. **AAAS Science Book List Supplement.** Washington, American Association for the Advancement of Science, 1978. 457p. index. $16.50. LC 78-6540. ISBN 0-87168-218-4.

For almost 20 years, science teachers and librarians have used the *AAAS Science Book List* to select the best science books for students from junior high school through the second year of college. This supplement (2,842 entries) updates the third edition (1970) with entries from 1969 to 1977. It relies heavily on books reviewed in *Science Books: A Quarterly Review* (now titled *Science Books and Films*). The book is classified by Dewey class number (18th ed.), and each entry has a brief descriptive annotation, grade level, complete bibliographic description, and price. Publishers' addresses have been omitted so that more titles could be included within the same number of pages. As the majority of publishers' addresses are easy to locate, the change seems worthwhile. Excellent author, title, and subject indexes provide important means of access. The subject approach is very useful since specific topics are often difficult to locate in the Dewey Decimal Classification System.

The major change in this volume is the expanded subject coverage. Because of the continued trend toward interdisciplinary treatment of a topic, social and behavioral science materials are now included (140, 150s, 170s, 300-301.6, 310, 333, 339, 350.855, 361, 362, 364, 370.1, 371.4, 371.9, 389, 410-419, 711, 721, 771, 778, 796.5, 904.5, 910, 912, 915-919.98, 930.1-930.19). Some inclusions are very logical, such as the conservation sections of the 333s and science and government (350.855), while other areas are rather questionable, such as ethics, ethnology, or geography. If some of these areas had been omitted, more actual science titles could have been incorporated. But without question, this supplement is needed and will be welcomed as a major aid in building quality science collections. [R: ARBA 79, p. 639; BL, 1 Apr 79, p. 1234; LJ, 1 Jan 79, p. 94; SLJ, Feb 79, p. 31]

G. Edward Evans

DICTIONARIES AND ENCYCLOPEDIAS

717. **Chambers Dictionary of Science and Technology.** Edinburgh, W & R Chambers; distr., New York, Two Continents, 1978. illus. (Chambers Paperback Reference Books). $25.00; $10.95pa. ISBN 0-8467-0520-6; 0-8467-0530-3pa.

For over 30 years the *Chambers Technical Dictionary* has been acknowledged as one of the most comprehensive single-volume dictionaries of its kind. The 1972 edition, completely revised and expanded, was published in hardcover by Barnes and Noble. In 1976 Chambers reissued the dictionary in paperback. This edition, now distributed by Two Continents in paperback or hardcover, is highly recommended for libraries as well as for home use.

The dictionary covers dozens of fields ranging from acoustics to zoology. The terms are arranged alphabetically in letter-by-letter order with compound or modified words grouped under the first component, although a few biological terms (such as respiration, aerobic; respiration, anaerobic; respiration, external; and respiration, internal) have been inverted. Each definition is labeled to indicate its field. If a term is used in more than one field, the definitions are arranged alphabetically by the label (i.e., *Acous., Bot., Inst.,* etc.). Trade names, when used, are also noted. The volume has many appendixes, including "Table of Chemical Elements," "Periodic Table," and tables of classification for "Igneous Rocks," "Sedimentary Rocks," "The Plant Kingdom," and "The Animal Kingdom." Most important are tables of physical concepts and standard values in SI (Système International d'Unités), the international metric system.

All in all, this dictionary achieves its goal, which is to reflect "honestly and adequately the level of vocabulary required by those interested in understanding the scientific and technological developments and problems in our lives today." Robert J. Havlik

718. Lapedes, Daniel N., ed.-in-chief. **McGraw-Hill Dictionary of Scientific and Technical Terms.** 2nd ed. New York, McGraw-Hill, 1978. 1771p. illus. $39.50. LC 78-18265. ISBN 0-07-045258-X.

The first edition of this comprehensive dictionary of some 100,000 terms was published in 1974. This compendium was prepared by an outstanding editorial staff and group of consultants, and it was highly recommended for libraries of all types. The second edition of this standard work adds some 8,000 new definitions and 200 new illustrations. Many definitions in this new edition are substantially revised, especially in such areas as electronics, computer science, physics, and chemistry. The appendix is also updated and revised to cover such topics as SI conversion tables, mathematical notations and symbols, etc. A section has been added with over 1,000 biographical entries on many of the individuals associated with the laws, reactions, and phenomena that are defined in the dictionary. Along with *Chambers Dictionary of Science and Technology*, the *McGraw-Hill Dictionary of Scientific and Technical Terms* is highly recommended for libraries of all types as one of the most comprehensive single-volume dictionaries of its kind. [R: ARBA 79, p. 641; WLB, Feb 79, p. 473]

719. **McGraw-Hill Encyclopedia of Science and Technology.** Daniel N. Lapedes, ed.-in-chief. New York, McGraw-Hill, 1977. 15v. illus. (part col.). index. $497.00/set. LC 76-44232. ISBN 0-07-079590-8.

This one-of-a-kind encyclopedia, intended for high school and college students, has adequate coverage of all areas of science and technology. It will also be useful for graduate students who may need information on a topic not in their field. The first edition of the *Encyclopedia* was published in 1960, and the revised edition (with only minor changes), in 1966. The third edition, published in 1971, was substantially expanded and revised, and contained some 7,600 articles written by more than 2,500 scientists and engineers.

The present edition also shows substantial revision and updating, with 1,240 out of the 7,600 articles revised and 200 articles added, expanding the *Encyclopedia* by 790 pages and 500,000 words. This edition contains 3,600 black-and-white illustrations, 9,500 illustrations in two colors, and 72 full-color pages. There is a double-column format; and many drawings, diagrams, graphs, and charts are functionally integrated in the text. An excellent, easy-to-use index volume contains 140,000 entries (the 1971 edition covered 130,000). It contains a list of contributors and their affiliations, along with articles written, and a section on scientific notation that presents the scientific conventions used in the *Encyclopedia*. Within the index, entries are arranged on a word-by-word basis with an adequate number of cross references. As in previous editions, the index is analytical, and all information on a given topic appears together under one broad subject heading. The topical index groups the 7,800 article titles under about 100 major subject headings, providing an excellent overview of information covered by the *Encyclopedia*. Two well-designed booklets, *Reader's Guide* and *Study Guide*, serve as an introduction to the *Encyclopedia* both as a reference work and as a means of studying a given subject through the various articles.

In examining the broad topic of mental health, we found a number of related subjects – i.e., abnormal behavior, aggression, emotion, human genetics, mental deficiencies, mental illness, etc. The article on mental deficiencies (volume 8, pp. 285-86) has the following divisions – diagnosis, classification, degrees of intelligence, and prevention and treatment. We compared this encyclopedia's treatment of mental illness and related topics with the 1976 edition of *Encyclopedia Americana* and found that *Americana* has a much longer article on mental health (volume 18, pp. 639-43), presenting a somewhat clearer picture of the subject and having longer and more recent bibliographic citations. In the same volume of *Americana* (pp. 643-49), there are also separate articles on mental disorders and mental retardation, both with extensive bibliographies. Judging from this and several other brief comparisons, one can make the assumption that in dealing with more general topics, adult encyclopedias such as *Americana* provide more in-depth and up-to-date treatment.

In examining a number of articles relating to pollution, we found in *McGraw-Hill* extensive material on such topics as air-pollution control, atmospheric pollution, ozone, and water treatment. The in-depth article on atmospheric pollution (volume 1, pp. 695-702A) is subdivided under several subheadings – sources and types, effects of stratospheric pollution, pollution controls, etc., and is enhanced by a number of graphs and charts as well as statistical tables. A rather comprehensive bibliography includes a number of more recent imprints. We found in *Encyclopedia Americana* one short paragraph under the general topic of pollution with cross references for air pollution, ecology, environment, water pollution, etc. McGraw-Hill's coverage of this subject is much more technical and precise indicating that the value of this encyclopedia is amplified when topics of a particular scientific nature are examined.

This latest edition of the *McGraw-Hill Encyclopedia of Science and Technology* is an authoritative work, providing detailed information on specialized topics, primarily in the area of technology. In view of the substantial updating of this fourth edition, many librarians will be interested in acquiring this set. [R: ARBA 78, p. 619; BL, 1 Jan 78, p. 767; Choice, Jan 78, p. 1480; LJ, 1 Apr 78, p. 723]   Susan C. Holte
                                                                                    Bohdan S. Wynar

720. **Van Nostrand's Scientific Encyclopedia.** 5th ed. Ed. by Douglas M. Considine. New York, Van Nostrand Reinhold, 1976. 2370p. illus. $69.50. LC 76-18158. ISBN 0-442-21629-7.

From Aa to Zymolytic Reaction, this fifth edition of a standard, one-volume science encyclopedia is impressive in size, format, completeness, and price. Even though it is a large volume, the binding is sturdy and should hold up to heavy use. The editor should be congratulated on maintaining a standard that was begun in 1938, with the first edition. However, 18 years is a long time to wait for a new edition, when one considers how drastically science has changed in the last 10 years. It is hoped that the next edition will be published sooner. The editor claims to have over 7,200 entries, 8,000 cross references, 2,450 diagrams, graphs, and photographs, and 550 tables. From the size of the volume, these claims appear to be true. The emphasis is on "scientific fundamentals and the logical ordering and classification of information." The broad range of users is constantly kept in mind, so the text is not highly technical and thus is a useful reference work for anyone. The length of the text for an entry may be only a couple of lines or several pages. After it has been defined, a term may then be discussed in broader terms, with numerous references to other terms within the encyclopedia. "Science" in this work includes earth and space sciences, life sciences, mathematics and information sciences, energy technology, materials science, and physics and chemistry. In the area of energy, terms associated with the topical subjects of chemical fuels, fossil fuels, geothermal energy, hydropower, nuclear energy, solar energy, and tidal and wind energy are covered. This is truly a masterpiece—useful for the home, office, and library; a library with a limited budget can have a comprehensive science encyclopedia without too much expense. This is a highly recommended reference book that should be available in all libraries. [R: ARBA 77, p. 629]

H. Robert Malinowsky

BIOGRAPHY

721. **American Men and Women of Science: Physical and Biological Sciences.** 14th ed. Ed. by Jaques Cattell Press. New York, R. R. Bowker, 1979. 8v. index. $50.00/v.; $385.00/set. LC 6-7326. ISBN 0-8352-1118-5(set). ISSN 0065-9347.

Now expanded from seven to eight volumes in order to include the engineering sciences, the fourteenth edition of *American Men and Women of Science* provides entries for 130,500 scientists, 13,000 of them new to this edition. Selection criteria remain the same as in earlier editions—"achievement by reason of experience and training, of a stature in scientific work equivalent to that associated with the doctoral degree, coupled with presently continued activity in such work" or "research activity of high quality in science as evidenced by publication in reputable scientific journals, or, for those whose work cannot be published because of governmental or industrial security, research activity of high quality in science as evidenced by the judgment of the individual's peers" or "attainment of a position of substantial responsibility. . . ." The information is based on data forms submitted by the biographees. Included are living U.S. and Canadian scientists in all physical and biological fields as well as engineers, mathematicians, and computer scientists.

The eighth volume of the set serves as an index to the first seven volumes, with work locations of the biographees used for geographic indexing. There is also a discipline index, where scientists may be indexed under one or two subjects.

American Men and Women of Science is a well-established and reliable reference source, useful to libraries of all types as an important fact-finding tool for biographical data for most scientists in this country and Canada. Most research libraries should have a standing order for this publication. [R: ARBA 81; LJ, 1 Mar 80, p. 602]   Susan C. Holte

722.   **Dictionary of Scientific Biography.** Charles Coulston Gillispie, ed.-in-chief. New York, Scribner's, 1970-1980. 16v. $695.00/set. LC 69-18090.

The index, volume 16 of the *Dictionary of Scientific Biography*, marks the completion of the set, a 20-year project published under the auspices of the American Council of Learned Societies. This monumental dictionary, closely patterned after the *Dictionary of American Biography* and the *Dictionary of National Biography*, covers all periods from classical antiquity to the present and includes only deceased scientists, a total of more than 5,000 biographies (representing more than 90 countries) and topical articles. Selection criteria are influenced by "contributions to science . . . sufficiently distinctive to make an identifiable difference to the profession or community of knowledge." Although the scope is international, some countries are not as well represented as Western countries because of the limited availability of scholarship, as acknowledged in the preface.

Entries first give places and dates of birth and death (when known) and a very brief summary of the individual's contributions to science. The body of each article presents in-depth coverage of the subject's career and scientific accomplishments; personal biography is intentionally minimized. Articles vary in length, but all have selective bibliographies which include both primary and secondary references. The article on Aristotle runs to 31 pages, 2 of which are devoted to bibliographical information. Although a balanced selection of Eastern scientists has been precluded, an eleventh-century Chinese mathematician and astronomer, Shen Kua, is discussed in 25 pages, nearly 3 pages of which are bibliography. Not all subjects receive such lengthy treatment, but the remote past is not skimmed in favor of more recent developments.

Volume 15 is a supplement to the parent set. Volume 16, a listing of important persons, concepts, movements, and theories, indexes more than 75,000 topics and subtopics.

The *Dictionary of Scientific Biography* has established itself as an indispensable work for serious science scholars as well as for the science historian. It is a well-balanced, scholarly biographical dictionary that could be a model for disciplines that still lack retrospective biographical coverage. [R: ARBA 71, p. 478; ARBA 75, p. 642; ARBA 76, p. 642; ARBA 77, p. 633; BL, 1 Nov 70, p. 201; Choice, Dec 73, p. 1526; Choice, July 73, p. 754; C&RL, Jan 71, p. 38; LJ, July 70, p. 2448; LJ, 15 Sept 76, p. 1845]

723.   Elliott, Clark A. **Biographical Dictionary of American Science: The Seventeenth through the Nineteenth Centuries.** Westport, CT, Greenwood Press, 1979. 360p. index. $45.00. LC 78-4292. ISBN 0-313-20419-5.

As so often noted before, biographical directories or dictionaries are an indispensable element in most reference collections. No matter how large the collection, the unique range of human endeavor invariably produces a request that cannot be answered by the resources at hand. However, this particular volume has a special value for most libraries since it is "deliberately designed as a retrospective companion to *American Men of Science*, which has been recognized as the chief directory of living scientists since its first edition appeared in 1906" (preface). The coverage of some 600 scientists who predate *AMS*, whose birth dates range from 1606-1867, with entries that average between 300 and 400 words, provides a useful synthesis of persons who "were noted for their contributions to scientific knowledge. . . . The term *science* has been somewhat narrowly defined to mean chiefly work in such areas as mathematics, astronomy, physics, chemistry, botany, zoology, geology, and their allied specialties, and including some aspects of applied science. In general, engineers, inventors, physicians, social scientists, cultural anthropologists, ethnologists, explorers, and the like have not been included" (preface).

Each major sketch includes standard biographical data: full name, birth and death dates, specialization, genealogy, education, honors, career data, society memberships, scientific contributions, works, and manuscripts and citations to resources used in the compilation of the biographical material. Needless to say, certain limitations are evident, such as restricting the number of publications cited, the actual assessment of the individual's scientific contribution, and, of course, omissions. The author, Clark A. Elliott, who is associate curator at the Harvard University Archives, with access to an impressive number of resources, both published and human, would readily admit his own key role in the selection and elimination of candidates for inclusion. There are a number of briefer entries that do not give an evaluation of the contribution or other significant biographical details; these entries provide an additional 300 names beyond the 600 longer articles noted above. As described in the preface, "these are persons who had reached a significant stage in their careers before 1900 and who therefore were closely identified with science in the late nineteenth century"; they *were* included in the first editions of *American Men of Science*, but are cross referenced or briefly noted here, e.g., Charles Loring Jackson and Washington Irving Stringham, respectively a chemist and a mathematician, who are covered in *AMS* and *DAB*.

Five useful appendices, arranged by year of birth, place of birth, education, occupation, and fields of science, give extra content access to the tool, while its well-designed layout and clear typography make visual use easy. There is an index that provides subject, publication, and other kinds of references as well as a list of abbreviations, an introductory analysis of the coverage, and a preface that precisely defines the scope of the volume. All in all, the tool is difficult to fault and should serve well as a basic reference source that effectively complements *American Men of Science*. [R: ARBA 80, p. 605; Choice, Oct 79, p. 992; LJ, 15 Dec 78, p. 2505; WLB, Sept 79, p. 65]   Laurel Grotzinger

724. Burington, Richard S. **Handbook of Mathematical Tables and Formulas.** 5th ed. New York, McGraw-Hill, 1973. 500p. illus. index. $10.50. LC 78-39634. ISBN 0-07-009015-7.

According to the author, "this book has been constructed to meet the needs of students and workers in mathematics, engineering, physics, chemistry, science, and other fields in which mathematical reasoning, processes, and computations are required." It consists of two parts. The first part includes the main formulas and theorems of algebra, geometry, trigonometry, calculus, vector analysis, sets, logic, matrices, linear algebra, numerical analysis, differential equations, some special functions, Fourier and Laplace transforms, complex variables, and statistics. The second part consists of tables of logarithms, trigonometry, exponential and hyperbolic functions, powers and roots, probability distributions, annuity, and other tables.

The readers to whom this book is directed will find it useful — particularly the part on mathematical tables. However, some chapters of part 1 might be incomprehensible to beginners. For example, the sections on plane areas and volumes by double integration (p. 67) are vague because no explanation is given about the limits of integration; the same is true of the section on homomorphic correspondence (p. 148); and the definition of convex surface (p. 117) is not exact. The chapter on partial differential equations is short (a little over two pages) and is therefore of little use to any reader. Despite the above, the book is a useful publication. [R: ARBA 74, p. 552; WLB, Mar 73, p. 609]   Elie M. Dick

725. Dorling, A. R., ed. **Use of Mathematical Literature.** Boston, Butterworths, 1977. 260p. index. (Information Sources for Research and Development). $29.95. LC 77-30014. ISBN 0-408-70913-8.

This is another title from the already well-known series Information Sources for Research and Development, edited by R. T. Bottle and D. J. Foskett. These are competent guides for graduate-level use, not belaboring the obvious but apportioning space intelligently with good analysis of major research and reference works. The present volume on mathematics shows the same clear structure, and all chapters are well documented. The first three chapters are concerned with the general character of mathematical literature — e.g., the structure of the discipline, major organizations and journals, and reference materials. Subsequent chapters, written by a group of specialists, cover specific aspects of mathematics, such as history, combinatorics, rings and algebras, group theory, measure and probability, topology, and mathematical programming. A well-executed volume. [R: ARBA 78, p. 627; Choice, Apr 78, p. 214]

726. **Encyclopedic Dictionary of Mathematics.** By the Mathematical Society of Japan. Cambridge, MA, MIT Press, 1977. 2v. illus. index. $150.00. LC 77-1129. ISBN 0-262-09016-3.

As every reference librarian is aware, numerous outstanding dictionaries and encyclopedias are lost to the English reading world because of a language barrier — especially if the language is from a Far Eastern country. An excellent mathematics encyclopedia, which has been available only in the original Japanese, has now been translated under the auspices of the Mathematical Society of Japan, the American Mathematical Society, and MIT Press. The original attempt to translate what Walford (3rd ed., p. 67) describes as "the most comprehensive mathematical dictionary" began in the late 1950s. Finally, in July

1968, *Iwanami Sūgaku Ziten* (*Iwanami Mathematical Dictionary*), which was published first in 1954 and revised in 1968, was formally contracted for translation. A distinguished number of Japanese and American mathematicians were involved in the effort so that absolute integrity and accuracy could be maintained.

The resulting two-volume translation has been reviewed in respective subjects by one group of subject specialists (e.g., set theory, algebra, geometry, topology, statistics, and history of mathematics); a second group of specialists "reviewed the whole manuscript, mainly from the linguistic standpoint" (preface to the English edition). The foreword to the translated work, written by the 1973-1974 president of the American Mathematical Society, notes that this is "an encyclopedia that contained effective and penetrating information about all the fields of advanced mathematical research. . . . We look forward to the fascination which we can now have in getting at this rich mine of information." Due to the time span actually involved in this translation, the manuscript was reviewed and updated to February 1976, so the user has access to a number of recent research efforts; however, the preface does note "that there are many things in the book which could be improved."

The text of the *Encyclopedic Dictionary* is composed of 436 articles, which are arranged alphabetically. Since each article has numerous subdivisions, a detailed subject index (pp. 1583-1750) gives expert, specialized access to all topics and tables. In addition, an equally detailed name index gives citations to references and key individuals. Furthermore, there are 23 specialized tables in Appendix A that range from algebraic equations, knot theory, conformal mappings, and interpolation to statistical hypothesis testing (pp. 1396-1490), as well as seven different numerical tables in Appendix B (including Bernoulli numbers, characters of finite groups, and coefficients of polynominal approximations). There is also a list of journals used in references, a list of publishers, a section on special notations used "commonly and frequently throughout the work," and a "Systematic List of Articles" that groups them under such categories as "logic and foundations," "group theory," "functional analysis," and "mechanics and theoretical physics." This systematic list is translated into French, German, and Russian as well. Preceding the name and subject indices is also an "Alphabetical List of Articles," and the names of both contributors and translators are given. Altogether, the supplementary appendices and indexes encompass over 350 pages of access points and supportive information.

The bulk of the dictionary (1,393 pages) consists of well-printed and arranged material. In addition to the major mathematical topics, there are biographical articles on such renowned mathematicians as Elie Cartan, Jean Baptiste Joseph Fourier, Felix Klein, Blaise Pascal, and John Von Neumann. Each major article, including the biographies, has references, and all terms that are defined in the text are printed in boldface. Any term found in the text and indexed is marked by the use of the dagger (†). In any given article, the number of such terms is substantial, a fact that supports a review published in *Library Journal* (1967), which states that this work "defines virtually every term used in mathematics today. . . ."

Any examination of major reference tools quickly reveals the fact that there are few superior mathematics dictionaries and encyclopedias. Without a doubt, this title is unique in terms of its comprehensive, but contemporary and basic, coverage of mathematics. The price is not to be ignored, but the tool may well in the coming years stand alone in terms of its scope and purpose. [R: ARBA 78, p. 628; Choice, Mar 78, p. 46; LJ, 15 Dec 77, p. 2492; WLB, Mar 78, p. 587]   Laurel Grotzinger

727.   James, Glenn, and Robert James. **Mathematics Dictionary.** 4th ed. New York, Van Nostrand Reinhold, 1976. 509p. illus. index. LC 76-233. ISBN 0-442-24091-0.

A standard reference work in the field of mathematics first published in 1949, this dictionary has proved an invaluable tool for librarians, mathematicians, students of mathematics, and the general reader. While definitions are longer than those found in a word dictionary, they are generally more concise than those in encyclopedias. As the preface points out, "it is a correlated condensation of mathematical concepts, designed for time-saving reference work." This fourth edition, which defines more than 8,000 terms, has expanded coverage in the fields of probability and statistics and also contains a significantly larger number of short biographic sketches of individuals who have contributed to the development of mathematics. A substantial number of definitions has been revised and/or expanded. An important adjunct is a multilingual index of mathematical terms in French, German, Russian, and Spanish. As compared to the third edition, published in 1968, the present work contains 24 additional pages of text but 7 fewer pages overall. Material that has been dropped consists of 31 pages of tables: logarithms, trigonometric functions, compound interest, and mortality. Other appendices that have been retained include those listing symbols, differentiation formulae, and tables of integrals. An essential acquisition for all reference collections. [R: ARBA 77, p. 634; BL, 15 May 77, p. 1452; Choice, Feb 77, p. 1572]   Jay K. Lucker

728.   Tuma, Jan J. **Engineering Mathematics Handbook: Definitions, Theorems, Formulas, Tables.** 2nd enl. and rev. ed. New York, McGraw-Hill, 1979. 394p. illus. bibliog. index. $21.95. LC 77-17786. ISBN 0-07-065429-8.

When the first edition of this basic handbook was reviewed, it was described as "a concise summary of the major tools of engineering mathematics . . . prepared with the intent to serve as a desk-top reference book for engineers, scientists, and architects." The 1979 second edition maintains both this purpose and the original five-part structure, and additionally has been revised to allow for use with a 10-digit display, four-register stack electronic pocket calculator.

Each of the parts of the text is grouped according to the type of mathematics covered: 1) algebra, plane and solid geometry, trigonometry, analytic geometry, and elementary functions; 2) differential calculus, infinite series, integral calculus, vectors, complex variables, Fourier series, and special functions; 3) ordinary and partial differential equations and related topics; 4) numerical methods, probability, and statistics, and related tables of numerical coefficients; 5) indefinite integrals. This reference text is thorough in its coverage, well-presented graphically, and competently indexed. It is highly recommended as a basic text in its field. [R: ARBA 80, p. 608; Choice, Nov 79, p. 1156]   Betty Gay

ATLASES

729. Moore, Patrick. **The Rand McNally New Concise Atlas of the Universe.** Chicago, Rand McNally, 1978. 190p. illus. (part col.). maps. index. $29.95. LC 74-421. ISBN 0-528-83031-7.

This revised edition of the highly acclaimed *Atlas of the Universe* (1970) continues the format of the former work. More an encyclopedia than an atlas, much of the book contains diagrams and photographs, mostly in color, accompanied by Patrick Moore's lucid text and a few excellent maps. Still divided into four atlases, 1) atlas of the earth from space, 2) atlas of the moon, 3) atlas of the solar system, 4) and atlas of the stars, most of the changes in the current edition are in the atlas of the solar system, which includes the 1976 photographs of Mars taken by the two Viking landers. The 1977 discovery of the five rings of Saturn is not mentioned.

The table of contents is still not broken down into any detail, but there is an adequate index so that individual topics can be located. Although we have become quite familiar with a number of the photographs taken from space, especially those of the earth, it is still a treat to see them all in one volume. Like its predecessor, the *New Concise Atlas of the Universe* will be a welcome addition to college and public library collections as well as a worthwhile purchase for home use. [R: ARBA 80, p. 609; BL, 15 Oct 79, p. 370; Choice, Mar 79, p. 58; LJ, 1 Feb 79, p. 394; WLB, Jan 79, p. 407]   Suzanne K. Gray

730. Yamashita, Yasumasa, Kyoji Nariai, and Yuji Norimoto. **An Atlas of Representative Stellar Spectra.** New York, John Wiley, 1978. 129p. illus. (A Halsted Press Book). $60.00. LC 78-535. ISBN 0-470-26315-6.

An Atlas of Representative Stellar Spectra is a valuable addition to previously published atlases of stellar spectra, providing a relatively large number of spectra with different dispersions from those of spectra found in earlier atlases. It consists of 45 plates containing spectra of 197 MK standard stars and 19 plates of 77 peculiar stars. Photographic reproductions are of high quality. There are two tables: one listing standard stars and one listing peculiar stars. Spectrograms were obtained over the past two years by the use of a Cassegrain spectrograph attached to a 91cm telescope at the Okayama Astrophysical Observatory, University of Tokyo. The spectra of the MK standard stars are grouped according to spectral type as O- and B- type stars, A- and F- type stars, G- and K- type stars, and M- type stars. Arrangement within these groups is first by temperature sequence, then by luminosity class (supergiants, giants, and main sequence stars). Published literature is cited to identify prominent spectral features. Especially valuable is the inclusion of energy level diagrams throughout the atlas. This is a publication many astronomers would like for their personal libraries, but, unfortunately, its high price will make it generally available only in libraries with strong collections in astronomy. [R: ARBA 79, p. 651; Choice, Dec 78, p. 1395]   Virginia E. Yagello

DICTIONARIES AND ENCYCLOPEDIAS

731. **The Cambridge Encyclopaedia of Astronomy.** Ed.-in-chief, Simon Mitton. New York, Crown, 1977. 481p. illus. (part col.). index. $35.00. LC 77-2766. ISBN 0-517-52806-1.

By virtue of its superb illustrations (photographs, diagrams, charts) and the credentials of its contributors (most are affiliated with Cambridge's astronomy program), this is a standard source for both beginners and advanced amateurs. It will have value as a reference for professionals, but is not technical enough to be the ultimate word for advanced research. As Sir Martin Ryle notes in the foreword, steering the middle course editorially was done deliberately, a decision reflected in the thematic approach rather than an alphabetical subject approach such as that employed in Satterthwaite's *Encyclopedia of Astronomy* (St. Martin's, 1971). The first of 23 chapters surveys the universe as an introduction to the study of it. The next six chapters cover stars and the nature of cosmic matter. Following that are five chapters dealing with our sun, the solar system, and its members. The next six chapters deal with intergalactic space and the galaxies, including radio galaxies. Two chapters covering cosmology and life in the universe are followed by the final three chapters, which detail the state of astronomy up to 1977.

The articles vary somewhat, reflecting the multiple (but anonymous with respect to specific sections) authorship. Generally, though, they provide clear, focused discussions of the topic at hand, and cross references aid in tying together scattered points. The illustrative matter amply supplements the text, as it is drawn from a wide variety of sources. The work reflects the interests of the Cambridge team, which should come as no surprise, but this in no way diminishes the value of the work. It is more current than Satterthwaite, a factor not to be ignored lightly in such a fast-changing field, and it provides extended discussion rather than quick answers or definitions. Using the two in concert would be an excellent introduction or extended survey, as Satterthwaite has only the simplest of illustrations. Its appended star atlas (based on data from the Smithsonian Astrophysical Observatory) covers 14 pages, and an "Outline of Physics" provides a glossary of physics as it relates specifically to astronomy and astrophysics. A useful index indicates both major explanations (boldface type) and passing references. In sum, then, anyone with an interest in astronomy will want to consult this volume, and libraries should give every consideration to purchase of it, especially if their holdings are older than Satterthwaite. [R: ARBA 79, p. 649; Choice, July 78, p. 666; LJ, 1 Apr 78, p. 762] Koert C. Loomis, Jr.

732. Hopkins, Jeanne. **Glossary of Astronomy and Astrophysics.** Chicago, University of Chicago Press, 1976. 169p. $12.50. LC 75-14799. ISBN 0-226-35172-6.

A comprehensive dictionary of astronomical and astrophysical terms. Started originally by Ms. Hopkins (while she was copyeditor of the *Astrophysical Journal*) as a list of terms unfamiliar to the author, the glossary is now the most comprehensive list of astronomical terms available. The main value of a dictionary such as this is that it contains the most current terms in use in a fast-moving field of knowledge. Ms. Hopkins uses an excellent system for filing complex astronomical terms, and the work can be used as a model for such filing by librarians and others. One small list of constellation abbreviations is found under the term *Constellations*; unfortunately, there are no other such helpful lists of abbreviations. No illustrations, tables, or photographs accompany the work. The volume, which is unique in its scope, could be improved substantially by more photographs, charts, tables, diagrams, lists, and general graphic arts expertise. The definitions given range from a simple explanation for the novice to complex astrophysical formulae. The work is a must for all libraries that have patrons interested in astronomy, astrophysics, and science fiction. [R: ARBA 77, p. 636; Choice, Sept 76, p. 798; RQ, Summer 77, p. 347] Ralph L. Scott

733. Illingworth, Valerie, ed. **The Facts on File Dictionary of Astronomy.** New York, Facts on File, 1979. 378p. illus. $17.50. ISBN 0-87196-326-4.

The *Facts on File Dictionary of Astronomy* is intended to serve as a personal reference book for both students and for specialists practicing in the field. It contains information not found in other astronomy dictionaries and is valuable for its currency. Alphabetical entries are brief and well formatted. It is, however, somewhat frustrating to use as a reference source.

In the body of an entry, a word may appear preceded by an asterisk to indicate that there is a separate entry for this word in the alphabetical sequence. On occasion, however, these entries merely provide a cross reference to a third entry, where the definition of the asterisked word appears. Words that are very briefly defined within a lengthy entry are italicized. Some of these italicized words also appear in the alphabetical sequence, but there is no further definition, only a reference to the lengthy entry in which they are included.

The alphabetical sequence is arranged on a letter-by-letter basis, ignoring spacing, so that "Gemini Project" appears after "Geminids," which is also tricky for quick reference use. Tables and line drawings appear throughout the text. In addition, 12 tables appear at the end of the dictionary sequence. Although they are referenced at the end of appropriate alphabetical entries as "backmatter," there is no table of contents which lists them.

In spite of these inconveniences, an up-to-date astronomy dictionary is needed. This one serves as a good companion to Satterthwaite's *Encyclopedia of Astronomy*. [R: ARBA 80, p. 609; LJ, 1 Dec 79, p. 2557]   Betty Gay

734. Weigert, A., and H. Zimmermann. **Concise Encyclopedia of Astronomy.** 2nd English ed. London, Adam Hilger; distr., New York, Crane, Russak, 1976 (c1975). 532p. illus. $19.75. ISBN 0-85274-099-9.

This encyclopedia contains over 1,500 entries on all aspects of astronomy as well as on such related topics as astrophysics and space travel. Entries include the names of noted astronomers, names of celestial bodies, astronomical instruments, and topics such as the history of astronomy, cosmogony, and cosmology. The 10 tables give a variety of useful information (e.g., some double stars, solar eclipses from 1975 to 1990) as well as 16 black-and-white photographic plates. Three star charts and cut-outs to make a simple planisphere are attached to the inside cover of the book.

Length of entries varies from a single sentence to as many as 12 pages. Although the compilers chose the dictionary format so that a reader does not have to "study a lengthy chapter" to find an answer, slightly over 100 entries account for over 60% of the pages of the encyclopedia. However, these articles are very well written and are easy to understand. The encyclopedia is addressed to interested laypersons; consequently, mathematical formulae were kept to a minimum, and illustrations, photographs, and tables are extensively used throughout the encyclopedia.

The second English edition is considerably revised and enlarged, and the physical format is much better than its earlier pocket-sized edition. This excellent encyclopedia should be in all astronomy collections. [R: ARBA 78, p. 636; Choice, Sept 77, p. 837]   Rao Aluri

HANDBOOKS

735. Baker, David. **The Larousse Guide to Astronomy.** New York, Larousse, 1978. 288p. illus. (col.). index. $15.95; $7.95pa. LC 78-56270. ISBN 0-88332-095-9; 0-88332-094-0pa.

The *Larousse Guide* is an excellent general introduction to the world of astronomy. Written primarily for a British audience, the volume is well illustrated with color charts, photographs, and paintings of astronomical phenomena. Complex cosmological theories are described and illustrated in a simple straightforward manner. Starting with a general introduction to amateur telescopes, the volume continues with a discussion of stellar dynamics, properties of the solar system, galactic theory, and concludes with a brief history of celestial observation by man. A narrative and visual portrayal of the heavens in 88 sky maps (with detailed notes on each constellation), together with charts of the moon and Mars, comprises about one-quarter of the work. This highly useful compendium is without equal in its modest price range. Most libraries will find it essential for answering amateur astronomy reference questions. The artwork in the guide is excellent, and in some cases breathtaking; the layout of the volume is well planned; and the typography is well executed. In short, the volume is a visual and textual delight. The only drawback is the volume's decided British slant. British imprints and astronomical societies are frequently cited, where North American users would no doubt benefit by their New World counterparts. [R: ARBA 80, p. 610; BL, 1 Dec 79, p. 574; LJ, 15 Sept 78, p. 1757]   Ralph L. Scott

736.   Barker, Edmund S. **Webb Society Deep-Sky Observer's Handbook, Volume 3: Open and Globular Clusters.** Webb Society, comp.; Kenneth Glyn Jones, ed. Hillside, NJ, Enslow Publishers, 1980. 206p. illus. bibliog. $8.95pa. LC 78-31260. ISBN 0-89490-034-X.

This new volume has the same format and arrangement of content as the previous two volumes (vol. 1, *Double Stars*, and vol. 2, *Planetary and Gaseous Nebulae*, published in 1979), but is a completely independent coverage of its topic. The foreword by Professor Helen Sawyer Hogg, foremost astronomical observer of star clusters to whom this volume is dedicated, attests to the excellence of the guide. Most of the text, which provides historical and theoretical background as well as useful hints on observing techniques and recording methods, is by Edmund Barker, director of the Nebulae and Clusters Section of the Webb Society, who directed many of the observations recorded in the catalogs which make up a major portion of the volume.

Star clusters are studied to obtain an understanding of their evolution and to relate their evolution to the overall structure and evolution of the galaxy. Readers are given comprehensive information on the different visual aspects and physical characteristics of open star clusters which are relatively young and near to our galaxy and those of globular clusters which are older and at a greater distance. Clusters covered range from well-known deep-sky objects such as the Pleiades to lesser-known but equally interesting ones. Expert guidance is given on the selection, location, and classification of the various types of open and globular clusters. Amateur astronomers are encouraged to strive for qualitative and comprehensive observation of these beautiful deep-sky objects, which requires great skill and patience at the telescope and great visual acuity for accuracy of results. Reference is made to the various classification schemes and to important comprehensive catalogs of star clusters. There is detailed discussion of the relation of clusters to the galaxy, of their morphology, their stellar populations, magnitudes, and distances; color magnitude diagrams are given.

The catalogs are selective compilations of observational data on 205 open clusters, 176 with drawings; and of 63 globular clusters, 53 with drawings compiled from observations made by Webb Society members over a period of years. Attention is focussed on those clusters for which a great deal of information can be obtained with relatively inexpensive instruments: for open clusters—telescopes of 60 to 3-inches aperture and 15x80, 20x50, 10x50, and 7x35 binoculars; for globular clusters—telescopes of 40 to 3-inches aperture and 15x80, 20x50, and 7x35 binoculars.

Five appendixes on Class 7 open clusters, on six additional open clusters received too late to be included in the main catalog, on distances of clusters, on photographic sources, and a classified bibliography complete the volume.   Virginia E. Yagello

737. Lang, Kenneth R., and Owen Gingerich, eds. **A Source Book in Astronomy and Astrophysics, 1900-1975.** Cambridge, MA, Harvard University Press, 1979. 922p. illus. index. (Source Books in the History of the Sciences). $50.00. LC 78-9463. ISBN 0-674-82200-5.

One of the series of monographs presenting original (source) articles and papers illustrating advances in the sciences, this voluminous book is aimed at the astronomer who is unaware of, or may have forgotten, the discoveries which shaped modern astronomy. In all, there are 132 articles from both scientific journals and popular magazines, with an emphasis on the former. This book differs substantially from its two predecessors, *A Source Book in Astronomy* (Harlow Shapley and Helen E. Howarth, McGraw-Hill, 1929) and *Source Book in Astronomy 1900-1950* (Harlow Shapley, ed., Harvard University Press, 1960), which were intended for the general reader and did not, for the most part, include technical papers or much mathematics.

The *Source Book* is divided into eight chapters, each of which is presented in rough chronological order: 1) New Windows on the Universe [instrumentation]; 2) The Solar System; 3) Stellar Atmospheres and Stellar Spectra; 4) Stellar Evolution and Nucleosynthesis; 5) Variable Stars and Dying Stars; 6) The Distribution of Stars and the Space between Them; 7) Normal Galaxies, Radio Galaxies, and Quasars; and 8) Relativity and Cosmology. Each article begins with a page or so of introduction in which the editors explain why the selection is important; citations to earlier works by other astronomers are included. Herein lies the book's usefulness: not only does it give insight into important discoveries and ideas, but it also provides background to put the selection in perspective. The selections themselves are generally two to six pages long, although some papers are longer. Each is abridged (to save space) and annotated. There are generally no review-type articles, although some pieces do have extensive lists of references appended. Extensive subject and author indexes conclude the volume.

The science historian will especially appreciate this work. Although it is not the type of book that would be of much use on the ready reference shelf, it should be seriously considered for the science reference collection. Some librarians will affix a reference label, while others will place the book in the history section; either use is appropriate. In any case, the volume is most appropriate for the observatory and academic library.

Robert A. Seal

738. Murdin, Paul, and David Allen. **Catalogue of the Universe.** New York, Crown Publishers, 1979. 256p. illus. (part col.). index. $17.95. LC 79-492. ISBN 0-517-53616-1.

The authors of this work have chosen to approach astronomy in a nontraditional manner. Rather than use a "nuts and bolts" basic textbook-type of arrangement, the *Catalogue* describes individual astronomical objects and goes on to show how these objects illustrate theories and concepts. The work is not a traditional atlas, dictionary, catalog, or textbook guide to the heavens. The study of specific astronomical concepts is used by the authors to teach the subject "the way research is done." Concepts covered are broad to begin with (galaxies, quasars, stars, constellations, double star, the solar system), but soon focus on specific objects (Shakhbazyan I, Sirius, Sagittarius, Algol, Jupiter). A background history of each object is given, followed by the current theory as to why astronomers find the object of importance. From each specific object, basic general principles of astronomy are taught.

The volume is well illustrated with excellent black-and-white and color photographs. On the whole, the work is well thought out, and the narrative makes fascinating reading. The index is a little sparse, however, and fails to include some of the topics covered. While there is some material included on the solar system, the bulk of the text deals with stellar dynamics. Some readers may find the topical method a little confusing at first glance, but this reviewer liked this novel approach to the traditional study of astronomy. The work was written with the layperson in mind, but professional astronomers will find it useful in areas outside their specialities. Amateur astronomers will enjoy reading and referring to the work often. A beginner will find portions of the volume tough going at first, but with a little effort may become quite knowledgeable by the time the text is completed. An excellent new approach to an ancient subject. [R: ARBA 80, p. 612; LJ, 1 Dec 79, p. 2557]

Ralph L. Scott

31 CHEMISTRY

BIBLIOGRAPHIES

739. Antony, Arthur. **Guide to Basic Information Sources in Chemistry.** New York, John Wiley, 1979. 219p. bibliog. index. (Information Resources Series; A Halsted Press Book). $15.95. LC 79-330. ISBN 0-470-26587-6.

This is an up-to-date, clearly written, and well-organized first resource for the chemistry student or librarian needing a guide to literature in the field of pure chemistry. Antony approaches the subject logically, beginning with an annotated list of the other guides to the subject and progressing from this general coverage to more specialized topics. His purpose is to focus the user's approach to the field, not to provide exhaustive lists of available materials. For example, the chapter on "Periodicals and Lists of Periodicals" briefly describes the value of the information to be found in periodicals, refers the reader to earlier guides containing briefly annotated lists, and provides a description of five specialized bibliographies of chemical periodicals. No specific periodical titles are listed.

Chapter divisions are specific and practical, such as: Bibliographic Searching by Computers; Nomenclature; General Compilations of Data; Specialized Data Compilations; Guides to Techniques; Safety Manuals and Guides; Style Manuals and Guides for Authors; Biographies and Directories of People; and Product, Service, and Company Directories. The *Guide* closes with a discussion of chemical information search strategy.

Guide to Basic Information Sources in Chemistry is an excellent, pragmatic reference source for pure chemistry. It substantially updates *A Guide to the Literature of Chemistry* (E. J. Crane, Austin M. Patterson, and Eleanor B. Marr, John Wiley Publishers, 1957), although its coverage is not as detailed. [R: ARBA 80, p. 614; Choice, Sept 79, p. 795]

Betty Gay

740. Maizell, Robert E. **How to Find Chemical Information: A Guide for Practicing Chemists, Teachers, and Students.** New York, John Wiley, 1979. 261p. bibliog. index. (A Wiley-Interscience Book). $20.95. LC 78-23222. ISBN 0-471-56531-8.

A comprehensive, up-to-date, and systematic guide to the literature of chemistry, the book covers both printed and computer-stored sources and is noteworthy for the extensive descriptive and evaluative citations of reference materials. The author, a manager of information services for a major chemical company, emphasizes the practical aspects of utilizing chemical information, so that the volume will be particularly useful to chemists working in industry.

Following introductory chapters on the organization of chemical information and search strategy, Maizell covers such topics as current awareness programs, access to primary sources, the publications and other programs of the Chemical Abstracts Service, other abstracting and indexing services, computer-based systems, reviews, encyclopedias, patents, safety and related topics, locating information on physical properties of materials, and, finally, chemical marketing and business information. All sources cited are fully referenced, including addresses of publishers and other issuing bodies. This is an excellent general guide to the literature of chemistry and should be acquired by special libraries covering the field and by the science collections of academic and large public libraries. [R: ARBA 80, p. 615]

Jay K. Lucker

DICTIONARIES

741. Concise Chemical and Technical Dictionary. 3rd enlarged ed. Ed. by H. Bennett. New York, Chemical Publishing, 1974. 1175p. illus. $56.50.

No technical library should lack this dictionary, first published in 1947 and since expanded to list about 75,000 definitions. H. Bennett, who is also the editor of *Chemical Formulary*, added some 15,000 new entries — new trademark products, chemicals, drugs, and terms.

A special feature of this work is the compilation of thousands of trade names of proprietary products in chemistry and related trades. Since this is a "concise" dictionary, brevity rather than extended definition has been the rule. For those who need more detailed treatment of a subject, a short list of references is attached.

Other useful features are the names of formulae of radicals occurring in organic compounds, the pronunciation of chemical words, and appendixes that cover conversion tables, indicators, important ring systems, and various symbols. The dictionary will be useful to scientists and technicians as well as to technical librarians. [R: ARBA 76, p. 648; WLB, Feb 75, p. 461]

Vladimir T. Borovansky

742. Dictionary of Organic Compounds, Fourth Edition: Fifteenth and Cumulative Supplement. J. B. Thomson, ed. New York, Oxford University Press, 1979. 1058p. index. $198.00. LC 65-8133. ISBN 0-19-520165-5.

The fifteenth (third cumulative) supplement completes the fourth edition (1965-1979) of the *Dictionary of Organic Compounds* by listing information up through 1978 on new compounds synthesized since the tenth cumulative supplement, plus correcting errors in earlier volumes. It includes a formula index of all new compounds covered since the fifth cumulative supplement as well as corrected formulas.

The *Dictionary* is a useful means of quick access to structural formulas, physical data, and literature references for natural products and common organic compounds of industrial importance most frequently mentioned in *Chemical Abstracts*. Trivial and trade names as well as systematic nomenclature (IUPAC-IUB) in an alphabetic dictionary arrangement are used with no inversion of entry. Entries in the fifteenth supplement follow the same pattern as those of the main work and earlier supplements, viz., literature sources and, wherever possible, full structural formulas drawn in conformity with the practice of the Chemical Society of London, physical and chemical properties for each compound or the first of a group of isomers. References are mainly to methods of preparation, summaries, and bibliographies. Derivatives and accompanying descriptive data are listed under parent compound names, and there is liberal use of cross references. As a rule, acyl derivatives, acetates, and benzoates are listed without formulas in the *Dictionary* and are accordingly not in the formula indexes.

Annual supplements (1964 [sic]-1979) updated the main work of five volumes published in 1965. A fifth cumulative supplement (1971) and a formula index, plus the tenth and now the fifteenth cumulative supplements, supersede the earlier intervening annual supplements. Symbols in the fifteenth supplement link corrections and additional data to the earlier main work and the fifth and tenth cumulative supplements. The *Dictionary* is a concise, convenient tool for use when a more detailed search or a search for a less common organic compound in the *Beilsteins Handbuch der Organischen Chemie* is not required.

Virginia E. Yagello

743. Hawley, Gessner G. The Condensed Chemical Dictionary. 9th ed. New York, Van Nostrand Reinhold, 1977. 957p. illus. $32.50. LC 76-19024. ISBN 0-442-23240-3.

This most recent edition of a classic chemical dictionary (the eighth edition was published in 1971) continues the format of recent editions. Described by its editors as a compendium of technical data and descriptive information which includes 1) technical descriptions of chemicals, raw materials, and processes; 2) expanded definitions of chemical entities, phenomena, and terminologies; and 3) description or identification of a wide range of trademarked products used in the chemical industries. Entries are listed alphabetically, with the most commonly accepted name as the key entry, formula (usually molecular or atomic, occasionally also structural), main physical and chemical properties, source or occurrence, derivation (stressing current industrial methods of preparation), grades commercially available, containers (unit types), hazards (e.g., flammability and toxicity ratings, uses and shipping regulations). Proprietary chemical names are identified as trademarks (or brand names), with superscript number referring to the numerical list of manufacturers at the end of the volume. This has been an important feature of the last several editions of this work.

Revision of entries shows continued concern for environmental and safety hazards. While the definition for amaranth (red dye number 2) in the eighth edition mentions a possible toxicity, the ninth edition calls it a suspected carcinogen, with restricted use in foods and drugs. Similarly, diethylstilbestrol (DES) is listed in the eighth edition as used in research, medicine, and animal feeds; the ninth edition lists it only as used in biochemical research and as an emergency contraceptive, pointing out also that its use is prohibited in cattle feeds.

Entries dealing with many energy-related topics have been enlarged or updated in the ninth edition. The entry for coal, for instance, reflects renewed interest in its wider use as an energy source as well as a raw material for a variety of derivatives. The above are important bonuses for the user of the *Condensed Chemical Dictionary*. It is, however, the conciseness of its entries and the wealth of information it contains that make the ninth edition, like its predecessors, one of the most useful reference sources for all kinds of information related to chemistry and chemical technology for all types of libraries. [R: ARBA 78, p. 640; Choice, Sept 77, p. 827; WLB, Sept 77, p. 84]   Suzanne K. Gray

744.   Stenesh, J. **Dictionary of Biochemistry.** New York, Wiley-Interscience, 1975. 344p. $29.00. LC 75-23037. ISBN 0-471-82105-5.

This dictionary updates *The Encyclopedia of Biochemistry*, edited by R. J. Williams and E. M. Lansford (Reinhold, 1967. 876p.), which is more comprehensive but not as up to date. Stenesh contains some 12,000 entries covering general and specific topics in chemistry, physics, metabolism, biophysics, genetics, biochemistry, molecular biology, etc. Entries are not as long or as detailed as in *The Encyclopedia of Biochemistry*. [R: ARBA 77, p. 646; Choice, June 76, p. 500]

ENCYCLOPEDIAS

745.   Bard, Allen J., ed. **Encyclopedia of Electrochemistry of the Elements. Volumes 1-8, 10-14.** New York, Marcel Dekker, 1973-1980. 13v. illus. charts. bibliog. index. $88.00/v.(vols.1-8, 10, 11, 13, 14); $108.00(v.12). LC 73-88796.

The purpose of this multivolume encyclopedia is to provide a critical, systematic, and comprehensive review of the electrochemical behavior of the chemical elements and their compounds. This unique reference work is designed to bring together in one convenient source the descriptive aspects of inorganic and organic electrochemistry. The *Encyclopedia* is divided into two parts: part I, Inorganic Electrochemistry; part II, Organic Electrochemistry.

The initial volumes cover the inorganic elements and their compounds. The basic classification of elements and their compounds is the same as that used by *Gmelins Handbuch der anorganischen Chemie*. Each chapter, written by a leading authority on the particular subject, is divided into five sections: 1) Introduction and Standard Potentials; 2) Voltammetric Characteristics; 3) Kinetic Parameters and Double-Layer Properties; 4) Electrochemical Studies; 5) Applied Electrochemistry. The first section discusses introductory material and the standard potentials in aqueous, nonaqueous, and fused salt mediums. Polarographic and other voltammetric research is presented in the second section. The third section explores such topics as rate constants, exchange current densities, transfer coefficients, potential of zero charge, and double-layer capacities. The fourth section surveys the electrochemical reactions of the element and its compounds, reaction mechanisms, reaction orders, current efficiencies, oxidation and reduction products, passivation phenomena, oxide films, and anodization. The last section discusses the use of electrochemistry in the isolation and/or purification of the element, the electrochemical production of compounds, and the use and behavior of the element and its compounds in electrochemical devices. At the end of each chapter there is an extensive bibliography covering references to the primary literature on all data and reactions.

In the volumes in part II, Organic Electrochemistry, the organic compounds have been classified according to their electroactive groups. These have, for the most part, been ordered in the manner used in Beilstein's *Organische Chemie*.

The primary value of this work is that it integrates much of the information that is known about the electrochemistry of the elements and their compounds into a handbook of data that is well organized and easy to use. In addition, extensive bibliographies serve as a starting point for updating information and suggesting areas wherein further research is needed. The compilers represent a significant portion of the literature available in this area. Publication of volume 9 will complete the set.

Robert K. Dikeman
Andrew G. Torok

746. Encyclopedia of Polymer Science and Technology: Plastics, Resins, Rubbers, Fibers; Supplement Volume 2, Adhesive Compositions to Transitions and Relaxations. Herman F. Mark, chairman, ed. board. New York, Interscience Publishers, a division of John Wiley, 1977. 870p. illus. index. $65.00. LC 64-22188. ISBN 0-471-56998-4.

Since the first volume of this unique encyclopedia was published in 1964, its reputation has grown apace with the developments in macromolecular science and biochemistry. Volume 15 of the original set, along with a supplement, was published in 1971. The first major supplement was published in 1976, with this volume following one year later; both cover new discoveries as well as update earlier articles relating to the amazing world of plastics, resins, rubbers, and fibers.

The title noted here is organized into 29 topics, which include, for example, albumins and globulins, dental applications, fire retardancy, microphase structure, polynucleotides, and pullulan. As the "preface to supplement volume 2" states, the work continues the editors' efforts "to keep the *Encyclopedia* current with descriptions of important new achievements. These include many biologically related subjects . . . ; environmental aspects continue to be of critical importance . . . ; new polymers or new versions of existing polymers that have been synthesized are covered . . . ; applications of these polymers are discussed . . . ; the supermolecular structure of block and graft copolymers and a mathematical treatment of melt processing can be found . . . ; [and] well-characterized polymers suitable as standards for molecular-weight determination, etc., are described. . . ."

The volume is well bound, well designed, and easy to use through its introductory section on "Abbreviations and Symbols" and a 30-page index. Illustrations are used extensively, and each major article (e.g., "Cationic Polymerization," with 140 specific references and a bibliography of some 30 citations, and "Thermodynamics of Polymerization," with 318 specific references plus general references to several review articles) maintains the same high standard of authority and currency noted in the original *Encyclopedia*. "See also" references to the multivolumed set add to this supplement's value as an updating but interrelated tool. It is an essential addition to any library serving the scientific community. [R: ARBA 80, p. 616] Laurel Grotzinger

747. Hampel, Clifford A., and Gessner G. Hawley, eds. **The Encyclopedia of Chemistry.** 3rd ed. New York, Van Nostrand Reinhold, 1973. 1198p. illus. index. $42.50. LC 73-244. ISBN 0-442-23095-8.

The third edition of this excellent one-volume encyclopedia exhibits the quality and usefulness of its predecessors, which were edited by Clark and Hawley. The new senior editor is well known for his work with other one-volume reference books in chemistry. Although many articles remain unchanged, or nearly so, the extensive additions and revisions reflect advances and new emphases since the second edition was published in 1966. Of particular interest are new topics in environmental chemistry and the chemistry of life processes including, for example, biomaterials, genetic code, psychotropic drugs, and sea water chemistry. The maintenance of approximately the same number of articles (more than 800) was accomplished by deletion of those of less interest to chemists, such as Mössbauer Effect, and by appropriate combination of topics previously listed under two or more separate headings. An especially noteworthy improvement is the inclusion of bibliographic references to additional literature on specific topics. An accurate and detailed index is provided. [R: ARBA 74, p. 557; WLB, Nov 73, p. 264] Julie Bichteler

748. **Kirk-Othmer Encyclopedia of Chemical Technology, Volumes 1-9, 11 & 12.** 3rd ed. Martin Grayson, executive ed. New York, John Wiley, 1978-1980. 11v. index. (A Wiley-Interscience Publication). $145.00/v. LC 77-15820.

All articles in this new edition have been completely revised and updated, and new subjects have been added to reflect recent changes in chemical technology. The *Encyclopedia* treats topics of concern to chemists, scientists, and engineers—industrial products, natural materials, and processes in fields such as chemical engineering; agricultural chemicals; ecology; fibers, textiles, and leather; industrial organic and inorganic chemicals; metals, metallurgy, and metal alloys; fermentation and enzyme technology; fossil fuels and derivatives; etc. Articles are written or updated by specialists and are signed. The emphasis is on American technology. SI units are now used simultaneously with traditional units, and Chemical Abstracts Service registry numbers are provided.

Twenty-five volumes are planned for this edition, with an average of four volumes published every year. [R: ARBA 81; ARBA 80, p. 617]

BIOGRAPHY

749. Miles, Wyndham D., ed. **American Chemists and Chemical Engineers.** Washington, American Chemical Society, 1976. 544p. index. $30.00. LC 76-192. ISBN 0-8412-0278-8.

This biographical dictionary provides information about 517 prominent men and women who have made significant contributions to chemistry and related fields in America. Covering a span of 300 years, from alchemists of early colonial times to chemists who have died recently, entries include educators, editors of professional journals, influential writers, consultants, and persons who have applied chemistry to other professions. Biographies range from 200 to 1,000 words and were prepared by authoritative persons with knowledge of the subject field. Selected references appended to the biographies document the writer's data and provide sources for additional information. Indexes include a list of contributors and a list of persons mentioned in the biographies.

Considering the broad range of activities and occupations represented, a subject index would have lent greater value to the work. The volume attempts to cover too broad an area and presents information that could be found more readily in standard biographical reference sources or major indexes such as *Chemical Abstracts*. Selection of entries is quite subjective and serious omissions occur due to failure of contributors in meeting publication deadlines. Biographical information about the contributors would also have been desirable, since many of them have already gained prominence in their respective fields.

On the positive side, the volume offers insight into the personal lives of chemists and provides good coverage of American Nobel Prize winners in chemistry and related fields. [R: ARBA 78, p. 645; Choice, Oct 76, p. 955; RQ, Summer 77, p. 353]   Andrew G. Torok

32   PHYSICS

750.   Besançon, Robert M., ed. **The Encyclopedia of Physics.** 2nd ed. New York, Van Nostrand Reinhold, 1974. 1067p. illus. index. $42.50. LC 73-17022. ISBN 0-442-20691-7.

The 344 articles in this encyclopedia, which are designed to give uniform coverage, are written on three different levels: those on the main divisions of physics are intended for readers with little background in the subject; those on the subdivisions are aimed at readers with more knowledge; and those on the more finely divided areas are geared toward readers with fairly sound backgrounds in both physics and mathematics.

This plan seems to be rather successful in the execution. There are a number of sections on mathematical techniques such as vector physics, tensors and tensor analysis, Fourier analysis, and a rather terse section on differential equations in physics. Descriptions of chemistry and chemists written by physicists are often the source of mild amusement; the results here, however, are a pleasant surprise—the Chemical Physics section is particularly succinct. One might wish for even a small discussion of a topic such as flames, which has no index entry; this subject must have been judged to be beyond the periphery of physics proper.

The articles sampled on each of the three levels provide appropriate weighted combinations of introductory material, references for further study, and clear and sometimes even provocative suggestions as to where future research in some areas may be headed. All teachers of beginning students will remember new insights that they have gained into a subject by looking at things from the perspective of the beginner; and so it is here with many of the first-level articles.

Among the numerous contributors are many leaders in their areas. One finds that equations, figures, and diagrams all seem to have been carefully set. The binding is strong, which is good, because the volume would seem to be in for a lot of use.

Ed. note: The information contained in the Van Nostrand Reinhold *Encyclopedia* is updated by the Addison-Wesley one-volume *Encyclopedia of Physics*, edited by Rita Lerner and George Trigg (1980 [c1981]. 1157p. $99.50). [R: ARBA 75, p. 655; Choice, Jan 75, p. 1602; WLB, Dec 74, p. 318]   John R. Riter, Jr.

751.   **Dictionary of Physics and Allied Sciences.** Ed. by Charles J. Hyman, and Ralph Idlin. New York, Frederick Ungar Publishing, 1978. 2v. $25.00/v.

Except for 23 pages of new words in the German-English volume and 28 pages of new words in the English-German volume, this is a reprint without revision of the two-volume set published in 1958-1962. It is a comprehensive work covering, in addition to physics, terms in the related sciences of mathematics, astronomy, chemistry, meteorology, mineralogy, geology, and geophysics. This is an essential acquisition for any collection in physics that contains foreign-language material, but it is questionable whether libraries owning the original version should expend additional funds on this, given the small amount of added material. [R: ARBA 79, p. 659; Choice, Nov 78, p. 1192]   Jay K. Lucker

752.   Gray, H. J., and Alan Isaacs, eds. **A New Dictionary of Physics.** 2nd ed. New York, Longman, 1975. 619p. illus. $38.00. ISBN 0-582-32242-1.

Substantially revised, updated, and expanded, Longman's *New Dictionary of Physics* is an invaluable tool for students, teachers, scientists, and the general reader in need of relatively simple explanations of the terms and concepts used in contemporary physics. The dictionary, which is alphabetically arranged, covers all branches of physics. It reflects all modern developments in particle physics, solid-state physics, and closely related fields.

The first edition's lengthy articles on the elements were dropped in order to accommodate new materials. Some key concepts are still treated at length, but most technical terms are given brief definition. Even with this new feature, the new edition is 65 pages longer than the first. The problem of British terminology for the American user has been almost completely solved by the new developments in solid-state technology and elimination of terms like "valve" or "vacuum tube," etc.

Each article consists of a self-contained description of the subject, accompanied, in some cases, by a diagram. Articles on leading physicists give brief biographical information, useful to a reader who comes across names in using the literature of physics. All quantitative information is given in SI units, and 16 tables, which give a wide range of information, are at the end of the dictionary. [R: ARBA 76, p. 652; Choice, Nov 75, p. 1142; WLB, Sept 75, p. 72]   Vladimir T. Borovansky

753.   Thewlis, J. **Concise Dictionary of Physics and Related Subjects.** 2nd ed., rev. and enl. New York, Pergamon Press, 1979. 366p. $49.50. LC 79-40209. ISBN 0-08-023048-2.

The well-known editor of the *Encyclopaedic Dictionary of Physics* (Pergamon, 1961-1964, with five supplementary volumes 1966-1975) has produced a second edition of this *Concise Dictionary*, consisting of over 7,200 short definitions of terms which are restricted primarily to individual concepts and directed toward students and nonspecialists. The scope covers not only physics proper, but to various degrees such related areas as astronomy, astrophysics, aerodynamics, biophysics, geophysics, hydraulics, mathematics, meteorology, photography, physical chemistry, etc. An attempt has been made to fill gaps in the first edition, and to update entries which now would be incomplete or inaccurate in light of recent research development and discoveries. The order of the entries is strictly alphabetical, and cross references from individual terms to related terms are noted to assist the reader. Appendixes include the Periodic Table and symbols of the elements; a new comprehensive table listing SI units, conversions, and equivalents; and values of some fundamental physical constants, including the latest recommended values. Throughout the text the numerical values of physical quantities given in the first edition, ranging from fundamental physical constants to experimentally determined values, have been reviewed and replaced with current values as necessary.

A useful dictionary which should appeal to those with wide-ranging interests — i.e., industrialists who employ scientists, politicians, teachers, scientific editors, and writers — as well as interested laypersons and physics students.

GENERAL WORKS

754. Bottle, R. T., and H. V. Wyatt, eds. **The Use of Biological Literature.** 2nd ed. Hamden, CT, Archon, 1971. 379p. index. (Information Sources for Research and Development). $39.95. ISBN 0-208-01221-4.

One of the best introductions of its kind. The literature of biology assumes a shape in 20 bibliographic chapters. Multiple changes in biology information caused the authors to rewrite and thoroughly revise the first edition (1966). Ecology, genetics, and teaching/laboratories now have whole chapters, and bibliographies have been updated (although not as much as one might have hoped). New questions have been added to the exercises, and the illustrations have been retained. Bottle and colleagues adequately survey the field: government publications, patents, abstracts, bibliographies, and such subjects as taxonomy, zoology, and agriculture. The index is impaired due to a decision to cite only important abstracts and reference books.

British this book is, but American libraries and budding biologists will find it viable. [R: ARBA 73, p. 549]   Peter Doiron

755. Smith, Roger C., W. Malcolm Reid, and Arlene E. Luchsinger. **Smith's Guide to the Literature of the Life Sciences.** 9th ed. Minneapolis, MN, Burgess Publishing, 1980. 223p. illus. index. $12.95pa. LC 79-55580. ISBN 0-8087-3576-4.

This book is more than a guide to life science literature: it is a manual on the pursuit of a professional career as a life scientist, with a major emphasis on library experience. Included are discussions of professional societies, their functions, requirements for membership, etc., how to write a research proposal, make an oral presentation, sources of funds for research and how to obtain them. In fact, the book assumes some subject knowledge but no familiarity with library organization.

It is an extraordinarily useful manual for the publishing academic. It deals with his/her problems beginning with doctoral candidacy, discussing such topics as selection of a research committee, ways to discover a research topic and how to proceed from there, including experimentation, preparation of a laboratory notebook, style of dissertations, development and proper presentation of a bibliography, with illustrations of citation forms. There is a whole chapter on scientific writing which describes the process step by step in great detail and even includes discussion of the complex and political problems of authorship, style, divising of a title, and editorial marking.

The book can be used as a self-study guide for the researcher-to-be or as a text for a literature course given by the biology department. Each chapter contains library exercises designed to give the student a hand-on experience in the use of library resources.

This edition is larger than the previous one by 50 pages. It has undergone considerable reorganization and includes new features such as a section on preparation of project proposals and preparation for writing theses and dissertations. The section on literature searching is expanded to include online services. The *Guide* defines library terms, describes library organization, mechanisms of bibliographic control, classification systems, etc. Since it is not directed primarily to librarians or library science students, its bibliographies are not as complete as other sources.

A few small errors filtered into the *Guide*. Nevertheless, this is a fine reference book, well organized, concise, informative, and useful.   Miriam Pollet

BIBLIOGRAPHIES

756.   Smit, Pieter. **History of the Life Sciences: An Annotated Bibliography.** New York, Hafner Press, 1974. 1036 cols. + pp. 1037-1071. index. $55.00. LC 74-12091. ISBN 0-02-852510-8.

The bibliography originated as an extension of those parts of George Sarton's *Guide to the History of Science* (Chronica Botanica, 1952) that deal with the life sciences. It is intended to serve primarily the historian of science, but also scholars in biology and medicine, and librarians. Over 4,000 entries containing full bibliographical information for all entries are included; summary reviews are given for nearly all the entries. Coverage is highly selective for the earliest writings and extends to publications issued through mid-1971.

The physical organization of the volume is somewhat unusual. Also, since the chapter listings in the table of contents do not correspond exactly to the chapter numbering in the text, the user will encounter some difficulties. The entries are set out in double columns on each page and each column is numbered; in contrast, the pages, not the columns, of the index are numbered. In addition to the two main chapters, there is a separate section – "Selected List of Biographies, Bibliographies, etc., of Famous Biologists, Medical Men, etc., Including Some Modern Reissues of Their Publications" – plus an index of personal names. The "Selected List" is labelled chapter III in the text but is not identified as a chapter in the table of contents.

Chapter I, General References and Tools, contains four main subsections treating philosophy and methodology of history, comprehensive works on the history of science and civilization, comprehensive bibliographies and biographical dictionaries, and recommended encyclopedias, chronologies, historical dictionaries, taxonomic indexes, and other reference works. Chapter II, Historiography of the Life and Medical Sciences, the main portion of the bibliography (columns 149-862), contains first a brief list on the philosophy of the life sciences, followed by a section on historiography, ancient and medieval periods, chronological and ethnographical (columns 157-558), and historiography, Renaissance and later periods, according to subject (columns 559-862). The "Selected List" cited in the text as chapter III lists entries in alphabetical order by author without any subdivisions (columns 863-1036). The index of personal names is on regularly numbered pages. It is unfortunate that title references were not added to listings for prolific authors; some of these require an extensive search in order to locate the desired title.

The retrospective bibliography, which is international in coverage, will be a valuable addition to the bibliographical sources on the life sciences. [R: ARBA 76, p. 654]

Christine Gehrt Wynar

DICTIONARIES AND ENCYCLOPEDIAS

757.   Gray, Peter, ed. **The Encyclopedia of the Biological Sciences.** 2nd ed. New York, Van Nostrand Reinhold, 1970. 1027p. illus. map. tab. bibliog. index. $34.50. LC 77-81348. ISBN 0-442-15629-4.

The second edition has the same purpose as the first (1961): "to provide succinct and accurate information for biologists in those fields in which they are not themselves experts." Thus it is a valuable reference for the generalist librarian. The editor wisely excluded the applied biological sciences but does include what he describes as "developmental, ecological, functional, genetic, structural, and taxonomic aspects" of biology – thereby giving it a wide subject base. The signed topical articles average two to three pages in length, but biographical entries are brief – often only half a column – and lack references. The coverage is uneven, but the explanations are lucid and seem relatively complete—although comparison with other encyclopedias is recommended. References, as a source for further data, are quite undependable; for example, an entry under *Ebenales*, a relatively small order, has 27 citations, while Platyhelminthes, a major phylum, has only four references. The illustrations are limited in number and poorly reproduced, as is the text, which is printed in a small type. Despite these limitations, Gray has produced the only comprehensive, one-volume biological encyclopedia in the field today. [R: ARBA 71, p. 493; Choice, Sept 70, p. 818; LJ, 15 May 70, p. 1826]   Laurel Grotzinger

758.   **McGraw-Hill Dictionary of the Life Sciences.** Daniel N. Lapedes, ed.-in-chief. New York, McGraw-Hill, 1976. 907p. illus. $19.95. LC 76-17817. ISBN 0-07-045262-8.

This handy reference book contains definitions of more than 20,000 terms. The definitions are very basic, thumbnail definitions, usually only one sentence. A great deal of this book is comprised of white paper. The definitions take up about two-thirds of the printed page; the remaining one-third is reserved for illustrations. There are some 800 of these and they are a very good feature; however, one could wish for many more of them since there are many pages with only one or none at all. Some of them are relatively fatuous. For instance, next to each element is the periodic chart of the elements with an arrow indicating the element in question. One chart would have sufficed, perhaps as an appendix. There are useful appendices covering other areas: U.S. Customary System and the metric system, the International System (SI), conversion factors for the measurement systems, symbols and atomic numbers for the chemical elements, fundamental constants, spectrum of antibiotic activity, normal clinical chemistry and cytology values, plus animal, bacterial, and plant taxonomy. This is primarily a derivative work, most of the material having been drawn from the *McGraw-Hill Encyclopedia of Science and Technology*. Higher level researchers will undoubtedly want a dictionary or one-volume encyclopedia more extensive than this one. But for undergraduates, the public, and others interested in definitions with a "clear and simple style" (p. vii), this dictionary should be a fine base for the beginning of an understanding and knowledge of biological terms. [R: ARBA 77, p. 653; Choice, June 77, p. 514; LJ, 15 Feb 77, p. 474; LJ, 1 Mar 77, p. 546; WLB, Feb 77, p. 538]

Henry T. Armistead

34 BOTANY

BIBLIOGRAPHIES

759. Swift, Lloyd H. **Botanical Bibliographies: A Guide to Bibliographic Materials Applicable to Botany.** Minneapolis, Burgess, 1970. 804p. index. LC 70-106633. ISBN 0-8087-1960-2.

This excellent guide to bibliographies of botany and of the manifold subjects allied to botany covers a stupendous range. It is divided into five main parts. Part I, General Bibliography, includes sections on library classifications, periodicals, book reviews, and abstracts. Part II, Background Literature for Botany, includes sections on mathematical and physico-chemical background literature as well as on life-science background literature. Part III, Botanical Literature, includes general and reference literature, taxonomic botanical literature, plant-kingdom literature, and ecological and physiological botanical literature. Part IV, Literature of Applied Areas of Plant Study, includes literature of economic aspects of plant study and literature of plant cultivation. Part V, Literature of Areas Auxiliary to Botany, includes bibliographic keys for literature on style, botanical illustration, photography, foreign works, etc. No book of this size can be definitive, and Dr. Swift states in his preface that his offering is "a guide and not a catalog. It enumerates selected lists and catalogs, but is not a compendium for their data. . . . The guide is planned primarily for beginning graduate students in botany, but it should be useful to all classes of users of botanical literature." [R: ARBA 71, p. 497; Choice, Apr 71, p. 208; LJ, 1 June 71, p. 1963; RQ, Fall 71, p. 84]   Elizabeth C. Hall

DICTIONARIES

760. Little, R. John, and C. Eugene Jones. **A Dictionary of Botany.** New York, Van Nostrand Reinhold, 1980. 400p. illus. bibliog. $18.50. LC 79-14968. ISBN 0-442-24169-0.

What can you ask of a dictionary? Well, that it be reasonably complete in coverage, that the definitions are clear, adequate, and non-circular (e.g., no "pit = hole; hole = pit"), that it is well illustrated where necessary, and that the definitions provided are correct. This book, with over 5,500 separate entries, fulfills most of these criteria. It is up to date, with many words of recent origin, and in this respect is an improvement over Delbert Swartz's *Collegiate Dictionary of Botany* (Ronald Press, 1971). The authors have also avoided the circularity which haunts some of Swartz's definitions, but some of their explanations are so terse as to potentially confuse the beginning student or amateur. They have also excluded many archaic and infrequently used terms, which is unfortunate, as a dictionary is often of greatest aid in unraveling the terminology in little-encountered or older works. This dictionary is well illustrated, although the choice of what to illustrate seems a bit arbitrary on occasion. One of the commendable aspects of the work is the number of cross references, which permit one to compare or contrast various terms and conditions. The book is well bound and will stand up to hard use.

The above criticisms and limitations aside, this is a useful book and worthy of purchase. It might be best used in conjunction with Swartz's *Collegiate Dictionary* for fullest coverage. Also, since neither book includes scientific or common names of plants, both should be supplemented with H. K. A. Shaw's *Dictionary of the Flowering Plants and Ferns* (8th ed., Cambridge University Press, 1973) and F. N. Howe's *Dictionary of Useful and Everyday Plants and Their Common Names* (Cambridge University Press, 1974).

Bruce H. Tiffney

CULTIVATED PLANTS

761. Howes, F. N. **A Dictionary of Useful and Everyday Plants and Their Common Names; Based on Material Contained in J. C. Willis: A Dictionary of the Flowering Plants and Ferns (6th Edition, 1931).** New York, Cambridge University Press, 1974. 290p. $27.50. LC 73-91701. ISBN 0-521-08520-9.

A Dictionary of Useful and Everyday Plants and Their Common Names is also a dictionary of products from plants. The late F. N. Howes, the author and former keeper of the museum, Royal Botanic Garden, Kew, compiled this dictionary to complement the seventh edition of J. C. Willis' *Dictionary of Flowering Plants and Ferns* (Cambridge University Press). The seventh edition, though revised and enlarged, was restricted in its scope to generic and family names; therefore, Howes undertook the task of enlarging and updating the more general information of the sixth edition into this new dictionary. For more than 70 years, Willis' work had been the most comprehensive plant dictionary available. Because of Howes, the encyclopedic approach of the early editions of Willis remains available. The eighth edition of Willis was published in 1973 (see entry 763).

Howes' emphasis is on common names, trade names, and economic or commercial plant products throughout the world where English is spoken. Definitions of such words as "grafting" and "germination" are given, but, in general, botanic terms and Latin names are left to other dictionaries or manuals of classification. The entries for common names or plant products give Latin names, country of each plant's origin, and practical uses. For such terms as "aquarium plants," "bee plants," "Bible plants," "bonsai," "classification," "gourds," "snakebite remedies," "tannin," and "timber," Howes provides concise but comprehensive essays, a unique and most helpful type of entry. In these essays, he lists plants that are, for example, suitable for aquariums, mentioned in the Bible, most popular to dwarf, and so on, as well as providing citations to published articles and books that readily open avenues to further research. A bibliography of major botanic dictionaries and manuals, titled "Some Useful Reference Works," concludes the dictioanry. Howes' work is a respected standard reference tool. [R: ARBA 75, p. 660; Choice, Jan 75, p. 1606; LJ, 1 Dec 74, p. 3124; LJ, 1 Mar 75, p. 452]   Amity Doering

762. Usher, George. **A Dictionary of Plants Used by Man.** New York, Hafner Press, 1974. 619p. $15.95. LC 74-2707. ISBN 0-02-853800-5.

All plants and trees used for commercial purposes are listed according to their botanical families. Usher used the classification adopted in Willis' *Dictionary of the Flowering Plants* (8th ed. revised by H. K. A. Shaw). The main reference for each plant (in italics) includes a brief description of its genus, total number of species included in it, authorities for the name, vernacular name, country of origin, and uses. Botanical descriptions have not been included. The reader may also find a plant by its vernacular name (in capitals) and learn the genus. This arrangement facilitates use by laypersons, students, and scholars.

Usher, author of *Dictionary of Botany* and *Textbook of Practical Biology*, is a recognized plant pathologist and teacher. The book was originally printed in Great Britain in 1973. F. N. Howes' *Dictionary of Useful and Everyday Plants* (see entry 761) is limited to plants that occur only in English-speaking countries, while Usher's is worldwide in scope. The undergraduate and graduate student may find it useful to combine the factual content of Usher's book with the *Oxford Book of Food Plants* (B. E. Nicholson and others), for its very clear colored illustrations, which show the plant parts most involved in food production at relevant stages of maturity. Usher's book is more inclusive, however, since it is not limited to food plants. [R: ARBA 76, p. 663]   Doris Flax Kaplan

763.   Willis, J. C. **A Dictionary of the Flowering Plants and Ferns.** 8th ed. Rev. by H. K. Airy Shaw. New York, Cambridge University Press, 1973. 1245p. index. $71.00. LC 72-83581. ISBN 0-521-08699-X.

First published in 1897, this important botanical dictionary at first included concise entries (A to Z) on the family and generic names, common names, and botanical terms and products. The seventh edition eliminated much of that material but did attempt to include every published generic name from 1753 onwards.

This eighth edition provides substantial additions and amends many of the errors in the 1931 (seventh) edition. One new feature is an alphabetical list of accepted plant family names with their equivalents in Bentham and Hooker's *Genera Plantarum* and in the latest edition of Engler's *Syllabus.* The list of generic names in this work includes all variant spellings and intergeneric hybrids. In many cases, brief characteristics of subfamilies are given. This comprehensive and recognized reference tool is well known to botanists and is important to scholarly collections of science materials. [R: ARBA 74, p. 573; Choice, Mar 74, p. 66]   Andy Armitage

ENDANGERED PLANTS

764.   Ayensu, Edward S., and Robert A. DeFilipps. **Endangered and Threatened Plants of the United States.** Washington, published jointly by the Smithsonian Institution and the World Wildlife Fund, Inc., 1978. 403p. maps. bibliog. $19.95. LC 77-25138. ISBN 0-87474-222-6.

This publication is a veritable gold mine of information for those concerned with any aspect of endangered and/or threatened plant species in the United States, Puerto Rico, or the Virgin Islands. The book is divided into roughly five portions. The introduction delimits the scope of the problem and the nature of the response provided to it in this book. It includes definitions of the status "endangered and threatened," together with a consideration of some of the conditions that lead to this status and a survey of the available mechanisms of conservation and governmental protection. The physical bulk of the book is provided by lists of endangered and extinct plant species, arranged in several groupings, e.g., by plant family, by state, etc. This is followed by a short section that describes the participants involved in the compilation of this data. The fourth section contains a series of very useful bibliographies on endangered plant species of the United States and of the world, their significance, and their conservation. The citations are up to date and would be of value to research workers. The last section provides a description of the methods by which the data used in the book were assembled; this includes examples of computer programs, maps, and data sheets used in the study. The volume contains information of potential interest to conservation commissions and the like, while also providing much of the background necessary for the continuing accumulation of such information. [R: ARBA 80, p. 628; Choice, Nov 79, p. 1196]   Bruce H. Tiffney

FLOWERS

765.   Hutchinson, John. **The Families of Flowering Plants Arranged According to a New System Based on Their Probable Phylogeny.** 3rd ed. New York, Oxford University Press, 1973; repr., Monticello, NY, Lubrecht & Cramer, 1979. 968p. illus. index. $90.00. ISBN 3-87429-160-X.

This is a great and scholarly work, the result of a long lifetime of study by one of the most outstanding botanists of the twentieth century. In 1926 Dr. Hutchinson, of the Royal Botanic Gardens, Kew, England, published the first volume of the first edition, which was followed in 1934 by the second volume. In 1959 appeared the second edition. The 1973 edition does not depart drastically from the evolutionary sequences presented in the previous ones. The change in the position of the family *Lythraceae* is the most notable change. New features include 67 drawings as well as notes on the chief orders, additional keys, and miscellaneous notes. In addition, for the first time, the parts dealing with the Dicotyledones and the Monocotyledones are contained in one volume.

At the time of Dr. Hutchinson's death the third edition was in page proof. The proofs were checked and minor corrections and emendations were made by Dr. William T. Stearn of the British Museum and by Dr. Bernard Verdcourt of the Royal Botanic Gardens, Kew. Botanical science does not stand still, as is well illustrated by the number of plant classification systems proposed both before and after Linnaeus. Two of the best known of these are those of Bentham and Hooker (1862-1883) and Engler and Prantl (1887-1898). One cannot expect everyone to agree with all of Dr. Hutchinson's views, but no botanical library should be without this outstanding contribution. [R: ARBA 75, p. 665; Choice, July 74, p. 786]   Elizabeth C. Hall

766.   Klimas, John E., and James A. Cunningham. **Wildflowers of Eastern America.** New York, Knopf, 1974. 273p. illus. (col.). bibliog. index. $17.95. LC 74-942. ISBN 0-394-49362-1.

767.   Orr, Robert T., and Margaret C. Orr. **Wildflowers of Western America.** New York, Knopf, 1974. 270p. illus. (col.). bibliog. index. $17.95. LC 74-943. ISBN 0-394-49363-X.

The logical approach to assessing these two works is to treat them as a set, and we would recommend that library catalogers consider entering them under a title entry: Wildflowers of America: vol. 1, Eastern America; vol. 2, Western America.

The volumes, identical in pattern, are descriptive guides based on a special identification system similar to that developed by the Royal Horticultural Society, whereby flowers are keyed by a symbol representing a color grouping. In this case, the color groupings for flowers are: white-green; yellow-orange; red-pink; blue-violet; and brown. Each is represented by a special symbol. The text is set out by color groupings identified by running titles at the head of the page; the plant descriptions are arranged numerically by plate numbers. The plates, in turn, are also keyed by the color-grouping symbols repeated as running heads; further subdivision is provided by season (for eastern America) or by locale (for western America).

The volume for eastern America contains an introductory chapter that is equally applicable to the western American volume. It discusses the definition of wildflowers, when and where to look for them, the source for common names, and folklore and uses. A "how to use this book" explanation appears in both volumes. Both volumes then have identical pictorial representations for identification of flower parts and leaves, and a duplicated glossary.

The texts are arranged non-alphabetically by the most widely used common name. For each flower is given its proper name, its family, a botanical description, and a paragraph of general information. Each color grouping begins with a simplified key relating the plants to the drawings of flower parts and leaves, to their season (for eastern America) or to their habitat (for western America). The key is followed by the superb color photographs, 304 for eastern America and 291 for western America.

Each volume then has a section describing the plant families included and a useful and informative chapter of wildflower recipes. The volume for eastern America, in addition, has a section giving edible parts of plants and a separate listing of poisonous and potentially poisonous plants, the lack of which in the western America volume leads one to believe either that western America wildflowers won't harm you if you ingest them, or that no one would eat them anyway. Both volumes have short select bibliographies and dual indexes of both common and proper names.

Other than the fact that either volume is perhaps a little heavy to pack for a hike through the woods, they are both extremely useful and easy to use. The organization of the books makes it quite easy to identify any particular wildflower. One imagines that the pair shall remain the standard work on United States wildflowers for some time to come. [R: ARBA 75, p. 666; BL, 15 May 75, p. 973; LJ, 15 Jan 75, p. 111; WLB, Apr 75, p. 596]

Ann Skene-Melvin
David Skene-Melvin

768.   Niering, William A., and Nancy C. Olmstead. **The Audubon Society Field Guide to North American Wildflowers, Eastern Region.** New York, Alfred A. Knopf, a division of Random House, 1979. 863p. illus. (part col.). index. (A Chanticleer Press Edition; A Borzoi Book). $9.95pa. LC 78-20383. ISBN 0-394-50432-1.

769.   Spellenberg, Richard. **The Audubon Society Field Guide to North American Wildflowers, Western Region.** New York, Alfred A. Knopf, a division of Random House, 1979. 862p. illus. (part col.). index. (A Chanticleer Press Edition; A Borzoi Book). $9.95pa. LC 78-20383. ISBN 0-394-50431-3.

Of outstanding value is the very extensive geographical range which these compact, pocket-size, profusely illustrated books offer. The demarcation line approximately parallels the 100th meridian. Each volume covers more than 600 species of wildflowers, with notes on 400 others, that are endemic to western or eastern North America. There are two major divisions to these books. The first presents photographs of the wildflowers arranged by color, and the second is a full descriptive text arranged by families. The access to the description is through the color arrangement. For each species there are included vernacular and scientific name, full description with height of plant and size of flower, flowering dates, habitat, range, fascinating comments on outstanding characteristics, origin of name, historical facts, plant lore, and poisonous and edible qualities. One drawback is the separation of illustrations from the text, which necessitates frequent page turning. Nevertheless, these are most attractive, authoritative publications, recommended highly for wildflower enthusiasts, high school, college, university, and public libraries. [R: ARBA 80, pp. 630, 631]

770.   Polunin, Oleg. **Flowers of Europe: A Field Guide.** New York, Oxford University Press, 1969. 662p. illus. 192 plates. map. bibliog. $49.00. LC 70-410049. ISBN 0-19-217621-8.

Flowers of Europe describes 2,600 common wildflowers in Europe. Arrangement is by families, and entries provide adequate identification with information on habitat and uses. Some 1,000 plants are illustrated by color photographs in the appendix. Also included are a glossary and lists of common French, German, and Italian names of well-known species. [R: ARBA 70, v.2, p. 121; Choice, Dec 69, p. 1372; LJ, 1 Nov 69, p. 4015; WLB, Nov 69, p. 329]

771.   Rickett, Harold William. **Wildflowers of the United States.** New York, McGraw-Hill, 1966-1975. 6v. plus index. illus. index. $69.50/v. (v.1, 2, 3, 5); $79.95(v.4); $74.50(v.6); $32.50(index). LC 66-17920. ISBN 0-07-052614-1(v.1); 0-07-052630-3(v.2); 0-07-052633-8(v.3); 0-07-052636-2(v.4); 0-07-052640-0(v.5); 0-07-052643-5(v.6); 0-07-052647-8(index).

Published for the New York Botanical Garden, these volumes provide the most comprehensive treatment of the subject available. The first six volumes are: volume 1, The

Northeastern States; volume 2, The Southeastern States; volume 3, Texas; volume 4, The Southwestern States; volume 5, The Northwestern States; and volume 6, The Central Mountains and Plains. An index volume, which lists both the common and botanical names for each flower, concludes the set. Each of the first six volumes is arranged in broad categories and subdivided according to genus and species. A wealth of detailed yet comprehensible information about flowers and their habitats is offered. Botanical terms are explained, and both Latin and common names are listed. Illustrations include many line drawings and thousands of strikingly beautiful color photographs, many showing the flowers in their natural habitats. [R: ARBA 70, v.2, p. 122; ARBA 74, p. 580; BL, 15 Sept 74, p. 111; Choice, Apr 70, p. 218; Choice, June 74, p. 581; WLB, Mar 74, p. 594]

GRASSES

772. Hitchcock, A. S. **Manual of the Grasses of the United States.** 2nd ed. Rev. by Agnes Chase. Washington, GPO, 1950; repr., New York, Dover, 1971. 2v. illus. index. $6.00pa./v. LC 70-142876. ISBN 0-486-22717-0(v.1); 0-486-22718-9(v.2).

A welcome reprint is this second revised edition of a monumental work on the native and introduced grasses of the United States (published by the U.S. Government Printing Office in 1950 as USDA Misc. Publ. No. 200). The first edition was published in 1935. Professor Hitchcock was the chief botanist in charge of systematic agrostology for the U.S. Department of Agriculture, and Agnes Chase was research associate, U.S. National Museum, Smithsonian Institution — both recognized authorities on the enormous and vastly important group of plants, the grasses. This unabridged republication includes 1,199 line drawings, identification keys, comprehensive descriptions of each species and variety (with scientific and vernacular names), range of distribution, the common uses, and over 200 pages devoted to synonymy — names of grasses that have previously appeared in botanical literature. This definitive work is invaluable to both the amateur and the professional botanist. [R: ARBA 72, p. 574; Choice, June 72, p. 527]   Elizabeth C. Hall

HERBS

773. Stuart, Malcolm, ed. **The Encyclopedia of Herbs and Herbalism.** New York, Grosset & Dunlap, 1979. 304p. illus. (part col.). bibliog. index. $35.00. LC 78-58101. ISBN 0-448-15472-2.

This magnificent work on the growing, preservation, uses, history, folklore, and chemistry of herbs is stupendous in weight (five pounds), in size (9x11½-inches), in superb quality of color photographs, drawings, and diagrams, and in the authentic text written by leading British authorities. The following partial list of chapter headings and the names of some of the contributors are revealing: The History of Herbalism, by Kay Sanecki and Christopher Pick; The Biology and Chemistry of Plants, by Allen Paterson and Peter Hylands; The Medicinal Uses of Plants, by Peter Hylands and Malcolm Stuart; Herbs in the Kitchen, by J. Audrey Ellison and Christopher Pick; The Domestic and Cosmetic Uses of Herbs, by Kay Sanecki; Cultivation, Collection, and Preservation of Herbs, by Kay Sanecki; Reference Section, by Malcolm Stuart; Glossary; Conversion Tables; Organizations; Bibliography; General Index; Index of Plants. This is the herb book of the year. Highly recommended.   Elizabeth C. Hall

MOSSES AND FUNGI

774. Miller, Orson K., Jr. **Mushrooms of North America.** New York, E. P. Dutton, 1977. 368p. illus. (part col.). $15.95; $9.95pa. LC 72-82162. ISBN 0-525-16166-X; 0-525-47482-Xpa.

This is a superb field guide to fleshy Basidiomycetes and Ascomycetes. Thus, not only are mushrooms in the strict sense included, but bracket fungi, puffballs, earthstars, tongue fungi, and many other less familiar groups are treated as well. The physical production of the book is outstanding. My only complaint is that it is perfect bound rather than sewn. Experience has shown that perfect binding and field use do not mix. I hope to be proven wrong.

About one-third of the species are illustrated by extraordinary photographs. These are uniformly of the highest quality, well chosen to demonstrate the characters of the species illustrated. The book is easy to use; there are numerous keys (picture and dichotomous), a standard glossary, and an illustrated one. Each species is described clearly (but technically — the reader must learn the appropriate terminology), any information available on edibility or toxicity is indicated, and geographic range and habitat are discussed. Here and there, suggestions for cooking are provided the reader. Introductory sections discuss fungal biology, the use of scientific names, techniques for collection and study of fungi, and the chemistry of toxins. The bibliography is brief but useful, helping the enthusiast to make the jump from "mushroom collector" to mycologist.

Miller's book is certain to be the standard in this field for many years to come. [R: ARBA 78, p. 664; BL, 15 June 78, p. 1638; RQ, Summer 78, p. 365; WLB, Dec 77, p. 348]

Javier Peñalosa

775. Mycological Society of America. Mycological Guidebook Committee. **Mycology Guidebook.** Ed. by Russell B. Stevens. Seattle, University of Washington Press, 1974. 703p. illus. bibliog. index. LC 73-17079. ISBN 0-295-95313-6.

This definitive and indispensable manual, the combined work of a host of eminent mycologists, is intended for those who teach introductory mycology. Part I covers field observations of fungi and discusses techniques of collecting and preserving; part II deals with the taxonomic groups; part III covers the ecological aspects; part IV, entitled "Fungi as Biological Tools," surveys fungus physiology and genetics. Most useful is the information offered in the appendixes, such as the quarantine and shipment of biological materials, culture collections, stains, reagents, media, and films and film loops. As stated in the preface, "the key objective . . . is not drastically to alter mycology courses but to provide resources whereby instructors may substantially improve them." [R: ARBA 75, p. 670; Choice, Sept 74, p. 972]

Elizabeth C. Hall

776. Snell, Walter H., and Esther A. Dick. **A Glossary of Mycology.** Rev. ed. Cambridge, MA, Harvard University Press, 1971. 181p. illus. bibliog. $10.00. LC 77-134946. ISBN 0-674-35451-6.

First published in 1936 under the title *Three Thousand Mycological Terms.* This is a completely revised edition, with some 7,000 terms defined. It will supplement Ainsworth and Bisby's *Dictionary of Fungi* (5th ed., 1963). [R: ARBA 72, p. 569; Choice, Sept 71, p. 813]

TREES

777. Bean, W. J. **Trees and Shrubs Hardy in the British Isles.** 8th ed. fully rev. George Taylor, general ed. London, John Murray, 1970. 3v. illus. index. £15.00(v.1 & 2); £7.50(v.3). ISBN 0-7195-1790-7.

First published 65 years ago, this monumental work is in the truest sense a classic, indispensable to every serious student of temperate-region trees and shrubs. Among the several outstanding dendrologists Great Britain has produced, none outshines — and probably none equals — William Jackson Bean. From 1883 until his death in 1947 he was employed at the Royal Botanic Gardens, Kew, for many years as curator in charge of all living plants, and before that in charge of the Arboretum. Bean lived at Kew; he knew intimately every tree and shrub of the vast collection there. His Kew experience was fortified by his many travels and by the unexcelled opportunity he enjoyed of corresponding with and meeting others who shared his interests. Bean's is a facile pen. His writings are not rehashes of the writings of others, nor are they merely skeletons of botanical terminology, lacking the flesh of simple descriptive English. Every description breathes of his intimate knowledge of the plant of which he writes, but his facts have been carefully checked against library and herbarium records. He writes clearly and succinctly, so that even non-experts can understand.

These volumes well reflect the capabilities of the team that has been engaged in bringing Bean's work up to date. It is a tribute to their integrity that they have succeeded in adding descriptions of new plants, updating certain information about others, and most importantly, bringing nomenclature into line with modern botanical thinking. To have done less would have failed their purpose, to have done more would have been as disastrous as for a modern artist to over-paint a Gainsborough or a Titian. But they have given us Bean as Bean was—unchanged in character or spirit, but reflecting changes necessitated by the passing years. No better horticultural book has ever been revised. [R: ARBA 75, p. 671]   Elizabeth C. Hall

778.   Leathart, Scott. **Trees of the World.** New York, A & W Publishers, 1977. 224p. illus. (part col.). index. $19.95. LC 76-52282. ISBN 0-89479-000-5.

Leathart's work introduces the subject with basic information about the structure, places where different types of trees grow (according to local geographic conditions), and about their relationship with man and wildlife. The major portions of the book are sections on conifers and on broadleafs. Beautiful colored illustrations and clear diagrams indicate tree shapes, leaf shapes, arrangement on stems, buds, leaves, needles, flowers, and fruit. For each tree, the following are presented: family, genus, and explanation of the language, if foreign; natural habitat plus other areas where it is found; general description of size and distinguishing features; and related species and their general characteristics. Although this is listed by the publisher as "a completely illustrated guide to the world's most familiar trees," the adverb "most" is a limiting factor. The wealth of information (although not all U.S. trees are included) allows this to compare favorably with the *Oxford Book of Trees* (Oxford University Press, 1975). The index is very useful, and the author is well qualified for his subject. [R: ARBA 79, p. 674; BL, 15 July 78, p. 1764; Choice, Dec 78, p. 1397; LJ, 1 Nov 77, p. 2268]   Doris Flax Kaplan

779.   Little, Elbert L., Jr. **Atlas of United States Trees, Volume 5: Florida.** Washington, GPO, 1978. 1v. (unpaged). illus. (part col.). maps. bibliog. index. (Forest Service Miscellaneous Publication, No. 1361). $4.25pa. LC 79-653298. S/N 001-000-03728-5.

This is the fifth volume of an atlas showing the natural distribution or range of the native tree species of the continental United States. The other four volumes include: vol. 1, *Conifers and Important Hardwoods* (1971, USDA Misc. Pub. no. 1146); vol. 2, *Alaska Trees and Common Shrubs* (1975, USDA Misc. Pub. no. 1293); vol. 3, *Minor Western Hardwoods* (1976, USDA Misc. Pub. no. 1314); and vol. 4, *Minor Eastern Hardwoods* (1977, USDA Misc. Pub. no. 1342). A sixth volume, a supplement on hawthorns, is planned.

Florida merited separate coverage from other region-species volumes because it has more native tree species than any other state (except Hawaii, which is outside the scope of the *Atlas*). Altogether, some 256 outline maps of the state have been color-coded to show the range of 262 species of conifers, temperate hardwoods, and tropical hardwoods native to Florida. In addition, 6 general maps showing such matters as county names, county seats, physical features, location of national forests and parks, and plant hardiness zones have been provided for background. Most maps are scaled 1:10,000,000, although a few larger maps are 1:4,000,000. Also included are "Selected References" and separate indexes by common and scientific tree names. [R: ARBA 80, p. 638]   Walter L. Newsome

780.   Polunin, Oleg. **Trees and Bushes of Europe.** New York, Oxford University Press, 1976. 208p. illus. (part col.). index. $14.95. LC 76-381275. ISBN 0-19-217631-5.

Oleg Polunin has compiled a well-produced and easy to use guide to the trees and bushes of Europe. Identification of unknown trees is simplified by the use of a leaf shape checklist. This list names all the genera and species that fall under each leaf shape category and the pages on which to find their respective descriptions and illustrations. Because of variations of leaf shape within some species, the list includes genera and species under all applicable shapes. After examination of the excellent photographs, drawings, and descriptions, the reader will easily be able to determine the identity of the unknown tree. Dichotomous keys to genus or individual tree are provided where there are several important genera in a family or many European species in a genus. Symbols denoting geographical distribution also help in the identification of an unknown tree.

Besides its use as a guide, the book contains a wealth of information on the study of trees and bushes. An illustrated glossary that includes all botanical terms used in the text is just one of several extras. The main body of the work gives descriptions of major families and genera of trees and bushes, which gives the reader a better grasp of their taxonomy. Included in the appendix are other extras: a section of photographs of barks of some European trees and a section on human use of selected trees and bushes. [R: ARBA 78, p. 667; Choice, May 77, p. 404; LJ, 1 Jan 77, p. 91]   Martin Kesselman

35 ZOOLOGY

ENCYCLOPEDIAS

781. Burton, Maurice, and Robert Burton, eds. **The International Wildlife Encyclopedia.** New York, Marshall Cavendish; distr., New York, Purnell Library Service, 1969-1970. 20v. illus. index. LC 78-98713.

Published simultaneously in England and the United States, this 20-volume encyclopedia aims to cover all animal life throughout the world. Each 8½x12-inch volume contains about 140 pages (the set is continuously paged). All volumes are lavishly illustrated with many full-page color photos, smaller photos, drawings, and distribution maps—a total of some 2,500 illustrations. The text, in three-column arrangement, is clearly printed and well edited. Entries are specific—e.g., amoeba, anchovy, badger, pack rat. Two indexes are contained in volume 20—an animal index and a systematic index. The animal index is especially important for locating, as an example, the names of all bees that are included. Entries range in length from one page to four or five pages. Each article includes information on the geographic distribution (a small map is provided for many of the animals). At the end of each article the scientific classification according to class, order, family, genus, and species is printed in boldface. Articles are broken down under such rubrics as breeding, conservation, feeding habits, habitat, enemies and defense, life cycles, and distribution.

The text is highly informative but at the same time makes enjoyable reading. The photographs, a delight to the eye, reveal a good amount of additional information about the animals. A close-up shot of a bearded lizard eating a stag beetle is nearly like being present at the meal. If small animals are shown larger than life size, the photograph is accompanied by a scale in millimeters and inches or by an indication of the number of times the subject is enlarged. A few photographs of ultra-tiny details, such as the teeth on an abalone's radula, were obtained by using a deep field scanning electron microscope (SEM). Most of the pictures show the animal, close up, in his natural habitat, which adds to the educational value of the work.

The International Wildlife Encyclopedia is quite similar to *The Illustrated Encyclopedia of the Animal Kingdom* (Danbury Press, 1972). The latter is arranged by animal groups and has a simpler, less detailed text. The index in the former work, however, is better, and the illustrations are all as good as those in the *Illustrated Encyclopedia*—perhaps even somewhat better. While specialists will prefer a work such as *Grzimek's Animal Life Encyclopedia* (see entry 782) for its more thorough treatment, *The International Wildlife Encyclopedia* is a good choice for general readers and certainly will be a valuable reference source in schools. [R: ARBA 73, p. 568; BL, 15 Oct 72, p. 153]   Christine Gehrt Wynar

782. **Grzimek's Animal Life Encyclopedia.** Bernhard Grzimek, ed.-in-chief. New York, Van Nostrand Reinhold, 1972-75. 13v. illus. (part col.). index. $34.95/v. LC 79-183178. ISBN 0-442-22944-5(v.1); 0-442-22942-9(v.2); 0-442-22943-7(v.3); 0-442-22933-4(v.4); 0-442-22938-0(v.5); 0-442-22939-9(v.6); 0-442-22934-8(v.7); 0-442-22935-6(v.8); 0-442-22936-4(v.9); 0-442-22930-5(v.10); 0-442-22931-3(v.11); 0-442-22932-1(v.12); 0-442-22938-0(v.13).

Originally published in Germany in 1967, this encyclopedia is now published in an English edition. The 13 volumes include: volume 1, Lower Animals; volume 2, Insects; volume 3, Mollusks and Echinoderms; volume 4, Fishes 1; volume 5, Fishes 2 and Amphibians; volume 6, Reptiles; volume 7, Birds 1; volume 8, Birds 2; volume 9, Birds 3; volume

10, Mammals 1; volume 11, Mammals 2; volume 12, Mammals 3; volume 13, Mammals 4. Volume 1 contains two introductory chapters for the whole set, summarizing basic concepts of zoology.

Articles were prepared by nearly 100 international authorities in various specialties, and a list of these contributors to the series is at the beginning of each volume. Material in each volume is arranged by animal orders and families. The text discusses the evolution of each group of animals and indicates physical description, range and habitat, feeding and mating habits, and other behavioral characteristics. Articles vary in length from less than a page to a full chapter. The writing is highly descriptive and detailed, presenting a large amount of information in concise form. As is almost inevitable in works of multiple authorship, there are occasional repetitions, conflicting interpretations, and differences in approach (e.g., a few contributors tend to focus on European or North American representatives of the group of animals being described, while others have no geographic emphasis). Overall, the accounts are accurate and accessible to the nonspecialist.

Illustrations consist of line drawings and color plates (both photos and paintings). The effectiveness of the latter is occasionally diminished by poor placement and reproduction from dirty or poor plates. At the end of each volume is a systematic classification index to the volume, showing page numbers as well as references to color plates. There is also a detailed index that includes common and scientific names. An additional feature is a four-way animal dictionary in English, German, French, and Russian. A common name can be located in any of the languages, and the corresponding word is provided in each of the other three languages. A short selective bibliography of English and German titles is appended. [R: LJ, July 72, p. 2375; LJ, 15 Apr 73, p. 1244; LJ, 15 June 73, p. 1904; BL, 1 June 73, p. 916; Choice, May 74, p. 412; Choice, Apr 75, p. 196; Choice, Jan 75, p. 1604; BL, 15 July 76, p. 1618; ARBA 76, p. 674; ARBA 76, p. 675]

783. **Grzimek's Encyclopedia of Ethology.** Ed.-in-chief, Bernhard Grzimek. New York, Van Nostrand Reinhold, 1977. 705p. illus. (part col.). bibliog. index. $39.50. LC 76-9298. ISBN 0-442-22946-1.

This excellent survey volume of ethology should be useful to students of animal behavior. However, the book has a decidedly European ethological slant and should not be considered as an authoritative volume on animal behavior. Forty-three contributors have provided articles covering the history, goals, organization, and methods of ethology: the structure and function of the nervous system and sense organs, the operation of the major senses, biological clocks, migration and orientation, displacement activities, sexuality and courtship, social behavior, the development and evaluation of behavior. These articles are in the most part clear and understandable, and some, like Wolfgang Wiehler's on the evaluation of behavior or that by Heinroth on the history of behavior, are excellent and give ample coverage of the subject. Others, however, are somewhat superficial and dogmatic in treatment. For example, the article on biological clocks fails completely to give an adequate presentation of exogenous clock theories and, instead, summarily dismisses such theories on the basis of experiments involving so-called constant conditions. These experiments are by no means as definitive as portrayed here and are in fact open to alternate interpretation. This treatment does not fully or accurately treat exogenous timing by factors other than light, temperature, or tidal rhythm. This is not meant to imply that either the exogenous or endogenous theory is correct, only to point out the unfortunate tendency of this article to present theory as proven fact and to neglect or gloss over viable alternate explanations. In science, where absolute proof does not exist, such superficial coverage is most unfortunate.

Of special interest and usefulness are the several articles dealing with sexuality, courtship, pair bonding, and sociality. Taken together, these articles provide an excellent overview and accurate coverage of animal sociality, including valuable contrasts of insect and primate social systems and the functional significance of social behavior. In conclusion, this is an excellent book. For a single volume, it does a very good job in covering a vast amount of material and theory. [R: ARBA 78, p. 670; BL, 1 Oct 78, p. 317; Choice, Mar 78, p. 45; WLB, Feb 78, p. 503]

784. **The Illustrated Encyclopedia of the Animal Kingdom.** 2nd English ed. New York, Danbury Press (Grolier), 1972. 20v. illus. (most col.). maps. charts. index. LC 71-141898. ISBN 0-7172-8100-0.

This major reference set was first published by Fabbri of Milan in 1968 as *Gli animali e il loro mondo*, edited by Antonio Valle; the first English-language edition under the current title was published by Danbury in 1971 under the editorial direction of Percy Knauth. This revised second edition was edited by Herbert Kondo and Jenny E. Tesar, with the advice of a group of outside consultants. The pictorial matter, which constitutes about 60% of the total content, has remained essentially the same in all three editions, but the text has undergone extensive rewriting.

The coverage is the entire animal kingdom from the amoeba to man, but, as is typical of comprehensive zoological works for the nonspecialist, there is a pronounced emphasis on the larger, more colorful forms. This is easily demonstrated by the contents: vol. 1, general introduction to vertebrates; vols. 2-6, mammals; vols. 7-8, birds; vols. 9-10, reptiles and amphibians; vol. 11, fishes; vols. 12-13, arthropods other than insects; vols. 14-16, insects; vol. 17, mollusks; vols. 18-19, other invertebrates; vol. 20, endangered species and the general index. This distribution bears no relationship to absolute numbers of species or individuals in the various phyla, but it does quite accurately reflect economic importance and predictable reader interest, if not exactly vindicating the claim in the advertising matter that this work is "a complete library of all the animals . . . in the world." Some imbalances of treatment within groups are also apparent—e.g., about one and three-fourths volumes of the five devoted to mammals are given over to the carnivores, while the far more abundant (both in species and in individuals) rodents rate only about half a volume. Similarly, the sharks are given a more extended and detailed treatment, at the expense of some other orders of fishes, than their actual importance would seem to warrant. Both examples doubtless reflect the peculiar fascination that large dangerous creatures have for the average man, a phenomenon that may be readily observed at any zoo.

The illustrations, mostly photographs but including some paintings and drawings, are almost without exception outstanding, and the printing is of very good quality. Certainly it is the illustrations that are the work's greatest asset; they will answer many reference questions, but at the same time they provide a temptation to mutilation that librarians should be aware of.

The concise text covers the morphology, behavior, and distribution of the animals treated, without extensive detail or use of difficult terminology. While some taxonomic interpretations presented are not universally accepted, overall the work is accurate.

Each volume is indexed separately, and the whole work is covered by the general index in the final volume. Although the indexes are much improved over the first edition, a serious weakness which has not been corrected in this edition is the total lack of bibliographic references that would lead the interested reader to more specialized treatises.

The page design is pleasing, and the printing is clear and acceptably free from typographical errors. The binding is sturdy enough for library use, and the attractive pictorial covers will draw the attention of prospective users. The work is not too difficult for better students in the upper elementary grades, nor too simple for the college undergraduate or the general adult reader without a background in biology. [R: ARBA 73, p. 570; BL, 15 Oct 73, p. 181]   Paul B. Cors

BIRDS

785.   **The Audubon Society Field Guide to North American Birds: Eastern Region.** John Bull and John Farrand, Jr., eds. New York, Alfred A. Knopf, 1977. 775p. illus. (part col.). index. (A Chanticleer Press Edition; A Borzoi Book). $9.95. LC 76-47926. ISBN 0-394-41405-5.

786.   **The Audubon Society Field Guide to North American Birds: Western Region.** Miklos D. F. Udvardy, ed. New York, Alfred A. Knopf, 1977. 855p. illus. (part col.). index. (A Chanticleer Press Edition; A Borzoi Book). $9.95. ISBN 0-394-41410-1.

Regional field guides for the identification of birds have traditionally been arranged taxonomically and illustrated with paintings or drawings; these titles, designed to be of particular use to the inexperienced birder, break with tradition in being arranged by the habitats in which the species most commonly occur and in being illustrated exclusively with color photographs. Twenty habitats are defined for the western region, 12 habitats for the eastern region.

The first half of the books contain color photographs arranged by groups of birds with similar appearances and further subarranged by color. With few exceptions the photography is first-rate. Species accounts make up the second portion of the volumes. Each species account includes description, common and scientific names, voice, habitat, range, nesting, and miscellaneous information. The indexes of common and scientific names cover both text and plates. Bindings are suitably sturdy for field use.

These volumes do not supplant the existing regional and state guides, but complement them nicely. They belong in any library serving birders. [R: ARBA 78, pp. 675, 671; BL, 15 Oct 78, p. 403; Choice, Mar 78, p. 51; Choice, June 78, p. 523; LJ, 15 Apr 78, p. 818]

Paul B. Cors

787.   Campbell, Bruce. **The Dictionary of Birds in Color.** American consultant ed., Richard T. Holmes. New York, Viking Press, 1974. 352p. illus. (col.). (A Studio Book). LC 73-17954. ISBN 0-670-27225-6.

An authoritative author and compiler and a topic of major interest to thousands of individuals occasionally come into happy conjunction and produce an excellent reference book: *The Dictionary of Birds in Color* is such a volume. This is a scholarly, comprehensive text that deals with more than a thousand different species distributed in six main geographical regions of the world: the Palaearctic, the Nearctic, the Oriental, the Australasian, the Ethiopian, and the Neotropical. The author provides a general introduction, which describes the six faunal regions, origins and species, bird anatomy, and classification; this last section includes an annotated sequence of orders and families developed first by Sir Landsborough Thomson and used widely by J. L. Peters and his successors. Each entry in this section briefly notes the relationship of orders and families, gives key physical characteristics, and cites examples. This section also includes a few line drawings that illustrate some of the exemplary species.

The bulk of the volume consists of an alphabetical dictionary arranged by the scientific general bird names – printed in boldface type. Entries, which average 150 to 200 words, include the common English name, approximate length in inches, and the zoogeographical region where the species breeds. The descriptive entry also notes breeding and wintering distribution and breeding habitat, gives colors of adults of both sexes, briefly comments on habits and behavior (including displays, voice, and principal foods), and usually cites each breeding season and details of nest, eggs, incubation, and fledglings. Complementing this section (and preceding it in physical placement) is a unique collection of color photographs. Although some artificial light was occasionally used in order to gain the needed clarity, the plumage of each bird is represented with considerable accuracy due to the excellent printing and processing used by the publishers. Access to these photographs is gained through the dictionary section, where each entry has a reference, also in boldface type, to the accompanying illustration. Each plate notes the scientific name.

For the average user, numerous cross references from the common names to the correct scientific terminology are provided in the dictionary section. No special index is needed because of this extensive cross referencing, but a brief glossary and some abbreviations and notes are included in the opening pages of the volume. British spelling is used throughout.

The volume is well bound, and the excellent paper, typography, and design give it overall quality. It makes it "possible for ornithologists and bird lovers alike to study the detailed beauty of nearly every living [bird] family in its natural surroundings in full-colour photographic close-ups." [R: ARBA 76, p. 679; BL, 15 Apr 75, p. 871; Choice, May 75, p. 367; WLB, Mar 75, p. 529]   Laurel Grotzinger

788.   Cramp, Stanley, chief ed. **Handbook of the Birds of Europe, the Middle East and North Africa: The Birds of the Western Palearctic, Volume I, Ostrich to Ducks.** New York, Oxford University Press, 1978. 722p. illus. (part col.). bibliog. index. $85.00. ISBN 0-19-857358-8.

789.   Cramp, Stanley, chief ed. **Handbook of the Birds of Europe, the Middle East and North Africa: The Birds of the Western Palearctic, Vol. II, Hawks to Bustards.** New York, Oxford University Press, 1980. 695p. illus. (part col.). maps. bibliog. index. $85.00. ISBN 0-19-857505-X.

These are the first two of what is to be a seven-volume set. The first volume includes the general introduction to the set and taxonomically arranged species accounts covering the orders Struthioniformes through Anseriformes. Volume II covers the subsequent orders Accipitriformes (hawks, vultures, eagles, and ospreys), Falconiformes (falcons), Galliformes (grouse, partridges, quails, pheasants, and guinea fowl), and Gruiformes (button-quails, rails, cranes, and bustards). The geographic area covered is all of Europe (including the Soviet Union west of the Urals and the Caspian Sea), Turkey and the Fertile Crescent (including Kuwait), Africa south to approximately 20° N. latitude, and the adjacent islands of the Arctic and northeast Atlantic oceans (excluding Greenland, but including the Cape Verde chain). General discussions of each family are followed by a detailed description of each of the species covered – scientific name, field characters, habitat, distribution, population, movements, food, social patterns and behavior, voice, breeding, etc. Extensive references, glossaries, and indexes are provided.

It is a joy to have so many paintings in color for each species in different stages from downy young to adults in flight, as well as egg plates. There are also fascinating behavioral black-and-white drawings.

One notes with regret the $30 list price increase in the two-year interval between volumes. Nevertheless, it must be viewed as a necessary investment, since this will surely remain the preeminent English reference in the field for at least a generation. [R: ARBA 79, p. 679; Choice, Dec 78, p. 1348; LJ, 1 May 78, p. 962; ARBA 81]   Paul B. Cors
                                                                                        Syd Schoenwetter

790.   Harrison, C. J. O., consultant ed. **Bird Families of the World.** New York, Harry N. Abrams, 1978. 264p. illus. (col.). $25.00. LC 77-25916. ISBN 0-8109-0706-2.

This is the latest of its genre, a lavishly illustrated, authoritative overview of the world's birds. It joins such illustrious predecessors as *Birds of the World* (O. Austin and A. Singer, Golden Press, 1961); *The World of Birds* (James Fisher and Roger Tory Peterson, Doubleday, 1964 – condensed version by the same authors, Crown, 1977); *The World*

Atlas of Birds (Sir Peter Scott, Random House, 1974); not to speak of *Birds of the World: Their Life and Habits* (Paul Barruel, Oxford University Press, 1975).

The present volume will appeal to those who prefer a tidy presentation. There are straightforward descriptions of each of the world's extinct and living 176 families (Fisher/Peterson list 199), with sections, as warranted, on distribution, behavior, feeding, courtship, nesting and the young, and economic importance, and there are fine color pictures on every page. In addition to its more thorough treatment of extinct orders, it has the present advantage of being the latest and thus most up to date. Even so, the book still uses some obsolete common names: e.g., the great egret referred to as the American egret, the renamed Wilson's storm petrel, common yellowthroat, and wood stork called respectively Wilson's petrel, yellowthroat, and wood ibis.

There are other sharp differences of opinion besides the number of families. Fisher/Peterson list Sphenisciformes (penguins) as the first order having living species, whereas Harrison prefers Struthioniformes (ostriches); Fisher/Peterson show the extinct moas in the same order as the living kiwis, but Harrison has moas and kiwis as separate orders; Scott, on the other hand, perhaps appropriately for an atlas, doesn't list extinct orders at all; etc. For this reason, though much of the same information appears in all these volumes, the point of departure, arrangement, and emphasis differ sufficiently to warrant interest in each. [R: ARBA 81]   Syd Schoenwetter

791.   Harrison, Colin. **A Field Guide to the Nests, Eggs, and Nestlings of North American Birds.** Cleveland, William Collins Publishers, 1978. 416p. illus. index. $11.95. LC 77-19361. ISBN 0-529-05484-1.

Here is an excellent new guide, the most ambitious yet attempted for the nest-egg-young syndrome among North American birds. Other books have been limited to eggs (*North American Birds Eggs*, by Chester A. Reed, Dover, 1965); nests (*A Complete Field Guide to Nests in the United States*, by Richard Headstrom, Ives Washburn, 1970); or nests and eggs of the eastern United States (*A Field Guide to Birds' Nests Found East of the Mississippi River*, by Hal H. Harrison, Houghton Mifflin, 1975). In 1975, Colin Harrison published another fine book, identical in format to the present one, entitled *A Field Guide to the Nests, Eggs, and Nestlings of British and European Birds.*

The North American book has 64 color plates (48 of eggs, 16 of nestlings, illustrating 622 eggs and 147 nestlings) plus 59 line drawings. In addition to this rich illustrative material, the text has sizeable species accounts with sections on habitat, nest, breeding season, eggs, incubation, nestling, and nestling period. Hal Harrison's book has the advantage of illustrating in color the eggs *and* the nest, but is otherwise much more limited in scope. Reed goes into much greater detail on the eggs, as does Headstrom on nests. A comprehensive library on the subject really requires all four American titles. In the convenient manner of modern field guides, the present volume sensibly groups the 48 egg plates in one section of the book, rather than dispersing them throughout the phylogenetic sequence of the text. The field guide size is another good feature of this most valuable addition to ornithological literature. The author is to be commended for condemning egg collecting and for urging caution (avoidance if possible) in the presence of breeding birds, which are easily disturbed.   Henry T. Armistead

792.   Palmer, Ralph S., ed. **Handbook of North American Birds. Volume 2, Waterfowl (Part 1). Volume 3, Waterfowl (Part 2).** New Haven, CT, Yale University Press, 1976. 2v. illus. (part col.). index. $35.00/v. LC 62-8259. ISBN 0-300-01902-5(v.2); 0-300-01903-3(v.3).

These encyclopedic volumes are the result of the concerted efforts of 32 authors, who have compiled and synthesized an enormous amount of literature and data, both published and unpublished, on the Anatidae. The descriptions for both sexes of each species cover plumage at all ages and in all seasons, measurements, weight, hybrids, and geographical variations. Field identification, voice, habitat, distribution, migration, banding status, reproduction, survival, habits, and food are also included. Not included are such topics as " . . . controlling waterfowl damage to agricultural crops, habitat movement, hunting methods, aviculture, domestication, parasites, diseases, lead poisoning, biocide studies, navigation, internal anatomy, genetics."

The introductory matter describes the very extensive research involved in preparing this work, tells the conventions used in the text, and includes some terminology definition. Reference is made to acknowledgments, general remarks, and a color chart in the front matter of the earlier volume (*Volume 1, Loons through Flamingos.* Yale University Press, 1962. $35.00) which is relevant to but not repeated in these volumes. Although the dust jacket describes the contributors as "experts," it would have been helpful if degrees, titles, affiliations, and perhaps even some background had been given for these authorities, in addition to their names. The editor is state zoologist, New York State Museum and Science Service. The *Handbook* is sponsored by the American Ornithologists' Union and the New York State Museum and Science Service.

The extensive bibliography is 26 pages long, single-spaced, in the telegraphic, run-on style typical of the German *Handbücher*—not the most easily readable format. The citations do not include article titles, and journal titles are abbreviated. The decision to omit author initials "except when there is a need to distinguish among different authors having the same surname" is an unfortunate one that might at times cause difficulty in identifying and locating these documents.

The *Handbook* is definitely not part of the popular ornithological literature. Its attention to scientific accuracy has not, however, resulted in an overwhelmingly technical text that might otherwise discourage the serious birder from consulting the wealth of information contained. This is an impressive production—exhaustive, yet concise—that will likely become the definitive source on waterfowl for biologists and environmentalists. [R: LJ, 15 Apr 76, p. 999; ARBA 77, p. 671; Choice, Dec 76, p. 1276]   Lorraine Schulte

793.   Todd, Frank S. **Waterfowl: Ducks, Geese & Swans of the World.** 1st ed. New York, Harcourt Brace Jovanovich, 1979. 399p. illus. (col.). bibliog. index. (A Sea World Press Publication). $45.00. LC 79-63521. ISBN 0-15-004036-9.

This is a book with an appeal so broad as to win enthusiastic endorsement from people so diverse as Walter Cronkite to some of the most respected experts in the field—Jean Delacour, Paul Johnsgard, S. Dillon Ripley, Roger Tory Peterson, and others. It earns this approval by the uniqueness of its 788 color photographs and by the clarity, readability, and authenticity of the accompanying text.

Most such volumes rely heavily on paintings and drawings, which highlight features and help in identification, but photos come closer to showing the birds as one sees them in real life with all their diversity of behavior. Without denigrating its other features, this is the work's major achievement. The industry that went into amassing so many pictures of such overall good quality is simply staggering.

There are 16 chapters, with pictures on almost every page. The first chapter of 51 pages is a general introduction to waterfowl, followed by a 2-page chapter on classification. Todd goes with the old standard Delacour-Mayr classification of 10 tribes rather than the recent modification to 13 tribes by Johnsgard. Each of the next 11 chapters is devoted to a single tribe, except for geese and swans, which are divided into two chapters. There follow then a chapter on screamers (whose inclusion in this family is questionable, but which adds interest to the book), a chapter on wildfowl in captivity and propagation, and a chapter on the future of waterfowl. Finally, there are two useful appendices—a chart summarizing all species and subspecies, and a discussion of techniques for photographing waterfowl in the field — and a helpful glossary.

Ornithologists, birders, aviculturists, nature lovers and photographers, hunters, and sports enthusiasts should find this volume fascinating and informative, a treasure in anyone's library. [R: ARBA 81; LJ, 15 Nov 79, p. 2474]   Syd Schoenwetter

FISHES

794.   Wheeler, Alwyne. **Fishes of the World: An Illustrated Dictionary.** Thomas H. Fraser, advisory ed. New York, Macmillan, 1975. 366p. illus. (part col.). $12.98. LC 75-6972. ISBN 0-02-626180-4.

Alwyne Wheeler, a noted British marine biologist and consultant to Unesco, has succeeded in preparing an excellent dictionary on fishes. This illustrated work contains 500 color photographs, 700 line drawings, and descriptions of over 2,000 species of fish. In addition, the introduction presents a brief and pertinent analysis of the various categories of fish, thus providing the user, and especially the layperson, with a general overview of living fishes found in the waters of the earth. A glossary of terms adds to the usefulness of this dictionary.

The 500 color plates, which are grouped in a special section, are arranged in a systematic order by families, so that closely related groups are brought together. Within each family group the plates are arranged alphabetically.

The dictionary section also utilizes an alphabetical arrangement. Separate entries for families are also included and are cross referenced to the genera.

Each fish species is under its scientific name, although vernacular names are also given and cross-indexed. Entries provide information on geographical range, size, habitat, commercial use, biological data, and behavior patterns. The dictionary is of value not only to the professional but also to the amateur ichthyologist. [R: ARBA 76, p. 688; BL, 1 June 76, p. 1424; Choice, May 76, p. 352; LJ, 15 Jan 76, p. 328; LJ, 15 Apr 76, p. 970; WLB, Mar 76, p. 554]   Anna T. Wynar

INSECTS

795.   Leftwich, A. W. **A Dictionary of Entomology.** London, Constable; New York, Crane, Russak, 1976. 360p. $22.50. LC 75-27143. ISBN 0-09-460070-8(Constable); 0-8448-0820-2(Crane, Russak).

The scope of this book is well described in the preface: "it is primarily intended for amateur entomologists, for naturalists with an interest in insects and for students of zoology who may have a special leaning towards this branch of their studies. The author has omitted definitions of general biological terms that may be found in other dictionaries, except where these have a special significance in relation to insects; anatomical terms such as abdomen, heart, eye, etc., have been defined only in terms of the body of an insect." Over 3,000 species are defined, "including many of agricultural, medical or veterinary importance and others with interesting habits or other special features." About 700 definitions deal with anatomical and physiological terms, and an equal number define families and larger groups. Overall there are in excess of 4,000 definitions. The author admits that this dictionary has a somewhat European bias. In addition to the dictionary part, there are a brief bibliography and a classification outline. The emphasis is on English nomenclature where feasible, but many Latin generic names are necessarily included. Running heads indicating the coverage of each page appear at the top. This very fine dictionary is recommended for all libraries with an interest in entomology. [R: Choice, June 76, p. 496; LJ, 1 Apr 76, p. 880; WLB, May 76, p. 746; ARBA 77, p. 674]   Henry T. Armistead

796. Linsenmaier, Walter. **Insects of the World.** Tr. from the German by Leigh E. Chadwick. New York, McGraw-Hill, 1972. 392p. illus. (col.). index. $25.00. LC 78-178047. ISBN 0-07-037953-X.

Linsenmaier is first a painter, then an entomologist, so it is not surprising that the 160 color plates are this book's most striking feature; many of them, both in rendering and in reproduction, rank among the finest colored illustrations of insects ever published. However, this is no mere picture book for the dilettante, since the extensive and accurate text provides an excellent conspectus of the huge and complex class Insecta, useful both to the professional zoologist and to the serious amateur naturalist. Following a general introduction on insect biology, the various orders are taken up in detail, with salient points illustrated both by the color plates and by numerous black-and-white drawings within the text. The arrangement is systematic, except that social insects and aquatic insects are each treated in separate chapters. The emphasis is on the insect as a living organism; economic and medical aspects of entomology are not overlooked, but they are not emphasized. There is a slight bias toward the two orders that contain the greatest number of strikingly beautiful species—Coleoptera and Lepidoptera—but not to the point of imbalance. Two minor weaknesses must be noted: the separation of the captions from the plates to which they refer is awkward, and the indexing could be somewhat fuller. [R: ARBA 74, p. 597; Choice, May 73, p. 490; LJ, 1 Mar 73, p. 755; LJ, 15 Apr 74, p. 1100]   Paul B. Cors

797. Swan, Lester A., and Charles S. Papp. **The Common Insects of North America.** New York, Harper and Row, 1972. 750p. illus. (part col.). bibliog. index. $17.50. LC 75-138765. ISBN 0-06-014181-6.

This introduction to the insects of the continental United States and Canada is written for the reader with some background in general biology but no previous special knowledge of the subject. While technical terminology is necessarily used, the terms are carefully defined, and the amateur naturalist should have no difficulty understanding the concepts presented. A brief general section on insect biology is followed by concise accurate accounts of about 2,400 species (most illustrated by a black-and-white drawing; eight illustrated by a color painting). The emphasis is noticeably on species of economic importance, both harmful and beneficial. Appendixes include charts of insects arranged by geological periods, orders, and families. There are an adequate glossary, an extensive bibliography, and good indexes to common and scientific names and to subjects. One slightly questionable practice is the providing of common names for all species, some of which are coinages (e.g., "guttate scymnus") of little use, but this is a minor weakness.

The only similar work, Donald Borror and Richard White's *A Field Guide to the Insects of America North of Mexico* (Houghton Mifflin, 1970. $9.95), is a guide for identification of families, with few individual species described; the two titles complement rather than duplicate each other. A most useful introduction to a complex subject. [R: ARBA 73, p. 577; BL, 1 Feb 73, p. 502; BL, 15 Feb 73, p. 570; Choice, Mar 73, p. 66; LJ, 15 Feb 73, p. 556; LJ, 15 Apr 73, p. 1245; RQ, Summer 73, p. 410; WLB, Mar 73, p. 609]
Paul B. Cors

798. Watson, Allan, and Paul E. S. Whalley. **The Dictionary of Butterflies and Moths in Color.** New York, McGraw-Hill, 1975. 296p. illus. (col.). bibliog. $39.95. LC 74-30433. ISBN 0-07-068490-1.

This excellent book contains 405 color photographs. "In this book we have illustrated examples of nearly every currently accepted family of the insect group Lepidoptera . . . " (p. vi). The quality of the photographs is good. Many of them illustrate specimens, some with 20, 25, or more species. Others show wild, live examples of one species only.

The dictionary section of the book (pp. 147-296) is an alphabetical arrangement with some 2,000 entries listing genera and families. Within these two groups selected species are also described, stressing unusual ones and/or those illustrated in the photo plates. These are conveniently referenced to the plate number if illustrated. The bibliography is good, and there is a helpful glossary also. Both authors are associated with the Department of Lepidoptera of the British Museum, which has the largest collection of these insects in the world. [R: ARBA 76, p. 690; BL, 1 Sept 76, p. 54; Choice, May 76, p. 351; LJ, 1 Feb 76, p. 539; LJ, 15 Apr 76, p. 970]   Henry T. Armistead

MAMMALS

799.   Mochi, Ugo, and T. Donald Carter. **Hoofed Mammals of the World.** New ed. New York, Scribner's, 1971. 268p. illus. bibliog. index. $9.95. LC 75-169790. ISBN 0-648-12382-7.

When this book was first published in 1953, its combination of scientific informativeness, in Carter's precise, accurate text, and artistic excellence, in Mochi's superb illustrations, made it an immediate success, and it has long been a choice collector's item. It is now back in print, and remains an outstanding work; it is still the only good general handbook of the ungulates in English, covering all living species, many subspecies, and a few recently extinct forms; and Mochi's illustrations still arouse the greatest admiration – nominally silhouettes, each being knife-cut from a single piece of black paper, they are astonishingly detailed, three-dimensional, and lifelike. The principal change in this edition is in format: the awkward folio size of the original has become a more convenient standard octavo, with the illustrations dispersed in the text rather than on separate plates. Textual revision consists of a new introduction, updating of African and Asian geographical names, and changes in the nomenclature of some species. The bibliography is unaltered, but the index is a welcome new feature. This splendid combination of art and science belongs in all academic and public libraries, though libraries owning the original edition may not find it absolutely essential to acquire this reissue. [R: ARBA 72, p. 593; BL, 15 Dec 71, p. 356]   Paul B. Cors

800.   Truitt, Deborah, comp. **Dolphins and Porpoises: A Comprehensive, Annotated Bibliography of the Smaller Cetacea.** Detroit, Gale, 1974. 582p. index. $65.00. LC 73-19803. ISBN 0-8103-0966-1.

This work attempts to list everything ever published on dolphins and porpoises, defined as all members of the families Delphinidae and Platanistidae except the genera Feresa, Globicephala, Orca, and Pseudorca. Perhaps it does not include everything, but it does contain some 3,549 entries, ranging chronologically from 560 B.C. through 1972, citing books, the report literature, and journal articles. Most of the titles are scientific works, but fiction, mythology, and even children's stories are included. The arrangement is by subject; there are 15 major categories, most of them subdivided into smaller subject areas, for a total of 72 sections; under each, the subarrangement is first chronological, then alphabetical by author. Titles in the roman alphabet are cited in the original language; titles in non-roman alphabets are translated into English. Each entry includes a concise but complete bibliographic description; most include a brief descriptive annotation as well. Works not seen by the compiler are so indicated, with a note on the basis for their inclusion if the title does not make this obvious. There are indexes of authors, taxonomic names (including some vernacular names if these are all that appear in the work indexed), and subjects. This comprehensive, well-organized, and well-printed book completely supersedes the few earlier works of similar scope. [R: ARBA 75, p. 688; LJ, 1 Nov 74, p. 2832]   Paul B. Cors

801. Walker, Ernest P., and others. **Mammals of the World.** Rev. for 3rd ed. by John L. Paradiso. Baltimore, Johns Hopkins University Press, 1975. 2v. illus. bibliog. index. $45.00. LC 74-23327. ISBN 0-8018-1657-2.

Mammals of the World is the long-awaited third edition of the late Ernest Walker's classic and highly acclaimed mammalogical work. This revision by John L. Paradiso differs from earlier editions in that the third volume, which was a classified bibliography of worldwide literature, has been dropped because of the monumental task of updating it.

The present edition includes more than 2,000 black-and-white photographs and descriptions of 1,050 genera of mammals, with 270 new photographs by such wildlife photographers as Leonard Lee Rue, III. Ten new genera are included, and most material has been updated. John Paradiso, chief of the branch of biological data, Office of Endangered Species, USFWS, spent more than five years updating and revising this monumental work.

The text describes the size, weight, coloration, food, mating habits, care of the young, and economic importance of each genus. Also included are descriptions of interesting behaviors. Many of the animals are photographed in their natural habitat, although the text still includes many photographs of stuffed specimens, museum skins, or captive animals when better material could not be found. This is especially true of the rarer species. In this respect, the edition is a major improvement over earlier editions. Distinctive features such as webbed claws, snouts, tails, and skeletal features are illustrated. Of special interest are descriptions of various endangered species such as rhinos, leopards, whales, wolves, and the vicuña. Each volume is indexed, and a 24-page world distribution chart greatly aids in locating any genera in the world.

No other single work includes such diverse information on the world's mammal fauna in such a readily accessible format. [R: Choice, Oct 75, p. 984; LJ, 15 May 75, p. 972; ARBA 76, p. 692; BL, 1 Dec 75, p. 528]   John C. Jahoda

MOLLUSKS

802. Abbott, Robert Tucker. **American Seashells: The Marine Mollusca of the Atlantic and Pacific Coasts of North America.** 2nd ed. New York, Van Nostrand Reinhold, 1974. 663p. illus. (part col.). bibliog. index. $49.50. LC 74-7267. ISBN 0-442-20228-8.

This second edition is substantially larger in size and broader in scope than the original edition of 1954, and is now aimed at the needs of the research malacologist rather than the amateur shell collector, though it is not beyond the comprehension of the serious amateur who has mastered the basic concepts and terminology of molluscan biology. It is a complete catalog of all the marine mollusks of North America (including nudibranchs and cephalopods, which are not normally thought of as "seashells"); approximately 2,000 species are described in detail, and 4,500 more are listed without descriptions. The geographic area covered is not clearly described, but it is essentially Canada, the continental United States (including Alaska), Bermuda, and northwest Mexico (Baja California, Sonora, and Sinaloa); however, some West Indian and even Brazilian species are included. The text is supplemented by about 4,000 black-and-white photos and drawings, and 24 well-done colored plates; there is a 65-page index of generic, specific, and common names. The extensive bibliography of the first edition has been replaced with a brief list of the major references used by the author in compiling the work. This will be a basic reference for all research libraries in the field, and, though expensive, it should also be considered by public libraries in areas where there is an interest in shell collecting. [R: ARBA 75, p. 688; WLB, Apr 75, p. 596]   Paul B. Cors

REPTILES AND AMPHIBIANS

803.   Cochran, Doris M., and Coleman J. Goin. **The New Field Book of Reptiles and Amphibians.** New York, Putnam, 1970. 359p. illus. photos. (part col.). bibliog. index. (Nature Field Book). $7.95. LC 69-18168. ISBN 0-399-10292-2.

This is the most comprehensive identification manual yet published in its subject area, providing, as it does, concise and accurate, yet not overly technical, descriptions of every species and subspecies, native and naturalized, of amphibian and reptile so far recorded within the United States (including Alaska and Hawaii). While its intended audience is primarily the amateur naturalist, it will be useful to professional herpetologists as well, especially for its information on distribution and systematics; the treatment of subspecies, in fact, is more appropriately the concern of professional taxonomists than of amateurs.

The textual descriptions are brief but adequate, but the book's use for field identification is hampered by inadequate illustrations; many forms described are not illustrated at all, and for those that are, the black-and-white photos don't always show markings clearly, while the color photos are too small (mostly about 3.5x5.5cm.) and too few (96) to suffice. There are glossaries for each of the six categories. For first purchase, the corresponding titles in Houghton Mifflin's Peterson Field Guide Series (Roger Conant, *A Field Guide to Reptiles and Amphibians of Eastern and Central North America*, 1975; and Robert C. Stebbins, *A Field Guide to Western Reptiles and Amphibians*, 1966) are preferable because of their superior colored illustrations, but this will be a necessary supplemental work. [R: ARBA 76, p. 516; BL, 1 Oct 70, p. 122; Choice, Oct 70, p. 1013; LJ, Aug 70, p. 2700; LJ, 1 Mar 71, p. 790; LJ, 15 Apr 71, p. 1328]   Paul B. Cors

804.   Conant, Roger. **A Field Guide to Reptiles and Amphibians of Eastern and Central North America.** 2nd ed. Illus. by Isabelle Hunt Conant. Boston, Houghton Mifflin, 1975. 429p. illus. (part col.). maps. index. (The Peterson Field Guide Series, No. 12). $10.95; $6.95pa. LC 74-13425. ISBN 0-395-19979-4; 0-395-19977-8pa.

This much-expanded edition is an important handbook for the amateur herpetologist. It identifies species and subspecies of turtles, crocodiles, alligators, lizards, snakes, salamanders, newts, frogs, and toads. Each family and genus is introduced with a brief description, followed by information on distinguishing features, habitat and range for each species, and a brief note on the appearance and range of subspecies. Handy information on such things as collecting and transporting of specimens, care in captivity, and first aid for snakebite is also included.

The expansion over the first edition (1958) is noticeable in many ways. Geographically, the range has been extended into western Texas as well as into the western parts of the states to the north and adjacent Canada—that is, beyond the 100th meridian (the first edition covered east of the 100th only). This was done in order to close the gap between the first edition and R. C. Stebbins' *Field Guide to Western Reptiles and Amphibians* (Houghton Mifflin, 1966), number 16 of the Peterson Field Guide Series. This expanded range, as well as new species within the range of the first edition, has increased the number of species from 391 to 474. The second edition has 48 plates (32 in color) as compared to 40 plates in the first. This edition includes measurements in both inches and metric equivalents, which the earlier edition did not.

The things that remain the same are good. The authority (Dr. Conant is a well-known expert on herpetology), the careful organization, and the comprehensiveness are good recommendations for this edition as a fine basic reference for identification of North American reptiles and amphibians. [R: ARBA 76, p. 693; BL, 1 May 76, p. 1291; Choice, Jan 76, p. 1420]   David Isaa'

805. Ernst, Carl H., and Roger W. Barbour. **Turtles of the United States.** Lexington, University Press of Kentucky, 1973. 347p. illus. (part col.). maps. bibliog. index. $25.00. LC 72-81315. ISBN 0-8131-1272-9.

This is the first comprehensive work in more than two decades on the turtles of the United States (including Hawaii) and the adjacent oceans; it will undoubtedly be the standard reference for some time to come. After a short introduction on general characteristics of turtles, the bulk of the work consists of detailed species accounts emphasizing ecology, behavior, and conservation, including a distribution map and good photographs. There are about 500 illustrations, of which 60 are color photographs. The data, which are derived both from the authors' own researches and from a thorough search of the literature, reflect recent taxonomic thought. Appendixes include a discussion of the evolution of American turtles; notes on the care of turtles in captivity; a list of the parasites, symbionts, and commensals reported from the species included; a glossary of scientific names; and an extensive bibliography emphasizing, but not strictly limited to, the period 1950 through 1970. The good index covers subjects and common and scientific names. Overall, the treatment is thorough enough for the professional zoologist, but it is within the understanding of the amateur naturalist who has a good basic knowledge of vertebrate zoology. [R: ARBA 74, p. 598; BL, 1 Sept 73, p. 17; LJ, July 73, p. 2127; Choice, Feb 74, p. 1891; LJ, 15 Apr 74, p. 1099]   Paul B. Cors

BIBLIOGRAPHIES

806. Hammond, Kenneth A., George Macinko, and Wilma B. Fairchild, eds. **Sourcebook on the Environment: A Guide to the Literature.** Chicago, University of Chicago Press, 1978. 613p. index. $22.00. LC 77-17407. ISBN 0-226-31522-3.

The rapidly expanding literature on the environment is discussed in this volume of 24 bibliographic essays. The book was developed with the aid of a government contract from original work by the Association of American Geographers. Twenty-six specialists, mainly geographers, but also including ecologists, geologists, and urban planners, participated in writing the essays.

The book is arranged in three major sections: environmental perspectives, case studies, and "major elements of the environment." Each essay is followed by a bibliography, current through 1976. Many essays appear to have been published elsewhere, but there is little duplication of information due to careful editing. A fourth section contains further study aids: a briefly annotated list of 100 pertinent periodicals; a list of environmental organizations; a review of federal environmental legislation since 1785; plus notes on helpful bibliographies, abstracts, and indexes. Because of the format, access to specific information must be gained through the subject index.

This work is not intended to be an exhaustive study of environmental literature, but is surprisingly comprehensive, covering the range of popular and technical works. The *Sourcebook* serves not only as a guide to the literature, but as an introduction for the nonspecialist to current environmental concerns. It will be useful to students, researchers, and educators. [R: LJ, Aug 78, p. 1498; BL, 15 Nov 78, p. 577; LJ, 1 May 79, p. 1007; RQ, Winter 78, p. 205; ARBA 80, p. 651]   Janet H. Littlefield

DICTIONARIES AND ENCYCLOPEDIAS

807. Allaby, Michael. **A Dictionary of the Environment.** New York, Van Nostrand Reinhold, 1977. 532p. $17.95. LC 77-12190. ISBN 0-442-20288-1.

This dictionary contains about 6,000 words and phrases currently in use in various fields that touch environmental concerns. Some disciplines covered include botany, zoology, chemistry, physics, geology, meteorology, and biology, as well as others. The words chosen for inclusion are given current meaning as they relate to the environment, and any new or specialized meanings are given. Definitions vary in length, ranging from a brief sentence to a lengthy paragraph; all are concise, well worded, and to the point without sacrificing comprehension. The information tends to be technical; when a term may have more than one meaning, all are provided. Many acronyms, both British and American English, as well as some of UN and international origin, are included. A few proper names, organizations, and laws are also defined. The arrangement is, of course, alphabetical, and there are no illustrations. An appendix lists organizations concerned with the environment in the United Kingdom.

A slight British emphasis is obvious but does not detract from the usefulness of the book. One confusing factor appears until the user realizes that one-word definitions are essentially the same as "see" references. For example, for "glass fibre," the definition is simply the word "Fiberglass." There is a separate entry under "Fiberglass." For "glass fibre reinforced cement," the definition reads "See cement." The user must discover alone that one-word definitions usually have a separate entry under that term; but "see" references are also included at the end of long definitions to alert the user to similar or related terms. Allaby and a panel of experts in various fields have taken a complex, multifaceted subject and created a coherent, broad-based dictionary of terms on which environmentalists can base further growth and understanding of the vocabulary unique to this field. This book is very useful. [R: WLB, Oct 78, p. 187; ARBA 79, p. 691; BL, 15 Sept 79, p. 146; Choice, Nov 78, p. 1191]   Susan Ebershoff-Coles

808. **Encyclopedia of Environmental Science and Engineering.** Eds., James R. Pfafflin and Edward N. Ziegler. New York, Gordon and Breach, 1976. 2v. illus. index. $258.00/set. LC 72-89286. ISBN 0-677-14670-1.

Encyclopedia of Environmental Science and Engineering is an attempt to combine an overview of key environmental areas with a treatment in some depth of specific subjects within these fields. For the environmentalist and the practicing engineer, the *Encyclopedia* will provide general insight into disciplines closely related to their own and will further a general appreciation of the environmental sciences. Answers to some specific questions will be found also within these pages. For the interested and sophisticated layperson, the *Encyclopedia* may prove interesting and rewarding reading.

The work has an international outlook: one editor is Canadian, the other American, and the contributors are drawn from Canada, the United States, and Great Britain. Subjects covered are arranged alphabetically, and cross references are provided where appropriate. References are given at the end of each article, and an index is also included. Unfortunately, there is no table of contents. Though this is to be expected in an encyclopedia, we believe that a table of contents might have helped in this instance to show the general scope of the work.

There is no doubt that this is a useful reference work. Individual articles are generally well written and concise. The length of the articles has been limited to avoid overspecialization and to maintain readability. [R: Choice, Sept 77, p. 830; LJ, 1 Apr 77, p. 785; ARBA 78, p. 686]   Harry Weihs

809. **Grzimek's Encyclopedia of Ecology.** Bernhard Grzimek, ed.-in-chief. New York, Van Nostrand Reinhold, 1977 (c1976). 705p. illus. (part col.). bibliog. index. $39.50. LC 76-9297. ISBN 0-442-22948-8.

This is not strictly an encyclopedia in terms of format, and some libraries might find it most useful in the circulating collection, but it may earn the title on the basis of its comprehensive coverage. A translation of a work first published in Switzerland in 1973, it consists of a collection of 51 essays by 43 authors (all but one German or Austrian) divided into two groups: "The Environment of Animals" and "The Environment of Man." The overall quality of the contributions is high, and all should be accessible to the reader with a basic knowledge of biology; the first section tends to be more detached and objective than the second, which is frankly polemic in approach.

The regular use of Old World, especially European, species and localities to illustrate specific points is hardly unexpected in view of the book's authorship and original audience, but could limit its usefulness for some American readers. Metric measurements are used throughout; conversion tables to and from Anglo-American units are provided. The work is liberally illustrated with color plates (most of superior quality), line drawings in the text, and a few maps. The selective bibliography includes titles in English and German, some published as recently as 1976. The index consists mainly of English and scientific names of animal families and species, with few topical entries, so it is of limited reference help. A few typographical errors were noted, and on page 405 a spotted skunk (Spilogale) is mislabelled a striped skunk (Mephitis), but these are minor blemishes in a generally accurate and readable work. [R: LJ, Aug 77, p. 1626; WLB, Oct 77, p. 186; ARBA 78, p. 686; BL, 1 Mar 78, p. 1128; LJ, 1 Mar 78, p. 509]   Paul B. Cors

810.   Hunt, V. Daniel. **Energy Dictionary.** New York, Van Nostrand Reinhold, 1979. 518p. bibliog. $22.50. LC 78-9707. ISBN 0-442-27395-9.

The *Energy Dictionary* contains definitions of some 4,000 terms related to the production, conservation, and environmental aspects of energy. Definitions are generally brief, averaging 2 to 3 lines, although some 10 to 15% are more extensive, with the maximum being 10 to 12 lines. The book also includes a brief overview of the energy situation (17 pages), as well as a glossary of acronyms, conversion factors, and an extensive bibliography. The level of technicality is moderate, and the definitions should be comprehensible to the educated layperson as well as to students and others interested in energy.

This book is by no means a substitute for more detailed reference tools like McGraw-Hill's *Encyclopedia of Energy* (see entry 811), but will be valuable for quick identification of terms. It is similar in focus and level to the *Energy Reference Handbook* (Government Institutes, 1977. $18.50). Of a sample of 35 terms, 11 that appeared in the *Energy Reference Handbook* were not in Hunt, and 11 that appeared in Hunt were not in the *Handbook*. The remaining 13 are terms defined in both books, and 6 of the definitions are identical, leading one to assume that some of the same source material was used in both compilations. There are a few omissions that detract from the overall worth of the *Dictionary*; for example, while the glossary lists most of the acronyms cited in the text, there are no citations for STE (solar thermal electric), PVC (poly vinyl chloride), or TF (thermal factor), even though these appear in the body of the text. ERDA is neither defined nor listed in the glossary. Given current interest in energy, this dictionary should be a useful addition to the reference collections of public and academic libraries. [R: ARBA 80, p. 648; Choice, Sept 79, pp. 798-800; LJ, 15 May 79, p. 1127; WLB, June 79, p. 728]

Jay K. Lucker

811.   Lapedes, Daniel N., ed.-in-chief. **Encyclopedia of Energy.** New York, McGraw-Hill, 1976. 785p. illus. index. LC 76-19026. ISBN 0-07-045261-X.

The stated purpose of the McGraw-Hill *Encyclopedia of Energy* is to "provide students, librarians, scientists, engineers, teachers and the general public with a better understanding of the issues surrounding energy and its use." To meet this goal, new material written especially for this volume was combined with articles selected from the *McGraw-Hill Encyclopedia of Science and Technology* and its yearbooks.

The encyclopedia is divided into two sections. The first, "Energy Perspectives," analyzes current energy policy in terms of economic, political, and technical issues in six essays. The second section, "Energy Technology," follows standard encyclopedic form, with an alphabetical arrangement of technical articles.

An excellent overview of the "energy crisis" is presented in the six essays, each written by a practitioner in the field. The development of different forms of energy is placed in historical perspective through discussions of the effects of economic influences, changing political alignments, and scientific developments on current energy policy and use. While they may be somewhat dated now, these essays provide both the layperson and the specialist with an overall look at the issues of today. Cross references link the essays to each other and to the technical articles that follow.

The technical articles range in length from a paragraph to several pages. Each begins with an attempt to define the topic, followed by a technical discussion and, in most cases, a bibliography. Because of the complexity of many of these articles, the layperson and nonspecialist will find this part of the volume more difficult to understand. But students, librarians, and others with some technical background should find this a highly useful compendium on energy.

While originally skeptical of another one-volume encyclopedia culled from the pages of a more extensive work, I have found this volume to be superbly designed, clearly written, and amply illustrated. It will serve as an important and useful reference source for students, librarians, teachers, and others involved in solving today's energy problems.

Susan Thorpe

812.   Parker, Sybil P., ed. **McGraw-Hill Encyclopedia of Environmental Science.** 2nd ed. New York, McGraw-Hill, 1980. 858p. illus. maps. index. $34.50. LC 79-28098. ISBN 0-07-045264-4.

As a reviewer noted in 1974 when the first edition of the *Encyclopedia* was published, this is "authoritative, complete, and easy to use. It is probably the best general work on the environment" (*American Reference Books Annual 75*, entry 1533). The second edition merits the same comments and even additional praise since it is substantially updated and revised. The structure and format of the volume are comparable to the earlier edition and, indeed, to all McGraw-Hill dictionaries and encyclopedias that are spin-offs from the larger tools which encompass science and technology in general. In this instance, the fourth edition of the *McGraw-Hill Encyclopedia of Science and Technology* (1977) is the base, but the articles are supplemented and analytically indexed within this volume. Moreover, the majority of the articles have bibliographies, and a selected sampling indicated that numerous citations from 1975 through 1979 have been included. Certain weaknesses in coverage have also been corrected, although some data, such as specific references to commonly known examples of environmental concerns, e.g., Love Canal, are not located through the index even though found in an article (cf. Industrial Waste). At the same time, earlier weaknesses such as incomplete listing of laws and outdated articles have been corrected.

The familiar editorial direction of Daniel N. Lapedes has been replaced by that of Sybil P. Parker, but, as suggested above, there are no resultant problems. As she notes in the "Preface," "more than 250 articles are organized in two sections—a section containing five feature articles on topics of broad, general interest, and a section of alphabetically arranged articles dealing with the basic scientific and technical concepts. Each article was prepared by a specialist. Many were written especially for this volume. . . . There are 650 photographs, diagrams, charts, graphs, and line drawings to supplement the text. . . . " It is clear from the preceding comments that the volume has a valuable breadth of coverage in a field of immense significance at this time: the entire spectrum of technology, conservation, waste management, climate and weather components, ecological interactions, pollution, and management of environmental problems is covered. The five feature articles are "Environmental Protection," "Precedents for Weather Extremes," "Environmental Satellites," "Urban Planning," and "Environmental Analysis." In particular, the first three titles have extensive bibliographies and contemporary data illustrated appropriately.

The audience for such an encyclopedia is obviously mixed. It is a useful tool for the general public, especially if the more expensive multivolumed encyclopedia is not available. Moreover, its detailed, easy-to-use index and internal cross referencing serve effectively to locate the general entry as well as subsets of relevant information. Although most college-level individuals would not find its contents difficult to comprehend, at least in the opening sections of each article, the *Encyclopedia* is not directed to the reader who has a largely non-scientific vocabulary and a rudimentary understanding of technology. The work would also be of value to professionals in the business and scientific communities who want concise and accurate syntheses of topics encompassed by environmental science.

Laurel Grotzinger

813.   **The World Energy Book: An A-Z Atlas and Statistical Source Book.** David Crabbe and Richard McBride, consultant eds. and principal contributors. New York, Nichols Publishing, 1978. 259p. $25.00. LC 78-50805. ISBN 0-89397-032-8.

Essentially, this is an encyclopedia of energy containing about 1,500 terms, which has appended to it an atlas (24 maps) of energy resources and 24 statistical and miscellaneous tables (conversions, timescales, etc.). The A-Z section, which forms the largest part of the work, is well designed with easy to see, boldface headings. The diagrams and line drawings that help explain things and/or concepts are well done and are located close to the related term. The definitions and descriptions are readable and nontechnical. The text includes cross references printed in italics. The maps in the atlas section (all black and white) are generally clear and uncluttered. While some maps (e.g., location of coal fields) give information readily obtainable elsewhere, others seem to be unique, at least in the way in which the concepts are presented. The same holds true for the statistical tables. All in all, this is a rather handy source for basic information on energy. As mentioned earlier, the work is nontechnical and, as such, will probably appeal more to the interested layperson or student than to the specialist and research worker. [R: ARBA 79, p. 691; Choice, June 79, p. 514; LJ, 15 Jan 79, p. 180; RQ, Summer 79, p. 401; WLB, Apr 79, p. 589]   David Isaak

DIRECTORIES

814.   Crowley, Maureen, ed. **Energy: Sources of Print and Nonprint Materials.** New York, Neal-Schuman Publishers, 1980. 341p. index. $17.95. LC 79-26574. ISBN 0-918212-16-2.

Nearly 800 organizations providing information on energy are covered in this informative reference guide. Comprised primarily of U.S. organizations, emphasis is placed on material of interest to the nonspecialist. Included are governmental organizations, businesses, professional, civic, and educational groups.

The book is arranged by type of organization. Each entry contains the name, address, and telephone number of the organization; a description of its major activities and programs; and a list of representative publications. Whenever possible the price, date of publication, and number of pages are noted. Particularly noteworthy is the inclusion of free and inexpensive material. An appendix of names and addresses of grass roots groups arranged by state and very complete sources, title, and subject indexes complete this volume.

Comparable to *Energy: A Guide to Organizations and Information Resources in the United States* (Public Affairs Clearinghouse, 1978), this directory is easier to use and more complete. With interest continuing to grow in the energy field, this book will be a worthwhile acquisition for most libraries.   Barbara M. Howes

HANDBOOKS

815.   Considine, Douglas M., ed.-in-chief. **Energy Technology Handbook.** New York, McGraw-Hill, 1977. 1v. (various paging). illus. index. $58.50. LC 76-17653. ISBN 0-07-012430-2.

"This Handbook concentrates on those fundamental technologies which relate to energy sources, energy reserves, energy conversion, energy transportation and transmission." Over 140 experts in the field have put together explanations of well-established practices and reviews of the more important progress made over the past years.

The impressive handbook is divided into nine sections—coal technology, gas technology, petroleum technology, chemical fuels technology, nuclear energy technology, solar energy technology, geothermal energy technology, hydrogen technology, and power technology trends. Each section is complete in itself, covering all the information that is needed, from definitions to historical background to current practices to future predictions. Numerous charts and graphs and excellent photos and diagrams make this handbook one of the best available. The book was intended for scientists, engineers, and technologists, but it is also a very good reference source for librarians, legislators, government leaders, economists, planners, social reformers, politicians, and the public information media. [R: LJ, Aug 77, p. 1626; ARBA 78, p. 688; Choice, Jan 78, p. 1478; LJ, 1 Apr 78, p. 722; SLJ, Jan 79, p. 21]   H. Robert Malinowsky

816.   Loftness, Robert L. **Energy Handbook.** New York, Van Nostrand Reinhold, 1978. 741p. illus. maps. index. $49.50. LC 77-18190. ISBN 0-442-24836-9.
    This comprehensive handbook presents in graphic and narrative form a well-selected portion of the published information on energy. Hundreds of sources were consulted, and pertinent bits of information were pulled from each source and reprinted with the full citation of the source given so that the reader can consult the original document. Some of the data and projections are controversial, since equally qualified authorities may have reached different conclusions. In cases such as this, both views are given.
    The data, arranged in 16 chapters, covers: energy and man; fossil and mineral energy resources; renewable energy resources; energy consumption trends; energy consumption projections; recovery of fossil fuels; nuclear power; geothermal energy; solar energy; energy conversion and storage; energy efficiency and conservation; energy transport; environmental aspects of energy use; environmental control of energy; energy costs; and energy futures. Each chapter is further subdivided, making it easy to find the topic that is being researched. This is fortunate, since the index is only two and one-half pages and rather inadequate for a book of over 700 pages. The graphs, charts, and diagrams are extremely well reproduced, but the photographs, in many instances, are not too clear. In spite of these failings, this is one of the better handbooks that has been published and should prove to be quite useful as a major resource on energy. [R: ARBA 80, p. 650; Choice, Sept 79, p. 802; LJ, 1 Apr 79, p. 816; WLB, Apr 79, p. 589]   H. Robert Malinowsky

817.   McRae, Alexander, and Janice L. Dudas, eds. **The Energy Sourcebook.** Howard Rowland, consulting ed. Germantown, MD, Aspen Systems, 1977. 724p. illus. index. (A Publication of The Center for Compliance Information). LC 77-99086. ISBN 0-89443-030-0.
    In this hefty volume, one may find answers to a large number of energy-related questions. McRae and Dudas have compiled a comprehensive, but somewhat practically oriented, work that consolidates information from a wide variety of sources to provide "background information and guidelines . . . to facilitate sound energy management and prudent corporate decisions." Although it is well suited for elements of the academic community, this book will be equally valuable for the practicing technical professional or business executive. The *Energy Sourcebook* covers all forms of energy, both renewable and non-renewable, quantitatively describing in detail the origin of the energy crunch, forecasts of the supplies of the various alternative resources, and projections of consumption. The presentation is accurate and unbiased throughout. It makes perfectly clear, however, the dilemma the country faces and, with it, the urgency of greater conservation as well as expansion of new technologies.
    In the first two chapters, the Carter administration's national energy plan is discussed and the outlook from the present to the year 2000 is developed using comparative "scenarios" based upon that program. In each scenario, the recurrent price-supply-governmental regulation theme nicely conveys the proper perspective so badly needed today by everyone. The heart of the book is chapter 3, in which some 42% of the text is

devoted to analyses of 15 individual sources. The appropriate emphasis here is given to coal. Solar is also strong, but nuclear is neglected to a slight degree. The processes and economics of utilization of each source are included. Other chapters furnish energy-usage data for nine industries and list numerous specific suggestions for improved energy management by industry and commerce. In addition to the above information, the volume contains three appendices; these give a complete reprint of Public Law 95-91 (the "Department of Energy Organization Act"), a synopsis of conservation approaches in the states, and a summary of national issues, with the roles of the various federal agencies in each.

The book has footnote references to source documents of all kinds, many of which are government-generated. There is an abundance of crisply reproduced and easily readable tables, charts, graphs, diagrams, and maps. The index is quite commendable since it incorporates cross references effectively. Insufficient editorial control is evident in two chapters, where the numbering of figures implies that some have been omitted. At any rate, the identification of all the illustrations should be redone for clarity and consistency. The absence of a key to the abbreviations is also an impediment, but a minor one. Overall, the book should be a useful acquisition for academic libraries with technical patronages. [R: ARBA 79, p. 687; LJ, 1 May 78, p. 962]   Philip H. Kitchens

37 EARTH SCIENCES

ENCYCLOPEDIAS

818.   Fairbridge, Rhodes W., ed. **The Encyclopedia of Geochemistry and Environmental Sciences.** New York, Academic Press, 1972. 1321p. illus. index. (Encyclopedia of Earth Sciences Series, Vol. IVA). $82.50. LC 75-152326. ISBN 0-12-786460-1.

This volume of the Encyclopedia of Earth Sciences Series covers the chemistry of the earth and its compositional evolution. Minerals are mentioned only briefly. Environmental science is included with geochemistry because of the geologist's current concern about the pollution of our air and water. The detailed entries provide clear, concise discussions, with all the needed chemical and mathematical notations, graphs, charts, and illustrations needed. This is a highly recommended encyclopedia for those in the fields of geochemistry, geology, and chemistry. References for additional reading and cross references to other entries in this volume and to entries in other volumes of the series are included at the end of each discussion. This makes it mandatory to have the complete series. [R: ARBA 73, p. 587; Choice, Feb 73, p. 1572]   H. Robert Malinowsky

819.   Parker, Sybil P., ed.-in-chief. **McGraw-Hill Encyclopedia of Ocean and Atmospheric Sciences.** New York, McGraw-Hill, 1980. 580p. illus. index. $34.50. LC 79-18644. ISBN 0-07-045267-9.

This work is a companion to the *McGraw-Hill Encyclopedia of the Geological Sciences* (see entry 825). Both are essentially off-shoots of the popular *McGraw-Hill Encyclopedia of Science and Technology* (4th ed., 1977), retaining many of the articles (presumably intact) from that comprehensive source, while adding others written specifically for the present volumes. There are no indications as to which articles are new and which represent the older material — a distinct drawback for science readership. However, even with the carry-over from the 1977 *Encyclopedia of Science and Technology*, the *Encyclopedia of Ocean and Atmospheric Sciences* is a useful and informative volume to have on hand for the general science audience. Its 236 major articles are authoritative, and present hard facts in a very readable format. The 500 photographs, drawings, maps, and graphs enhance the text. Included are a listing of the 200 international authorities who contributed to the book, a subject index, and numerous cross references. [R: ARBA 81; BL, 1 Nov 80, p. 410; Choice, June 80, p. 520; LJ, 1 Feb 80, p. 395; WLB, Mar 80, p. 464]   Dederick C. Ward

820.   **The Planet We Live On: Illustrated Encyclopedia of the Earth Sciences.** Ed. by Cornelius S. Hurlbut, Jr. New York, Harry N. Abrams, 1976. 527p. illus. (part col.). $40.00. LC 75-29977. ISBN 0-8109-0415-2.

This reviewer is not aware of a *single-volume* English-language encyclopedia of the earth sciences published since the now very old *Larousse Encyclopedia of the Earth* (Prometheus, 1961) — so we are long overdue to receive the present work, and it is a good one! The editors and contributors are well known, and the articles reflect their expertise at including the salient points and writing for the layperson without sacrificing technical necessities. Articles are signed and vary in length according to the topic discussed. There are approximately 600 black-and-white photographs and diagrams, including a colored photo essay discussing earth history and the generalities of the subjects making up earth science. An appendix includes an index to the entries by subject (in the main body, entries are arranged alphabetically in a single sequence), a table of mineral properties, and tables of statistics concerning the principal physical features of the earth. The cross references in the text are keyed by an asterisk to other entries in the encyclopedia. The metric system is adopted, except that English equivalents are given where helpful.

With respect to its content, this encyclopedia should appeal to high schools, public libraries of every size, and undergraduate college libraries; but because the articles are so readable, professionals on any level will find this work fascinating. [R: LJ, 1 Nov 76, p. 2268; WLB, Nov 76, p. 263; ARBA 77, p. 690; BL, 15 Apr 77, p. 1293; Choice, Apr 77, p. 182; LJ, 1 Mar 77, p. 548; LJ, 15 Apr 77, p. 876; RQ, Winter 76, p. 186]

Dederick C. Ward

GEOLOGY

821. American Geological Institute. **Dictionary of Geological Terms.** Rev. ed. Garden City, NY, Anchor Press/Doubleday, 1976. 472p. $3.95pa. LC 73-9004. ISBN 0-385-08452-8.

In 1972 the American Geological Institute published *Glossary of Geology*, edited by Margaret Gary as the first comprehensive dictionary on this subject. It contained some 33,000 entries. This abridgment contains 8,500 of the more common definitions found in the glossary, plus 1,000 new definitions that update the basic volume. There are terms that deal with recent advances in earth sciences, such as environmental geology, plate tectonics, and sea floor spreading. Also included are brief definitions of such areas as stratigraphy, sedimentation, petrology, volcanology, geochemistry, geomorphology, geophysics, nuclear geology, invertebrate paleontology, and mineralogy. This is by far the best dictionary of geology available in paperback. [R: ARBA 77, p. 690; WLB, Nov 76, p. 262]

Bohdan S. Wynar

822. Challinor, John. **A Dictionary of Geology.** 5th ed. Cardiff, University of Wales Press; New York, Oxford University Press, 1978. 365p. index. $14.95. LC 78-4530. ISBN 0-19-520063-2.

Compared to the 33,000 terms in the American Geological Institute's *Glossary of Geology* (1972), the number of terms in Challinor's *Dictionary of Geology* (1,500) seems meager. But the number is all that's meager. The definitions are rich and clear and flavored with quotations and citations to significant discussions. With the exception of a few British terms, most of the 1,500 entries should be familiar to anyone with a bachelor's degree in geology. Terms are not only defined but placed in relation to other terms and concepts; they are also set in the context of their historical usage, providing helpful information for both those who are familiar with the terms and those who are not.

Rather than a simple dictionary, Challinor has written a book which probes geology "by examining the meaning and usage of names and terms that stand for the more significant things, facts and concepts of the science" (preface, 1st ed.). Special features include a list of prefixes and suffixes used in geology and a classified index of terms.

Nancy J. Pruett

823. **The Encyclopedia of World Regional Geology, Part I: Western Hemisphere (Including Antarctica and Australia).** Ed. by Rhodes W. Fairbridge. New York, Academic Press, 1975. 704p. illus. index. (Encyclopedia of Earth Sciences Series, Vol. 8A). $48.00. LC 75-1406. ISBN 0-12-786461-X.

The previously published volumes in the Encyclopedia of Earth Sciences Series, under the general editorship of Fairbridge, have all been of value in earth science collections; the present volume will be needed as well. Part II of this volume will cover the Eastern Hemisphere. If readers approach the reference shelf and pick up part I, whose spine stamping tells them that it covers the Western Hemisphere, they may be surprised at finding a resume of the geology of New Caledonia on page 365. A quick look in the preface explains all: Antarctica, Australia, and the Australasian islands are here because of space problems — the editors apparently wished to keep the two parts nearly equal in size. With this explanation of the rather cavalier manner in which Dowden, Hutchinson, and Ross have demarcated the world (shades of Pope Alexander VI!), we proceed with a description of the volume at hand.

The various geographical areas are arranged alphabetically, beginning with American Samoa and ending with the Windward Islands. The entries vary greatly in length: that for the Cocos (Keeling) Islands is only about one-fourth of a page; that for the United States is much longer. Generally, an entry contains a brief geographical introduction and notes, longer or shorter as required, on such topics as rock units, geologic regions, geological history, mineral deposits, orogenic history, paleontology, and the like. The illustrations (all in black and white) consist of geologic and other maps, stratigraphic correlation charts, geologic cross-sections, and some photographs. Geologic maps in black and white do not do the best job, of course, but their use is quite adequate in the present context.

The longer entries are divided in some appropriate manner: Australia, for example, is described as a whole and then by each state; the United States is divided into its major physiographic provinces. Each entry also contains a list of references for further reading and a few cross references to lead the reader to other entries. In the entry for Grenada, for example, we are told to check the entries for two nearby islands and "West Indies" for an overview. Overall indices for author and subject are provided. Through the latter, one may find all the references to gold or to fossil names, etc.

This volume satisfies a great need. An overview of the geology of the American Great Plains may not be too difficult to find elsewhere, but try finding the same for Paraguay or Norfolk Island! As a reference tool, this encyclopedia will help the errant geologist avoid quite a few artful bibliographical ploys. Highly recommended. [R: Choice, Mar 76, p. 43; ARBA 77, p. 691]   R. G. Schipf

824.   Fairbridge, Rhodes W., and Joanne Bourgeois, eds. **The Encyclopedia of Sedimentology.** Stroudsburg, PA, Dowden, Hutchinson & Ross; distr., New York, Academic Press, 1978. 901p. illus. maps. index. (Encyclopedia of Earth Sciences Series, Vol. 6). $65.00. LC 78-18259. ISBN 0-87933-152-6.

An extremely well-written and designed addition to the Encyclopedia of Earth Sciences Series, this volume provides broad coverage of the field of sedimentology. There are short (usually one to three pages), basic articles on specific subjects, arranged alphabetically. The articles, written by qualified specialists, discuss current and historical issues on such topics as argillaceous rocks, base-surge deposits, biostratinomy, carbonate sediments — diagenisis, crude-oil composition and migration, grain-size studies, submarine canyons, and fan valleys. Martian and lunar sedimentology are also included.

These basic discussions are followed by extensive references to more detailed information, and there are cross references at the end of each article to lead the user to related topics. Along with the 27-page index, these make it very easy to locate the correct subject entry. There are numerous diagrams and photographs that illustrate important concepts in the text. Of interest to sedimentologists, petroleum and coal geologists, social scientists, hydrologists, and archaeologists, the *Encyclopedia* is highly recommended to academic or special libraries serving such scientists. [R: ARBA 80, p. 655; Choice, Apr 79, p. 202]

Barbara A. Rice

825. Lapedes, Daniel N., ed.-in-chief. **McGraw-Hill Encyclopedia of the Geological Sciences.** New York, McGraw-Hill, 1978. 915p. illus. index. $29.50. LC 78-18425. ISBN 0-07-045265-2.

Due to the environmental movement of the 1960s and the energy problems of the 1970s, interest in the study of the earth has increased. This encyclopedia provides a comprehensive treatment of the geological sciences, including geology, geochemistry, geophysics, and related aspects of oceanography and meteorology. The often extensive articles, which are listed alphabetically, were selected by a board of consulting editors and either have been taken from the *McGraw-Hill Encyclopedia of Science and Technology* (4th ed., 1977) or have been written especially for this volume. A detailed analytical index provides easy access. The popular approach is enhanced by over 700 photographs, maps, tables, drawings, graphs, and diagrams. An alphabetical list of contributors and their affiliations and a "Table of Accepted Mineral Species" (giving chemical formula, crystallography class, hardness, and specific gravity) complete this most welcome addition to geologic literature.   Judith G. Gerber

826. Sarjeant, William A. S. **Geologists and the History of Geology: An International Bibliography from the Origins to 1978.** 1st ed. New York, Arno Press, 1980. 5v. index. $350.00. LC 77-78075. ISBN 0-405-10469-3.

The field of "geology" or earth sciences with its many interrelated disciplines and sub-disciplines has not been an area in which comprehensive reference sources are prolific. Although several national and international bibliographies exist, each has suffered from one or more problems related to coverage, currency, and authority. This contribution to the field does not fill the total need which obviously exists, but it does attempt "to bring together details of all those works written in languages using the Latin alphabet which deal with the history of geology" (general introduction, p. 5). This includes "the origin and growth of geology, of its societies, associations and collections, of the history of the petroleum industry, . . . and of the lives of the men and women whose endeavours have built the science of geology. . . . In concept at least, the bibliography embraces all books, journals and articles published before December 31, 1978. . . . There are undoubtedly serious inadequacies in coverage of relevant items published during that year [1978] and even during the later part of 1977" (general introduction, p. 5). The compiler then goes on to estimate that he probably includes references to between 50 and 60% of the books and journal articles which might exist. Regardless, this five-volume set does give a broad picture of the literature of the field, and benefits greatly from the 20 years of effort which William A. S. Sarjeant has devoted to his labor of love. Dr. Sarjeant is well known for his primary research in various aspects of the history of geology, has published several books, and is a fellow of the Explorers Club in New York.

In addition to the data explaining the coverage of the work, the first volume outlines the "Sources of Information Employed," "Details Concerning the Presentation of Information," which covers arrangement and contents of entries, the "List of Serial Publications Comprehensively Researched," and a note about supplements which indicates Sarjeant's plan to produce five-year updates of the subject matter.

The five-volume set does present a unique picture of both geologists and their writings. Volume I contains five sections: 1) General Introduction, 2) General Works, 3) Historical Accounts of Societies, Museums and Other Institutions Concerned with Geology, 4) Histories of the Petroleum Industry, and 5) Accounts of Events Significant in the History of Geology. Each section has an explanatory introduction and then the bibliography. Volumes II and III contain the biographical studies of the individual geologists arranged alphabetically by name plus, in volume III, a section on prospectors, diviners, and mining engineers. Volume IV has two indexes: 1) by nationality and country, and 2) by specialty.

Finally, volume V has a comprehensive index of authors, editors, and translators. The total pages in the five volumes number 4,526.

The major weakness, but also the factor which made the volumes possible, lies in the fact that the final typeset is computer-produced and reproduced. The last section of volume V describes the nature of the computer technique, including programming, general project problems, and solutions. This gives the potential bibliographer a quick overview of the use of the computer in a compilation as massive as this one, since there is a discussion of text processing, data entry and coding, and the selected solutions. The final product is not impossible to use effectively: it has been spatially designed to provide visual clarity; the typeface is one that reflects the regular alphabet; and much care has been given to cross references through the index. In addition, the volumes are well bound although four of the five are over two inches thick and therefore not easy to handle. Rebinding would be difficult given the narrow margins, but should not be necessary under normal use.

In summary, this undoubtedly can be described as a "landmark bibliography." There are an estimated 30,000 entries arranged by subject with a detailed author, editor, and translator index. Citations are not abbreviated, and an internal breakdown sets them within a chronological pattern as well as by subject. The two large biographical volumes contain narratives about the geologists, their contributions, autobiographical and biographical works. As noted earlier, there are omissions, but the many years of compiling and the general extent of its coverage justify its inclusion in every library serving the wide community of geologists, historians, and researchers in related disciplines. [R: ARBA 81; LJ, 15 Oct 80, p. 2191]   Laurel Grotzinger

HYDROLOGY

827.   Geraghty, James J., and others. **Water Atlas of the United States.** 3rd ed. Port Washington, NY, Water Information Center, 1973. 1v. (unpaged). illus. maps. $40.00. LC 73-76649. ISBN 0-912394-03-X.

A good general visual guide to the water situation in the United States, including Alaska and Hawaii. The information is presented in 122 maps arranged on a common base, so that the data can be compared from map to map. The data cover all aspects of precipitation, surface water, and ground water, plus new material on water pollution, water quality, water conservation/recreation, and water law. The text that accompanies each map defines the subject (e.g., water hardness) and gives facts and statistics necessary to cover the subject. A good companion to water facts in tabular form as presented in the *Water Encyclopedia* (Water Information Center, 1970. 550p. $40.00). [R: ARBA 75, p. 711; Choice, Sept 74, p. 919; WLB, Apr 74, p. 674]   Dederick C. Ward

METEOROLOGY

828.   **Climates of the States: National Oceanic and Atmospheric Administration Narrative Summaries, Tables, and Maps for Each State.** 2nd ed. Detroit, Gale, 1980. 2v. maps. $68.00. LC 80-22622. ISBN 0-8103-1036-8.

This reprints a U.S. government document originally issued in 51 separate parts at $0.25 each between 1976 and 1978. Appended are the maps which appeared in the first edition of the series, but dropped from the second. Volume 1 includes Alabama to North Dakota. Volume 2, Ohio to Puerto Rico and the Virgin Islands. Volume 2 also includes the atlas hurricane data and a review of the State Climatologist Program, which ran from 1954 to 1973, with the status of the states' programs as of February 1980 and a list of National Weather Service personnel who served in the program.

The following material is included for each state: physical description, general climatic features, temperature, precipitation, floods, snowfall, winds and storms, other climatic elements, climate and the economy, and a bibliography. Tables show means, extremes, degree days, precipitation, humidity, wind, freeze data, etc.

The tables have been reprinted in a facsimile of the original. The narratives have been reset and slightly revised from the original 1960 edition. Names of the original authors, the state climatologists, have been dropped. Running headlines on each page showing the name of the state would have been helpful.

This is a useful compilation, although one may wonder at the price for a reprint of a government document.

Ed. note: See also the *Weather Atlas of the United States* (Gale, 1975. 262p. $30.00).

David W. Brunton

829. Ruffner, James A., and Frank E. Bair, eds. **The Weather Almanac: A Reference Guide to Weather, Climate, and Air Quality in the United States and Its Key Cities, Comprising Statistics, Principles, and Terminology**. . . . 2nd ed. Detroit, Gale, 1977. 728p. illus. index. $35.00. LC 73-9342. ISBN 0-8103-1043-0.

Weather Almanac is a comprehensive compilation of weather and climatic data throughout the United States. Comprised of numerous tables, charts, maps, and diagrams, this volume provides such information as severe weather conditions, health and safety rules, yearly weather records for selected U.S. cities, air quality data, marine weather, retirement and health weather, and round-the-world weather.

Considerable effort has been made in the second edition to update and revise the 1974 edition. Most weather records of the 108 selected U.S. cities have been extended to cover the period 1936-1975. The "U.S. Weather in Atlas Format" section has been revised to incorporate data from 1941-1970 as well as major revisions to sections on air pollution, cloud genera, and marine weather. New additions to this volume include information on heat wave dangers, a temperature-humidity index, a livestock safety index, jet lag fatigue, weather fundamentals, heating and cooling degree data, weather of the Alaska pipeline route, and a much-needed glossary and index. [R: ARBA 78, p. 691; WLB, Feb 78, p. 503]

Barbara M. Howes

MINERALOGY

830. Arem, Joel E. **Color Encyclopedia of Gemstones.** New York, Van Nostrand Reinhold, 1977. 147p. illus. (col.). bibliog. index. $37.50. LC 77-8834. ISBN 0-442-20333-0.

Arranged alphabetically according to mineral species, this encyclopedia lists basic mineralogical and gemological data on every known species and variety of gemstone. Information on each gem includes chemical formula, crystal structure, colors, luster, hardness, density, cleavage, optics, spectral data, luminescence, and sizes; the book does not cover history and lore of stones or cutting techniques.

Of the 210 mineral species covered, 185 are illustrated in spectacular color photographs, clearly the result of the author's technical competence in gem photography. Each photo simultaneously captures the best cut and brilliance of each gem while displaying the exact color of the faceted stone. Also included are an introduction, a bibliography, a refractive index graph and index. Many cross references from familiar gem names to the species name are included. This encyclopedia is of practical interest to gemologists, but valuable also to the layperson, who would do well to consult this reference before purchasing gems. [R: LJ, 15 Mar 78, p. 673; WLB, Apr 78, p. 651; ARBA 79, p. 703]

Dederick C. Ward

831. Hamilton, W. R., A. R. Woolley, and A. C. Bishop. **The Larousse Guide to Minerals, Rocks and Fossils.** New York, Larousse, 1977. 320p. illus. (part col.). index. $15.95. LC 77-71167. ISBN 0-88332-079-7.

A well-organized, elegantly illustrated guide for the serious collector of rocks, minerals, and fossils, this volume is an important addition to the reference literature of the geological sciences. Each of the three sections—minerals, rocks, and fossils—consists of a general introduction followed by detailed information respectively on 220 minerals, 90 rocks, and approximately 300 fossils. A typical entry for a mineral includes chemical formula, crystal system, specific gravity, hardness, cleavage, fracture, color and transparency, streak, luster, distinguishing features, and occurrence. Rocks are identified in terms of color, grain size, texture, structure, mineralogy, and field relations. Fossil descriptions include geologic period, occurrence, and physical characteristics. Each specimen is accompanied by a full-color photograph taken from specimens in the British Museum (Natural History) and chosen for typicality rather than as spectacular examples. There is an excellent index.

Although most American libraries will already have Pough's *Field Guide to Rocks and Minerals* this handbook is highly recommended as a complementary volume because it covers rocks and fossils as well as minerals (Pough is primarily a guide to minerals) and because it is a beautifully illustrated, excellently edited and organized, and relatively inexpensive guide to a popular field. [R: ARBA 78, p. 694; BL, 15 Oct 78, p. 408; LJ, 15 Oct 77, p. 2149; WLB, Feb 78, p. 503]   Jay K. Lucker

832. Pough, Frederick H. **A Field Guide to Rocks and Minerals.** 4th ed. Boston, Houghton Mifflin, 1976. 317p. illus. (part col.). bibliog. index. (The Peterson Field Guide Series, No. 7). $10.95; $5.95pa. LC 75-22364. ISBN 0-395-24047-6; 0-395-24049-2pa.

Those who know the second or third edition of this work will find no surprises in the latest one. The organization is the same, with the first part given over to chapters on how to find and arrange specimens, followed by brief chapters giving summaries of the various kinds of rocks. Short chapters describing the physical and chemical attributes of minerals, the crystal classification, and home laboratory techniques close off the first section.

The second and largest part describes, in an individual and structured pattern, 270 minerals grouped according to chemical composition—i.e., carbonates, sulphides, oxides, halides, etc. This is as it was in the third edition, and the arrangement in itself is a great aid to classification.

As in the earlier editions, and as expected, illustrations play a great part in this type of book. The fourth edition has 268 photographs, 156 of them in color and 143 entirely new, including one plate of photomicrographs. Also as before, each mineral pictured has corresponding drawings of its crystal forms on the facing legend page.

Generally the extent of revision is not great. A few extra rare minerals have been added and localities of occurrences have been updated. As mentioned above, there are many new photographs, but these are not necessarily better than the ones replaced. Libraries that have a third edition in good condition can probably get along without this one. However, it is an authoritative and well-organized guide. [R: ARBA 77, p. 695; BL, 1 Sept 77, p. 67]   David Isaak

833. Roberts, Willard Lincoln, George Robert Rapp, Jr., and Julius Weber. **Encyclopedia of Minerals.** New York, Van Nostrand Reinhold, 1974. 693p. illus. (col.). $69.50. LC 74-1155. ISBN 0-442-26820-3.

The *Encyclopedia of Minerals* is an authoritative compendium of information on the mineral kingdom. It provides chemical, physical, crystallographic, x-ray, optical, and geographical data on over 2,200 authenticated mineral species. The mineral names are arranged alphabetically so as to be available to a wide audience not familiar with the more refined structural/chemical arrangements of the researcher. For each mineral is given: crystal system, class, space group, lattice constant, three strongest diffraction lines, optical constants, hardness, density, cleavage, habit, color-luster, mode of occurrence, and the best reference in English (i.e., most complete and handiest). The latter feature is an outstanding bibliographic aid not available in former compilations.

As mineralogists know, many mineral species are described in the published literature by conflicting data. In this volume, the compilers have chosen to include what they believe to be the most correct data from a variety of sources. The phrase "inadequately described mineral" is used to accompany mineral names when tentative data are the only kind presently available.

Because minerals can be so well documented visually, the *Encyclopedia* contains nearly 1,000 spectacular full-color photomicrographs by Julius Weber, of the American Museum of Natural History. Weber chose this method to illustrate minerals because photographs of micro-crystals offer a wealth of details not captured by the naked eye, and because specimens of similar or equal quality are available to all mineral collectors.

This definitive and beautifully illustrated reference volume has quickly gained wide acceptance by a broad audience of scientists, museum curators, students, teachers, and mineral collectors at all levels. [R: ARBA 75, p. 713; Choice, Feb 75, p. 1759; Choice, Nov 75, p. 1146; LJ, 1 Jan 75, p. 42; WLB, Jan 75, p. 354; BL, 1 Feb 76, p. 811]

Dederick C. Ward

834. Woolley, Alan, consultant ed. **The Illustrated Encyclopedia of the Mineral Kingdom.** New York, Larousse, 1978. 240p. illus. (part col.). bibliog. index. $19.95. LC 77-90038. ISBN 0-88332-089-4.

Almost all Larousse publications are carefully designed and lavishly illustrated with color plates; this volume is no exception. Four of the British Museum's geology/mineralogy experts and four other British scientists prepared this volume for the layperson. In addition to the introduction and an annotated bibliography, there are eight sections: "Minerals, Rocks, and Their Geological Environment," "Crystals," "Properties and Study of Minerals," "The Mineral Kingdom," "Gemstones," "Economic Minerals," "Building a Collection," and "A Guide to the Literature on Minerals." Every geological/mineralogical term used is carefully defined, and concepts are described in a straightforward text that includes dozens of illustrations and photographs.

The heart of the book is the 70-page section on "The Mineral Kingdom." Descriptions of 300 of the most common minerals are given in the usual mineralogical categories: identification of chemical composition; crystal system; habit; twinning; specific gravity; hardness; fracture; color and transparency; streak; lustre; distinguishing features; formation and occurrence; and economic use. The book's coverage is similar to that of *Minerals of the World* (Golden Press, 1974). If you have the *Encyclopedia of Minerals* (see preceding entry) in your reference collection, you might consider this volume for your circulating collection. This is a fine basic book on minerals for the layperson. [R: LJ, Aug 78, p. 1497; ARBA 79, p. 705; BL, 1 May 79, p. 1390; Choice, May 79, p. 364; LJ, 1 Mar 79, p. 547]

G. Edward Evans

OCEANOGRAPHY

835. Groves, Donald G., and Lee M. Hunt. **Ocean World Encyclopedia.** New York, McGraw-Hill, 1980. 443p. illus. maps. index. $29.95. LC 79-21093. ISBN 0-07-025010-3.

This encyclopedia of oceanography is written for the nonspecialist by two staff members of the National Academy of Sciences—National Research Council. Subjects covered include physical, geological, chemical, and biological oceanography; oceanographic instrumentation; hurricanes; international marine sciences organizations;

and famous oceanographers. There is a separate article on each of the five oceans, on the 60+ seas, and on all the major ocean currents.

The over 400 articles appear in alphabetical order, with liberal use of "see" and "see also" references. These articles offer clear and concise subject coverage, serving as an excellent introduction to each topic. The authors have addressed their text to the high school and college student and have succeeded in presenting a large amount of material very well. The text is preceded by an introduction to SI units with instructions for conversion and by a list of basic abbreviations used in the book. All measurements used in the text are given in customary U.S. units of measure with the metric equivalent in parentheses. There is also a detailed 25-page index for further access. This is an excellent and basic reference text in its field. [R: ARBA 81; LJ, 1 June 80, p. 1292; RQ, Summer 80, p. 395; WLB, June 80, p. 670] Betty Gay

836. Tver, David F. **Ocean and Marine Dictionary.** Centreville, MD, Cornell Maritime Press, 1979. 358p. $18.50. LC 79-1529. ISBN 0-87033-246-5.

Ocean and Marine Dictionary fills the premise suggested by its title. The author has compiled an excellent attempt to provide short, concise, yet informative, definitions on a variety of marine subjects. Tver does not attempt to be all things to all people — he admits the impossibility of defining every marine term, but he certainly has managed to cover a good deal of oceanographic terminology. Sailing nomenclature, ships, weather, currents, ancient terminology, seashells, marine biology, and nautical terms are all covered. Several tables have been included at the end of the book — area, volume and mean depth of oceans and seas, salt present in the sea, velocity of sound in sea water, composition of sea water, mineral matter in river and sea water, and temperatures of the oceans. This well-done volume will be of interest to the layperson as well as helpful to the professional. Tver has compiled a book which will be of use in most general reference collections and certainly in all oceanographic and marine libraries. [R: ARBA 81; BL, 1 Sept 80, p. 71; Choice, Sept 80, p. 70; WLB, Apr 80, p. 529] Charla Leibenguth Banner

SOIL SCIENCE

837. Fairbridge, Rhodes W., and Charles W. Finkl, Jr., eds. **The Encyclopedia of Soil Science: Part I: Physics, Chemistry, Biology, Fertility, and Technology.** Stroudsburg, PA, Dowden, Hutchinson & Ross; distr., New York, Academic Press, 1979. 646p. illus. index. (Encyclopedia of Earth Sciences Series, No. 12). $62.50. LC 78-31233. ISBN 0-87933-176-3.

Another excellent addition to the Encyclopedia of Earth Sciences Series. Material for this volume on soil science has been grouped into two parts in accordance with the seven commissions of the International Society of Soil Science. Part I, this volume, covers physics, chemistry, biology, fertility and plant nutrition, and technology. Part II, to be published, will cover soil morphology, genesis, classification, and geography. The arrangement is alphabetical by fairly broad terms such as acidity, buffers, capillary pressure, imbibition, information systems, and moisture management. Discussions range from 2 to 12 pages on each topic and summarize up-to-date as well as historical information on the subject.

Each article is extensively cross referenced to other articles in this and other published volumes in the series. Numerous references are given at the end of each discussion. There are a comprehensive subject index and an author index which includes both contributors and cited authors. A concise and thorough discussion of the bibliography of soil science appears in the preface. [R: ARBA 81; Choice, Mar 80, p. 48] Barbara A. Rice

38 PSYCHOLOGY

BIBLIOGRAPHIES

838. Viney, Wayne, Michael Wertheimer, and Marilyn Lou Wertheimer. **History of Psychology: A Guide to Information Sources.** Detroit, Gale, 1979. 502p. bibliog. index. (Psychology Information Guide Series, Vol. 1; Gale Information Guide Library). $28.00. LC 79-9044. ISBN 0-8103-1442-8.

This volume contains nearly 3,000 entries (40% of which are annotated), and, as with other numbers in the Gale Information Guide Library, the titles included are in English only. This is a drawback (as the authors freely admit in their preface), but it is compensated by excellent and clear organization, worthwhile though brief annotations, and proper indexing (names, titles, subjects). The work is divided into five sections: "General References" (not necessarily in psychology); "General Works on the History of Psychology" (e.g., major periodicals, historiography); "Systems and Schools of Psychology"; "Works in Selected Content Areas of Psychology" (e.g., social psychology, learning, personality); and "Histories of Related Fields." There are references to materials published as late as the middle of 1978.

The Gale volume follows by a year the publication of another reference book on the same subject (Robert Watson, *The History of Psychology and the Behavioral Sciences: A Bibliographic Guide*), which is broader in scope but lists fewer works in psychology. Watson's book gives long annotations but contains no index. The Gale volume is very well suited to both researchers and undergraduates, and it should be in all collections. [R: ARBA 80, p. 664]   Michael Stuart Freeman

839. Watson, Robert I., Sr., ed. **Eminent Contributors to Psychology: Volume I, A Bibliography of Primary References.** New York, Springer, 1974. 469p. $29.50. LC 73-88108. ISBN 0-8261-1450-4.

840. Watson, Robert I., Sr., ed. **Eminent Contributors to Psychology: Volume II, A Bibliography of Secondary References.** New York, Springer, 1976. 1158p. index. $80.00; $95.00/set. LC 73-88108. ISBN 0-8261-1780-5; 0-8261-2081-4(set).

The first volume of this important reference book (*Eminent Contributors to Psychology: Volume I, A Bibliography of Primary References*) lists 12,000 publications produced by 538 individuals living between 1600 and 1967, an average of 23 references per person, with a range from 1 to 80. The second volume contains about 55,000 selected secondary references to the work of the same contributors. The contributors are listed alphabetically; information given for each includes full name, dates of birth and death, the country (or countries) where the principal work was done, major field of endeavor, and eminence rating score derived for this bibliography. Listings of bibliographical citations follow (John Dewey, for example, has four pages).

This bibliography has several laudable purposes. Its goal is to make available for quick reference a list of major publications of and by eminent contributors to psychology without the inconvenience of accumulating lengthy lists from *Psychological Index* and *Psychological Abstracts*. This is indeed one of the more interesting projects in psychology today. [R: ARBA 75, p. 716; Choice, Mar 75, p. 52; RQ, Winter 75, p. 181; LJ, 15 Dec 76, p. 2560; ARBA 77, p. 698; Choice, Feb 77, p. 1577; RQ, Summer 77, p. 364; WLB, Mar 77, p. 602]   Bohdan S. Wynar

DICTIONARIES AND ENCYCLOPEDIAS

841. Goldenson, Robert M. **The Encyclopedia of Human Behavior: Psychology, Psychiatry, and Mental Health.** Garden City, New York, Doubleday, 1970. 2v. $24.95. LC 68-18077. ISBN 0-385-04074-1.

Some insatiable achievement-oriented enthusiast is reported to have said "the difficult we do right away; the impossible takes a little longer." Goldenson's Herculean efforts tell us such a task may take considerable time. Many previous efforts up to the level of the eight-volume *Encyclopedia of the Social Sciences* are deficient in special areas and often of little use to the expert. In like manner, Dr. Goldenson's work must fall short of its avowed goals.

Knowledge is growing at disciplinary interfaces, and it is here that this encyclopedia runs into serious difficulty. The decision to stay in the mainstream of an area necessitates losing much information of importance to psychologists and psychiatrists. It is literally impossible to define where the efforts of the latter end and those of sociologists, anthropologists, and other social scientists begin. To illustrate, terms such as "alienation," "anomia," and "anomie" are either ignored or poorly treated in the present work.

If, however, we attempt to stay within the center of psychology, just as the clinical domain seems exceptionally well treated, so is the perceptual one seriously slighted. We find listed among the references the seminal works of Ames, Bruner, Sherif (Brunswik is left out), but no index citations are made to these scholars or their views—Transactional Functionalism, Directive-State Theory, Hypothesis Theory, Probabilistic Functionalism, and Frame-of-Reference Theory. Similarly, considerations of Perceptual Defense and Vigilance are not present. One can match these with weaknesses in the motivational area (e.g., Surgency, Regnancy, Succorance, Nurturance) and with learning—the distinction between primary and secondary stimulus generalization.

It is not difficult to multiply similar examples, but pebble-picking an effort such as this is really the height of trivialization. Goldenson has accomplished more than could have been expected of one man, or even one computer. In addition, the depth and clarity of the writing afforded the many concepts presented here cannot be lightly treated. A number of articles include case histories and illustrations. There is a good general index. For laypersons and professionals alike, this encyclopedia may offer a valuable entrée to the field of behavioral study. [R: ARBA 71, p. 527; LJ, 15 Apr 71, p. 1329]   Bernard Spilka

842. **International Encyclopedia of Psychiatry, Psychology, Psychoanalysis & Neurology.** Ed. by Benjamin B. Wolman. New York, published for Aesculapius by Van Nostrand Reinhold, 1977. 12v. illus. index. $675.00. LC 76-54527. ISBN 0-918228-01-8.

This encyclopedia represents a tremendous effort (on the level of *International Encyclopedia of the Social Sciences*) in its comprehensive treatment of psychology and related subjects. In comparison to such works as Eysenck's *Encyclopedia of Psychology* or even Robert M. Goldenson's *Encyclopedia of Human Behavior: Psychology, Psychiatry, and Mental Health*, this work is much more comprehensive.

In preparation for eight years, it contains survey articles by a number of internationally known scholars, with adequate cross references and bibliographical citations. Some 1,500 contributors and 300 editor/consultants participated in this 12-volume, 5,000,000-word project. The result is impressive, with the possible exception of biographical materials. The index volume, computer produced, has a number of deficiencies, primarily in its failure to link related topics. Nevertheless, this encyclopedia will be a standard source of information in these areas for years to come. [R: LJ, 1 Oct 77, p. 2048; ARBA 78, p. 697; BL, 1 Oct 78, p. 318; Choice, Apr 78, p. 210; LJ, 15 Apr 78, p. 817]   Bohdan S. Wynar

843. Kinkade, Robert G., ed. **Thesaurus of Psychological Index Terms.** 1974 ed. Washington, American Psychological Association, 1974. 362p. $12.00. LC 74-13190.

The uncontrolled proliferation of psychological terminology in the past decades has been an annoying source of difficulties and problems for psychologists in theoretical and applied fields as well as for professionals in related areas. In responding to this problem, the American Psychological Association has published its *Thesaurus*, which, for the users, represents an authorized systematic list of terms in the discipline and thus, indirectly, an attempt at codification.

The volume is divided into three sections, each serving a different purpose. The Relationship Section forms the essential part; here each alphabetically listed term is cross referenced and presented with its broader, narrower, and related concepts. In order to facilitate rapid selection of a search term, as well as verification of its spelling, thesaurus terms are listed alphabetically in the Alphabetic Section. In the Hierarchical Section, the concepts, represented by 17 major classification categories used in *Psychological Abstracts*, are placed at the highest level. Subsequently, all associated concepts are listed hierarchically as subcategories; the hierarchical structuring of terms was produced by computer and is listed in descending order, based on broader and narrower term designation. The technical aspects related to the development of the *Thesaurus* (such as the selection of candidate terms) are described in the introductory part. No definition or explanation of the meaning of any listed psychological term is provided. Evidently, the user is expected to be familiar with the conceptual spheres within the discipline.

The *Thesaurus* is a highly technical reference instrument. It is an essential guide for many search and indexing operations. The attempt of the American Psychological Association to stabilize terminology in psychological sciences is commendable.

Ed. note: A 1977 edition of the *Thesaurus* (spiral binding) was unavailable for review.
[R: ARBA 76, p. 714]   Miluse Soudek

844. Wolman, Benjamin, ed. **Dictionary of Behavioral Science.** New York, Van Nostrand Reinhold, 1973. 478p. $24.50. LC 73-748. ISBN 0-442-29566-9.

This comprehensive dictionary, which briefly defines some 20,000 terms, was compiled and edited by Dr. Wolman, a well-known author of several psychology books. Some 30 consulting editors also participated in this project. The scope of the dictionary is rather broad. It covers psychology, psychiatry, psychoanalysis, neurology, psychopharmacology, endocrinology, and related disciplines. Among the categories of psychology covered are experimental and developmental psychology, personality, learning, perception, motivation, and intelligence. In terms of applied psychology, the reader will find here definitions of terms used in diagnoses and treatments of mental disorders, and in social, industrial, and educational psychology. In general, definitions are brief but adequate for a beginning student. Some terms have a number of different definitions depending on their use in a particular discipline (see, for example, "functional unity").

In addition to definitions of terminology, there are some biographical sketches, primarily of leading psychologists. The length of an article does not necessarily reflect the relative importance of a given individual. Compared to older works, however, e.g., English and English's *A Comprehensive Dictionary of Psychological and Psychoanalytical Terms* (McKay, 1958. $15.95pa.), it is not only more up to date but also much more comprehensive. [R: ARBA 74, p. 614; Choice, May 74, p. 416; LJ, 15 Apr 74, p. 1100; WLB, Mar 74, p. 596]   Bohdan S. Wynar

MENTAL HEALTH

845. Rifken, Hal, ed. **The Selective Guide to Publications for Mental Health and Family Life Education.** 4th ed. Prepared by the Mental Health Materials Center. Chicago, Marquis Academic Media; Marquis Who's Who, 1979. 912p. $34.50pa. LC 78-71071. ISBN 0-8379-5001-5.

The Mental Health Materials Center (MHMC), publisher of the selective guides, was established in 1953 for the purpose of facilitating the most effective dissemination and utilization of the "best" mental health program aids to help program planners in this field. These aids, whether books and pamphlets or techniques and ideas, are carefully evaluated. Each must meet certain criteria such as authoritativeness, integrity as an educational tool, substantive content, well-balanced presentation, and its utility in a mental health or family life education program. The details of these principles of selection are described in several key chapters in the *Guide.*

Materials recommended are found under 21 principal subject headings, ranging from various phases of child growth and development, adults and family life, to special problems such as alcoholism, drug abuse, and suicide and crisis intervention. The information for each entry includes the title and bibliographic facts, the primary audience for which the item was intended by the publisher, a concise abstract, an evaluation by MHMC, and the target audiences and uses for which the piece is appropriate. The final page of each section identifies other relevant suggestions under "Cross References."

This fourth revised edition is substantially larger than its predecessor in the number of new entries. It also includes three new subject categories—child abuse, community care, and death and dying. A very useful index at the end of the volume provides access to publications in more than 100 categories. [R: ARBA 80, p. 664; LJ, 1 Oct 79, p. 2086]

Lorraine Mathies

PARAPSYCHOLOGY AND THE OCCULT

846. Cavendish, Richard, ed. **Encyclopedia of the Unexplained: Magic, Occultism and Parapsychology.** New York, McGraw-Hill, 1974. 304p. illus. (part col.). bibliog. index. $19.95. LC 73-7991. ISBN 0-07-010295-3.

The editorial approach of this much-needed reference work is one of "sympathetic neutrality" toward three overlapping categories: parapsychology, magic and the occult, and divination. Consultant J. B. Rhine, noted expert and author on psychic research, stresses that much of this information has previously been hidden from the layperson and that now the reader can decide for himself about the topics, which range from systems that have no reliable proof to those that have accumulated a body of evidence.

Because of space limitations, there is a concentration on the nineteenth- and twentieth-century West. Arrangement is alphabetical; length of articles varies greatly, but many of the longer ones are signed by authorities on the subject and are accompanied by bibliographies. The helpful index of names and book titles occasionally misses briefly mentioned people. The article on yoga fails to mention Swami Yogananda, who brought yoga to the United States, and his world organization, Self-Realization Fellowship. The bibliography of over 500 books and articles, which is otherwise complete, fails to mention his books and, for some reason, those of L. Ron Hubbard. There is no mention of Scientology, although, according to the preface, the *Encyclopedia* does not shy away from exposés. The societies that are included are mostly those of European origin.

Tiny flaws aside, this interestingly written and beautifully illustrated work will throw much light on many previously unknown or little-known secrets and research. [R: LJ, Aug 74, p. 1925; ARBA 75, p. 728; BL, 15 July 75, p. 1205; Choice, June 75, p. 509; LJ, 1 Mar 75, p. 452; LJ, 15 Apr 75, p. 732; WLB, Dec 74, p. 318]

Margaret Kaminski

847.   Eberhart, George M., comp. **A Geo-Bibliography of Anomalies: Primary Access to Observations of UFOs, Ghosts, and Other Mysterious Phenomena.** Westport, CT, Greenwood Press, 1980. 1114p. map. index. $59.95. LC 79-6183. ISBN 0-313-21337-2.

   This unique work lists published sources of information about some 22,100 strange and unexplained events that have occurred in or near some 10,500 American and Canadian cities, towns, military installations, and archaeological sites. The compiler's conception of such anomalous events is extremely broad (being listed and defined in a 13-page glossary) and includes many archaeological, geological, and historical anomalies in addition to those centered on parapsychology, UFOs, and survival after death. Place name entries are arranged alphabetically under the name of the state or Canadian province, but the states are grouped into six regions rather than being listed alphabetically. Each place name entry is followed by a subject heading(s) for the type(s) of anomaly, the date of the anomaly, the name of the observer, and the name, date, and page of the magazine, newsletter, newspaper, or book in which that anomaly is described and discussed. The 16-page subject index, the 56-page observer index, the 2-page ship index, and the 2-page ethnic group index greatly facilitate the location of desired information.

   The major weaknesses of this work are its failure to list the books and newspapers used in its compilation (only 28 of the journals and newsletters used are identified in a separate list of "journal sources indexed") and its failure to specify the criteria by which books, magazines, and newspapers were selected for geographical indexing of their reports of anomalous events. (Did the compiler index only the most reliable account, the lengthiest account, the original account, or the only account of the anomalous event?). In addition, most libraries are not likely to have the magazines, special newsletters, newspapers, or paperback books cited by the place entries. Nevertheless, this massive, carefully executed and unique reference work will greatly expedite the finding of published information about an enormous number of strange and unusual events, and should thus be available in most medium and large public and university libraries. [R: ARBA 81; LJ, 15 Sept 80, p. 1799]

Joseph H. Cataio

848.   Pritchard, Alan. **Alchemy: A Bibliography of English-Language Writings.** Boston, Routledge & Kegan Paul; London, Library Association, 1980. 439p. index. $75.00. ISBN 0-7100-0472-9.

   A truly comprehensive bibliography of works about alchemy written in English from 1597-1978. Within the over 3,400 entries, compiler Alan Pritchard claims to have listed all primary and secondary works, including theses. He can do this by keeping strictly to the subject and not allowing any digressions into the occult or chemistry. The result is a definitive bibliography of alchemy. Pritchard, whose background includes chemistry as well as library and information science, is well prepared to undertake this task. His work reflects his competence in these fields. He has clearly defined the scope of his work and systematically researched it. His format is clear.

   The work is divided into primary and secondary source sections, which are subdivided by country. Secondary sources are further subdivided by subject. Annotations are used only for occasional clarification, but many entries have contents notes which greatly increase their usefulness. The preface contains a careful explanation of arrangement as well as a short history of alchemy and a synopsis of bibliography in the area to date. The index is quite thorough, though more cross references would have been useful.

   Since the only other extensive bibliographies of alchemy are collection catalogues like John Ferguson's *Bibliotheca Chemica*, Pritchard's work is indisputably the best bibliography now available in the field.

Cleon Robert Nixon, III

849. Shepard, Leslie, ed. **Encyclopedia of Occultism & Parapsychology.** Detroit, Gale, 1978. 2v. index. $74.00/set. LC 77-92. ISBN 0-8103-0185-7.

The subtitle of this encyclopedia is *A Compendium of Information in the Occult Sciences, Magic, Demonology, Superstitions, Spiritism, Mysticism, Metaphysics, Psychical Science and Parapsychology, with Biographical and Comprehensive Indexes.* This edited work is basically based on articles appearing in Lewis Spence's *Encyclopaedia of Occultism* (1934, reprinted 1966) and Nandor Fodor's *Encyclopedia of Psychic Science* (1934, reprinted 1966). There are over 4,000 entries in the two Shepard volumes, with over 3,000 articles directly extracted from Spence and Fodor. The typeface of the *Encyclopedia* incorporates the small typefaces of both Spence and Fodor. Consequently, one can nearly detect by the printing what is old and what new articles have been added in this rather uneven, typographically patched format.

The editor indicates that by merging the basic two encyclopedias and bringing the articles up to date, a contemporary work has been created in the fields of occultism and parapsychology. Unfortunately, there are vast problems in this claim. First, occultism as a term has not been redefined, nor has new information been added. The definition of occultism is taken from Fodor and indicates that the practical side of occultism relates to psychical phenomena. This definition is obscure, since the occult arts (such as astrology, alchemy, the study of the Kabala, etc.) may have nothing to do with psychical phenomena but stand as occult philosophical subjects. On the other hand, a new entry for parapsychology does not show it as a subject closely related to occultism. Issuing an encyclopedia for the two subjects may not contribute to a serious study of either one. Second, the editor frequently has not given credit to Fodor or Spence in extracting from their articles. One must determine this either by the smaller print or by comparing the entry with those in Fodor or Spence, or both.

Third, the editor has promised to update the older articles, but frequently, this has not occurred. For example, articles on death, gnoticism, magic, neoplatonism, demonology, Paracelsus, occult fiction, mysticism, and Kabala are not updated, but are frequently extracted word-for-word without attributing the entry to Fodor or Spence. In addition, major articles have very little information attached to the older article (e.g., astrology, devil, and hypnotism). Fourth, there is doubt as to the propriety of including non-occult, non-parapsychology articles (e.g., Zen, Jehovah's Witnesses, Kathryn Kuhlman, EST, Hare Krishna, Yoga) in the *Encyclopedia.* Fifth, there are many articles for occult and parapsychology periodicals that do not give birth and death dates for them and, consequently, imply they are still published (e.g., *Spiritual Age* and the *Spiritual Clarion*).

Frequently many new articles added follow popular trends, such as "Rosemary's Baby," "Alex Sanders," "Morey Bernstein," and do not seriously contribute to a careful objective approach. However, there are articles (this is particularly true for persons involved in parapsychology) that would be difficult to locate elsewhere. Nevertheless, Fodor and Spence emerge as primary contributors to the *Encyclopedia.* There are special indexes to the two-volume encyclopedia, and they cover paranormal phenomena, periodicals, and societies and organizations. An updating service, entitled *Occultism Update*, is available (4-issue subscription—$45.00pa.). [R: ARBA 79, p. 714; LJ, 15 May 78, p. 1050; WLB, June 78, p. 813]   Jerome Drost

850. White, Rhea A., and Laura A. Dale, comps. **Parapsychology: Sources of Information Compiled under the Auspices of the American Society for Psychical Research.** Metuchen, NJ, Scarecrow, 1973. 303p. index. $9.50. LC 73-4853. ISBN 0-8108-0617-7.

This comprehensive book provides many sources of information on parapsychology. There are 282 annotated entries of the best books in the field, covering 24 topics (e.g., altered states of consciousness, critical review of literature, experimental research, mediums and sensitives, precognition and retrocognition, survival, unorthodox healing). The books were selected on the bases of scientific merit as well as interest value, and they should help beginning and serious students and librarians to select materials wisely from the mass of literature published. The annotations accurately reflect the contents of the books and are clearly written. Other important contributions of this source book are the sections that describe 1) parapsychological topics in encyclopedias; 2) parapsychological organizations, including their addresses and functions; 3) parapsychological periodicals, including addresses and information pertaining to their editorial policies; 4) various sources of scientific recognition of parapsychology (e.g., academic institutions that have sponsored courses and research); and 5) a glossary of terms. Other sources of information include very detailed indices of names, topics, books and periodicals in the field, and bibliographical references. This source book is clearly the best to date; it provides a wealth of information for persons with differing interests and levels of experience in parapsychology. [R: WLB, Nov 73, p. 263; ARBA 74, p. 619; Choice, Feb 74, p. 1850; LJ, 15 Jan 74, p. 126; RQ, Fall 74, p. 72; Choice, Sept 75, p. 808]   Gregory T. Fouts

BIBLIOGRAPHIES

851. Andrews, Theodora. **A Bibliography of the Socioeconomic Aspects of Medicine.** Littleton, CO, Libraries Unlimited, 1975. 209p. index. $13.50. LC 74-34054. ISBN 0-87287-104-5.

Divided into two major sections, general reference sources and source material by subject area, this bibliography presents 569 annotated references to socioeconomic aspects of medicine. Social, political, and economic implications are the linking factors to medicine. Limited to mostly American sources, the books are mainly those written after 1969.

Entries are complete with pagination, price, and book numbers. The length of annotation varies from two sentences to several paragraphs. The information is complete enough to indicate audience, useful material and facts, and the purpose of the author. Occasionally, an annotation reflects the annotator's personal opinion.

Government publications are included as well as general information sources. The 65 periodicals listed represent a good cross section of the area. Under source material by subject area appear health care delivery; ethics; hospital and nursing homes; mental health; drug abuse, alcoholism, and tobacco; the environment; and patent medicine, quackery, and questionable belief. But don't expect to find malpractice or dying. In all, this title is intended for use by laypersons, librarians, and personnel involved in the health sciences field. [R: ARBA 76, p. 723]   Roylene G. Cunningham

852. **Bibliography of Bioethics, Volumes 1-3.** Ed. by LeRoy Walters. Detroit, Gale, 1975-1977. 3v. $44.00/v. LC 75-4140. ISBN 0-8103-0978-5(v.1); 0-8103-0980-7(v.2); 0-8103-0982-3(v.3).

Walters, director for the Center for Bioethics of the Kennedy Institute at Georgetown University, has compiled and edited these volumes (the first three of a series of annual publications) on a multidimensional subject that has received national and international attention. The volumes cover references on medical ethics, research ethics, and social questions relating to biomedical and behavioral technology, physician-patient relationships, contraception, abortion, reproductive technologies, genetic intervention, human experimentation, and death and dying.

The *Bibliography* is comprehensive in English-language publications, includes non-print materials, and covers a variety of literary forms such as journal and newspaper articles, monographs, essays in books, court decisions, bills, and unpublished documents. The basic part of the volumes consists of a thesaurus or list of subject headings used and a subject entry section where the citation is given. Also included are lists of journals cited (with ISSNs) and title and author indexes. This is a professionally produced bibliography of high quality, and is both timely and indispensable for all academic and health sciences libraries. [R: ARBA 76, p. 726; Choice, Nov 76, p. 1120; LJ, 15 Dec 75, p. 2316; WLB, Jan 76, p. 408; RQ, Winter 76, p. 187; WLB, Sept 77, p. 92; BL, 1 Dec 77, p. 632; ARBA 78, p. 706]
Theodora Andrews
James E. Bobick

853. Green, Lawrence W., and Connie Cavanaugh Kansler. **The Professional and Scientific Literature on Patient Education: A Guide to Information Sources.** Detroit, Gale, 1980. 330p. index. (Health Affairs Information Guide Series, Vol. 5; Gale Information Guide Library). $28.00. LC 80-19649. ISBN 0-8103-1422-3.

With the emphasis on consumer protection and satisfaction impacting on all aspects of society, there has been a recent explosion in the literature relating to patient education. Green and Kansler's annotated bibliography of journal and monographic publications allows the public, scholar, and librarian to readily access the new material.

The authors selected material from the fields of public health, policy analysis, and hospital literature, written by experts from the health care professions, behavioral sciences, and the health education area. These citations come from the Health Education Retrieval System (HEIRS) at Johns Hopkins University, and the large majority of these items come from the mid-1970s, though there is an introductory historical section. The subject index lists 576 topics examined in this study, which are divided into chapters covering health problem analysis, behavioral problem analysis, factors influencing patient behavior, staff development, and communication and organization concepts. One of the authors' stated goals is to illustrate the state of the literature in patient education; regrettably, this intention has led to the inclusion of a number of poor quality studies, while some worthwhile publications are omitted.

Valuable reference material is included in the three appendices. In the first appendix is a compilation of addresses of institutions, agencies, and companies which provide health education materials. The next appendix contains an annotated list of newsletters produced by commercial, federal, and private sources which cover national health activities. Finally, there is a listing of accredited schools of public health which can provide patient education consultants from their faculty.

Each chapter contains an introductory essay explaining the nature of the material presented. Author and subject indexes make this volume easy to use. Hospital, health care, and large public libraries will find this volume a useful reference tool to begin unraveling the confusing mass of patient education literature currently available.   Jonathon Erlen

854. Lunin, Lois F. **Health Sciences and Services: A Guide to Information Sources.** Detroit, Gale, 1979. 614p. index. (Management Information Guide, 36). $28.00. LC 77-80614. ISBN 0-8103-0836-3.

This volume is an annotated inventory of information resources including publications, data bases, and organizations of the disciplines that comprise the health sciences. The major sections are: 1) general health sciences and services, including history and education; 2) basic health science, i.e., the preclinical sciences such as anatomy, biochemistry, physiology, etc.; 3) clinical sciences, i.e., the medical and surgical specialties (the 37 divisions [e.g., dermatology, hematology, pediatrics, etc.] that comprise this section cover 225 pages); 4) dentistry; 5) nursing; 6) public health; 7) veterinary medicine; 8) allied health sciences; 9) hospitals and nursing homes; 10) health insurance; 11) pharmacy and the pharmaceutical industry; and 12) the communication of health information.

Each section contains the following items: 1) definition or scope; 2) publications arranged by form of literature, i.e., dictionaries, bibliographies of periodicals, handbooks, atlases, directories, indexing and abstracting publications, serials, audiovisual materials, etc.; 3) data bases, including files, services, and user aids; and 4) organizations, including libraries and special collections. The remaining sections of this guide are: core libraries; addresses for publishers, data base distributors, and suppliers; sources used; and author, title, and subject indexes.

Lunin has done an admirable job of collecting, organizing, and annotating the major sources of health sciences information. This volume should, unquestionably, be in all medical library reference collections and in the personal libraries of both medical library practitioners and educators. [R: ARBA 80, p. 677]   James E. Bobick

855. Morris, Dwight A., and Lynne Darby Morris. **Health Care Administration: A Guide to Information Sources.** Detroit, Gale, 1978. 264p. index. (Health Affairs Information Guide Series, Vol. 1; Gale Information Guide Library). $28.00. LC 78-53431. ISBN 0-8103-1378-2.

Since 1960, no area in health-related literature has expanded more rapidly than the complex field of health care administration. The Morrises' new indexing and abstracting tool on this subject is the first in a forthcoming 18-volume series from Gale Research Company that will cover a broad spectrum of biomedical topics, including social gerontology, health statistics, and bioethics. If the future volumes equal this initial work, librarians and researchers will be extremely grateful.

The present volume contains over 1,100 citations, mostly annotated, on health care administration issues concerning mental health facilities, long-term care institutions, hospitals, and ambulatory care facilities. References are drawn from the following sources: journals, manuals, bibliographies, indexes, abstracts, proceedings, series, directories, and encyclopedias. Citations refer only to entire works, rather than to individual journal articles or book chapters. Besides complete author-title and subject indexes, extensive appendices cover ongoing information sources through libraries, associations, graduate schools, audiovisual centers, and other publishers in the health fields. While most of the listed references are from post-1960 secondary sources, a few primary references date back to 1935. Citations are arranged by overall function, rather than by types of institutions covered. Because of the increasing interest in health care administration, this research tool is a necessity for all health-related libraries and institutions, and this reviewer eagerly awaits future volumes in this important new series. [R: ARBA 80, p. 678; LJ, 15 Mar 79, p. 718]   Jonathon Erlen

856. Weise, Frieda O. **Health Statistics: A Guide to Information Sources.** Detroit, Gale, 1980. 137p. index. (Health Affairs Information Guide Series, Vol. 4; Gale Information Guide Library). $28.00. LC 80-12039. ISBN 0-8103-1412-6.

This well-annotated guide should serve as a useful introduction to a very complex field. Weise is head of the Public Services Unit of the Reference Section of the National Library of Medicine and has taught courses in health statistics. The guide includes an introductory chapter citing general sources—textbooks, directories, dictionaries and handbooks, catalogs, bibliographies, machine-readable files, as well as a survey of vital and health statistics. Subsequent chapters deal with sources of birth and death data, statistics on major diseases, health care costs, and population characteristics. The major emphasis is on national and regional data; state agencies are listed in one of the appendices. Although the majority of statistics cited are compiled by government agencies, the guide also includes those released by private organizations. The annotations are brief, precise, and up to date; cross references link related series. Among the several appendices is a helpful glossary defining the most important terms used in health statistics. Although there have been a number of new guides to the literature published in the field of health care and medicine, the area of statistics is usually neglected. Ms. Weise's work is a welcome addition to a very confusing field.   Suzanne K. Gray

DICTIONARIES AND ENCYCLOPEDIAS

857. **Black's Medical Dictionary.** 31st ed. By William A. R. Thomson. New York, Barnes and Noble, 1976. 950p. illus. (part col.). $17.50. LC 59-167. ISBN 0-06-490443-1.

Black's Medical Dictionary, now in its thirty-first edition, is a standard reference source in medicine. The thirtieth edition was completely reset and incorporated extensive textual revisions; in addition, illustrations in that edition were for the first time placed on text pages instead of being included on separate plates.

The thirty-first edition has not been reset, of course, but it has added numerous new articles to reflect new developments or changed emphases. Among these new articles are those on shin splints, Lassa fever, tattooing, and vasectomy. The new article on the Sudden Infant Death syndrome is entered under the heading "cot deaths," with no cross reference from SID or crib deaths—terms that are more likely to be searched in the United States. Besides adding new articles, this 1976 edition has extensively revised certain articles, including those on frostbite, death, prostaglandins, sleep, and transplantation.

The two-column format of the dictionary is clear and easy to read, and the black-and-white illustrations amplify the definitions. The two colored plates at the back of the book show general front and back views of the abdominal and thoracic viscera.

Black's Medical Dictionary is successful in its goal of providing "a reasoned account of healthy living, of disease, and how to recognize it, avoid it and treat it." [R: ARBA 76, p. 727; ARBA 77, p. 710; LJ, 15 Dec 76, p. 2560]

858.   Critchley, Macdonald, ed. **Butterworths Medical Dictionary.** 2nd ed. Woburn, MA, Butterworth Publishers, 1978. 1942p. $125.00. LC 77-30154. ISBN 0-407-00061-5.

Although numerous medical dictionaries are available at the present time, few have attained the stature and respect of the original edition of this work. Published first in 1961 as the *British Medical Dictionary*, and edited by the distinguished Sir Arthur S. MacNalty, the volume was highly lauded by the profession. Butterworth acquired the rights in 1963, and spent nearly 15 years revising and updating the material. (A "revised edition" was published by Butterworth in 1965, but it included new terms only as a special supplement.) The editor-in-chief, Macdonald Critchley, is a renowned medical authority who has involved the services of over 50 other medical specialists as contributors and consultants to the second edition, which builds, of course, on the earlier contributions of some 100 other authorities. As a result, this edition contains 8,000 new entries and much revision of original terms. Nearly 60,000 entries provide coverage of basic medical terminology, chemical nomenclature, anatomical vocabulary, pharmaceuticals, and eponymous terms. Pronunciation, etymological derivation, variant definitions, individuals, and many subentries (subsidiary terms relative to the headword) are included along with the basic definition. The arrangement is alphabetical according to the rules of the British Standards Institution.

The volume includes a carefully written and illustrated set of explanatory notes, a section on abbreviations and symbols, and an appendix on anatomical nomenclature that gives the Nomina Anatomica term, the Birmingham Revision (or English Equivalent), and the definition location. In addition, a special dictionary entry under the term "test" identifies "the most important clinical, biochemical, chemical, physiological and psychological tests, arranged in alphabetical order of the ordinary names by which they are known," and a second list "of comprehensive cross-references to all tests for specific substances or purposes" (explanatory notes).

Butterworth has an excellent reputation as a publisher of medical sources, and both the content and format of this volume support their reputation. The volume is well designed, well printed, and well bound. It is easy to use and comprehensive in its coverage, so it should be a valuable addition to the medical reference section of any major public or academic library. [R: ARBA 79, p. 724]   Laurel Grotzinger

859.   **Dorland's Medical Dictionary.** Shorter ed.; abridged from the 25th ed. of *Dorland's Illustrated Medical Dictionary.* Philadelphia, Saunders Press, a division of W. B. Saunders, 1980. 741p. illus. (col.). $12.95. LC 79-67113. ISBN 0-7216-3142-8.

This dictionary is an intermediary work that stands between the classic comprehensive medical dictionaries such as *Stedman's Medical Dictionary* or *Dorland's Medical Dictionary* (from which it is abridged), and the pocket dictionaries such as *Blakiston's* or *Dorland's*.

The introduction explains why a work such as this is needed. The general public, for whom it is primarily intended, is getting increasingly involved in health care. The laity has been introduced into the decision-making process regarding public policy in health care. The citizen must become acquainted with the language of medicine to do this. The introduction also points out that the language of medicine is far more difficult to understand, far more elaborate, and more difficult to spell than the jargon of other professions or trades.

The work contains 45,000 definitions in comparison to 100,000 items found in the comprehensive *Dorland's*. Pronunciation is indicated. Special features include: 16 pages of color illustrations portraying the structure and function of the body; tables that offer comparative data on arteries, bones, chemical elements, muscles, nerves, temperature equivalents, fetal positions, veins, and weights and measures; a special section listing forms by which words are combined from Greek and Latin roots; pharmaceutical trade names and abbreviations used in prescriptions are interpreted; and acronyms are identified.

It is presumed that the dictionary will be especially useful to students in the sciences, attorneys, insurance agents, medical suppliers, copy writers, secretaries, hospital administrators, politicians, and any others involved with health care concerns. It is a work of high quality. [R: ARBA 81; WLB, Sept 80, p. 61]   Theodora Andrews

860.   Dox, Ida, Biagio John Melloni, and Gilbert M. Eisner. **Melloni's Illustrated Medical Dictionary.** Baltimore, Williams & Wilkins, 1979. 530p. illus. (col.). $18.95. LC 77-2952. ISBN 0-683-02642-9.

This new dictionary defines approximately 25,000 terms and includes about 2,500 good illustrations that complement the text. The scope of the work is not as comprehensive as that of the Dorland or Stedman volumes, but it is more inclusive than the abridged medical dictionaries. The definitions in the new work are fairly easily understood and are more suitable for the general reader than those in the other medical dictionaries. An attempt has been made to use terms in the definitions that do not require additional reference.

Major anatomic terminology groupings, such as arteries, bones, muscles, nerves, and veins, are presented in illustrated tables alphabetized within the text. Tables of measurements, conversions, dosages, etc., are graphically presented on the pages where the subject terms of the calculations are located. Commonly used chemical compounds and drugs have been included as defined entries. Brand names are frequently cited at the ends of the definitions but are not included as separate defined entries. Synonyms of defined terms, however, are cited in the definitions and are also included as cross reference entries to the defined terms. This work fills a void among medical dictionaries and should prove very useful to students in the health sciences as well as to the general public. [R: ARBA 80, p. 681; LJ, July 79, p. 1441]   Theodora Andrews

861.   Duncan, A. S., G. R. Dunstan, and R. B. Welbourn, eds. **Dictionary of Medical Ethics.** London, Darton, Longman and Todd; distr., Atlantic Highlands, NJ, Humanities Press, 1977. 335p. $13.75pa. ISBN 0-232-51302-3.

Few if any fields cover as diverse a range of topics as biomedical ethics, with its concerns overlapping the disciplines of medicine, philosophy, law, and theology, among others. This outstanding reference tool edited by Duncan, Dunstan, and Welbourn admirably surveys the main ethical issues found in contemporary biomedical sciences.

Relying on contributions from 116 eminent professionals drawn from the above-mentioned disciplines, the editors present the reader with a solid, compact, British view of biomedical ethics, arranged alphabetically with no index of terms but excellent cross references. Though some of the items covered are strictly British in nature, like the General Medical Council, most are of universal interest to bioethicists, such as euthanasia and confidentiality.

Throughout this work, the editors maintain objective treatment of sensitive topics and provide brief bibliographies on each item, though these listings tend to be slightly dated. The coverage of topics ranges from a few sentences to several pages in length, with the latter type including historical, legal, religious, and philosophical materials concerning the issue at hand. There is excellent treatment of the major religions' ethical viewpoints toward medicine, as well as the complete texts of the leading twentieth-century medical ethics codes. After reading this work, this reviewer only hopes that America will produce a similar study of equal stature in the near future. [R: LJ, July 78, p. 1424; ARBA 79, p. 725; Choice, Nov 78, p. 1192]   Jonathon Erlen

862.   Larson, Leonard A., ed., and Donald E. Herrmann, asst. ed. **Encyclopedia of Sport Sciences and Medicine.** Under the sponsorship of the American College of Sports Medicine, the University of Wisconsin, and in cooperation with other organizations. New York, Macmillan, 1971. 1707p. $52.00. LC 70-87898.

This publication, which is international in scope, summarizes the scientific literature of this interdisciplinary field and serves as a definition of the sports medicine field, which is somewhat in the development stage.

The *Encyclopedia* contains over 1,000 signed articles that present data on all the influences that affect the human organism before, during, and after participation in sports. Since the editors felt that any force, stress, or environmental factor that influences the human being in such instances is within the scope of sport sciences and medicine, the context of physical activity has been enlarged to include the social, emotional, physical, and intellectual characteristics, abilities, and capabilities of the individual independently, the individual within the group, and the group as a whole. Consequently, the coverage of the *Encyclopedia* is quite broad. Such areas as the environment, emotions and the intellect, drugs, prevention of disease, safety, rehabilitation, and physical activity and the handicapped individual are included, along with the more obvious areas. Some detailed information is also included regarding individual sports — the basic skills required, evaluation, and skill measurement.

Over 500 writers, authorities in science and medicine, contributed to the *Encyclopedia.* Numerous approaches, including experimental, clinical, and theoretical approaches, were used. For instance, certain articles have been written theoretically because of a lack of research data.

The publication is impressive and well written, and it has considerable value as a general reference book. It is organized in 10 general areas. References are included in most cases. Articles vary in length from about a quarter of a page to two or three pages. The detailed subject index makes it easy to locate material on specific topics. The author index includes the names of authors of the articles and also the names of the authors in the citations. The publication is unique in that no other work of this kind and scope is available. [R: ARBA 72, p. 614]   Theodora Andrews

863.   **Stedman's Medical Dictionary: A Vocabulary of Medicine and Its Allied Sciences, with Pronunciations and Derivations.** 23rd ed. Baltimore, Williams and Wilkins, 1976. 1678p. illus. (part col.). index. $29.50. LC 75-4993. ISBN 0-683-07924-7.

This volume is a revision of a classic work that first appeared in 1911. Stedman's dictionary has long held its place of top rank among medical dictionaries along with *Dorland's Illustrated Medical Dictionary*, and probably ahead of *Blakiston's Gould Medical Dictionary*. However, some may prefer the latter, since its definitions are somewhat less technical and require less knowledge of medical terminology than do those of the other two compilations.

In this edition of *Stedman's* the range of vocabulary has been expanded, and a greater degree of integration and coherence has been attempted. There has been a search for elusive synonyms and a correlation of supplementary information. There are 15,313 new entries, of which 10,322 are new definitions and 4,991 new cross references for synonyms. In addition, 13,094 definitions have been revised. The new edition contains 1,678 pages as compared to 1,533 in the twenty-second edition. There has been considerable revision of neuroanatomy terms, reflecting the expanding literature in this area. In the combined areas of biochemistry and pharmacology more than 1,000 new entries have been supplied, covering drugs, enzymes, pharmacognosy, and toxicology. Another area of expansion is that of bacteria, viruses, and parasites.

As with earlier editions, this work continues to group multiple-word terms as subentries under governing noun main entries. For example, typhoid fever is defined as a subentry under the main term "fever." An appendix serves as a "master" cross referencing system for adjectival or descriptive terms in the vocabulary in lieu of such cross referencing within the vocabulary. It works very well, although some users prefer *Dorland's* approach, which provides cross references in the main vocabulary.

Several useful special sections have been provided: instructions for use of the work, medical etymology (containing a root word list), blood groups, a glossary of common Latin terms used in prescription writing, symbols and abbreviations, and results of laboratory analyses.

This is an impressive, comprehensive work of high quality. [R: ARBA 77, p. 712]

Theodora Andrews

864. **Taber's Cyclopedic Medical Dictionary.** 13th ed. Ed. by Clayton L. Thomas. Philadelphia, F. A. Davis, 1977. 1v. (various paging). illus. (col.). $14.50; $15.95(thumb-indexed). LC 76-19064. ISBN 0-8036-8505-7; 0-8036-8304-9(thumb-indexed).

Taber's Cyclopedic Medical Dictionary is compiled primarily for a nursing and allied health professional audience. Current medical terms and phrases are defined, and approximately 150 two-color line drawings are included. Words are arranged alphabetically, letter-by-letter, using American spellings. Compound terms are usually listed under the adjective rather than the noun, but may be listed under both. Related words are sometimes listed as subentries in alphabetical order. Synonyms are incorporated into definitions. Phonetic spellings are included for most entries, as well as abbreviations where appropriate. Brief first-aid information is given with entries for forms of accidents, and brief biographies are included also. An appendix of 179 pages includes a variety of useful information, including: units of measurement; abbreviations; Latin and Greek nomenclature; lists of muscles, joints, arteries, veins, etc., with brief descriptions of functions; basic dietary information; brief descriptions of medical emergencies and their treatment; poison control centers in North America and other miscellaneous addresses; and lists of common health-related questions and answers, translated into five languages. *Taber's* is well organized and easy to read and use. It will be useful to the health professional and, in many cases, to the layperson. [R: ARBA 78, p. 712]

Brett A. Kirkpatrick

DIRECTORIES

865.   Jaques Cattell Press, comp. **Biographical Directory of the American Academy of Pediatrics, 1980.** 1st ed. New York, R. R. Bowker, 1980. 940p. index. $95.00. LC 80-65349. ISBN 0-8352-1282-3.

This typical Bowker medical biographical directory lists over 18,000 pediatric specialists. The biographies are arranged geographically, first by state then by city or town. Also represented are the Canal Zone, Puerto Rico, the Virgin Islands, and a variety of other countries. The profiles list name, membership status, year of election to the Academy, pediatric specialty, birthplace and date, date of marriage, number of children, education, past professional experience, professional and academic activities, honors and awards, and mailing address and telephone. There are a few entries on each page which contain only a mailing address.

There are several very specific medical biographical directories on the market today, but their prices tend to run high. This book is no exception. Except for large medical collections with unlimited budgets, this type of volume is becoming too costly for the small library. These smaller collections will be better served by a more general directory such as *Directory of Medical Specialists*, by Marquis Who's Who, or *American Medical Directory*, by the American Medical Association.   Charla Leibenguth Banner

866.   Wasserman, Paul, ed. **Health Organizations of the United States, Canada and Internationally: A Directory of Voluntary Associations, Professional Societies and Other Groups Concerned with Health and Related Fields.** 4th ed. Jane K. Bossart, associate ed. Ann Arbor, MI, Anthony T. Kruzas, Associates; distr., Ann Arbor, MI, Edwards Brothers, 1977. 327p. $36.00. LC 77-79000. ISBN 0-686-27874-7.

This work lists 1,460 organizations, societies, foundations, associations, and other nongovernmental bodies concerned with health care. The fourth edition is an expansion of the earlier work, attesting to the growth of the field. Only organizations considered voluntary or unofficial in character are included. Described are national, international, and regional organizations concerned with medicine, hospitals, pharmacy, dentistry, and many other related areas. The book is in two parts. The first, the bulk of the work, lists the organizations arranged alphabetically by the official name. Each entry usually includes the following information: address, phone number, year of establishment, names of officers and/or executive director, a statement of the aims of the organization, membership, financial information, meeting dates, awards given, publications, affiliations, and occasionally information about the organization's library. The second part of the volume lists the organizations under subject headings that relate to their activities and functions, thus supplying a kind of subject index.

The associations included in the work provided the details about their characteristics themselves through replies to questionnaires. The book gives rather comprehensive coverage of health organizations, and the information included appears to be accurate and well edited. Librarians and many others interested in the health care field will find the book of considerable value, as it is a convenient source of information. [R: BL, 1 May 78, p. 1452; WLB, Dec 77, p. 348; ARBA 79, p. 729]   Theodora Andrews

867.   **Who's Who in Health Care.** 1st ed. New York, Hanover Publications, 1977. 764p. index. $60.00. LC 77-79993. ISBN 0-918710-00-6.

This reference work provides biographical information for more than 8,000 professionals in all areas of the health care industry. Included are medical school educators, researchers, consultants, government and public health officials, hospital and nursing home administrators, HMO and PSRO directors, foundation executives, and pharmaceutical and insurance personnel. The preliminary material consists of the preface; the names and affiliations of the book's editorial advisory board; admission standards that centered on 1) position of responsibility held, and 2) meritorious contributions to the health care field; a biographical reference key; an explanation of alphabetical practices; and a table of abbreviations. Entries are arranged alphabetically and cross referenced by name, state, current affiliation, and professional field. Information varies in length from five lines to almost one-half page (e.g., in the latter case, entries for Michael DeBakey and Milton Halpern) and probably averages 20 lines per individual. Attractive, with easy-to-read typeface and clear format, this volume assembles data on noteworthy individuals who may not be included in other biographical sources and is, therefore, an excellent candidate for appropriate reference collections. [R: Choice, May 78, p. 380; LJ, 15 Mar 78, p. 676; ARBA 79, p. 730]   James E. Bobick

HANDBOOKS

868.   **Standard Medical Almanac.** 2nd ed. Chicago, Marquis Academic Media; Marquis Who's Who, 1979. 711p. illus. maps. index. $39.50. LC 79-87624. ISBN 0-8379-4002-8.

This is the second edition of a valuable sourcebook of socioeconomic statistics of the U.S. health care industry. It extracts and coordinates recent information from more than 40 sources, including professional associations, other organizations, and the government. Sources are credited with each presentation. Much of the data presented are in tabular and graphic form, but text material is also included.

The *Almanac* is in six parts plus the index section. Part 1, on expenditures, explores private and government expenditures, costs to patients/consumers, and cost containment. Part 2 deals with personnel, identifying specific occupations and providing distribution. Further, it contains articles on foreign medical school graduates and future needs for health manpower. Part 3, "Education and Licensure," gives state regulations for licensure for each profession and provides education statistics for each. Professions covered are: chiropractic, dentistry and dental auxiliaries, medicine, nursing, optometry, osteopathy, pharmacy, physical therapy, podiatry, public health, veterinary medicine, and allied health professions.

Part 4, on facilities and ancillary services, covers hospital regulations, and location, size, type, and services provided. Dental services, nursing homes, the drug industry, and medical instruments and supplies industries are featured. In addition, there are articles on the ethical pharmaceutical industry and the controversy surrounding the use of generic drugs in place of brand-name products. Part 5, "Disease, Disability, and Health Status," provides information on vital statistics, morbidity and mortality, environmental factors, measures of health, and preventive medicine. There are specific articles on blacks, adolescents, smoking, costs of cancer, asbestos exposure, and socioeconomic differentials in U.S. mortality. Part 6, on the government and health care, covers governmental interaction, federal programs and policies, veterans administration, and professional standards review organization.

A great deal of useful material is brought together in this work in a succinct and convenient format. The volume concludes with subject, organization, and geographic indexes. [R: ARBA 81; LJ, 1 May 80, p. 1072]   Theodora Andrews

POPULAR MEDICAL GUIDES

869.   Fenwick, R. D. **The Advocate Guide to Gay Health.** 1st ed. New York, E. P. Dutton, 1978. 240p. illus. bibliog. index. $10.95. LC 78-6577. ISBN 0-525-05050-7.

One of the most valuable works to come out of the gay movement thus far, the *Advocate Guide to Gay Health* can be of immense value to both health professionals and their gay patients. For the first time, health problems confronting primarily gay men (the primary focus of this work, despite the inclusiveness of the title) are confronted matter-of-factly, in language that can be comprehended by the average layman. Seven chapters cover: sources of health care; sexually transmitted diseases; hazards of sex; sexual dysfunction; drugs (including alcohol, old number one); aging; and holistic health and preventive medicine. Appended matter includes a list of gay community services, a list of sources, a list of works on preventive medicine, and a bibliography of professional reading. The index is comprehensive and useful.

Within the various chapters are questions or topics (in boldface, for easy location), lists, anecdotes (always well selected and to the point), and direct advice. Whether a topic arises from a question or an item on a list, it is handled in easily understood fashion. Prose is simple but not at all simplistic, and complex topics are broken down, with each component part receiving scrutiny until an entire answer has been formulated. The only probable bias is a tendency to advocate more of a vegetarian stance on diet, but this is hardly the main thrust, and the advice might well do a great many people some good. In sum, this book should be in the hands of health professionals as well as available to patients. It represents a milestone in the gay movement in that, at last, we have begun to take care of our own by building on our own knowledge and experiences. [R: ARBA 80, p. 689; LJ, 15 Oct 78, p. 2126]   Koert C. Loomis, Jr.

870.   Homan, William E. **Caring for Your Child: A Complete Medical Guide.** New York, Harmony Books, a division of Crown Publishers, 1979. 192p. illus. index. $10.95; $5.95pa. LC 79-8044. ISBN 0-517-53957-8; 0-517-53910-1pa.

A pediatrician and the editors of *Consumer Guide* have joined forces to offer parents remarkably understandable information about handling many of their children's health-related problems. The introduction contains wise advice about approaching these problems calmly, and discusses the parent/physician partnership, the importance of fever immunizations, the lymph nodes as infection fighters, and the recommended contents of the home medicine chest. There is also a helpful chart of symptoms.

The text covers some 150 topics, arranged alphabetically, one to a page. A brief description of the condition noted, such as "dizziness," is followed by possible diagnosis, home treatment, some precautions that might lead to calling or seeing the doctor, mention of what treatment might be given, and some related topics to check. This information is clearly and simply stated, and intended to alert rather than alarm the reader. Parents are urged to browse through this handy book before a real emergency arises, so that they can more readily refer to it when needed. The utterly charming illustrations by Nan Brooks help to make this truly pleasurable, and may even serve a mnemonic function.

Among the many current pediatric manuals, this one stands out for its clarity and ease of presentation, and its reassuring but not patronizing tone. Although not as comprehensive as Robert Pantell's *Taking Care of Your Child — A Parent's Guide to Medical Care* (Addison-Wesley, 1977. $10.95), or as accident-oriented as Martin J. Green's *A Sigh of Relief — The First-Aid Handbook for Childhood Emergencies* (Bantam, 1977. $7.95pa.), it does contain a great deal of helpful and even lifesaving information for parents caring for young children and adolescents. [R: ARBA 80, p. 691]   Harriette M. Cluxton

871.   **The New Illustrated Medical Encyclopedia for Home Use: A Practical Guide to Good Health.** Ed. by Robert E. Rothenberg. New York, Abradale Press, 1974. 4v. illus. (part col.). index. $50.00. LC 67-14553. ISBN 0-8109-0284-2.

The questions that patients or their families would like to ask are often not asked, frequently because patients are afraid to impose on the busy doctor's time; and even those questions that are asked sometimes remain unanswered, because the doctor's explanation is not fully understood. But knowledge of one's medical problem and access to accurate information about health and disease are rights that everyone has.

Recognized medical specialists have collaborated with Dr. Rothenberg in this encyclopedic compilation of such questions, with succinct, authoritative answers. Medical terms are clearly explained at the end of the fourth volume, which also contains a detailed index. The extensive table of contents in the first volume outlines the whole set. It is thus very easy to locate individual items. Each chapter starts with cross references to related topics, considerably enlarging coverage of each subject.

Senior citizens will appreciate the large readable type in this revised edition. Illustrations are exceptionally attractive and informative.

This is not a do-it-yourself medical book; helpful explanations of conditions and problems of health and disease at all stages of human existence are expertly presented. Coverage is remarkably wide. Useful for health educators and students as well as consumers of health care. [R: ARBA 76, p. 736]   Harriette M. Cluxton

872. Stewart, Felicia Hance, and others. **My Body, My Health: The Concerned Woman's Guide to Gynecology.** New York, John Wiley, 1979. 566p. illus. (part col.). bibliog. index. (A Wiley Medical Publication). $13.95; $5.95pa. LC 78-31499. ISBN 0-471-04517-9; 0-471-04515-2pa.

This book is based on the authors' clinical experiences with obstetrical, gynecological, and family planning patients. The writers intend for the work to be used as a guide for teaching and counseling women about their anatomy and physiology and related health concerns and problems. Physicians as well as other health care providers will find this book of practical value in meeting the educational needs of female patients. Because the volume is written not only in language readily understandable by the general public but also in a factual, unbiased manner, it can be used by patients in learning more about themselves and their personal health problems.

The authors utilize the philosophy that providing complete information is essential to informed consent, and discuss the implications of informed consent for health care practitioners. The book includes current information on various birth control measures, decision-making regarding birth control options, sexuality, signs and symptoms of pregnancy, self breast examination, pelvic examination, health problems related to the female reproductive system, and various medical and surgical approaches which can be used in treating those problems. The various illustrations are useful teaching aids. The bibliographies at the ends of many of the chapters, along with a suggested, briefly annotated reading list at the end of the book, are helpful.

This work will be a valuable teaching guide for health care providers as well as a quick reference source for individuals wanting information related to women's health. Both medical and public libraries will find it useful as a reference tool for their clientele.

                    Judith Ann Erlen

PHARMACOLOGY

873. **AMA Drug Evaluations.** 4th ed. Prepared by the AMA Department of Drugs, in cooperation with the American Society for Clinical Pharmacology and Therapeutics. New York, John Wiley, 1980. 1580p. index. $48.00. ISBN 0-471-08125-6.

This updated and expanded edition is a cooperative effort on the part of the AMA Department of Drugs and the American Society for Clinical Pharmacology and

Therapeutics (ASCPT). It includes over 90% of prescribed drugs, with individual evaluations of some 1,300 drugs, including 57 new entities. Other products and their composition and manufacturers are listed as well. Drugs are broken down into therapeutic categories with information on dosage, actions, and uses, contraindications, and adverse reactions. Structural formulas are provided for most single-entity drugs. There are brief introductions to each of the major categories.

While the volume is comprehensive in scope and well written, it is not a quick reference book on drugs. It requires the extensive use of the excellent index to gain a complete overview of a drug. For quick reference, one should consult the *Physician's Desk Reference* or the *National Formulary*.

Susan Holte
Mary Ann Mills-Evans

874. Glasby, John S. **Encyclopaedia of Antibiotics.** 2nd ed. New York, John Wiley, 1979. 467p. (A Wiley-Interscience Publication). $76.25. LC 78-13356. ISBN 0-471-99722-6.

Since the first edition of the *Encyclopaedia* appeared in 1977, a large number of new antibiotics have been described in the scientific and patent literature. Over 400 of these have been added to this new edition, and the structures of several of the substances previously described have been revised in the light of more recent investigations, particularly into their stereochemistry. The format of the second edition is similar to that of the first, and the arrangement is alphabetical. For each antibiotic are given: the formula, structure, melting point, elaborating organism, methods of preparation and purification, those organisms against which the antibiotic is effective, toxicity, and literature and/or patent references. The work is of particular value for workers in the fields of medicine, pharmacology, microbiology, chemistry, and biochemistry.

Theodora Andrews

875. **Handbook of Non-Prescription Drugs.** 5th ed. Washington, American Pharmaceutical Association, 1977. 388p. illus. index. $12.50. LC 68-2177. ISBN 0-917330-08-0.

When the first edition of this excellent publication appeared in 1967, there were virtually no other reference works available that gave information on non-prescription drugs. Although a few works since then have purported to be guides to home remedies and over-the-counter drugs, particularly for laypersons, there are no others as comprehensive and authoritative as the volume under consideration. The *Handbook* is not intended for the lay public, but rather is designed to assist pharmacists and other health professionals in providing information and professional advice to the patient. However, much of the material included can be understood by and is of interest to the educated layperson. Information has been included on product formulas, indications/contraindications, safety, and appropriate use of specific non-prescription drugs. Much of the material is presented in tabular form, although text discussions and literature references have also been included. More than 1,500 drug products are covered. It is estimated that these represent 90% of the dollar market in over-the-counter drugs.

The *Handbook* is made up of 32 chapters, each on a different type product (such as antacid products, acne products, cold and allergy products, etc.). This edition contains 11 new chapters: emetics/antiemetics, ostomy care, asthma products, infant formulas, stimulants, contraceptives, feminine cleansing and deodorant products, otic (ear) products, contact lens products, sunscreen and suntan products, and topic anti-infectives.

The *Handbook* was compiled with the help of a group of authors, an advisory committee, and a review panel, all made up of distinguished members of the pharmaceutical and/or health science professions. The work is extremely useful and is much needed, as the lay public continues to use large amounts and varieties of self-prescribed medications. [R: ARBA 78, p. 731]

Theodora Andrews

876. Jones, Judith K. **Good Housekeeping Guide to Medicines and Drugs.** New York, Good Housekeeping Books; distr., New York, Hearst Books, 1977. 288p. $9.95. LC 77-072363. ISBN 0-87851-021-4.

The author of this work, who is a physician and pharmacologist, points out that there is a growing interest by drug consumers in obtaining full and accurate information about drug effects. The book is based on the premise that a patient who is well informed can obtain better medical care in the traditional medical system, and that eventually this may allow for joint decisions between patients and doctors on the proper medication to be prescribed. The author has two major goals. The first is to provide general information on drugs, and the second is to present in easily understood fashion detailed information about the most commonly prescribed drugs, particularly their therapeutic actions, possible adverse effects, and interactions.

The work is in three parts. Part I, an introduction, describes what drugs are in general and how they work in the body. Part II, called "A Brief Introduction to the Different Types of Drugs," considers drugs according to the conditions or diseases for which they are used. There are about 40 brief sections (or subsections), e.g., "Drugs for Gastrointestinal Disorders." Part III, which makes up more than one-half of the work, is an alphabetical guide to over 200 of the most frequently prescribed drugs. The drugs are listed either by trade (brand) name or by generic name with cross references from the other form or forms. In addition, each drug is cross referenced to the chapter in part II that discusses that class of drugs in general. With each individual drug description is given: other brand names for the drug, the actions, side effects, precautions, and interactions.

The number of drugs included in this work is limited, but well selected. The *Guide* should serve its intended purpose very well, and the quality of the material presented is high. As a bonus, a good deal of information is included about the diseases treated by the specific drugs discussed. [R: ARBA 79, p. 737; BL, 1 Oct 78, p. 325; LJ, 15 Mar 78, p. 676]

Theodora Andrews

877. **National Formulary XIV.** 14th ed. Prep. by the National Formulary Board with the Approval of the Board of Trustees, by authority of the American Pharmaceutical Association. Washington, American Pharmaceutical Association; distr., Easton, PA, Mack, 1975. 1123p. illus. index. $24.00. LC 55-4116. ISSN 0084-6414.

This publication (known as the *NF*) and the *United States Pharmacopeia* (the *USP*) are the two compendia that list drugs with official status in the United States. The publications do not duplicate one another; official drugs are designated as either USP or NF. In recent years, the publications have come out at about the same time and at approximately five-year intervals. The compendia are produced by volunteer medical and pharmaceutical scientists, and their basic aim is to set forth standards of identity, strength, quality, purity, packaging, storage, and labeling of drug and related articles. A primary objective of official compendium standards is to ensure uniformity of drug products from lot to lot and from manufacturer to manufacturer.

The largest section of the book (about three-fourths of it) is made up of short monographs (about half-a-page in length) on each of the therapeutic agents. They are arranged alphabetically by generic name. The rest of the book presents sections on 1) General Tests, Processes, Techniques, and Apparatus; 2) Reagents, Test Solutions, and Volumetric Solutions; and 3) General Information. There is also an interesting section on the history of the *National Formulary*.

The first edition of the *NF* appeared in 1888, although the *USP* was established in 1820. It is of note that, although there have long been two official U.S. compendia, most countries have only one or have adopted that of another country. This is the last edition of the *NF* to be prepared as it has been. Steps have been taken to unify the two drug standards, setting compendia under one organization. The *United States Pharmacopeia: National Formulary XV*, 20th ed., was to have been published in 1980 by Mack ($65.00. ISBN 0-912734-30-2). [R: ARBA 76, p. 739]   Theodora Andrews

878.   Osol, Arthur, and Robertson Pratt. **The United States Dispensatory.** 27th ed. Philadelphia, Lippincott, 1973. 1287p. bibliog. index. $45.00. LC 73-2673. ISBN 0-397-55901-1.

This monumental work is a new edition of an old classic. Basically, the dispensatory presents a collection of articles, alphabetically arranged, about individual drugs. Articles are longer than in most drug compendia – one page to several pages, as compared to about half a page in the *U.S. Pharmacopeia* or the *National Formulary*. The articles contain such information as: chemical, generic, and brandname nomenclature; chemical structure; a summary of method of synthesis or other form of preparation; pharmacologic action; therapeutic uses; contraindications; untoward effects; warnings and precautions; drug interactions; dosage; and dosage forms. There are also general articles on classes of drugs, such as antibiotics, antihistamines, etc. The work is planned to provide pharmacists with a source of information so that they may better help the physician, other health professionals, and their patients with proper information on the use of drugs. Much of the information included came from scientific journals, and the references are included in the text.

The older editions of the *USD* (up to the 26th) were much larger volumes. The reduction in size was brought about by deleting older drugs, botanical descriptions, and explanations of physical and chemical tests and assays for drugs. The older editions are sometimes consulted for this material. [R: ARBA 74, p. 643]   Theodora Andrews

879.   Wigder, H. Neil. **Wigder's Guide to Over-the-Counter Drugs: A Critical Comparison of the Effectiveness, Cost, and Safety of the Most Popular and Widely Advertised Brands.** Los Angeles, J. P. Tarcher; distr., New York, St. Martin's Press, 1979. 224p. index. $10.00. LC 79-54749. ISBN 0-312-90489-4.

Wigder is associate director of the Emergency Medicine Department at Christ Hospital in Oak Lawn, Illinois. For over 15 major product categories (allergy medications, sleeping pills, antacids, etc.) he provides up-to-date ingredient information, price comparisons, critical evaluations of advertisers' product claims, comparisons of the effectiveness of a drug for its intended use, and material on side effects, interactions, and contraindications. There are summary charts for each category which include recommended child and adult dosages and a comparison of common brands. A unique feature of this volume is a three-star product rating system, with a "Doctor's Choice" heading the list and a "not-recommended" category. Another special feature is the "Doctor's Prescription" for specific brands in each drug category for those who wish to stock a medicine chest. In the last several years there has been a plethora of books on non-prescription drugs for the layperson; overall, this scientifically sound and extremely informative reference volume is perhaps the best. [R: ARBA 81; LJ, 15 Nov 79, p. 2448; WLB, Apr 80, p. 529]

BEVERAGES

880. Lichine, Alexis. **Alexis Lichine's New Encyclopedia of Wines & Spirits.** 2nd ed. New York, Alfred A. Knopf, 1974. 716p. illus. maps. bibliog. index. (A Borzoi Book). LC 74-7734. ISBN 0-394-48995-0.

Wine merchant Lichine has here produced *the* definitive basic book about wines, in a revision of his well-received 1967 book. His superb and well-written introductory material covers history, health, cellars, vinification processes, and viticulture. The main body is alphabetical in arrangement and self-indexing. He covers geographic areas with the types of vines, wines, aperitifs, and locally applied technical terms (much more of the latter for this revision). Sketch maps have been reduced in size to accommodate more text, but for good maps one should consult Hugh Johnson's *World Atlas of Wine* (Simon and Schuster, 1978. $29.95).

Most entries are long, especially for French and German wine-growing areas, and chateaux or specific appellations are also given their own alphabetical entries. Appendixes include classifications of Médoc, Pomerol, Graves, St. Emilion, and other Bordeaux areas (including Bourg and Blaye for the first time), plus German wines, a new feature; container information; tables of spirit strength and conversions; updated vintage charts through 1973; pronouncing glossary; and a good historical bibliography through 1973. In fact, all parts of the book have been thoroughly revised through 1973. Other changes: upgrading of wine qualities (e.g., the Italian Abruzzi has changed from 1967's "pleasant but unimportant" to 1974's "agreeable"); new material on the United States (from 31 columns to 54, plus three more maps); many additional entries; and primary measurements now in "hectares" instead of the previous edition's "acres." This is a well-organized book that is also very enjoyable to read. [R: BL, 15 Mar 75, p. 774; LJ, 1 Jan 75, p. 45; WLB, Jan 75, p. 357; ARBA 76, p. 744]   Dean Tudor

881. Schoonmaker, Frank. **Frank Schoonmaker's Encyclopedia of Wine.** Rev. and expanded by Julius Wile. New York, Hastings House Publishers, 1978. 473p. $12.95. LC 78-9563. ISBN 0-8038-1947-1.

The first edition (1964; revised in 1965, 1968, 1969, 1973, and 1975) was favored by two French wine book prizes (in 1965 and 1966). Its authority is unimpeachable; Schoonmaker, at the time of his death in 1976, was America's foremost wine expert. In reviewing previous editions, I slammed the book because revision was so very minimal, except in vintage charts. The average library could get by with the fourth edition from 1969, or choose from either Grossman's or Lichine's competitive wine encyclopedias—both of which were extensively revised in the 1974-1975 period. *But* Schoonmaker's *Encyclopedia* has at last been brought up to date, by his friend Julius Wile, a well-known and respected wine merchant.

On the positive side: statistics generally are current through 1976; new material has been added (changing terminology, charts of the 100 largest U.S. wineries in 1977, a table of vineyard temperatures, listings of all the grape varieties and how they perform); tasting notes are for vintages from around the world (by country and district) as related by a committee—right through to a cautious (understandably) 1977 report; explanations of new wine laws in Germany, Italy, and France (especially the October 24, 1977 elevation of Côtes de Provence from V.D.Q.S. to A.O.C.); and modification to the pronunciation system. On the negative side: a smaller typeface has been used to accommodate the new material, and Schoonmaker's vibrantly humorous style has been eliminated (e.g., the Bernkastel Caveat Emptor classification). The alphabetical format remains: 2,000 terms defined in brief statements from "Abboccato" (an Italian term for semi-sweet) to "Zymase" (the enzymes of yeast), complemented by about 100 maps and wine labels. [R: ARBA 79, p. 751]

Dean Tudor

882.   Tudor, Dean. **Wine, Beer and Spirits.** Littleton, CO, Libraries Unlimited, 1975. 196p. index. (Spare Time Guides, No. 6). $11.50. LC 74-80964. ISBN 0-87287-081-2.

Which books on wine are worth purchasing and which are not? This sixth volume of the Spare Time Guides series provides some answers. Separate chapters of this annotated bibliography cover reference works, wines (subdivided by geographical regions), beers, spirits, brewing and winemaking at home, audiovisual sources of information, and "ancillary aspects" (cocktails, cookery and food, crafts and collecting, health, history, literary and musical references, "personal notes of contemplation," pubs and inns, and tasting and evaluation guides). The cut-off date for inclusion was 1973. The final four chapters of the book provide annotated lists of periodicals; associations and clubs; museums, libraries, and contacts; and publishers and supply sources. Chapters are subdivided where necessary, and entries are arranged alphabetically by author within these divisions. Information given for each entry includes author, title, place and date of publication, publisher, pagination, price, LC number; the lengthy annotations are both descriptive and critical. An author-title-subject index concludes the book. [R: LJ, 1 May 75, p. 837; RQ, Fall 75, p. 82; WLB, June 75, p. 756; ARBA 77, p. 732]

DOMESTIC ANIMALS

883.   **The Complete Dog Book: The Photograph, History and Official Standard of Every Breed Admitted to AKC Registration, and the Selection, Training, Breeding, Care and Feeding of Pure-Bred Dogs.** 16th ed. New York, Howell Book House, 1979. 768p. illus. index. $11.95. LC 79-1490. ISBN 0-87605-462-9.

This standard reference has a new look for its golden anniversary edition — color photographs of 113 different breeds. These photographs are excellent, and depict the different qualities and traits of each breed. The chapter on dog sports has been expanded, as has the glossary; and there is a list of AKC films and services available. In addition, 21 breed standards have been corrected and revised since the 1975 edition, and 35 breed histories revised for greater accuracy. Three new breeds — the bearded collie, the Ibizan hound, and the Norfolk terrier — are presented for the first time. As before, the histories and standards of the 124 recognized breeds are covered in detail, and there are chapters on dog care, health and nutrition, diseases, and first aid. Since this is still the only authoritative and complete reference to nearly all breeds of dogs, public libraries should have the latest edition. [R: ARBA 80, p. 700]

Joy Hastings

884.   Dangerfield, Stanley, and Elsworth Howell, eds. **The International Encyclopedia of Dogs.** With special contributions by Maxwell Riddle. New York, McGraw-Hill, 1971. 480p. $19.95. LC 70-161547. ISBN 0-07-015296-9.

The editors describe this book as an international work, stating that contributors were commissioned from the appropriate countries to write with authority on breeds, kennel clubs, shows, and specialist subjects. A list of contributors is at the front; American articles are written by Maxwell Riddle, an AKC judge and newspaper columnist. The book was produced by Rainbird Reference Books, Ltd., London, and published in the United States and Canada by McGraw-Hill in association with Howell Book House.

The *Encyclopedia* covers dog care; training and management; diseases; all breeds recognized by Kennel Clubs of America, United Kingdom, Canada, Australia, and New Zealand; some breeds from other countries; genetics and biology; international shows; and other topics. Arrangement is alphabetical beginning with Aberdeen Terrier and Abortion, ending with Yorkshire Terrier and Zygoma. British spellings and names are used, with cross references under alternative names. Small caps are used within articles to signal related articles where additional information may be found. Every page contains one or more black-and-white photos or sketches, over 600 in all. A photo accompanies almost every article on a particular breed. In addition, 126 full-color plates present champions of nearly every important breed. The double-column pages are easy to read, entries are simple to locate, and the whole is handsomely illustrated. Articles on various breeds discuss the origin, development, and use of dogs, physical characteristics, and special traits, qualities, or defects; articles end with a summary: essentials of the breed. While the articles are highly informative, they are well written and do not display the impersonal, dull writing characteristic of over-edited reference works. This is an attractive and easy-to-use reference book covering a wide range of topics of interest to dog lovers and experts. [R: ARBA 72, p. 265; LJ, 1 Feb 72, p. 484; LJ, 15 Apr 73, p. 1244]   Christine Gehrt Wynar

885.   Ensminger, M. E. **The Complete Encyclopedia of Horses.** Cranbury, NJ, A. S. Barnes; London, Thomas Yoseloff, 1977. 487p. bibliog. illus. (part col.). $29.50. LC 74-9282. ISBN 0-498-01508-4.

The author claims this is the most complete horse encyclopedia presently available, and it does appear to be much more comprehensive than most books claiming this distinction. Ensminger, a well-known and respected authority in the livestock field, has used his knowledge and expertise to write an in-depth book on all aspects of the horse. Anatomy, diseases, riding and hunting terms, equipment, clothing, breeds, colors, feed, stabling, racing, etc.; little, if anything, seems to have been overlooked. Most of the entries are brief, one or two paragraphs, but there are some lengthier and more detailed articles on "Law and Horses," "Pastures," "Protein," "Horse Insurance," "Management," "Income Taxes," and "Vitamins," to name just a few. Many of the articles have accompanying photos, charts, tables, or diagrams. Appendices provide further information on addresses of breed associations, horse publications, recommended horse books, and agricultural colleges. While information in some of the tables (racing and horse shows) is current only to 1971 and 1974, this minor flaw should in no way detract from the quality of content or coverage of this book. Superior to both Hope's *Encyclopedia of the Horse* and Self's *Horseman's Encyclopedia*, and wider in scope than Taylor's *Harper's Encyclopedia for Horsemen*, this volume will supplant all three as the finest horse encyclopedia in print. [R: ARBA 78, p. 742; Choice, May 78, p. 372; LJ, 15 Mar 78, p. 675; WLB, Apr 78, p. 648; BL, 15 Jan 79, p. 824]   Joy Hastings

886.   Henderson, G. N., and D. J. Coffey, eds. **The International Encyclopedia of Cats.** New York, McGraw-Hill, 1973. 256p. illus. (part col.). $19.95. LC 72-10958. ISBN 0-07-027163-7.

Cat lovers, owners, and breeders will appreciate this nontechnical, authoritative encyclopedia, which covers every aspect of owning and caring for cats. Photographs (over 60 in color and 100 in black and white) of exceptionally fine quality enhance the visual appeal of this fine volume on the cat.

The more than 700 alphabetical entries contain explicit and useful advice on buying, breeding, grooming, genetics, the cat in the home, sickness, and health. There are descriptions and photographs of all well-known breeds, newly developed species, and the larger wild cats, plus articles on the role of the cat in different countries, periods, religion, art, music, literature, legend, and lore.

Encyclopedic in format, with many cross references (but no index), it includes articles on such diverse topics as achondroplasia (defective cartilage formation before birth); brain disorders; diaphragmatic hernia; the Jaquarondi (which has a remarkable resemblance to the family that includes badgers, martens, weasels and otters); parasites; the Royal College of Veterinary Surgeons; tongue disorders; and warts. The line drawings liberally scattered throughout the volume consist primarily of anatomical bisections and silhouettes of the cat structure and skeletal makeup. [R: ARBA 74, p. 652; BL, 15 Oct 74, p. 250; LJ, 15 Jan 74, p. 125; WLB, Dec 73, p. 277]   Judy Gay Caraghar

FOODS AND COOKING

887.   Fitzgibbon, Theodora. **The Food of the Western World: An Encyclopedia of Food from North America and Europe.** New York, Quadrangle/New York Times Book Co., 1976. 529p. illus. bibliog. $25.00. LC 74-24279. ISBN 0-8129-0427-3.

Ms. Fitzgibbon is the acclaimed author of the cookbook series *A Taste of* . . . (Wales, Scotland, Ireland, West Country, London, Paris, and Rome), published in Britain by J. M. Dent, with some titles available in the United States through Houghton Mifflin. This current title, about 15 years in the making, compares quite favorably with Ruth Martin's *International Dictionary of Food and Cooking* (New York, Hastings House, 1974. $9.95), which is itself a British book of some 5,000 short definitions. There are, of course, the inevitable duplications, and while Fitzgibbon's work does not have typical encyclopedia-length articles, it does contain a fuller treatment of the material. Even some 3,000 recipes appear from 300 books originally published in several languages. These are conveniently laid out in a narrative style that encourages confidence in use and application, and they are presented naturally under the heading of the major ingredient. Martin's work contains no recipes but does include several entries lacking in Fitzgibbon's book. Thus, the two complement each other.

Thirty-four Western countries are covered here, tracing the gastronomic interrelations and the histories of diverse foods and travel patterns. The 15,000 entries have black-and-white illustrations where appropriate, although they are not up to the calibre of the *Larousse Gastronomique*, which should still be consulted for the French manner of presentation. The obvious use of Fitzgibbon's opus is to translate and define traditional and common terms, for she has chosen foods that have been eaten for at least a hundred years. Unfortunately, this cuts out a lot of American traditions, unless she made an exception. A quick check reveals no entries or cross references to New Orleans coffee (Venezuelan beans plus chicory), Winnipeg gold-eye fish, moose, or even French Canadian tortière pie, which has a long tradition. Certainly the "Gateau Basque" from France is worthy of consideration also, but there is no listing for it. Thus, not everything will be found here, but most items relating to a strong European background will be described. Recommended. [R: BL, 1 June 76, p. 1389; BL, 15 July 76, p. 1617; Choice, Oct 76, p. 957; ARBA 77, p. 741; LJ, 15 Apr 77, p. 877]   Dean Tudor

888.   **The New Larousse Gastronomique: The Encyclopedia of Food, Wine & Cookery.** By Prosper Montagne. American ed., Charlotte Turgeon. New York, Crown, 1977. 1064p. illus. (part col.). index. $25.00. LC 77-9905. ISBN 0-517-53137-2.

For years recognized as the bible of fine cooking, the *Larousse Gastronomique* is also a history of cookery and wine with definitions of terms in current usage. Special material in this alphabetically arranged (by English-language term) work includes sections on diagnoses of wine "illnesses" and how to correct them (not found elsewhere, to my knowledge), a large entry on "culinary methods" to delineate cooking styles of roasting, broiling, sauteeing, etc., and—new to this second English-language edition—a section on "International Cookery" that describes the similarities and differences among the world's cuisines. There are 46 full-size color photographs. Structurally, the entries have copious cross references for British, French, and American terms, and all quantities are noted in metric (SI, often referred to here as French, a distinct error), Imperial, and American measurements. Since the first English translation in 1961 (from the 1938 French original), there has been a shrinkage of 34 pages. The index, now in four columns, was reduced by nine pages, but is now French/English, which is a distinct improvement over the original American edition, which was only indexed in French. The bibliography has also been eliminated, as well as several wine charts (including vintage tables), and the book is still weak in its treatment of liqueurs.

On the other hand, revision has indeed been thorough. There is completely new material on crock pots, microwaves, cuisine minceur, dietetics, the Cuisinart®, and the wok. The cross references are now indicated by actual words instead of the confusing asterisk previously employed. Some slight, older commentary has been dropped, e.g., the entry *Zakusi* no longer refers to the fact that this food *used* to be served in a room apart from the dining room; the entry for *quiche* no longer refers to its bread paste origins; the entry *quartanier* (French, for a four-year-old wild boar) has been dropped, as has *quassia-amara* (a bark from Surinam). The entry title "Irish Stew (English Cookery)" is now "Irish Stew (British Cooking)" but that *still* is not correct. "Italian past*es*," though, was changed to "Italian past*a*." New illustrations have been added, as under "quail"; older ones, dropped or shuffled; but the picture on page 499 of Les Halles (which no longer exists as a market in downtown Paris) is not identified as a historical photograph and may confuse some readers. There are new entries, at random, such as "xylopia" (a fruit), "worcestershire sauce," "ice," "ierchi" (Russian fish), and "intoxication"; new recipes such as "confit of quail" or "quail terrine" or the several listed under "zabaglione" are included, but some have been excised or combined with others. Nutritional data has been updated, as under the now-long entry for "yeast," and the wine section has been completely rewritten. All foreign terms (mainly French) have now been placed in italics. Turgeon, the second editor (Nina Froud did the first edition), should be congratulated on a job well done, for maintaining the brevity of the approximately 8,500 narrative-form entries on preparations and recipes. Readers, though, are again cautioned that the proportions of food are approximate and that the techniques demand skill. Considering the prices paid for cookbooks these days, this book *is* a bargain. [R: ARBA 78, p. 747; BL, 15 July 78, p. 1760]

Dean Tudor

889. Ockerman, Herbert W. **Source Book for Food Scientists.** Westport, CT, AVI Publishing, 1978. 926p. illus. $75.00. LC 77-17406. ISBN 0-87055-228-7.

This comprehensive collection of facts and figures on food-stuffs is organized in two parts. Part 1, the "Source Book," is a 306-page dictionary containing entries for plants, animals, vitamins, spices, additives, units of measurement, and other terms used in food science and technology. Entries give definitions, descriptions, composition analyses, chemical formulas, and other pertinent information. Ample cross references link entries in both parts. Part 2, "Food Composition, Properties and General Data," consists of 615 pages of charts, tables, and diagrams reprinted from government publications and other reference works (sources are fully documented). By consulting this section, the reader can obtain an abundance of useful information on such subjects as grades of canned vegetables, equivalents of various can sizes, cooking procedures for various cuts and grades of meats, grain analyses, properties of food acidulants, sources of vitamins and minerals, fruit growing seasons, harvest dates, and storage life. Also included are food lists for sodium- and gluten-restricted diets, breeds of animals and their characteristics, and even more esoteric subjects, such as the number of drops in a teaspoon of water. The endpapers contain a table for temperature conversion from Fahrenheit to Celsius or vice versa and a set of metric conversion charts for units of weight, liquid measure, volume, and oven temperatures. The work should be useful in both general reference and subject collections. [R: ARBA 79, p. 755; Choice, Feb 79, p. 1687]   Shirley L. Hopkinson

890. Peterson, Martin S., and Arnold H. Johnson. **Encyclopedia of Food Science.** Westport, CT, AVI Publishing, 1978. 1005p. illus. index. (Encyclopedia of Food Technology and Food Science Series, Vol. 3). $75.00. LC 77-17873. ISBN 0-87055-227-9.

This is a companion volume to AVI's previously published *Encyclopedia of Food Engineering* (Carl W. Hall, et al. 1971. $75.00) and *Encyclopedia of Food Technology* (also edited by Johnson and Peterson, 1974. $75.00). The *Encyclopedia of Food Science* contains more than 250 signed entries written by food specialists and authorities, and it covers the entire spectrum of the food sciences. General articles outline the composition, attributes, and deteriorative factors of common foodstuffs; describe manufacturing processes; and analyze food laws and regulations. Specific entries define or describe topics such as ribonucleases, alkaloids, or low fat/low cholesterol diets. Subjects of interest to food scientists from related disciplines are included, as are entries on the methods and tools of scientific research.

Articles range in length from the less-than-one-page entry on auxins to a 56-page essay on vitamins. Most entries contain bibliographies of varying lengths, and many include cross references to related topics. Articles that describe the food science programs of representative countries are gathered in a supplementary section; they stress the nation's food industry, research programs and organizations, and major publications on food science. The comprehensive subject index provides rapid reference access to very specific topics, and a glossary of food science terms and a three-page temperature conversion chart complete the volume. [R: ARBA 79, p. 756; Choice, June 79, p. 507]

Shirley L. Hopkinson

HORTICULTURE

891. **The Encyclopedia of Organic Gardening.** By the staff of *Organic Gardening* Magazine. New rev. ed. Emmaus, PA, Rodale Press, 1978. 1236p. illus. $19.95. LC 77-25915. ISBN 0-87857-225-2.

With over 550,000 copies of the first edition in print, the *Encyclopedia of Organic Gardening* (new revised) by the staff of *Organic Gardening* magazine, is a well-known work. This massive book is an outgrowth of the many new organic methods and developments that have come along since this work was first published in 1959. For instance, the rewritten greenhouse section brings the reader improved methods of construction and recently developed techniques for cutting heating costs. There is also a new entry on raised-bed gardening, a concentration planting method that will be most useful to city gardeners and others with limited space.

The work is organized in a standard encyclopedic format, with over 2,000 entries devoted to identification, cultivation, and use of specific fruits, grains, nuts, vegetables, and ornamentals. In addition, significant emphasis is given to practical how-to's, such as companion planting, composting, greenhouse construction and maintenance, insect control, and soil testing and improvement. Plants are listed first by their common name for layman reference use, and this is followed by their botanical name in italic typeface. The large print makes the clearly written text pleasent to read, and extensive cross referencing provides easy access to all of the material. The reader seeking information on *Helianthus*, for example, is directed by cross reference to "sunflower." When a plant has no common name it is listed under its botanical name. Botanical names are given in the standard binomial manner, with the genus followed by the species, and where necessary, the variety. Cultivars are distinguished by single quotation marks. For the most part, the international rules of botanical nomenclature have been followed, so the plant names used conform with those in Bailey's *Hortus Third* (Macmillan, 1976). There are numerous clearly presented line drawings, black-and-white photographs, and reference tables, 400 of which are new to this edition. It is unfortunate that in a work of this quality, color plates were not used. Both illustrations and textual material about them are located on the same page, thereby eliminating a complaint that I have had about many reference manuals. When open, the book lies flat, and its sturdy binding should keep it serviceable for many years. With 1,236 pages, this big, handsome volume should be a fine base for the beginner or seasoned organic gardener. It is a real buy for anyone who believes that "there exists a strong direct relationship between the health of our bodies and the health of the soil in which we grow our food" (introduction). [R: LJ, 1 Oct 78, p. 1997; ARBA 79, p. 758; BL, 1 Mar 78, p. 1117]   David R. Caraghar

892.   Everett, Thomas H. **The New York Botanical Garden Illustrated Encyclopedia of Horticulture, Volume 1: A-Be.** New York, Garland, 1980. 355p. illus. (part col.). $525.00/10-vol. set. LC 80-65941. ISBN 0-8240-6308-0/set.

The first extensive encyclopedia of horticulture to be published since Macmillan's *Standard Cyclopedia of Horticulture* (1914-17), the *New York Botanical Garden Illustrated Encyclopedia of Horticulture* will undoubtedly become a standard work. The 10-volume set is illustrated with over 10,000 photographs, with several hundred in color. Approximately 20,000 species and varieties of plants are described and, based on the contents of the first volume, illustrated with one or more photographs. Some 900 additional entries deal with subjects other than plant genera; 2,500 cross references and descriptions of 260 plant families complete the set. Thomas H. Everett, the author, has been the senior curator of education at the New York Botanical Garden since 1932, and has written many other books on horticulture.

The typical entry is under scientific name, with popular names listed. Pronunciation is provided when necessary. The plant or plants are described, and scientific names of varieties are provided. Areas of native habitation are outlined, and, in many cases, suitable areas of adaptation for the United States are mentioned. Most articles conclude with descriptions of garden and landscape uses, cultivation, and diseases and pests affecting the plant. More general discussions, for example, of annuals, air layering, or "April, gardening reminders for," make the set more valuable for the gardener. Articles on topics such as annual rings and army worms round out the coverage and make the work more than an encyclopedia of plant species. Entries average one column of a three-column page, although multi-page articles are common. The black-and-white photographs are crisp, but some of the bushier plants, shrubs, and grasses are somewhat difficult to distinguish. The color photographs are grouped on one-sheet insets at intervals throughout the volumes, containing alphabetically arranged illustrations.

The *Illustrated Encyclopedia of Horticulture* satisfies users needing practical information as well as those interested in botanical descriptions. The work is a necessary acquisition for most general collections.   Janet H. Littlefield

893.   Hay, Roy, and Patrick M. Synge. **The Color Dictionary of Flowers and Plants for Home and Garden.** Compact ed. Published in collaboration with The Royal Horticultural Society. New York, Crown, 1975. 584p. illus. (col.). $14.95; $6.95pa. LC 76-75086. ISBN 0-517-52458-9; 0-517-52456-2.

This dictionary of flowers and plants is accompanied by bold colored plates. It will supplement the *Dictionary of Gardening*, prepared by the Royal Horticultural Society, which has no colored plates. The plates have been arranged into six main sections: alpine and rock garden plants; annual and biennial plants; greenhouse and house plants; hardy bulbous plants; perennial plants; trees and shrubs (with climbers and conifers separately grouped within the section). Preceding the photographs are general cultural notes for each section and some helpful techniques on photographing flowers for vivid color and composition. The 2,048 brilliant color plates, in the first 344 pages, are alphabetical by the botanical names within the six main sections. Each of the six plates per page is accompanied by a number and the correct botanical name.

The last 200-plus pages of the volume are the dictionary text, arranged alphabetically by the botanical name with complete cross references from the common names. Here a compact, complete description of the plant is given, noting the identification, flowering time, foliage, soil, hardening, pruning, geographic location, color, and illustration number referring to the plate for the color illustration. This comprehensive collection of plants in color, published by the Royal Horticultural Society, is of outstanding quality. [R: ARBA 76, p. 754]   Mary Clotfelter

894.   **Reader's Digest Encyclopaedia of Garden Plants and Flowers.** London, Reader's Digest Association; distr., New York, W. W. Norton, 1977 (c1975). 799p. illus. (part col.). $22.50. ISBN 0-393-08780-8.

Here we have a most attractive, authoritative gardening work, covering over 2,000 plants, profusely illustrated in color. It is a British publication, written for British gardeners, but a goodly proportion of the plants presented are grown in American gardens. The publishers of this American edition are to be congratulated for their foresight in furnishing a supplementary leaflet with the U.S. equivalents of the proprietary British trade names of the recommended insecticides and fungicides, as well as the special potting soils which are more familiar to the English gardeners. The format, the comprehensive text, and the color illustrations all contribute to making this encyclopedia of considerable use to gardeners on this side of the Atlantic. [R: LJ, 1 May 77, p. 1004; ARBA 78, p. 755; BL, 1 Dec 77, p. 640]   Elizabeth C. Hall

895.   Riker, Tom. **The Healthy Garden Book: How to Control Plant Diseases, Insects, and Injuries.** New York, Stein and Day Publishers, 1979. 224p. illus. maps. index. $11.95; $7.95pa. LC 78-8407. ISBN 0-8128-2515-2; 0-8128-6009-8pa.

Because of the numerous publications on how to grow plants that have appeared in the past few years, this is a timely guide, dealing with plant pests, diseases, and controls (be they natural or chemical). Steps are discussed for the preventative controls of diseases and insects. A comprehensive listing is given of all the major pests and the damage they cause; pests included are insects, plant diseases, weeds, and pest animals. The chapters covering pests on vegetables and fruit trees are arranged alphabetically by the name of the plant, with a verbal description of the pest, damage done, and geographic location of the pests. Excellent illustrations of the insects (many enlarged for easier identification), with larva, and damage to horticultural specimens, accompany each plant. Insects and plant diseases of deciduous trees, shrubs, evergreens, flowers, peony blight, and fireblight of ornamentals are clearly described and illustrated.

Other chapters, all in similar format, deal with roses, bulbs (both summer and fall), house plants, lawns, and air pollution damage to plants. One chapter defines pesticides, explains how they work, and gives instructions on application, discusses health hazards, and provides general information on insecticides and fungicides. The next chapter tells how to control pests without chemical pesticides by employing beneficial insects, organic insecticides, and companion planting. In addition to the detailed index, space for the gardener to record the conditions in the garden (insects and/or diseases), yearly control program, and soil conditions should be helpful for future reference. The work is an offset from typescript with black-and-white woodcuts and steel engravings. All illustrations complement the clear, comprehensive text, and the arrangement is easy to follow. Highly recommended for gardeners and libraries with collections on plants and their problems. [R: ARBA 80, p. 708; BL, 1 Jan 79, p. 726] Mary Clotfelter

896. Wyman, Donald. **Wyman's Gardening Encyclopedia.** Rev. and expanded ed. New York, Macmillan, 1977. 1221p. illus. (part col.). $25.00. LC 76-49114. ISBN 0-02-632060-6.

This revised edition still remains one of the best, most up-to-date gardening encyclopedias available, offering complete information on most major horticultural practices as well as on a wide variety of plant species. Although not an extensive revision, additions such as recent recommendations concerning pesticides, herbicides, fungicides, and insecticides; a greater varietal list of vegetables, fruits, and flowers; and a new table of contents make this a most worthwhile edition. Interestingly though, it is mentioned in the section on house plants that both *Hedera helix* and *Ficus elastica* do well in areas with a minimum amount of light. These species ideally require a good quantity of light (4,000-8,000 footcandles) in order to retain their best, robust appearance. Still, this work remains an indispensable tool for those wishing to increase their knowledge in almost every aspect of gardening. [R: ARBA 78, p. 756] Sarah E. Kuhlman

VETERINARY MEDICINE

897. West, Geoffrey P., ed. **Black's Veterinary Dictionary.** 13th ed. London, Adam & Charles Black; distr., Totowa, NJ, Barnes & Noble Books, a division of Littlefield, Adams, 1979. 906p. illus. maps. $27.50. ISBN 0-7136-1951-1.

Through the years, *Black's* has become an acknowledged reference in the field of veterinary medicine, and a reliable source to consult for information relating to diseases and conditions of various types of animals. The fact that *Black's* is constantly updated adds to its usefulness and reliability as a reference. As with previous editions, certain sections have been revised, in this case those on bloat, eye diseases, and laminitis, while there are new entries on contagious equine metritis, parasitic moths, and the dog's diet. Language is straightforward and largely nontechnical; diseases and problems are described in such a manner that symptoms are recognizable, and diagnoses are easily understood. The articles on fractures, genetics and breeding, muscles, and parasites are particularly good. Line drawings and photographs accompany many articles. *Black's* is one of the most complete veterinary dictionaries in print. Those libraries which have not purchased an earlier edition published in this country under the title *Encyclopedia of Animal Care* (Williams and Wilkins, 1977. 867p. $24.00) and desire an all-animal, all-encompassing dictionary have found it here. Joy Hastings

CHEMICAL ENGINEERING

898.   Considine, Douglas M., ed. **Chemical and Process Technology Encyclopedia.** New York, McGraw-Hill, 1974. 1266p. illus. index. $48.50. LC 73-12913. ISBN 0-07-012423-X.

This one-volume encyclopedia covers many facets of chemical and process technology—inorganic, organic, and physical chemistry and chemical, metallurgical, and process engineering. Arranged alphabetically, it includes many cross references. Topics include equipment, materials, processes, products, and theory. There is a substantial subject index that includes, for example, some 120 references under steel and two references to barbiturates. In addition to the expected traditional topics, there is material that will be of interest to rather diverse groups of workers: medicinal chemists and metallurgists, electronics engineers, and design specialists. The few entries tested almost at random yielded rather detailed and extensive discussions. Many entries include brief bibliographies. The illustrations seem to be helpful and are of good quality. [R: ARBA 75, p. 784; Choice, Dec 74, p. 1453; LJ, 15 Apr 75, p. 735]   John R. Riter, Jr.

CONSTRUCTION

899.   Putnam, R. E., and G. E. Carlson. **Architectural and Building Trades Dictionary.** 3rd ed. Chicago, American Technical Society, 1974. 510p. illus. $15.95. LC 74-75483. ISBN 0-8269-0402-5.

This third edition of a very comprehensive dictionary has been completely updated since the 1955 publication of the second edition. Definitions have been revised where necessary, and many new terms have been included. The clear, simple line drawings, diagrams, and photographs illustrating many of the definitions are well placed in relation to the text and successfully expand the meaning of many of the terms. The section of legal terms has been retained, and an alphabetical listing of building material sizes has been added. This is a thoroughly useful volume for students, professionals, and the general public. [R: ARBA 75, p. 447]   Joan E. Burns

900.   Stein, J. Stewart. **Construction Glossary: An Encyclopedic Reference and Manual.** New York, John Wiley, 1980. 1013p. index. (The Wiley Series of Practical Construction Guides; A Wiley-Interscience Publication). $60.00. LC 79-19824. ISBN 0-471-04947-6.

Each discipline, each industry has developed its own terminology and jargon which to the initiated facilitate and speed communication; to the uninitiated they are frequently a mystery. *Construction Glossary: An Encyclopedic Reference and Manual* is an attempt to provide a comprehensive glossary for those involved, or about to become involved, in the construction industry.

The work is intended to serve the needs of "the working constructor" as well as "engineers, architects, planners, specification writers, project managers, superintendents, materials and equipment manufacturers and the source of all these callings, instructors and their students." All of these will find it a useful tool. Explanations of terms are precise and concise, yet sufficiently detailed to be easily understood.

The major part of the work is divided into 16 divisions conforming to the Masterformat of the Construction Specification Institute. These divisions cover the various parts of a construction project (e.g., site work, concrete, furnishings, mechanical, electrical, etc.), and the terms used in the particular field are defined under the appropriate division.

Two Onform-Divisions contain definitions, explanations, and data on professional services and technical, scientific, and related fields. There is a section of reference data sources, a list of abbreviations, a table of weights and measures, all of it capped by an extensive index.

The author, J. Stewart Stein, AIA, FCSI, is well known and respected in the industry.

Harry Weihs

COMPUTER TECHNOLOGY

901. **Encyclopedia of Computer Science and Technology. Volumes 1-14.** Executive eds., Jack Belzer, Albert G. Holzman, and Allen Kent. New York, Marcel Dekker, 1975-1980. 14v. illus. $75.00/v.(v.1-12); $88.00/v.(v.13 & 14). LC 74-29436.

According to the executive editors, this set was projected for at least 15 volumes. This editorial decision has been revised, and the current projection is 20 volumes, including more than 2,000 articles. The *Encyclopedia of Computer Science and Technology* finds its *raison d'être* in the fact that, hitherto, there has been no encyclopedic survey of computer science addressed to the broad spectrum of its component subfields. One major category of potential users consists of the various kinds of computer scientists, such as program analysts, operations researchers, and mathematicians. Secondly, it is addressed to those who use the products of computer technology, a category that definitely includes librarians. There are, of course, several one-volume works on this subject, e.g., Ralston's *Encyclopedia of Computer Science*. None of them, obviously, approach the scope of this project.

The completion of this authoritative set will be anxiously awaited. In the meantime, as prices do go up, we would recommend standing orders for librarians interested in a comprehensive treatment of computer technology. [R: ARBA 76, p. 770; ARBA 78, p. 768]

ELECTRICAL ENGINEERING

902. Graf, Rudolf F. **Modern Dictionary of Electronics.** 5th ed. Indianapolis, IN, Howard W. Sams, 1977. 832p. illus. $18.95. LC 77-71678. ISBN 0-672-21314-1.

The *Modern Dictionary of Electronics* defines approximately 20,000 terms. All terms from the previous edition were reviewed and revised as necessary, and in addition, some 3,000 new terms were added. Three tables follow the body of the dictionary: the International System of Units (SI), schematic tables, and the Greek alphabet. Graf has extensive experience in the electronics field as a teacher, consultant, and salesman. As in previous editions, the definitions are clearly written. In comparison with the *Electronics Dictionary*, by John Markus, Graf's definitions are fuller, more informative. Frequently Graf gives several definitions for a term, while Markus has only one. Both dictionaries provide accurate, up-to-date information. In choosing an electronics dictionary, one must consider the needs of the user. As a quick tool, Markus will be adequate for the informed reader. But if the dictionary is to be used by a broad spectrum of people with varying degrees of electronics expertise, Graf provides more complete information. [R: ARBA 79, p. 772]

Susan Thorpe

MECHANICAL ENGINEERING

903. Baumeister, Theodore, ed.-in-chief. **Marks' Standard Handbook for Mechanical Engineers.** Eugene A. Avallone, and Theodore Baumeister, III, associate eds. 8th ed. New York, McGraw-Hill, 1978. 1v. (various paging). index. $44.50. LC 16-12915. ISBN 0-07-004132-7.

First published as *Mechanical Engineers' Handbook* (1st-6th eds., 1916-1958), *Standard Handbook for Mechanical Engineers* (7th ed., 1967), *Marks' Standard Handbook for Mechanical Engineers* continues its long tradition of being one of the most widely used and acclaimed handbooks in the field of technology. This extensively revised edition covers such traditional topics as properties and handling of materials, machine elements, fuels and furnaces, power generation, pumps and compressors, and shop processes. In addition, new material is presented in the areas of industrial engineering, instrumentation, and environmental control with special reference to the impact of OSHA and EPA. The encyclopedic topical format successfully established in previous editions is continued, with each topic or subtopic arranged within broad subject chapters. Each topic is authored by a subject specialist or a team of subject specialists. References through 1977 are included as required in order to provide both the practicing engineer and the student with the latest information on a widely divergent subject field. In conjunction with the widespread interest in the conversion to the metric system in the United States, where appropriate and realistic, SI units are presented along with the U.S. Customary System units. Extensively illustrated with line drawings, graphs and tables, the *Handbook* also provides a detailed subject index. [R: ARBA 79, p. 776]   Robert K. Dikeman

TRANSPORTATION

904. **The Illustrated Encyclopedia of Aviation.** Anthony Robinson, executive ed. Reference ed. New York, Marshall Cavendish, 1979. 20v. illus. (part col.). index. $229.50. LC 78-12408. ISBN 0-85685-318-6(set).

Originally published in England by Orbis Publishing Ltd., this work was simply titled *Wings* and it appeared in 120 weekly parts, beginning in 1977. The magazine format remains obvious in the present edition, and we presume that the same arrangement is followed, as has been done in similar works. The illustrations are profuse and include both photos and drawings; many of each are in color. Two complaints about the illustrations: many planes are mentioned without there being even a small drawing, and many illustrations span the gutters, losing much of their effectiveness.

This being an encyclopedia, the entries are arranged alphabetically, but this is not immediately apparent. In each volume the articles are grouped under these headings: Trailblazers, War in the Air, Theory of Flight, Famous Aeroplanes, and Fighting Airmen. Within each group, things are alphabetized through the 20 volumes even though the table of contents headings are not alphabetical. Perhaps it sounds more confusing than it actually is! There is a British bias, as one might expect in a British magazine, but other nations are pretty well represented.

The entries cover the whole of aviation history in this century. They vary from a page or two to articles of 20 or so pages. The longer entries are generally for the more famous aircraft such as the Lancaster, Spitfire, Hurricane, Thunderbolt, Bf 109, and Mustang. A good deal of technical data is supplied, and much is made of the history of several companies and of the development of the more important planes. The biographical information includes material about designers as well as pilots.

The entries chosen for this work obviously represent the interests of the contributors and the availability of data, but the range is excellent and the detail is astonishing; there is much here that the reviewer had not seen before. Unfortunately, there is very little about the training of aviators in the several air services, and there is no mention of the Nomonhon Incident of 1939, which showed the world (very few people noticed it!) that the Japanese had capable planes and determined and excellent pilots.

There is an index bound into the last volume, but a duplicate is also supplied as a separate item. This is a very nice feature in any multi-volume set. All in all, there is a truly marvelous amount of information in this work, and the whole is excellently written and beautifully illustrated. Highly recommended for all aviation collections, the set deserves to be well used. [R: ARBA 81; WLB, May 80, p. 590]   R. G. Schipf

905. Kemp, Peter, ed. **The Oxford Companion to Ships & the Sea.** New York, Oxford University Press, 1976. 971p. illus. (part col.). $39.95. ISBN 0-19-211553-7.

A reference book this good does not need a long review. Its 3,700 articles, arranged alphabetically and well supplemented with halftones and line drawings, fulfill the promise of the title in every respect. The coverage is international and ranges from earliest recorded times to the present. It is rich in biographies, seamanship definitions, battles, famous ships, navigation terms, lore, and almost everything connected with ships and the sea except flora and fauna.

The writing is clear and authoritative, the editing experienced and intelligent. Appendices present equivalent military ranks, the international code of signals in color, rules of the road, buoyage, and units of measurements. This book should prove so informative and entertaining that its binding will not withstand the heavy usage. [R: BL, 15 Sept 77, p. 228; Choice, Apr 77, p. 182; LJ, 15 Jan 77, p. 188; RQ, Summer 77, p. 357; WLB, Feb 77, p. 540; ARBA 78, p. 779]   David Eggenberger

906. Rolfe, Douglas. **Airplanes of the World, 1490-1976.** Rev. and enl. ed. New York, Simon and Schuster, 1978. 482p. illus. index. $11.95. LC 77-16105. ISBN 0-671-22684-3.

This new edition of an old classic aircraft reference brings the state-of-the-art into the picture. The volume is divided into 12 parts, spanning aviation history from the time Leonardo da Vinci made his drawings of heavier-than-air craft during the fifteenth century. Each part has an introduction, which is followed by drawings of particular aircraft. Each drawing has a description containing pertinent physical characteristics, and significant events concerning the aircraft are mentioned, such as the Douglas Skyrocket, the first aircraft to fly at twice the speed of sound. The key to the information is the index, which enables the user to get at a particular aircraft through the manufacturer, the nomenclature, or even the aircraft's nickname. This is a good, inexpensive reference book that should be found in all general library collections. [R: ARBA 80, p. 724; WLB, June 78, p. 811]

Steven J. Mayover

ALMANACS

907. Dupuy, Trevor N., Grace P. Hayes, and John A. C. Andrews. **The Almanac of World Military Power.** 3rd ed. New York, R. R. Bowker, 1975. 387p. illus. maps. index. $27.50. LC 74-7578. ISBN 0-8352-0730-7.

The noted military historian Trevor N. Dupuy and his associates have expanded and updated this valuable reference work, which provides essential information on the strategic situation and defense structure of 154 countries throughout the world, both large and small. Divided into 10 regions, such as North America and Western Europe, the *Almanac* provides a survey describing the military geography of the region, discusses its strategic significance and regional alliances, and includes a chronology of recent intra- and extra-regional conflicts. The survey is followed by a section for each country within the region, which summarizes its power potential statistics (including area, population, total armed forces, GNP, and military budget); describes its defense structure, military assistance programs, and alliances; and analyzes its politico-military policy and strategic problems. Detailed statistics on the armed forces of each of the countries include strength, organization, and armament; in most cases, the information is current as of mid-1974. The uncolored maps that are provided for each region and country are considerably improved from previous editions, being larger and providing more detail. A glossary of military terms includes operating characteristics of major types of aircraft, ships, and armaments.

Ed. note: The fourth edition of the *Almanac* was published in 1980 by Presidio Press (488p. $40.00. LC 80-11844), but was unavailable for review at the time of this writing. [R: BL, 15 Oct 75, p. 323; WLB, May 75, p. 675; ARBA 76, p. 790]   LeRoy C. Schwarzkopf

ATLASES

908. Banks, Arthur. **A Military Atlas of the First World War.** Commentary by Alan Palmer. New York, Taplinger, 1975. 338p. illus. maps. index. $29.95. LC 77-179660. ISBN 0-8008-5242-7.

For the student of the military history of World War I, this very complete collection of maps, charts, diagrams, and tables relating to the slaughter of 1914-1918 will be a necessity. The organization and scope of the book are shown by the following list of sectional headings: The Pre-War Situation; War on the Western Front in 1914; War on the Eastern Front in 1914; The Gallipoli Campaign; The War in 1915; The War in 1916; The War in 1917; The War in 1918; The Peripheral Campaigns; Weapons; The War at Sea; The War in the Air.

Although detailed maps of battles and campaigns predominate, the work has numerous features not commonly associated with atlases, an example of which is the technical explanation of how the Royal Navy overcame the German U-Boat menace by relentless surface tracking and, consequently, exhausting the German submarines' batteries. Such technical explanations as this appear routinely throughout the book as parenthetic adjuncts to maps. The maps are clearly drawn in such a manner as to render the chaotic movements of armies intelligible even to those innocent of military knowledge. [R: ARBA 76, p. 175; Choice, Jan 76, p. 1419; LJ, 1 Dec 75, p. 2245; RQ, Spring 76, p. 263]

909. Davis, George B., Leslie J. Perry, and Joseph W. Kirkley. **The Official Military Atlas of the Civil War.** Comp. by Calvin D. Cowles. New York, Arno Press; New York, Crown

Publishers, 1978. 1v. (various paging). illus. (col.). maps. $60.00. LC 78-16801. ISBN 0-405-11198-3(Arno); 0-517-53407-X(Crown).

One of the greatest publication projects carried out by any government was *The War of the Rebellion: A Compilation of the Official Records of the Union and Confederate Armies, 1861-1865*. Published serially by the U.S. Government Printing Office from 1880 to 1901, the celebrated *Official Records* ran to 70 volumes in 127 books of documents, plus a general index volume and an atlas. It is the atlas that is reproduced here in a sturdy, handsome facsimile volume measuring approximately 13x16-inches, which gives a 10% reduction of the original. It consists of 821 maps, arranged in rough chronological order; 106 engravings, chiefly of fortifications; and 209 drawings of weapons, logistical equipment, uniforms, and federal corps flags. These 1,136 graphics are grouped into 178 double-spread pages, called plates. Some of these plates carry a single, large map, while others have as many as 40 small maps (some of which may be there because of grouping by a single cartographer or a single commander, e.g., General Sheridan in the Valley).

The OR *Atlas* was prepared to complement the written documents. Except for a few maps drawn after the war for historical purposes, the field operations maps in plates 1-135C were prepared "on the spot" to show strategy and tactics down to details of redoubts, picket positions, signal stations, and lines of march. In maps that erred in understanding the ground or troop deployments, the original was allowed to stand. These are graphic reminders of how battles are fought with varying degrees of guesswork, misapprehensions, and downright wrong intelligence (and often won with courage as blind as a commander's battle plan).

Following the field operations plates are general topographical maps (plates 136-161), military divisions and departments (plates 162-171), and miscellaneous drawings (plates 172-175). The front matter carries a new introduction, together with the original preface, table of contents, a correlation of the maps with volumes of the OR, a list of 406 credits for the cartographic work, and an index of the maps' internal contents (the latter must be used with care because of the many imprecise references). There is also a list of maps and sketches that appear in the first 53 volumes of text.

(A microfilm edition of the *Official Records* is available from the National Archives; a five-volume guide-index to the OR is available from the National Archives/Government Printing Office.) [R: ARBA 80, p. 727] David Eggenberger

910. Young, Peter, ed. **Atlas of the Second World War.** Cartography by Richard Natkiel. New York, Putnam, 1974. 288p. illus. maps. index. $17.95. LC 73-78626. ISBN 0-399-11182-4.

This reference work covers every important aspect of the military operations of the war, including battles and campaigns on land and sea and in the air. Arranged according to major theaters or campaigns, and within these by major battles, the book also provides succinct explanatory texts to accompany the 215 detailed maps. Longer narrative introductions precede each main section and provide more general information regarding the forces, the commanders, and the tactical, geographical, and logistical problems involved. Though still somewhat brief, these sectional introductions enable the reader to have enough of an overview so as to be able to understand the sequence and importance of the subsequent battle and campaign maps.

A check of the maps with other sources reveals them to be quite accurate. The text pertaining to each of the maps provides good capsulized descriptions. Interspersed, where appropriate, are informative balance charts that show the relative strength of opposing forces. Photographs relating to the area covered are also included, lending an aura of realism to the maps and text.

The work is comprised of the following sections: "Germany Strikes in the West," "The War in the Mediterranean," "The North African Campaign," "Operation Barbarossa," "The Japanese Offensive," "The Italian Campaign," "The Pacific War," "The Burma Campaign," "Russia Fights Back," "The War in North-West Europe," "The Naval War," "The War in the Air." The index is well done; within the alphabetical sequence, military forces are arranged by nationality, and within this grouping by theater and size of unit.

One could wish for longer and more detailed explanatory texts, but, on the whole, this is an excellent work with clear, concise, and precise maps and texts. A good succinct bibliography would have been an excellent addition. [R: ARBA 75, p. 817; LJ, 1 Oct 74, p. 2477; BL, 15 July 75, p. 1198; Choice, Dec 74, p. 1462; LJ, 15 Apr 75, p. 733]

Hans H. Weber

BIBLIOGRAPHIES

911. Higham, Robin, ed. **A Guide to the Sources of British Military History.** Sponsored by the Conference on British Studies. Berkeley, University of California Press, 1972. 630p. $34.50. LC 74-104108. ISBN 0-520-01674-2.

An outstanding bibliography compiled by Higham with the assistance of a score of American, British, Canadian, and other experts in the field. Subject oriented, the work ranges from English defense policy to military developments to strategic and tactical historical accounts, with special emphasis on the economic, scientific, and technological background thereof. Each of the chapters is prefaced by an explanatory essay of greater length and more in-depth informational value than are customarily found in most full-fledged bibliographies. Entries following the essays are for published works, journal articles, unpublished official works (to include staff studies), government documents, private papers, manuscripts, and archival materials. Within each category, entries are numbered consecutively, arranged alphabetically by author, editor, or other source, and include standard minimal bibliographic data. All titles are conveniently italicized. Updating addenda help the reader identify those works and articles issued just prior to going to press. The vast majority of citations cover material published only in English, although some few major untranslated works of foreign origin and especial interest are noted. [R: ARBA 73, p. 169; Choice, May 72, p. 353]

Lawrence E. Spellman

912. Higham, Robin, ed. **A Guide to the Sources of United States Military History.** Hamden, CT, Archon Books, 1975. 559p. LC 75-14455. ISBN 0-208-01499-3.

This well-planned, useful volume is modelled on the longer *Guide to the Sources of British Military History* (see preceding entry), but it takes into account technology and science as well as modern military and naval medicine. It begins with the European background of American military affairs and proceeds chronologically from Colonial Forces 1607-1766 to the Department of Defense and its components 1945-1973. Eighteen author/experts assisted Professor Higham, who is editor of the journals *Military Affairs* and *The Aerospace Historian*.

After contributing general sources to the introduction, each author had about 4,500 words and 300 entries to survey the broad sources in his field (or period), cover key subtopics, list applicable archives, and suggest further research. The plan worked very well. The volume ends with a 12-page bibliographic essay on museums as historical resources. A solidly compiled and well-manufactured sourcebook. [R: ARBA 76, p. 789; BL, 15 July 76, p. 1619; Choice, Apr 76, p. 204; WLB, Mar 76, p. 551]

David Eggenberger

913. Nebenzahl, Kenneth. **A Bibliography of Printed Battle Plans of the American Revolution, 1775-1795.** Chicago, published for The Hermon Dunlap Smith Center for the History of Cartography at the Newberry Library by University of Chicago Press, 1975. 159p. index. bibliog. $12.00. LC 74-16679. ISBN 0-226-56958-6.

A listing and description of the battle plans of the War of Independence. Over 200 maps are cataloged in chronological order and are provided with an excellent index and supplemented with a list of cartobibliographies and references consulted. Maps relating to the Revolutionary War have been taken from many different types of publications, such as broadsides and almanacs published both in the colonies and in England. The emphasis is on published material, since the bibliography does not include manuscript maps.

The volume is the work of one of the nation's foremost authorities on rare books and maps, Kenneth Nebenzahl, and is the outgrowth of research he has done for other books. It is published under the auspices of the Hermon Dunlap Smith Center for the History of Cartography at Newberry Library. The union list (partial) is compiled from first-hand sources and is presented in a format consistent with the principles of the Anglo-American Cataloging Rules. Additional information, primarily of a military nature, is added to satisfy questions about variant editions, related battles, and copy description.

A first-rate bibliography, the volume is of primary importance to the military historian. It is nonetheless an excellent addition to the cartographic bibliography. [R: AR-BA 76, p. 182; RQ, Winter 75, p. 178]   William Brace

DICTIONARIES AND ENCYCLOPEDIAS

914. Dupuy, R. Ernest, and Trevor N. Dupuy. **The Encyclopedia of Military History: From 3500 B.C. to the Present.** Rev. ed. New York, Harper and Row, 1977. 1464p. illus. bibliog. index. $29.95. LC 74-81871. ISBN 0-06-011139-9.

Dupuy and Dupuy's *Encyclopedia of Military History* is without question the standard reference work on the history of armed conflict, comprehensive, authoritative, and well organized. The *Encyclopedia* is divided by chronologically arranged periods into 21 chapters. Each chapter begins with a discussion of contemporary military trends, outstanding leaders, military organization, weaponry, logistics, tactics, and strategy. Following are a chronology of major conflicts in the time period, and a variant chronology organized by regions. Nearly 200 black-and-white maps and numerous drawings and photographs are included. The general bibliography contains nothing more recent than 1970. There are three outstanding indexes: a general index (events, subjects, persons), an index of battles and sieges, and an index of wars, civil wars, rebellions, and colonial conflicts.

Despite some faults, the *Encyclopedia of Military History* is the indispensable source of information on the topic. The very limited changes of the second edition from the first (1970) bring into question its value to small collections owning the first edition. [R: ARBA 78, p. 178; Choice, July 77, p. 654; LJ, 1 Apr 77, p. 788; WLB, June 77, p. 813]
                                                            Arthur H. Stickney

915. Gunston, Bill, consultant ed. **The Encyclopedia of World Air Power.** New York, Crescent Books, a division of Crown Publishers, 1980. 384p. illus. (part col.). index. $17.95. LC 78-25599. ISBN 0-517-53754-0.

This newest entry in the military aircraft reference market has all the marks of a coffee table volume, but turns out to be a very good reference book. The most striking feature is the extensive use of color photographs and renderings of aircraft. This alone makes it an attractive alternative to Taylor's *Military Aircraft of the World* and *Jane's All the World's Aircraft.*

The work is divided into three sections: air forces, aircraft, and air-launched missiles. The air forces section is arranged alphabetically by continent and provides both photos of representative aircraft and the insignia (roundel and fin flash designs). An appropriately sized narrative gives details of the functional organization of forces, with numbers and types of planes assigned and some mention of bases and condition. Aircraft occupy 304 pages illustrating some 400 examples arranged alphabetically by manufacturer. Virtually all planes have a color photograph, three-way drawing, and/or color profile showing the application of national color schemes and insignia. The most important planes are shown in detailed cutaway drawings with key and in large color renderings of top, side, and front views. There is a narrative sketch of each craft's development, production, functions, and modifications, as well as a tabular presentation of: type, powerplant, performance, weights, dimensions, armament, and countries using. Sixty-nine air-launched missiles are similarly described and about half pictured in relation to carrying aircraft.

An index provides access by number code and common names such as foxbat and phantom. Descriptions show no discrepancies from Jane's aircraft and weapon systems volumes, although the latter's are fuller. Overall, this is a handsome volume, priced reasonably and with good reference qualities. Recommended.   Leon J. Stout

916.   **The Illustrated Encyclopedia of 20th Century Weapons and Warfare.** Bernard Fitzsimons, ed. Milwaukee, WI, Purnell Reference Books, a division of Macdonald Raintree, 1979. 24v. illus. (part col.). index. $249.50. LC 78-26585. ISBN 0-8393-6175-0.

This authoritative military weapons encyclopedia is beautifully and accurately illustrated with over 7,000 black-and-white photographs, color drawings and photographs, line drawings, cutaway drawings, and exploded views. It covers all significant military weapons that were used in substantial numbers by regular armed forces during the twentieth century, as well as weapons that were developed in the last half of the nineteenth century and had major impact after 1900. Also included are weapons that have had an impact on the development of modern armaments without actually seeing service, as well as projects that were never realized but are notable for their influence on subsequent developments.

Coverage includes the following major types of weapons: aircraft, armoured fighting vehicles, artillery, missiles, ships, and small arms. Aircraft types include airships, bombers, early warning and electronic, fighters, helicopters, maritime patrol and ASW, reconnaissance, trainers and transport. Coverage of naval vessels is especially comprehensive and includes the following classes: aircraft carriers, amphibious assault ships, capital ships, cruisers, destroyers, escorts, gunboats, minelayers and minesweepers, monitors, motor torpedo boats, and submarines. Capital ships and significant warships have their own entries; small warships are discussed in classes.

Entries are alphabetical, except that artillery weapons are covered in separate sections at the end of each volume. Weapons are generally entered under their official name. Thus, the famous Japanese World War II fighter aircraft "Zero" is entered under "A6M Zero-sen Mitsubishi." However, this presents no problem since there are numerous cross references. There is also an excellent index broken down by major types of weapons and their subtypes. The index has direct page references to both "Zero" and "A6M."

The *Encyclopedia* appears to be intended primarily for general reference, and should be especially valuable for that purpose. However, military buffs will appreciate the comprehensive coverage and the analytical, critical, and concise entries (although they would probably like more detail). Entries were prepared by acknowledged experts in the fields represented. They provide background on early development of the weapon, modifications and revisions, general physical and operating characteristics, employment of the weapon, and significant events or contributions to warfare. Entries provide excellent analysis, not only in selection of facts presented, but also in critical evaluation of the weapon compared to other weapons.

The *Encyclopedia* is not intended to be a military history, and does not discuss major wars, battles, or military tactics and strategy. Its main shortcoming is inadequate coverage of the ammunition used by these weapons or used independently, such as grenades. There is limited coverage of artillery ammunition, but practically nothing on aerial bombs. Atomic weapons are not covered, although much information is now unclassified. Another shortcoming is the slimness of individual volumes. The 24-volume set includes 2,685 pages, an average of 112 pages per volume. Compressed to 10 or less volumes, the set would be easier to use, and probably less expensive. Despite these minor shortcomings, this is a valuable and outstanding compilation of useful and authoritative information on military weapons of the twentieth century. [R: ARBA 81; RQ, Summer 80, p. 393]

LeRoy C. Schwarzkopf

917. Parrish, Thomas, ed. **The Simon and Schuster Encyclopedia of World War II.** Chief consultant ed., S. L. A. Marshall. New York, Simon and Schuster, 1978. 767p. illus. (part col.). maps. bibliog. index. (A Cord Communications Book). $29.95. LC 78-9590. ISBN 0-671-24277-6.

We are used to claims that a book is the ultimate in a certain field, and certainly the *Simon and Schuster Encyclopedia of World War II* makes these claims—with good reason. Consider the statistics: 4,000 entries, 700,000 words, a comprehensive index; 200 maps and photographs. It maintains that the treatment of strategy, campaigns, battles, heroes, traitors, generals and admirals, statesmen, and scientists is comprehensive, and this is true. There are copious notes on code names, intelligence secrets, and double agents, but with the revelations from ULTRA, the book is well behind this history. Of course this may be an unfair comment, because with its exquisite map diagrams, superb photographs, and a formidable list of consulting editors and contributing writers, this book could not fail. It answers all the questions that the reference desk would expect to get, and as such is a must for most libraries. It is a huge book, but beautifully designed and printed. [R: ARBA 80, p. 165; BL, 1 May 79, p. 1399; Choice, June 79, p. 512; LJ, 1 Jan 79, p. 94; WLB, May 79, p. 652]

P. William Filby

918. Quick, John. **Dictionary of Weapons and Military Terms.** New York, McGraw-Hill, 1973. 515p. illus. bibliog. $27.50. LC 73-8757. ISBN 0-07-051057-1.

A copiously illustrated compendium of military hardware from the dawn of history to the present, with succinct definitional notes on the development, physical characteristics, and use of such hardware. Over 1,200 black-and-white photographs, judiciously selected and of high clarity, portray mankind's martial armory from the earliest edged weapons to the latest nuclear missile. The geographic span is international, with special emphasis on the United States and its NATO allies. Also included are military terms used in intelligence, training, combat, and logistical operations. Technical words and phrases are defined, as well as acronyms, code names, and slang expressions of all the armed services. Cross referencing is extensive. The source of each photograph is indicated.

Summation: an accurate, well-written, and wide-ranging reference work of particular interest to instructors, students, and hobbyists concerned with military history. [R: ARBA 75, p. 814; BL, 1 Oct 74, p. 196]

Lawrence E. Spellman

DIRECTORIES

919. Hewish, Mark, and others. **Air Forces of the World: An Illustrated Directory of All the World's Military Air Powers.** New York, Simon & Schuster, 1979. 264p. illus. (part col.). index. $24.95. LC 79-15255. ISBN 0-671-25086-8.

This is a beautifully illustrated guide that surveys the organization and aircraft inventory of 125 air forces. The authors, all recognized authorities in the field, also describe the missions and role of each air force within its nation's armed forces, defense and attack capabilities, deployment of units, training, and future plans. This book has two notable features: a map section showing the location of air bases of virtually every country, and a technical directory of current aircraft with two view line drawings of each type. The numerous color photographs make for fascinating browsing, even for those with only a marginal interest in military aviation.

The text is arranged in 13 major geographical regions and then alphabetically by country. Each country section includes data about the state's area, population, gross national product, and defense expenditure. Many of the country sections contain air force orders of battle. Although the book contains little material about missiles, it is a most comprehensive reference that is well organized, excellently researched, and available at a remarkably reasonable price. One can only hope that the work will be updated at regular intervals, for it is sure to become a standard reference source on military aviation. Highly recommended for all major libraries. [R: ARBA 81; BL, 15 July 80, p. 1692; LJ, 15 Jan 80, p. 210]

Alexander S. Birkos

BIOGRAPHY

920. **Webster's American Military Biographies.** Springfield, MA, G. & C. Merriam, 1978. 548p. (A Merriam-Webster). $12.95. LC 77-18688. ISBN 0-87779-063-9.

This valuable reference book presents 1,033 biographies of men and women who have figured notably in the military history of the United States. Arranged in alphabetical order, the subjects served the nation (or fought against it) from the Pequot War of 1636-1637 to the evacuation of South Vietnam in 1975. The average length of entries is 450 words; the information is detailed and accurate. Happily, the publisher allowed editor Robert McHenry to define "military" in its broadest sense. Thus the book covers the expected battlefield heroes — Eisenhower, Pershing, Grant, York, Murphy — but also such welcome additions as Confederate spy Belle Boyd, astronaut Neil Armstrong, inventor Richard Gatling, Swiss adventurer Henry Bouquet, historian Samuel Eliot Morison, and naval hero Robert Smalls.

Following the biography of Admiral Elmo Zumwalt are 50 pages of useful and interesting addenda — lists of the secretaries of war, navy, and defense; tables of major commanders in the major wars; chronological listings of wars, battles, expeditions, etc., together with the biographies associated with that particular event. There are also lists of various career categories from adventurers to veterans' officials. The book is well designed and sturdily manufactured. It should be mentioned in all appropriate despatches. [R: Choice, Oct 78, p. 1032; LJ, 15 June 78, p. 1259; WLB, Sept 78, p. 88; ARBA 79, p. 783]

David Eggenberger

INDEX

A. E. Nordenskiöld collection in the Helsinki Univ library, 294

AAAS science book list suppl, 716

Abbott, R. T., 802

Abbreviations and acronyms, 59-60

Abbreviations dictionary, 5th ed, 60

Abdullah, O., 213

Accounting, 395-96

Ackroyd, P. R., 549

Acronyms, initialisms, and abbreviations dictionary, 6th ed, 59

Actors and actresses, 510-12, 514, 521

Adams, C. J., 529

Adams, J. T., 173

Adhesives, 746

Adler, M. J., 51

Advertising, 397

Advocate gd to gay health, 869

Africa, 91-92, 129-31, 286, 190-91

African encyclopedia, 129

Aging, 362

Air forces, 915, 919

Air forces of the world, 919

Airplanes, 906, 915, 919

Airplanes of the world, 1490-1976, rev ed, 906

ALA world encyclopedia of library & information services, 97

Album of American history, 173

Alchemy, 848

Alden, D. W., 702

Alexander, G. L., 290, 300

Alexis Lichine's new encyclopedia of wines & spirits, 2nd ed, 880

Allaby, M., 807

Allen, C. G., 249

Allen, C. J., 548

Allen, D., 738

Allen, N., 515

Alloway, D. N., 312

Almanac of world military power, 3rd ed, 907

Alternative culture, 35, 61

AMA drug evaluations, 4th ed, 873

American Academy of Pediatrics, 865

American & British genealogy & heraldry, 2nd ed, 224

American art, 410, 416, 425

American Assn of Law Libraries, 269-70

American authors & books, 1640 to the present day, 3rd ed, 679

American book of days, 3rd ed, 573

American book publishing record cumulative 1950-77, 8

American bottles & flasks & their ancestry, 448

American chemists & chemical engineers, 749

American Contract Bridge League, 345

American culture, 573-74

American drama, 512, 633

American drama criticism, 1890-1977, 2nd ed, 497

American film directors, 525

American Film Institute catalog of motion pictures: 1961-70, 522

American Geological Institute, 821

American governors & gubernatorial elections, 1775-1978, 257

American heritage dictionary of the English language, 579

American historical fiction, 3rd ed, 686

American Indian & the U.S., 221

American Library Assn., 118

American Library Assn Govt Documents Round Table, 258

American literature, 684

American literature, 215, 679-81 – bibliography, 629, 631-32, 682-88; biography, 689

American Medical Association, 873

American men & women of science, 14th ed, 721

American music, 488

American Pharmaceutical Association, 875, 877

American place names, 301

American political dictionary, 5th ed, 251

American prints in the LC, 419

American Psychological Assn, 843

American Revolution, 175-76, 183, 913

American seashells, 2nd ed, 802

American Society for Clinical Pharmacology & Therapeutics, 873

American theatrical arts, 505

American women writers, 371

Amphibians, 803-804

Amy Vanderbilt complete book of etiquette, rev ed, 576

Analytical concordance to the Rev. Standard Version of the New Testament, 556

Anatomy of wonder, 672

Anderson, G. H., 540

Anderson, M., 494

Andors, S., 134

Andrews, E. L., 663

Andrews, J. A. C., 907

Andrews, T., 851

Andriot, J. L., 62

Animals, 781-84

Annals of opera, 1597-1940, 3rd ed, 480

Anniversaries & holidays, 3rd ed, 572

Annotated bibliog of selected Chinese reference works, 3rd ed, 133

Anthologies, 51

Anthropology, 374-75, 377-78

Antibiotics, 874

Antiquarian books, 39

Antique American country furniture, 439

Antiques, 436-40

Antony, A., 739

Apel, W., 472

Applied & decorative arts, 432

Arab Islamic bibliog, 150

Arabic language dictionaries, 605

Arata, E. S., 215

Arbingast, S. A., 288

Archaeological atlas of the world, 159

Archaeology, 155-59

461

Architectural & building trades dictionary, 3rd ed, 899

Architecture, 417-18, 899

Archives, 108, 186, 223, 366

Area Studies—Africa, 129-31; Asia, 132-36; Australasia, 137-38; Canada, 139-40; China, 133-35; Developing countries, 128; Eastern Europe and the Soviet Union, 141-45; Great Britain, 146; India, 136; Latin America, 147-49; Middle East and North Africa, 150-52; U.S., 153-54

Arem, J. E., 830

Arnold encyclopedia of real estate, 403

Art—bibliography, 404-406; biography, 414-16; dictionaries, 407-409, 422, 426-27; directories, 423; encyclopedias, 410-12; filmographies, 524; handbooks, 424-25, 428; indexes, 413

Art books, 1950-79, 404

Art galleries and museums, 404

Art industries and trade, 432-35; 453

Art libraries, 109, 111

Art library manual, 111

Artists, 412-16, 422, 426

Artists' & illustrators' encyclopedia, 2nd ed, 412

Arts, 6

Arts in America, 406

Ash, B., 674

Ash, L., 100

Asia, 132, 193

Associations, 209

Astronomy—atlases, 729-30; dictionaries and encyclopedias, 731-34; handbooks, 735-38

Astrophysics, 732, 737

Atkins, B. T., 609

Atlas of . . . Africa, 286; African history, 2nd ed, 190; American history, rev. ed, 177; Central America, 288; early American history, 176; early man, 372; medieval man, 165; representative stellar spectra, 730; the American Revolution, 175; the Second World War, 910; the universe, 729; U.S. trees: Florida, 779

Atlases—Africa, 286; archaeological, 159; Asia, 193; bibliography, 290, 294-96; Canada, 287; Central America, 288; China, 289; economic, 384; historical, 163-66; oceans, 281; religion, 530-31; U.S., 175-78, 284-85; world, 277-80, 282-83

Atmospheric sciences, 819

Auchard, J., 684

Audiovisual equipment, 331

Audubon Society field gd to North American birds, 785-86

Audubon Society field gd to North American wildflowers, 768-69

Australia, 23, 84, 138

Australian bibliography, 23

Australian dictionary of biography: 1891-1939, 84

Author biographies master index, 72

Authors, 34, 72, 215, 371, 646-47, 649, 651, 664-66, 679, 683, 689, 697, 699

Authors & printers dictionary, 11th ed, 34

Authorship, 70

Avallone, E. A., 903

Avery, C. B., 202, 570

Aviation, 904, 906

Avi-Yonah, M., 155

Awards, honors, & prizes: U.S. & Canada, 4th ed, 50

Axford, L. B., 460

Ayensu, E. S., 764

Bain, R., 689

Bair, F. E., 829

Baker, C., 604

Baker, D., 735

Baker's biographical dictionary of musicians, 6th ed, 490

Baker's dictionary of Christian ethics, 538

Bakewell, K. G. B., 402

Bakó, E., 141

Baldrige, L., 576

Ballet, 501

Banking, 398

Banks, A., 908

Barbour, R. W., 805

Bard, A. J., 745

Barker, E. S., 736

Barnhart, C. L., 585, 603

Barnhart dictionary of new English since 1963, 603

Baronetage, 232

Baroque art, 428

Barraclough, G., 163

Barrett, H., 477

Barron, N., 672

Barron's gd to the two-year colleges, rev ed, 323

Barrow, G. B., 225

Barzun, J., 160, 604

Baseball, 339-40

Baseball encyclopedia, 4th ed, 340

Basic school edition, 587

Basketball, 341

Basler, R. P., 154

Bateson, F. W., 629, 692

Battles, 178, 913

Baumeister, T., 903

Bawden, L., 516

Baylen, J. O., 85

Beale, S., 34

Beall, K. F., 419

Bean, W. J., 777

Beer, 882

Behavioral science, 844

Belch, J., 330

Bellot, H. H., 201

Belzer, J., 901

Bennett, H., 741

Benson, M., 620

Bereavement, 363

Berke, B., 458

Berlitz, C., 602

Bernstein, J. E., 363

Besançon, R. M., 750

Besford, P., 356

Best in children's books . . . 1973-78, 659

Best of the best, 2nd ed, 656

Besten der Besten, 2nd ed, 656

Betteridge, H. T., 611

Bible, 547-58

Bible lands, 155

Bibliographia Canadiana, 195

Bibliographical gd to the study of Southern literature, 685

Bibliography, 149, 561

Bibliography, national—Australia, 23; Germany, 24, 25; Great Britain, 20-22; South Africa, 26; U.S., 8-19

Bibliography of . . . American children's books printed prior to 1821, 660; American literature, 682; bioethics, 852; British history 1789-1851, 198; crime fiction, 1749-1975, 668; geography, 291;

Bibliography of (cont'd) . . .
Latin American bibliographies published in periodicals, 149; maps & charts published in America before 1800, 295; medieval drama, 2nd ed, 498; philosophical bibliogs, 561; printed battle plans of the American Revolution, 1775-95, 913; research studies in education, 1926-40, 314; the socioeconomic aspects of medicine, 851; songsters printed in America before 1821, 469
Biggerstaff, K., 133
Bill of Rights, 273
Biochemistry, 744
Bioethics, 562, 852
Biographical dictionaries & related works . . . 2nd suppl, 71
Biographical dictionaries master index, 73
Biographical dictionary of . . . American educators, 329; American science, 17th through 19th centuries, 723; film, 521; modern British radicals: 1770-1830, 85; Republican China, 86; the Comintern, 261
Biographical directory of the American Academy of Pediatrics, 1980, 865
Biographical directory of the U.S. executive branch, 1774-1977, 2nd ed, 259
Biographical ency & who's who of the American theatre, 512
Biographical register of the Confederate Congress, 189
Biography — Africa, 91-92; Australia, 84; authors, 371, 644-51, 662, 664-66, 689, 697, 699; Canada, 88; China, 86; Communist countries, 93, 261; Great Britain, 85, 90; India, 89; international, 53, 71-81, 93, 168; Ireland, 87, 90; Jews, 219; librarians, 124; military, 920; scientists, 721-23, 749; social scientists, 127; U.S., 82-83, 189, 259
Biology, 754-58
Biomedical subject headings, 2nd ed, 110
Bird families of the world, 790

Birds, 785-93
Birnbaum, M., 324
Bishop, A. C., 831
Black, H. C., 271
Black American reference book, 216
Black American writers past & present, 215
Black genesis, 229
Black music, 217
Black playwrights, 1823-1977, 213
Blackburn, G. M., III, & L. A., 661
Blacks, 211-17, 229
Blacks in films, 526
Black's law dictionary, 5th ed, 271
Black's medical dictionary, 31st ed, 857
Black's veterinary dictionary, 13th ed, 897
Blanck, J., 682
Blom, E., 473
Blues who's who, 492
Boatner, M. M., III, 183
Bobinski, G. S., 124
Bock, H., 349
Bogart, G. L., 642
Boger, L. A., 455
Bond, H. L., 436
Bond, O. F., 622
Bondanella, J. C. & P., 707
Book collecting, 37-39
Book collector's hndbk of values: 1978-79, 3rd ed, 37
Book publishers directory, 2nd ed, 35
Book review digest: . . . index 1905-74, 27
Book reviews, 27, 116-17
Book selection, 95, 116-23, 206
Bookman's gd to Americana, 7th ed, 38
Books and reading, 121, 315
Books for college libraries, 2nd ed, 118
Books for secondary school libraries, 5th ed, 119
Books in series in the U.S., 2nd ed, 1
Books to help children cope with separation & loss, 363
Boorman, H. L., 86
Borchardt, D. H., 23
Borklund, E., 645
Bossart, J. K., 866
Botanical bibliogs, 759
Botany — bibliography, 759; cultivated plants, 761-63; dictionaries, 760;

Botany (cont'd) — endangered plants, 764; flowers, 765-71; grasses, 772; herbs, 773; mosses & fungi, 774-76; trees, 777-80
Botterweck, G. J., 547
Bottle, R. T., 754
Bottles, 448
Bourgeois, J., 824
Boutell's heraldry, rev ed, 233
Bower, A. S., 366
Boyer, R. H., 673
Boylan, H., 87
Brace, E. R., 344
Bradley, V. A., 37
Brandon, S. G. F., 536
Brauer, J. C., 534
Breed, P. F., 506
Breen, W., 441
Brewer, A. M., 35
Brewer's dictionary of phrase & fable, centenary ed, 564
Brewton, J. E., 661
Brickman, W. W., 321
Bridge (card game), 345
Briggs, K., 565-66
Britannica encyclopedia of American art, 410
British art, 427
British bibliog & textual criticism, 691
British drama, 633
British Library general catalogue of printed books to 1975, 20
British literature, 629, 631-32, 690-97
British medical dictionary, 858
British periodicals & newspapers, 1789-1832, 146
British writers, 697
Broadcast communications dictionary, rev ed, 625
Broadman Bible commentary, 548
Broderick, R. C., 545
Bromiley, G. W., 552-53
Brooke-Little, J. P., 233-34, 236
Brooks, R. A., 702
Brown, C., 557
Brown, L., 624
Brown, L. G., 120
Brown, L. M., 198
Bruccoli, M. J., 683
Bruce, C. R., II, 442
Brun, C., 295
Bruntjen, C. & S., 10-12
Bryant, L. E., 49

Bryforiski, D., 627-28
Buchanan, W. W., 63
Buchanan-Brown, J., 635
Budge, E. A. W., 608
Building, 899-900
Building ethnic collections, 206
Bulas, K., 618
Bulgarian literature, 711
Bull, J., 785
Burchfield, R. W., 592
Burgess, J., 192
Burington, R. S., 724
Burke, J. B., 235
Burke, W. J., 679
Buros, O. K., 302-11
Burton, M. & R., 781
Bush, G. P., 40
Business — bibliography, 385-86; dictionaries & encyclopedias, 390; directories, 391-94
Business information sources, 385
Business services, 394
Butler, J. P., 188
Butterflies and moths, 798
Butterworths medical dictionary, 2nd ed, 858
Buttlar, L., 206, 209
Byrne, P. R., 179

Cabeen, R. M., 450
Caenegem, R. C. van, 167
California Indians, 379
Cambridge bibliog of English literature, 692
Cambridge encyclopaedia of astronomy, 731
Cambridge history of the Bible, 549
Cambridge Italian dictionary, 615
Campaigns of the American Revolution, 178
Campbell, B., 787
Canada, 88, 139-40, 195, 287, 698
Canadian artists, 415
Canadian Centre for Films on Art, 524
Canadian literature, 698
Canadian reference sources, 139; suppl, 140
Cannons' bibliography of library economy, 1876-1920, 96
Cappon, L. J., 176
Card games, 346
Caribbean, 147
Caribbean literature, 699

Caribbean writers, 699
Caribbeana 1900-65, 147
Caring for your child, 870
Carlson, G. E., 899
Carpentry, 462
Carrington, D. K., 299
Carroll, D., 601
Carter, T. D., 799
Cartographers, 298
Cass, J., 324
Cassell's encyclopaedia of world literature, rev ed, 635
Cassell's German-English, English-German dictionary, rev ed, 611
Castillo, C., 622
Cataloging and classification, 106-107, 110, 114-15
Catalogue of American portraits, 425
Catalogue of the universe, 738
Catholic church, 532, 545-46
Catholic encyclopedia, 545
Catholic Univ of America, 546
Cats, 886
Cavendish, R., 846
Central America, 288
Central Europe, 143
Ceramics, 455-56
Chadwick, L. E., 796
Challinor, J., 822
Chambers, C. A., 366
Chamber's biographical dictionary, rev ed, 77
Chambers dictionary of science & technology, 717
Chan, L. M., 106-107
Chapel, C. E., 446
Chapman, R. L., 597
Charles-Picard, G., 156
Chase, A., 772
Checklist of American imprints, 1820-29: Index, 9; 1831, 10; 1832, 11; 1933, 12
Chemical & process technology encyclopedia, 898
Chemical engineering, 898
Chemistry — bibliography, 739-40; biography, 749; dictionaries, 741-44; encyclopedias, 745-48
Chemists, 749
Chess, 344
Chi-Bonnardel, R. V., 286
Childhood in poetry: 2nd suppl, 654
Children, 363, 870
Children's books in the rare book division of the LC, 655

Children's dictionary, 582
Children's literature, 121, 652-53 — authors and illustrators, 420, 664-66; bibliography, 654-60; indexes, 661-63
Children's literature . . . 2nd suppl, 121
China, 86, 133-35, 289
Chinese-English dictionary of modern usage, 606
Chinese language dictionaries, 606
Choice: a classified cumulation, 116
Christianity, 534-35, 537-38, 540-41
Christie, I. R., 198
Chronologies in New World archaeology, 158
Chronology, historical, 158, 168-70, 191-92
Chronology of . . . African history, 191; Indian history, 192; world history, 2nd ed, 169
Civil War, U.S., 189, 909
Clabburn, P., 457
Clapp, J., 429
Clarendon Press, 384
Clarke, J. A., 634
Classical literature, 700-701
Classification of books, 107, 114-15
Climates of the states, 2nd ed, 828
Climatology, 828-29
Cline, H. F., 378
Clotfelter, C. F., 350
Clothing and dress, 458
Clute, J., 675
Cochran, D. M., 803
Coffey, D. J., 886
Cohen, R., 377
Coins, 441-42, 444-45
Collecting — antiques, 436-40; coins and money, 441-45; dolls, 451; firearms, 446-47; glass, 448-49; stamps, 444, 450
Collection development, 515
College and university libraries, 118
College blue book, 17th ed, 325
Colleges and universities, 323-26
Collins, F. H., 34
Collins encyclopedia of music, 475
Collins-Robert French-English, English-French dictionary, 609

Collocott, T. C., 77
Colonialism in Africa, 1870-1960, 130
Color dictionary of flowers & plants for home & garden, compact ed, 893
Color encyclopedia of gemstones, 830
Colton, V., 459
Comic books, 667
Comitas, L., 147
Commager, H. S., 174
Commire, A., 664
Common insects of North America, 797
Communication, 625
Communism, 93, 260-63
Communism in the U.S., 262
Community colleges, 323
Compact edition of the Oxford English dictionary, 589
Comparative gd to American colleges, 9th ed, 324
Complete color encyclopedia of antiques, rev ed, 437
Complete dog book, 16th ed, 883
Complete ency of horses, 885
Complete ency of ice hockey, rev ed, 349
Complete gd to heraldry, rev ed, 236
Complete illustrated ency of the world's firearms, 447
Complete outdoors encyclopedia, 337
Comprehensive dissertation index, 1861-1972, 327
Comprehensive index to English-language little magazines 1890-1970, series one, 643
Comprehensive Persian-English dictionary, 617
Computer science, 901
Conant, I. H. & R., 804
Concise Cambridge Italian dictionary, 615
Concise chemical & technical dictionary, 3rd ed, 741
Concise dictionary of . . . American biography, 3rd ed, 82; physics & related subjects, 2nd ed, 753; the Christian world mission, 540
Concise encyclopedia of antiques, 440
Concise encyclopedia of astronomy, 2nd ed, 734

Concise Oxford companion to the theatre, 496
Concise Oxford dictionary of . . . ballet, 501; current English, 6th ed, 593; French literature, 704; music, 2nd ed, 474; opera, 2nd ed, 482
Condensed chemical dictionary, 9th ed, 743
Congress & the nation, 1973-76, 252
Congressional Quarterly, 252, 255
Congressional Quarterly's gd to Congress, 2nd ed, 253
Congressional Quarterly's gd to the U.S. Supreme Court, 268
Connoisseur, 437
Connolly, M. J., 271
Connor, B. M. & J. M., 507
Considine, D. M., 720, 815, 898
Construction, 899-900
Construction glossary, 900
Consultants & consulting organizations directory, 4th ed, 394
Contemporary artists, 414
Contemporary dramatists, 2nd ed, 513
Contemporary games, 330
Contemporary literary criticism, 627
Contemporary literary critics, 645
Contemporary novelists, 2nd ed, 647
Contemporary popular music, 487
Contests, 46
Continental Congress, 188
Cooking, 888
Cooper, M. F., 9
Copyright, 40-41
Cordasco, F., 312
Core media collection for elementary schools, 2nd ed, 120
Cotterell, A., 567
Coughlan, M. N., 121
Coulson, J., 591
Country music, 483, 488
Cowie, A. P., 594
Crabbe, D., 813
Crafts, 452-54, 459
Crafts business encyclopedia, 453
Crafts for today, 452
Cramp, S., 788-89
Crawford, E. D., 665

Creative Canada, 415
Crime fiction, 668-69
Critchley, M., 858
Critical bibliog of French literature, v. 6, 702
Critical gd to Catholic reference books, 2nd ed, 532
Cross, F. L., 541
Cross, R. W., 172
Crowell's hndbk of . . . classical mythology, 571; contemporary drama, 494; Elizabethan & Stuart literature, 693
Crowley, E. T., 59, 391-92
Crowley, M., 814
Cuddon, J. A., 636
Cultural anthropology, 377
Cummings, P., 416
Cumulative subject gd to U.S. govt bibliogs, 1924-73, 64
Cumulative subject index to the monthly catalog of U.S. govt publications, 1900-71, 63
Cunningham, J. A., 766
Curley, D. N., 680
Cyclopedia of education, 321
Czechoslovakian language dictionaries, 607
Czechoslovakian literature, 711

Daily, J. E., 98
Dale, L. A., 850
Dance, 501
Dangerfield, S., 884
Daniells, L. M., 385
Darby, H. C., 164
Data bases, 36
Davids, L. E., 400
Davies, J. G., 535
Davis, G. B., 909
Davis dictionary of the Bible, 4th ed, 550
Days, 573
Debrett's peerage & baronetage with Her Majesty's Royal Warrant Holders 1980, 232
DeConde, A., 250
Decorative art, 407, 432-35, 438
DeFilipps, R. A., 764
De Ford, M. A., 168
de Gámez, T., 621
Deighton, L. C., 317
DeLaura, D. J., 690
Dellar, F., 483
Delpar, H., 148
de Montreville, D., 665

De Sola, R., 60
Detective fiction, 668-69
Developing countries, 128
Devers, C. M., 28
Diagram Group, 478
Diamant, L., 625
Dick, E. A., 776
Dickinson, A. T., Jr., 686
Dictionary & glossary of the Koran, 543
Dictionary buying gd, 578
Dictionary for accountants, 5th ed, 396
Dictionary of . . . advertising terms, 397; American history, rev ed, 184; American library biography, 124; American penology, 365; American slang, 2nd ed, 595; architecture, rev ed, 417; behavioral science, 844; biblical theology, 2nd ed, 555; biochemistry, 744; biographical quotation of British and American subjects, 53; birds in color, 787; botany, 760; British folk-tales in the English language, 565; British miniature painters, 422; British portraiture, 427; business & management, 390; butterflies & moths in color, 798; Canadian biography, 1771-1800, 88; comparative religions, 536; contemporary American artists, 3rd ed, 416; education, 3rd ed, 319; entomology, 795; fictional characters, rev ed, 639; film makers, 519; films, 518; foreign terms, 2nd ed, 602; foreign terms in the English language, 601; geological terms, rev ed, 821; geology, 5th ed, 822; German history 1806-1945, 196; insurance, 400; international finance, 399; international law & diplomacy, 272; Irish biography, 87; Islam, being a cyclopaedia . . . of the Muhammadan religion, 539; Italian literature, 707; literary terms, 636; literature in the English language from Chaucer to 1940, 640; liturgy & worship, 535; medical ethics, 861; modern written Arabic, 3rd ed, 605; national biography, 89;

Dictionary of (cont'd) . . . national biography, compact ed, 90; 19th century antiques & later objets d'art, 438; non-Christian religions, 542; occupational titles, 4th ed, 401; organic compounds, 4th ed, 742; Oriental literatures, 709; philosophy, 560; physics & allied sciences, 751; plants used by man, 762; political economy, 389; politics, rev ed, 243; Russian historical terms from the eleventh century to 1917, 204; scientific biography, 722; statistics, 4th ed, 383; the Czech literary language, 607; the decorative arts, 434; the environment, 807; the flowering plants & ferns, 8th ed, 763; the history of ideas, 563; the natural environment, 297; tools used in the woodworking & allied trades, c1700-1970, 462; 20th century art, 408; useful & everyday plants & their common names, 761; weapons & military terms, 918; word & phrase origins, 590; world literary terms, rev ed, 641; world mythology, 567; world pottery & porcelain, 455
Diplomacy, 272
Directories, 45-46
Directory of . . . American Jewish institutions, 219; American scholars, 7th ed, 328; archives & manuscript repositories in the U.S., 186; directories, 45; special libraries and information centers, 5th ed, 101; of world museums, 48
Dissertations, academic, 327
Divorce in the U.S., Canada, & Great Britain, 364
Documents of American history, 9th ed, 174
Dogs, 883-84
Dolls, 451
Dolphins & porpoises, 800
Domestic animals, 883-86
Dorland's medical dictionary, shorter ed, 859
Dorling, A. R., 725
Doskey, J. S., 331

Doubleday Roget's thesaurus in dictionary form, 596
Douglas, J. D., 537
Dowell, A. T., 114
Dox, I., 860
Drachkovitch, M. M., 261
Drama—bibliography, 213, 497-98; biography, 513-14; dictionaries & encyclopedias, 499-500, 502-503; directories, 504; handbooks, 494, 496; history, 495; indexes, 506-509
Dramatic criticism, 497, 506
Dramatic criticism index, 506
Dramatists, 648
Dramatists, 213, 512-14, 646, 648
Dreyfuss, R. H., 40
Drugs, 873-79
Drury's gd to best plays, 3rd ed, 504
Duckett, K. W., 108
Duckles, V., 467
Dudas, J. L., 817
Duignan, P., 130
Duncan, A. S., 861
Dunmore-Leiber, L., 27
Dunning, J., 626
Dunstan, G. R., 861
Dupuy, R. E., 914
Dupuy, T. N., 907, 914
Dyson, A. E., 694
Dyson, A. J., 696

Early American proverbs & proverbial phrases, 58
Earth & man, 277
Earth sciences—encyclopedias, 818-20; geology, 821-26; hydrology, 827; meteorology, 828-29; mineralogy, 830-34; oceanography, 835-36; soil science, 837
East Central Europe, 143
Eastern Europe, 142-44
Eastman Kodak, 463
Eberhart, G. M., 847
Eberly, J. E., 182
Ebershoff-Coles, S., 352
Echols, J. M., 614
Ecology, 809
Economics, 384, 388-89
Eddleman, F. E., 497
Editing, 70
Education—bibliography, 302-16; biography, 328-29; dictionaries and encyclopedias, 317-22; directories, 323-26; indexes, 327; instructional media, 330-34

Educational research, 314, 316, 318
Educational tests and measurements, 302-11
Educators, 328-29
Edwards, P., 559
Eggenberger, D. I., 79
Egyptian hieroglyphic dictionary, 608
Ehresmann, D. L., 405, 432
Ehrlich, E., 583
Eichelberger, C. L., 687-88
Eichholz, A., 229
Eisner, G. M., 860
Elections, 256
Electrochemistry, 745
Electronics, 902
Elementary school library collection, 12th ed, 122
Elliott, C. A., 723
Eminent contributors to psychology, 839-40
Emmens, C. A., 523
Encyclopaedia Africana dictionary of African biography, 91-92
Encyclopedia buying gd, 2nd ed, 42
Encyclopaedia Judaica, 218
Encyclopedia of . . . accounting systems, 395; American foreign policy, 250; American history, 5th ed, 185; anthropology, 374; antibiotics, 2nd ed, 874; antiques, 436; archaeological excavations in the Holy Land, v. 4, 155; Australia, 138; banking & finance, 7th ed, 398; bioethics, 562; business information sources, 4th ed, 386; chemistry, 3rd ed, 747; China today, 134; computer science & technology, 901; crafts, 454; decorative arts 1890-1940, 435; education, 317; educational media communications & technology, 322; educational research, 4th ed, 318; electrochemistry of the elements, 745; energy, 811; environmental science & engineering, 808; fairies, 566; food science, 890; football, 16th ed, 343; geochemistry & environmental sciences, 818; herbs & herbalism, 773; human behavior, 841; information systems & services, 3rd ed, 104; Latin America, 148;

Encyclopedia of (cont'd) . . . library & information science, 98; military history, rev ed, 914; minerals, 833; motor sport, 353; mystery & detection, 669; occultism & parapsychology, 849; occupational health & safety, 387; organic gardening, rev ed, 891; Papua & New Guinea, 137; philosophy, 559; physics, 2nd ed, 750; polymer science & technology, 746; pop, rock, & soul, rev ed, 486; practical photography, 463; sailing, rev, 354; science fiction & fantasy through 1968, v. 1-2, 676; sedimentology, 824; social work, 17th ed, 360; sociology, 361; soil science, 837; southern Africa, 6th ed, 131; sport sciences & medicine, 862; sports, 6th ed, 336; swimming, 2nd ed, 356; the American Revolution, 183; the biological sciences, 2nd ed, 757; the Third Reich, 197; the Third World, 128; the unexplained, 846; world air power, 915; world history, 5th ed, 170; world literature in the 20th century, 637-38; world regional geology: Western Hemisphere, 823; world soccer, 342; world theater, 499; Zionism & Israel, 151
Encyclopedias — general, 43-44; selection aids, 42
Encyclopedic dictionary of mathematics, 726
Encyclopedic directory of ethnic newspapers & periodicals in the U.S., 2nd ed, 210
Encyclopedic directory of ethnic organizations in the U.S., 209
Endangered & threatened plants of the U.S., 764
Energy, 810-11, 813-17
Energy dictionary, 810
Energy hndbk, 816
Energy: print & nonprint matls, 814
Energy sourcebook, 817
Energy technology hndbk, 815
Engineering and technology — bibliography, 715; chemical engineering, 898;

Engineering and technology (cont'd) — computer technology, 901; construction, 899-900; electrical engineering, 902; handbooks, 728; mechanical engineering, 903; transportation, 904-906
Engineering mathematics hndbk, 2nd ed, 728
Engineers, 749
English-Indonesian dictionary, 614
English language — dictionaries, 578-93; foreign terms, 601-602; grammar and usage, 603-604; idioms and colloquialisms, 594-95; synonyms and antonyms, 596-600
English literature, 631, 633, 640, 692
English novel, 694
English novel explication, 696
English-Serbocroatian dictionary, 620
English tests & reviews, 302
Ensminger, M. E., 885
Entomology, 795
Environmental engineering, 808
Environmental science, 297, 806-809, 812, 818
Eponyms dictionaries index, 76
Ernst, C. H., 805
Espenshade, E. B., Jr., 278
Ethics, 538, 562
Ethnic studies — comprehensive works, 206-210; blacks, 211-17; Jews, 218-19; Native Americans, 220-21; Puerto Ricans, 222; Slavic Americans, 223; USSR, 207; U.S., 208-10
Ethnographic bibliog of North America, 4th ed, 373
Ethnology, 373, 375
Ethology, 783
Ethridge, J. M., 45
Etiquette, 575-76
European Assn of Information Services, 36
Eusidic, 36
Evans, C. F., 549
Evans, I. H., 564
Everett, T. H., 892
Ewen, D., 491

Fables, 564
Facts on File dictionary of astronomy, 733

Fadum, A. M., 220
Fage, J. D., 190
Fairbridge, R. W., 818, 823-24, 837
Fairchild, W. B., 806
Fairchild's dictionary of textiles, 6th ed, 461
Fairies, 566
Fairy tales, 568
Families of flowering plants arranged according to a new system based on their probable phylogeny, 3rd ed, 765
Family, 363, 845
Fantasy, 527, 673, 676
Fantasy literature, 673
Far Eastern serials, 132
Farish, M. K., 468
Farrand, J. Jr., 785
Faruqi, I. R., 531
Fascism, 264
Fashion production terms, 458
Fellmann, J. D., 292
Fenwick, R. D., 869
Ferguson, A. D., 205
Ferns, 761, 763
Ferris, S. P., 470-71
Fest, W., 196
Festivals, 46
Fiction, 639, 642, 686-88, 694-96
Fidell, E. A., 508
Field gd to . . . reptiles & amphibians of eastern & central North America, 2nd ed, 804; rocks & minerals, 4th ed, 832; the nests, eggs, & nestlings of North American birds, 791
Filby, P. W., 224
Film directors and producers, 519, 521, 525
Film libraries, 515
Film programmer's gd to 16mm rentals, 3rd ed, 528
Film study collections, 515
Films — general, 515-17; dictionaries and encyclopedias, 518-21; filmographies, 522-28; indexes, 510
Films on art, 524
Finance, 398-99
Fine arts, 2nd ed, 405
Fine arts — bibliography, 404-406; biography, 414-16; dictionaries, 407-409; encyclopedias, 410-412; indexes, 413
Finkl, C. W., Jr., 837
Firearms, 446-47
First printings of American authors, 683

Fisher, M., 652
Fisher, M. L., 211, 269
Fisher, R. T., Jr., 204-205
Fishes of the world, 794
Fishing, 350-51
Fitzgibbon, T., 887
Fitzsimons, B., 916
Flags & arms across the world, 237
Fleischmann, W. B., 637
Fleming, J., 417, 434
Flew, A., 560
Flexner, S. B., 595
Flora, J. M., 689
Flowers, 761, 763, 765-71, 892-94
Flowers of Europe, 770
Focal dictionary of photographic technologies, 465
Focal encyclopedia of film & television techniques, 520
Folk music, 488
Folklore, 564-66, 568-69
Follett, W., 604
Food of the Western world, 887
Foods and cooking, 887-90
Football, 343
Ford, G. H., 695
Forecasting, 61
Foreign language tests & reviews, 303
Foskett, D., 422
Fossils, 831
Foster, D. W. & V. R., 708
Foundations (philanthropic), 47
Fourth book of junior authors & illustrators, 665
Fowler, H. W., 591
Fox-Davies, A. C., 236
Frame by frame, 526
Frank Schoonmaker's encyclopedia of wine, rev ed, 881
Fraser, T. H., 794
Freeman, W., 639
Freeman-Grenville, G. S. P., 169, 191
Freidel, F., 180
French art, 424
French language dictionaries, 609-10
French literature, 702-704
French painters & paintings from the fourteenth century to post-impressionism, 424
Frey, R. L., 345
Friedberg, A. L., I. S., & R., 443
Friedman, L., 275
Friedrich, G., 553
Fry, P. E., 109

Fullard, H., 164
Fungi, 775-76
Funk & Wagnalls comprehensive standard international dictionary, bicentennial ed, 580
Funk & Wagnalls standard dictionary of folklore, mythology, & legend, 569
Furniture, 439
Future: . . . information sources, 2nd ed, 61

Gadney's gd to 1800 international contests, festivals & grants in film & video, photography, TV-radio broadcasting, writing, poetry, playwriting, journalism, 46
Galaxies, 736
Gamboa, M. J., 272
Games, 330, 346
Gann, L. H., 130
Ganshoff, F. L., 167
Garcia, F. L., 398
Gardening, 891-96
Gardner, R. K., 116
Garfield, A. M., 471
Garland, H. & M., 705
Garner, P., 435
Gassner, J., 500
Gaustad, E. S., 530
Geelan, P. J. M., 289
Gehman, H. S., 551
Geils, P., 25
Geiser, E. A., 35
Geisinger, M., 495
Gems, 830
Genealogies in the LC, 226; suppl 1972-76, 227
Genealogist's gd, 225
Genealogy — general, 225-27; Great Britain, 224, 230, 232; Scotland, 231; U.S., 224, 228-29
General armory of England, Scotland, Ireland, & Wales, 235
Genesis, 558
Geo-bibliog of anomalies, 847
Geochemistry, 818
Geography — atlases, 277-89; bibliography, 290-91, 294-96; dictionaries, 297-98; directories, 299; serials, 292
Geologists & the history of geology, 826
Geology, 821-26
Georgano, G. N., 353

Georgi, C., 386
Geraghty, J. J., 827
German language dictionaries, 611-13
German literature, 705
Germany — bibliography and imprints, 24-25; history, 196-97
Gesamtverzeichnis des deutschsprachigen Schrift-tums (GV), 1700-1910, 25; 1911-65, 24
Gidwani, N. N., 136
Gifted student, 313
Gillispie, C. C., 722
Gingerich, O., 737
Gioello, D. A., 458
Glare, P. G. W., 616
Glasby, J. S., 874
Glashan, R. R., 257
Glass, 448-49
Glossary of astronomy & astrophysics, 732
Glossary of mycology, rev ed, 776
Goin, C. J., 803
Goldenson, R. M., 841
Golf, 347-48
Golf Magazine's encyclopedia of golf, rev, 347
Good, C. V., 319
Good Housekeeping gd to medicines & drugs, 876
Good reading, 21st ed, 315
Goode's world atlas, 15th ed, 278
Goodwin, J., 540
Gorzny, W., 24-25
Gossman, N. J., 85
Government publications, 62-69
Governors, 257
Graf, R. F., 902
Graff, H. F., 160
Granger's index to poetry, 1970-77, 671
Grant, M., 700
Grants-in-aid, 46
Graphic arts, 419-21
Graphic arts encyclopedia, 2nd ed, 421
Grass roots music, 488
Grasses, 772
Gray, H. J., 752
Gray, P., 757
Grayson, M., 748
Great Britain — bibliography and imprints, 20-22, 146, 198, 201; biography, 85, 90; government publications, 68; history, 198-201, 911
Great treasury of western thought, 51

Greek & Latin authors, 800 B.C.-A.D. 1000, 700
Greek art, 431
Greek literature, 700-701
Green, D. B., 483
Green, L. W., 853
Greenberg, M., 251
Greenberg, R. M., 187
Greenwald, D., 388
Greenwood, V. D., 228
Gregory, R. W., 572
Grenville, J. A. S., 265
Griffin, C. C., 203
Grimwood-Jones, D., 150
Gropp, A. E., 149
Grove, G., 473
Groves, D. G., 835
Grove's dictionary of music & musicians, 5th ed, 473
Grumm, P., 116
Grzimek, B., 782-83, 809
Grzimek's animal life ency-clopedia, 782
Grzimek's encyclopedia of ecology, 809
Grzimek's encyclopedia of ethology, 783
Guerry, H., 561
Guide to . . . atlases, 290; basic information sources in chemistry, 739; British govt publications, 68; critical reviews of U.S. fiction, 1870-1910, 687-88; English & American literature, 3rd ed, 629; foreign language courses & dictionaries, 3rd ed, 577; foreign language grammars & dictionaries, 577; Hungarian studies, 141; reference books, 9th ed, 2-3; reference books for school media centers, 123; reference material, 3rd ed, 4-6; reference materials on India, 136; sources of educational information, 316; special issues & in-dexes of periodicals, 2nd ed, 28; state legislative materials, 269; the sources of British military history, 911; the sources of medieval history, 167; the sources of U.S. military history, 912; the study of the U.S.A.: suppl 1956-65, 154; the study of U.S. imprints, 14; UN organization, docu-mentation, & publishing for students, researchers, librar-ians, 266; U.S. govt pub-lications, 1978-79 ed, 62

Gun collector's hndbk of values, 13th ed, 446
Gunston, B., 915
Guralnik, D. B., 587-88
Guth, D. J., 199
Gynecology, 872

Hajnal, P. I., 266
Hall, H. W., 677
Halliwell's filmgoer's compan-ion, 7th ed, 517
Halsey, W. D., 584
Hamilton, W. R., 831
Hamilton-Edwards, G., 230-31
Hammond, K. A., 806
Hammond, N. G. L., 701
Hammond citation world atlas, 279
Hampel, C. A., 747
Hamsa, C. F., 38
Handbook of . . . American Indians, 376; American popular culture, 574; black librarianship, 212; major Soviet nationalities, 207; mathematical tables & formulas, 5th ed, 724; method in cultural anthro-pology, 377; Middle Ameri-can Indians, 378; non-prescription drugs, 5th ed, 875; North American birds: waterfowl, 792; North American Indians, 379; pseudonyms & personal nicknames, 56-57; the birds of Europe, the Middle East & North Africa, 788-89
Hanson, P. K. & S. L., 630
Harewood, Earl of, 481
Harper's dictionary of Hin-duism, 544
Harrap's new standard French & English dictionary, 610
Harris, C. D., 291-92
Harris, S., 492
Harris, W. H., 43
Harrison, C., 791
Harrison, C. E., 179
Harrison, C. J. O., 790
Harrison, F. L., 475
Harrod, L. M., 99
Hartnoll, P., 496
Harvard concise dictionary of music, 472
Harvard dictionary of music, 2nd ed, 472
Harvard gd to American his-tory, rev ed, 180

Harwell, A. J. & R. M., 452
Hatch, J. M., 573
Hatch, J. V., 213
Haviland, V., 121
Havlice, P. P., 413, 476, 644
Hawkes, J., 372
Hawley, G. G., 743, 747
Hay, R., 893
Hayes, G. P., 907
Hazeltine, M. E., 572
Heads of State, 247-49
Health care administration, 855
Health organizations of the U.S., Canada & internationally, 4th ed, 866
Health sciences & services, 854
Health statistics, 856
Healthy garden book, 895
Heard, J. N., 38
Heise, J. O., 293
Heizer, R. F., 379
Helsinki Univ Library, 294
Henderson, G. N., 886
Henderson, R., 354
Henry, C. F. H., 538
Henshaw, R., 342
Heraldic alphabet, 234
Heraldry, 224, 233-37
Herbert, I., 511
Herbert, M. C., 74
Herbs, 773
Herdeck, D. E., 699
Herman, V., 246
Hernon, P., 258
Herrera, D., 222
Herrmann, D. E., 862
Hewish, M., 919
Hieroglyphic dictionaries, 608
Higginbotham, D., 175
Higham, R., 911-12
Higher education, 320
Hinding, A., 366
Hinduism, 544
Hinson, M., 479
Historian's hndbk, 162
Historical atlas of . . .
religion in America, rev ed, 530; South Asia, 193; the religions of the world, 531
Historical biographical dictionaries master index, 74
Historical fiction, 686
Historical research, 160-62, 180, 204
Historical sites, 187
Historical statistics of the U.S.: . . . to 1970, 381
History — general, 161-62; Africa, 190-91; ancient, 372; archaeology, 155-59;

History (cont'd) —
Asia, 192-94; atlases, 163-66; bibliography, 5, 167; Canada, 195; chronologies, 168-69; encyclopedias, 170-72; Germany, 196-97; Great Britain, 198-201; Italy, 202; Latin America, 203; medieval, 165, 167; modern, 164, 171-72; Russia, 204-205; U.S., 173-89; world, 160-63, 166, 168-70
History of . . . American presidential elections, 1789-1968, 256; psychology, 838; the life sciences, 756
Hitchcock, A. S., 772
Hochman, S., 525
Hockey, 349
Hodge, F. W., 376
Hodson, H. V., 47
Hogarth, G. A., 420
Hogg, I. V., 447
Holidays, 572-73
Hollander, Z., 341, 349
Holmes, R. T., 787
Holzman, A. G., 901
Homan, W. E., 870
Homosexuality, 869
Honour, H., 417, 434
Hoofed mammals of the world, new ed, 799
Hoover, J. H., 38
Hopkins, J., 732
Hopwood, D., 150
Horak, S. M., 142
Horecky, P. L., 143-44
Horn, M., 667
Horror films, 527
Horses, 885
Horticulture, 891-96
How to find chemical information, 740
Howard-Hill, T. H., 691
Howe, W. D., 679
Howell, E., 884
Howes, F. N., 761
Howes, W., 181
Howland, M. S., 162
Hoyle up-to-date, rev, 346
Hubin, A. J., 668
Hudson, K., 48
Hughes, M. M., 369
Hughes, T. P., 539
Humanities, 2nd ed, 95
Hungarian authors, 706
Hungary, 141
Hunt, L. M., 835
Hunt, V. D., 810
Hunter, D. E., 374
Hunting & fishing, 350
Hurlbut, C. S., Jr., 820

Hutchinson, J., 765
Hydrology, 827
Hyman, C. J., 751

Idea (philosophy), 563
Idlin, R., 751
Iggers, G. G., 161
Illingworth, V., 733
Illustrated dictionary of . . . ceramics, 456; chess, 344; glass, 449
Illustrated encyclopedia of . . . aviation, reference ed, 904; country music, 483; mankind, 375; rock, 484; the animal kingdom, 2nd ed, 784; the mineral kingdom, 834; 20th century weapons & warfare, 916
Illustrated inventory of famous dismembered works of art, 423
Illustrators, 412, 420, 664-65
Illustrators of children's books, 1967-76, 420
Immroth's gd to the LC classification, 3rd ed, 106
Imperialism, 130
In search of British ancestry, 3rd ed, 230
In search of Scottish ancestry, 231
Index, the papers of the Continental Congress, 1774-89, 188
Index to . . . artistic biography, 413; British literary bibliog, 691; fairy tales, 1949-72, 568; literary biography, 644; plays in periodicals, rev ed, 509; poetry for children & young people 1970-75, 661; young readers' collective biographies, 2nd ed, 662
India, 89, 136, 192
Indians of Middle America, 378
Indians of North America, 220-21, 373, 376, 379
Indonesian language dictionaries, 614
Information centers, 101-104
Information market place 1978-79, 36
Information networks, 36
Information on music, v. 1, 470-71
Information science, 97-99
Inge, M. T., 574
Insects, 795-98

Insects of the world, 796
Instructional materials centers, 119-20, 122-23
Instructional media, 330-34
Insurance, 400
Intelligence tests & reviews, 304
International agencies, 266
International encyclopedia of . . . cats, 886; dogs, 884; higher education, 320; psychiatry, psychology, psychoanalysis & neurology, 842; statistics, 382; the social sciences biographical suppl, 127
International foundation directory, 2nd ed, 47
International hndbk of historical studies, 161
International Labour Office, 387
International law, 272
International list of geographical serials, 3rd ed, 292
International maps & atlases in print, 2nd ed, 296
International relations, 250, 265, 267
International relations dictionary, 267
International standard Bible encyclopedia, rev ed, 552
International thesaurus of quotations, 52
International wildlife encyclopedia, 781
Interpreter's one-volume commentary on the Bible, 554
Introduction to . . . cataloging & classification, 6th ed, 114; reference work, 3rd ed, 94; U.S. documents, 2nd ed, 65
Ireland, N. O., 568
Ireland, 21-22, 87, 90
Irvine, B. J., 109
Isaacs, A., 752
ISIS cumulative bibliog, 1913-65, 714
Islam, 150, 152, 539, 543
Islamic Near East & North Africa, 152
Israel, 151
Italian art, 428
Italian language dictionaries, 615
Italian literature, 707
Italy, 202
Iwanami mathematical dictionary, 726

Jackson, J. S., 168
Jackson, K. T., 177
James, E. T., 83
James, G. & R., 727
Japan, 194
Jaques Cattell Press, 328, 721, 865
Jazz, 489
Jazz music, 485, 489
Jazz records 1897-1942, 4th ed, 485
Jews, 218-19
Johnson, A. H., 890
Johnson, D. B., 254
Johnson, J., 116
Johnson, N. P., 270
Jones, C. E., 760
Jones, D. B., 384
Jones, J. K., 876
Jones, K. G., 736
Jones, T., 613
Jordan, A. H. & M., 96
Josey, E. J., 212
Judaica, 128
Judges, 275
Junior book of authors, 665
Junior colleges, 323
Justices of the U.S. Supreme Court, their lives & major opinions: the Burger Court, 1969-78, 275

Kaminkow, M. J., 226-27
Kane, J. N., 300
Kanely, E. M., 63-64
Kansler, C. C., 853
Kaplan, F. M., 134
Karpel, B., 406
Katz, B., 29
Katz, D. B., 28
Katz, W. A., 94
Katz, Z., 207
Keckeissen, R. G., 2
Keller, D. H., 509
Kemp, P., 905
Kenin, R., 53
Kent, A., 98, 901
Kernig, C. D., 260
Kingman, L., 420
Kingman, L., 653
Kings and rulers, 247-49
Kinkade, R. G., 843
Kirkley, J. W., 909
Kirk-Othmer encyclopedia of chemical technology, 3rd ed, 748
Kirkpatrick, D. L., 648-50, 666
Kister, K. F., 42, 578
Kittel, G., 553
Kleeberger, P., 223

Klimas, J. E., 766
Klotman, P. R., 526
Knauth, P., 784
Knowles, A. S., 320
Koegler, H., 501
Kohler, E. L., 396
Kondo, H., 784
Koran, 543
Kościuszko Foundation dictionary, 618
Krafsun, R. P., 522
Kramer, E. F. & M., 680
Kruskal, W. H., 382
Kruzas, A. T., 104
Kubijovych, V., 145
Kunitz, S. J., 651
Kurian, G. T., 128
Kusnet, J., 403

La Beau, D., 72-73, 510
Labor, 387, 401
Lamar, H. R., 153
Lancour, H., 98
Landau, S. I., 580, 596
Lang, K. R., 737
Langenscheidt's comprehensive English-German dictionary, 612
Langer, W. L., 170
Languages, 577
Lapedes, D. N., 718-19, 758, 811, 825
Laqueur, W., 243, 264
Larousse encyclopedia of archaeology, 156
Larousse gd to astronomy, 735
Larousse gd to minerals, rocks & fossils, 831
Larson, L. A., 862
Late-medieval England, 1377-1485, 199
Latin America, 203
Latin America, 147-49, 203
Latin American literature, 708
Latin language dictionaries, 616
Laubenfels, J., 313
Law, 268-76
Laymon, C. M., 554
Lazitch, B., 261
Leach, M., 569
Leaders in education 1974, 328
Learmonth, A. M. & A. T., 138
Leary, L., 684
Leathart, S., 778
Ledésert, M. & R. P. L., 610
Lee, J., 97

Lee, W., 527
Leftwich, A. W., 795
Legends, 569-70
Legislative bodies, 246
Legislative histories, 270
Leibenguth, C. A., 352
Lerner, R., 750
Levey, J. S., 43
Levy, F., 78
Lewanski, R. C., 105
Lewytzkyj, B., 93
Librarians, 124
Librarians' glossary of terms, 4th ed, 99
Libraries and librarianship —
general, 94-95; bibliography, 96; biography, 124; dictionaries and encyclopedias, 97-99; directories, 49, 100-105, 223, 299, 366; handbooks, 106-14, 212; periodicals, 115; selection aids, 116-23; special collections, 100, 105
Library administration, 111
Library information networks, 36, 104
Library of Congress, 655
Library of Congress, 226-27, 419, 655
Library of Congress cataloging service bulletins 1-125, 115
Library of Congress classification, 106
Library of Congress subject headings, 107
Library resources, 100, 105
Library service to the handicapped, 113
Lichine, A., 880
Life sciences, 755-56, 758
Linguistics, 6, 577
Linsenmaier, W., 796
Liquor, 880, 882
Literary characters, 652
Literary criticism, 627-28, 630, 687-88, 691, 696
Literary critics, 645
Literary history of the U.S., 4th ed, 681
Literary magazines, 643
Literary prizes, 653
Literary research gd, 631
Literature — general, 627-28; American, 679-89; bibliography, 6, 220, 629-34; biography, 644-51; British, 690-97; Canadian, 698; Caribbean, 699; children's, 652-66; classical Greek & Roman, 700-701;

Literature (cont'd) — comics, 667; dictionaries and encyclopedias, 635-41; French, 702-704; German, 705; Hungarian, 706; indexes, 642-44; Italian, 707; Latin American, 708; mystery & crime fiction, 668-69; oriental, 709; poetry, 670-71; science fiction and fantasy, 672-78; Slavic, 710-11; Spanish, 712
Literature by & about the American Indian, 2nd ed, 220
Little, E. L., Jr., 779
Little, R. J., 760
Little, W., 591
Littlefield, D. W., 152
Livingstone, E. A., 541
Local government, 258
Loeb, C., 370
Loewenberg, A., 480
Loftness, R. L., 816
Logan, N., 484
London bibliog of the social sciences: 12th suppl 1977, 125
Lovejoy's college gd, 14th ed, 326
Lowens, I., 469
Lu, D. J., 194
Lubin, M. A., 699
Luchsinger, A. E., 755
Lunin, L. F., 854

Macinko, G., 806
Mackey, M. G. & M. S., 238
Mackin, R., 594
Macmillan dictionary for children, 584
MacNalty, A. S., 858
Magazines for libraries, 3rd ed, 29
Magic, 846
Magill's bibliog of literary criticism, 630
Maillard, R., 430
Mainiero, L., 371, 638
Maizell, R. E., 740
Major international treaties 1914-73, 265
Makers of America, 208
Malinowsky, H. R., 715
Mammals, 799-801
Mammals of the world, 3rd ed, 801
Management, 390, 393, 402
Management principles & practices, 402

Mandeville, M. S., 39
Mansion, J. E., 610
Manual of style, 12th ed, 70
Manual of the grasses of the U.S., 2nd ed, 772
Manuscripts, 108, 186, 366
Map collections in the U.S. & Canada, 3rd ed, 299
Maps, 294-96, 298-99
Marco, G. A., 470-71
Marine sciences, 836
Mark, C., 358
Mark, H. F., 746
Marks' standard hndbk for mechanical engineers, 8th ed, 903
Marlow, C. A., 45
Marr, W., 214
Marshall, D. W., 178
Marshall, J. K., 30
Marshall, S. L. A., 171
Marxism, communism & Western society, 260
Mass media, 625
Masterson, J. R., 182
Mathematical Society of Japan, 726
Mathematics, 724-28
Mathematics dictionary, 4th ed, 727
Mathematics tests & reviews, 305
Matlaw, M., 503
Mawson, C. O. S., 602
Maxims, 58
McAleese, R., 322
McBride, R., 813
McCabe, J. P., 532
McClane's new standard fishing encyclopedia & international angling gd, rev ed, 351
McDavid, B., 120
McGraw-Hill dictionary of . . . art, 407; modern economics, 2nd ed, 388; scientific & technical terms, 2nd ed, 718; the life sciences, 758
McGraw-Hill encyclopedia of . . . environmental science, 2nd ed, 812; ocean & atmospheric sciences, 819; science & technology, 719; the geological sciences, 825; world biography, 79; world drama, 502
McIlvaine, E., 2
McKearin, H., 448
McLean, J., 50, 394
McNeil, B., 74

McRae, A., 817
Mechanical engineers' hndbk, 903
Media equipment, 331
Medical care, 854-55, 866
Medical ethics, 852, 861
Medical libraries, 110
Medical statistics, 856
Medicine — bibliography, 851-56; dictionaries & encyclopedias, 857-64; directories, 865-67; handbooks, 868; pharmacology, 873-79
Medicine, popular, 869-72
Meighan, C. W., 158
Melloni's illustrated medical dictionary, 860
Mendel, F., 246
Mendelson, P. C., 628
Menke, F. G., 336
Mental health, 841, 845
Mental Health Materials Center, 845
Mental Measurements Yearbook, 302-11
Meserole, H. T., 629
Messinger, H., 612
Meteorology, 828-29
Methodist church, 533
Methodist union catalog: pre-1976, 533
Mickwitz, A., 294
Microforms, 112
Micrographics, 112
Middle Ages, 165, 167, 199
Middle East, 150, 152, 155
Miekkavaara, L., 294
Mihailovich, V. D., 710-11
Miles, W. D., 749
Military atlas of the First World War, 908
Military history, 911-12, 914
Military science — almanacs, 907; atlases, 908-10; bibliography, 911-13; biography, 920; dictionaries and encyclopedias, 914-18; directories, 919
Miller, E. W., 211
Miller, J. K., 41
Miller, O. K., Jr., 774
Miller, R. W., 451
Mineralogy, 830-34
Minorities, 222
Mitchell, J., 44
Mitton, S., 731
Mochi, U., 799
Modern American literature, 4th ed, 680
Modern American usage, 604
Modern Chinese society, 135

Modern dictionary of electronics, 5th ed, 902
Modern encyclopedia of basketball, 2nd ed, 341
Modern English-Yiddish, Yiddish-English dictionary, 623
Modern French literature, 703
Modern Latin American literature, 708
Modern manuscripts, 108
Modern researcher, 3rd ed, 160
Modern Slavic literatures, 710-11
Modern world drama, 503
Mollusks, 802
Money, 443
Monkhouse, F. J., 297
Monographic series, 1
Monroe, P., 321
Montagne, P., 888
Montague-Smith, P., 232
Monthly Catalog of U.S. Government Publications, 63-64, 67
Mooney, J. E., 13
Moore, P., 729
Moquin, W., 208
Morehead, A. H., 346
Morehead, J., 65
Morrill, J. S., 200
Morris, C. G., 584
Morris, D. A. & L. D., 855
Morris, J. B., 185
Morris, M., 590
Morris, P., 518-19
Morris, R. B., 185
Morris, W., 579
Morris, W., 590
Morrison, C., 556
Morrison, J. L., 278
Mossman, J., 239
Motorsports, 352
Motorsports, 352-53
Mott-Smith, G., 346
Muehsam, G., 424
Muench, E. V., 110
Mulhall, M. G., 383
Municipal govt reference sources, 258
Munn, G. G., 398
Murdin, P., 738
Murdock, G. P., 373
Museums, 48, 223
Mushrooms of North America, 774
Music — general, 466; bibliography, 467-71; biography, 490-93; dictionaries and encyclopedias, 472-75; discography, 217, 485; indexes, 476

Music, popular, 476, 483-89, 492
Music reference & research materials, 3rd ed, 467
Musical instruments, 477-79
Musical instruments of the world, 478
Musicians, 473, 490-93
Musicians since 1900, 491
My body, my health, 872
Mycological Society of America, 775
Mycology, 775-76
Mycology guidebook, 775
Myers, B. S. & S. D., 407-408
Myers, C. F., 215
Myers, R., 640
Mystery fiction, 668-69
Mythology, 567, 569-71

Nairn, B., 84
Names, geographical, 300-301
Names, personal, 238-41
Nariai, K., 730
Naroll, R., 377
National Assn of Independent Schools, 119
National atlas of Canada, 4th ed, 287
National atlas of the U.S., 285
National Formulary XIV, 14th ed, 877
National index of American imprints through 1800, 13
National party conventions 1831-1976, 255
National party platforms, rev ed, 254
National register of historic places, 1976, 187
Native Americans, 220-21, 373
Natkiel, R., 910
Naval science, 905
Navalani, K., 136
Naylor, C., 414
Nebenzahl, K., 175, 913
Needham, R., 355
Needlework, 457, 459
Needleworker's dictionary, 457
Negro almanac, 214
Negro in America, 2nd ed, 211
Neill, S. C., 540
Neiswender, R., 142
Neurology, 842
New Cambridge bibliog of English literature, 692
New Cambridge modern history: atlas, 164

New Catholic encyclopedia, 546
New century hndbk of Greek mythology & legend, 570
New century Italian Renaissance encyclopedia, 202
New college encyclopedia of music, 475
New Columbia encyclopedia, 4th ed, 43
New dictionary of . . . American family names, 240; modern sculpture, 430; physics, 2nd ed, 752; statistics, 383
New Emily Post's etiquette, 14th ed, 575
New field book of reptiles & amphibians, 803
New Grove dictionary of music & musicians, 473
New gd to popular govt publications, 66
New Guinea, 137
New illustrated medical encyclopedia for home use, 871
New information systems & services, 104
New international dictionary of New Testament theology, 557
New international dictionary of the Christian church, rev ed, 537
New Kobbé's complete opera book, rev, 481
New language of politics, 245
New Larousse gastronomique, American ed, 888
New Oxford atlas, rev ed, 280
New Sabin, 15-19
New serial titles: . . . 1950-70 cumulative, 31; subject gd, 32
New special libraries, 102
New Westminster dictionary of the Bible, rev ed, 551
New York Botanical Garden illustrated encyclopedia of horticulture, 892
New York Historical Society, 425
New York Times atlas of the world: concise ed, 283
New York Times book review index, 1896-1970, 117
New York Times encyclopedia of television, 624
Newbery & Caldecott medal books, 1966-75, 653
Newman, H., 449, 456
Newsome, W. L., 66

Newspapers, 146, 210
Nicholls, A., 48
Nicholls, P., 675
Nicholsen, M. E., 75
Nicknames, 56-57
Nicknames & sobriquets of U.S. cities, states, & counties, 3rd ed, 300
Niering, W. A., 768
Nineteenth-century painters & painting, 426
Nolan, J. R., 271
Norback, C. & P., 362
Norimoto, Y., 730
Norman, G., 426
North Africa, 152
Notable American women 1607-1950, 83
Notable names in the American theatre, 512
Novelists, 647, 649
Novelists & prose writers, 649
Novels, 694, 696
Nunn, M. E., 335

Oberschelp, R., 24
Obituaries from The Times 1951-60, 80
Obituaries on file, 78
Occult, 846-47, 849
Occupational safety, 387
Occupations, 75, 401
Ocean & marine dictionary, 836
Ocean world encyclopedia, 835
Oceanography, 819, 835-36
Oceans, 281
Ockerman, H. W., 889
Official encyclopedia of baseball, 10th ed, 339
Official encyclopedia of bridge, 3rd ed, 345
Official military atlas of the Civil War, 909
Ohles, J. F., 329
Older American's hndbk, 362
O'Leary, T. J., 373
Olmstead, N. C., 768
Olton, R., 267
Opera, 480-82
Orchestral music in print, 468
Organic chemistry, 742
Organic Gardening magazine, 891
Oriental literature, 709
Ormond, R., 427
Orr, M. C. & R. T., 767
Osborn, J., 114

Osborne, H., 433
Osol, A., 878
Ottemiller's index to plays in collections, 6th ed, 507
Outdoor recreation, 337
Owens, J. J., 558
Oxford American dictionary, 583
Oxford classical dictionary, 2nd ed, 701
Oxford companion to . . . film, 516; French literature, 704; German literature, 705; music, 10th ed, 466; ships & the sea, 905; Spanish literature, 712; the decorative arts, 433
Oxford dictionary of . . . current idiomatic English, 594; English Christian names, 3rd ed, 241; quotations, 3rd ed, 54; the Christian church, 2nd ed, 541
Oxford economic atlas of the world, 4th ed, 384
Oxford English dictionary, 589, 591-92
Oxford-Harrap standard German-English dictionary, 613
Oxford junior companion to music, 2nd ed, 466
Oxford Latin dictionary, 616
Oxford Russian-English dictionary, 619
Oxford Univ Cartographic Dept, 280

Pacey, P., 111
Painting, 422-28
Palgrave, R. H. I., 389
Palmer, A., 908
Palmer, A. M., 49
Palmer, H. H., 696
Palmer, M. A., 393
Palmer, P., 336, 339, 343
Palmer, R. S., 792
Paper money of the U.S., 9th ed, 443
Paperback books, 7
Papp, C. S., 797
Papua New Guinea, 137
Paradiso, J. L., 801
Parapsychology, 850
Parapsychology and the occult, 846-50
Parker, H. T., 161
Parker, S. P., 812, 819
Parliamentary government, 246

Parliamentary practice, 242
Parliaments of the world, 246
Parrinder, G., 542
Parrish, T., 171
Parry, P. J., 464
Partnow, E., 367
Patai, R., 151
Patient education, 853
Patterson, M.C., 631
Pearson, J. D., 150
Peckham, H. H., 178
Peerage, 232
Penguin dictionary of decorative arts, 434
Penology, 365
Penrice, J., 543
Penzler, O., 669
People in books . . . 1st suppl, 75
Periodicals and serials —
   bibliography, 96, 132, 146; directories, 28, 31-33, 210; indexes, 27, 509, 643; selection aids, 29-30
Persian, Arabic, & English dictionary, 617
Personality tests & reviews II, 306
Pery, L. J., 909
Pescow, J. K., 395
Peter's quotations, 55
Peterson, M. S., 890
Pevsner, N., 417
Pfafflin, J. R., 808
Phaidon dictionary of twentieth-century art, 2nd ed, 409
Phi Delta Kappa, 319
Philosophy, 5, 559-63
Photo-atlas of the U.S., 284
Photography, 463-65
Photography index, 464
Physicians, 865, 867
Physics, 750-53
Piano in chamber ensemble, 479
Pickles, J. D., 692
Place names, 300-301
Planet we live on, 820
Plano, J. C., 244, 251, 267
Plants, 761-65, 891-94
Platt, C., 165
Play index 1973-77, 508
Plays, players & playwrights, 495
Ploski, H. A., 214
Poetry, 654, 661, 663, 670-71
Poets, 650
Poets, 646, 650
Polish language dictionaries, 618
Polish literature, 711

Political economy, 389
Political parties, 254-55
Political science — general, 242; communism, 260-63; dictionaries, 242-45, 251; encyclopedias, 250, 260; fascism, 264; handbooks, 246-49; international relations, 265-67; U.S., 250-59
Political science dictionary, 244
Pollard, A. W., 21
Polunin, O., 770, 780
Polymers, 746
Popkin, D. & M., 703
Popular culture, 574-76
Popular song index, 1st suppl, 476
Porcelain, 455
Porpoises, 800
P-Orridge, G., 414
Porter, C. L., 46
Post, E. L., 575
Postage stamps, 444, 450
Pottery, 455
Pough, F. H., 832
Poulton, H. J., 162
Praeger encyclopedia of art, 411
Prakken, S. L., 632
Pratt, R., 878
Precious stones, 830
Prelinger, R., 528
Preminger, A., 670
Presidents, 256
Princeton encyclopedia of classical sites, 157
Princeton encyclopedia of poetry & poetics, enl ed, 670
Printers, 34
Prints, 419
Prisons, 365
Pritchard, A., 848
Private presses, 35
Professional & scientific literature on patient education, 853
Pronunciation of 10,000 proper names, 238
Proverbs, 58
Prusek, J., 709
Przebienda, E., 67
Pseudonyms, 56-57, 239
Pseudonyms & nicknames dictionary, 239
Psychiatry, 841-42
Psychologists, 839-40
Psychology — bibliography, 838-40; dictionaries and encyclopedias, 841-44; mental health, 845

Public services (libraries), 113
Publishers and publishing, 34-36, 713
Puerto Ricans & other minority groups in the continental U.S., 222
Purnell's history of the 20th century, 172
Pushkarev, S. G., 204
Putnam, R. E., 899

Quick, J., 412, 918
Quimby, H., 420
Quinn, E., 500
Quinquennial cumulative personal author index 1971-75, U.S. govt publications monthly catalog, 67
Quotable woman 1800-1975, 367
Quotations, 51-55, 58, 367

Radio, 626
Ramsey, L. G. G., 437
Rand McNally atlas of the oceans, 281
Rand McNally concise atlas of the earth, 282
Rand McNally new concise atlas of the universe, 729
Randel, D. M., 472
Random House encyclopedia, 44
Rapp, G. R., Jr., 833
Rare books, 37-39, 655
Rare plants, 764
Reader's adviser, 12th ed, 632-34
Reader's Digest complete gd to needlework, 459
Reader's Digest encyclopedia of garden plants & flowers, 894
Reader's encyclopedia of the American West, 153
Reader's encyclopedia of world drama, 500
Reader's gd to the great religions, 2nd ed, 529
Reading tests & reviews II, 307
Real estate, 403
Recreation and sports — baseball, 339-40; basketball, 341; bibliography, 335; dictionaries and encyclopedias, 336-38; football, 343; games, 344-46; golf, 347-48; hockey, 349; hunting and fishing, 350-51;

Recreation and sports
(cont'd) — motorsports,
352-53; sailing, 354; skiing,
355; soccer, 342; swim-
ming, 356; tennis, 357
Redgrave, G. R., 21
Reference books, general, 1-7
Reference books in paper-
back, 2nd ed, 7
Reference gd to fantastic
films, 527
**Reference services (libraries),
94**
Regan, M. M., 28
Reich, W. T., 562
Reichler, J. L., 340
Reid, J. M. H., 704
Reid, W. M., 755
Religion — general, 529;
atlases, 530-31; Bible stud-
ies, 547-58; bibliography,
5, 532-33; dictionaries,
534-44; encyclopedias,
545-46
Renaissance, 202
**Reptiles and amphibians,
803-805**
Research centers directory,
6th ed, 49
Researcher's gd to American
genealogy, 228
Reynolds, B., 615
Richards, B. G., 29
Richards, J. M., 418
Richardson, J. M., 715
Richter, G. M. A., 431
Rickett, H. W., 771
Riddle, M., 884
Rifken, H., 845
Riker, T., 895
Ringgren, H., 547
Robert, H. M. & S. C.,
242
Roberts, F. C., 80
Roberts, J. M., 172
Roberts, W. L., 833
Robert's rules of order,
newly rev, 242
Robinson, A., 904
Rock music, 484, 486, 493
Rocks, 831-32
Rodgers, F., 68
Rogers, A. R., 95
Rogers, M., 427
Roget's international the-
saurus, 4th ed, 597
Rolfe, D., 906
Roman baroque painting, 428
Roman literature, 700-701
Romanofsky, P., 359
Rose, J., 229

Rosenberg, J. K., 658
Rosenberg, J. M., 390
Rosenberg, K. C., 331
Rosenthal, E., 131
Rosenthal, H., 480, 482
Rosichan, R. H., 444
Ross, J. M., 347
Ross, M., 247
Rothenberg, R. E., 871
Rowe, K. E., 533
Royal Historical Society, 201
Royal Horticultural Society,
893
Rubin, L. D., Jr., 685, 689
Ruffner, J. A., 76, 829
Rulers & governments of the
world, earliest times to
1491, 247; 1492-1929, 248;
1930-75, 249
Rules of order, 242
Ruoff, J. E., 693
Rush, T. G., 215
Russia, 142, 204-205
Russia, the USSR, & Eastern
Europe: 1964-74, 142
Russian-English dictionary,
rev ed, 619
**Russian language diction-
aries, 619**
Russian literature, 710
Rust, B., 485
Ryan, P., 137
Ryder, D. E., 139-40

Sader, M., 643
Sadoul, G., 518-19
Saffady, W., 112
Safire's political dictionary,
245
Sailing, 354
Salaman, R. A., 462
Salem, J. M., 504
Sanders, J. B., 36
Sarjeant, W. A. S., 826
Saunders, N., 249
Savage, G., 438, 456
Savage, H., 115
Scarne's ency of games, 346
Scharff, R., 354
Scherf, W., 656
Schlesinger, A. M., Jr., 256
Schmittroth, J., Jr., 104
Scholars, 328-29
Scholes, P. A., 466, 474
Schön, G., 445
School libraries, 119-23
Schoonmaker, F., 881
Schwartz, B., 273-74
Schwartzberg, J. E., 193
Science & engineering litera-
ture, 3rd ed, 715

Science and technology —
general, 713; bibliography,
4, 714-16; biography, 721-
23; dictionaries and ency-
clopedias, 717-20; history,
714
Science fiction, 527, 672-78
Science fiction book review
index, 1923-73, 677
Science fiction encyclopedia,
675
Science fiction story index,
1950-68, 678
Science tests & reviews, 308
Scientific books, libraries,
& collectors, 3rd ed, 713
Scientific libraries, 713
**Scientific literature, 713,
715-16**
Scientists, 721-23
Scotland, 21-22
Scott, M., 453
Scott, Foresman advanced
dictionary, 585
Scott, Foresman intermediate
dictionary, 585
Scott-Kilvert, I., 697
Screen, J. E. O., 577
Scullard, H. H., 701
Sculpture, 429-31
Sculpture & sculptors of the
Greeks, 4th ed, 431
Sculpture index, 429
Seashells, 802
**Secondary school libraries,
119**
Sedimentology, 824
Seidman, J., 262
Selecting materials for instruc-
tion, 332-34
Selective gd to publications
for mental health & family
life education, 4th ed, 845
Sell, B. H. & K. D., 364
Sen, S. P., 89
**Serbo-Croatian language
dictionaries, 620**
Serials for libraries, 30
Serle, G., 84
Serving physically disabled
people, 113
17th century Britain, 1603-
1714, 200
Sewing, 457-58
Sex discrimination, 369
Sexual barrier, 369
Seymour-Smith, M., 646
Shadily, H., 614
Shadwell, W. J., 425
Shannon, B., 357
Sharp, H. S., 56-57
Shaw, H. K. A., 763

Shaw, J. M., 654
Sheehy, E. P., 2-3
Shells, 802
Shepard, L., 849
Shepherd's historical atlas, 9th ed, 166
Shera, J. H., 124
Shevchenko Scientific Society, 145
Shipley, J. T., 641
Ships, 905
Shipton, C. K., 13
Shockley, A. A., 212
Short stories, 523, 642
Short stories on film, 523
Short story index: suppl 1974-78, 642
Short-title catalogue of books printed in England, Scotland, & Ireland & of English books printed abroad 1475-1640, 2nd ed, 21; 1641-1700, 22
Shorter Oxford English dictionary on historical principles, 3rd ed, 591
Showers, V., 380
Showman, R. K., 180
Siemon, F., 678
Silverman, J., 662
Simon & Schuster encyclopedia of World War II, 171
Simon & Schuster world coin catalogue 1979-80, rev ed, 445
Simon & Schuster's international dictionary: English/Spanish, Spanish/English, 621
6,000 words, 581
Ski Magazine's encyclopedia of skiing, rev ed, 355
Skinner, G. W., 135
Slavic ethnic libraries, museums & archives in the U.S., 223
Slavic literature, 710-11
Slavic studies, 223
Slide libraries, 2nd ed, 109
Slides, 109
Slocum, R. B., 71
Slonimsky, N., 490
Small, J., 297
Small presses, 35
Smirnitsky, A. I., 619
Smit, P., 756
Smith, D. B. F., 663
Smith, E. C., 240
Smith, R. C., 755
Smith, W., 237
Smith, W. J., 671

Smith's gd to the literature of the life sciences, 9th ed, 755
Smythe, M. M., 216
Snell, W. H., 776
Sniderman, F. M., 506
Snyder, L. L., 197
Sobel, R., 259
Sobin, J. M., 134
Soccer, 342
Social sciences — bibliography, 5, 125-26; biography, 127; encyclopedias, 127
Social service, 359-60
Social service organizations, 359
Social studies tests & reviews, 309
Sociology — aging, 362; bibliography, 312, 358; directories, 359; encyclopedias, 360-61; marriage and the family, 363-64; prisons, 365
Sociology of America, 358
Sociology of education, 312
Soil science, 837
Something about the author, vol. 17, 664
Songs, 469, 476
Sopher, D. E., 531
Soul music, 486
Source book for food scientists, 889
Source book for Russian history from early times to 1917, 205
Source book in astronomy & astrophysics, 1900-75, 737
Sourcebook on the environment, 806
Sources of . . . compiled legislative histories: 1st-94th Congress, 270; information in the social sciences, 2nd ed, 126; Japanese history, 194; serials, 33
South African bibliog to the year 1925, 26
South Asia, 193
Southeastern Europe, 144
Southern literature, 685, 689
Southern writers, 689
Spanish language dictionaries, 621-22
Spanish literature, 712
Sparano, V. T., 337
Special libraries, 101-104, 109, 111

Spellenberg, R., 769
Spencer, D. A., 465
Spiller, R. E., 681
Spinning, 460
Sports, 335
Sports, 335-36, 338, 352-53
Sports medicine, 862
Spottiswoode, R., 520
Spuler, B., 248-49
Stambler, I., 486
Stamps & coins, 444
Standard catalog of world coins, 1981 ed, 442
Standard hndbk for mechanical engineers, 903
Standard hndbk of stamp collecting, rev ed, 450
Standard medical almanac, 2nd ed, 868
Stars, 730, 736
State government, 257, 269
Statistics, 380-83, 856
Statutes, 274
Statutory history of the U.S., 274
Stedman's medical dictionary, 23rd ed, 863
Stein, J. S., 900
Steinbrunner, C., 669
Steingass, F., 617
Steinmetz, S., 603
Stenesh, J., 744
Stensland, A. L., 220
Stephenson, R. W., 299
Stern, E., 155
Stevens, R. B., 775
Stevenson, G. A., 421
Stewart, F. H., 872
Stewart, G. R., 301
Stewart, T. D., 378
Stillwell, R., 157
Stineman, E., 370
Storey, J., 716
Stratman, C. J., 498
Stroynowski, J., 93
Strunsky, R., 425
Stuart, M., 773
Stutley, J. & M., 544
Style manuals, 70
Subject collections, 5th ed, 100
Subject collections in European libraries, 2nd ed, 105
Subject directory of special libraries & information centers, 5th ed, 103
Subject headings, 110
Subject index to poetry for children & young people, 1957-75, 663
Sullivan, L. V., 104

Supplement to the Oxford companion to Canadian history & literature, 698

Supplement to the Oxford English dictionary, 592

Sutherland, Z., 659

Swan, L. A., 797

Swift, L. H., 759

Swimming, 356

Sworakowski, W. S., 263

Sykes, J. B., 593

Synge, P. M., 893

Sypher, F. J., 633

Taber's cyclopedic medical dictionary, 13th ed, 864

Tanselle, G. T., 14

Tanur, J. M., 382

Tarbert, G. C., 73

Taylor, A. J. P., 172

Taylor, G., 777

Taylor, R. E., 158

Technology, 4, 741, 748

Technology and copyright, 40

Technology and the law, 40

Television, 510, 520, 624

Teng, S., 133

Tennis, 357

Tesar, J. E., 784

Tests in print II, 311

Textiles, 460-61

Tezla, A., 706

Theatre—biography, 511-12, 514; dictionaries and encyclopedias, 499-500; directories, 505; handbooks, 496; history, 495; indexes, 510

Theatre, film & television biographies master index, 510

Theological dictionary of the New Testament, 553

Theological dictionary of the Old Testament, 547

Theologisches Begriffslexikon zum Neuen Testament, 557

Theology, 555, 557

Thesaurus of psychological index terms, 1974 ed, 843

Thewlis, J., 753

Thibault, C., 195

Third world, 128

Thomas, C. L., 864

Thompson, L. S., 15-19

Thompson, R., 483

Thompson, S. C., 339

Thomson, D., 521

Thomson, J. B., 742

Thomson, W. A. R., 857

Thorndike, E. L., 585

Thorndike-Barnhart advanced dictionary, 585

Thorndike-Barnhart high school dictionary, 585

Thorne, J. O., 77

Thornton, J. L., 713

Three thousand mycological terms, 776

Times (London), 80

Times atlas of . . . China, 289; the world: comprehensive ed, 283; world history, 163

Todd, F. S., 793

Tooley's dictionary of mapmakers, 298

Torbet, L., 454

Toye, W., 698

Trade names dictionary, 2nd ed, 391; company index, 392

Training & development organizations directory, 393

Transportation, 904-906

Travel guidebooks in review, 3rd ed, 293

Treat, R., 343

Treaties, 265

Trees & bushes of Europe, 780

Trees and shrubs, 777-80

Trees & shrubs hardy in the British Isles, 8th ed, 777

Trees of the world, 778

Trigg, G., 750

Tripp, E., 571

Tripp, R. T., 52

Truitt, D., 800

Tuck, D. H., 676

Tudor, D., 217, 487-89, 882

Tudor, N., 217, 487-89

Tully, R. I. J., 713

Tuma, J. J., 728

Tune in yesterday, 626

Turgeon, C., 888

Turkin, H., 339

Turner, J. B., 360

Turtles of the U.S., 805

Tver, D. F., 836

20th century, 172

20th-century children's writers, 666

20th-century literary criticism . . . 1900-60, 628

Twitchett, D. C., 289

Tymn, M. B., 673

Udvardy, M. D. F., 786

UFOs, 847

Ukraine, v. 2, 145

Ukrainian literature, 711

Unbegaun, B. O., 619

Unesco, 423

Ungar, F., 638

Union of Soviet Socialist Republics, 142, 207

United Nations, 266

U.S.—general, 153-54; armed forces, 920; atlases, 284-85; bibliography and imprints, 8-19, 38; biography, 74, 82-83; ethnic groups, 208-12, 214, 216, 221-23; foreign relations, 250; history, 173-89, 368, 381, 909, 912-13; politics and government, 250-59, 262

U.S. Bureau of the Census, 381

U.S. Congress, 252-53

U.S. Constitution, 273

U.S. copyright documents, 41

U.S. dispensatory, 27th ed, 878

U.S. Employment Service, 401

U.S. Executive Branch, 259

U.S. Geological Survey, 285

U.S. govt publications, v. 1: author index . . . pre-1956, 69

U.S. Library of Congress, 154

U.S. National Archives & Records Service, 186, 188

U.S. National Historical Publications & Records Commission, 186

U.S. National Park Service, 187

U.S. Office of Education, 314

U.S. Supreme Court, 268, 275

U.S. Tennis Association official encyclopedia of tennis, rev, 357

University of Chicago Press, 70

University of Chicago Spanish dictionary, 3rd ed, 622

University of Victoria. McPherson Library, 415

Unwin, D., 322

Urdang, L., 397

Urquhart, F., 639

Use of biological literature, 2nd ed, 754

Use of mathematical literature, 725

Used book price gd . . . 1977 suppl, 39

Usher, G., 762

U.S.iana (1650-1950), rev ed, 181

Van Caenegem, R. C., 167
Vanderbilt, A., 576
Van Doren, C., 51
Van Nostrand's scientific
  encyclopedia, 5th ed, 720
Velleman, R. A., 113
Vernadsky, G., 204-205
Veterinary medicine, 897
Victorian fiction, 695
Victorian prose, 690
Viney, W., 838
Vinson, J., 513, 647-50
Viola, 2nd ed, 477
Visual encyclopedia of
  science fiction, 674
Vocal music, 469
Vocational education, 393
Vocational tests & reviews,
  310
Voss, T. M., 439

Wadia, B., 430
Wakeman, J., 651
Walford, A. J., 4-6, 577
Walker, E. P., 801
Wallace-Homestead price gd
  to dolls, 2nd ed, 451
Walmsley, J., 399
Walter Breen's encyclopedia
  of U.S. & colonial proof
  coins 1722-1977, 441
Walters, L., 852
Ward, A., 156
Ward, J. O., 466, 474
Ward, P., 712
Ward, W. S., 146
Ward-Thomas, P., 348
Warfare, 916
Warner, E. J., 189
Warrack, J., 482
Washburn, W. E., 221
Wasserman, P., 50, 386, 393-
  94, 866
Water, 827
Water atlas of the U.S.,
  3rd ed, 827
Water birds, 792-93
Waterfowl, 793
Waterhouse, E., 428
Watson, A., 798
Watson, G., 692
Watson, R. I., 839-40
Weapons, 916, 918
Weather almanac, 2nd ed,
  829
Weaver, K., 528
Weaving, 460
Weaving, spinning, & dyeing,
  460
Webb, A. D., 383

Webb Society deep-sky
  observer's hndbk, v. 3, 736
Weber, J., 833
Weber, J. S., 315
Webster's American military
  biographies, 920
Webster's biographical dic-
  tionary, 81
Webster's collegiate thesaurus,
  598
Webster's new collegiate dic-
  tionary, 586
Webster's new dictionary of
  synonyms, 599
Webster's new world diction-
  ary for young readers, 587
Webster's new world diction-
  ary of the American lan-
  guage, 2nd ed, 588
Webster's sports dictionary,
  338
Webster's students thesaurus,
  600
Webster's third new interna-
  tional dictionary, 581
Wedgeworth, R., 97
Wehr, H., 605
Weigert, A., 734
Weinreich, U., 623
Weise, F. O., 856
Weiss, I., 679
Welbourn, R. B., 861
Welch, d'A. A., 660
Wentworth, H., 595
Wertheimer, M. & M. L.,
  838
West, G. P., 897
West, The, 153
Westminster dictionary of
  church history, 534
Westminster dictionary of
  worship, 535
Westrup, J. A., 475
Whalley, P. E. S., 798
Wheat, J. C., 295
Wheeler, A., 794
White, C. M., 126
White, R. A., 850
Whitehouse, D. & R., 159
Whitfield, F. J., 618
Whiting, B. J., 58
Whitrow, M., 714
Whitten, P., 374
Who was when? A dictionary
  of contemporaries, 3rd ed,
  168
Who was who in the theatre,
  1912-76, 514
Who's who in . . . Ameri-
  can Jewry, 1980 ed, 219;
  American law, 2nd ed, 276;

Who's who in (cont'd) . . .
  architecture from 1400 to
  the present, 418; children's
  books, 652; health care,
  867; rock music, 493;
  the socialist countries, 93;
  the theatre, 16th ed, 511;
  20th century literature, 646
Wiener, P. P., 563
Wigder's gd to over-the-
  counter drugs, 879
Wildflowers, 766-71
Wildflowers of eastern
  America, 766
Wildflowers of the U.S., 771
Wildflowers of western Amer-
  ica, 767
Wile, J., 881
Williams, V. L., 365
Willis, J. C., 763
Willison, I. R., 692
Wills, G., 440
Wilson, C., 475
Wilson, K. M., 448
Winch, K. L., 296
**Wine and wine making, 880-
  82, 888**
Wine, beer & spirits, 882
Wing, D., 22
Wingate, I. B., 461
Wings, 904
Winkel, L., 122
Wintle, J., 53
Wit and humor, 55
Withycombe, E. G., 241
Witt, E., 268
Woffinden, B., 484
Wolff, K., 716
Wolman, B., 842-44
Women, 83, 179, 366, 371
Women in American history,
  179
Women's history sources, 366
Women's studies, 370
**Women's studies — general,
  366-67; bibliography, 368-
  70; biography, 371**
Woodbury, M., 316, 332-34
Woodworking, 462
Woolley, A., 834
Woolley, A. R., 831
World atlas of golf, 348
World authors, 1970-75, 651
World communism . . . 1918-
  65, 263
World encyclopedia of
  comics, 667
World energy book, 813
World facts & figures, 380
World Future Society, 61
World War I, 908
World War II, 171, 910, 917

Woy, J., 386
Writings on American history, 1961, 182
Writings on British history 1901-33: v. 5, 1895-1914, 201
Wyatt, H. V., 754
Wyman's gardening encyclopedia, rev ed, 896
Wynar, A. T., 209-10
Wynar, B. S., 7, 114, 124
Wynar, C. L., 123
Wynar, L. R., 206, 209-10, 223

Xavier, L., 555

Yacht Racing/Cruising, 354
Yamashita, Y., 730
Yearns, W. B., 189
Yiddish language dictionaries, 623
York, W., 493
Young, H. C. & M. L., 101-103
Young, P., 910
Young, W. C., 505
Young adult literature, 658, 661-63

Young people's literature in series, 1973-75, 658
Yugoslav literature, 711
Yutang, L., 606

Zahorski, K. J., 673
Ziegler, E. N., 808
Zimmermann, H., 734
Zionism, 151
Zoology – birds, 785-93; encyclopedias, 781-84; fishes, 794; insects, 795-98; mammals, 799-801; mollusks, 802; reptiles and amphibians, 803-805